Modern Thai Buddhism and Buddhadāsa Bhikkhu

A Social History

Modern Thai Buddhism and Buddhadāsa Bhikkhu

A Social History

Tomomi Ito

NUS PRESS
SINGAPORE

Published by:

NUS Press
National University of Singapore
AS3-01-02, 3 Arts Link
Singapore 117569

Fax: (65) 6774-0652
E-mail: nusbooks@nus.edu.sg
Website: http://www.nus.edu.sg/nuspress

ISBN 978-9971-69-572-9 (Paper)

National Library Board, Singapore Cataloguing-in-Publication Data

Ito, Tomomi, 1971-
Modern Thai Buddhism and Buddhadāsa Bhikkhu : a social history / Tomomi Ito. – Singapore : NUS Press, c2012.
p. cm.
Includes bibliographical references and index.
ISBN : 978-9971-69-572-9 (pbk.)

1. Phra Thēpwisutthimēthī (Ngūam), 1906-1993 – Political and social views. 2. Buddhism – Thailand. 3. Buddhism – Social aspects – Thailand. 4. Theravāda Buddhism – Thailand. 5. Theravāda Buddhism – Social aspects – Thailand. 6. Buddhism and politics – Thailand. I. Title.

BQ566
294.309593 -- dc22 OCN709556467

Cover image courtesy of Mr. Metta Phanit, one of Buddhahāsa's nephews and current President of the Dhammadāna Foundation.

Typeset by: Forum, Kuala Lumpur, Malaysia
Printed by: Mainland Press Pte Ltd

Contents

List of Illustrations

Maps*

**Adapted by the author from Wikipedia via the following links*:

<http://en.wikipedia.org/wiki/Thailand>
<http://en.wikipedia.org/wiki/Surat_Thani_Province>
<http://en.wikipedia.org/wiki/Chaiya>

Figures

† *Drawn by the author based on interview data collected from Buddhadāsa's relatives*

Notes on Romanization of Thai Words and Names

In this book, the Romanized spelling of Thai words basically follows the method described in "ALA-LC Romanization Tables", available at <http://www.loc.gov/catdir/cpso/roman.html>.

For the names of individuals and organizations that have particular Romanization in English publications or suggest one in their business cards, brochures or websites, those spellings are used in the main text of this book. However, when referring to authors of publications in Thai, this book follows the ALA-LC Romanization method and provides the author's own spelling in brackets.

For the names of monks, their original lay given names are spelt in accordance with the ALA-LC system, unless they have their own particular Romanized spelling, whereas their ordination names (Thai: *chaya*), which are given to them in Pāli, are thus written in Pāli in the main text of this book, rather than a transcription of the Thai pronunciation.

For monastic titles (Thai: *samanasak*) and titles bestowed by the Thai court (Thai: *bandasak*) and indicating a rank, the ALA-LC method is used, unless there is a particular Romanized spelling by which the individual is commonly known.

For the titles of Thai books, sermons and lectures, English translations are used in the main text and the original Thai titles are provided either in brackets or in footnotes.

Thailand used to be called Siam, and the country's name was officially changed to Thailand on 24 June 1939 by the government of Field Marshal Phibun Songkhram. In this book, the country and its people are basically called "Thailand" and "Thais" throughout the history, except for some cases prior to the time of official change of the country's name, or in some organizations which use the words "Siam" and "Siamese."

Acknowledgements

The publication of this book marks the end of my long journey in Thailand and Australia, away from my home country, Japan. With no personal connection to either Thailand or the Western world, I embarked on the study of a Thai Buddhist monk, the report to be written in English. It was necessary to learn many things, in particular the languages, basic cultural assumptions and common practices of both Thailand and the West, contemporary Buddhism as it is lived, and extensive specific knowledge about Buddhadāsa's thought and the historical context of his time. In the course of my research and writing, I had the benefit of the inspiring thought of many people and the kind help of many more.

I was motivated to explore Buddhadāsa's world by the inspiration gained from reading extensive studies on Buddhadāsa by three Western scholars: Prof. Donald K. Swearer, Dr. Peter Jackson, and Dr. Louis Gabaude. Prof. Swearer's English translation was the first of Buddhadāsa's sermons which I read during my undergraduate exchange study in Canada. When my command of the Thai language was still very limited, I learned more about Buddhadāsa from Dr. Jackson's book and Dr. Gabaude's thick French volume, for which the study of yet another language was required. Without the benefit of those scholars' studies, it would have been much more difficult to grasp the deep philosophy of Buddhadāsa.

As I consolidated my academic foundation, I found invaluable advice from great scholars of Thai Buddhism and history: the late Prof. Yoneo Ishii, Dr. Craig Reynolds, and Prof. Eiji Murashima. With his broad scholarship supported by joyful enthusiasm in Thailand and Southeast Asia, Prof. Ishii taught me how to depict an invisible past in a clear structure. Dr. Reynolds offered his precious time to read all of my earliest, still somewhat confused drafts, providing many insightful comments and great encouragement. Prof. Eiji Murashima gave me generous research support and advice based on his vast knowledge on modern Thai history, acquired through his life of dedication to thorough and precise research.

In Thailand, more than a hundred people kindly offered opportunities for interviews; among them especially Khun Metta Phanit, Achan Dr. Soemsap Damrongrat, and Achan Chitsai Phadungrat at Suan Mokkh; also Achan Sulak Sivaraksa, Pracha Hutanuwatr, and Venerable Phra Paisal Visalo, who kindly read the sections in which they appeared and offered encouraging comments about publishing the study as a book. I regret that this volume does not include a chapter on interreligious dialogue due to limitations of word count and time, even though the topic is of great significance in Buddhadāsa's thought and in the Thai Buddhist public sphere. I have to apologize to those people, including Prof. Suwanna and Chaiwat Satha-Anand, for their kind advice and/or interviews for my research on this issue.

Also in Thailand, Achan Malinee Kumsupa helped my understanding of Thai and my collection of materials, especially at the beginning stage of my research. In Australia, Dr. Royce Wiles offered his advice on religious and academic aspects of Buddhism, including Pāli, and also took on the burden of editing my thesis, from which this book has developed. Back in Japan, my colleagues in Kobe University, particularly Prof. Ken'ichi Sudo, Prof. Kyoichi Ishihara, Prof. Wang Ke, Prof. Mamoru Hagihara, Prof. Sachiko Kubota, and Prof. Yasushi Sadayoshi, kept supporting my work and provided moral support for this publication. Furthermore, Prof. Lawrie Hunter kindly proofread the final version of this long manuscript. Most importantly, Prof. Paul Kratoska's support was essential for publishing this study in book form. Without his thoughtful understanding, this might never have become a reality.

I would also like to express my deep gratitude to all those whose kind advice and generous cooperation in my interview research were the superb sources for my exploration of the modern Thai Buddhist public sphere and enabled me to complete the long process of preparing the manuscript.

Finally, I sincerely thank my family, Takayuki Ito, Kikue Ito, and Chiyomi Ito, who were always supportive in allowing me to take frequent long overseas trips and to spend much time at my computer. I owe the completion of this study very much to them.

Tomomi Ito
Kobe, Japan
February 2012

Introduction

Anyone who visits a bookstore in Bangkok and takes a look at the English book section may find a considerable number of books on Buddhism there. Because Bangkok is an important hub for international travelers exploring Asia, and because Buddhism is one of the most intriguing Asian spiritualities, bookstores in Bangkok plan their stock to meet the demand of their international customers. Looking specifically at the store's selections on Buddhism, there will be general manuals by both scholars and Buddhist monks of Western origin, as well as English editions of a variety of books by famous teachers from different Buddhist traditions, including the 14th Dalai Lama of Tibet, Thich Nhat Hanh of Vietnam, and Mahasi Sayado of Burma. Together with those books by teachers outside Thailand, there are Thai Buddhist teachers' books translated into English, especially books by the Venerable Buddhadāsa Bhikkhu (1906–1993). Even a brief look at English translations of his books will reveal a rich array of publications, suggestive of Buddhadāsa's extensive teaching activities and the popularity of his thought, which attract the attention of the international Buddhist audience. More than a decade after his death, Buddhadāsa remains one of the most respected and internationally best known Thai Buddhist monks.

If, in the same bookstore, a person with knowledge of Thai shifts his or her eyes to Thai books, he or she may find a rather large section on Buddhism, and in the Buddhism section, at least a shelf or two, or in some cases even a whole bookcase, full of Buddhadāsa's works. His many books range from small booklets which might be read through in a short break, to collections of his sermons printed in thick, beautiful bindings, looking like an encyclopedia or a modern printing of Buddhist scriptures. Pick up one of the small booklets, the photo shows the late Buddhadāsa: an old monk with a wise face and a good constitution, wearing glasses, sitting calmly in the meditation posture in front of a Buddha image in the middle of the forest. The image of Buddhadāsa in a Thai bookstore could never be enough to reveal his significance today, but could maybe hint at it; many of the sermons this sagacious monk gave in his lifetime are still highly respected and well received among both casual and serious readers in Thailand.

For a few decades already, Buddhadāsa has been studied with great interest by both scholars and Buddhist practitioners. His life and thought were introduced to the West as early as the 1930s; more attention seems to have been given since the 1970s. Among the many who committed themselves to studies of Buddhadāsa and to English translations of his sermons and biography are Jack Kornfield, Louis Gabaude, Peter A. Jackson, Donald K. Swearer, Sulak Sivaraksa, Santikaro (formerly Santikaro Bhikkhu; no longer a monk but still teaching and translating under his ordination name), and Kamala Tiyavanich.[1] Their publications have indicated that Buddhadāsa's thought has "modern" characteristics: rationality, a scientific and demythologizing approach, scant interest in traditional rituals and "unscientific" beliefs, and an emphasis on causality in mind.

In *A Modern Buddhist Bible*, Donald S. Lopez, Jr. lists Buddhadāsa as one of the 31 figures who contributed to the formation of "modern Buddhism".[2] In his study of "Buddhist modernism," David L. McMahan also refers to Buddhadāsa as a prominent contemporary Asian Buddhist leader.[3] In archetype modern Buddhists, including Colonel Olcott, Anagārika Dharmapāla, Yang Wen-hui, T'ai Hsu, Shaku Soen, D.T. Suzuki, Mahasi Sayadaw, and the 14th Dalai Lama, Lopez identified a common tendency to dismiss rituals that interfere with the natural order, and a tendency to aim at ending suffering through a rational approach, particularly meditation practice.

Because of its transcendent character, modern Buddhism is regarded as a universal religion, transcending differences of regional forms, languages, sectarian affiliation, gender, and even the traditional roles of monks and lay people. Consequently, Lopez pointed out that the door to the traditionally elite monastic realm of scriptural study and meditation practice has been opened to lay people and even people from traditionally non-Buddhist countries, particularly from the West. According to Lopez, "… modern Buddhists were very much products of modernity, with the rise of the middle class, the power of the printing press, the ease of international travel." He suggested that modern Buddhism is "… an international Buddhism that transcends cultural and national boundaries, creating in the following generation a cosmopolitan network of intellectuals, writing most often in English"; it is "… itself a Buddhist sect. There is Thai Buddhism, there is Tibetan Buddhism, there is Korean Buddhism, and there is Modern Buddhism".[4]

Roughly speaking, Buddhadāsa's thought and his historical context do coincide with the general picture of "modern Buddhism," and he may have been one of the agents of "Buddhist modernity." Yet, unlike the typical Asian modern Buddhists, such as Dharmapāla, D.T. Suzuki, and the 14th Dalai Lama, who traveled vigorously all around the world and spoke fluent English in their interaction with Western and other audiences outside their native countries, Buddhadāsa worked predominantly in Thai in Thailand. Although some of Buddhadāsa's works were translated into English and he openly welcomed foreigners for *dhamma* conversations, Buddhadāsa contributed much more significantly to Thai Buddhists in Thailand than to Western Buddhists who typically followed the "modern Buddhist" teachings of several teachers from a variety of traditions in Buddhist Asia. Even if Buddhadāsa's teaching appealed universally to modern Buddhists around the world, "modern" characteristics are only part of his thought. Modernity tends to be understood as a homogeneous force in the contemporary world, and modern science and technology drastically changed Thai people's lifestyle from traditional to modern; however, the drive of modernity did not transform Buddhadāsa and contemporary Thai Buddhism on the same scale. There were some social forces which to some extent prevented Buddhadāsa's modern rational teaching from becoming an exclusive, dominant new standard of contemporary Thai Buddhism.

A group of Buddhadāsa's followers in Thailand referred to Buddhadāsa's thought as "radical conservatism,"[5] meaning that in one sense Buddhadāsa was "conservative," as he aimed at following the Buddha's essential teachings; and that at the same time he was "radical," never hesitating to reject seemingly inessential rituals or even to criticize some traditional scriptures and their exegeses, particularly those relating to the Abhidhammapiṭaka scriptures. Furthermore, Buddhadāsa's intellectual pursuits were well beyond the scope of orthodox Theravāda Buddhist textual grounds; his sermons included notions of Zen, Christianity, and even socialism, in which he found some commonalities with and aspects helpful to an understanding of Buddhist concepts.

In fact, the abovementioned character of Buddhadāsa has met with both positive and negative evaluations. On the one hand, many Thai and Western religious intellectuals appreciate Buddhadāsa's rational and scientific view as relevant to the present time and his liberal attitude and insightful interpretations as something helpful to their lives. On the other hand, Buddhadāsa was not free from criticism of his independent development of Buddhist thought. Some experts of classical text studies referred to him in Pāli as *attanomati*, which means a personal opinion of the teacher, at a distance from the most reliable doctrinal authority, the "original" Buddhist texts. Some Thai Buddhist intellectuals even more harshly criticized him, calling him a "heretic" (Thai: *diarathi*) and "communist," for destroying Buddhism.[6] When Buddhadāsa's unique thought, with its contradictory reputation, is studied only textually, through a comparison to some standard exegesis of traditional Theravāda Buddhism, he would likely be summed up with the all-too-common critical remarks on his departure from orthodoxy or tradition.

One approach of examining Buddhadāsa's position in the Thai social context was to identify some particular social groups which supported his unconventional teaching; they could then be considered bearers of new change in modern Thai Theravāda Buddhism. One social group which might take up the change brought about by Buddhadāsa and some other burgeoning Buddhist groups would be the middle class.[7] After the late 1980s, accompanying Thailand's achievement of economic growth and political stability, the middle class, with a fair standard of living and education, came to the fore as a new group appearing to support democracy and social fairness as a rational choice. Buddhadāsa's rational and liberal character seemed a good fit to the general image of the middle class, rather than to the rural and urban commonalty, who were often characterized by poor education, hardships of life, a random lifestyle, ignorance of righteousness, and unthinking fascination with magic.

It appears that a significant portion of Buddhadāsa's followers come from the well-educated class rather than the lower, less educated class; however, religious preference does not arise simply from educational background and social category. Among those belonging to the middle class, some are skeptical about the supernatural, while others are enthusiastic amulet collectors and frequent visitors to fortunetellers.[8] Moreover, as the following chapters of this book will reveal, not just Buddhadāsa and his followers, but his keen opponents as well, came from middle-class backgrounds; thus, it is quite unlikely that their conflicts over doctrinal interpretation represented class interests.

Venturing a simplified remark on Buddhadāsa's place in contemporary Thai Buddhism, I consider his main contribution to be his rediscovery of *lokuttara dhamma* (supra-mundane Buddhist teaching) in the classical scriptures and his popularization of it for practical use by general Thai Buddhists who knew Buddhism only as *lokiya dhamma* (mundane teaching), particularly the notion of *kamma* (causality of one's actions) — do good, receive good results; do evil, receive evil results.[9] Yet the purpose of this book is neither to retrace messages in Buddhadāsa's teaching about previously unknown Buddhist doctrines, nor to evaluate the accuracy of his interpretation through comparison with the original passages in the classical scriptures, to do which requires a philological method beyond the scope of this volume.

The focus of this book is rather on social controversy revolving around Buddhadāsa's stimulating teaching. Overall, as a great reformer in modern Thai Buddhism, Buddhadāsa appears to have enjoyed much more respect than criticism; yet he got into trouble from time to time for his straightforward speech. In a way, Buddhadāsa's regal posture and his lack of fear of confrontation attracted people who were challenging the existing social order politically, and their support made him look even more polemical. Furthermore, his image as a challenger was intentionally twisted by his opponents to make him appear politically troublesome. A look at the controversies in which Buddhadāsa was involved will reveal Thai Buddhists' lively but tricky debates. Buddhadāsa is in fact the best figure to tell a rational current in contemporary Thai Buddhism, a trend which intends to transcend conventional Buddhist practice and reclaim the spiritual depth of original Buddhism in classical scriptures, but is accompanied by unreasonable mundane intentions. Such a phenomenon in contemporary Buddhism requires a new research perspective, an alternative to anthropological studies of popular religious practices and philological studies of classical texts.

A key notion in this book is that of the Buddhist public sphere, inspired by Jürgen Habermas' notion of the public sphere.[10] Habermas' notion captures the phenomena in which, through newspapers and coffeehouse discussions, people engaged in critical political debate opposing the government. The public sphere concept is rooted in the historical rise of the modern bourgeoisie toward the end of the absolute monarchy in Europe from the late 17th century through the 18th century, around the time of Britain's establishment of the parliamentary cabinet system and 1789 French Revolution. The bourgeois public sphere is also a normative model of democratic participation in contemporary political life. Habermas considered that later on, the public sphere underwent a structural transformation, becoming a sphere of mass control through the use of mass media; it no longer functions as a critical sphere for the examination of government decisions or the formation of a consensus through rational debates, but rather, serves as a public relations device for conveying some already determined matters, or as yellow journalism, as the substance for gossip and cultural consumption.

Habermas' notion of public sphere was intended to integrally comprehend the beginning of a new era marked by the economic growth of the bourgeoisie, their participation in critique of the arts, literature and government policy, which were previously dominated by the aristocratic class, and the new authority of publicly extended reasonable political critique. Non-aristocrat bourgeoisies were admitted, as cultivated "common human beings," on an equal footing to critical debates in the public sphere in the world of letters. According to Habermas, the bourgeoisie's accomplishment of consciousness as "humanity" was reflected in the political realm. Private persons who had autonomy in love, freedom, and cultivation in the sphere of the bourgeois family and inside the person were considered to have autonomy in private property based on ownership, and thus their economic and political interests were thought to be respected as the freedom of the individual in general.[11] Therefore, their interests, such as emancipation from mercantilist rule promoted by absolute monarchy, were considered to be reflected in the government policymaking. Habermas' model of the public sphere is composed of private persons who came from different social strata to hold discussions in salons and coffeehouses in a manner presupposing equality of status, welcoming open participation, freely considering topics previously under the authority of church and state.[12]

What then of the Buddhist public sphere, the key notion through which this book attempts to develop an understanding of Buddhadāsa and his world in 20th-century Thailand? Unlike Habermas' public sphere, the Buddhist public sphere is not an all-embracing notion for looking at every significant occurrence in the dawn of modernity, including the rise of inner consciousness as humanity, of the bourgeoisie, of capitalism, of democracy, and of mass communication. Nor does it have the same vision as the "public sphere in the world of letters," in which experiences Habermas considered that the bourgeoisie had found a "humanity" in common with ruling-class aristocrats and which in extension, became their political appeal of "equality" and "liberty."

Rather than linking Buddhist discussions to public political opinions, the notion of the Buddhist public sphere in this book looks at the general populace's public expressions of doctrinal interpretation of Buddhism. It highlights Thai Buddhists' discussions of doctrinal interpretation, which took place in places such as Buddhist journals, Buddhist associations, town corners and temple yards, and public expression of opinion by the mass media. The Buddhist public sphere is the arena for a variety of contesting interpretations to attempt to gain broad public recognition of their appropriateness, or to win hegemony over the many other interpretations being offered.

Theravāda Buddhism is known for its adherence to the "words of the elders" faithfully passed on from the Buddha to successive generations, and the Thai Saṅgha is centralized just as is the state's provincial administration; however, in reality, Thai Theravāda Buddhism is not as dogmatic as it looks, but rather it tolerates coexistence of a range of plural opinions which sometimes conflict and are extensively debated.[13] Justin McDaniel identified an important point: "Scribes were creatively engaged and constantly altered manuscripts. Mimetic fidelity was not an ideal. These teachers and students were not merely amanuenses. They willingly and frequently changed the content and structure of Buddhist texts in the process of teaching and translating them."[14] Such convention in the transmission of Buddhist thought did contribute to the pluralization of doctrinal interpretations and did tolerate a variety of decodings of scriptural texts. 20th-century modern print and mass communication technology exposed the variety of positions in existence in the Buddhist public sphere.

Just like the Catholic Church, the National Saṅgha of Thailand (hereafter also called "the Thai Saṅgha") is hardly monolithic; it embraces many sub-groups which promote different doctrinal emphases and distinctive practices — particularly methods of meditation practice — developed rather privately by influential teachers. Those sub-groups, which are even smaller units than the two institutionalized formal orders (the Mahanikai and the Thammayut) include, among many, Wat Pak Nam Bhasicharoen originating from Luang Pho Sot (Sot Candasaro Bhikkhu, 1884–1959); Wat Nong Pah Pong and its numerous branches following Luang Pho Chah (Cha Subhaddo Bhikkhu, 1918–1992); and the group of Luang Pho Thian (Thian Cittasubho Bhikkhu, 1911–1988). In Thailand, there are even more Buddhist groups led by lay and *mae chi* (female practitioners consistently observing eight precepts) teachers who are not members of the Thai Saṅgha, which consists of only male monks (*bhikkhu*) and novices (*sāmaṇera*). The diversity of doctrinal emphases and meditation methods existed even before the emergence of prominent new groups such as the Santi Asoke group and the Dhammakāya Foundation, which receive the attention of several scholars.[15] It should be noted, then, that diversity does not always trouble the Thai Saṅgha.[16]

In fact, some influential senior monks who are closely involved in the Thai Saṅgha administration expressed in interviews with me in the early 2000s their concerns about the appropriateness of diversified Thai Buddhist practices and hinted at a concern that the Saṅgha's attitude not be interpreted as arbitrary. The more prominent a newly emerging group becomes, the less it can remain unconcerned about the Saṅgha elders' recognition; group leaders frequently visit and invite influential elders in order to ingratiate themselves with them. New groups are seriously concerned about the Saṅgha elders' favor; yet the Saṅgha does not look so rigorously committed to the resolution of every doctrinal argument in Thai Buddhism. The coexisting diversity of alternative teachings and methods of practice in Thai Buddhism may not be simply the result of the Saṅgha elders' tolerant and merciful attitude toward differences, possibly because of the difficulty of doctrinal judgment of acceptable options. Whatever the reasons, as long as the Thai Saṅgha does not clarify its position on conflicting interpretations, doctrinal debates continue in the Buddhist public sphere.

In the 20th century, it seems that the doctrinal distinction between acceptable variations and "delusive" ones is becoming even more difficult. The modernized monastic education system and the devoted efforts at Thai translation, with the help of the print media, afford a wide range of people access to Buddhist doctrines which had traditionally been passed on among a relatively small group of highly learned religious specialists who had mastered the classical language, Pāli.[17] Consequently, more people can now freely examine their means of doctrinal understanding based on their direct experiences of religious practice. Rediscovery of the "rational" aspect of Buddhist teaching, which can be experimentally proven in meditation practice, through one's physical and mental senses without involving miracles or supernatural interventions, does not restrict the variety of Buddhist practice to a single logically coherent doctrinal authority; the testability of Buddhist doctrine has even pluralized expressions of experience.

Furthermore, the persistence of conventional Thai Buddhist beliefs in miracles and the supernatural increases the complexity of the situation. Those beliefs do not easily give in to the rational current; they continue to coexist side by side with rational Buddhist teaching; miracles and the supernatural do attract people. For example, as we shall see in Chapter 5 of this book, one group promoted a study of the Abhidhamma, which is considered the most "orthodox" doctrine in Theravāda Buddhism, yet at the same time, they piqued people's curiosity through the use of fraudulent magic. As will be examined in detail in that chapter, it should be noted that the group's reference to the Abhidhamma and their use of magic was not necessarily interlinked by tradition and traditional religious faith; after their magic was exposed as a fake and criticized, the group's leader confessed that his intention was to bring the Abhidhamma to people's attention. In contemporary Thai Buddhism, the notion that magic and supernatural phenomena are believed and practiced exactly in accordance with a "tradition" is questioned. Magic and the supernatural can rather be renewed and utilized to stimulate people's curiosity, to mobilize a large number of followers, and to collect ample donations, because through a display of the substantial support, a religious group can secure the recognition of the public and the authorities.

Unlike Habermas' normative model of the bourgeois public sphere, the Buddhist public sphere model presented here does not focus entirely upon rational, critical debates, despite the fact that the main character here, Buddhadāsa, was rational and critical. Buddhadāsa's rational presentation of "original Buddhism" — or perhaps "modern Buddhism" — was a convincing notion which appealed to many people, but this never meant that Buddhadāsa's modern teaching established itself as a new doctrinal authority, pushing aside all the other interpretations. In this volume, the notion of the Buddhist public sphere is taken as a sphere for the discussion of Buddhist doctrines and many different coexisting interpretations. Among those many ideas, none are regarded as infallible dogma; rather, at any given time, one persuasive notion gains support and wins hegemony, whilst less persuasive ones provide as optional views. Unlike secular politics, in which a dominant public opinion is revealed by democratic election, a dominant thought in the Buddhist public sphere is seldom proven mathematically. Therefore, a certain notion's hegemony or dominance, which is rooted in popular support, is quite often vague and easily changeable.

In the Buddhist public sphere, people do not necessarily support the most rational, scientific view that appears to be the most convincing at a given time. As Michael Walzer indicated in his critique of liberalism, passion is an important part of people's preferences.[18] Rationality aside, the people would respect and support a teacher if he or she could overwhelmingly demonstrate precise knowledge of doctrine (such as Kittivuḍḍho Bhikkhu, discussed in Chapters 4 and 5), could solve complex problems of doctrine in scripture based on psychological experience in meditation practice (such could the forest monks in Isan and Naep Mahaniranon, as mentioned in Chapter 5), or could give a comical yet eloquent talk which could entertain audiences (as is the case for many common monks who speak at temple fundraising events).

Moreover, expressions in the Buddhist public sphere are not always as beautiful as true Buddhism ought to be. In the public sphere of Buddhism, as in other societal groups, reputation bears great significance. When colored by defilements or mundane concerns, Buddhist debates are not pure matches of doctrinal refutation or contests of validity. In order to produce a reliable, positive public image, a newly prominent religious group often approaches royal family members or the Saṅgha's elder monks, just as politicians and other secular notables in Thailand often do for the same purpose. Photos of a royal or holy audience can effectively convey a message to the public that the group has gained the acknowledgement of the establishment. On the other hand, when attempting to defame opponents, a religious group can devote a huge amount of money to the spread of damaging rumors, the distribution of handbills, and radio broadcasting; sometimes even the mobilization of raucous mobs to lead a negative campaign. Through ill intention, information in the public sphere can be easily manipulated, and in the face of a vicious campaign, a public figure's reputation or credibility is fragile enough to be at least shaken, if not totally destroyed.

Quite similar to the public sphere in 18th-century Britain, as observed by the historian John Brewer, in Thai society, people enjoy observing both serious debates and scandalous gossip with great excitement.[19] For them, Buddhism is not just a religion to be practiced, but in a way, it is also a philosophy which is familiar enough for discussion and for the exploration of its unrevealed depths. Famous monks are of course religiously respected, but in a sense, their popularity and reputation have a common character with that of public figures such as politicians, whose public image is of crucial importance to their credibility. Slapstick controversies in the Thai Buddhist public sphere are a Buddhist aspect of the intellectual history and social history of Thailand.

The significance of exploration of the public sphere of Southeast Asia and religious publications has already been indicated by Shawn McHale in his study on Vietnam from the 1920s to 1945.[20] The number of religious and other publications in early 20th-century Thailand is as impressive as that in Vietnam around the same time. In Bangkok in the late 1990s and early 2000s, when research for this study was conducted, second-hand bookstores in the Chatuchak weekend market and roadside vendors heaped up old Buddhist booklets covered with black dust and sold them at dirt-cheap prices. Since Buddhist booklets were printed in large runs for free distribution on such merit-making occasions as funerals and celebrations, or for the purpose of religious propagation, a number of copies ended up in those bargain shops. Even though they looked no better than rubbish, thanks to the lasting value of their religious messages, they were still marketable and read by people on the street who wanted to remind themselves of religious lessons for life. They were hardly ever considered materials for scholarly research. I, too, would never have been motivated to fully explore the piles of countless Buddhist publications without having had a focus on Buddhadāsa.

The number of publications by Buddhadāsa alone were initially perceived to be a big challenge for a foreign researcher with only a limited command of Thai. It was fortunate for me that Phra Pracha Pasannadhammo (now disrobed and known as Pracha Hutanuwatr), a brilliant disciple of

Buddhadāsa in his later years, thoroughly interviewed Buddhadāsa in the mid-1980s and published the essentials of the interview as *Lao Wai Mua Wai Sonthaya* (*Talking in the Twilight Years*) in 1988, well before I started my PhD study in 1997.[21] Pracha's book offered me indispensable insights into Buddhadāsa's course of life, his intellectual associates, important debates, opponents and followers, as well as his fundamental viewpoints. Based on his extensive reading of Buddhadāsa's old letters and memoirs collected in Suan Mokkh archives in Chaiya, Pracha, the conscious former student activist, questioned the reverend frankly and drew out many interesting episodes about his life and work. Following the details provided in Pracha's book, I traced Buddhadāsa's publications, including his tri-monthly journal, books and booklets, collected in Suan Mokkh library and in the National Library of Thailand in Bangkok, and found in second-hand bookstores. In addition, I interviewed, as many as possible, the important followers and keen opponents of Buddhadāsa mentioned in Pracha's book, and collected their publications.

Although I could never articulate the depth of Buddhism presented in Buddhadāsa's publications any better than his own words have done, my research led me to a portrayal of Buddhadāsa as he was likely seen through the eyes of Thai Buddhists in the turbulent 20th century, and to picture the actuality of contemporary Buddhism through Thai Buddhist discussions involving Buddhadāsa, his followers and his opponents. I understand that contemporary Buddhism is spiritual and reasonable, as do the many contemporary Western Buddhists who find it helpful to their lives; yet it may be simplistic to label it "rational," "scientific," and "modern" — such characteristics are sometimes even plausibly associated as a threat to traditional popular beliefs, such as animism. Hopefully, the method applied in this study provides a scientific enough picture of an aspect of contemporary Buddhism, which has been distanced by scholars who are happy to be "fair" and "objective" toward religions of the "Other," but hardly adopt the same attitude toward a teaching which possibly dazzles their eyes.

Chapters 1 and 2 will examine the time when the young Buddhadāsa had a strong impact on Thai Buddhist intellectuals with the launch in 1933 of the quarterly journal *Buddhism* in the provincial town Chaiya; reasons for that impact are sought in Buddhadāsa's and his journal readers' words, and a new current of Buddhist thought in the early 20th century is presented through comparative readings of articles in Buddhadāsa's and other Buddhist journals in circulation during the same period.

Chapters 3, 4, and 5 will consider the period when Buddhadāsa became well known as a respected Buddhist thinker and started to encounter challenges to and criticism of his unconventional teaching; in these chapters, the processes of Buddhadāsa's establishment and doctrinal confrontations regarding the notion of "empty mind" and the book of Abhidhamma are traced in the development of his thought and propagation, not just concerning his own effort and provocative expressions, but also that of his keen followers and opponents who promoted his teaching publicly through their own interpretations. Those chapters will consider related parties' intentions toward and relationships to Buddhadāsa in the socio-political context of Thailand during the Cold War period. The nature of their doctrinal debates will be revealed to have been not always purely doctrinal, but sometimes rather aspired by political urge to damage his public face. Buddhadāsa's controversial character was developed through confrontations in doctrinal debates, and his challenging image promoted a political expectation supportive of radical change.

Chapter 6 will examine Buddhadāsa's intellectual exchanges, which involved some of the most famous Thai intellectuals, leaders in their specialized fields in the secular realms; for example, Pridi Phanomyong, a highly esteemed socialist politician who had served as Prime Minister and as regent of King Ananda Mahidol; Kulap Saipradit, a respected journalist and writer also inspired by Marxism; and Samak Burawat, a pioneer of mining engineering in Thailand and the author of lasting works on Marxism, science and Buddhism. Chapter 7 will look at the acceptance of Buddhadāsa's thought outside his acquaintances and frequent personal contacts, particularly among student activists in the early 1970s, who were prompted to work for radical social change and read Buddhadāsa's sermons as a guiding principle in their lives. These chapters will consider Marxism's impact on Buddhadāsa's thought and the significance of Buddhadāsa's teaching in the lives of the Marxist intellectuals of different generations. Their political activities and the internal conflict between Marxism and Buddhism will shed light on an important aspect of the intellectual history of Thailand.

Finally, Chapter 8 will observe a notable turn in Buddhadāsa's thought in the last stage of his life, i.e., regarding women's rights in Buddhism. In Thai Buddhism, it has long been quite apparent that women are serious participants in Buddhist practice but they are not allowed to fully perform the monastic role that male monks do. However, the claim for gender equality reform in Buddhism has not been welcomed by the public, and even Buddhadāsa in his early years was not fully supportive of this matter, contrary to some women practitioners' expectations. The late Buddhadāsa's proposed resolution to this issue was his rare commitment to social issue, and it hints at his fundamental method for social change.

CHAPTER 1

A New Era in Thai Buddhism

Buddhadāsa's early 20th-century contribution to Buddhist teaching was *lokuttara dhamma*, the path to *nibbāna*. *Lokuttara dhamma* was not Buddhadāsa's invention but a discovery from traditional scriptures which began to be more widely studied rather than being upheld as sacred. From the late 19th century to the early 20th century, increasing numbers of Western intellectuals from the non-Buddhist background became interested in Buddhism, a mysterious Eastern religion. At a time when science was convincing more and more intellectuals, the Buddhism which attracted Western intellectuals of that time was not the Buddhism of merit accumulation in combination with supernaturalism that was widely believed and practiced among Buddhist population in Asia; it was the teaching about transcending the state of suffering, a teaching that did not require beliefs in the supernatural and did not contradict science. In the colonial period, when the West had gained hegemony in world politics and culture, it is not difficult to imagine that Asian Buddhists felt proud that their spiritual traditions were receiving the attention of Western intellectuals. Through the leadership of both Western and Asian intellectuals, new interest in *lokuttara dhamma* was promoted and shared among wider Buddhist audiences in the West and Asia through English print media, the new lingua franca of the world.

Buddhadāsa certainly played a part in that intellectual current of his time; for many Thai people, he was the teacher who restored "authentic" Buddhism to contemporary Thailand. The purpose of this chapter is to examine movements which were new in the time of Buddhadāsa's youth, the limitations of those earlier movements as perceived by Buddhadāsa, and Buddhadāsa's attempts at new directions. This chapter begins with Thai Buddhism's reformative movements in the Saṅgha and among lay Buddhist intellectuals before the 20th century, and the international current of interest in Buddhist doctrine which reached Thailand. It then examines Buddhadāsa's family background, which introduced him to progressive elements in Buddhism. The chapter finally focuses on how young Buddhadāsa and his younger brother worked together in an attempt at reform. Many of the background stories in this chapter are based on Buddhadāsa's statements in a biographical interview with his disciple Phra Pracha Pasannadhammo in the early 1980s, when Buddhadāsa was in his late seventies.[1] Buddhadāsa's statements in Phra Pracha's interview provide much more information than his own biographical stories. Combined with further details found in materials mentioned by Buddhadāsa, this chapter overviews the intellectual setting of early 20th-century Thai Buddhism.

Buddhist Reforms before Buddhadāsa

Even before the modern era, reforms of Buddhism did exist in Thai history. Through the studies by historians of Thailand, we know that notable reforms in the pre-modern period were Buddhist's kings' intervention in the monastic realms. Although in theory, royalty and religion should be independent and should not interfere with each other, Buddhist kings had a great concern in the Saṅgha's monastic conduct. At a time of power transition, for instance, one king invited respected elder monks to the new capital, ordered them to collect Buddhist manuscripts to copy, and promoted Buddhist scholarship, in order to demonstrate that the new power offered better rule than the previous. In underpopulated Mainland Southeast Asia, kings were also interested in the unused male labor of Buddhist monks who were exempted from corvée labor. Some kings examined monks' reading of Pāli scriptures, and the monks who failed were forced to disrobe and do heavy labor for the government.[2] Buddhist reforms in the dawn of the modern period were different from kings' reforms of the Saṅgha recorded in earlier history, reforms in the 19th and 20th centuries were a proactive commitment by both monastic and lay Buddhists searching for "true" Buddhist teaching and practice.

Reforms in the Saṅgha

(i) Prince Mongkut and Thammayut Order

The most notable reformative movement was in the 1830s led by the famous monk-prince Mongkut (1804–1873). By applying the monastic practice of the Mons of Lower Burma, which he perceived as a better embodiment of the original tradition from the Buddha's time, Prince Mongkut distinguished his reformative group from the conventional practice of monks; he named it the Thammayut, which later became sanctioned as a new monastic order in Siam. Mongkut's reform is often characterized as rationalist, and his skepticism toward mythical cosmology is regarded as a precursor of Buddhadāsa's demythologizing interpretation.[3] From the bird's eye view of historians, the rational spirit of the time may not have been limited to Mongkut as an individual, but may have extended among the Siamese elite of that time and on to the generation of Buddhadāsa in the 20th century.[4]

The impetus of Mongkut's movement had an impact on Buddhadāsa, although in fact the order in which Buddhadāsa ordained was not Mongkut's Thammayut Order, but the more conventional Mahanikai Order. Just like Buddhadāsa, who ordained in 1926, a century earlier, Mongkut did not simply accept Buddhism in Siamese tradition as authentic. After he ordained and had studied scriptures for a few years, Mongkut became disappointed with his fellow monks' lax discipline, their selling of religious items, and providing of services based on supernatural beliefs.[5] After meeting a respected elder from Pegu, Mongkut turned to the Mon monastic tradition as the one inheriting the original Buddhism. Not just adopting the Mon style of ordination, of wearing of robes, of holding of the alms bowl, and of pronunciation of Pāli, Mongkut sought out a complete version of Pāli *Tipiṭaka*, borrowing a copy from Ceylon because the one then available in Siam was incomplete.[6] He also installed a printing press in his monastery — probably the first one in Siam outside the control of Christian missionary. Substituting the traditional palm-leaf religious manuscript written in Cambodian characters, Mongkut used the printing press to publish the Patimokkha and Buddhist teaching books, first in the new script, *ariyaka* which he invented; later giving up the use of *ariyaka* and using Thai script. According to a study by Lingat, Mongkut was a popular preacher of his monastery, Wat Bowonniwet. Lingat wrote that Mongkut "composed in Pāli many hymns for daily worship at morning and evening, and formulate for the devotions of the laity."[7] Mongkut explained the legendary stories and miraculous events in the life of the Buddha as parables, and on each *uposatha* day and each important Buddhist day, he gave sermons in simple language so that his audience could understand the message. In a sense, Mongkut's efforts to recover and popularize "true" Buddhist teaching laid a foundation for Buddhadāsa's work.

Interestingly, however, contrary to historians' observations, Buddhadāsa's comment on Mongkut's reform was not very positive. In his biographical interview, when his disciple asked if he were influenced by Mongkut's reform, Buddhadāsa answered, "It had no direct impact on me. There was an impact on politics, so the Thammayut Order was established.

Problems arose because of having two orders."[8] In the mid-19th century after the Thammayut group was officially sanctioned as a distinctive monastic order of the national Saṅgha in Siam, all the monks who did not belong to the Thammayut Order were categorized as belonging to the Mahanikai Order. Nearly a century after the establishment of the Thammayut group, in the 1920s and 1930s, Buddhadāsa witnessed strife between the two orders near his hometown in Southern Thailand.[9] Buddhadāsa referred to one of the respected meditative monks in his locality who was asked to reordain in the Thammayut Order; the monk rejected the request by suggesting that entering the Thammayut Order could never solve the problem of erection in monks observing the celibacy precept.[10] Buddhadāsa saw the reform of the new order rather as a source of political problems; he did not appreciate it as a philosophical shift which could guide him to a rational way of thinking.

Buddhadāsa's attitude toward Mongkut's reform can be interpreted as showing that Buddhadāsa did not place much value on the rational hermeneutics of supernaturalism and traditional religious cosmography, one area where his and Mongkut's thoughts coincided. Or, put another way, both Mongkut and Buddhadāsa were interested in rational aspects of Buddhist teaching, but Buddhadāsa seems to have seen a limitation in Mongkut's understanding of Buddhism. Although Buddhadāsa did not explicitly mention the name of Mongkut in his biographical interview by Phra Pracha, Buddhadāsa said, "Aside from the revisions of the scriptures, I skimmed through the history of religious reforms in the Rattanakosin period. I did not find much of importance and I believe that those revisions were useless. They followed the old style of merit and *kamma*".[11] For Buddhadāsa, Buddhist beliefs in merit and *kamma*, or the teaching of *lokiya dhamma*, were nothing new; what he found fascinating was *lokuttara dhamma*, the teaching for transcending the conditions of *kamma* to reach the state of *nibbāna*.

Was Buddhadāsa's understanding of reforms by Mongkut and other Buddhist intellectuals in Rattanakosin period relevant? Were their thoughts really limited to the teaching of merit and *kamma*? Griswold, who studied Mongkut's life and thought, described Mongkut's "new Buddhism" as follows:

> He [Mongkut] was fond of saying that there is nothing in it that conflicts with modern science. But what of the belief in transmigration, which seems so fanciful to westerners? He did not reject it, but gave it a more philosophic interpretation. He could point to the laws of physics to show that given causes produce given effects. If there laws govern the material universe, was it not reasonable to assume that similar ones govern the moral domain, so that every deed, whether good or evil, is

> inevitably followed by its appropriate consequence, either in this life or the future? Though there was no "soul" to be reborn, the "energy of action" was everlasting.[12]

This was not just Mongkut's conception. Chao Phraya Thipakorawong, one of Mongkut's Buddhist intellectual confidants, expressed a similar view in his famous book *Kitchanukit*, written in response to Christian missionaries with whom he had discussed modern science and the relevance of religious teaching. Reynolds explained the new cosmography of *Kitchanukit* as follows:

> Approximately halfway through the book, the author [Thipakorawong] — through his imaginary master and pupil — addressed himself to religion, specifically to such fundamentals of Theravāda Buddhism as *karma*, merit, rebirth, giving, and the precepts … In replying to a question about the existence of heaven and hell, for example, the master examined Christianity, Islam, Hinduism/Brahmanism, and Buddhism and concluded that all religions have heaven to entice and hell to threaten. Since the idea of *karma* was taken as a basic premise, it followed that heaven and hell must exist as destinations for the consequences of good and bad deeds.[13]

As far as the question of Buddhism's rationality, the law of *kamma* or the teaching of *lokiya dhamma* was coherent enough with modern science. Like science, the law of causality is the foundation of *lokiya dhamma. Lokiya dhamma* teaches morality via causal logic and promotes the doing of good; in return for a good deed, an individual can receive merit and happiness; it teaches the avoidance of evil doing, as one's evil deed will result in demerit and suffering.

Mongkut's reform and the establishment of the Thammayut Order marked a new beginning, questioning conventional Buddhism in Siam and promoting its found alternative as the "true" Buddhism. However, what was offered as an alternative, which coincided with the rational logic and modern Western science, did not very much impress Buddhadāsa and some later Buddhist intellectuals in Thailand. Along similar lines to that of Buddhadāsa, Phra Paisal Visalo, one of the monks who leads contemporary Buddhist social engagement, expressed his concern about simple acceptance of the view linking science and rationality with Buddhism. Paisal wrote,

> Even though the scientific worldview made it clearer that Buddhism is based on reason, at the same time it made Buddhism to place more emphasis on *lokiya dhamma*, and less on *lokuttara dhamma* (for instance, *nibbāna*). This tendency had already appeared in the time of

> King Rama IV [Mongkut], but it became clearer later, especially in the Buddhist principles taught and propagated by the Thammayut Order under the leadership of Prince Patriarch Wachirayan Warorot.[14]

Buddhadāsa's and Paisal's view on the Buddhist reforms in the 19th century urge historians to reconsider the significance of "rational Buddhism" as encountered in modern history. It is easy to assume that people in the last few centuries became skeptical of a traditional worldview and convinced by modernity and rationality, but this stereotype is not uniformly accurate. Buddhist intellectuals became skeptical of the supernatural premises of religious teaching not simply because they were not satisfied with any teaching that should be demythologized in light of empirical phenomena. They wanted something more, something that motivated their religious commitment. At least for Buddhadāsa and his followers, it was *lokuttara dhamma*, the Buddhist teaching of transcendence, with which many of them had been unfamiliar, and had rediscovered in ancient scriptures.

(ii) Standardization of Monastic Education

Mongkut's reform was followed by the work of Prince Patriarch Wachirayan Warorot (1860–1921), a son of Mongkut, after Mongkut disrobed and ascended to the throne as King Rama IV.[15] Wachirayan played a significant role in expanding the reform of ecclesiastical education. In particular, Wachirayan's Pāli grammar book greatly facilitated the improvement of doctrinal understanding. Before he wrote his textbook, monks in Siam and the neighboring regions studied Pāli using a traditional grammar book, *Munkatchai* (Pāli: *Mūla Kaccāyana*). However, as Buddhadāsa recalled, the old textbook was too difficult, and after five or ten years of study, many could still not understand anything, but became "crazy" instead.[16] Wachirayan's reform unified all Buddhist monks within the boundaries of the state of Siam, and its impact even expanded beyond the border into Laos and Cambodia. According to a Laotian elder monk, the new grammar book was also introduced as an epoch-making innovation in Laos by monks who had studied in Bangkok.[17]

With the assistance of textbooks written by Wachirayan, the Mahamakut Buddhist Academy, which was established in 1893, became a center of ecclesiastical education for monks and novices in the Thammayut Order. From this academic center in Bangkok, monastic education in Buddhist doctrine expanded to the provinces through the basic doctrinal textbooks and the journal, *Thammachaksu* (*Eye of the Dhamma*). In 1894, this journal began publishing Thai translations of parts of the Pāli scriptures, as well as Wachirayan's and other famous monks' sermons.[18] Through these textbooks and the journal, Siamese Buddhists were able to acquire a sound scriptural understanding of Buddhism, replacing the previous vague understanding seen in local daily practice.

Scriptural knowledge became more accessible for monks and novices in the provinces, thanks to the introduction of the *nak tham* ecclesiastical examination. The examination was originally established to provide objective criteria for the identification of "novices who know the *dhamma*," who along with monks were exempted from military conscription, as determined by the Royal Edict on Military Conscription in 1905.[19] With amendments made by later Pāli scholars, Wachirayan's textbooks provided the syllabus for the *nak tham* examinations, which evolved into the third, second and first grades, in 1912, 1917, and 1921 respectively.[20] The examination became far more popular than was originally envisaged, not only among monks and novices, but also among lay Buddhists who wanted to learn the *dhamma*, the contents of which had been unfamiliar to them but which had always been respected as sacred. In 1929, a similar ecclesiastical examination for lay Buddhists, *thammasuksa*, was introduced to replace the questions on the *bhikkhu*'s 227 *vinaya* rules with questions on the eight lay precepts. This also became very popular. In order to promote Buddhist education for monks and novices, the Mahamakut Buddhist Academy spent an annual budget of 10,000 baht to support local teacher monks who taught *nak tham* with *nithayaphat*, or monastic salary for monks with official titles and duties.[21]

As a result, candidates for the *nak tham* examinations grew from 44,167 in 1931, to 50,922 in 1932, and 54,397 in 1933;[22] and those for the *thammasuksa* increased to 3,512 in 1931, 4,779 in 1932, and 6,525 in 1933. The applicants expanded into every province in Siam as well as to Phnom Penh in Cambodia. Since the *nak tham* examinations began, the number of applicants increased in number every year for 20 years, with yearly increases ranging from a few hundred to several thousand. Phra Maha Thongsup Charuwanno, who provided these statistics and who was then the director of the textbook bureau at the Mahamakut Buddhist Academy, observed that these numbers included a few novices who were attempting to escape from military service, but that most of the applicants genuinely wanted to study the *dhamma*.[23] Sanya Dhammasakdi, who was ordained in 1927, was deeply impressed by *Nawakowat* (one of the textbooks written by Prince Patriarch Wachirayan Warorot for the third grade *nak tham*), and called it *pramuan chiwit* (a compendium, or guidelines, for life).[24] Such popular enthusiasm for the study of basic Buddhist doctrines was an important feature of the early decades of the 20th century, and as will be seen below, Buddhadāsa was also enthusiastic about the study of *nak tham* textbooks.

Activities of Lay Buddhist Intellectuals

One of the most remarkable developments in the early 20th century was the vigorous involvement of lay Buddhist intellectuals in discussions of the *dhamma*. From the late 19th century onward, there were some non-royal intellectuals who through their publications expressed opinions, criticism and ideas for the reform of Thai society, politics and religion. K.S.R. Kulap[25] (1834–1913), Thianwan (a.k.a. T.W.S. Wannapho)[26] (1842–1915), and Narin Phasit[27] (1874–1950) were famous examples of these well-to-do commoner intellectuals. These thinkers based their opinions on their experience working for foreign and local trading firms, which had provided them with a good income. Through their work, they acquired extensive knowledge of the languages, societies, histories and cultures of other countries. In addition, their early experiences of ordination as novices and monks had provided them with a basic education. Their publications inspired young Buddhadāsa.

The activities of these lay Buddhist intellectuals included criticism of contemporary Buddhism in Thailand and attempts to reform it. In 1900, K.S.R. Kulap and his two sons produced a weekly journal in order "to provide 'alms of knowledge' to monks and poor people."[28] Thianwan, whose sermons were very popular among palace residents during his five years as a young monk, presented his critical analysis of Buddhist practice in his journal, *Thulawiphak Phochanakit*.[29] Buddhadāsa remarked that Thianwan was, like Prince Patriarch Wachirayan Warorot, an intellectual who interpreted the *dhamma* in a contemporary way in the late 19th century, and his *sati paññā* or wisdom should have been expanded among some groups of monks. However, Buddhadāsa continued, Thianwan had to resort to shocking the monks with his words, because the monks had not reached the level of knowledge of Thianwan.[30] Narin Phasit attempted a more explicit Buddhist reform movement, in combination with his political proposals and campaigns. In 1912, Narin established the Association of Buddhists (*Phutthaborisat Samakhom*), and published a journal, *Sara Tham* (*Essential Dhamma*), in which he severely criticized the inappropriate behavior of monks. Narin sought a common approach to the overcoming of suffering without excluding any Buddhists, ordained or non-ordained, male or female, and he also sought to restore the *bhikkhunī* ordination for Buddhist women, which had fallen out of practice in Theravāda Buddhism.[31] These progressive movements and speeches were led by lay Buddhist intellectuals who did not depend on the authority of the Saṅgha or on individual monks; those lay Buddhist intellectuals implied that most monks would not work for progress because they did not wish to jeopardize their comfortable lifestyles or take up rigorous ascetic practice.

Although the goodwill and higher purposes of these lay intellectuals gained a certain support, even from a few monks, their outspokenness against the existing religious order met with resistance. Yet no matter how shortlived these movements by non-elite lay intellectuals were, dissatisfaction with the current religious order and a demand for true Buddhism continued to exist in Thai society into the early 20th century. The number of less confrontational lay Buddhists from elite circles who wanted to demonstrate an ideal Buddhist practice, which was not always apparent in daily custom, continued to grow. Buddhadāsa identified as deeply perceptive four influential intellectuals: No. Mo. So., Khru Thep (also known as Chao Phraya Thammasakmontri), Prince Wan Waithayakon, and Luang Wichit Wathakan.[32] They all presented their views in depth from a critical point of view. Later on, the Buddhist Association of Thailand (established as *Phuttha-Tham Samakhom* in February 1934, renamed a few years later *Phuttha Samakhom haeng Prathet Thai*) and The Young Buddhist Association (*Yuwaphutthika Samakhom*, established in January 1949) became significant meeting places for lay Buddhists seeking Buddhist teachings from both ordained and lay teachers. Buddhadāsa was to become one of those teachers who responded to this new demand on the Buddhist establishment, which was unprecedented in the daily practice of lay Buddhist life.

Arrival of International Buddhist Movements in Thailand

Another important trend in the background of Buddhadāsa was the international Buddhist movements, especially the activities of the Mahā Bodhi Society led by Anagārika Dharmapāla[33] (1864–1933) from Sri Lanka. By the early 20th century, inspired by the activities of the Mahā Bodhi Society, there were a number of Buddhist journals published in English and distributed worldwide. Among the English journals, those which reached Buddhadāsa and his brother[34] in the south of Thailand included: *The Mahā Bodhi*, published in India from January 1892 onward; *Buddhist Annual of Ceylon* published in Sri Lanka from 1920; *The British Buddhist* published by the British Mahā Bodhi Society in England starting from 1926; and *The Young East* published by the International Buddhist Society in Japan from 1925.[35] The articles in these journals had at least two defining characteristics. First, there were many stories and reports on Westerners' conversion to Buddhism, and on activities of Buddhist associations and groups in Europe, America, and Asian countries. Second, the Western and Asian authors of the journal articles often discussed major concepts in Buddhism, such as *nibbāna*, *anattā* and the four noble truths, as well as the history of Buddhism in different local traditions. These Buddhist topics had to be explained philosophically and historically for new converts with a high level of education. The philosophical concepts and the teachings of other traditions of Buddhism were not necessarily familiar to the Buddhists in Asia. Those Asian intellectuals who could read and understand these English journals were driven intellectually to inquire more and more into the philosophy and history of their own religion, to which educated Westerners had converted, abandoning their native Christianity.

In fact, Siamese intellectuals especially should have felt pride and a degree of responsibility for this phenomenon, because their country, Siam, was given an honorable position in the international Buddhist movement in the early 20th century. In the British Mahā Bodhi Society,[36] of which Anagārika Dharmapāla and Mrs. Mary Foster were patrons and the Siamese ministers in London, Prince Wan Waithayakon[37] and Prince Damras Damrong Devakula[38] after him, were the presidents. After the deaths of Mrs. Foster in 1931 and of Dharmapāla in April 1933, the position of Society Patron was passed on to the then king of Siam, or King Prajadhipok.[39] Why was the honorary position in the international Buddhist society, which had originated in Sri Lanka and India, conferred on a Siamese monarch? An article introducing Prince Wan related the prestigious position of Siam as follows:

> Siam alone stands to-day as an ideal Buddhist State ruled by an enlightened Buddhist King whose government represents a unique combination of modern democratic methods with the principles of *Rajadharma* of bygone times.[40]

Among the colonized Asian Buddhist countries, Siam was the only country that maintained independence and rule by a Buddhist monarchy.

After it was demanded in June 1932 that King Prajadhipok accept the constitution and democratic government by the People's Party, the Mahā Bodhi Society in Calcutta sent a telegram to congratulate the King of Siam, who had accepted the demands "in a statesmanlike manner."[41] The new constitution of Siam was published in full in the September 1932 issue of the journal, *The Mahā Bodhi*.[42] The change in the Siamese regime to democracy under a Buddhist constitutional monarchy was viewed as an ideal model for Buddhists who sought independence from colonial rule. Although Siam was prestigious in the international community of Buddhist Asia, King Prajadhipok could not have been very happy to accept congratulatory messages regarding the change. The position of Patron of the British Mahā Bodhi Society suddenly became vacant in January–March 1934.[43] In January

1934, King Prajadhipok went to Europe for dental work and eye surgery, leaving Siam in despair at the dictatorial rule of the People's Party. Then, in March 1935, the King abdicated the throne; he died in May 1941.

Despite the fate of King Prajadhipok, Siamese Buddhist intellectuals who read those English journals felt a sense of pride in the Buddhism of their home country and how it had attracted educated Westerners.[44] Because of a sense of responsibility arising from this acclaim, together with the inspiring discussions of Buddhist philosophy in the international journals, Siamese intellectuals were determined to work for Buddhism of their country in order to present a good model for foreign Buddhists. The activity of Buddhadāsa and his brother was also inspired by these international Buddhist movements.[45]

Buddhism in Siam/Thailand was gradually shifting away from conventional local practice. Buddhist education was systematized and spread among Thai people through the pedagogical efforts of the Saṅgha. However, lay intellectuals were not satisfied with the existing state of monks' daily behavior and the ritualistic, incomprehensible sermons in Pāli. In journals, lay intellectuals expressed their critical insights into the world and life, and some even examined alternatives for reform. International Buddhist movements gave more incentive to the study of doctrine and to the achievement of ideal Buddhism so that Siam/Thailand could contribute to the world. Buddhadāsa's own thinking was developed in the wake of such trends in Buddhism in the early 20th century.

2. Buddhadāsa's Early Background

Chaiya, where Buddhadāsa was born and spent his ascetic life, is now one of the districts in the Surat Thai province, southern Thailand. It is a historic city located on the Gulf of Thailand coast near the famous island resort, Ko Samui. There are old Mahāyāna Buddhist ruins in this area, and Chaiya is thought to have been one of the centers of the Sri Vijaya Empire from the eighth to the 13th century. Over time, people from different ethnic and religious origins, including Chinese and Muslims, settled in this region. After the fall of the Sri Vijaya Empire, Muang Chaiya was the local base of Ayutthaya rather than Nakhon Si Thammarat, to which the area belonged.[46]

Although Chaiya is known for its Mahāyāna ruins, Theravāda Buddhism penetrated the area. When King Vajiravudh visited this area in 1915–1916, he was impressed by the elegant manner of the people who upheld *sīla dhamma* (morality) and practiced Buddhism. He gave a new

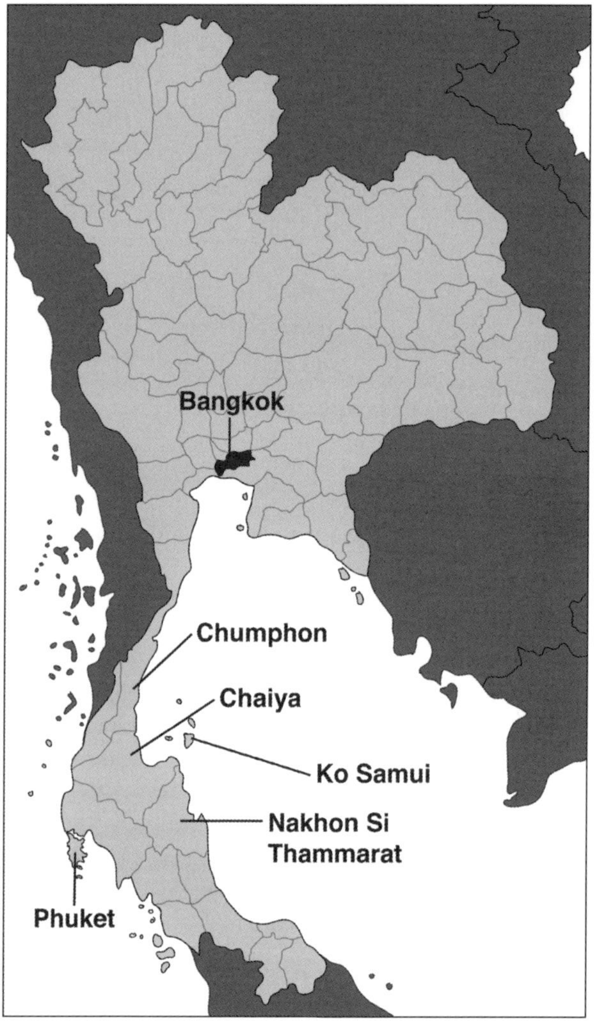

Map 1.1. Thailand

name to Monthon Chaiya: "Monthon Surat Thani" (The State of Elegant People).[47]

Most of the people in Chaiya were rice growers, and their high-quality rice traded at a good price in Bangkok, in cities in Southern Thailand and in Malaysia.[48] The city market area was a Chinese quarter, and over the generations, new migrants from China continued to assimilate by marrying Thais and local Chinese descendants.[49] In the early Rattanakosin period, some Muslim groups also migrated to Chaiya.[50]

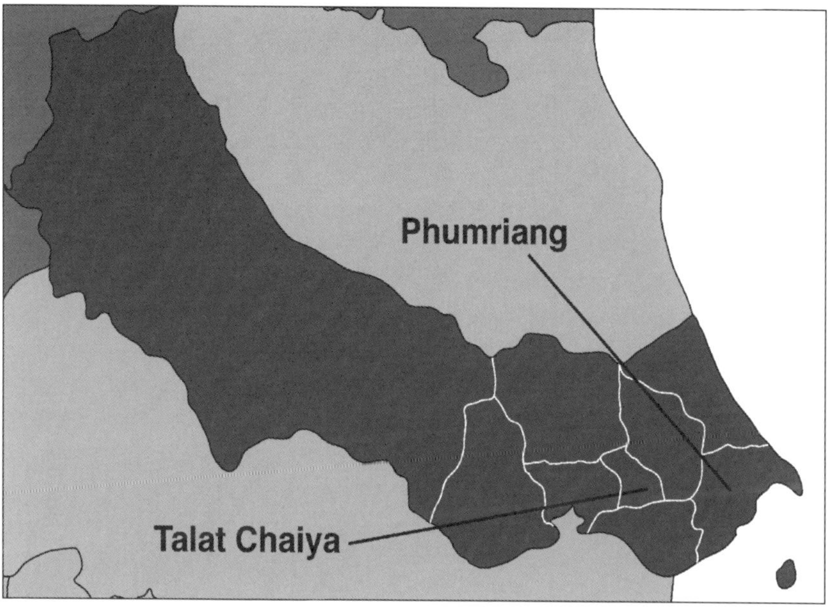

Map 1.2. Subdistricts in Chaiya District

Phumriang, which is located six kilometers east of the present Chaiya district office and only a kilometer from the coast, was a city inhabited by Chinese traders, Thai Buddhist artisan weavers of *bai lan* (palm leaf) hats, and the so-called white Muslim community engaged in fishing and was famous for its silk weaving.[51] Phumriang village was then the center of Muang Chaiya, and transport to and communication with the nation's capital, Bangkok, was not overtly difficult.[52] It was in this place that Buddhadāsa was born.

Buddhadāsa's Family

Buddhadāsa's father, Siang Phanit (1873?–1922), was among the second generation of Chinese migrants born in Phumriang. He dealt in rice, salt, and dried foods at his local shop, and was also a carpenter capable of building a ship. Buddhadāsa's mother, Khluan (1875–1948), was an ethnic Thai from the Tha Chang District. Buddhadāsa was born the first child of the family in 1906, and was named Nguam. He had a younger brother, Yikoei[53] (who later named himself Dhammadāsa[54]) (1909–2000), and a younger sister, Kimsoi (1911–1989).

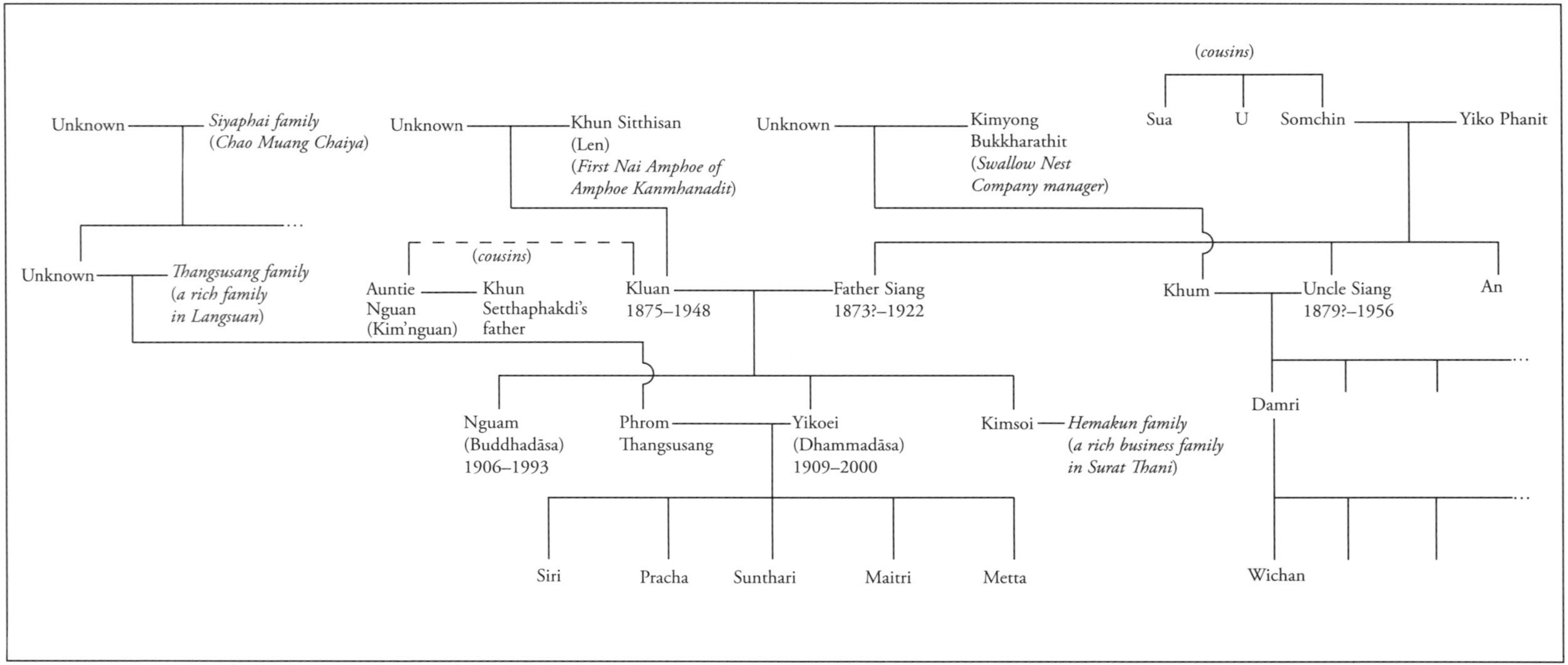

Figure 1.1. The family of Buddhadāsa

Buddhadāsa's father's family[55] originated in China, but was assimilated into Thai culture by marrying into local families and adopting Thai Buddhist culture. Buddhadāsa's grandfather, Kho Yiko (許二哥?), was born in Taechew and had lived for some time in Hokkien.[56] He came to Thailand as a brewer artisan, invited by a concession (*sampathan*) brewer in Chaiya. When King Rama VI ordered that all the Thai population have family names, he was given the Thai family name, Phanit, which means "trading," because his was the only family engaged in commerce in the region.[57] Yiko married a third-generation Chinese descendant, Somchin, and had three sons: Father Siang (Buddhadāsa's father), Uncle Siang[58] (1879?–1956), and An (?–?). It appears that Somchin's family had already been assimilated into local Thai culture, as her two cousins ordained Theravāda Buddhist monks throughout their lives. One of them, Luang Pho U, was the abbot of Wat Mai Phumriang, and both Buddhadāsa's father and uncle were for some time ordained.

Yiko died when Father Siang was 13 and Uncle Siang was seven, so the brothers were not able to learn Chinese from their father. Father Siang, who was skilled, especially at shipbuilding, could earn a good income in addition to the profits from his retail rice and dry goods business. While the youngest brother, An, died young, the second brother, Uncle Siang, had a great influence on Buddhadāsa and Dhammadāsa. Uncle Siang was an ordained novice from age seven to 20, and an ordained monk until the age of 32. He then became the manager of a trading ship sailing between Bangkok and Chumphon. Uncle Siang was the abbot of Wat Mai Phumriang for four years, and he studied in Bangkok for the last three years of his ordination in 1909–1911. While in Bangkok, Uncle Siang was in the position of *phra baidika*,[59] and secretary to the abbot of his temple, Wat Pathumkhongkha,[60] which indicates that his ability was recognized by his elders.

This background of Buddhadāsa's father's family suggests that their Chinese origin inclined them to commerce, but in a cultural and intellectual sense, Buddhadāsa's father's generation had already taken to Thai Buddhism rather than maintaining Chinese customs.[61] Buddhism played a very important role for Chinese migrants as a vehicle for assimilation into Thai culture. Other famous monks, such as Kittivuḍḍho Bhikkhu[62] and Sujīvo Bhikkhu (who later disrobed and took the name Suchip Punyanuphap),[63] have similar Chinese backgrounds.

On the other hand, according to Buddhadāsa, his mother, Khluan, a pure ethnic Thai, was a daughter of Khun Sitthisan (Leng), the first district governor (*nai amphoe*) of the Kanchanadit District[64] in old Muang Chaiya. Clearly, Khluan was from an influential local family. According to

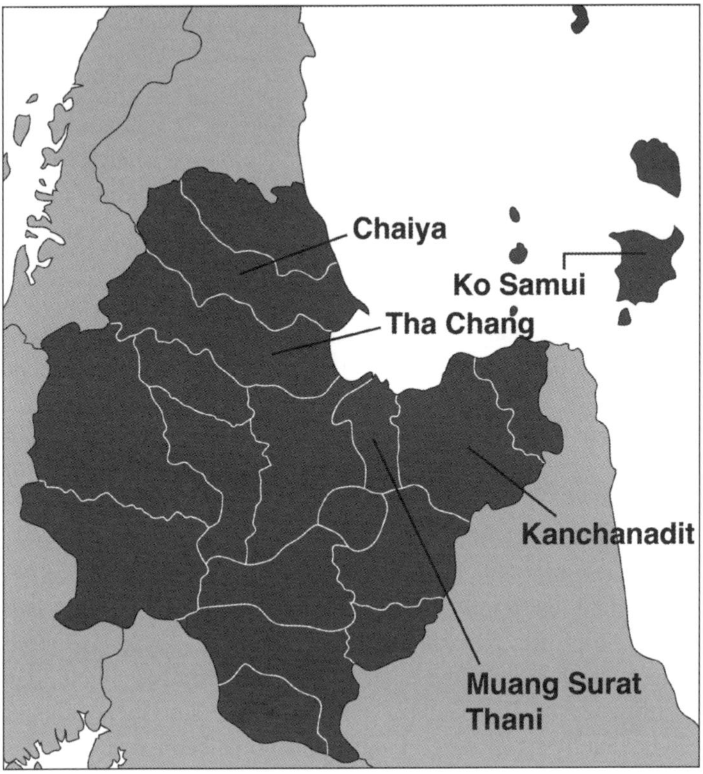

Map 1.3. Districts in Surat Thani Province

Dhammadāsa and his eldest son, Siri Phanit,[65] their shop in Chaiya, *Ran Chaiya Phanit* (Chaiya Trading Shop of the Phanit Family), was owned by Buddhadāsa's mother, and although she did not own much land, she had sufficient assets to lend money to people in town. She had a cousin, Kim'nguan, or Auntie Nguan (auntie for Buddhadāsa and Dhammadāsa), who became one of the wives of Phraya Patinanphumirak, the ninth president of the Chinese Chamber of Commerce and father of Khun Setthaphakdi, a prominent and prosperous Chinese merchant from the Surat Thani region.[66] Although Buddhadāsa's mother was rather thrifty in nature, their family fortune supported the non-profit religious propagation activities of Buddhadāsa and Dhammadāsa.

In Chaiya, Buddhadāsa's family was quite wealthy and well-respected (in Thai, *thana di*), though they were not the wealthiest in the town of Phumriang.[67] Their local status is suggested by the marriage partners of Dhammadāsa and the youngest sister, Kimsoi, who were both from local influential families. Dhammadāsa's wife was a granddaughter of the Siyaphai family, the old Chao Muang Chaiya. Kimsoi married into the Hemakun family, which was a very rich merchant family in Surat Thani. In the early 20th century, the Phanit family and other provincial noteworthies and upper-middle commoners produced children who were highly motivated intellectually to seek knowledge through the print media and to write about their ideas.

Early Intellectual Influence

Some members of Buddhadāsa's family took great delight in seeking knowledge.[68] The brothers, Father Siang and Uncle Siang, were close friends; Uncle Siang, who had more opportunities to learn new ideas through his monastic experience in Bangkok, kept his elder brother, who had never been to Bangkok in his life, well supplied with ideas and information. Uncle Siang always found new books in Bangkok, including the journals of Thianwan and K.S.R. Kulap, to which he subscribed, and he sent them to Father Siang. Through those collections of his father and uncle, Buddhadāsa also had a chance to read the works of these distinctive intellectuals. He also heard stories about those intellectuals from Uncle Siang, who had talked with them when he was in Bangkok.[69]

The former monk uncle, Uncle Siang, had a Buddhist intellectual foundation; he was able to read palm leaf writings in Pāli fluently, and could even write them. After disrobing, Uncle Siang developed an interest in the secular world in addition to his Buddhist education. He became a clerk of a company that dealt in swallow nests, one of the special products of Southern Thailand. He married a daughter of his company manager, who trusted him and recognized his ability, and settled in Chumphon. The eldest son of Uncle Siang reports that Uncle Siang had a good collection of books at home, including books on Buddhism, law, and medicine, some of which were printed by Dr. Bradley, who first introduced the printing press in Thailand.[70] Uncle Siang was a provincial businessman of Chinese descent, and a Buddhist intellectual with new secular knowledge. Uncle Siang was the most influential intellectual for the brothers, Buddhadāsa and Dhammadāsa, who lost their father when they were 16 and 13 respectively.

Buddhadāsa and Dhammadāsa had the same thirst for knowledge as their uncle. Their enthusiasm for intellectual inquiry and passion for discussion was the source of many of their later activities in Buddhism. As a result of their relatively advanced education, they investigated specialized areas of Buddhism.

According to one of the biographers of Buddhadāsa, one thing that Buddhadāsa inherited from his father and uncle (and which his brother did not) was the ability to write Thai poetry.[71] This ability enhanced the popularity of his preaching. Intellectual ability had to be supported by good rhetoric in order to be received widely. Buddhadāsa's works became far more popular than Dhammadāsa's, not only because of his ordained status, but also because of his power of expression.

3. Buddhadāsa and Dhammadāsa: The Brothers' Interest in Buddhism

Although Buddhadāsa[72] became more famous and respected as a monk, the development of his thoughts and activities was always supported by the intellectual partnership of his lay brother, Dhammadāsa.[73] They both became interested in Buddhism through separate, but similar, channels and experiences.

Buddhadāsa (1906–1993) was two years older than Dhammadāsa (1909–2000) according to the Thai calendar,[74] but Dhammadāsa went to school a year ahead of Buddhadāsa. At the age of eight, Buddhadāsa started his primary education, learning to read and write Thai, as a temple boy (*dek wat*) in his family temple, Wat Mai Phumriang. It seems that his interest in Buddhism was not noticed when he was a temple boy, since he expressed more interest in traditional medicine that the monks were practicing.[75] Buddhadāsa started his first grade of formal primary school at the age of 11, attended until Grade Three, and then moved on to secondary school.[76] On the other hand, Dhammadāsa started formal primary education at the age of seven, finished four years in primary school, and continued his studies in secondary school. When their father died in 1922, Buddhadāsa was in the third year of secondary school, and Dhammadāsa was in the fourth. The brothers seem to have become intellectually mature together.

Upon the death of their father, the elder brother Buddhadāsa became the manager of his mother's shop in Phumriang, while Dhammadāsa was ordained as a novice, with the merit incurred to be dedicated to their late father. Their worlds began to drift apart, but both found an interest in Buddhism in their respective places in society. Although Buddhadāsa was only 16 when his father died, he took full responsibility for the shop (which dealt with daily commodities, such as rice, dried foods, oils, and books), buying goods and selling and delivering them to customers. Buddhadāsa said that he enjoyed that business.[77] The most significant experience for Buddhadāsa during this time was the discussion of the *dhamma* in his shop front with local customers. An old man who worked at the provincial office liked to slip away from his work for an hour to talk about the *dhamma* at Buddhadāsa's shop, and people raised questions about the *dhamma* whenever he appeared. Most of the *dhamma* discussion members were old, while Buddhadāsa was still a young boy. He had to prepare for these discussions by means of the *nak tham* textbooks and other books on Buddhism that his father had collected at home, including those of Thianwan and K.S.R. Kulap. As a result of his study, Buddhadāsa was confident that his explanations were more correct than other people's, which were based purely on speculation. In 1925, when Buddhadāsa was 19, a *nak tham* school opened in Wat Photharam, Phumriang, and everyone was stimulated to talk about the *dhamma*.[78] Buddhadāsa's time as a lay Buddhist shopkeeper in a provincial town seems to have been the beginning of his interest in the *dhamma* and Buddhism.[79]

While Buddhadāsa was running the shop, Dhammadāsa continued his education as a novice in Surat Thani and found interest in Buddhism in his own circle. After several months of his novitiate at Wat Mai Phumriang, Dhammadāsa moved to Wat Traithammaram in Surat Thani and resumed his high school studies. In the temple in Surat, Dhammadāsa met a novice friend who was writing and circulating a newsletter on Buddhism within the temple. Dhammadāsa liked the "argumentative newspaper" (*nangsuphim thiang*), to which he also contributed. He continued pursuing Buddhism after disrobing, even during his further study in Grade Seven and Eight at Suan Kulap High School in Bangkok, and during his first year in the medical school preparatory course at Chulalongkorn University. Dhammadāsa became fluent in reading English through lessons given by Western teachers at the elite high school and university. He came across Buddhist journals in English, such as *The Young East* and *The Mahā Bodhi*, in the library of Chulalongkorn University, and he discovered Thai books and journals on Buddhism published in Bangkok, including *Suksa Thammada* (*Ordinary Education*).[80] Dhammadāsa cultivated his interests through lay Buddhist movements both in foreign countries and in Bangkok until he left school to take over the family business in place of his then ordained brother.

The education of Buddhadāsa and Dhammadāsa must be viewed in the context of that time. After his father's death, Buddhadāsa had to stop his formal education in the third year of secondary school in order to run the family's shop. According to the statistics of the Ministry of Public Instruction, in 1926, in all of Thailand, there were only 2,844 students enrolled in the third year of secondary school, among whom only 1,938 passed the final exam.[81] Dhammadāsa, after completing the sixth grade in secondary school in Surat Thani, completed Grade Seven and Eight in order to matriculate; as a result, he was among the elite of the country. According to similar statistics for the whole of Thailand, there were only 305 students enrolled in the eighth grade of secondary school, and among them only 72 passed the graduation exam.[82] Although Dhammadāsa had to stop his studies because of his brother's ordination, he was one of the few selected students of his time. The brothers' educational accomplishment should not be compared with the standards of the 21st century.

Buddhadāsa's Ordination and Monastic Education

In 1926, at the age of 20, the qualifying age for full ordination, Buddhadāsa became a monk, Phra Nguam Indapañño, at his family temple, Wat Mai Phumriang, which belongs to the Mahanikai Order. Buddhadāsa and his family followed the Thai tradition for Buddhist males to be ordained for three months before getting married, but Buddhadāsa never disrobed.[83] In his first two years as a monk at Wat Mai Phumriang, he voluntarily gave sermons[84] and wrote an internal newspaper.[85] These were the most basic methods for holding *dhamma* discussions in local corners of the Buddhist public sphere, as Dhammadāsa had experienced in Surat Thani.

Buddhadāsa's attitude toward the study of Buddhism became serious after he experienced the monastic life in Bangkok in his third year of ordination in 1928. After passing the third- and second-grade *nak tham* examinations in Phumriang, Buddhadāsa was persuaded by Uncle Siang to study in Bangkok at Wat Pathumkhongkha, the temple where Uncle Siang used to be *phra baidika*. Buddhadāsa was disappointed with the *vinaya* offences of Bangkok monks, whom he once thought of as excellent and *arahant*. After a few months' stay in Bangkok, Buddhadāsa felt like disrobing because he was about to start behaving like the other monks. Buddhadāsa returned home in Phumriang, but it was not an appropriate time for disrobing, so he spent time by himself, read books including foreign journals and the works of lay intellectuals that Dhammadāsa gave him, and he passed the first-grade *nak tham* at the end of the rains retreat.[86] The study was so engaging that he forgot about disrobing.

In 1930, during his fifth year of ordination, after his experience as a teacher at a *nak tham* school founded at Wat Phra Boromathat Chaiya by his wealthy aunt, Kim'nguan (Nguan) Setthaphakdi,[87] Buddhadāsa decided to study Pāli in Bangkok in order to investigate Buddhism more deeply. This time, Buddhadāsa ignored the transgressions of other Bangkok monks. He had private Pāli lessons with Phra Khru Chayaphiwat (Klan), who was a disciple of Uncle Siang while he was in robes. He studied English using Linguaphone records, and played with cameras and typewriters.[88] Buddhadāsa passed the foundation third level of the Pāli examination on the *Dhammapada* in 1930 without much difficulty, but he felt too tired to study the fourth level, which dealt with a very short section of the *Tipiṭaka*, the *Maṅgala Sutta*, and its extensive commentary, *Maṅgalatthadīpanī*, on which the teachers based their explanations. Buddhadāsa still expected to pass the fourth level, though he found it rather difficult to agree with the teachers and other students.[89] After he failed the fourth level of Pāli examination at the end of 1931, he decided to return home in Chaiya in order to start to follow a direction that he believed to be correct. In May 1932, Buddhadāsa went into seclusion in an abandoned temple, Suan Mokkhabalārāma, which was renovated as his place of *dhamma* practice.

Although Buddhadāsa's formal ecclesiastical education ceased at the third level of the Pāli examination, this did not mean that his scriptural studies remained at a basic level. Even before his study of Pāli in Bangkok, his philosophical understanding of Buddhism was advanced. The young Buddhadāsa's intellectual maturity was demonstrated in his sermon in 1930, *Buddhism at the Level of Unenlightened Ordinary People* (*Phra Phutthasasana Chan Phuthuchon*), which was published and distributed by his aunt, Kim'nguan Setthaphakdi, to inaugurate the opening of her new *nak tham* school, where Buddhadāsa taught for a year. It was at a time when Buddhist philosophy was not yet commonly understood by monks or well explained in books; the sermon very logically explained key Buddhist concepts, and is perhaps much less accessible than his later popular sermons.[90] Furthermore, Buddhadāsa studied Pāli by himself after he abandoned the ecclesiastical examinations. Buddhadāsa's early works, in which he translated and edited Pāli scriptures, such as *The Life of the Buddha in His Own Words* (*Phutthaprawat chak Phra Ot*), were highly respected even by *pariyatti* monks in Mahamakut Buddhist Academy. *The Life of the Buddha in His Own Words* was chosen as a sub-textbook.[91] Buddhadāsa was respected as a Pāli *pariyatti* scholar, and his academic standard cannot be judged by the level of his formal education.

Mutual Support of the Brothers on Their Different Paths

While Buddhadāsa as a monk pursued his study of Buddhism in the Pāli scriptures, his lay brother Dhammadāsa investigated Buddhism through foreign Buddhist journals in English. After his return home from Chulalongkorn University, Dhammadāsa met Sirisena, a Sinhalese traveler staying in Chaiya, and learned in detail about the work of Anagārika Dharmapāla and the Mahā Bodhi Society. Dhammadāsa became more interested in Buddhist movements around the world and he began subscribing to Buddhist journals in English such as *Mahā Bodhi*, *The British Buddhist*, and *Buddhist Annual of Ceylon*. Dhammadāsa gave some of those journals to Buddhadāsa to read, but Buddhadāsa said that he did not understand them very well.[92] Although Buddhadāsa studied English on his own, it seems that it was not until the mid-1940s that he was able to translate English works. English literature was Dhammadāsa's specialty thanks to his formal training. The brothers exchanged views and respected each other's knowledge, and Buddhadāsa's Pāli and Dhammadāsa's English complemented each other.[93]

Dhammadāsa started translating some of the English articles about Buddhism for publication in Thai newspapers, such as *Sri Krung*, *Daily Mail* (Thai: *Deli me*), and *Thai Khasem*, and after 1929, he started using his penname "Dhammadāsa," meaning a slave of the *dhamma*, instead of his given name, Yikoei.[94] Following his brother's lead, Buddhadāsa named himself "Buddhadāsa," which means a slave of the Buddha. Using that name "Buddhadāsa," he contributed some articles of religious criticism to the daily newspaper, *Krungthep Daily Mail* (*Krungthep Deli me*),[95] in the days before he established Suan Mokkh. Dhammadāsa was corresponding with news figures such as Narin Phasit (1874–1950)[96] and Phra Lokanatha (1897–1966),[97] an Italian *bhikkhu* whose world Buddhist mission project created a sensation in Thailand in 1933–1934. Buddhadāsa met these luminaries through Dhammadāsa; it appears that Dhammadāsa's interest in contemporary Buddhist movements was a stimulus for Buddhadāsa.

Being a monk, Buddhadāsa was more involved than Dhammadāsa in the monastic world. The books that impressed Buddhadāsa and which influenced him most were not only those of lay Buddhist thinkers, but also those of the Saṅgha's doctrinally most influential figure, Prince Patriarch Wachirayan Warorot. Buddhadāsa in fact collected all the works by Wachirayan, since an anthology of his works had not yet been published. Buddhadāsa said that he liked Wachirayan's style of writings, which

> ... had the principles of a *nak prat* [philosopher, a person with wisdom]. We can consider that he was a pioneer of modern/up-to-date interpretation of the *dhamma* (*phu bukboek kan-tikhwam thamma hai than samai*). He interpreted miracles comprehensively.[98]

Buddhadāsa felt that the reforms undertaken by Wachirayan had yielded significant progress. However, the problems of the Saṅgha being outdated could still be seen in conservative elder monks who did not see any necessity to catch up with the changing world. He said,

> The period of Somdet Phra Maha Samana Chao [i.e., Wachirayan] can be considered as a certain level of pioneering and moving toward quite a few further changes. However, there were few who continued it, who were as smart as him, or as capable as him. Thus, the reform did not go beyond inflexible rules, as far as he had established them. People were not brave enough to touch or change even a word. Problems existed like this in the circle of religion.[99]

Through this critical view of conservative monks, Buddhadāsa implied that his work was to make further progress based on the achievement of Wachirayan's reform.

When he looked at the harsh attacks on corrupt monks made by notable lay Buddhist activists, Buddhadāsa was rather skeptical, as were the elder monks in the Saṅgha and conservative circles.[100] For example, Dhammadāsa and some other lay members of the Dhammadāna Group supported Narin Phasit's critical campaign against the existing state of Buddhist practice and favored his plan to revive *bhikkhunī* ordination. On the other hand, Buddhadāsa considered Narin "half crazy, half intoxicated" (*khrung ba, khrung mao*), "seeking fame by complimenting the four Buddhist groups,"[101] which in the Thai Theravāda tradition had lost *bhikkhunī* out of the *bhikkhu* (ordained men), *bhikkhunī* (ordained women), *upāsaka* (laymen), and *upāsikā* (laywomen).

Also, Buddhadāsa was not as enthusiastic as Dhammadāsa was about Phra Lokanatha. Dhammadāsa was very excited about the news of Lokanatha's project of a Buddhist world missionary tour, which had been advertised in *The Mahā Bodhi Journal* and in both English and Thai journals along with related news and articles about Lokanatha.[102] On the other hand, Buddhadāsa did not agree to join Lokanatha's world *dhamma* mission to Bodhgaya, Jerusalem, and Rome. When Lokanatha was still at the peak of his popularity, Buddhadāsa wrote an article, "Why I Did Not Go with Lokanatha" under another pseudonym "Parien Dek" (A Boy with the Pāli Qualification) in a daily newspaper, *Prachathipatai* (24 November 1933).[103] Among the four reasons that Buddhadāsa pointed out for not going with Lokanatha, the first one seems to be the most important.[104] Buddhadāsa wrote that he was engaged in *pariyatti dhamma* or scriptural studies, but not much involved in *samana dhamma* (ascetic practice). It would be difficult to have solitude, which is appropriate and necessary for practicing *samana dhamma*, during a big campaign. Unlike his lay brother, who was excited by the dissemination of the Buddhist *dhamma* as something to be expanded,

Buddhadāsa, a monk, was more concerned with his own experience of the path to *arahantship* in order to teach other people about its nature.

In a similar vein, Buddhadāsa did not completely believe in or agree with the mission of Anagārika Dharmapāla which Dhammadāsa respected and took as a model for his own activities. Although Dhammadāsa translated Dharmapāla's writings and activities extensively to introduce them in Thailand, Buddhadāsa considered that though some of his works were good, some others were reckless (*ba bin*). In Buddhadāsa's view, the Dharmapāla's academic standard did not reach the ultimate level of the *dhamma*, and his spirituality was less than perfect. Buddhadāsa indicated that Dharmapāla still believed in rebirth just as common, uneducated people do, and pointed to the case of Dharmapāla striking the head of a Westerner who entered a temple *vihāra* without taking off his shoes. Buddhadāsa criticized Dharmapāla for being worldlier rather than religiously-oriented.[105] In fact, Dharmapāla was not well received by the Thai elite and wealthy classes when he came to Thailand on a fundraising trip for the purchase of historical Buddhist sites in India from landowners. Prince Damrong's analysis was that because Dharmapāla's attitude was hateful and critical of the destruction of Buddhism in India for the past 700 years, Thai people did not feel that they would receive merit from this Buddhist restoration, which instead might turn out to be merely an act of revenge based on *micchādiṭṭhi* (wrong views).[106] Buddhadāsa held an attitude closer to the common sense view of the Thai elite, although he appears to have favored protest and reformist campaigns.

The brothers both came to be strongly interested in Buddhism in their respective circles, but their ways of looking at things were not always the same, partly due to their differences in educational backgrounds (which gave them access to different languages), and in their ordination status. However, their different ordination status and roles proved necessary for the development of their activities: Suan Mokkh for *dhamma* practice, and the Dhammadāna Group for material and propagation support. Both lent support to the production of the journal, *Phutthasasana* (hereafter referred to as *Buddhism*).

4. Establishment of Suan Mokkh and the Dhammadāna Group

Buddhadāsa gave up his studies in Bangkok and returned to Phumriang in March 1932. Dhammadāsa's group found and renovated an abandoned temple, Wat Traphangchik, for Buddhadāsa's solitary ascetic practice. On 12 May 1932, Buddhadāsa entered the temple for *vipassanā* meditation, and named it Suan Mokkhabalārāma, which means "A Place Having Power for Liberation"; people call it by its shortened name, "Suan Mokkh."[107] In July 1932, the Dhammadāna Group, which consisted of ordinary town commoners of Chinese descent, came together as a group.[108] They opened a room for monks' sermons.

Buddhadāsa and Dhammadāsa asked their mother, Khluan, for seed money for their Buddhist activities. In June 1932, after the establishment of Suan Mokkh, their mother agreed to draw up a legal will to make the foundation fund of the Phanit family (*thun ton takun phanit*) using her savings of 6,368 baht.[109] This amount, called in their Thai dialect, *ngoen phuan phi* (literally "money of a ghost's friend"), was for the treatment of illness in old age and for making merit before death. Khluan had originally intended to build either a temple or a monastery hall with her personal savings in order to accumulate good merit for her future lives, a common action of old people in Thailand who were about to leave this world. The brothers persuaded their mother, saying that spending her money on the construction of a hut for monks and the publication of a journal would make more merit than building ten beautiful monastery halls. They explained that their way was more meritorious because some people would become clear about the teachings of the Buddha and some might become eager to practice the *dhamma* of the Buddha, while ten beautiful monastery halls would never give rise to such feelings.[110] Through the interest that they gained from their mother's fund, approximately 500 baht per year,[111] they could pay for the initial cost of supporting the monks at Suan Mokkh and publishing the journal, until their activities attracted sufficient support from other donors.

At first glance, it would appear that the brothers took traditional roles, one an ordained Buddhist, the other a lay Buddhist. Buddhadāsa, a monk, needed appropriate support for his religious practice. As an ordained monk, he had to avoid breaking his precepts through actions such as handling money, as he had seen monks do in the temple in Bangkok. His lay brother prepared ideal conditions for his retreat, and provided only the necessary food and basic survival materials for Buddhadāsa's pursuit of the *dhamma* that would lead him to religious attainment.[112] From the beginning, Buddhadāsa and the monks in Suan Mokkh received material support from the Dhammadāna Group, and the lay group received *dhamma* teaching from the ordained monks. This reciprocal relationship corresponds to the traditional exchange of *vatthu-dāna* (material offering) for *dhamma-dāna* (offering of the *dhamma*) between monks and laity.

However, it should be emphasized that Dhammadāsa and the Dhammadāna Group seldom expected to make merit for achieving a better state of being, as commonly believed among Thai Buddhists, through their support for Buddhadāsa and Suan Mokkh. Both Buddhadāsa and Dhammadāsa were interested in the Buddhist teaching for overcoming suffering, which ultimately leads to *nibbāna*. Dhammadāsa, who lived as a lay Buddhist, could not entirely devote himself to religious practice, but he trusted his ordained brother's seriousness to discover how the Buddha taught and practiced, and to actually follow the prescription of the classical scriptures.[113]

Buddhadāsa and Dhammadāsa carefully started their new project. When they began renovations of the abandoned temple for Buddhadāsa's retreat, they drew up a legal contract to rent the place from the government in order to obtain the legal rights to occupy the land.[114] Buddhadāsa also reported the purpose of his activities in Suan Mokkh to the chief monk of the Saṅgha's provincial administration (*chao khana changwat*).[115] Their prudence in preparation seemed to be partly a result of what they had learned from the experiments of Narin Phasit (1874–1950; who founded various religious reform groups before Buddhadāsa),[116] which were so controversial that the goodwill of his movement was difficult for the general public to credit.[117] Overall, in order to carry out a plan that they believed to be true and good, Buddhadāsa and the Dhammadāna Group took great care not to set themselves at odds with the public or the religious authorities. Although just as Narin, Buddhadāsa was also from a well-to-do commoner background, unlike Narin, it did not mean that Buddhadāsa and the Dhammadāna Group overtly challenged the status quo as representatives of the middle class confronting the authoritarian control of the absolute monarchy or the Saṅgha.

Coincidentally, in 1932, the same year that Buddhadāsa launched Suan Mokkh, the so-called Constitutional Revolution occurred on 24 June, when the People's Party demanded that King Prajadhipok sign a constitution that granted sovereignty for the people. Buddhadāsa commented on this coincidence as follows:

> Therefore, the calendar of Suan Mokkh is easiest to remember in a short phrase: "the same year of the change of political system". We consider this point as a sign of a new change in order to make things better to the utmost of our abilities.[118]

Despite its taking place at the same time as the Constitutional Revolution, for Buddhadāsa, the establishment of Suan Mokkh signaled a shift in his personal focus to a commitment to ascetic practice, rather than to a political or organizational reform of religion. He said,

> By reading Pāli scriptures published in *Thammachaksu* [in Pāli, *dhammacakkhu*; the oldest Buddhist journal in Thailand published by

> Mahamakut Buddhist Academy — note by Ito], at that time I knew what were good and right practices. I never intended it to be [a reform] for the nation and the state. It was rather a private attempt. This was because I felt that we could not do much more than just our own things, and also that other things which other people might be interested in were not very important.[119]

Even though Buddhadāsa and the Dhammadāna Group had nothing to do with this political change in Bangkok, the historical significance of the launch of Suan Mokkh was Buddhadāsa's reaffirmation of the accessibility to *nibbāna*. As a matter of fact, Buddhist intellectuals of his time tended not to consider the path to *nibbāna* as a realistic goal of their life. According to Buddhadāsa, Phra Khru Chayaphiwat, his Pāli teacher in Bangkok, considered *vipassanā* (the traditional Buddhist meditation method to attain *nibbāna*) to be outdated. Buddhadāsa explained his thinking at the beginning of Suan Mokkh as follows:

> If we speak in the aspect of doctrinal studies (*pariyatti*), it is not related to practice (*paṭipatti*). I thought that the works of Prince Patriarch Wachirayan Warorot were already good and sufficient. Although I didn't think of the ultimate end yet, I thought that I had to do something further ... In Bangkok everything was restricted; I could do nothing, so returned home to enter the forest. Honestly speaking, it was nothing serious; I just took my chances on it and moved on ahead. But, I had only one principle: that was, the restoration of Buddhist practice which had already disappeared. Therefore, from its inaugural issue up until today the journal *Buddhism* indicates on its front cover that there are three sections: promoting doctrinal studies, promoting practice, and propagating religion. These were the things to restore and reform with the small wisdom I had. The aspect of practice was the most difficult to attempt.[120]

The uniqueness of Buddhadāsa's reform was his unusual combination of doctrinal studies and meditation practice. He said, "I became a forest monk working on *Tipiṭaka*; I assume that there were few such monks."[121] Usually, forest monks specialized in meditation practice, but many of them did not have good knowledge of doctrines in the scriptures. On the other hand, usually urban monks extensively studied doctrines, but only a small number of them were interested in putting the theory of Buddhist doctrines into practice. Buddhadāsa borrowed Pāli volumes *Tipiṭaka* from another temple in his neighborhood, read them in his forest hut, and actually experimented with the practice just as the Buddha had taught.[122] He recalled the early days in Suan Mokkh:

> … it was like trying to do practice, at the same time, trying to do research [in scriptures]. Reading *Tipiṭaka*, I found a lot about meditation. Things became further clearer later. In the beginning I did it considering by researching. Thus, [the whole process] itself was meditation while considering and researching each day by day; because each item needed deep considerations. So, consideration of each item was equivalent to do *vipassanā.*[123]

Buddhadāsa's teaching of the *dhamma* was based on such personal experiences. He considered how each concept was relevant to reflection on his body and mind.[124] Therefore, Buddhadāsa's teaching was not mere philosophy of Buddhism; it was rather an advice to observe what was happening in one's mind by comparing to what the Buddhist theories say. Through Buddhadāsa's teaching, people were urged to understand, for instance, the nature of their suffering, the cause of suffering, the cessation of suffering, and the paths leading to the cessation of suffering. In other words, Buddhadāsa convinced many people that Buddhist teachings were actually practical means of overcoming suffering and reaching the transcendent state of *nibbāna*.

The extent of Buddhadāsa's influence went beyond those who stayed close to him in his territory. The propagation of the *dhamma* as realized by Buddhadāsa was conducted as the inseparable joint activity of Buddhadāsa in Suan Mokkh, and Dhammadāsa and the other lay supporters in the Dhammadāna Group. They propagated the *dhamma* through the print media and speeches. Publishing their journal *Buddhism* and setting up occasions for *dhamma* talks and lectures at gatherings were the most common activities of Suan Mokkh and of the Dhammadāna Group.

As a result of the inspirational value of the *dhamma* that Buddhadāsa delivered, later more people — both ordained and lay Buddhists, and even some non-Buddhists — came to learn religious practice from Buddhadāsa and support the delivery of his messages. Accordingly, Suan Mokkh had to be expanded. Suan Mokkh began in 1932 as a place for Buddhadāsa's solitude, but the old Suan Mokkh in Phumriang became too small for the increasing numbers of monks and lay people who came to do *dhamma* practice. So, in 1944, they moved to the present site in Chaiya, where many disciple monks and practitioners could be accommodated. Even after Buddhadāsa's death in 1993, Suan Mokkh had continued to be important as a place for serious Buddhists to observe their state of mind. The mission of Buddhadāsa and the Dhammadāna Group was different from the proselytizing tradition of Christian missionaries, who attempted to convert believers of other religions to Christianity. For Buddhadāsa and the

Dhammadāna Group, the propagation of the *dhamma* meant the promotion of a Buddhism that teaches the overcoming of suffering here and now, even to those who were born as Buddhists but never realized that they could better face their problems of life by practicing the teaching of Buddhism. Regardless of one's ordained status or religious identity, Buddhadāsa was a model teacher for those who wanted to overcome suffering by practicing the "true *dhamma*" that should replace popular Buddhist beliefs. Buddhadāsa's followers insisted that his teaching was the "true *dhamma*," the "authentic," "original" Buddhism; whereas prevailing Buddhist practices which involved fortunetelling or sales of magical items were not. It was this *dhamma* that Buddhadāsa urged the Buddhist movements of the new period to seek out and disseminate.

CHAPTER 2

Early Development of Buddhadāsa's Work and Growing Influence

After the establishment of Suan Mokkh in May 1932, Buddhadāsa committed himself fully to *dhamma* practice along with his study of the *Tipiṭaka* scriptures. However, his inner practice in the abandoned temple in the south Thailand forest never led to his total separation from secular society. Rather, it was an experiment to articulate his state of mind with reference to the scriptures and to explain how classical Buddhist theories of psychological transitions were relevant for people in the modern era to overcome their suffering. Buddhadāsa shared his interpretation and experience of the scriptures with his audiences through religious teaching activities he called "*dhamma* propagation" (in Thai, *kan-phoei-phrae tham/thamma*). Dhamma propagation was not just an important aspect of Buddhadāsa's individual work, but was also his significant contributions to the Buddhist public sphere, where people discussed the "authentic" teaching of Buddhism.

This chapter traces the early development of Buddhadāsa's *dhamma* propagation activities and identifies his position in and impact on the Buddhist public sphere in Thailand in the 1930s and 1940s. Rather than specifically examining the contents of Buddhadāsa's articles and *dhamma* lectures, the chapter looks more broadly at Buddhadāsa's work in the intellectual environment of his time, referring to the lives and work of those who lent their support to Buddhadāsa. By widening the focus and viewing Buddhadāsa together with other Thai Buddhists, I would like to lay out the characteristics of Buddhadāsa's thought as seen through the eyes of the people who lived in that society.

1. The Journal *Buddhism*

The propagation of the *dhamma* by Buddhadāsa and the Dhammadāna Group started with the journal *Buddhism* (in Thai, *Phutthasasana*). It has been published every three months since May 1933 under an official publication permit. In order to distribute this newly launched journal, the Dhammadāna Group advertised and had a free distribution coupon for *Buddhism* printed in the weekly journal, *Thai Khasem News*.[1] The first issue of *Buddhism* was distributed free to the 133 people who replied with the free coupon and a postage stamp, and the second issue was sent to 14 people who replied too late for the first distribution.[2]

Buddhism was circulated widely throughout Thailand, far beyond Buddhadāsa's native region, Chaiya in Southern Thailand. In the beginning, usually 1,000 copies of *Buddhism* were printed and distributed free.[3] The journal was mailed to subscribers, and payment was made by money order. In order to reduce the cost of sending money orders, the Dhammadāna Group contracted with shops in other provinces such as Bangkok, Nakhon Ratchasima, Nakhon Si Thammarat, Songkhla, and Phisanulok to become payment agents.[4] By November 1933, the provincial agent shops had expanded in number to seven, including shops in Roi Et and Chonburi. According to these shops' advertisements in *Buddhism*, most of the agents were provincial textbook shops which dealt in textbooks for schools and monasteries and in foreign language books. In Bangkok, the Mahamakut Buddhist Academy's bookshop also retailed the journal, but sales were few.

Apart from mail order subscribers, many copies of *Buddhism* were ordered by faithful wealthy readers, who would give copies away to propagate the *dhamma*. Copies of the journal were popularly given at cremations and other memorial ceremonies, as part of the merit-making custom in contemporary Thailand. Since journal publishing was a non-profit activity of the Dhammadāna Group, such big orders for distribution were an important contribution both in terms of finance and spreading the message.

Furthermore, *Buddhism* was read by Thai students in foreign countries such as Britain, India, China, and the Philippines,[5] as can be seen in some article contributors' backgrounds. It seems that Dhammadāsa sent some copies to the Mahā Bodhi Society in Calcutta so that Sāmaṇera Karuna Kusalasai, then a Thai novice who was studying in India, could read and contribute to *Buddhism*.[6] Also, it appears that Thai students abroad read copies of the journal sent by their families in Thailand. Famous intellectuals such as scientist and Marxist philosopher Samak Burawat, and socialist thinker Sot Kuramarohit were inspired by the journal and produced some works and articles related to Buddhism while they were in Britain and China, respectively.[7] This response from highly-educated Thai students abroad indicates the quality standard of the journal; it was worth reading overseas.

The distribution of the journal suggests the geographical range of circulation and readership. Even though Buddhadāsa and his brother were writing, editing and printing their articles in a provincial town in Southern Thailand, they could communicate with an intellectual audience all over the country and abroad through their journal. The journal itself was a very public space for Buddhist discussion, created for Thai intellectuals by Buddhadāsa and the Dhammadāna Group in 1933, a year after the Constitutional Revolution.

Buddhism is probably one of the best materials for the study of the development of Buddhadāsa's works, because series of his articles have been collected chronologically from the beginning. However, Buddhadāsa did not develop his original ideas alone and divorced from the discussions of other Buddhist intellectuals. Buddhadāsa's intellectual position becomes clear when his works in *Buddhism* are compared with the discussions of Buddhist intellectuals in which Buddhadāsa himself was involved. Buddhist journals, including Buddhadāsa's *Buddhism*, often recorded important Buddhist discussions that took place in the form of panel discussions and lecture gatherings; therefore, they are rich resources of modern Thai Buddhist thought for historians to study. An analysis of major Buddhist journals including *Buddhism* will reveal discussion trends in contemporary Thai Buddhism and the ideological position of Buddhadāsa.

Characteristics of Buddhism: Comparison with Thammachaksu

In Thailand, from 1933 to the end of the Second World War, apart from *Thalaengkan Khana Song*, the journal of the Saṅgha's official announcements, there were three major journals devoted to discussions of Buddhism. These three were the Mahamakut Buddhist Academy's *Thammachaksu* (*Eye of the Dhamma*), the Dhammadāna Group's *Buddhism*, and the Buddhist Association of Thailand's *Phuttha-tham* (*Buddha-dhamma*). Coincidentally, one of Thailand's oldest journals, *Thammachaksu*, was restarted in 1933, the same year *Buddhism* was launched, while *Phuttha-tham* was first published in 1934. In terms of intellectual standards, *Thammachaksu* and *Buddhism* were more important than *Phuttha-tham* until the end of the Second World War. Every book and journal had to reduce its print run toward the end of the war, because paper for publishing books was very expensive and difficult to obtain.

In order to examine the development of Buddhadāsa's thoughts in the context of his contemporary discussion of Buddhism, I will compare *Thammachaksu* and *Buddhism* until the late 1950s. From 1933, throughout the Second World War and to the 1950s, the two intellectual Buddhist journals, *Thammachaksu* and *Buddhism*, formed the major intellectual currents of Buddhism in Thailand. Although both offered opportunities for intellectual exchange and together they created a discussion space, they had their own distinctive characteristics in basic structure and content. *Thammachaksu* contained articles such as translations of Pāli scriptures into Thai, transcribed sermons, essays, prizewinning questions on the *dhamma*, and news. On the other hand, *Buddhism* was originally constructed of three sections: the general knowledge section, which included articles, prizewinning *dhamma* questions and news; the *Tipiṭaka* translation section; and the *dhamma* prac-tice promotion section.

The two journals each had a Pāli *Tipiṭaka* translation section, but their orientations were quite different. *Thammachaksu* intended to translate all the Pāli scriptures little by little through its series of translations,[8] whereas *Buddhism* selected special verses of wit and epigrams usually only found in the inaccessible world of Pāli. Buddhadāsa's selections included harsh criticism of monks' corrupt practices and incomplete insight into the *dhamma*; such criticism already existed within the Buddhist scriptures. Buddhadāsa drew attention to the *dhamma* in Pāli scriptures for non-Pāli specialist Buddhists to apply to their ordained or lay lives without having to read all the scriptural texts.

In *Thammachaksu*, there was little concern for the aspect of practice, while *Buddhism* provided a special section for it. For the section promoting *dhamma* practice, Buddhadāsa translated and edited verses from the Pāli *Tipiṭaka* which related to the practice for overcoming suffering to reach perfect sainthood. The early series in this section was named "Following the Footprints of the *Arahant*,"[9] and became one of the first recognized works of Buddhadāsa. Similarly, though it was published in the scripture translation section, Buddhadāsa wrote "The Life of the Buddha in His Own Words,"[10] in which he translated and edited the Buddha's life of *dhamma* practice toward enlightenment. Buddhadāsa did not have any particular meditation teacher, unlike the case of forest monks in Northeastern Thailand; instead, he examined the methods that were documented in the Pāli scriptures. Just like those academic monks who contributed to *Thammachaksu*, he started as a scholarly *pariyatti* monk by studying Pāli and reading as many books as he could find. However, what he found in the scriptural studies was the forest monk practice of *vipassanā* meditation, an element of Buddhism often ignored by the *pariyatti* monks in Bangkok. Buddhadāsa's special mission was to practice *vipassanā* meditation, following the descriptions in the scriptures. The academic monks in Mahamakut Buddhist Academy and the elders in the Saṅgha acknowledged that Buddhadāsa had revived the reputation of *vipassanā* meditation in Pāli scriptures.

Comparing the two journals' general articles and sermon sections, in the beginning, they had at least three distinctive characters. First, for a couple of years after *Thammachaksu* was re-launched in October 1933, the sermon section in *Thammachaksu* was dominated by transcribed sermons and sermons written by monks. Thus, in *Thammachaksu*, which was the creation of academic monks, there was little place for lay Buddhists to express their opinions. If any lay people were involved, they were likely to have been formerly ordained and to have passed ecclesiastical examinations. In this context, the overwhelming religious authority of the journal contributors was quite apparent; it is not surprising if ordinary lay Buddhists found the sacred sermons in a printed form to be somewhat distant from the thoughts and emotions they experienced in their daily lives. On the other hand, *Buddhism* was run by an ordained person, Buddhadāsa, and a layman, his brother, Dhammadāsa. Dhammadāsa expressed his excitement for and concerns about Buddhism as a lay Buddhist with a higher education in secular society. Dhammadāsa began a column called "For Young Students" in order to show how the teachings of Buddhism could help the life of young intellectuals who lived outside monasteries, and who were going to be leaders of the country. For example, Dhammadāsa argued that the four noble truths (suffering, the cause of suffering, the cessation of suffering, and the way to the cessation of suffering), are a necessary study for human beings, because other school subjects never teach this.[11] In this form of presentation, the journal *Buddhism* responded directly to the concerns of lay Buddhist intellectuals as well as those of the ordained.

The second distinctive character of *Buddhism* was its wealth of infomation about Buddhist movements in foreign countries, centered on the concerns of newly converted educated Western Buddhists. *Thammachaksu* only started reporting news in October 1936 and publishing translations of foreign language articles in September 1937. Although *Thammachaksu* introduced numerous translations of foreign authors' articles from *The Mahā Bodhi* journal after 1937, such translated articles became limited in number by the end of 1942. An opening announcement in the January 1942 issue suggests that there seemed to be some dissatisfaction from a conservative faction about including so many articles by foreigners.[12] On the other hand, *Buddhism* had competent translators of English articles, including Dhammadāsa in the first few years, Bhikkhu Bunchuan Khemaphirat, who had returned from Lokanatha's tour in India, and Sāmaṇera Karuna Kusalasai, who contributed from the Mahā Bodhi Society in Sarnath. These translated articles in *Buddhism* dealt with the expansion of Buddhism in Europe and America, the present situations in Buddhist countries around the world, and histories of Buddhism in ancient India and in Mahāyāna Buddhist countries.

Those translated articles in Thai journals inspired Thai Buddhists to catch up on the contemporary international movements and to take part in and contribute their tradition of Buddhism. These translators and other readers of foreign articles must have received some influence from Western Buddhists; however, it must not be ignored that on the other hand, Thai Buddhists were proud of their religion, which was becoming more accepted in the Western world, rather than acquiring in a humble way about any Western interpretation of Buddhism.[13] In 1934, the Dhammadāna Group introduced themselves in *The British Buddhist*, an international journal in English.[14] The Group expressed a wish to translate the works of Thai authors into English in order to contribute to the propagation of Buddhism in other countries; yet the wish does not appear to have been so easy to fulfill.

The third characteristic feature of *Buddhism* was its call for argumentative exchanges of different opinions on controversial issues. *Thammachaksu* also featured prizewinning questions on the *dhamma* as a method of encouraging the readers to participate in the journals and to present their different interpretations, but discussions in *Buddhism* were livelier.[15] Apart from the *dhamma* questions, *Buddhism* liked to discuss controversial issues, such as vegetarianism, which the Italian monk Lokanatha Bhikkhu brought to Thailand, and interpretations of the key Buddhist concept, *anattā* (non-self), which is difficult to realize in everyday experience. There were various responses from the readers: expressions of agreement, disagreement and uncertainty. Sometimes, the editors, Dhammadāsa and Buddhadāsa, wrote an open letter under their pseudonyms to raise questions and provoke responses from readers.

One such example was Dhammadāsa's open letter, under his pseudonym, A'ngun On,[16] worrying whether he should ordain as a monk or remain a layman. A'ngun On wrote that he was bored with the social incidents about which he wrote as a newspaper reporter, but he still wanted to depend on himself rather than on alms, to retain his freedom outside the 227 precepts, and was not sure whether monks might exploit fellow countrymen.[17] The two responses to A'ngun On were published in *Buddhism*. The first response, from Khaisaeng, pointed out that A'ngun On's desire to eat whatever he wanted without depending on alms was a *kāma taṇhā* (thirst after sensual pleasure), and defended the true way of living of a monk as thrifty enough not to disturb lay supporters' lives. Khaisaeng insisted that the renounced life is a method to achieve the overcoming of suffering, not a restriction of freedom, and recommended the Buddha's teachings for lay people who are satisfied with the worldly life.[18]

The other response was from Sot Kuramarohit, a communitarian socialist then studying in Beijing. Sot interpreted A'ngun On's question of whether to ordain or not was actually intended to criticize ordained monks' way of living as firstly selfish, lazy and exploitive of the general population, and secondly as contradicting human nature in matters such as not being allowed to marry. Sot defended the monks' way of living from his communitarian point of view that every occupation has some necessary function and that all occupations are of equal value in society. Sot understood that the duty of monks is to maintain the Buddha's teaching and succeed in keeping the 227 precepts. This duty of monks cannot be perfected by people such as physicians, politicians and soldiers who have other, worldly duties. For those who are willing to accept this duty, the 227 precepts were not something that deprives them of the freedom of human beings. Also, Sot argued that when monks do their duty by succeeding in Buddhism and teaching what they have achieved to other people, their role is fair participation in society, not exploitative.[19] These discussions in *Buddhism* indicate that the journal had reached a respectable standard, given that it was presenting a discussion of concern to educated Buddhists based on reasonable arguments.

Buddhism and Thammachaksu in the Post-Second World War Period

After the serious paper shortage eased at the end of the Second World War,[20] the discussions in both journals, *Thammachaksu* and *Buddhism*, became more active and developed a variety of issues. The changes in *Thammachaksu* were remarkable. Three new characteristics appeared in the post-war *Thammachaksu*: first, the return of translated articles from English-language Buddhist journals; second, more frequent participation of lay intellectuals; and third, growing concern about other Buddhist traditions and other religions' ideologies. *Thammachaksu* also started publishing English-language articles in order to transmit its ideas to foreign readers as well. These new trends reflected the substantial growth of lay Buddhist groups, such as the Buddhist Association of Thailand (*Phutthasamakhom haeng prathet thai*) and the Young Buddhist Association of Thailand

(*Yuwaphutthika samakhom haeng prathet thai*). The intellectual members of these lay Buddhist associations, including Samak Burawat and Sathian Phothinantha, introduced philosophical and historical discussions of Buddhism into the traditional Buddhist academia dominated by scripturally expert monks. The role of lay intellectuals, particularly those in the Young Buddhist Association, was supported by Sujīvo Bhikkhu (who later disrobed and took the name Suchip Punyanuphap), a young Pāli scholar monk in Mahamakut Buddhist University. The post-war period, especially at the end of the 1950s, was one of the most prosperous eras of *Thammachaksu*.

During this period, *Buddhism* also continued vigorous discussions which addressed the same intellectual trends appearing in *Thammachaksu*. Although *Buddhism* had already had two of those three elements, the ideas of foreign Buddhists' and lay people's participation from the beginning, *Buddhism* in the post-war period began to respond to discussions in *Thammachaksu*. For example, after *Thammachaksu* published a translation of Christmas Humphreys' article, "Twelve Principles of Buddhism" in June–October 1946,[21] Buddhadāsa published his translation of the same article in *Buddhism* in February 1947.[22] This translation was probably Buddhadāsa's first translation of a long English essay, which indicates the improvement in his English by then, and he became very famous for his beautiful Thai phrases that conveyed the original message better than the translation in *Thammachaksu*.[23]

More important was that *Thammachaksu* and *Buddhism* together created an intellectual enthusiasm about Mahāyāna Buddhist philosophy, especially Zen Buddhism, among Thai Buddhists whose interest in Buddhism had originated in the Pāli scriptures. In the popularity of Mahā-yāna Buddhism from the late 1940s, the ethnic Chinese in Thailand, especially Tan Mo Siang (陳慕禪) and Sathian Phothinantha, played significant roles. Tan Mo Siang was a Taechew-speaking Chinese Zen Buddhist lay preacher at the Institute for Studies of Chinese Buddhism (中華佛學研究社). Sathian Phothinantha, who was perfectly bilingual in Chinese and Thai, often translated Tan Mo Siang's sermons. Even though general ideas about the history of Mahāyāna Buddhism had been translated from English articles and published in *Buddhism* and to some extent in *Thammachaksu* before the end of the war, other philosophical ideas from Mahāyāna Buddhism would not have been so accessible without these two Chinese-Thai intellectuals.

Tan Mo Siang and Sathian were essential to Buddhadāsa's interest in and translation into Thai of an English text on Mahāyāna Buddhism. In February 1947, *Buddhism* published Buddhadāsa's public lecture at the Institute for Studies of Chinese Buddhism, entitled "Points that Should be Known about Different Schools of Buddhism."[24] This indicates Buddhadāsa's concern for Buddhist ecumenism. In the next issue, *Buddhism* started publishing Buddhadāsa's famous translations from English into Thai of the Zen Buddhist *Sutra of Wei Lang*.[25] For this translation, Buddhadāsa sought the advice of Tan Mo Siang about the original Chinese concepts of Zen Buddhism. It should be noted that Buddhadāsa was not at odds with his contemporary Thai Buddhist academic monks, although some scholars have indicated that a Mahāyāna element is a characteristic of Buddhadāsa's thought, which deviated from the orthodox Theravāda Buddhism of Thailand. On the contrary, one of the most orthodox Thai Buddhist academics in Mahamakut Buddhist University was also excited about the new knowledge of another school of thought in Buddhism. Sathian's articles, in particular his translations, were frequently published in *Thammachaksu*. Buddhadāsa said that his translations of English texts on Mahāyāna Buddhism were appreciated by everyone because they helped to illuminate a previously unknown philosophy.[26]

Aside from other traditions of Buddhism, Buddhadāsa and other Thai intellectual Buddhists expressed their interest of other religions, especially Hinduism, in the journals. In the 1930s, Thai people who were unaware of Indian cultural influence on ancient Thai culture received a strong impact from Swami Satyananda Puri, a Hindu philosopher who had migrated from India to Thailand. Swami Satyananda Puri was often invited to give public lectures, which were published in *Thammachaksu* until the early 1940s,[27] and Buddhadāsa also visited him for private lessons.[28] However, Swami's interpretation of Buddhism was not welcome to Thai Buddhists. In one of his speeches at Chulalongkorn University in 1932, entitled "The Origin of Buddhist Thought," Swami characterized Buddhism as a part of Hindu philosophy.[29] Some of the leading Thai Buddhist intellectuals, such as Prince Wan[30] and Phra Ratchathamnithet,[31] responded critically in Chulalongkorn University's journal, *Mahawitthayalai* (*University*).

Articles published in Buddhist journals in Thailand suggest that in the early 1940s, Thai Buddhists reacted antagonistically to adherents of Catholicism. Because of the nationalist sentiment during the Thai-French Indochinese conflict, both *Buddhism* and *Thammachaksu* became critical of Roman Catholicism as represented by French missionaries. Buddhadāsa seems to have been affected by this atmosphere, and he wrote a critical article on Roman Catholicism in *Buddhism*, "Answering Questions of a Catholic Father" in November 1939–February 1940.[32] An article with a similar reaction is found in *Thammachaksu* in February 1940.[33]

After the Second World War, Thai Buddhists revitalized their interest in the thoughts of other religions by comparing them with Buddhism. In Mahamakut Buddhist University, Sujīvo Bhikkhu started teaching "Comparative Religions" as a new subject for student monks around 1946. He published his lecture notes as a textbook in 1961.[34] Also, it seemed to be in the post-war period that Buddhadāsa, after his initial prejudice against Christianity, started to be interested in interreligious dialogue. In August 1948, *Buddhism* reprinted an article from the Catholic journal, *Udomphan*, which was edited by a promoter of interreligious dialogue, Father John Ulliana.[35] By the early 1960s, Buddhadāsa had developed intellectual associations with other religions, such as Catholicism through John Ulliana (mentioned above), and Islam through Haj Prayun Wathayanakun. *Buddhism* published an article by Prayun in 1953[36] and one by Buddhadāsa in 1963 on whether the *dhamma* is "God."[37]

Summarizing the development of Buddhadāsa's interest in the current of philosophical interests expressed in Thai Buddhist journals, he seems to have shared the concerns in the Buddhist public sphere at that time, rather than deviating from the Buddhist academics in the Mahamakut Buddhist University, the main contributors to the journal *Thammachaksu* up until the early 1950s, who worked closely with the Saṅgha administration during that time. However, Buddhadāsa and the academics at *Thammachaksu* gradually came to have differing interests around the late 1950s and early 1960s. From the period onward, Buddhadāsa further developed his understanding of the world and religion on the basis of Theravāda Buddhism through dialogues with other traditions of Buddhism and with other religions. On the other hand, during the 1960s and 1970s, in the midst of the Cold War period, *Thammachaksu* took up political incidents and variations of Buddhism, such as Buddhism in Vietnam as related by Kukrit Pramoj.[38] Those articles indicate that *Thammachaksu* became closer to such politicians as Kukrit, who was politically supportive of the status quo.

From the early 1950s, *Buddhism* became a less significant journal for discussions in the Buddhist public sphere, as did *Thammachaksu* in the late 1950s. In their place, *Phuttha-tham*, a journal of the Buddhist Association of Thailand, and *Phutthachak*, a journal of Mahachulalongkorn Buddhist University, became more substantial from the 1950s and the late 1960s respectively. During the Cold War period in the 1960s and 1970s, *Phutthachak* incor-porated social issues into Buddhism, especially after 1969, and around the same time, a group of socially engaged Buddhists, including Sulak Sivaraksa, started contributing to the journal.[39] *Buddhism* became smaller in terms of number of pages and had fewer articles from around the 1960s, but Buddhadāsa's lectures and interviews were very often published in *Phuttha-tham* and *Phutthachak* to represent a Buddhist point of view in the midst of social turmoil.

When the journal *Buddhism* became less significant, Buddhadāsa had already become an important figure in the Buddhist public sphere. Buddhadāsa said that *Buddhism*'s editors became tired of working on the journal, and it gradually took on the role of merely a newsletter of the Dhammadāna Group.[40] Buddhadāsa was invited to talk at the Buddhist Association of Thailand in Bangkok from 1940, and famous newspaper reporters summarized Buddhadāsa's lectures at the Buddhist Association in their papers. Also, the Suwichan Bookshop opened in Bangkok in 1953 specifically to publish and retail Buddhadāsa's books. In other words, by the early 1950s, these other places provided more opportunities than his journal for Buddhadāsa to propagate his understanding of the *dhamma* in the Buddhist public sphere in Thailand.

2. Buddhadāsa's Impacts on Monastic Intellectuals

In order to determine Buddhadāsa's impact and position in the Buddhist public sphere, it is important to identify those who gave support to his interpretation. As we shall see below, among the members of the Saṅgha, Buddhadāsa and his journal *Buddhism* received positive responses, particularly from intellectual elders and young progressive monks and novices who had had monastic experience outside Thailand. More than simple generalizations, this section explores the personal background of those monastic intellectuals and their meetings with Buddhadāsa's teaching. The details of their association with Buddhadāsa can reveal the reality of the people who revitalized Thai Buddhism together with him.

Saṅgha Elders and Academic Monks

From the 1930s to the late 1940s, Buddhadāsa was given a number of honors by elder Thammayut monks. One of the most supportive elders was Somdet Phra Phutthakhosachan (Charoen Yanawaro, 1872–1951) at Wat Thepsirin. Charoen was born in the Chonburi province and studied Thai script at Wat Khao Bang Sai, the temple of Chao Khun Chonlathopmakhunnamuni (Punnako Phut). The abbot of this Thammayut temple had good connections with King Mongkut and King Chulalongkorn.[41] When Charoen ordained as a novice and studied higher *pariyatti dhamma* (scriptural studies), he was introduced to a school at Wat Ratchabophit, whose principal also had connections with a prince.[42] After he ordained as a monk in 1902, Charoen came in first at every level of the Pāli ecclesiastical examination at Mahamakut Buddhist Academy. Charoen's ability was recognized by Prince Patriarch Wachirayan Warorot, and he was appointed to the Pāli school at Wat Thepsirin. In 1908, at the age of 28, he was also appointed director of education of Monthon Prachinburi, and in January 1909, he was appointed abbot of Wat Thepsirin.[43] After that, he held a number of positions in which he was responsible for ecclesiastical education and examinations, as well as for ecclesiastical administration. He was highly respected for his devotion to duty and thriftiness, and his sermons at Wat Thepsirin were very popular among well-educated lay Buddhists in Bangkok.[44] Among elder monks in the Saṅgha, he was known as the most progressive and the best acquainted with Westerners.[45] In January 1932, he was elected chairperson of the Elders' Council, and was acting Supreme Patriarch until 1938.[46]

In June 1937, while Charoen was the acting Supreme Patriarch, Buddhadāsa had the honor to receive a visit from him and have him stay overnight at Suan Mokkh. Charoen visited them after an inspection trip to the Southern provinces. Buddhadāsa went to welcome him at the Surat Thani station and accompanied him to Chaiya station. Over 70 monks and novices, 52 students at the Phuttha Nikhom high school, of which Dhammadāsa was the principal, and many more people in the region turned out to welcome Charoen. Charoen gave copies of his books to some people, and gave a pamphlet about meditation to each person. Even though his leg was not in good shape, he took two hours to walk all the way the five or six kilometers from the station to Suan Mokkh. Charoen gave a sermon for two hours, and listeners filled the temple premises. Charoen gave several sets of his own printed *dhamma* sermons, poems and Chinese sermons to Suan Mokkh and Dhammadāna Group, and talked with Buddhadāsa in the evening and the following morning. Buddhadāsa wrote that through their talk on practice, scriptural study, and translation, he learned countless new things. He had the impression that Somdet Charoen strictly adhered to the precepts just like a newly ordained monk who had entered the order yesterday.[47] Charoen's visit was only five years after the establishment of Suan Mokkh and in Buddhadāsa's 11th year as a monk. Considering their difference in age and status in the Saṅgha, this was a tremendous honor for Buddhadāsa.

After Charoen's first visit, Buddhadāsa recalled that Charoen had assisted with funds for Dhammadāna Group's publications, but he had never given special support to Buddhadāsa's promotion to ecclesiastical titles or ranks. Every time Buddhadāsa went to Bangkok, he visited Charoen at Wat Thepsirin. Charoen gave Buddhadāsa the honor of conversing in his private room. In their talks, Charoen told Buddhadāsa that it was too early to teach people about *anattā* (non-self), but according to Buddhadāsa, he liked to talk to Buddhadāsa about hidden *dhamma* as he understood it. Charoen expected Buddhadāsa to propagate his ideas of the *dhamma* because Buddhadāsa was able to express things very clearly. Buddhadāsa sometimes wrote about Charoen's unusual interpretations in his journal, and was even criticized by other elder monks. Buddhadāsa did not always agree with Charoen, but these were no serious difficulties. He never argued with Charoen. Charoen called Buddhadāsa "Maha Nguam, he who fits with my character."[48]

Charoen's personal background suggests that he worked to promote Wachirayan's reform of ecclesiastical education. Buddhadāsa was also inspired by Wachirayan's textbooks and sermons as being innovative for the new era. Based on the common ground of basic doctrinal understanding, which was standardized by the uniform textbooks and examinations, both Charoen and Buddhadāsa were pursuing religion at deeper levels. From the point of view of a Saṅgha elder such as Charoen, Buddhadāsa's interpretation was not perceived as "deviant" (*diarathi*), as his opponents later called him, but rather as a good attempt. Beyond the level of the standard formulae, there was room for exploration. At this level, people had freedom of individual interpretation, and their opinions did not have to coincide on every point. Charoen, as a high-level elder of the Saṅgha, was seldom overtly criticized, while Buddhadāsa, who carried out individual activities in his province, was more open to public discussion of his ideas. Buddhadāsa was always ready to face up to disagreements from the Buddhist public sphere, in which people could express their own understandings, which differed from the standard formulae of the modern ecclesiastical education system.

Buddhadāsa also had intellectual exchanges with academic monks at Mahamakut Buddhist Academy, then the most advanced academic institute for Buddhism in Siam. In 1937, the Academy adopted Buddhadāsa's work, *The Life of the Buddha in His Own Words*, as a textbook for the Academy's students.[49] Phra Maha Thongsup (Suphamak), the head of the textbook bureau of the Academy, was a good academic friend of Buddhadāsa. Buddhadāsa said that they probably knew each other through the journal, *Buddhism*. Buddhadāsa bought an extra copy of *Communism* in the Home Library series for Thongsup to read. He explained that because communism was then well known as an enemy of Buddhism, they should have some knowledge of it, and he wanted to know what Thongsup would think.[50]

Apart from their intellectual communication, Buddhadāsa was introduced through Thongsup to another elder monk in the Saṅgha, Somdet Phra Wachirayanawong, the Supreme Patriarch and the chair of the committee of Mahamakut Buddhist Academy residing at Wat Bowonniwet. Wachirayanawong often visited the textbook bureau at Mahamakut in the evening to talk with monks working there. Thongsup spoke to Wachirayanawong about Suan Mokkh before Buddhadāsa's meeting with him. When Buddhadāsa was accused of being a "communist" by Phra Thipparinya, Wachirayanawong did not take the matter seriously, but said instead, "I would like to stay with you at Suan Mokkh. Here it is too busy."[51] At the suggestion of Thongsup, Wachirayanawong even bought the complete set of the *Tipiṭaka* for Suan Mokkh, because up to then, Buddhadāsa could only afford to buy 20 volumes of it, and he had to borrow the rest from Wat Boromathat Chaiya, a noted historical temple in Chaiya.[52]

In Buddhadāsa's biography, no episode is found of troubles with Saṅgha elders about his own doctrinal interpretations. At the beginning of his activities, these elder Thammayut monks were supportive of Buddhadāsa. Another Thammayut elder, Phra Sasanasophon (Plot) at Wat Rachathiwat, also defended Buddhadāsa from Phra Thipparinya's accusation, and assisted in Buddhadāsa's promotion to ecclesiastical titles and administrational appointments, such as to the head of the Propagation Unit (*Ongkan phoeiphae*) of the Surat Thani province, and of the fifth region, under the 1941 Saṅgha Act.[53] Buddhadāsa also had a good relationship with an elder in the Mahanikai Order, Phra Phimolatham (Aat) at Wat Mahathat, who gave him the honor of speaking at the sixth council in Burma as a representative of the Thai Saṅgha. Buddhadāsa's ability was recognized by the elders in the Saṅgha. Buddhadāsa's originality of interpretation was seen as rather controversial, not by the Saṅgha elders, but by other participants in the Buddhist public sphere, which became increasingly active from the 1930s to the middle of the century.

Progressive Monks and Novices

Aside from the monastic elites of the Thai Saṅgha, Buddhadāsa's interpretation of the *dhamma* was welcomed by young progressive monks and novices, especially those who followed the Buddhist world mission led by the Italian monk, Phra Lokanatha, in the early 1930s. As indicated in Chapter 1, Buddhadāsa was critical of Lokanatha's mission, but Buddhadāsa's original approach to search for the *dhamma* attracted young Buddhists who were inspired by Lokanatha's grand attempts.

At the beginning, Lokanatha's initiative was perceived as honorable work for the religion and was supported by many Thai people of high status, including King Prajadhipok and important government officials connected to the People's Party. Lokanatha called his members "lion-hearted *bhikkhus* and *sāmaṇeras*" as they dedicated themselves to the propagation of Buddhism in Bodhgaya, Jerusalem, and Rome. But the group also included those who were simply interested in traveling all over the world.[54] In the face of difficulties encountered on the way from Northern Thailand to Burma, through Tak, Mae Sot, and up to Yangon, Lokanatha soon lost control of the more than 100 followers of his idealistic project. When they went through the jungle, quite a few members either became ill or dropped out even before leaving the territory of Siam. In May 1934, when the group arrived in Yangon, Burmese people told them that in the previous year, Lokanatha took about 300 Burmese monks and novices on a very difficult journey to India, where a number of them died. Therefore, only a few Burmese people respected and supported Lokanatha and his Thai followers. Most Thai monks abandoned Lokanatha to return to Thailand, and only about ten young novices remained to continue the journey in India.[55] Among the monks who left Lokanatha in Yangon, there were two future co-workers of Buddhadāsa's *dhamma* propagation activities, Phra Pan Padumuttaro (known as Paññānanda Bhikkhu; 1911–2007) and Phra Bunchuan Khemaphirat (1907–1988). On the other hand, among those who followed Lokanatha, there was Sāmaṇera Karuna Kusalasai, who remained in India and corresponded with Buddhadāsa in Siam.

Ten monks from the South, including Pan and Bunchuan, went ahead of the main group, and Lokanatha sent a telegram to someone in the town where they were heading. After leaving Bangkok, they practiced real *dhutaṅga* (ascetic practice), which included sleeping only in the open air, sometimes in a graveyard, and keeping a vegetarian diet. They even gave sermons in English for Burmese people, because as a schoolteacher, Bunchuan knew English, and Pan had learned it in his secondary school, which was unusual in Siam at that time.[56] This was a very adventurous experience for them. However, when Lokanatha lost control of nearly 100 newly ordained, uneducated monks who started fighting each other because of the fatigue of the journey, he accused the ten monks from the South of splitting from the group. After the splitting of the group in Yangon, Pan returned to Siam, and Bunchuan went to India by himself.[57]

Although in the beginning, those monks were admired for their aspirations, when the members returned from Burma, Thai people were disappointed by Lokanatha's unsuccessful mission. Abbots of temples in Bangkok even rejected the returnees.[58] At the suggestion of a friend, Pan went south to Songkhla province, where he gained tremendous popularity as an excellent preacher of the *dhamma*. It was in Songkhla that Pan first read Buddhadāsa's journal, *Buddhism*. The biographer of Pan wrote:

> Most articles [in *Buddhism*] were the works of Venerable Buddhadāsa. He encouraged and stimulated readers to feel like doing *dhamma* practice. He [Pan] read [the journal] and felt very satisfied with it. He thought, "Ah, Venerable Buddhadāsa should have been in the group of Phra Lokanatha."[59]

After the splitting of Lokanatha's group, Bunchuan went on to stay in India for two years. There, he also read the journal *Buddhism*, and in May 1936, he started contributing many articles and translations from English journals.[60] Because of his foreign experience and his ability to translate English, his contributions brought previously unknown information to Thai Buddhist readers, and enriched the discussions in the journal. Bunchuan was given a special introduction in the issue in August 1936 by the journal editor, Dhammadāsa.[61]

Returning from India in 1936, Bunchuan asked Pan to spend the rains retreat at Suan Mokkh. In that year, there were only four monks and one novice staying at Suan Mokkh. They saw that Buddhadāsa was writing *Following the Footprints of Arahant* by translating into Thai Pāli scriptures that had appeared as a series of articles in *Buddhism*. In the evening, they discussed the *dhamma* in all aspects, including scriptural studies, practice, and propagation. According to Pan's biographer, Bunchuan often expressed disagreement and argued with Buddhadāsa, but Buddhadāsa explained his views and gave his reasons. Pan, who was still younger than Bunchuan and Buddhadāsa, listened rather quietly, and gained considerable insight from these discussions. After the rains retreat, Buddhadāsa recommended that Pan study Pāli in Bangkok in order to work further for Buddhism.[62]

Although Bunchuan and Pan never had another chance to spend a rains retreat with Buddhadāsa in Suan Mokkh, they continued to share ideas and cooperate with each other. Bunchuan later became involved in the Saṅgha administration, was appointed to the head of the Chumphon province ecclesiastical division, and was given the title Phra Ratchayanakwi. Pan became known as Paññānanda Bhikkhu for his sermons on the *dhamma*. At the cremation of Bunchuan, Buddhadāsa commented on the relationship between the three:

> We say that the three of us are brothers. Venerable Bunchuan, Venerable Paññānanda and I called each other three brothers, because we have the same purpose in life.[63]

Among the members of Lokanatha's mission, there was another who was referred to by Buddhadāsa as his "brother in the *dhamma*." This was Sāmaṇera Karuna Kusalasai (1920–2009). Karuna was just turning 14 when Lokanatha's group came to his town in Nakhon Sawan province. Because he was an orphan, Karuna thought that this tour would give him a better chance for an education abroad. In February 1934, he was ordained as a novice by Lokanatha and joined the world mission.[64]

When the group split up in Yangon, Karuna, along with about ten novices, followed Lokanatha to India. Lokanatha took them to Almora, a town in the Indian Himalayas, where Dr. Jina, a Burmese physician and disciple monk of Lokanatha, was doing *dhamma* practice. Lokanatha left the Thai monks with Dr. Jina and went to Sri Lanka to organize Sinhalese monks and novices to join his world mission. In the winter, the group had to move to a warmer place. On their way to Sarnath, they visited the Buddhist holy places of Lumbini and Kusinara. During that journey, they had to face difficulties with wild animals and malaria. After the group's leader Dr. Jina became seriously ill and was taken back to Burma by his family, most of the remaining Thai disciples of Lokanatha also decided to return to Siam. Karuna was the only one who had to stay at the Mahā Bodhi Society in Sarnath, because he was seriously ill with malaria. When he had recovered, the secretary-general of the Mahā Bodhi Society allowed him to study under their novice education program for the world Buddhist mission.[65]

In India, Karuna had an unusual opportunity for Buddhist education as a Thai novice. From 1935 to 1939, Karuna studied together with Sinhalese monks and novices at the Mahā Bodhi Society in Sarnath. He learned Hindi and English from an Indian teacher with the assistance of a pocketbook edition of McFarland's English-Thai Dictionary, and he also learned Pāli using Sinhalese script. His study of Hindi was assisted by Dr. Bhadanta Ananda Kausalyayana, a famous Indian *bhikkhu* who was propagating Buddhism in Europe. After two years of study, Karuna took first place in all India in the Hindi examinations, and he was able to write articles in Hindi journals. In 1938, his Hindi was evaluated as equivalent to that of a high school graduate. He also studied English through a correspondence course from Bennett College in England, and after four years, he received a diploma in English, equivalent to the London Matriculation or Senior Cambridge level. He gave up studying Pāli in Sinhalese script having achieved only the elementary level, because he knew that he would be able to study Pāli in Thailand. Instead, he started to learn Sanskrit, which is important for Thai literature and culture, but which was difficult to study in Thailand. From 1940, Karuna continued his study in Vishavabharati Shantiniketan

University, which was founded by Rabindranath Tagore. He was majoring in Indology, and studied Sanskrit with Pandit Hazari Prasad Dwivedi.[66] The knowledge Karuna acquired in India was, for most Thai Buddhists at the time, very interesting and almost inaccessible.

Moreover, before he left Thailand with Lokanatha, Karuna had already completed the third year of secondary school, so he was able to translate his new knowledge into Thai. When he was in the Mahā Bodhi Society at Sarnath, he found two Buddhist journals there, *Buddhism* and *Thammachaksu*, which had been sent to the Mahā Bodhi Society as a companion organization working for the propagation of the *dhamma*. Karuna discovered an interest in the "modern" Buddhism that *Buddhism* introduced, so in early 1936, he sent a letter to the Dhammadāna Group together with some English books that the Mahā Bodhi Society had published, as well as some writings by Phra Lokanatha, and postcards of the Buddhist sites in India.[67] Correspondence between Buddhadāsa and Karuna began in this way.

Under the pseudonym, "A Thai Sāmaṇera in Sarnath," Karuna contributed 11 articles to Buddhadāsa's journal *Buddhism* between February 1936 and February 1942.[68] These articles by Karuna included up-to-date news about Buddhist movements in India, such as that of Dr. Ambedkar, and translations of both English and Hindi articles about the history of Buddhism and Buddhism in other traditions. Karuna not only enriched Buddhadāsa's journal with news and information, but also sent Buddhadāsa English books available in India and connected him to important Indian monks such as Ananda Kausalyayana and Rahula. Karuna said that sometimes Buddhadāsa asked Karuna to seek advice from Ananda on good books about certain Buddhist topics. Karuna bought the books that Ananda recommended, and sent them to Buddhadāsa.[69] Karuna helped Buddhadāsa to keep up with international movements and scholarship.

By the same token, Buddhadāsa's advice and encouragement were very supportive for Karuna, who was an orphan and a Thai novice alone in India. Buddhadāsa himself also studied Sanskrit and Indian philosophy with Swami Satyananda Puri, a Hindu scholar who settled in Siam and often gave lectures in Thai, but he encouraged Karuna to revive Sanskrit in Siam and to write a Hindi language textbook for Thais. Buddhadāsa also sent good Thai books to Karuna, and informed him of the current situation of Buddhism in Siam, such as Luang Wichit's nationalistic thoughts and the conflict between Thammayut and Mahanikai Orders. Buddhadāsa attempted to share ideas on contemporary Thai Buddhism with Karuna, whom he regarded as a co-worker for the same objective.[70]

Karuna was introduced by Buddhadāsa to a contact person on the editorial board of *Thammachaksu*, to which he contributed four articles between May and October 1939.[71] He also wrote a number of short reports about Buddhist and other movements in India for a Thai daily newspaper *Prachachat*, of which Kulap Saipradit and Malai Chupinit were the editors. He received copies of the newspapers in return. Karuna brought new knowledge from India to the intellectual Buddhist community of Siam.

Unfortunately, Karuna had to terminate these activities because of the outbreak of the Second World War. As an ally of Japan, Siam declared war against Britain and the United States on 25 January 1942. On 8 February, Karuna was arrested and sent to a concentration camp as a citizen of an enemy nation of India's suzerain state, Britain.[72] Although the war interrupted the exchange between Karuna and Buddhadāsa, their correspondence in all likelihood contributed to the development of Buddhadāsa's understandings and to his own thoughts on Buddhism.

3. Buddhadāsa's Impact on Lay Elite Intellectuals

Buddhadāsa's *dhamma* propagation never targeted ordained Buddhists alone. Buddhadāsa worked closely with lay people, such as his brother Dhammadāsa, to spread the same *dhamma* to both ordained and lay people. Lay Buddhist readers of *Buddhism* responded well, as did monastic readers. Soon after the launch of *Buddhism*, Buddhadāsa received extensive support from his lay audience, among whom were two judges: Sanya Dhammasakdi and Phraya Latphli Thammaprakhan (Wong Latphli), who played important roles in the expansion of Buddhadāsa's *dhamma* propagation.

Sanya Dhammasakdi (1907–2002) is known for having the trust of the present king, King Bhumibol, who selected and appointed him interim Prime Minister after the 14 October uprising in 1973, and chair of the Privy Council. Sanya has played a significant role in Buddhist circles. While he was studying law in London from 1930 to 1933, Sanya was excited to find at the British Mahā Bodhi Society that many Western people were interested in Buddhism. He also attended *dhamma* lectures there every week. The lecture method of teaching the *dhamma* seems to have been of interest to Sanya, perhaps in contrast to the solemn sermons read from traditional palm leaf texts by Thai monks in high preaching seats in monastery halls. Sanya wrote an article about the activities of the British Mahā Bodhi and published it in *Thai Khasem News*, a weekly newspaper in Thailand. Eventually, Buddhadāsa read Sanya's article and sent a letter to him in London, informing him of the activities of the Dhammadāna Group, which was effective in propagating the principle of the *dhamma* directly to the people. Sanya saw this as a new attempt, different from that of ordinary monks, and he replied to Buddhadāsa.[73] Even before reading Sanya's article, Buddhadāsa would have come across the idea of *dhamma* propagation through reading the English journals of international Buddhist movements; he had already put it into practice in the Dhammadāna Group. Sanya developed enthusiasm similar to that of Buddhadāsa for the propagation of the *dhamma* by direct participation in the activities of the British Mahā Bodhi Society in London. Sanya's experience became an impetus for him to lead the lay Buddhist activities of the Buddhist Association of Thailand, which he, together with other elite bureaucrats in high positions, helped to establish after his return from England. These two Thai intellectual Buddhists had parallel interests in *dhamma* propagation though they arrived through different paths.

Sanya and Buddhadāsa met for the first time in late 1933 or early 1934. When Phra Lokanatha, the Italian monk who organized the world Buddhist mission, gave a public lecture at Wat Bowonniwet in order to call for participants, Sanya, who had just returned from England and was interested in Buddhism, acted as interpreter. From the audience, one young monk asked many questions of Lokanatha about his philosophy of the world mission. In the end, Lokanatha saw that the monk had asked good questions so he must be very interested in the propagation of Buddhism. Lokanatha asked the young monk to join his tour. The young monk smiled and said he would prefer to work in Thailand first. After the question and answer period, the young monk introduced himself to Sanya as the one who had sent him a letter in England.[74]

After this first meeting, the relationship between Sanya and Buddhadāsa became important for their activities. Sanya invited Buddhadāsa into his circles, such as the Buddhist Association of Thailand and the Ministry of Justice, where Sanya asked Buddhadāsa to give lectures on Buddhism to trainee judges. Both institutions were socially regarded as elite, and Buddhadāsa was deemed an appropriate teacher for those highly-educated bureaucrats and notables. In contrast to the old days when monks and temples were respected as holders of knowledge, in the 20th century, lay people in the secular world were often much better educated than those who spent their lives in monasteries. Many monks felt hesitant to teach the lay elites, feeling that their knowledge was insufficient. Buddhadāsa was one of the few monks who could teach religious messages which have no equivalent in secular areas of study. Instead of just performing the conventional rituals, Buddhadāsa investigated Pāli scriptures and English works on Buddhism and adapted his understanding of Buddhism for people to apply to their lives.

Sanya, who perceived the relevance of Buddhist teachings to lay social life and who actually was a member of the elite, helped connect Buddhadāsa to new audiences. In other words, Sanya opened up more channels through which Buddhadāsa could play his role in the Buddhist public sphere.

The other important lay intellectual associate of Buddhadāsa was Phraya Latphli Thammaprakhan (Wong Latphli, 1894–1968; hereafter referred to by the shortened form, Phraya Latphli). Before becoming acquainted with Buddhadāsa, Phraya Latphli had already had a successful career as an elite judge. From 1913 to 1917, he studied at the City of London College. In 1917, he returned to Thailand and graduated as a first-class barrister-at-law at the top of his class. By the time he read Buddhadāsa's journal in 1933, he was already the director of the criminal court, the foreign case court, and the appeal court. Toward the end of his career as a judge, in 1941 he became president of the Supreme Court, and from 1953 to 1957 he was appointed Minister of Justice in the cabinet of Field Marshal Phibun Songkhram. As a judge in highly responsible positions, he had a much higher salary than that of other government officials.[75]

Sanya Dhammasakdi, who studied law with Phraya Latphli (his *bandasak* title was Phra Inthapanya duing the period 1922–1928; he was given the title Phraya from August 1928), reported that everyone admired Phraya Latphli as an intelligent, energetic teacher who had just completed studies in England. He was known as an excellent tennis player, and even received trophies as a golf player, as a result of his natural tendency to practice intensively until he was proficient. Sanya wrote that Phraya Latphli pursued *dhamma* study and practice with the same energy.[76]

Buddhadāsa called Phraya Latphli "the firstborn comrade among all the folks in the Dhammadāna Group" (*sahai thammathan khon hua pi haeng chao khana thammathan thang lai*), or "the number one comrade of the Dhammadāna Group." Buddhadāsa considered the intellectual exchanges with Phraya Latphli to be the most important stimulus for his thought and activities. Phraya Latphli was one of the first lay elite intellectuals who supported the activities at Suan Mokkh. Buddhadāsa recalled:

> … when we started the activities of the Dhammadāna Group and Suan Mokkh, [our activities were looked on] suspiciously, as those of such crazy people as Narin Klung, who was working about the same time, because everything [we did] was out of the ordinary, and of the nature that they did not believe that we could do. However, [Phraya Latphli] extended a helping hand when he found out about us, even from the very first year of the tri-monthly journal *Buddhism*, which was launched in 1933.[77]

Phraya Latphli even offered to abandon his career as a returnee from overseas education and as an elite bureaucrat in order to work for the Dhammadāna Group's *dhamma* propagation activities. Buddhadāsa replied that the activities were not significant enough for someone to do such a thing. Instead of taking that action, Phraya Latphli became the best friend with whom Buddhadāsa could discuss his thinking and the best supporter of the Dhammadāna Group and Suan Mokkh.[78] In terms of material support, Phraya Latphli funded the construction of enough *kuti* for the increasing numbers of monks at Suan Mokkh; he also provided robes for each monk, and brown sugar every month for the monks there to drink in the evening. His financial support was helpful for Suan Mokkh, which until then was funded only with the savings of the mother of Buddhadāsa and Dhammadāsa.[79]

In 1938, Phraya Latphli first visited Suan Mokkh, together with his judicial colleagues, Phraya Pharotratchasuphit (Choi Hemachan; 1885–1970; hereafter referred to as Phraya Pharot) and Sanya Dhammasakdi.[80] This was only a year after the visit of Phra Phutthakhosachan (Charoen), and was one of the first occasions for Buddhadāsa to receive a visit from lay elite intellectuals from Bangkok.[81] Buddhadāsa commented that these three were all good readers of his works and of the journal *Buddhism*, and that, inspired by Phraya Latphli, the number of good readers had increased.[82]

Phraya Latphli was also very important for Buddhadāsa's intellectual development. Every time Phraya Latphli bought books, he bought two copies: one for himself and the other for Buddhadāsa. For example, he bought the books of Krishnamurti, and the *Complete Works of Vivekananda*, who was the teacher of Swami Satyananda Puri, a renowned Hindu scholar settled in Thailand.[83] Also, Phraya Latphli introduced Buddhadāsa to famous religious teachers in Bangkok, including Phra Phatthanta Wilasa, a Burmese Abhidhamma teacher, and Swami Satyananda Puri, with whom Buddhadāsa discussed Vedanta philosophy and the history of Indian philosophy, and perhaps under whom he studied Sanskrit for awhile.[84] Moreover, Buddhadāsa's translations of the Zen books, the *Sutra of Wei Lang* and *The Zen Teaching of Huang Po*, were books first introduced to him by Phraya Latphli.[85]

According to Buddhadāsa, what Phraya Latphli wanted was

> … the "*dhamma*", not Buddhism. Studying Buddhism was [for Phraya Latphli] to acquire or to reach what is called the "*dhamma*", which does not belong to any particular religion.[86]

Phraya Latphli was especially interested in Krishnamurti, who, according to Buddhadāsa,

> … taught the *dhamma* which is a salvation for human beings by not necessarily being concerned with religion, [so] ultimately abolishing attachment to any religion, ideology, association, or group.[87]

Because of the influence of Krishnamurti, Phraya Latphli's understanding of Buddhism was unique. Buddhadāsa explained his understanding as follows:

> To sink deep into the liberal/liberated ideas, just as the thought of Krishnamurti, was the foundation of thought and desire of the mind or spirit of [Phraya Latphli]. [It was also] used in the search for the "*dhamma*" of Buddhism, which is not limited to Theravāda, Mahāyāna, or others, which were reformed as Zen Buddhism and the like.[88]

These characteristics of Phraya Latphli's understandings of Buddhism, religious teachings, and the *dhamma* somewhat coincided with those of Buddhadāsa. Buddhadāsa's leap from the Theravāda Buddhist scriptures to his own integration of various ideas from other schools of Buddhism and other religions may have been related to those intellectual exchanges with Phraya Latphli. In this way, Buddhadāsa's thought was enriched by non-Theravāda schools and consequently became somewhat controversial in the Buddhist public sphere of Thailand.

Phraya Latphli and Buddhadāsa seem to have been excited to talk with each other about these topics. Buddhadāsa said that they corresponded every week for many years, and when Buddhadāsa went to Bangkok, they escaped from other visitors to talk just by themselves.[89] Although unfortunately their letters seem to have been lost by the time Buddhadāsa wrote his memoir of Phraya Latphli when the latter died in 1968, their intellectual exchanges were most significant for the development of Buddhadāsa's thought. Phraya Latphli was one of the most important discussants discovered by Buddhadāsa in the Buddhist public sphere through the publication of his journal. Also, based on the inspiration gained from their discussions, Buddhadāsa further developed his own thoughts and expressed them to the public.

4. The Buddhist Association of Thailand

The Buddhist Association of Thailand (*Phutthasamakhom haeng prathet thai nai phra boromrachupatham*) created significant opportunities for Buddhadāsa's *dhamma* teaching to become known to intellectuals in Bangkok. Although the Association was not an organization aimed solely at propagating Buddhadāsa's preaching, the most central figure of the association Sanya Dhammasakdi, who has been elected president many times, related the personal significance of Buddhadāsa for the association as being, "The inspiration by which I accepted the load of working for the Buddhist Association until today was the inspiration that I received from Buddhadāsa Bhikkhu, though it was indirect."[90] Moreover, the interest of the people involved in this, the longest-lived and most substantial lay Buddhist association in Thailand was similar to their interest in Buddhadāsa's teaching, which indicated a way for lay people to overcome suffering, the highest goal of Buddhism. The Buddhist Association of Thailand promotes the idea of giving the laity a more active role in Buddhism, which has traditionally been represented by the Saṅgha, the association of ordained monks.

The Establishment of the Buddhist Association of Thailand

The Buddhist Association of Thailand[91] was established on Māgha Pūjā Day, 28 February 1934, by a group of bureaucrats under the rule of the People's Party who were interested in Buddhism. The establishment of the Buddhist Association was discussed among five people: Luang Siriratmaitri (former secretary of the Embassy of Thailand in London and a member of the People's Party), Luang Woraphakphinit (secretary-general of the Board of Audit), Phra Ratchathamnithet (Phian Ratchathamnithet; 1891–1965; the director of the Department of Religious Affairs), Luang Ronasitthiphichai (the director of the Department of Publicity and a member of the People's Party), and Sanya Dhammasakdi (then an assistant judge at the Civil Court).[92] Among the 33 original committee members for the establishment of the Buddhist Association, Sanya regarded Phra Ratchathamnithet as the most important supporter. He was the director of the Department of Religious Affairs and provided the meeting place.[93]

While they were working and studying in London, Luang Siriratmaitri, Luang Woraphakphinit, and Sanya Dhammasakdi were impressed by the work of the British Mahā Bodhi Society. They felt that they would like to create a lay Buddhist association that contributed to the propagation of Buddhism, especially in order to support the Italian monk, Phra Lokanatha, who brought the idea of sending a Buddhist mission of 100 monks and novices from Thailand out to the world in February 1934. Sanya explained that the atmosphere of that time was excitement about an attempt to start something new after the Constitutional Revolution in 1932, and curiosity about the white foreign monk, Phra Lokanatha.[94]

The establishment of a lay Buddhist association gave rise to a degree of skepticism among the Saṅgha. Originally, the name of the association was "Phuttha-tham Samakhom," or the "Buddha-Dhamma Association."

As far as Sanya remembered, this name was chosen because of the association's commitment to adhere to the *dhamma* of the Buddha and propagate it to the people. However, the association was criticized for ignoring the Saṅgha because the Saṅgha was the only one of the three gems of Buddhism excluded from the name. A few years later, they changed the name to "Phuttha-samakhom," or literally the "Buddha's Association," and once the association's activities were underway, such misunderstandings disappeared.[95]

The recognition of the Buddhist Association can be understood in terms of the situation after the Constitutional Revolution in 1932. As a result of the Revolution, some important Thammayut members of the Elders' Council from royalist backgrounds felt threatened.[96] Perhaps the prestige of the Saṅgha was shaken or at least less certain than under the absolute monarchy which had been supporting the Saṅgha. On the other hand, some other important members of the Buddhist Association had connections with the People's Party, which had overthrown the absolute monarchy. The lay Buddhists in the Buddhist Association belonged to the new politically powerful elite, which became more confident when the Saṅgha's authority was somewhat shaken.

In fact, the Buddhist Association of Thailand caused few problems for the Saṅgha, unlike the preceding lay Buddhist association of Narin Phasit, who often challenged the authority of the Saṅgha in debates over understandings of texts and through his innovative attempts to restore the female monastic order. The actual activities of the Buddhist Association were largely in cooperation with the Saṅgha. Sanya wrote,

> … this association never thought to compete with the *bhikkhu*'s Saṅgha, which has had the duty to propagate the *dhamma* of the Buddha. Instead, this Association works as a disciple of the monks, serves monks, and invites those [lay people] who do not respect monks to respect monks.[97]

The Association's activities had two dimensions: one was the enforcement of the traditional lay role of *dāna* to the monks; the other was propagation, a new role for lay Buddhists. As for the first activity, the Buddhist Association organized an almsgiving ceremony on Visākha Pūjā Day in 1934. On this occasion, the Association invited 1,250 monks and novices, headed by the Supreme Patriarch, to the schoolyard of Suan Kulap High School. Since the following year, 1935, the Buddhist Association has been assigned the almsgiving ceremony on New Year's Day at Sanam Luang (Phrameru Ground).[98] Apart from ceremonial alms giving, the Buddhist Association also supported the welfare of monks and novices by providing textbooks on *vinaya*, meeting their medical expenses, and making practical arrangements when they had to escape from bomb damage during the Second World War.[99] These activities were a systematization of the traditional lay role of support for monks, but were not as innovative as the other role, the propagation of the *dhamma*, through newly developed communication technologies.

For the propagation of the *dhamma*, the Buddhist Association staged various activities: publishing journals, free distribution of books, holding schoolchildren's essay competitions,[100] giving regular public lectures, radio broadcasting of *dhamma* talks,[101] and arranging religious instruction in schools.[102] From the beginning, publication of Buddhist journals was one of the most important propagation activities of the Association. The Buddhist Association published the monthly journal *Phuttha-tham* from May 1934 until it was faced with a financial deficit in May 1935. The Association then replaced *Phuttha-tham* with the tri-monthly journal *Ramruk* from 1935 to 1939. When *Ramruk* experienced financial difficulties, they published instead *Newsletter of the Buddhist Association* (in Thai, *Nangsu thalaengkan khong phutthasamakhom*) until 1942. After the period of commodity shortages during the war, they restarted publication in October 1951 with the monthly journal *Phuttha-tham*, which continues to this day.[103]

Regular public lectures were the other propagation activity that the Buddhist Association conducted from 1934 onward. The regular public lectures were not very popular in the beginning, so the preachers were not very happy to give lectures to audiences of as few as ten.[104] Sanya identified the reason for this unpopularity:

> … there were not many speakers who could accept to expound the *dhamma* for '*phu-ru*', or knowledgeable people. This was very unusual at that time.[105]

In other words, the preachers were not as educated as the main committee members of the Buddhist Association, who were the country's elite bureaucrats, some of whom had even been educated in Europe. However, later the Association's lectures became very prestigious, and it was a point of pride to be invited to address the Buddhist Association.[106] It was only after the Second World War that the lecture series gained popularity, when the Buddhist Association held the lectures at the library of Mahamakut Buddhist University. During that time, listeners filled the library to overflowing capacity and the membership of the Association grew.[107] Buddhadāsa was one of the popular lecturers in the period of expansion of the Buddhist Association's lecture series.

Buddhadāsa's Lectures at the Buddhist Association of Thailand

Buddhadāsa was first invited to preach at the Buddhist Association in 1940[108] by Sanya Dhammasakdi. It was Buddhadāsa's first appearance in person in the society of Buddhist intellectuals and the elite of Bangkok. Buddhadāsa had already become known among Buddhist intellectuals, having published the journal *Buddhism* for seven years. The Buddhist Association advertised Buddhadāsa's first lecture in daily newspapers. Buddhadāsa recalled that 200 to 300 people attended his first lecture.[109]

Buddhadāsa's first *dhamma* lecture at the Buddhist Association, "The Way to Reach the Buddha *Dhamma*" (in Thai, *Witthi haeng kan-khao thung phuttha-tham*), was a tremendous hit among Bangkok intellectuals. Buddhadāsa, a self-taught young intellectual monk from the provinces, exhibited his extensive knowledge of the theory of Buddhist practice as written in the scriptures, which until then had attracted little attention in Thailand, and explained it to the lay Buddhist public.

In this lecture, Buddhadāsa aimed to share *phuttha-tham*, the Buddha's *dhamma*, with lay Buddhist intellectuals by cooperating with the propagation activities of the Buddhist Association of lay Buddhists. He opened his lecture by saying:

> Although I am not a member of the Buddhist Association, since this association does not have ordained members, I am a member of this association in spirit. This is because this association has the same purpose that I have — that is, to propagate the Buddha's *dhamma*.[110]

Buddhadāsa articulated the word *phuttha-tham* in three ways. According to Buddhadāsa, *phuttha-tham* means first, "the teaching of the Buddha" or the *pariyatti dhamma* (scriptural study); second, "the *dhamma* that makes us become a buddha" or the *paṭipatti dhamma* (practicing the *dhamma*); and third, "the normality of the Buddha … or "'the thing' that the Buddha found out," or the *paṭivedha dhamma* (realization of the *dhamma*).[111] Among these three, Buddhadāsa examined in his lecture the third meaning of *phuttha-tham*, the *paṭivedha dhamma*. Buddhadāsa reasoned that if we define *phuttha-tham* in the first and second meanings, only a few people could reach the Buddha's *dhamma*, particularly the ordained monks. Instead, in the third meaning, Buddhadāsa said:

> You do not have to go either through the *Tipiṭaka* or through ascetic meditation practice in order to reach the Buddha *dhamma* … The Buddha *dhamma*, or the thing that the Buddha found out, was a public thing that is available to everyone, it exists everywhere, and is ready to touch every person in every moment.[112]

In other words, Buddhadāsa was teaching the essence of Buddhism to lay Buddhists in the secular world, those who had until then been considered as too far away to reach the Buddha *dhamma*. This was in fact what interested the lay intellectuals in the Buddhist Association.

The lecture further expanded on the actual ways of reaching the Budddha's *dhamma*, based on Buddhadāsa's extensive scriptural studies. Buddhadāsa explained that in order to reach the Buddha's *dhamma*, we have to rid ourselves of our attachments to worldly matters which are impermanent, give rise to suffering, and have no self. People consider these things as permanent, pleasurable, and self-entities because of *avijjā* (ignorance), and therefore are attached to them. Buddhadāsa prescribed three steps to overcome these wrong conceptions. By *paññā* (wisdom) we have to examine: first, visible objects, sounds, smells, tastes, and bodily sensations that our instinct tends to become attached to; second, attachment to any ideologies, which disturb the freedom of the mind that can distinguish *nibbāna* and the Buddha's *dhamma*; and third, attachment to self.[113] Buddhadāsa examined these ways of overcoming the attachments that prevent us from attaining the Buddha's *dhamma*. Buddhadāsa prescribed training of the mind through meditation which is thoroughly described in the scriptures.[114] In this path, Buddhadāsa thought that ordained monks could make good achievements faster than those practicing in lay worldly life. Buddhadāsa considered ordained monks as "more advanced models that lay people can follow to practice for accomplishing the perfect state of mind."[115]

Buddhadāsa's first lecture at the Buddhist Association had a great impact on lay Buddhist intellectuals in Bangkok. The Buddhist Association recorded Buddhadāsa's lecture in shorthand, and it was first published in his journal *Buddhism* in November 1940 with some of Buddhadāsa's own editorial corrections. Subsequently, it was published as a cremation volume first by Phraya Pharot, an important member of the Buddhist Association and one of the three judges who visited Buddhadāsa at Suan Mokkh for the first time in 1938. This cremation volume reached the hands of Chao Phraya Thammasakmontri (1877–1944; pseudonym: Khru Thep), known as a poet and as "a teacher of schoolteachers." He wrote many school textbooks and worked for the Ministry of Education and Religion until the early 1930s.[116] Chao Phraya Thammasakmontri commented on Buddhadāsa's lecture in the cremation volume, "This book will never die."[117] The lecture was reprinted in many cremation volumes, and made the depth of Buddhist teaching known to the people. This lecture led to Buddhadāsa being acknowledged among elite intellectuals as a scholarly monk.

After his first lecture, all Buddhadāsa's lectures at the Buddhist Association were recorded in shorthand for publication. The lectures attracted many intellectuals. His lecture at the Association in January 1947, "The Buddha's *Dhamma* and the Spirit of Democracy" was honored by the presence in the audience of Pridi Phanomyong (1900–1983), who was the regent of King Rama VIII.[118] Also, Kulap Saipradit (1905–1974), a leading intellectual journalist, attended every lecture by Buddhadāsa at the Association. He wrote a short summary of each lecture for his newspaper.[119] Another journalist, Wilat Maniwat (1924–2003),[120] who was born in Buddhadāsa's hometown, contributed articles on Buddhadāsa to Supha Sirimanon's weekly journal, *Nikon Wan Athit*. He indicated that Buddhism as presented by Buddhadāsa could endure critical examination by modern European philosophers.[121] Wilat regarded another famous lecture by Buddhadāsa to the Buddhist Association, "Mountainous Hindrance on the Way to the Buddha *Dhamma*," as the book that he would bring with him if he were banished to an island and only allowed one book.[122] Buddhadāsa's reputation was well established by his lectures at the Buddhist Association as well as by his journal *Buddhism*.

However, Buddhadāsa's stimulating lectures did not proceed without conflict. A former judge and an important supporter of Wat Mahathat, Phra Thipparinya (Thup Klamphasut) (1890–1977), reviled Buddhadāsa as a communist in both religious and political circles after hearing the lecture, "Mountainous Hindrance on the Way to the Buddha *Dhamma*" in June 1949. Phra Thipparinya criticized Buddhadāsa for regarding the Buddha as a hindrance to reaching the Buddha's *dhamma*, and promoted an extensive although unsuccessful campaign to censure Buddhadāsa's offence against the Buddha. Buddhadāsa was in trouble again in January 1965 for his lecture at the Buddhist Association in which he said that the Abhidhamma is not a written record of the Buddha's own speech. The Abhidhamma group in the Buddhist Association brought up his comment as a problem and attacked Buddhadāsa, claiming that he had defamed the Abhidhamma as not being the Buddha's words.[123] Because of this conflict with the Abhidhamma group, Buddhadāsa refrained from giving further lectures at the Buddhist Association.[124]

As one of the central entities of the Buddhist public sphere of Thailand, the Buddhist Association lent significant support to Buddhadāsa's propagation of the *dhamma*, but later on in the 1960s, Buddhadāsa was developing a reputation as a controversial thinker. The Buddhist Association, which began as an elite club in the early 1930s, gradually expanded its membership to include fairly well-off and quite well-educated urbanites, though they were not seen as intellectuals or members of the social elite. The expansion of the Buddhist Association's membership may have signaled heightening of interest in the deep Buddhist *dhamma* among the lay Buddhist masses, and broadening of the Buddhist public sphere as well. The more people became involved, the more interpretations of the *dhamma* emerged, along with increasing contestations and uncertainties. Similarly, as Buddhadāsa became more popular, more interpretations of his teaching emerged. As we shall see in the following chapters, it was unfortunate for Buddhadāsa, whose fame was established earlier, that the period of proliferation of free interpretations and uncertainties about his teaching coincided with the Cold War period with its political and ideological uncertainties.

CHAPTER 3

The Spread of Buddhadāsa's *Dhamma*

Buddhadāsa's mission to spread the transcendent truth of *lokuttara dhamma* was taken on by many of his followers who had realized its benefits in their lives. In the dissemination of *dhamma* — by which Thai people usually mean the wisdom of *lokuttara dhamma* — both ordained and lay Buddhists played active roles, with the lay Buddhists' involvement being particularly striking. As we shall see in this chapter, while Buddhadāsa's fellow monks such as Paññānanda played a central role in delivering the message of *dhamma*, some of Buddhadāsa's lay followers also committed themselves to offering their own interpretation of Buddhadāsa's sermons for further promulgation. Those lay Buddhists took up the work of spreading *dhamma* as an important religious mission well worth the dedication of their funds and labor. Through their contribution, they would not have denied the benefit of earning merit (good *kamma*), but for them it was even more relevant than the conventional method of merit-making; it meant a noble contribution to inform people the way to achieve "true" religious goal.

This chapter will trace the expansion of the propagation of Buddhadāsa's teaching by his lay followers, first, by the group of Chao Chun Sirorot at Wat Umong in Chiang Mai, a remote area with a different local tradition; second, by the Organization for the Restoration of Buddhism, which distributed many free copies of *dhamma* booklets in which Pun Chongprasoet printed his interpretation of Buddhadāsa's sermons; third, by the Sublime Life Mission, which published an inexpensive series of Buddhadāsa's influential sermons; fourth, through popular *dhamma* debates by urban commoners in temple grounds; and last, through involvement of more groups after the late 1960s and onward.

1. Taking the *Dhamma* Beyond Bangkok: Wat Umong in Chiang Mai

Not only did the propagation of Buddhadāsa's preaching of the *dhamma*, teaching which originated in Southern Thailand, have an impact on people in the nation's capital, it also was transmitted by his lay disciples to people in other regions of Thailand. Buddhadāsa also had devoted support in Chiang Mai Province in northern Thailand, where a distinctive local tradition of Buddhism had been practiced. In terms of both political and religious administration, the north had already been integrated into the nation-state of Siam/Thailand before Buddhadāsa's teaching arrived there toward the end of the Second World War. In contrast to Thammayut monks such as Chao Khun Ubalikhunupamachan (Chan Siricando; 1857–1932) and Phra Achan Man Bhūridatto (1871–1949), who were assigned the Saṅgha's administrative tasks in their teaching and education in provinces, Buddhadāsa and his group came to the north from a different region with private status, and Buddhadāsa's teaching was spread by means of newly developed mass communication techniques.[1] By that time, Buddhadāsa's group from Chaiya and the people from Chiang Mai in the north joined in the same public sphere for the exchange of intellectual expressions and opinions using a common language and script. The propagation activities of Buddhadāsa's group was developed along with geographical inclusion of outer regions into the Thai national Buddhist public sphere.

The Beginning of Buddhadāsa's Propagation in the North: Chao Chun Sirorot

For this geographical extension, Buddhadāsa had significant support from Chao Chun Sirorot (1896–1995)[2] for his propagation of the *dhamma*. Chun was the son of Chao Inthapat, who descended from a Lord of Chiang Tung, Chao Kramom, and his wife, Duang, who was from a Karen (a hill tribe) family. When Chun's father Chao Inthapat married Chao Mae Buaphan, who was also descended from a lord of Chiang Tung, his mother Duang left her first husband and returned to her parents' home with her children. Later, Duang married Kaew Rattanaphon, who was the janitor of a provincial government school, and who brought up Duang's sons, i.e., Chun and his brother. Even though he was called "Chao" (Lord) as a descendent of Chiang Tung's lord, Chun was not in a position to inherit the full family fortune and honor, but rather had to struggle to find his way as a commoner.

One important benefit that Chun gained from his noble family background was the opportunity for higher education. Since most farmers then considered the education of their children as a waste of work time,[3] Chun could not have had an education if he had been from a humble family. Chun was supported in his education by his father and his stepmother, Chao Inthapat and Chao Mae Buaphan, who also lived in Chiang Mai Province. He finished the fourth grade of secondary school, which few people attained, and was qualified to become a government official. After some work experience as a school clerk in Lampang, Chun continued his study in the agriculture teacher training school in Nakhon Pathom for two years, graduating in 1921. With this educational qualification, Chun established and managed a similar school in Chiang Mai, and later engaged in newly introduced cash crop agriculture, including tobacco farming.

Chun married Chao Surichai (a descendent of King Rama I from her father's lineage and of King Kawila of the Lanna Thai Kingdom from her mother's), with whom he had ten children. He had to struggle with his business, which was *dukkha* (suffering) for him. When Chun succeeded in the tobacco business in 1933–1943, and achieved stability and enough wealth, he became devoted to Buddhism after meeting Luang Pu Sim Buddhācāro, a *dhutaṅga* monk. Chun first met Sim in Amphoe Chomthong, Chiang Mai Province, where he stayed after being evacuated in the Second World War. Chun started learning about the nature of life as presented in the Buddhism preached by Sim.[4] Chun devoted his support to Sim's first settlement in Chiang Mai until increased support established a temple for Sim, Wat Santitham, which was the first forest school of the Thammayut temples in the north.[5] Apart from Sim's talk, Chun also listened to sermons by such famous forest monks as Phra Achan Man and Luang Pu Waen, both of whom often came to Chiang Mai for *dhutaṅga* ascetic practice and occasionally gave sermons to the people.[6]

A few years after he became interested in the *dhamma* through meeting Sim, Chun first read one of Buddhadāsa's books around 1944–1945. The book *Practicing the Dhamma* (*Kan-patibat tham*) had been sent to him by his brother in Bangkok. The aspects that Chun found most impressive in the book were that it "explains the meanings of the *dhamma* and [teaches how] to apply the *dhamma* in various aspects," and that it especially "makes readers understand Buddhism as science."[7] Chun became a life subscriber to Buddhadāsa's journal *Buddhism*. This was about 12 years after Buddhadāsa started his *dhamma* propagation in Suan Mokkh, Chaiya; by this time, elder monks and lay intellectuals in Bangkok already recognized him as a young monk scholar.

What difference did Chun find between conventional Buddhism in the north, the school of forest monks who belonged to Phra Achan Man, and Buddhadāsa's teaching? According to his daughter Phenchai Sirorot, who among his children had been assisting the most in Chun's *dhamma* propagation activities, the Buddhism that was commonly practiced in the north taught Chun to keep the precepts and to do good, meritorious acts. These teachings did not work for the overcoming of *dukkha* or suffering that Chun had in mind. Buddhadāsa's teaching targeted practice for the overcoming of suffering, which was exactly what Chun was working toward. Although he respected Khruba Siwichai for his *barami* (charismatic perfect state) that attracted people to work for his project of building a road to the mountain Doi Suthep in Chiang Mai,[8] Chun was too busy with his own business when Siwichai was active. Phenchai remembered that Chun respected Siwichai as a development-oriented monk (*phra nak phatthana*), but was not much interested in his teachings.[9]

On the other hand, Chun found significance in the teachings of forest monks in the school of Phra Achan Man, and he continued his support for Sim throughout his life; however, he considered Buddhadāsa's teachings were more suitable for contemporary society. The forest monk teachers taught that one should seclude oneself from secular society in order to specialize in meditation by closing the eyes and by reciting *phuttho*, which means "the Buddha," in order to concentrate on breathing in and out. Whereas in the teaching of Buddhadāsa, Phenchai explained, everyone can train his or her mind to be in the state of *sati*, or awareness, at any time and in any place, right in the middle of worldly life.[10] In other words, what Buddhadāsa extracted from the scriptures coincided with the needs of lay Buddhists who had responsibilities and duties in secular life.

In order to support Buddhadāsa's propagation of the *dhamma*, Chun basically imitated what Buddhadāsa had been doing for 15 years. After Chun visited Buddhadāsa at Suan Mokkh, and observed the activities of the Dhammadāna Group in Chaiya, in 1947 he renovated an abandoned temple in Chiang Mai, Wat Umong, which is estimated to have been built in the period 1380–1450,[11] the developing and prosperous age of the Lanna Kingdom.[12] Wat Umong is known for its *umong*, or brick cave, which was built by King Ku Na (r. ca. 1355–1385) and dedicated it to a scholarly ascetic monk, Thera Chan (1370?–1445), as a place to live and do meditation practice. According to one tradition, the monk Thera Chan read through the whole *Tipiṭaka* and commentaries on the *Vinayapiṭaka* within three and a half months, and was able to answer any kind of *dhamma* question. However, Thera Chan preferred to wander in the forest, so the king was unable to ask questions when he wanted. Then, King Ku Na built the cave as a place for Thera Chan to settle down in and do his ascetic practice.[13] The story of Thera Chan led Chun to choose Wat Umong as a place of work for the contemporary scholarly ascetic monk, Buddhadāsa and his group.

Also in 1947, Chun established a group of lay Buddhists for *dhamma* propagation, named the Phuttha Nikhom Group, just as Buddhadāsa and his brother had founded the Dhammadāna Group in Chaiya. Chun also opened an office and a printing house for the Phuttha Nikhom Group, for propagating the *dhamma* through publications. However, what the Phuttha Nikhom Group needed the most was a monk to provide leadership like Buddhadāsa did in Suan Mokkh. Chun invited Buddhadāsa to Chiang Mai in 1948, and asked him to stay there.[14] Buddhadāsa was not able to accept Chun's offer, but instead, he sent other monks from Suan Mokkh, including Phra Maha Phon Rattanasuan (1918–1993) and Phra Maha Chawiang Mitsiri. Chun further requested Buddhadāsa to send Padumuttaro Bhikkhu, who wrote an article in *Buddhism*, which was "direct and easily understood". The article, "A *Bhikkhu* and Begging" (*phiksu kap kan-riarai*), criticized monks who demanded that lay people support the building of their beautiful monasteries in return for merit.[15] Buddhadāsa contacted the monk author of the article in Penang to ask him to cooperate in the work of the Phuttha Nikhom Group in Chiang Mai. The monk finally arrived in Chiang Mai in April 1949, and introduced himself to Chun as Paññānanda Bhikkhu.[16] This was when Paññānanda adopted his most famous pseudonym.[17] The *dhamma* propagation activities of the Phuttha Nikhom Group became extremely popular in Chiang Mai because of the presence of Paññānanda Bhikkhu, a gifted oratory monk and Buddhadāsa's junior co-worker to popularize the *dhamma*.

Paññānanda Bhikkhu

Paññānanda Bhikkhu (1911–2007),[18] or Pan Sanecharoen before he was ordained, was from a well-to-do farmer's family in Phatthalung Province in Southern Thailand. At the time of his arrival in Chiang Mai at the age of 38, Paññānanda had not experienced ordinary ordained life. Pan attended secondary school up until the middle of the fourth year, which was quite an advanced level of education among his contemporaries, but he had to leave school because of his father's illness. After that, Pan worked in Phuket as a mine laborer. His biographer wrote that Pan preferred to spend his spare time with monks in a temple rather than visiting prostitutes, smoking and drinking as other laborers often did. Pan was ordained as a novice at the age of 18 in Ranong Province where he assisted an elder monk. He returned home to be ordained as a monk, Phra Pan Padumuttaro, at the age of 20 in 1931. By early 1934, when Pan was studying for the ecclesiastical examinations of *nak tham* and Pāli, and was training himself to be a *dhamma* preacher in Nakhon Si Thammarat, Lokanatha Bhikkhu, the Italian monk, came to Thailand to recruit monks and novices for his world Buddhist mission.[19] Pan decided to join Lokanatha's world mission as a leader of ten monks from the South. Pan went on foot as far as Rangoon in Burma, where Lokanatha lost control of the group of Thai monks.

After his return from Burma, Pan moved to Songkhla province. While he was in Songkhla, Pan first read Buddhadāsa's journal, and visited Buddhadāsa together with Bunchuan to spend the rains retreat at Suan Mokkh.[20] Pan started studying Pāli in Bangkok at the suggestion of Buddhadāsa, who said, "If you are going to work for the progress of Buddhism, you have to acquire Pāli and apply it in your work."[21] Pan stayed at Wat Samphraya in Bangkok for five years, until the end of 1941, and passed the third and fourth levels of the Pāli ecclesiastical examinations. While he was studying Pāli, Pan read a range of books, including those of Luang Wichit Wathakan, King Vajiravudh's *Preaching to the Wild Tiger Corps* (*Thetsana Sua Pa*) and *Encouraging the Wild Tiger Corps* (*Pluk Chai Sua Pa*), 500 stories of the *Jātaka*, and some of the works of Siburapha, Malai Chuphinit, and Sot Kuramarohit. Because of his devoted reading of Luang Wichit's works on history, Pan was called "the historian" by his fellow monks.[22] Moreover, Pan attended and listened to the sermons of famous preaching monks, and public lectures by lay intellectuals at Samakkhayachan Association, including the lectures of Luang Wichit.[23] This experience was essential for the future "star" preacher. As well as his oratorical ability, Pan drew on his skill and knowledge for his sermons.

After the Asia Pacific War started in December 1941, Pan decided to leave war-damaged Bangkok and evacuate to the south, to Phatthalung and Songkhla, but he found that the air raids were more severe in the south than in Bangkok. Eventually, he was recommended to look after a temple in Perak, Malaysia, and he decided to take this opportunity. At that time, Pan tried to teach himself English by reading an English Buddhist journal, *The Mahā Bodhi*, which had inspired Buddhadāsa and his brother for a long time. However, at the Malaysian Chinese temple in Perak, monks were expected to do rituals, blessing ceremonies and fortunetelling, and to make amulets. If they declined, people spoke ill of them, asking why they did not do these things despite having had long experiences of ordained life. After two years, Pan decided to move to Penang in order to study Chinese and to propagate the *dhamma* to Chinese people. In the more favorable environment in

Penang, where people had more interests in the *dhamma*, Pan was to study English and Chinese, but he received a letter from Buddhadāsa in 1948 inviting him to propagate the *dhamma* in Chiang Mai with Chao Chun Sirorot.[24] After the rains retreat of 1948, Pan took this opportunity to go to Chiang Mai together with his interpreter monk from Penang, Phra Wong Chanthanet, who later named himself Silananda.

Propagation Activities by the Phuttha Nikhom Group: 1949–1959

The *dhamma* propagation by Buddhadāsa's group in Chiang Mai started working full-scale when Chun and Paññānanda became partners. The material and practical support by the laity is essential for a preaching monk if he wishes to spread the *dhamma* to the mass of people in society because a monk's possessions are restricted by the *vinaya*. As in the case of Dhammadāsa and Buddhadāsa, the *dhamma* propagation activities in Chiang Mai became most effective and fruitful when Chun's support and Paññānanda's sermons were combined. No matter how adventurous Phra Pan's past experiences and his gifted oratory, he could not become a nationally known preacher until he came to work with Chun in Chiang Mai as Paññānanda Bhikkhu.

After inviting Paññānanda to stay at Wat Umong in Chiang Mai, the Phuttha Nikhom Group began to use the two major propagation methods of the Dhammadāna Group: *dhamma* lectures and journal publication. First, Chun rented land and a small building in the city center of Chiang Mai for a place for Paññānanda's *dhamma* lectures, and for a library and printing house. Chun considered that Paññānanda needed a special preaching space of his own instead of borrowing the premises of existing temples, because he expected that abbots of ordinary temples would not accept Paññānanda who did not restrain his criticism.[25] Also, this was an attempt to make Buddhist teaching more accessible for people outside the temples. In this new place, there was no stringent etiquette to make people hesitant to go to the temple, but the message of Buddhism was available for lay people to apply in their own lives. Paññānanda's style of sermons was symbolic of the new era of Buddhism which began to be propagated to the masses. Instead of sitting on the *thammat* (a traditional monk's preaching seat) with *bailan* (scriptures written on palm leaves) in Pāli reading slowly and solemnly, Paññānanda innovated by giving his sermons briskly, standing up, not reading any notes, just as lay lecturers do in their public speeches.[26] Paññānanda and his disciples believe that Paññānanda was the first monk to preach standing up.[27]

People in Chiang Mai felt Paññānanda's standing sermons were unusual,[28] but his methods became far more popular than the traditional ones. After his first four or five sermons, given regularly twice a week on Sunday morning and *uposatha* evening, the temporary hall for 70 persons could no longer accommodate his audience. After two months, another temporary hall for 150 persons collapsed because of too many people; eventually, his audience grew to 2,000.[29] By the time of Paññānanda's arrival in Chiang Mai in 1949, the Central Thai language that Paññānanda spoke in his sermons was not a problem for the ordinary people in the north because of the penetration of the national education system.[30] The audience included not only the local people, but also Indian and Chinese businessmen, as well as high-level government officials appointed by Bangkok, such as the governor of Chiang Mai Province and the director general of the fifth court region in the northern provinces.[31] It is said that on the days when Paññānanda preached, there were few people in the movie theaters.[32]

The tremendous popularity of Paññānanda's *dhamma* lectures was enhanced by Chun's propagation techniques. Chun bought a loudspeaker and a generator from Bangkok to prepare for Paññānanda's *dhamma* lectures, so that many people would be able to hear him.[33] Chun also drove around in a publicity car, which looked like the ones used for movie advertising, to invite people to attend Paññānanda's *dhamma* lectures. These were all first instances in Chiang Mai of the use of these means to support a monk's sermons.[34]

Apart from his style and propagation techniques, how was Paññānanda's message perceived by people? The content of Paññānanda's teaching is characterized as follows:

> he shifted from reading scriptures to expressing the *dhamma* by verifiable knowledge; instead of speaking of hidden depths, he talked of tangible reality in order to lead to a revolution in everyday life; he clearly pointed out many essential aspects of true Buddhism, without any reference to the supernatural or magic.[35]

Because of Paññānanda's radical attitude toward supernaturalism, Buddhadāsa named him "the revolutionist of supernaturalism" (*nak patiwat saiyasat*).[36]

Another important characteristic of Paññānanda's teaching was his unhesitating critical commentary about powerful authorities. One example was his lecture at a general meeting of Saṅgha administration heads of provinces (*chao khana changwat*) and districts (*chao khana amphoe*), held in Chiang Mai. Elder monks of the Saṅgha came from Bangkok to attend, and Paññānanda was invited as a guest lecturer. Paññānanda's lecture was entitled "A Thought on Propagation" (*kho-khit kan-phoei-phae*). In this lecture, Paññānanda harshly criticized lazy monks at all levels. He said:

> Monks who are appointed to propagation positions do not spread (*phoei-phae*) anything but lies while sprawled out (*non phae*) in their *kuti* (monks' huts).[37]

When Paññānanda was lecturing, an elder monk with the title of Somdet stood up, approached Paññānanda and stared at him in order to pressure him to stop speaking. However, Paññānanda did not stop but rather made his speech even stronger to the very end. The next morning, the newspaper, *Northern People* (*Chao Nua*), reported this incident in detail with the headline, "Venerable Paññānanda Hits a Tender Spot in the Tail of the King Serpent with an Iron Hammer."[38] This episode illustrates Paññānanda's critical comments about the realities of otherwise untouchable authorities, with whom ordinary commoners were always dissatisfied but were prevented from criticizing. People could only applaud when they heard a speech as radical as Paññānanda's.

Paññānanda's popular sermons were published in booklets and in *Buddhists* (*Chao Phut*), the Phuttha Nikhom Group's monthly journal and their second major medium for propagation of the *dhamma*. The journal was launched in May 1952 when Buddhadāsa was invited to Chiang Mai. He suggested starting a journal so that more people would be able to read Paññānanda's sermons.[39] In the journal, Paññānanda wrote different articles under various pseudonyms, just as Buddhadāsa did in the beginning days of his journal, *Buddhism*. For short stories for children, Paññānanda used the name Panyasara; for the application of the *dhamma* to economics, politics, and society, his pseudonym was Thammaphani; and for the *dhamma* and his travel reportage, he chose his most widely known name, Bhikkhu Paññānanda.[40] The journal *Buddhists* saw increased subscriptions from all over Thailand. The Phuttha Nikhom Group distributed the journal both in retail and for free.[41]

The *dhamma* propagation activities of the Phuttha Nikhom Group that Chun and Paññānanda started became so popular that the project was expanded to build a more solid and sophisticated public hall for giving *dhamma* lectures. The public hall was named the Chiang Mai Buddhist Hall (in Thai, *Phuttha Sathan Chiang Mai*). The project to build the Buddhist Hall was begun on 14 October 1951 by a joint gathering of the Buddhist Association of Thailand's Chiang Mai branch, the Phuttha Nikhom Group, and the Chiang Mai branch of the Young Buddhist Association. The new building complex included offices of these three Buddhist organizations, a large hall for *dhamma* lectures, a library, a museum, care facilities for aged people and orphans, a guesthouse, and charity project facilities.[42] The building, costly at 110,000 baht, was funded by donations from people who could afford only one baht for their share, as well as from the King, elder monks in the Saṅgha, foundations, rich officials and businessmen.[43] In February 1958, the main building opened, and the central committee for the establishment of the Chiang Mai Buddhist Hall was dissolved and became the Foundation for the Chiang Mai Buddhist Hall (in Thai, *Mulanithi phuttha sathan chiang mai*) that legally owns the estates and controls the funding for the Buddhist Hall.[44]

These purposes and activities in the Buddhist Hall were indeed an extension of the Phuttha Nikhom Group, of which Chun and Paññānanda were the main motivators. Sanya Dhammasakdi, one of the founders of the Buddhist Association of Thailand, moved to Chiang Mai upon his appointment as the director general of the fifth judicial court region in April 1951; Sanya became one of the persons most committed to the establishment of the Chiang Mai Buddhist Hall. Sanya said:

> Because this type of place that propagates the *dhamma* is not a temple, it can attract all kinds of ordinary people without any hesitation. Also, there is a new method of propagation that is not restricted by the rules and customs [as in temples] which prevent people from coming to listen to the *dhamma*.[45]

Another member of the central committee for the hall's establishment, Udom Bunyaprasop, the former governor of Chiang Mai Province, called the Buddhist Hall "a temple of lay people."[46] This remark suggests that the Buddhist Hall embodied the spread of the *dhamma* to lay people belonging to a wide range of classes, ethnicities, and occupations, and that gained the cooperation and encouragement of the Saṅgha.[47]

Nevertheless, in order to build a huge, enduring hall, the most significant resource was the alliance of the civil and military bureaucrats, businesspeople, and the King: in the commemoration book for the opening of the Buddhist Hall, only a very few gave recognition to the initiating role of Chun and the Phuttha Nikhom Group. Perhaps, wealthier, more influential people than Chun became dominant in the costly project of creating the permanent building. In the book commemorating the hall, an article contributed under the name "A Person in the Phuttha Nikhom" (*Chao phuttha nikhom*) related, "These days no one calls it the library of the Phuttha Nikhom, but the library of the Buddhist Hall. Such things as loudspeakers and other equipment for public lectures, as well as the persons of the Phuttha Nikhom who played important roles in informing people and urging them to attend, also belong to the Buddhist Hall … [When] the name of the Phuttha Nikhom has been absorbed and disappeared into the name of the Buddhist Hall, perhaps there will still remain the very work that the Phuttha Nikhom has been doing [in the Buddhist Hall]."[48] In contrast to the financially poorer Phuttha Nikhom Group and Chun, the Asia Foundation, which maneuvered to promote anti-communism in Thailand in connection with the CIA, donated an unequalled amount of money to the Buddhist Hall project, and the Samnakngan Thalaeng Khao Amerikan (probably, USIS) donated many books to its library.[49] In the political situation of Thailand in the 1950s, the project of the Chiang Mai Buddhist Hall could have been taken over for political purposes intended to utilize and promote Buddhism as an anti-communist ideology.[50]

In 1960, Paññānanda was invited to be abbot of Wat Chonlaprathan, a newly built temple in Nonthaburi Province dedicated by Mom Luang Chuchat Kamphu, the director of the Department of Irrigation. Chun did not oppose Paññānanda's move from Chiang Mai, because it was more convenient for Paññānanda, who was already a national figure, to settle in central Thailand near the capital.[51] After Paññānanda, a tremendously popular preaching monk, left for Wat Chonlaprathan, the current abbot of Wat Umong, Phra Khru Sukhanthasin, suggested that Wat Umong became more concerned with temple activities involving local visitors. He said that when Paññānanda was in Chiang Mai, Wat Umong only functioned as accommodation for monks; all the preaching took place outside Wat Umong, and there were only a few people visiting the temple for conventional merit-making and ceremonies, which are less significant in the teachings of Buddhadāsa and Paññānanda. Phra Khru Sukhanthasin started to give sermons in the northern dialect in the premises of Wat Umong during the rains retreat. Although Phra Khru Sukhanthasin came from Phatthalung Province in the south, which is in fact Paññānanda's home, the villagers did not like his sermons if they were not in the northern dialect.[52]

The activities of the Phuttha Nikhom Group continued up to March 1999, the time of research. The journal, *Buddhists*, was still being published, the library in Wat Umong, was in good condition, and since 1991, the camp for nurturing the virtues of schoolchildren (in Thai, *khai khunnatham*), has been organized by Dr. Phra Maha Chanya Suddhiñāṇo.[53] The *dhamma* propagation was expanded by monks and lay Buddhists funded by scholarships from Chun to study and complete degrees in India. These monks included Sīlānanda Bhikkhu and Vivekananda Bhikkhu, who went to teach Buddhism in Britain and America.[54] The situation at Wat Umong Suan Phuttha-tham indicated that the *dhamma* propagation activities of the Phuttha Nikhom Group, which adopted the style of Suan Mokkh, have maintained in the north.

2. Bringing the *Dhamma* to the Urban Masses: The Organization for the Restoration of Buddhism

The *dhamma* propagation of Buddhadāsa was assisted and promoted by many outside groups, especially after the 1950s. Numerous individuals and groups volunteered to spread Buddhadāsa's teaching independently through their own resources; some chose his sermon to print in a cremation volume and distribute it as a gift of *dhamma*, whereas more devoted followers printed Buddhadāsa's sermons in the form of small booklets for either free or at a handy price. Contributions to the *dhamma* propagation were largely welcomed and considered as meritorious acts.

Buddhadāsa's teaching was not simply duplicated for the mass propagation; it was also reinterpreted and transmitted to people by the words of his followers. When rearticulated by other people's phrases, it is not surprising if Buddhadāsa's sermons about the transcendent *dhamma* were not always identical to the original intention of Buddhadāsa. The same thing could have happened in the case of Paññānanda; yet any perceived interpretational differences were hardly taken up problematically for the monk established fame and popularity almost equivalent to Buddhadāsa. In other cases, some enlivened the Buddhist public sphere with their frank speech on the *dhamma*'s "truth" and "justice," at the same time they did cause waves in the name of Buddhadāsa.

Suwichan Bookshop

In the 1950s in Bangkok, the Suwichan Bookshop was one of the sources of significant contributions to Buddhadāsa's propagation of the *dhamma*. The owner, Sa'at Watcharaphai (1913–1987), renounced his job and successful educational careers[55] to open the shop in 1953 as "a kind of *dhamma* propagation in the form of book retailing."[56] Sa'at had sufficient family wealth to support himself and his family, so he could run a business which did not aim at making a good profit.[57] The Suwichan Bookshop was located in Samyot, near the Wangburapha area of Bangkok, where there are many shops dealing with books and educational equipment. Because of this location, schoolteachers and book lovers would often come across to Suwichan.[58] Important lay disciples of Buddhadāsa exchanged ideas and built networks through conversations with Sa'at, who liked to talk with his customers. Sa'at propagated the *dhamma*, particularly the teachings of Buddhadāsa, through committing himself to every aspect of the bookshop's management. Sa'at gave his customers advice about which books to read and listened to their queries about what kind of sermons would be published next time. He selected sermons for publication, did the proofreading by himself, and advertised his shop's books in leading magazines in Bangkok.[59] In the *dhamma* propagation work, Sa'at let Buddhadāsa take the role of teaching the *dhamma*. Except for a few introductory notes, Sa'at hardly put his comments or opinions into his publications of Buddhadāsa's books. Rather, he focused on the management of *dhamma* propagation. However, not everyone who volunteered to propagate Buddhadāsa's teaching of the *dhamma* shared Sa'at's attitude; Pun Chongprasoet in particular tended to disseminate his own interpretations as Buddhadāsa's teaching.

Pun Chongprasoet and the Establishment of the Organization

After the late 1950s, Buddhadāsa's teaching became further popularized among the urban masses; the publication of his sermons by the Organization for the Restoration of Buddhism was especially influential. The activities of the organization were supported by the enthusiasm and uniquely critical thought of Pun Chongprasoet (1915–1980),[60] the founder and in fact the only member of the organization.

Pun's educational and occupational career was a celebrated one. He graduated from an elite high school, Wat Thepsirin, subsequently received degrees from the nation's best universities, Chulalongkorn and Thammasat, and also qualified as a high-school teacher. In 1935, Pun was among the first generation of students to receive a full bachelor's degree from Chulalongkorn University, and was among the 134 students who completed the law degree program at Thammasat University in 1940.[61] In short, Pun was one of the few people to achieve the highest level of education available in Thailand at that time. After completing his education, Pun worked for the Ministry of Foreign Affairs. By the standard of Thai diplomats of his time, Pun's final positions were venerable: he served as the head of the Economic Division in the Department of the United Nations and the First Secretary of the Royal Thai Embassy in Cairo, Egypt.[62] In November 1961, he retired from his job at the Ministry of Foreign Affairs. After his retirement, Pun lived on a pension, which allowed him to devote himself to *dhamma* propagation activities through the Organization of the Restoration of Buddhism.

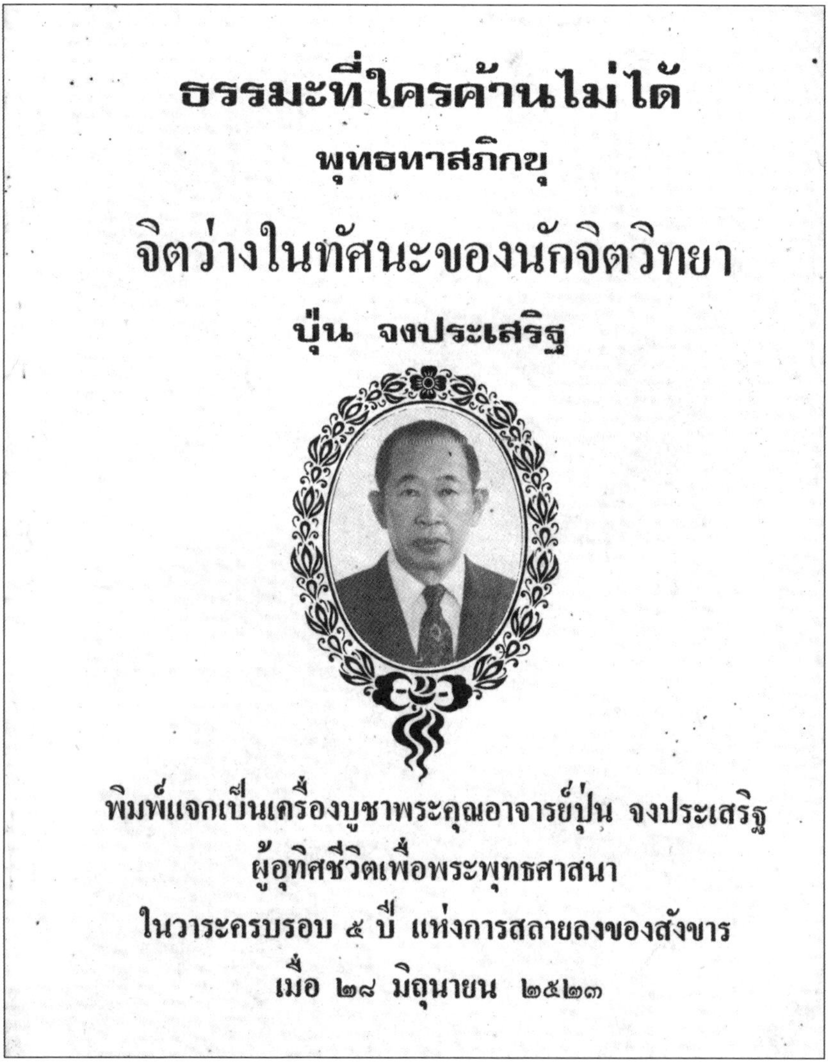

Figure 3.1. Pun Chongprasoet's portrait in one of his booklets

The establishment of the Organization for the Restoration of Buddhism arose from Pun's experience as the Secretary of the Royal Thai Embassy in India, near the end of his career. Pun resigned from his position in the embassy because he disagreed with a government project to build a Thai temple in India.[63] Pun was very disappointed with the fact that in India, where the Buddha had based his teaching of the *dhamma*, only a few people believed in Buddhism. Pun thought that Buddhism in India had been taken over by Muslims, whom he perceived as not very tolerant of other religions, and by Brahman scholars who had incorporated Buddhist philosophy into their system by defining the Buddha as an incarnation of the Hindu god, Vishnu. However, what was more important, according to Pun, were the beliefs of the Indian Buddhists, especially the teachings and practices of monks. Pun explained that monks imported beliefs in deities (*thewada*) and gods (*thepphachao*) and associated rituals from Brahmanism, and led Buddhists to believe in supernaturalism (*saiyasat*) instead of the teaching of the Buddha. Pun argued that these monks were largely responsible for the disappearance of Buddhism from India.[64] Pun's main concern was to criticize the elder monks who were intoxicated with wealth and the respect generated by belief in the supernatural in contemporary Buddhism, which he thought should be replaced by the true teaching of the Buddha.

Pun learned of Buddhadāsa's teaching by January 1956, at which time Buddhadāsa was traveling in India with Chao Chun Sirorot's group. Pun met Buddhadāsa during Buddhadāsa's stay in India, and was photographed with him.[65] In early 1959, Pun established the "Organization for the Restoration of Buddhism in India," and printed 50,000 copies of books on "true Buddhism" for free distribution to people in India and Thailand. These consisted of English works such as *Through Light to Peace* and *Golden Drops*, and Thai works that included an abridged version of Buddhadāsa's *A Treasure Trove from the Buddha's Words* (*Khumsap chak phra ot chabap yo*).[66] Pun's Organization for the Restoration of Buddhism in India either distributed books for free, or sold them at cost[67] in bookshops that specialized in Buddhism, such as Suwichan[68] and the bookshop at Mahamakut Buddhist University,[69] or he accepted orders to print his publications for distribution at celebrations for birthdays, of the receiving of ecclesiastical titles, of ordinations, or of *katin* robe offering ceremonies, or at cremation ceremonies.[70]

Pun's contribution to the propagation of Buddhadāsa's teaching was significant. In fact, one of Buddhadāsa's best known works, *A Handbook for Humankind*,[71] was actually a summary by Pun Chongprasoet. In 1957, the 2500th year of the Buddhist era, or the middle of it, Pun was temporarily ordained as a monk for four months, and spent the rains retreat at Suan Mokkh in order to celebrate the year 2500. During his stay at Suan Mokkh, Pun summarized, with advice from Buddhadāsa, Buddhadāsa's sermons for the assistant judges in May 1956, which was entitled *The Principles of Buddhism* (*Lak phra phutthasasana*). Pun published his summary as *A Handbook for Humankind* (*Khu mu manut*) using Buddhadāsa's name in the following year, 1958.[72] Buddhadāsa agreed with Pun's summary, as well as

Figure 3.2. The original edition of *A Handbook for Humankind*

his intention to begin *dhamma* propagation activities. In the congratulatory forward to *A Handbook for Humankind*, Buddhadāsa wrote:

> As far as I have examined the intention and practice, I would like to express my approval to the activities of the people who assist in the propagation of the *dhamma* as I have explained it through free distribution, using funds donated by people and groups with faith, rather than profit seeking.[73]

Many people read Pun's summary as the work of Buddhadāsa and became interested in Buddhadāsa's teaching. In fact, it was not just Pun Chongprasoet who did summaries of Buddhadāsa's sermons and published them as Buddhadāsa's; several other authors did the same thing.[74] Why did they have to summarize his sermons? Why were such summaries acceptable to the public? To these questions of mine, a famous engaged Buddhist activist who had studied closely with Buddhadāsa as his monastic disciple, answered that Buddhadāsa's publications contained insightful points, but because many of them were transcriptions of oral speech, Buddhadāsa repeated the same things over and over until he got to the point. This disciple indicated that people often find it boring to read the thick volumes of Buddhadāsa; rather they prefer to read his religious messages in a simplified handy booklet form.[75] Even in others' summarized editions, many Thai people can recognize some of the vocabulary particular to Buddhadāsa and accept those editions as the teaching of Buddhadāsa. Pun Chongprasoet's summary, *A Handbook for Humankind*, was readable because the Buddhist technical terms in Pāli and their formulaic Thai translations were simplified into plain language, so it was suitable as an introduction to Buddhadāsa's thought. Among the many publications of Buddhadāsa's sermons by the Organization for the Restoration of Buddhism, this was the least radical and most popular.

Radical Character of the Organization's Activities

The unique character of publications of the Organization for the Restoration of Buddhism was the result of Pun's commentary articles, which were added to Buddhadāsa's sermons and which functioned as authorization and support for Pun's own opinions. For example, *A Field-Guide for Monks and Their Precepts* (*Tamra du phra lae winai khong phiksu*), another popular Organization for the Restoration of Buddhism publication, was a work of Buddhadāsa edited and commented on by Pun. In the beginning of the book, Pun inserted part of the *Preaching to the Wild Tiger Corps* (*Thetsana sua pa*) by King Vajiravudh, which criticized monks who intend to gain offerings for a living, and argued that the only appropriate solution to the situation is for lay people to select monks worthy of respect.[76] After presenting the argument of King Vajiravudh as an authorized critique of unpraiseworthy monks, Pun wrote in his introduction that there are good texts in the *Tipiṭaka* that teach us how to distinguish monks who are worthy of support. The texts, which were originally translated from Pāli and edited as *A Treasure Trove from the Buddha's Words* (*Khum sap chak phra ot*) by Buddhadāsa, included for instance, Buddha's sermon that indicated the eight causes of deterioration of monks who have not yet completed their practice to achieve *nibbāna*. The eight causes were: 1) Being a person who is satisfied with the work of construction; 2) Being a person who is satisfied with chatting; 3) Being a person who is satisfied with sleeping; 4) Being a person who is satisfied with making comrades; 5) Being a person who does not control his/her eyes, ears, nose, tongue, body, and mind; 6) Being a person who does not know the limit in eating; 7) Being a person who is satisfied with an act that causes bodily sensation; and 8) Being a person who is satisfied to do several activities very slowly and waste a long time dillydallying.[77] Even though this passage was cited from the classical Buddhist text, most people who have ever lived in modern Thailand can recall the monks living in their neighborhood. It was as a kind of caution to his fellow monks when Buddhadāsa, a monk, referred to this passage; but it turned out to be very radical to the ordained when a lay believer, Pun, started propagating such stories.

Pun's activities in distributing *dhamma* books of this kind were certainly insulting for many monks. In 1978, Pun even started sending his *dhamma* books, including many radical publications, to elder administrative monks, such as ecclesiastical heads of provinces, districts (*amphoe*) and sub-districts (*tambon*; an administrative group of villages), all over Thailand as New Year's greetings. Pun rationalized his act by saying that although his organization had published and distributed 45 books to promote *lokuttara dhamma*, ordinary monks did not read the truth that would decrease their income. However, if monks and teachers misunderstood Buddhism as Brahmanism or animism, Pun envisaged that the teachings of the Buddha would be destroyed. Thus, Pun decided to distribute his publications to every high school in Thailand.[78] His act was challenging; it was similar in nature to the activities of Narin Phasit a few decades earlier, at the beginning of the 20th century.

Pun's radical *dhamma* propagation was not only in the form of book distribution. Pun explained the *dhamma* by showing slides of the religious situation in India. Pun called this "a new method of demonstrating

Buddhism."[79] Apart from showing the historical ruins of Buddhism, Pun's slides showed "superstitious" religious beliefs and practices in India,[80] where Buddhism had almost disappeared. According to one member of the audience who attended the slideshow, Pun showed a picture of the *linga*, which Hindus worship, and explained that the Thais should not be as "superstitious" as them.[81] For Pun, the "superstitious" beliefs and rituals of Hindu origin had been incorporated into the actual practices of Thai Buddhists, and had become a significant ideological justification for donations. Those slides, which would offend "superstitious" ritual caretakers, were brought by Pun to temples and schools, i.e., public places where everyone could enter, in order to show them to many people who passed by.[82]

Pun's activities were very radical and insulting to monks, but he was given some credit. For one thing, Pun was helped by his elite occupational career. Phra Sithawat, then a young novice and monk studying at Wat Mahathat and voluntarily helping Pun in his activities, believed that he would never be arrested for radical words because Pun must have been respected for his work at the Ministry of Foreign Affairs. Pun was once even allowed to talk on *tamnak* at Wat Mahathat, an honorable venue for giving a sermon.[83] Moreover, Pun's intentions and opinions were recognized by some progressive monks. Although Phra Sithawat had to keep it a secret that he helped Pun to show his slides, he liked Pun's determined commitment to the "true" teaching of the Buddha. Even the then abbot of Wat Mahathat, Phra Phimolatham (Aat), in his personal capacity praised and promoted Pun's activities. According to Phra Sithawat, who was then serving as Phra Phimolatham's personal secretary, Phra Phimolatham said, "There should be such a person as Pun. Then Buddhism will be clean and pure." However, the abbot could not allow Pun to do everything that he wanted in the temple, because Pun became a problem for the other elder monks. Pun was finally more or less prohibited from entering the premises of Wat Mahathat.[84]

On the one hand, Pun's outspokenness was supported by many people who donated money to his publications. For the urban masses gathered in Wat Mahathat at that time, one of the attractions of Pun's activities was perhaps a feeling of fun in hearing radical criticism of a corrupt authority from a just viewpoint supported by scriptural authenticity as explored by Buddhadāsa. With religious truthfulness, Pun spoke for the common people who were usually unable to speak up and confront their superiors. Pun functioned as a voice of the people in the Buddhist public sphere of Thailand. On the other hand, at the same time, as shall be discussed later, Pun's propagation of Buddhadāsa's teaching did cause trouble for

Buddhadāsa. Pun had to be partly responsible for Buddhadāsa being criticized as a "heretic" (*diarathi*), because of his reference to Buddhadāsa in the context of discussing his own extreme position on controversial topics of Buddhism.

3. Dhamma Discussion and Controversy at Lan Asok

The Lan Asok is a courtyard located in the premises of Wat Mahathat. Through the gate of the temple facing toward Phra Chan Pier, nowadays we find a car park between a building of Mahachulalongkorn Buddhist University on the right, and one of Abhidhamma Chotika College (*Aphitham chotika witthayalai*) on the left. Although the premises now appears quite narrow because of the crowd of cars, there are *asoka* trees that give shade from the strong sunlight. Beneath them, there are stone benches and also some traders sell drinks and fruit. People, especially book lovers, remember that at least until the end of the 1980s, many old book traders used to spread their wares on the ground for sale at very low prices every weekend and *wan phra*. They say that the din and bustle then resembled the present-day weekend market in Chattuchak. This place, called Lan Asok, used to be a space for talk and discussion of Buddhist matters by the commoners of Bangkok.

According to Phon Rattanasuan, one of Buddhadāsa's early monk disciples, then a popular lay lecturer at Mahachulalongkorn Buddhist University and the Buddhist Sunday School of Wat Mahathat, people used to visit the temple hall to listen to sermons and practice meditation, but they did not visit Lan Asok before 1956.[85] In December 1956, Phon started his *dhamma* lectures for schoolchildren on Sundays and during school holidays at a building which was later renovated as the Dhamma Research Division (*Phanaek thamma wichai*); this faces on to Lan Asok. After awhile, Phon's lectures became so popular that the classroom could no longer accommodate his audience, which included adults as well as children. For listeners outside the building, Pun Chongprasoet, who was a regular attendant of Phon's lectures, donated stone benches and loudspeakers.[86] Also around 1958, some political orators who were driven out of Sanam Luang, which is located just across the road from Wat Mahathat, moved to Lan Asok, changing their topic from politics to the *dhamma*.[87] Furthermore, Abhidhamma study was expanding, especially after two Burmese monks were invited to come and stay in Wat Mahathat and Wat Rakhang in 1952,[88] and after the opening of an Abhidhamma school at Wat Mahathat in 1959.[89] In the late 1950s, when people started to gather, vendors began selling food in the temple courtyard, and Lan Asok became a place like *talat nat*, a market that opens regularly on the weekend.[90]

In Lan Asok, various *dhamma* preachers representing different schools of Buddhist thought gave speeches, answered questions from the people, discussed and talked. Perhaps the most popular teachers at Lan Asok during that time were Sawai Kaewsom, a socialist and a lay disciple of Buddhadāsa, Naep Mahaniranon, a female lay teacher of Abhidhamma, and Sathian Phothinantha, an independent scholar of Mahāyāna Buddhism. Also, in the Dhamma Research Division building, there were lectures by Phon Rattanasuan, an early disciple of Buddhadāsa, who later developed his own idea of supernatural existence of *viññāṇa* (Thai: *winyan*) independent of Buddhadāsa's influence. In the Dhamma Research Division, there were also lectures by Kittivuḍḍho Bhikkhu, a very popular monk preacher of Abhidhamma, who was also an active anti-communist, and a harsh opponent of Buddhadāsa. Among their audience, there were future famous teachers of Buddhism, such as the present-day Samana Phothirak at Santi Asoke, Suchat Kosonkitiwong at Samnak Pu Sawan, Kovit Khemānanda and Phra Phayom Kalayaṇo, famous disciples of Buddhadāsa.[91] The audience included many more anonymous monks and lay people, and they entered discussion with, and put questions to, those teachers. Lan Asok truly functioned as a stage for urban commoners to exchange opinions about the *dhamma*; it was a key venue of the Buddhist public sphere in Thailand in the late 20th century.

Sawai Kaewsom's Propagation of Buddhadāsa's Teaching

For the study of the *dhamma* propagation activities of Buddhadāsa's school, one of the most important persons at Lan Asok was Sawai Kaewsom (1928–).[92] Sawai was from Phatthalung Province in the south; he graduated from Wat Benchamabophit High School and from the Navy School for non-commissioned officers, and started his work as a chief petty officer in the navy in 1951. Compared with Pun Chongprasoet with his high education and elite career, Sawai belonged to a social group of ordinary commoners, amongst whom he had a relatively high education for his generation.

Sawai's intellectual concerns started with political ideology, especially Marxism. Sent as a soldier into the Korean War in 1952–1953, Sawai thought that the war was promoted by the Americans in order to sell their weapons leftover from the Second World War. This promoted Sawai to study Marxism and political ideologies by reading the books of Thai Marxists such as Supha Sirimanon, Kulap Saipradit and Samak Burawat. Although as a navy officer, Sawai was not allowed to take part in any political movement such as the Peace Committee, he believed that he had the right to express his opinions. Sawai often spoke of politics among his navy colleagues, and went to Sanam Luang for socialist orations. Finally, suspected by his commander, he was investigated as a communist and was urged to resign from the navy, be ordained and stay out of politics. After three months of ordination without much concern with Buddhism, Sawai started to work for an oil company, and continued his public speeches at Sanam Luang.

Sometime after the takeover by Sarit Thanarat's anti-communist military dictatorship in October 1958, political assemblies and speeches were banned, and Sawai started going to Lan Asok in Wat Mahathat. Sawai said that since the abbot prohibited political speeches on the premises of the temple, he changed his topic from politics to Buddhism. In Wat Mahathat, Sawai found a book by Buddhadāsa, *Human Language and Dhamma Language* (*Phasa-khon — phasa-tham*), which was distributed by Wirot Siriat. Through Buddhadāsa's teaching, Sawai found out that conventional Buddhism in Thailand was intermingled with Brahmanism, which made Thai Buddhism "superstitious." Sawai read Buddhadāsa's books, and applied Buddhadāsa's ideas in his Lan Asok speeches about discussion of Buddhism.

In addition to Buddhadāsa's ideas, Sawai studied Abhidhamma theory and incorporated it in his explanations of the *dhamma*. Although there were several Abhidhamma teachers in Wat Mahathat, including Phra Satthamma Chotika Thammachariya and Phra Techin Thammachariya from Burma, Sawai did not have any lessons from these monk teachers. There was even a person who offered to pay for Sawai's tuition in Abhidhamma, but Sawai did not like to memorize the details of Abhidhamma theory, saying that they would make him "crazy" (*ba*). Instead, in order to explain his idea of *lokuttara dhamma* better, Sawai listened to and entered discussions with those who had studied Abhidhamma. Although he applied Abhidhamma, which was subscribed to by many teachers who opposed Buddhadāsa, Sawai said that the basic ideas of his *dhamma* propagation came from Buddhadāsa's school of thought. Sawai and other lay disciples of Buddhadāsa, such as Pun Chongprasoet and Wirot Siriat, often cooperated in propagating the *dhamma* through public discussion sessions on various temple premises and public lectures for teachers at schools.

Every Saturday, Sunday and public holiday, Sawai came to discuss the *dhamma* in Lan Asok, and he became an influential teacher there. Even though he did not have any degrees, he could explain the *dhamma* better than many other people who came to talk with him. Sawai said that to learn the nature of life requires neither the study of textbooks nor enrolment for a doctoral degree. According to Sawai's friend, many monks, perhaps including those who were studying at Mahachulalongkorn Buddhist University, felt ashamed listening to Sawai's speech since they had thought that they might disrobe in the future, most likely after completing their degrees. Kovit Khemānanda, who had studied at Sinlapakorn University, and who was to become one of the most famous disciples of Buddhadāsa, confessed to Sawai that he decided to be ordained as a monk because of the speeches of Sawai. A friend of Sawai said that many people could understand Buddhadāsa's teaching by listening to Sawai, although they could not understand it by reading his books.[93] Sawai's speeches were supported by his audience in Lan Asok, who provided him with a loudspeaker and other equipment.

Controversy over Kamma and Rebirth: Interpretations of Buddhadāsa, Pun and Sawai

Some publications and discussions by Pun and Sawai unfortunately involved Buddhadāsa in a Buddhist controversy, particularly regarding notions such as *kamma* and rebirth. In fact, the notion of *kamma* had been a controversial matter even in the Buddha's time. In India, before the Buddha started his teaching, people generally believed in the causal principle of *kamma*: good acts result in merit and the state of happiness, whereas evil acts result in demerit and the state of suffering. The causal relationship is believed to affect not only the future of one's present life, but also one's state of being in subsequent lives. The belief in *kamma*, therefore, is premised on the continuity of the self, which perpetuates the results of one's actions. When the Buddha taught *lokuttara dhamma*, the higher truth regarding suffering, impermanence and the non-self, his teaching appeared to contradict conventional belief about *kamma* because if there is no permanent self or soul to continue one life after another, no one can receive the merit or demerit of their past actions. However, the Buddha never rejected the popular belief in *kamma*; rather, he accepted it as *lokiya dhamma* for the masses, because it encourages people to adhere to morality. The Buddha regarded both views as wrong views (Pāli: *micchādiṭṭhi*): *sassata-diṭṭhi* (or *atta-diṭṭhi*), the view which premises the continuity of the self in the next lives, and *uccheda-diṭṭhi* (or *natthika-diṭṭhi*), the alternative view which insists on the discontinuity of the self, which ends and disappears at death, implying that after a person dies, he/she does not have to take any responsibility for his/her actions in the present life.

In Buddhadāsa's time, this same issue was still a serious concern for Thai Buddhists. Buddhadāsa promoted scriptural interpretations such as "birth" meaning the arising of attachment to the self and the possessions of the self, and "death" meaning the cessation of attachment to them, rejecting the literal understanding of those words.[94] Buddhadāsa knew that the annihilation of the self had to be considered a wrong view, so rather than discussing whether or not the self or the soul exists, he urged people to focus their attention on occurrences in the mind.[95] On the other hand, some other followers of Buddhadāsa, including Pun and Sawai, affirmed that according to Buddhadāsa's teaching of *lokuttara dhamma*, there would be no next life after death. When Pun published a booklet of Buddhadāsa's sermons, he excerpted only the part of the original sermon in which Buddhadāsa particularly emphasized the significance of overcoming suffering in the present life: he published it along with his editorial introduction, which insisted that no one would be born again. In his editorial note, Pun wrote,

> … the Buddha has never affirmed that a person would be reborn after his/her death, because what we call the body and the mind are never the self of someone; they are simply composed of some elements which are constantly changing, and one day they will be dissolved into their original components. Therefore, there is no self or thing belonging to the self that can be reborn. Buddhists still do not accept this argument, because they have never heard it … Therefore, it is appropriate to summarize Venerable Buddhadāsa's lecture entitled "After death, are we reborn or not?". I will publish this in order for those who have insight to correctly understand Buddhism, not for anyone to use [the belief of *kamma*] for deceiving people and making personal profit.[96]

Similarly, Sawai Kaewsom referred to Buddhadāsa and spoke of his interpretation of *kamma* in public spaces such as the temple grounds of Wat Mahathat, one of the most popular Buddhist gathering places in Bangkok. Sawai was firmly convinced that there would be no rebirth after death. In his free speech, Sawai consistently insisted,

> Ignorant people understand that the five aggregates are the individual or "I". As far as *avijjā* [ignorance] remains, they should keep insisting that the five aggregates are their possessions; so (having *upādāna* [clinging to existence]) they say that after death they will be reborn. However, when all kinds of *avijjā* have vanished (and *vijjā* [wisdom] has taken their place), there would be no such understanding (no *upādāna* exists) of the five aggregates as an individual. In other words, after death, everything vanishes; after we die, we will never be reborn.[97]

In an interview, Sawai told me that when listening to his speech at Lan Asok, an old man fainted away, so shocked was he that all his merit accumulated through his temple donations would simply disappear after his death.[98] In

Sawai's understanding, Buddhadāsa was not as definitive as Sawai and Pun because he was compassionate to such elderly people. On the other hand, Sawai said that he and Pun held rather to the principle of the "true" *dhamma* and taught people to correct their misunderstanding about *nibbāna*, which they consider as a heaven where their souls could be reborn after death.

Regarding Pun's and Sawai's interpretations of his sermon, Buddhadāsa expressed his troubled feeling in an autobiographical interview by his disciple. He said,

> [Pun] summarized some of [my sermons] but he did not clearly state [that it was his summary]. He incorporated only a part of my sermons and [his summary] led people to misunderstand [my message]. Those who liked to accuse others and those who were not well informed inflamed me. For example, regarding the question of whether or not one would be reborn after death, he [Pun] inserted his own opinion and made up his story. He did not seek my permission. I did not prohibit anything; I had no time to read Pun's books … There are people who criticized me for teaching *natthika-diṭṭhi* [skepticism, nihilistic view], i.e., no rebirth after death. In fact, that was all Pun's view. I found out about that after it became troublesome. Pun was also criticized extensively; he received anonymous abusive letters. Sawai Kaewsom was the same; he selected some parts and added his own conclusion. But I was not interested in who said what. I did not care. There is evidence of what I actually said in several books.[99]

Giving a third party point of view, Sathianphong Wannapok, a renowned Thai Buddhist scholar quite independent of the networks of Buddhadāsa's disciples, explained to me in an interview that Buddhadāsa's interests and emphasis were rather inclined toward *uccheda-diṭṭhi*, the view denying rebirth after death, although he could understand Buddhadāsa's teaching.[100] Sathiangphong indicated that Buddhadāsa was only concerned with the causal path that led to the cessation of suffering, and he never spoke of physical rebirth after death, although he never denied its possibility. In Buddhist scriptures, Sathianphong could see that there were numerous descriptions of the overcoming of suffering, just as Buddhadāsa taught, but many Thai people were so attached to the popular Buddhist belief in rebirth that they could not accept Buddhadāsa's innovative interpretation. He used the metaphor of the mangosteen; its thick husk is important to protect the inner fruit, but we eat only the fruit and discard the husk; the same thing should be done when people aim at *nibbāna*. Sathianphong also pointed out that among Buddhadāsa's disciples, the interpretations of Wirot Siriat and Ranchuan Inthrakamhaeng were correct, whereas Pun Chongprasoet and

Sawai Kaewsom distorted Buddhadāsa's teaching and misled people with their individual interpretations.[101]

When Buddhadāsa came to the discussion of *kamma* and rebirth, he was caught in a controversy. When his opponents seized on this issue and harshly criticized him, Buddhadāsa had already established his fame as a reformative modern thinker of Thai Buddhism for a few decades, but the timing was not good; this was just during the period of Cold War tension. As will be examined in the following chapters, Buddhadāsa's opponents spread an image of him as an unorthodox thinker who might have a connection to communists and thus might present a challenge to the traditional Buddhist institution. Buddhadāsa still kept inspiring younger generations, and there were people whose trust in Buddhadāsa was unshaken, but at the same time, there were also some who started to view him skeptically and distance themselves from him.

Sawai's Dhamma Speech After the 14 October 1973 Student Uprising

Sawai's speech in Lan Asok was so popular, and the monk students at Mahachulalongkorn Buddhist University, which is located beside Lan Asok, skipped their classroom lectures, preferring to attend Sawai's talks. The then vice-chancellor of the university pressured the abbot of Wat Mahathat not to allow Sawai to give his speeches at Lan Asok. On 14 October 1973, the day of the student uprising that overthrew the military dictatorship, Sawai was prohibited from giving a speech at Lan Asok in Wat Mahathat and was moved to a place beside the main auditorium of Thammasat University, which is adjacent to Wat Mahathat.[102]

Between 14 October 1973 and 6 October 1976, Sawai's public speeches and discussions sometimes involved politics as well as Buddhism. At that time, according to Sawai himself, a student of Marxism before 1958, he took the Buddhist position, and argued that his enemy was *kilesa* (difilements), not any kind of person. After the 14 October uprising, Sawai was often criticized as *patikiriya*, or a reactionary, by leftist students at Thammasat, a center of radical student activism. However, one of his political speeches during this time, "Who is a Terrorist?" (*Khrai? khu phu-ko-kanrai*),[103] presented a radical view that opposed American imperialism and rightist Thais' labeling of any disagreeable persons as "communist." Sawai listed the kinds of things a terrorist does, and concluded that those who had "terrorist" characteristics were not those who were called "communist," but in fact American imperialists. In his argument, Sawai supported the ideology of communism of the Communist Party although he did not have any position in the Communist Party of Thailand. Most ordinary pious Buddhists labeled Sawai as "leftist," but his Buddhist perspectives were considered as "rightist" by the radical students. This epitomizes the position of progressive Buddhists who were concerned with social issues in the 1970s.

Sawai's discussions of Marxism and Buddhism continued into the 1980s, especially when he was introduced to Prasoet Sapsunthon by his friends. Prasoet was an old friend of Buddhadāsa, and was once a member of the Central Committee of the Communist Party of Thailand, but after 1959, he became an advisor to the military, teaching the strategies of communists for application in counterinsurgency.[104] Sawai said that both Prasoet and Sawai agreed that even the highest teaching of Marxism does not reach the level of the highest teaching of the Buddha, and that by becoming a Buddhist, a Marxist can reach the summit. They understood that Marxism only teaches an aspect of materiality, but it is little concerned about spirituality and morality, and considers that people will be happy, good persons if their material environment, such as food and possessions, is improved. However, those who are affluent in terms of food, shelter, and clothing are not necessarily happy and morally good, because they also have *avijjā* (ignorance) and *kilesa* (defilements). Corresponding to the claims in the works of Buddhadāsa and Pun Chongprasoet, Sawai also argued that we do not need material goods more than are sufficient for our basic needs, but the pure mind that has overcome defilements can save the world. Sawai and Prasoet further agreed that communism cannot survive without incorporating Buddhism, and that in fact communism without Buddhism was in vain.[105]

This discussion by Sawai and Prasoet suggests how Thai intellectuals or *achan* (teachers) in town commoners' discussion circles elaborated their understandings in conflicting, but equally suggestive ideologies. Questions about and interest in Marxism were not just the domain of radical students and those related to the Communist Party. Questions about Buddhism were not exclusively the domain of monks and pious regular temple visitors. The discussions about political and Buddhist ideologies in their circle were very significant events in the public sphere of Thailand in the late 20th century.

Sawai stopped going to Thammasat University to give public speeches and take part in discussions after the bloodshed of the *coup d'état* on 6 October 1976, when the military returned to government with the massacre at Thammasat, and reactionary governments placed restrictions on political speech and activity. After that, Sawai was invited to teach in the projects of the Foundation for Sublime Life Mission and others, and he also visited schools and colleges to teach *lokuttara dhamma*. The public discussions in Lan Asok continued even after Sawai left in 1973, but Achan Naep

Mahaniranon, another popular teacher in Lan Asok, stopped going there in 1979 for health reasons. Perhaps the function of Lan Asok as a public space for Buddhist discussions by town commoners had to move to other places with other teachers and followers. In the next few decades, among numerous groups of Buddhadāsa's followers, the Foundation for Sublime Life Mission played a major role in the *dhamma* propagation.

4. The Sublime Life Mission

The Sublime Life Mission, or the *Mulanithi Phoei Phae Chiwit Prasoet* (abbreviation in Thai, Pho. Cho. Po.), was one of the most dedicated groups outside Suan Mokkh working to propagate Buddhadāsa's teaching. The Sublime Life Mission actually followed and cooperated in the activities of Pun in the beginning, took over some works of Pun after his death in 1980, and expanded *dhamma* propagation activities with other lay disciples of Buddhadāsa, including Sawai Kaewsom and Somsong Punyarit.

The Sublime Life Mission was founded by Wirot Siriat (1921–).[106] Wirot also had sound educational background and work experience before he started his *dhamma* propagation activities. He graduated from Thammasat University in 1946, and started working for a legal office as a lawyer in 1947. However, he could not find meaning in his life beyond eating, working, wandering, being intoxicated with sensual pleasures, and sleeping every day. Wirot felt that it would be better to die if he had to endure suffering in his life solely in order to live, eat and sleep. Wirot developed a mental disorder, and looked for an answer to questions such as why we were born, for what purpose we were born, and why we have life today. People told Wirot that he made a problem out of a non-problem, and called him crazy. In the beginning, Wirot did not look for his answers in religious teaching, because he thought that life is possible without relating it to a religion, and any relation with a religion would give him unnecessary burdens and expenses.[107]

At the end of 1958, Wirot came across a book by Pun Chongprasoet, *A Handbook for Humankind*. Wirot wrote that he would not have read it if he had known the book was a religious teaching, but he read it because he was interested in the life of human beings.[108] This was the book that eventually answered his questions.

How did *A Handbook for Humankind* answer Wirot? If we read the book with his questions in mind, the following passage is illuminating.

> Buddhism indicates that [desires] 'to get something' and 'to become something' are only transient things of this world, and exist through the power of ignorance (*avijjā*), because when we speak of the truth

> at the absolute and highest level, [we] cannot become anything. For what reason? It is because both a person who gets something and the thing that is gotten are impermanent, suffering, and do not belong to anybody … Desire arises because the person does not know that nothing is worth wanting. It is also because wrong assumptions have become attached to us as instincts from the time when we were in the womb. From childhood we feel that we want, and know that we will behave in accordance with the desire. Then, some kind of effect arises; the effect sometimes corresponds with the desire, sometimes does not. If the effect corresponds with the desire, we want it more. If the effect does not correspond with the desire, we continue to struggle in other ways until we can get a desirable result. When we do something, it generates some kind of effect again, and fuels the cycle of defilement. Such a cycle of an act and its effect ([in Pāli] *kamma* and *vipāka*) is called *vaṭṭa saṁsāra* … We have to bear suffering in this very cycle. If we are able to exit from this cycle, it is surely the overcoming of suffering. Regardless of whether one is a poor beggar, a millionaire, a king, an emperor, a *brahman*, or whatever, all the beings who are in this cycle have to have some kind of suffering, suitable to the person's desire. Therefore, we can say that this *vaṭṭa saṁsāra* is filled with great suffering. *Sīla dhamma* [morality] and *cariya dhamma* [proper conduct] are incapable of solving this problem. Thus, we have to rely on true Buddhism, which is a higher-level principle of the *dhamma* that can be applied to this problem in particular. We can see that suffering is derived from desire. The Buddha placed desire as the second item of the four noble truths as the cause of suffering.[109]

In other words, Pun's summary of Buddhadāsa's teaching indicated that satisfying human desires such as eating, sleeping, and seeking sensual comfort does not ultimately make a person happy. Rather, it is a part of the cycle of suffering in human life. There is a different way to overcome suffering. The book indicated that this is in fact the teaching of "true Buddhism." The true Buddhism is even different from the Buddhism that Thai people are familiar with, which deals with such aspects as moral and proper conduct, taught by ordinary monks at temples. What Wirot had to seek was the true Buddhism that he had never expected in conventional Buddhism, and he wrote as an answer to his questions of life, "We were only born in order to find non-suffering."[110] This is in fact what many of Buddhadāsa's followers indicate as most inspiring.

After Wirot had inquired into the works of Buddhadāsa that had been published by the Organization for the Restoration of Buddhism, and met Pun, he was motivated to propagate this Buddhism that people had not been exposed to. Wirot started propagating the *dhamma*, especially the teaching of Buddhadāsa about the way of overcoming suffering, by offering to cooperate with Pun's activities, such as publishing books, showing slides and organizing lectures at various temples.[111]

Around 1967, Wirot established his own group, The Group for the Propagation of the Sublime Way of Life (*Khana phoei phrae witthikan damnoen chiwit an prasoet*), with his friends. The group is so named on the advice of Buddhadāsa, and called in short, The Group of the Sublime Life Mission (in Thai, abbreviated as the Khana Pho. Cho. Po.). Perhaps the first and most important work of the Group of the Sublime Life Mission was the publication of a series of Buddhadāsa's sermons in booklet form, the *Looking Inside* series (*Ekkasan chut mong dan nai*). The name of the series was taken from the phrase "Looking at things happening inside" (*Kan-mong sing thang puang nai dan nai*), which Wirot found and liked in Buddhadāsa's teaching to the Buddhist club students at Chulalongkorn University, *The Dhamma, A Companion of Life* (*Thamma khu chiwit*). Wirot installed a picture entitled *Know Yourself!* (*Chong ruchak tua eng*),[112] at the Spiritual Amusement Theatre in Suan Mokkh. In the picture, a person is jumping into a lotus flower inside the self. Wirot realized that looking inside is nothing but *vipassanā* meditation.[113] The Group of the Sublime Life Mission published *Human Language and Dhamma Language* (*Phasa-khon — Phasa-tham*), the first issue of the series, around 1967,[114] and altogether one million copies of the 66 stories of Buddhadāsa in this series have appeared both for sale and for free distribution.

Dhamma book propagation by the Sublime Life Mission adopted the method of Pun's Organization for the Restoration of Buddhism. According to a report in the first printing of the second issue of the *Looking Inside* series, 10,000 volumes of *Human Language and Dhamma Language*, the first issue of the series, were published through public donation. The Sublime Life Mission spent 6,000 baht for printing and 750 baht for shipping. Of those 10,000 copies, the Sublime Life Mission donated 5,000 to Suan Mokkh for distribution to visitors, to monks in general, and to libraries. The Sublime Life Mission also encouraged people to buy its publications for distribution on occasions such as ordination ceremonies, cremations, festivals, house-building celebrations, and *katin* robe offering ceremonies, and for donation to libraries.[115]

The *dhamma* book distributions of the group of the Sublime Life Mission were further supported by the opening of its bookshop Thamma-bucha in 1969. This was when Sa'at Watcharaphai, the owner of the Suwichan Bookshop, became seriously ill, and the Sublime Life Mission took over the role of providing a bookshop that specifically dealt in low

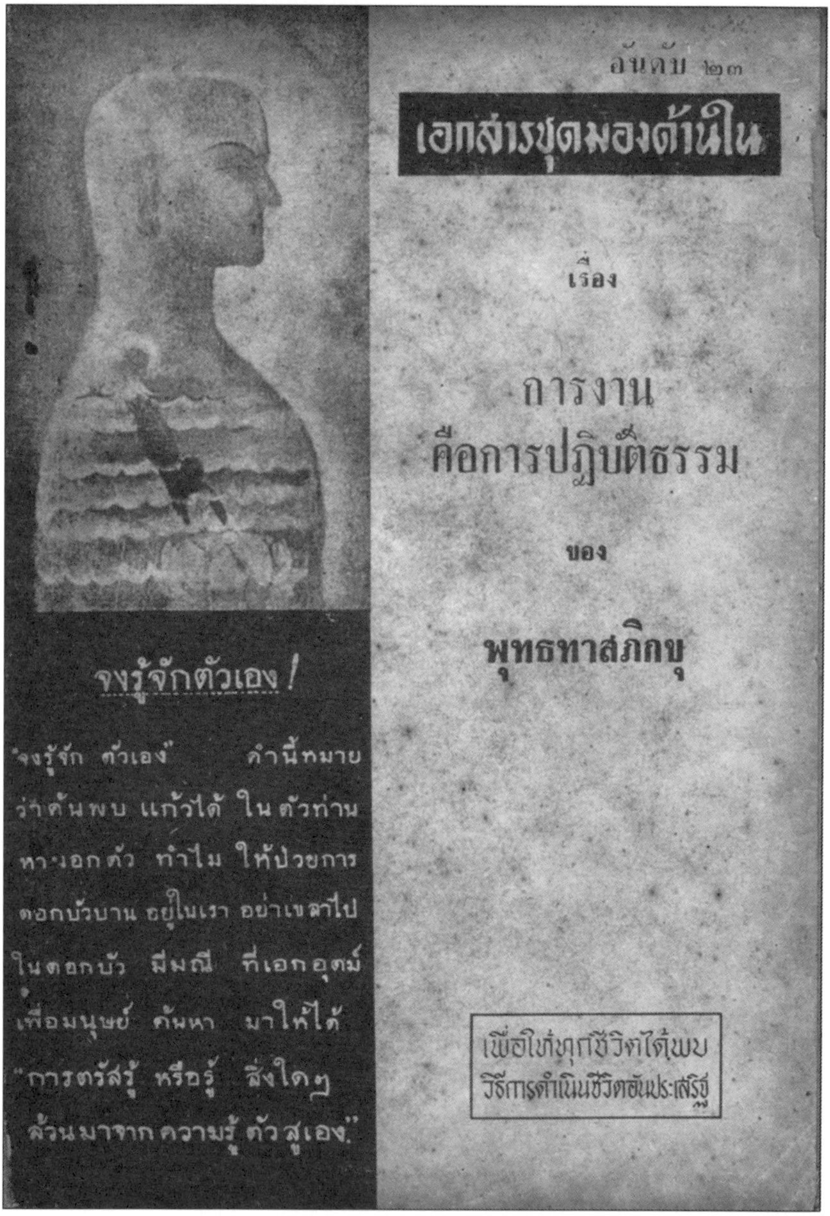

Figure 3.3. *Looking Inside* series booklet. The attached prose says: "Know yourself. This phrase means that you can seek and find a jewel inside yourself. Why do you look for it outside yourself? It is a waste of time. A lotus is in our self. Don't be a fool. In the lotus, there is the finest gem for a human being to seek and find. Enlightenment or knowledge of any kind of thing, all comes from the knowledge of yourself."

price publications on Buddhism as explained by the group of Buddhadāsa. Through the *dhamma* book distributions of the Sublime Life Mission, the influential *dhamma* orator Sawai Kaewsom first read a work by Buddhadāsa, *Human Language and Dhamma Language*. In addition, a number of student activists also investigated Buddhadāsa's Buddhist thought. For instance, Pracha Hutanuwatr read Buddhadāsa's book, *Empty Mind* (*Chit wang*), which was summarized by Pun Chongprasoet, for the first time, and bought copies of each of the books of Buddhadāsa at the Thammabucha Bookshop.[116] Another former student activist Weng Tochirakan helped Wirot to transcribe a sermon of Buddhadāsa in order to publish it as a book.[117] These examples suggest that the *dhamma* propagation activities of the Sublime Life Mission certainly brought the teachings of Buddhadāsa and Buddhism to those who were less familiar with traditional temple activities, such as keeping the eight precepts, meditation, and listening to monks' sermons.

Toward the end of the 20th century, the Sublime Life Mission further expanded its activities in accordance with the expansion of Wirot's interests and personal network; for instance, the group had a training program to help monks and novices to become skilful preachers and a preaching project for schoolteachers who taught morality classes. Although the details of the group's activities are omitted here, it should be stressed that Wirot and the group made a significant contribution to expanding access to Buddhadāsa's teaching. In other words, their activities represented an expansion of the range of concern in the Thai Buddhist public sphere, until then confined to morality teaching and conventional merit making, to include the teaching of the cessation of suffering.

5. Expansion after the Late 1960s and Onward

From the late 1960s through to the early 1980s, Buddhadāsa stressed issues in contemporary society to groups of people who came to Suan Mokkh to hear him preach and receive training in *dhamma* practice. Around the mid-1970s, in parallel with Buddhadāsa's concerns, a group which later started calling themselves "engaged Buddhists" became interested in Buddhadāsa's teaching of Buddhism that could be applied to social issues. Those organizations, particularly groups under the advisement of Sulak Sivaraksa, such as the Komon Khimthong Foundation (established in 1971) and the editorial board of the journal *Pacharayasan* promoted Buddhadāsa's social teachings in their publications. The group of engaged Buddhists also organized seminars and public panel discussions that were based on

Buddhadāsa's ideas on Buddhism and society, which they published in book form after some seminars.

Along with the publication of numerous booklets by many publishers, Buddhadāsa's sermons were compiled as the *Thammakhot* series; the thick, hardcover volumes look like encyclopedias. The series appears to have begun in 1956 for the purpose of collecting Buddhadāsa's sermons in substantial volumes so that they would not disappear as easily as small booklets. For the publication of these thick volumes, Buddhadāsa started to organize his sermons around certain topics and spoke them as a series for the same audience; for instance, he taught about *ānāpānasati* meditation for the dining hall lecture series and published it as *Ānāpānasati Complete Edition* (*Ānāpānasati chabap sombun*).[118] The fund for publishing the *Thammakhot* (literally translates "*dhamma* propagation") series was significantly supported by Phraya Latphli's considerable legacy after his death in 1968.[119] On the other hand, the actual work of transcription was done by Arunwati Suwannakanit and other women practitioners of high educational background staying at Suan Usom, a women's place of *dhamma* practice in Bangkok established by Buddhadāsa's women followers.[120] According to Metta Phanit, one of Buddhadāsa's nephews and the present head of the Dhammadāna Foundation, about 80 volumes were published as the *Thammakhot* series before May 2005. Buddhadāsa's disciples wanted to see 100 volumes compiled in the *Thammakhot* series before the 100th anniversary of Buddhadāsa in 2006; many people took tapes home and worked on transcription. They had already transcribed almost all the remaining Buddhadāsa's sermon tapes, but Metta said that editing would take even more time and work.[121]

After the 1980s, more publishers who put special emphasis on *dhamma* books by Buddhadāsa were established. In this period, Buddhadāsa's *dhamma* books became available in stylish layouts from more commercialized publishers through the book distribution network. Such a new type of *dhamma* book business included the Sukkhaphap Chai Publisher (established in 1982) and the Thammasapha Publisher, as well as the abovementioned publishers who were established through Sulak Sivaraksa's advice. The Arun Witthaya publisher also distributes Buddhadāsa's books on a comparatively small scale. In the late 1990s, some old type of *dhamma* propagation groups, such as the Sublime Life Mission and the Suan Usom, still supply booklets of Buddhadāsa's preaching either at a low price or for free. Other groups of this old type were newly established in the late 1980s, including the Group for Dhamma Studies and Practice, and the series of *Buddhadāsa's Works — For the Memory of Phra Dulayaphak* (*Phutthathat *bannalai — dulayaphak anuson*; this series has been published by a daughter of Phra Dulayaphak, a judge disciple of Buddhadāsa). There are also some individual writers who were inspired by Buddhadāsa to write their own books on the *dhamma*, such as Maj. Gen. Dej Tulavardhana, the author of the series of *An Intellectual Way of Studying Buddhism* (*Rian phutthasasana yang panyachon*). In the 1990s, new journals came out to follow on from and expand Buddhadāsa's ideas, for example, *Dok mokkh* (*mokkh* blossoms), and *Panithan* (Pāli: *paṇidhāna*; strong determination).

Buddhadāsa's teaching has now spread outside Thailand through translations and teachings by his foreign disciples, such as Santikaro in the United States. Buddhadāsa's teaching is also popular in Taiwan and Hong Kong through Chinese translations of his works. Recently, English and other language translations of Buddhadāsa's sermons have also been made available on websites.[122]

Metta said that even after Buddhadāsa's passing, increasing numbers of publishers were publishing his sermons.[123] He said that he knew of the recent increase because he had signed many printing permissions. Metta indicated two reasons for the recent popularity of Buddhadāsa's teaching. First, there are more people who find suffering in their business, so they want their business to deal with the *dhamma*. Second, recently *dhamma* books became marketable even at high prices. Metta said that people suffer a lot, so *dhamma* books sell well even at Seven-Eleven stores. Although they are reprinted editions of Buddhadāsa's sermons delivered some decades ago, Metta said that people would never be tired of the *dhamma*, as it could help release emotional distress.

Buddhadāsa's mission to spread the *lokuttara dhamma* in the modern world was passed on to many groups and individuals, and its wisdom is no longer a novel philosophy. Some say that nowadays many *dhamma* books are available in Thailand, a set of scriptures is published in Thai translation to serve the insight in it as "true, original Buddhism," so people do not necessarily refer to Buddhadāsa's pioneering role to revive the *dhamma* to be practiced in contemporary Thailand. Put in another way, with the help of *dhamma* propagation by many followers who were inspired by Buddhadāsa's sermons, perhaps more people had a chance to come across with the wisdom of the *dhamma*, practice it in their own lives, and express their interpretations of *dhamma* based on their experiences. In present day Thailand, the "ideology of merit" which S.J. Tambiah called the popular Thai Buddhism in practice is still very strong and persistent, but it cannot solely represent the present Thai Buddhism as a whole; the higher doctrines are also applied to people's suffering to be overcome.[124]

Buddhadāsa should have had no complaint about the popular expansion of *dhamma* practice without mention of his name, as his publications state that their author did not exercise copyright. Yet, when his disciples freely rearranged his sermons in a misleading way and published under the name of Buddhadāsa, his philosophy had to be questioned. Such a way of *dhamma* propagation was not totally free from problems, although their wholehearted devotion to *dhamma* propagation was probably difficult to be blamed. In a debate at the Buddhist public sphere, many ideas of a "true" Buddhism was vigorously proposed, but none of them could have hardly be established exclusively as an authoritative interpretation about unspecified extension of the texts of classical scriptures. In other words, even if having some problems, many optional interpretations about a "true" Buddhism can coexist for discussion. This chapter portrayed people who joyfully attended endless discussions about religious truth and justice, which enlivened contemporary Thai Buddhism.

CHAPTER 4

Debates on the Empty Mind

As indicated in earlier chapters, reading the classical scriptures written in Pāli, Buddhadāsa was fascinated with the teaching of *lokuttara dhamma*, or the teaching of *nibbāna*, which many Thai Buddhists in the early 20th century tended to consider unrealistic or unpractical. Buddhadāsa's interest in *lokuttara dhamma* was its teaching about "overcoming suffering," and his spiritual pursuit was not confined to the scope of *Tipiṭaka*, the classical scriptures of Theravāda Buddhism. For the purpose of overcoming suffering, Buddhadāsa found common ground in the notion of emptiness (Pāli: *suññatā*), which had developed later in the Mahāyāna tradition rather than Theravāda. Buddhadāsa freely created dialogue with people and thoughts from other religious traditions, and he was enthusiastic to discover and propagate teachings which Thai Buddhists had hardly ever heard of. The notions of emptiness and empty mind (Thai: *chit wang*) were among the most striking ideas that Buddhadāsa introduced to the Thai Buddhist public sphere. There were people who greatly appreciated Buddhadāsa for teaching these new ideas, but at the same time, those unfamiliar concepts became an object of criticism.

Earlier studies of Buddhadāsa also considered his proposal of emptiness and empty mind as characteristic of his thought. Gabaude indicated that emptiness was one of Buddhadāsa's criteria for determining the authenticity of the scriptures and Buddhist beliefs,[1] and Jackson implied that Buddhadāsa's promotion of empty mind was a modern, Protestant kind of abolition of the monk-laity distinction in order to afford wider access to *nibbāna*.[2] Both studies identified significant implications of Buddhadāsa's unique interpretive traits, and Jackson's study at least partly mentioned critical statements by Buddhadāsa's opponents about his thoughts, and indicated some problematic aspects of their arguments.[3] What has not yet been examined is people's general perceptions and discussions of

Buddhadāsa's teaching. In order to approach this aspect, it is not sufficient to study solely the content of Buddhadāsa's sermons and publications. High-profile public discussions and even the inflammatory nature of the negative campaigns would have had a strong impact on people's perception of Buddhadāsa's teaching. In the public sphere — probably not just that of Buddhism or of Thailand, but generally speaking — there are rumors, prejudgments, exaggerations, personal preferences and misunderstandings about well-known individuals. There have even been some intentional distortions of famous people's reputations in order to provide the public with inaccurate interpretations of their thoughts. Even though some of those attacks are based on unreasonable grounds, their impact on the public image or perception of an individual can be significantly large. In the case of Buddhadāsa, his public image was characterized as polemical by his opponents, especially through reference to his introduction of unconventional ideas: emptiness and empty mind. As we shall see in this chapter, Buddhadāsa's opponents used various tactics to manipulate public perception of him. Few previous studies have given consideration to the discourses of Buddhadāsa's opponents.

The aim of this chapter is not to present some interpretation of Buddhadāsa's teaching about emptiness and empty mind as a better alternative to existing studies, but rather to explore discussions in the Buddhist public sphere, which strove to characterize his teaching as controversial. In order to clarify this matter, the following four points will be examined: first, Buddhadāsa's and Thai Buddhists' encounter with new ideas in Zen through intellectual assistance from local Chinese migrants; second, the main points of Buddhadāsa's interpretation of emptiness and empty mind; third, Buddhadāsa's panel discussions with Kukrit Pramoj, through which the notion of empty mind became widely known; and fourth, *What is Right? What is Wrong?* (*Arai thuk, arai phit*), a book in the form of a debate over the issue. This chapter will demonstrate how Buddhadāsa's opponents manipulated public opinion to undermine his credibility, and how his followers defended the relevance of his teaching.

1. Buddhadāsa's and Thai Buddhists' Encounter with Zen Notions

Buddhadāsa's Thai translation of the English edition of a classical Chinese Zen text, *Sutra of Wei Lang*, which was first published in the journal *Buddhism* in 1947, was probably the first work to spread the unfamiliar ideas of Mahāyāna Buddhism widely among Thai Buddhists.[4] Buddhadāsa's lay friend, judge Phraya Latphli, introduced him to Wong

Mou-lam's English translation of this book.[5] Latphli suggested that Buddhadāsa translate the book into Thai and publish the chapters as a series in *Buddhism*, but initially Buddhadāsa was not confident of his language ability. Latphli insisted that the English in the book *Sutra of Wei Lang* was quite easy, but that it was rather more difficult to give the right interpretation of its teaching. He said that because the book was written in ordinary words and sentences but with deep meanings, it could not be translated properly without an understanding of the true *dhamma*.[6] In order to make the task easier for Buddhadāsa, Latphli made a draft translation of the first chapter, and let Buddhadāsa edit it and then continue to translate the rest by himself.[7]

In order for Buddhadāsa to translate the English edition of *Sutra of Wei Lang* into Thai, he sought further advice from Dr. Tan Mo Siang (陳慕禪; 1906–1993), a Chinese medicine physician and Chinese Zen preacher who taught in the Taechew dialect of Chinese at the Thai-Chinese Buddhist Association (*Samakhom phutthaborisat thai-chin pracha*; 中華佛學研究社) in Bangkok.[8] As a result of his fluency in three languages: Mandarin, the Taechew dialect, and Thai, Tan Mo Siang conveyed his accumulated knowledge of Chinese Buddhism and other Chinese religions, philosophies, and literatures to both local Chinese migrants and Thai intellectuals.[9] When Buddhadāsa became interested in Zen teaching, he became acquainted with Tan Mo Siang. Every time Buddhadāsa went to Bangkok, he visited Tan Mo Siang and talked with him for hours.[10] While assisting Buddhadāsa's translation of *Sutra of Wei Lang*, Tan Mo Siang indicated some mistakes in Wong Mu-Lam's English translation from Chinese, so in his translation into Thai, Buddhadāsa adopted the original meaning of the Chinese text suggested by Tan Mo Siang.[11] Thus, the Thai edition of *Sutra of Wei Lang* was the product of intellectual exchanges between these two prominent Buddhist teachers who represented two different Buddhist traditions in Bangkok, where many generations of people from China settled down and adopted local Thai culture.[12]

In contemporary Thailand, local Chinese intellectuals such as Tan Mo Siang and Sathian Phothinantha (1929–1966) played significant roles in specifically teaching Mahāyāna Buddhism in the mid-20th century. In addition to their work, Buddhadāsa made an equally significant contribution to Thai people's understanding of notions like emptiness that had developed in the tradition of Mahāyāna Buddhism. Buddhadāsa's Thai translations of Mahāyāna texts such as *Sutra of Wei Lang* and *The Zen Teaching of Huang Po* were reprinted many times by various individuals and publishers and were widely read.[13]

2. Features of Empty Mind Appeared in Booklets by Buddhadāsa

When Buddhadāsa taught the notion of emptiness, he did not intend to spread Mahāyāna Buddhism to his Thai audience, but rather, he introduced it as the most essential teaching of Buddhism regardless of schools, not just in Mahāyāna, because it is related to the state in which suffering is overcome. Buddhadāsa indicated that the idea of *suññatā* or emptiness is mentioned in the *Tipiṭaka*, the classical scriptures that underpin the views and practices of people in Theravāda tradition. Buddhadāsa referred to the *Dhammadinna Sutta*,[14] the *Mahāsuññatā Sutta* and the *Culāsuññatā Sutta*[15] in which the concept of emptiness is presented. In order to explain the significance of emptiness in the Theravāda scriptures, Buddhadāsa frequently cited the Pāli phrase in the *Dhammadinna Sutta*, *Ye te suttantā tathāgatabhāsitā gambhīrā gambhīratthā lokuttarā suññatapaṭisaṃyuttā*. This was a helpful reference for Buddhadāsa to support his teaching that the notion of emptiness was actually practical for lay Buddhists.[16]

The Theravāda also had the concept of emptiness in its canon, but it was not discussed in the traditional Theravāda commentaries as much as in the Mahāyāna schools, which expanded on it. According to a renowned Buddhist scholar, Étienne Lamotte, following Nāgārjuna, the Śrāvakayāna (or "Hīnayāna"), in which the Theravāda was included, teaches the emptiness of beings (*sattvaśūnyatā*), or non-self, while the Buddhayāna (or Mahāyāna) teaches both emptiness of beings and emptiness of things (*dharmaśūnyatā*), which means the world is as empty as the "self."[17] In other words, Lamotte also recognized that in Theravāda and other earlier schools, the notion of emptiness did exist, but that it indicated the state of mind of an individual human being; whereas in Mahāyāna schools developed later, the idea was expanded to discussion of the nature of the universe. Because contemporary Thai Theravāda Buddhists were uncertain whether this teaching was inherent in their form of Buddhism, emptiness became controversial when they came to know of it through Buddhadāsa, and especially so when he was attacked by his opponents.

Furthermore, Buddhadāsa did not explain the Pāli word *suññatā* (emptiness) alone; he delivered the idea by the Thai word *chit wang*, or "empty mind," in order to make the unfamiliar concept of emptiness easier to his audience. Tracing Buddhadāsa's widely read booklets about emptiness or empty mind, which had significant impact on popular understanding of his teaching, there are at least four points that became topics of discussion.

First, Buddhadāsa explained that empty mind is a state of mind freed from *kilesa* (defilements) and from *upādāna* (clinging), which sees things as *tua ku* (me, self) or *khong ku* (mine, possessions of the self).[18] According to Buddhadāsa,

> Empty mind is not a mind that does not feel anything. What is called *citta* (mind) has to have *kwam-rusuk* (feeling), because it is the nature of the mind. If the mind has a feeling of non-egoism, it is called '*chit wang*' (empty mind). If the mind has a feeling of strong egoism, it is called '*chit wun*' (unsettled mind).[19]

Buddhadāsa considered the state of mind that is free from attachment to the self and its possessions as the heart of Buddhism. He referred to the words of the Buddha,

> All kinds of *dhamma* (*dhammajāti* [nature])[20] are *anattā* (non-self). No one should become attached to any kind of *dhamma*.[21]

When there is no sense of attachment to a "self," or to things as the possession of a self, which in reality cannot be owned, suffering does not arise. Because the ultimate goal of Buddhism is to overcome suffering, Buddhadāsa identified emptiness or empty mind as the essence of Buddhism.

Second, Buddhadāsa explained that the mind is originally pure and empty, free from defilements. This argument of Buddhadāsa sounds like Zen, but he supported his idea with a Pāli phrase from the *Tipiṭaka*:

> *pabhassaram idaṃ bhikkhave cittaṃ āgantukehi upakilesehi upakiliṭṭhaṃ*

which means

> Bhikkhu[s], the mind is luminous. But, the mind becomes gloomy because *upakilesa* (imperfections) come as visitors.[22]

Thus, Buddhadāsa argued that the original mind (*chit doem thae*) does not have any defilement, so that it is always pure and luminous if we prevent defilements from arising by following the noble eightfold path (right view, right thinking, right speech, right action, right livelihood, right effort, right mindfulness, and right concentration). He explained,

> Mud is not a jewel, but luminosity is covered with mud. If we take away the mud, the jewel is luminous as it used to be. The mind is the same. Many sorts of *cetasika* come to it and deprive it of its luminosity.[23]

According to Buddhadāsa, defilements come to the original, pure mind in the following way. When a baby is born, it starts to have attachment. For example, when its eyes see a visual object, its ears hear a sound, its nose smells an odor, etc., it becomes interested in the visual object, sound, odor, taste, or body sensation, and either satisfaction (Pāli: *sukha vedanā*) or dissatisfaction (Pāli: *dukkha vedanā*) arises. Then, some kind of desire (Pāli: *tanhā*) arises, and then *upādāna* (clinging), or in other words, *tua ku* and *khong ku* (me and mine), arises. Since a little child does not have knowledge of the *dhamma*, *kilesa* easily arises because of its *avijjā* (ignorance). It soon starts to be attached to *sukha vedanā*, and that attachment produces suffering.[24]

However, Buddhadāsa thought that *tanhā* or *upādāna* does not occupy the mind for too long, perhaps several hours or minutes a day. If the mind were dominated by the sense of me and mine all the time, Buddhadāsa said, the person would become crazy. Any time when the mind is not interfered with by *kilesa*, the mind is at peace and is able to think with *sati paññā* (insight) and *sati-sampajañña* (full awareness).[25] Buddhadāsa's notion of empty mind, which is originally pure and freed from defilements and clinging, does not agree with the Abhidhamma theory of mind, so these points of disagreement became targets of criticism for the Abhidhamma groups, as is examined further in Chapter 5 of this volume.

Third, Buddhadāsa taught that empty mind is attainable and should be pursued by everyone, including lay people living in secular society. Since Buddhadāsa taught that the idea of empty mind or emptiness belongs to *lokuttara dhamma*, or the path of overcoming suffering, some people interpreted it as a teaching relevant to monks who aim at becoming *arahant* by renouncing the mundane world. However, Buddhadāsa found a scriptural foundation to support the practice of empty mind by lay people. Buddhadāsa often referred to the Pāli phrase,

> *Ye te suttantā tathāgatabhāsitā gambhīrā gambhīratthā lokuttarā suññatapaṭisaṃyuttā*,

which appears in the *Dhammadinna Sutta*.[26] In the story, the Buddha recommended the practice of emptiness when Dhammadinna sought advice that would benefit lay people. The Buddha answered,

> Then, Dhammadinna, thus must ye train yourselves: As to those discourses uttered by the Tathāgata, deep, deep in meaning, transcendental and concerned with the Void, from time to time we will spend our days learning them. That is how you must train yourselves, Dhammadinna.[27]

Through this scriptural authorization, empty mind or emptiness is encouraged for ordinary lay people who also have emptiness as the foundation of their mind, even though their mind is not always empty of defilements as is that of an *arahant*, hence *upādāna* often interferes with their mind.

Fourth, Buddhadāsa taught lay people to "work with empty mind" (*tham ngan duai chit wang*) in the midst of secular society. According to Buddhadāsa, when the mind is empty of egoism (*khwam-hen-kae-tua*), without the sense of me and mine, we work only in accordance with our duty. Also, when the mind is empty from clinging to me and mine, the mind is filled with *sati paññā* and *sati sampajañña*. Therefore, a person can fulfill their duty most perfectly when they have an empty mind. For example, Buddhadāsa said that when the mind is empty of attachment to the sense of "me" and "mine," a farmer can plough the field enjoyably even in the middle of the blazing sun, a hunter can shoot a target precisely, and a musician can play music in a most refined way.[28] Buddhadāsa promoted "work for work's sake," "work with empty mind," being forgetful of the benefit to oneself, especially with regard to work for society or for the nation. If there is egoism in the mind, the work will only be a means of unlawful benefit, and will not be done accurately.[29] However, Buddhadāsa taught that if a soldier has a sense of responsibility for the nation without any intention of doing unjust violence or killing people, the shooting by the soldier would not be a demerit, as it would be for those who have a sense of me and mine. This is compared to taking a medicine to excrete a parasitic worm. The person may know that the worm will be killed by the medicine, but the primary intention is not to kill, but to cure the body.[30] Buddhadāsa considered such acts as working with empty mind.

Because of Buddhadāsa's emphasis on this subject, the notion of emptiness was already familiar to Thai people in the 1960s. The more the notion of emptiness became popular, the more people were tempted to challenge Buddhadāsa regarding its relevance. In 1964, a dispute-ridden panel discussion about empty mind by Buddhadāsa and M.R.W. Kukrit Pramoj (1911–1995) gave rise to a lot to talk in the Buddhist public sphere of Thailand,[31] and even came to the attention of King Bhumibol.[32] In the following sections, I will examine how Buddhadāsa's notion of empty mind was discussed by his opponents and his followers.

3. Discussions with Kukrit Pramoj

From 1963 to 1965, the Teachers' Association (*Khurusapha*) had three series of panel discussions and a public lecture entitled "*Dhamma* as a Tool to Build a Person, to Build a Nation, and to Build the World," in which Buddhadāsa and M.R.W. Kukrit Pramoj were the main guest speakers.[33] This was an attractive event for Thai intellectual audiences because it involved two of the most respected intellectuals in Thailand, Buddhadāsa and Kukrit.[34] Buddhadāsa was a preacher who could seriously present essential Buddhist teachings which people in general had until then not been aware of in their ordinary Buddhist practice. He was a monk who had gained popularity not because of amusing jokes and funny stories, but because of the impressiveness of his religious message. On the other hand, Kukrit was a lay Buddhist and provocative public intellectual whose opinion was respected by many people.

As his title "Mom Ratchawong" (often abbreviated as "M.R.W.") suggests, Kukrit was a fourth-generation royal descendent, descending from King Rama II. He had a B.A. with honors in Philosophy, Politics, and Economics from Queen's College, Oxford. After his return from England in 1933, Kukrit demonstrated his ability in many areas, as a banker, a newspaper columnist, a novelist, and a politician. Before the early 1960s, Kukrit had been elected as an M.P. many times and had even served as a minister in the cabinet of Khuan Aphaiwong from 1947–1948. In 1950, he launched the newspaper *Sayam Rat* (*Siamese Nation*), which he owned and contributed to as a main columnist.[35] Kukrit was also popular for his skilful speech, through which he often made cynical comments and jokes about his discussant's arguments, inviting audience laughter and applause. Even though by blood he belonged to a royal lineage and was a royalist in terms of political ideology, Kukrit was one of the popular figures in democratic parliamentary politics and in the Thai public sphere.

The series' first panel discussion, "Work is a Practice of the *Dhamma*" (*Ngan khu kan-patibat-tham*), was held on 6 July 1963 with Buddhadāsa and three discussants invited: Kukrit Pramoj, Pui Rotchanaburanon, and Chanthit Krasaesin. This first discussion was broadcast nationwide on television and radio.[36] In the discussion, Buddhadāsa expressed his idea that the *dhamma* should not be left to the monasteries but should also be applied in everyday life. He said that when speaking of the *dhamma*, people should not consider it as abandoning or escaping from the secular world. Instead, the "true *dhamma*," said Buddhadāsa, teaches those who live in the secular world to "overcome the world," in other words, not to have suffering in the world.[37]

Basically, Buddhadāsa led the discussion by opposing the prevailing ethic, "Work is money, money is work"; he proposed an alternative idea, "Work is for work's sake" as the taking up of one's duty, which he regarded as a practice of the *dhamma*. He expanded this argument and said that if we work for money, conflicts between capitalists and laborers arise; on the other hand, if laborers are satisfied to practice the *dhamma* in their duty, there will be no conflict, thus such an ideology as communism would have never been born in the world.[38] Buddhadāsa insisted that:

> To practice the *dhamma* is to practice a duty. To practice a duty means to produce the beneficial [result] of the duty. This point is a pure *dhammajāti* (nature), and is the mind which is empty from [egotistical] attachment to self.[39]

One of the discussants, Chanthit, disagreed with Buddhadāsa's position regarding it as an idea only suitable for ordained people. He supported the truth of the prevailing saying, "Work is money, money is work that creates happiness" as the natural understanding of lay people who are attached to staying in the secular world.[40]

In the face of their disagreement, Kukrit supported Buddhadāsa's view in this first panel discussion. Kukrit said,

> [I] completely agree with Venerable Buddhadāsa who said that in our Buddhist religion the highest good that Buddhists should do is to act in accordance with duty. In general, for all who believe in Buddhism, who are not necessarily ordained persons, but farmers, government officials, army officers, and people in any other occupations including renunciates, the so-called good act is to do [one's] duty perfectly.[41]

After the session, Kukrit even wrote an article, "Work is to Practice the *Dhamma*," which supported this view of Buddhadāsa's in *Sayam Rat*, the newspaper that Kukrit owned.[42]

However, in the second discussion at Khurusapha, Kukrit and Buddhadāsa began to disagree. In the second discussion, only Buddhadāsa and Kukrit were invited to discuss the topic, "Work with Empty Mind (How Should We Understand the *Dhamma*?)."[43] In the beginning of their discussion, Kukrit agreed with Buddhadāsa, who criticized people's enthusiasm for memorizing scriptural passages and all the numbers of certain characteristics of mind in the Abhidhamma theory, which made it difficult to reach the real meaning of the *dhamma*, the overcoming of suffering.[44] However, when Buddhadāsa spoke of empty mind, Kukrit opposed Buddhadāsa with the insolently polite attitude of a royal descendent by calling Buddhadāsa "*tai thao*" (Your Excellency).[45]

By proposing "work with empty mind," Buddhadāsa argued that we should carry out all our duties with a non-egotistical mind, i.e., with no sense of self and possession by the self, because when the mind is free from egoism, the work will be well done. However, Kukrit said that he did not know how to work with empty mind in the secular world, and if his mind were empty from egoism, he would not work, but would instead ordain.[46] For Kukrit, work in secular society is contradictory to empty mind and the overcoming of suffering, because worldly happiness means suffering from the viewpoint of the *dhamma*, and success in work only makes sense in the secular world. Kukrit argued,

> Work is in a state of attachment. If someone cannot abandon *upādāna* (clinging) yet, the person has to continue working. It is a part of suffering. If I do my work with empty mind, I still do not find a way. This is perhaps because I have a narrow mind or eyes that do not discern the *dhamma*. I really cannot think of [how to work with empty mind] yet … I express true respect, but I do not understand, and would like to understand … These are [the different] expressions of a layman and a monk. We live in different worlds for just this reason.[47]

He also said playfully,

> If I determined only to make money in order to become rich, I would not be here today. I am not *wang* [empty/free].[48]

Kukrit's point was that the world and the *dhamma* cannot go together.

Their disagreement about "work with empty mind" was a difference of opinion as to whether it was appropriate to apply *lokuttara dhamma* (teaching indicating supramundane states) to lay people as well as to monks. *Lokuttara dhamma* contrasts with *lokiya dhamma* (teaching at the level of mundane states). Thai Buddhists have long been familiar with *lokiya dhamma*, which teaches that we should maintain morality by doing good and avoiding evil, but *lokuttara dhamma* has not been so well known. *Lokuttara dhamma* is usually regarded as teaching for those who wish to become *arahant*, in other words usually it is a teaching for renunciates, because it shows paths for transcending the mundane world so as to attain *nibbāna* by extinguishing defilements and suffering. Making the mind empty of defilements and clinging should be included in the teaching of *lokuttara dhamma* as the path of enlightenment and liberation, but Buddhadāsa promoted lay people's use of it in their lives, for instance, for farmers while they plough the fields.[49]

Buddhadāsa's keen proponent, Pun Chonprasoet, also recognized the difficulties in that proposal as pointed out by Kukrit. In his commentary written just after their panel discussion, Pun wrote that both Buddhadāsa and Kukrit were fair in their manner of discussion, but their disagreement derived from their different specializations, respectively in the *lokuttara* and the *lokiya*, and especially from Buddhadāsa's lack of expertise with the *lokiya* realm.[50] In other words, the disagreement between Buddhadāsa and

Kukrit at the Kurusapha discussion session was quite understandable; it did not appear to be a serious conflict between the two intellectuals.

Kukrit's Antagonism Toward Buddhadāsa After the Khurusapha Discussions

The true nature of the conflict appeared after the second Khurusapha discussion. Kukrit hated Buddhadāsa strongly, and became a prominent opponent of his teaching. According to stories reported by Pun Chongprasoet, on Kukrit's birthday in 1964 or 1965, which was either the same year or a year after they had the disagreement at Khurusapha, Kukrit received a book by Buddhadāsa as a birthday gift from poet Prakat Watcharaphon. Kukrit got very angry, and said that his birthday had become ill-omened. He threw Buddhadāsa's book onto the ground, and drove Prakat out of his house.[51] On another occasion, Kukrit said that if Buddhism consisted of only *lokuttara dhamma*, empty mind, and Zen, he would quit believing in Buddhism. Kukrit considered that all suffering could only be relieved by *mettā* (loving kindness), so he did not address *nibbāna*. Pun reported that Kukrit was of the opinion that "heaven is only a night club, *nibbāna* is only a tranquilliser, and Suan Mokkh is no different from Disneyland (i.e., an American town of puppets for the amusement of children)."[52]

Beyond his emotional antagonism toward Buddhadāsa, Kukrit wrote a number of essays, especially in his newspaper *Sayam Rat* opposing Buddhadāsa.[53] Kukrit used his position as a popular oratorical politician and columnist to link Buddhadāsa's propagation of *lokuttara dhamma* with the issue of national security during the Cold War period. According to Pun Chongprasoet, in May 1972, Kukrit wrote an article in *Duang Prathip* (*A Light*), a journal of the Department of Religious Affairs, criticizing the propagation of *lokuttara dhamma*. Pun summarized Kukrit's main arguments in his book.[54] In this article, Kukrit argued that if the teachings of *lokuttara dhamma*, including *suññatā*, spread to the people, Buddhism would become an evil obstacle to the development of the nation. Because *lokuttara dhamma* teaches people to extinguish defilements, craving, desires, sense of self, and clinging, people would lose interest in developing the country as a result of achieving empty mind and becoming *arahant*.

However, instead of rejecting the whole of Buddhism as useless, Kukrit felt that *lokiya dhamma* should be promoted as a pillar of national development. *Lokiya dhamma* teaches people the law of *kamma*: those who do good will receive good; those who do evil will receive evil. According to Kukrit, *lokiya dhamma* is based on the transient truth which considers that those who perform *kamma* have a self, so people can act in order to attain the fruit of the act for their own benefit or for that of others.[55] Thus, Kukrit regarded *lokiya dhamma* as beneficial for its potential as a principle of social development.

On the other hand, Kukrit explained that *lokuttara dhamma* is a teaching aimed at making one's actions *suññatā* or empty, so as not to cause any suffering to arise. In the state of emptiness, according to Kukrit, people could not remain in ordinary lay life, so they would have to escape from society; he regarded this as natural for the attainment of *nibbāna*.[56] Also, in *lokuttara dhamma* both the positive *kamma* and negative *kamma* of *lokiya dhamma* are to be avoided, because both of them mean "arising" (*khwam-koet*), which can lead to suffering. Thus, Kukrit argued in *lokuttara dhamma*,

> To struggle over whatever we consider good in the world, society and development is an act of demerit. Instead, an act, which does not cause anything to arise, and does not produce any fruit for society or oneself at all, is a right act in *lokuttara dhamma*.[57]

Kukrit understood that traditional secular authorities had restricted *lokuttara dhamma* from spreading to people because it was seen as a profoundly disquieting truth which would prevent the nation from developing.[58]

In Kukrit's understanding of Buddhism, those who follow the path of *arahant* are the ones who have abandoned the world for their own accomplishment, and they do not make a contribution to society. This view of *lokuttara dhamma* coincided with the Marxist criticism of religion as idealism useless for revolutionary change in society, despite the fact that Kukrit was known as a keen opponent of communism. As a liberal, but at the same time a conservative royalist politician, Kukrit did not totally reject Buddhism, but proposed to make use of Buddhism by instituting *lokiya dhamma* as an ideology for national development. By national development, in the political context of the late 1960s and the 1970s, he meant improved welfare for the people in order to prevent the penetration of communism into Thailand. Kukrit's viewpoint was that of a rightist politician, in which Buddhism had to be an attractive counter-ideology to Marxism to which people could become attached, rather than a means to achieve transcendent liberation by abandoning clinging to the self or the possessions of the self.

Buddhadāsa's view differed radically from Kukrit's. Buddhadāsa also felt that Buddhism was useful for the work of society, but by Buddhism, he meant *lokuttara dhamma*. Unlike Kukrit, Buddhadāsa did not see *lokuttara dhamma* as a religion only for those who abandon the world; rather he felt it provided a means to conduct secular duties most efficiently and enjoyably, and to produce the most desirable result.

Although in their second discussion at the Khurusapha, the significant conflict was regarding the appropriateness of such teaching for the unordained, the significance of this dispute should not be considered as equivalent to the ideological conflict between Catholic and Protestant in Christianity. In fact, it was Buddhadāsa, a monk, who urged that lay people practice *lokuttara dhamma*, which used to be the domain of only a few monks, and Kukrit, a layman, who was opposed to the possibility of opening it up to ordinary lay people. By his propagation of *lokuttara dhamma* to lay people, Buddhadāsa did not intend to lead a Protestant kind of movement to abolish the monk-lay distinction, which action would in turn negate the existing order of the Saṅgha.

Also, the conflict between Buddhadāsa and Kukrit should not be understood as an ideological conflict between commoners and members of royal high society. Buddhadāsa recalled that among the audience at the discussion with Kukrit, Mom Chao Suphasawat Sawatdiwat (Chin), a royal descendent who had even higher status and closer links with the recent kings than Kukrit did, encouraged Buddhadāsa rather than Kukrit.[59] There were quite a few Buddhadāsa supporters among the royal family, including the Queen Mother of King Bhumibol Adulyadej.[60]

Perhaps for Kukrit, who could not completely defeat Buddhadāsa in the Khurusapha discussion, one of the most efficient ways to keep face with the audience in the public sphere was to link their disagreement to differences in ideological and political positions. When Kukrit argued that Buddhadāsa's propagation of empty mind and *lokuttara dhamma* was problematic for national security, which was becoming an increasingly serious issue in the face of the escalating Vietnam War, he could give people the impression that Buddhadāsa might be an "unorthodox," dangerous monk. The disagreement between Kukrit and Buddhadāsa continued throughout the period of ideological conflict, and it was only when Buddhadāsa passed away in 1993 that Kukrit expressed his great respect for Buddhadāsa in his column, "Suan Phlu Lane" (*Soi suan phlu*).[61] That article marked the end of their conflict.

Pun Chongprasoet's Defense of Buddhadāsa and Empty Mind

The discussion about empty mind was not simply a personal conflict between Buddhadāsa and Kukrit. Especially after Kukrit's criticism made people skeptical of Buddhadāsa and empty mind, Buddhadāsa's lay disciples also reacted against Kukrit. Those disciples of Buddhadāsa who were committed to assisting in the propagation of his teaching spread not only Buddhadāsa's arguments and defenses; they also expressed their own views and understandings of empty mind. One of the most prominent persons in that group was Pun Chongprasoet, the president of the Organization for the Restoration of Buddhism.

Pun published a number of booklets that opposed Kukrit, using both the words of Buddhadāsa and his own essays and comments.[62] In one of those books, Pun stated that one purpose for publishing the booklet was:

> I liked the writings of M.R.W. Kukrit for a long time, and was never an opponent of his. However, when he expressed *micchādiṭṭhi* [wrong view] on the Buddha's teachings like this many times, I considered that it is not only a lot of verbal offence to Venerable Buddhadāsa, but also has the intention to distort the Buddha's teachings by speaking badly about teachings at the level of *lokuttara dhamma*, *suññatā*, and the accomplishing of the *nibbāna* of the Buddha. Also, there is no one who dares to challenge him at all. If [we] leave his smart expressions further unchecked, it is going to be dangerous to Buddhism, and it will make those who pay respect to him follow his deluded way. Thus, I think that it is appropriate for me to crush the *kilesa* of M.R.W. Kukrit in order to prevent it from becoming too active and a danger to society … [People] are deluded to be afraid only that communists will destroy Buddhism; [when] someone of the capitalist and *sakdina* [feudalist] class is openly destroying Buddhism in this way, no one knows and no one points it out. Is this love of the nation and religion? His mouth shouts to protect religion, but he himself does not know what the religion teaches, where it is, or how to protect it. These days there are only talkative people who [just] follow their feelings/emotions (Thai: *arom*) [but do not have a good understanding of Buddhism — complementary note by Ito].[63]

Such a reaction by Pun to Kukrit represented an expansion of the discussion about empty mind in the Buddhist public sphere of Thailand. Pun indicated that Kukrit was campaigning from his socially privileged position to promote Buddhism, the religion of the Thai nation, for national security against communism, but the politically motivated campaign was not necessarily based on a deep understanding of the content of the religion. When Kukrit called Buddhadāsa's propagation of empty mind and *lokuttara dhamma* a hindrance to national security, and Kukrit was accused of belonging to the "capitalist" and "*sakdina*" (feudalist) class, and the connotations of their conflict were twisted to align with the ideological conflict between the right and the left. Even though Kukrit was a secular intellectual without long monastic experience and could not be counted as representing any orthodoxy of Thai Buddhism, his conflict with Buddhadāsa significantly contributed to the Buddhist public sphere perception of Buddhadāsa as "unorthodox" and a radical preacher.

Aside from defending Buddhadāsa from Kukrit's criticism, Pun also played an important role in popularizing the idea of empty mind through his supplementary comments on Buddhadāsa's sermons.[64] Pun's explanation of empty mind appealed to Thai people's dissatisfaction with contemporary politics and society. In a booklet, following a sermon of Buddhadāsa entitled "Working with Empty Mind for Society," Pun wrote a supplementary essay, "What Should We Do to be Said to be Working with Empty Mind?"[65] In his essay, Pun explained the idea of working with empty mind by giving examples of several occupations, such as prime minister, governor, government official, judge, soldier, executioner, policeman, businessman, and renunciate. Those examples showed how empty mind works in secular society, even though the notion of emptiness, in which state the mind is freed from the defilements of greed, anger, delusion, craving and fear, and rather is filled with *satipaññā*, is too difficult for some people to understand. In the case of MPs, Pun commented as follows:

> If they [determine to] stand for election and [eventually] are elected in order to do their duty for people's benefit — not because they expect a monthly salary (15,000 baht per month) or seek indirect benefit for themselves — they can dare to say and do something in their duty gloriously with 'empty mind'. They do not sell themselves to capitalists or *sakdina* [feudalists], because they do not expect to gain more importance than as representatives of people. When they run for election, they do not become addicted to bribery, so-called 'vote-buying' as capitalists spend millions of baht with the expectation that if they can become Ministers, they might be able to gain more than they spent in a short period. MPs with 'empty mind' thus tend to be elected every time, even though they themselves do not have enough money to deceive anyone.[66]

Pun even insisted that communists should also have empty mind. Pun said,

> ... otherwise they are fake communists who still have thick *kilesa* [defilement] and intense *taṇhā* [craving], by which they only think to rob rich people of their fortune to make it their own; they want to kill capitalists or ordinary people who have not yet agreed with them; and have the intention to eradicate kings who have *dasarājadhamma* [ten kingly virtues]. They have not yet dedicated themselves to the public. They have not even given a thought to doing something for society. They only advertise their ideology with words, but they still cannot do it. They are provocative because they want to be famous, aspire to high

> positions, and then they will be able to look for a benefit for themselves as do all people with thick *kilesa*. Thus in the group of communists there are still mutual betrayals, competition for positions, and frequent murders. These are because they still do not have true 'empty mind.'[67]

When this booklet of Pun was published in 1975, the conflict between the communist insurgency and the government's counter-insurgency was becoming tense. It was true that people were sick of the *thorarat*, the three interrelated military dictators before the 14 October 1973 uprising, but politicians in the post-uprising democratic parliament did not exhibit many differences from the corrupt dictators on this issue. Among students and intellectuals, there was enthusiasm for communist theories of revolution and struggle, but the actual politics and human nature of international communist leaders did not meet people's expectations of fairness. People were never satisfied with the existing politicians, but at the same time, they feared a communist takeover of the existing order as had been repeatedly foretold by successive Thai governments. In such conditions, people could find diversion in Buddhadāsa's proposal of non-egotistical conduct of duty with empty mind, which supported and was supported by Pun's comical criticisms of the powerful authorities and equally frightening counter-authorities. Pun's discussions of empty mind were one of his contemporary expressions of and responses to people's demand for social justice in the Buddhist public sphere.

4. Debates between Buddhadāsa's Opponents and Followers

As a result of the Khurusapha discussions with Kukrit, Buddhadāsa's concept of empty mind became widely known among Thai Buddhists. More people started to talk about empty mind, and more opinions appeared in the Buddhist public sphere in the late 1960s and early 1970s.

What is Right? What is Wrong? (*Arai thuk, arai phit*) was a booklet in which Pun Chongprasoet collected both supporting and opposing arguments on empty mind. To focus debate on the issue, he contrasted his summary of Kukrit's article on empty mind[68] with three of Buddhadāsa's sermons, which were actually delivered five years before Kukrit's criticism, but which Pun considered to be apt responses to Kukrit's arguments.[69] Apart from the discussions by Kukrit and Buddhadāsa, in the appendix of the book, Pun reprinted a handbill, articles, a transcript of a public lecture and letters by other advocates. By juxtaposing the pro and the con opinions, Pun created in one book a *wethi*, or a public forum about empty mind. Also, by asking the readers, "Who is right? Who is wrong?" (*khrai thuk, khrai phit*),[70] Pun invited people to think about their position on this issue. The following is an exploration of the discussions that Pun reprinted in the appendix of the book.

Participants in the discussion forum were chosen from groups both opposing and supporting Buddhadāsa. Major opponents of Buddhadāsa were Kittivuḍḍho Bhikkhu (1936–2005), a popular Abhidhamma preacher and leader of an anti-communist mass movement), and "Khamhuno" (1924–2002), whose real name was Chamrat Duangthisan, a famous columnist for the *Sayam Rat* weekly magazine. Pun presented each of them with counter-arguments from ordinary citizens who were dissatisfied with their arguments against Buddhadāsa. Pun then introduced a public lecture by Sanya Dhammasakdi (1907–2002), who had served as Prime Minister, chair of the Privy Council, and president of the Buddhist Association of Thailand). Sanya, a socially respected figure, gave an opinion in support of Buddhadāsa's concept of empty mind. And moderator Pun concluded the discussion.

Kittivuḍḍho Bhikkhu versus "Prayut"

First, Pun introduced a handbill by Kittivuḍḍho criticizing Buddhadāsa's proposal of empty mind and emptiness.[71]

Scholars outside Thailand may remember Kittivuḍḍho as an anti-communist monk, and for his notorious speech: "Killing Communists is Not Demeritorious."[72] In the 1960s, Kittivuḍḍho was known as a young, capable Abhidhamma preacher at Wat Mahathat. He came from the third generation of a Chinese wholesaler's family in the Nakhon Phathom province. Although he and Buddhadāsa differed in age by 30 years, Kittivuḍḍho agreed in an interview with me that he and Buddhadāsa had some background in common. Both came from families originally from Hokkien province in China; they had the same Chinese family name Khou (許), and both families had been doing business in Thailand. When they were small, both of them helped with the family business and started to learn Buddhism by themselves.[73] By the age of 20, both of them could start preaching the *dhamma* immediately.

Kittivuḍḍho ordained in 1957, read the *Tipiṭaka* in a cave in Chumphon for six months, and studied Abhidhamma doctrines at Wat Mahathat with a Burmese monk Techin, and his Thai assistant monk Phra Khru Prakat-samathikhun. In 1960, only three years after his ordination, Kittivuḍḍho started his *dhamma* propagation on television and radio, and in 1965 he started a training project for novices and young monks to become preachers.[74] According to an Abhidhamma classmate of Kittivuḍḍho, Kittivuḍḍho was intelligent and his ability to memorize the complicated technical terms of Abhidhamma was beyond compare. Even though Kittivuḍḍho had little in formal or ecclesiastical education, his classmate reported that his ability to work for religion was encouraging for those monks who had not passed the Pāli ecclesiastical examinations.[75]

According to Pun, Kittivuḍḍho was strongly opposed to empty mind in his publications and *dhamma* lectures on radio from around 1964, only seven years after his ordination. Kittivuḍḍho lent his support to the critical campaign against Buddhadāsa led by Phra Thipparinya (Thup Klamphasut), one of the important lay supporters of Wat Mahathat and the first person who labeled Buddhadāsa a communist in 1948. In 1969, Phra Maha Khachit, who was then a novice studying under Kittivuḍḍho's project, witnessed Kittivuḍḍho burning Buddhadāsa's books because Kittivuḍḍho argued that they would disseminate a wrong view that did not correspond to Abhidhamma theory.[76]

Furthermore, Arun Wetchasuan (1946–), an ex-monk Buddhist writer,[77] said that in the mid-1970s many handbills making accusations about Buddhadāsa and distributed nationwide were assumed to be by Kittivuḍḍho. Arun saw many local monks posting those handbills, allegedly written by Kittivuḍḍho, on temple walls because they hated Buddhadāsa's rational teachings, which would interfere with their making a living through supernatural "services." Arun thought of two reasons why Kittivuḍḍho would author the handbills. One was because of Buddhadāsa's radical criticism of the Abhidhamma, upon which Kittivuḍḍho relied, as useless and so to be torn up and abandoned. The other reason, Arun suspected, was revenge on Buddhadāsa by the CIA, because he had declined to cooperate with their propaganda program. Arun assumed that the CIA had supervised and funded Kittivuḍḍho's anti-communist mass organization through which Kittivuḍḍho carried out his anti-Buddhadāsa campaign. Although these remarks were not well supported by evidence, Arun said that it was very likely.[78]

In the handbill that Pun reprinted in *What is Right? What is Wrong?*, Kittivuḍḍho critically examined the *Dhammadinna Sutta* in the *Tipiṭaka*, which Buddhadāsa often used to legitimize his teaching of emptiness. Buddhadāsa liked to relate the story that when Dhammadinna and 500 lay disciples went to ask the Buddha to give a suitable teaching for lay people, the Buddha recommended practicing emptiness that had been taught by the *Tathāgata* (perfect one). Buddhadāsa usually only related the first half of the story of the *Dhammadinna Sutta*, but Kittivuḍḍho introduced the rest of the story in his handbill: hearing the advice of the Buddha, Dhammadinna replied that they looked after their houses and children and handled gold and silver, so it was not easy for them to learn the discourses of the *Tathāgata*. Instead, he asked the Buddha to teach those who firmly followed the lay five precepts. The Buddha then taught them to have faith in the Buddha, the Dhamma, and the Saṅgha, and to conduct themselves with the virtues of the Ariyan (Noble Ones), all of which would lead to concentration. Dhammadinna answered that those conditions already existed in them. On hearing their statement, the Buddha affirmed their attainment of the fruit of stream-winning (Pāli: *sotāpattiphala*).[79]

By introducing the latter half of the story, Kittivuḍḍho insisted that neither this section of the *Tipiṭaka* nor the Theravāda School of Buddhism taught empty mind as "one teacher" (by which Kittivuḍḍho meant Buddhadāsa) understood, namely that the Buddha taught lay people to work or to have sexual intercourse with empty mind.[80] Kittivuḍḍho supported his criticism with an extract from the *aṭṭhakathā* (commentary), *Sārattathappakāsinī* containing phrases from the *Dhammadinna Sutta* to which Buddhadāsa frequently referred. According to Kittivuḍḍho's Pāli quotation,

> *lokuttarā[ti] lokuttaradīpakā asaṅkhatasaṃyuttādayo*
>
> (Kittivuḍḍho's Thai translation: *Plae wa bot lokuttara nan, dai kae asangkhata sangyut pen ton, an sadaeng attha pen lokuttara*)
>
> (An English translation of Kittivuḍḍho's Thai translation: *lokuttarā* which is given in *asaṃgatasaṃyuttā* etc. expresses the words of *lokuttara*)
>
> (An English translation from Pāli: *lokuttarā* stands for the meaning [of what is] beyond the world, i.e., connected with the uncompounded and so on),
>
> *suññatappaṭisaṃyuttāti sattasuññatādīpakā khajjanikasuttantādayo*
>
> (Kittivuḍḍho: *Bot wa sunyatappatisangyutta nan, dai kae sut tang tang, mi khatchanika sut pen ton, an sadaeng phawa thi wang chak sat*)
>
> (A translation of Kittivuḍḍho: *suññatappaṭisaṃyuttā* which is given in various *sutta*, such as the *Khajjanika Sutta*, expresses the state that is empty/free from animals/beings)
>
> (A translation from Pāli: *suññatappaṭisaṃyuttā* stands for emptiness of a living being, [like in] the *Khajjanika-suttanta* and so on).[81]

By citing the story of the *Dhammadinna Sutta* and these phrases in the commentary, Kittivuḍḍho argued that the Buddha never spoke of empty mind. He explained that by the word *lokuttara* the Buddha meant *asaṃkhata-dhamma*; by *suñña* he meant the five aggregates which are empty of/free from a person, as expressed in the *Khajjanika Sutta*.[82] Furthermore, Kittivuḍḍho insisted that the teaching of emptiness or empty mind belongs to Mahāyāna Buddhism, and does not belong to the *Tipiṭaka* and pure Theravāda Buddhism. Therefore, he concluded, "to cite an idea which developed in the tenth century after the extinction of the Buddha's speaking is not a merit at all. It does not help those who practice it. It is wrong to claim that it is the true word of the Buddha."[83]

In Kittivuḍḍho's criticism of empty mind, there are at least three points to note. First, as Kittivuḍḍho said, it is true that in the *Dhammadinna Sutta*, the group of lay people had the fruit of stream-winning (Pāli: *sotāpattiphala*) even though they said that they could not follow the teaching of emptiness as the Buddha recommended. In fact, Buddhadāsa also mentioned the latter half of the story in one of his sermons.[84] In Buddhadāsa's nuanced explanation, if *suññatā*, or emptiness, is too advanced to practice, then four items of practice are sufficient, namely unshakeable faith in the Buddha, the Dhamma, and the Saṅgha, and the observance of pure precepts, which are already commonly practiced, so people do not have to worry. Thus, Buddhadāsa said, "If [they] do not accept *suññatā*, there is nothing to add," by which he implied that lay people should be interested in *suññatā*, which is more than they are accustomed to, and also that it was recommended as suitable for them by the Buddha.[85] This remark by Buddhadāsa indicates his selective interpretation of the scriptures. Buddhadāsa still recommended that lay people practice emptiness, even though it was not a necessary condition for lay people's spiritual liberation: as the scriptures state, the Buddha still recognized they could arrive at *sotāpattiphala* simply by the common code of lay practice.

However, as for the second point of Kittivuḍḍho's argument, his concluding by citing this *sutta* and its commentary, namely that the concept of emptiness is not taught in the Theravāda *Tipiṭaka*, went too far. Although it is commonly known that, as Kittivuḍḍho pointed out, the ideas and discussions about emptiness developed in Mahāyāna Buddhism, the fact that it exists in the Theravāda *Tipiṭaka* cannot be denied. Aside from the *Dhammadinna Sutta*, in the *Culāsuññatā Sutta* and the *Mahāsuññatā Sutta*, the Buddha also taught Ānanda how to enter and abide in emptiness.[86]

Moreover, when it is more carefully examined, the *Sārattathappakāsini*, the traditional Theravāda commentary that Kittivuḍḍho cited, is also supportive of the point that often appeared in Buddhadāsa's teaching. The commentary explained the meaning of *suññatā* as "emptiness of a living being, [like in] the *Khajjanika-suttanta* and so on."[87] In the *Khajjanīka sutta*, instead of mentioning the word "emptiness," the Buddha was saying, "I say, every body should be thus regarded as it really is, by right insight: 'this is not mine; this am not I; this is not the Self of me.'"[88] In other words, the ancient commentator of the Theravāda School understood that *suññatā* was to be understood as "empty [of self]" or equivalent to non-self. Detachment from "me" and "mine" was one of the important teachings of Buddhadāsa.[89]

Third, Kittivuḍḍho's citation and his Thai translation of a Pāli commentary is perceived to be potentially very difficult for most ordinary people who are not used to technical terms of Buddhism in Pāli. In his Thai translation of the Pāli phrases, several Pāli words remained untranslated, and would not make sense to those in his audience who did not already have some knowledge of Buddhist technical terms. Clearly, when he used these almost incomprehensible Pāli terms fluently in his speech, people would have felt that Kittivuḍḍho was truly an expert of Pāli scriptures, an area they did not know well, and some would have felt great respect for him.

Furthermore, in his Thai translation, which contained a great number of Pāli words, the only comprehensible Thai phrase was "*wang chak sat*." This is a translation of the Pāli phrase, *suññatappaṭisaṃyuttā*, which actually means "emptiness of a living being," but for those Thais not specializing in Buddhist scriptures, Kittivuḍḍho's Thai translation was perceived as something like "not having a violent nature like an animal."[90] In other words, Kittivuḍḍho's Thai translation only served to give Thai people a vague impression that the emptiness in the Pāli scriptures was not at all as deep as Buddhadāsa was trying to say, but something to do with the nature of beasts. Especially when Kittivuḍḍho's speech was supported by rather trustworthy evidence, such as the latter half of the *Dhammadinna Sutta* and the Mahāyāna development of emptiness, people became more inclined to accept his main, false claim, i.e., that the concept of emptiness does not exist in the Theravāda *Tipiṭaka*. This was a shrewd technique by the eloquent preacher Kittivuḍḍho.

In the face of such arguments from Kittivuḍḍho, Buddhadāsa's followers reacted strongly. As a counter-argument to Kittivuḍḍho, although it was not directly about the handbill, Pun introduced a letter from "Prayut."[91] Prayut, who worked for the Irrigation Department, was perhaps an ordinary lay follower of Buddhadāsa but could not be said to be Buddhadāsa's personal acquaintance. He felt that he could not stand listening to Kittivuḍḍho's attacks on the radio against Buddhadāsa and empty mind, so he sent his letter of refutation, one copy to Kittivuḍḍho, and another to Pun, in order to share his view with other people.[92]

Prayut perceived that Kittivuḍḍho did not examine the empty nature of mind from his own experience and wisdom, but only followed classical commentaries written after the death of the Buddha. Prayut also pointed out that in the radio broadcast, Kittivuḍḍho distorted the fact that the concept of emptiness does exist in the *Tipiṭaka*, and manipulated the meaning of *suññatā* to be "total vanishing." He indicated that together with the extensive demonstration of the Abhidhamma theory, Kittivuḍḍho utilized his attractiveness as a young and skilful speaker to induce people to trust him. Because of these acts, Prayut criticized Kittivuḍḍho for uncritically following the *atthakathā* (commentary) teachers rather than using his own *satipaññā* (wisdom).[93]

Although Prayut's criticisms of Kittivuḍḍho stood to reason, perhaps Prayut had not studied scriptures as Kittivuḍḍho had done. The reason for Prayut accepting Buddhadāsa was not only out of respect for Buddhadāsa as an authority on interpretation, but also because he recognized the practicality of empty mind for overcoming suffering. Prayut wrote that he studied Buddhism as a *chao ban* (villager or ordinary commoner); he learned whatever teaching made his suffering lighter and increased his *paññā* (insight and understanding), no matter whether the teaching originated from the Mahāyāna or Theravāda, without "being deluded" by the *Abhidhammapiṭaka*.[94] This was the same way Buddhadāsa developed his thought. Such an impression by Prayut represents the acceptance of Buddhadāsa's unfamiliar concept of empty mind in contemporary Thailand as more authentic than traditional Theravāda Abhidhamma scholasticism.

"Khamhuno" versus Wai

Next, Pun introduced two articles by "Khamhuno," who criticized empty mind and wrote for *Sayam Rat* weekly magazine, which was run by Kukrit Pramoj. According to Pun, some people misunderstood, thinking that "Khamhuno" was Kukrit himself,[95] but in fact "Khamhuno" was a pseudonym of Chamrat Duangthisan.[96] Pun explained that Khamhuno used to be a monk at Wat Phichaiyat in Bangkok and had passed the seventh grade of the Pāli ecclesiastical examination, but by the time of the discussion, he had already disrobed and was working as a Buddhism columnist.[97] In the book *What is Right? What is Wrong?*, Pun collected Khamhuno's "A Farmer with 'Empty Mind'" (*Chao na 'phu chit wang'*)[98] and "Me and Mine" (*Tua ku lae khong ku*).[99] In both of these articles, Khamhuno elaborated on the arguments of Kukrit, his employer, who criticized the propagation of empty mind and *lokuttara dhamma*, and backed this up with his higher Pāli qualification, which was even higher than Buddhadāsa's.

In the first article, which is especially important, Khamhuno's aim was to connect the concept of empty mind with communism. Khamhuno argued that in Buddhism, there are two levels of teaching: the level of empty mind and the level of non-empty mind, namely *lokuttara dhamma* and *lokiya dhamma*. At one level, he wrote that the Buddha taught his disciples, for example, the *pañcavaggiya* (the five ascetics who first accompanied Gotama) in the *Dhammacakkapavattana Sutta*, not to be attached to anything, such as their wife, children, fortune, and rather encouraged them to feel bored with those things and leave them alone (*ploi wang*).[100] On the other hand, Khamhuno wrote,

> The Buddha taught ordinary people to be attached to their family, to society, eventually to the nation. In other words, everyone has a responsibility as a member of society, [so that they] cannot work as a person with 'empty mind' … In life, to survive, if [they] want to become wealthy, [they] have to be honest, be diligent, know [how to] guard and protect [themselves], plant rice in the field, and plant vegetables and fruits in the garden. So, they have to have a sense of the self as an owner. [They do] not plant with the power of the isolated 'empty mind', [which makes them] say 'This rice belongs to the government, this rice field is not mine, but is a collective field.'[101]

He pointed out that in worldly society, having a sense of ownership generates better results than considering oneself as a common owner, therefore the Buddha taught the mundane level of teaching, which does not speak against those who have the defilement of the sense of ownership. Khamhuno concluded that the system of collective farming and communes in communism was in vain because it tried to make farmers be persons with empty mind, who have no sense of being an own.[102]

This essay by Khamhuno developed Kukrit's point of disagreement with Buddhadāsa: the incompatibility of empty mind and *lokuttara dhamma* for lay people, which he intentionally connected with communism. As Pun rephrased it, Khamhuno's argument implied that the teaching of empty mind was a vehicle to bring communism into Thailand, and thus the teacher of empty mind, Buddhadāsa, was propagating communism, so the government should promptly eliminate him.[103] Even though Khamhuno provided no supporting evidence for Buddhadāsa's being a communist, those articles contributed to suspicions about Buddhadāsa's political and ideological intentions.

Khamhuno even made fun of empty mind, which is freed from a sense of me and mine, by saying,

> If someone picked up a pen which fell from the bag of a person who was thinking to become 'empty mind', and asked 'Whose pen is this?' then there would immediately be a voice in reply with *upādāna*, 'Mine.'[104]

These statements of Khamhuno suggest that his essays were written in order to discredit the notion of empty mind among his readers. Even without a rational argument, facile yet catchy impressions can have a strong impact in the public sphere of Thailand.

Consequently, reactions to Khamhuno were also emotional. Pun mocked Khamhuno, who had studied as a monk, as follows:

> He is recently adhering to the motto, 'Work is money, money as work creates happiness'. Thus, the mind of 'Khamhuno' cannot be empty, and has no way of understanding 'empty mind' at all. He used to stretch out in a temple for a long time in the way of 'empty mind'. He had no need to work for survival, but [just] relied on the people's support. When he studied higher *pariyatti* [scriptural studies], his mind started to be disquieted, thus he had to escape from the state of a renunciate to be a lay man. ... [Since he has] disrobed, he writes essays that destroy the most important teaching of Buddhism, again for the purpose of survival, or to please his employer, who also hates *suññatā*.[105]

Pun also published a letter from "Wai," who opposed Khamhuno strongly.[106] Describing himself as "a farmer with empty mind in the Songkhla province," Wai talked about his own experience as follows:

> I am a farmer who has been closely associated with rice planting until becoming an adult. I think that rice planting is not an easy task at all. But having a kind of empty mind helped me to do that task. 'Khamhuno' would not have grown rice, because he used to be a monk who for a long time begged from villagers to eat. [He did] not have to do any work, [but] ate and slept comfortably, so he does not know anything at all. Empty mind is, therefore, a foundation of life. If life is always repressed by *upādāna*, life is beyond enduring.[107]

Wai concluded his letter with a strong tone,

> Actually, at the level of [your] mind, when you [Khamhuno] do not understand Venerable Buddhadāsa clearly enough, is it appropriate for you to rush to state that Buddhadāsa talks about impossible things? ... Your level of knowledge of *dhamma* is still as far away from Buddhadāsa's as the sky is from the earth. Please know yourself somehow, and do not follow your employer to become crazy together.[108]

These quotations indicate that discussions in the mid-20th-century Buddhist public sphere of Thailand were not always rational or supported by evidence. There were rational arguments as Buddhadāsa demonstrated, but there were also many emotional statements, manipulations, exaggerations, speculations, and jokes. Evidence and facts were not so important as the general impressions that people received. Those who went on to the stage of public discussion tended to argue their discussant down, even using mere quibbles. Therefore, extensive campaigns, which were often supported by generous funding and famous people, were very influential.

However, whatever tactics were applied, as long as there was no official intervention from the government or the Saṅgha, it was hardly ever possible for one opinion to eliminate others from the public sphere. The only possible victory in the public sphere was for some opinions to gain hegemony over competing ones. In order for Buddhadāsa's teaching to gain hegemony, Pun collected and publicized the opinions of Buddhadāsa's ordinary followers, who attempted to counter-argue against his detractors. Also, by contrasting the opposing sides of the argument, Pun appealed to people's "rationality" to distinguish the "right view."

The other approach that Pun applied to increase Buddhadāsa's social credibility was to introduce the opinion of a socially respected lay disciple of Buddhadāsa, Sanya Dhammasakdi.

Sanya Dhammasakdi

Sanya was a highly respected judge, elected many times to the presidency of the Buddhist Association of Thailand, appointed by the King to be interim Prime Minister after the 14 October 1973 uprising, and Chair of the Privy Council in 1975.[109] Pun reprinted a public lecture by Sanya in which he related his own example of how empty mind helped him in his highly responsible tasks. In a public lecture, "The Buddhist *Dhamma* and Work Life," which he gave at the Chachoengsao branch of the Buddhist Association of Thailand on 9 September 1972, Sanya said,

> I myself have invited [empty mind] many times. I used it because there were strong tensions in some meetings which involved intense conflicts. If [the meeting] resolved this, one group would listen; if [it] resolved that, the other group would listen. [In such a case] how could we seek the best way out? I was the chair of such meetings. I took them as an exercise, simply switched off, and made my mind empty from considering anyone, but only considered reason. When [I found out that a] reasonable [decision] should be this, no matter who was going to be angry, hate it, or not listen to it, those were not issues to consider. Then it went well. Namely, we only held reasons, but were not considering people as "us" or "them."[110]

About the teaching of empty mind and *lokuttara dhamma*, which had been criticized as inappropriate for the laity, Sanya affirmed,

> It is really possible to have *anattā* (non-self) and empty mind. These principles of the *dhamma* are most useful [teachings] for us. I myself confess that at times of tension I have benefited very much from them.[111]
>
> If we do not become attached to anything as me and mine, we can overcome everything. Even death, which we are most afraid of in the world, or the things that we regard as the most important in the world do not have meaning. Property, status, children, wife, and honor are all characteristics of *sāmañña lakkhaṇa* [general characteristics of what is formed, i.e. impermanence, non-self, and suffering]. This is the peak of the *dhamma* in my knowledge and understanding. In this way the Buddhist *dhamma* can help while we are working, or for us to know that level, not just by making merit, respecting monks or dedicating robes on the occasion of *kathin* and *pha pa*. Although keeping five or eight precepts is good, if [we] would like the Buddhist *dhamma* to help us in our way of living and in our work, we have to study Buddhism to really reach its core (*lokuttara dhamma*). Then, [we] will think about it and test whether it is true or not. The Buddha did not teach us to believe in anyone, but taught people to examine whether something is true or not.[112]

These remarks by Sanya indicate that empty mind was actually being practiced, and *lokuttara dhamma* was considered as beneficial for worldly life by a lay Buddhist in Thailand, based on his understanding of it through Buddhadāsa's teaching. Sanya's son, Chakradharm Dhammasakdi, also said in an interview with the author that Sanya practiced empty mind while he was the interim Prime Minister after the 14 October 1973 uprising. After the military dictators had been expelled by the people, a great many demands were made of the successor government. Chakradharm said that Sanya used to be respected as a good person, but during the time when he was appointed as interim Prime Minister, he received a lot of unprecedented criticism. Sanya often told his family that he could not take on such a heavy task without the practice of empty mind.[113] In Pun's book, Sanya's story functioned as a good support of the validity of Buddhadāsa's teachings on empty mind and *lokuttara dhamma*, regardless of the frequent criticisms of those unfamiliar concepts.

Pun's Understanding of the Debates on Empty Mind

Pun, as a propagator of Buddhadāsa's teachings, concluded the discussion forum by contrasting Buddhadāsa's contribution to the Thai people with the problems that he perceived in statements by Buddhadāsa's opponents.

Pun was of the opinion that the purpose of Buddhism was not to argue over which teaching is good to follow, but rather to teach people to be able to overcome their suffering by restricting greed, anger, and delusion. Therefore, as Buddhadāsa presented it, Pun denied teachings which do not teach the overcoming of suffering, since they were not taught by the Buddha; it was unnecessary to be interested in them. By following Buddhadāsa's ideas, Pun insisted that the teaching of *suññatā*, empty mind, which enables one to overcome suffering, is unique to Buddhism, whereas *lokiya dhamma* is taught in all the other religions as well. He thus criticized Buddhadāsa's opponents who promoted only *lokiya dhamma* but rejected *lokuttara dhamma*, as follows:

> … it is natural for those who do not have *paññā* [insight] or who are not courageous enough to use their own *paññā* to understand the highest teaching of the Buddha. [They] do not have to proudly present themselves as teachers of scriptures, as *mahaparian* [persons with Pāli qualification], or as teachers of the Abhidhamma. [These people] are not different from those who are employed to keep cows, [but] have never tasted milk.[114]

Pun also criticized what they had done,

> If teachers, the kind who tend to make people veer away from Buddhism, stop arguing and competing about what is unjust in terms of reason, it is considered to be a kind of merit. Because of [preventing other people exploring the *dhamma*] they interfere in other people's business, from which they themselves get no return. When Thai people started to be interested in *suññatā* and empty mind, they used rhetoric to make people doubtful and stop believing in *suññatā*. The more chances someone has to explain the *dhamma* on the radio or in the newspaper, the more puffed up they are as great philosophers. Thus I [Pun] collected their thoughts to present here in order for readers to examine [them].[115]

In contrast to these opponents, Pun explained the contribution of Buddhadāsa's *dhamma* propagation. Pun understood that Buddhadāsa was highly respected by intellectuals, and was even invited by the Ministry of Justice to give religious instruction over a ten-year period, for the following reasons:

> He [Venerable Buddhadāsa] is the first monk in Thailand who introduced and widely propagated many teachings of the *sacca dhamma* [truth] that have been buried in the *Tipiṭaka*. Those who achieved even the ninth level [i.e., the highest level] of the Pāli qualification or teachers of the Abhidhamma had never discovered nor understood them … He [Venerable Buddhadāsa] does not have a high level of

> Pāli qualification and his ecclesiastical title is only at the level of Phra Ratcha Khana, because his purpose of ordination was not to serve the ecclesiastical administration, but to teach the people … Thus, he secludes himself in a forest and practices the way of renunciates by following the teachings of the Buddha. Still he translated parts of the [Pāli] *Tipiṭaka* into Thai, and codified a number of books, such as *A Treasure Trove from the Buddha's Words* [*Khumsap chak phra ot*], *The Life of the Buddha in His Own Words* [*Phuttha prawat chak phra ot*], and *Four Noble Truths from the Buddha's Words* [*Ariya sat chak phra ot*]. Who could have ever done such works, or done as well as he? Even though there are official [Thai translations of] the *Tipiṭaka*, almost no Thai people can understand what they mean. It is because they just put Thai words into Pāli style sentences … *Mahaparian* [Pāli qualification holders] or Abhidhammists have never read the Buddha's own words in the *Suttapiṭaka*, and do not know the truth. Thus, they cannot grasp the principle of Buddhism.[116]

Pun's impressions of Buddhadāsa can stand for the aspects of Buddhadāsa's teachings that appealed to Thai intellectuals. What Pun called the truth revealed by Buddhadāsa was *lokuttara dhamma*, which teaches people the way to overcome suffering. One of the central themes of Buddhadāsa's works was to indicate, among many other complex and detailed theories about the states of mind or paths for liberation, the messages in the *Tipiṭaka* that can teach people to reduce suffering. According to Buddhadāsa's teaching, all those detailed ideas in the *Tipiṭaka* make sense when they are viewed as supportive of the aim of overcoming suffering. Popularizing the ideas of *lokuttara dhamma* was Buddhadāsa's contribution to the Thai people.

However, Buddhadāsa's propagation of *lokuttara dhamma* was controversial in the Buddhist public sphere of Thailand. As a summary of all the above Thai Buddhists' discussions about *lokuttara dhamma* and the concept of empty mind, there were at least three points that made Buddhadāsa's teaching controversial.

The first point was whether or not *lokuttara* or supermundane level of teaching is relevant for the laity. If attachment is understood as the source of suffering, everyone, regardless of their ordained status, can remind themselves not to become attached to the self, which is only a misperception of the compound of aggregates, and to the things that do not belong to them as their possessions. What Buddhadāsa called empty mind, or the state of mind that is free from the sense of attachment, was considered by his lay followers to be useful in worldly life, which was always associated with greediness, anger, and delusion. Buddhadāsa identified having such an empty state of mind as a temporary liberation, or state of *nibbāna*, which is also attainable for lay people as well as renunciates. In fact, the *Tipiṭaka* gives many examples of lay people who accomplished the path of sainthood, and thus *lokuttara dhamma* is also open for lay Buddhists. However, the path for liberation has been considered too difficult for ordinary people in Thailand. They perceived that it is such a highly revered path, particularly for those forest monks who keep themselves away from worldly pleasures and conduct ascetic practices in order not to indulge in transient happiness, which is not true liberation. With this basic assumption, people found it difficult to imagine that they, who were satisfied with worldly happiness, could follow the path of the saint in their daily life. Therefore, in this context, Buddhadāsa's propagation of *lokuttara dhamma* was viewed by some as an authentic teaching of the Buddha, and by others as a teaching irrelevant for ordinary people.[117]

The second point was whether the concept of empty mind belongs to the Theravāda or the Mahāyāna. Buddhadāsa's teaching of emptiness, his proposal to practice empty mind was also regarded as a teaching for people to avoid suffering in the world. From this point of view, it is not important to Buddhadāsa, nor to those who support his teachings, where the teaching of emptiness originated, whether it was Mahāyāna or Theravāda, as long as it helped people to overcome suffering. As a matter of fact, the concept of emptiness actually exists in Theravāda scriptures; this fact was a strong support for Buddhadāsa and his followers to promote the practice of empty mind. However, at the same time, because of the fact that the concept was unfamiliar in traditional Theravāda commentaries, but was emphasized in the Mahāyāna, Buddhadāsa's proposal of empty mind could be attacked as unorthodox.

The third point was that opponents of Buddhadāsa created controversies about him through their written and oral debates. Along with Buddhadāsa's propagation and dissemination of his own ideas, these controversies in themselves served to expand and enrich the Buddhist public sphere in Thailand. Even though Buddhadāsa's teaching of *lokuttara dhamma* and empty mind were unfamiliar to Thai Buddhists in general, he had reasonable grounds supporting his ideas so that they were accepted by intellectuals in their daily practice. His opponents manipulated their interpretations, for example by claiming that *suññatā* does not exist in Theravāda *Tipiṭaka*, and by relating the practice of mind empty of "me" and "mine" to the communist policy of cooperative agriculture instead of private enterprise. They also used other methods, such as the fluent presentation of material from a Pāli commentary, jokes, and citing a higher Pāli qualification, to make people trust them or be attracted to them rather than Buddhadāsa. Some who could not by themselves follow the arguments in the Pāli *Tipiṭaka* or its commentaries became skeptical of Buddhadāsa, simply on the basis of negative rumors. In the 1960s and 1970s, although Buddhadāsa was already a well-established preacher, a suspicious image of Buddhadāsa as unorthodox and radical was generated and transmitted in the Buddhist public sphere, at least to a certain degree.

CHAPTER 5

Abhidhamma Controversies: The Supreme Doctrine in the Buddhist Public Sphere

The period from the Second World War to the 14 October Students' Uprising in 1973 was one of increasing liveliness in the Buddhist public sphere of Thailand. The expansion of education and the development of mass communication enhanced popular access and the sharing of new ideas transmitted by individuals to the public. Religious textbooks became available, enabling people to confirm the validity of their traditional beliefs and to clarify their vague interpretations of Buddhist symbols, concepts, sayings, and narratives. Scriptural specialists could no longer contain sacred knowledge among small circles of their disciples; rather, they publicized it for the benefit of pious Buddhists outside monasteries. Monks started to deliver their sermons in plain Thai, rather than just ritualistically reading palm leaf scriptures written in an inaccessible classical language, and admonished people to reflect on their attitudes, pointing to insightful stories or interpretations of Buddhist concepts. More and more people became interested in learning about the details of Buddhist doctrine beyond the basic levels of the Thai Saṅgha's ecclesiastical education. Buddhadāsa was one of the influential Buddhist preachers who explained complex Buddhist doctrines in an understandable way; he was highly respected by a wide range of people.

While Buddhadāsa's teaching was gaining popularity, the study of the Abhidhamma, the highly refined definitions and exegesis of Buddhist doctrines that had been developed in the Theravāda school, rapidly prevailed among Thai Buddhists in the 1950s and 1960s. An interesting phenomenon of Abhidhamma study in contemporary Thailand is its popularity among lay Buddhists, not just among monastic scholars and their novice students. Those lay Buddhists who attended lectures and classes to study the Abhidhamma included not only intellectuals who had become interested in the observation of the mind through meditation practice by following the Abhidhamma theory of mind, but also middling educated urban commoners who were not necessarily very wealthy. They were excited to discover the precise Buddhist doctrines in the Abhidhamma, which was knowledge previously unavailable to them.

The popularity of Buddhist doctrinal studies in the mid-20th century can be divided into two distinctive groups: one led by Buddhadāsa and his followers who focussed on the study of *lokuttara dhamma* and emptiness; the other composed of learners of the Abhidhamma theory. It is not surprising to find that rivalry arose between these two groups.

The Abhidhamma groups' harsh criticism of Buddhadāsa's unique interpretations of Buddhist doctrine gained the particular attention of scholars who had studied Buddhadāsa's thought. Studies by both Jackson and Gabaude contrasted the dichotomous characteristics of Buddhadāsa and the Abhidhamma groups and analyzed their different stances as the root of their conflict. Jackson was of the opinion that Buddhadāsa's opponents, most of whom were dedicated learners and teachers of the Abhidhamma, represented a "conservative" or "traditional" viewpoint, and thus it was difficult for them to accept Buddhadāsa's "progressive" or "innovative" interpretations.[1] Gabaude indicated that the distinct positions of Buddhadāsa and the Abhidhamma groups were respectively "interpretative" and "scholastic," "rationalist" and "supernaturalist."[2] Gabaude's dichotomous contrasts of Buddhadāsa and the Abhidhamma groups were based on Buddhadāsa's consistent tendency to demythologize supernatural religious narratives and to interpret them rationally as metaphors of psychological occurrences; this in opposition to studies of the Abhidhamma following a systematic summary of exegesis interpretations in the Theravāda Buddhist tradition. The theory of the Abhidhamma is supported by scholastically sophisticated texts and involves some stories and ideas dealing with supernatural phenomena such as rebirth in accordance with one's *kamma* (the consequences of one's past actions). Nevertheless, even though the *Abhidhammapiṭaka* and other later exegesis may have laid claim to the authority of "orthodoxy" in Theravāda Buddhism, as will be seen later in this chapter, the activities of Abhidhamma groups were run by enthusiastic individuals independent of the religious authority of the Saṅgha, a position from which someone could lay a claim to "orthodoxy."

The primary requirement for an understanding of the nature of conflict between Buddhadāsa and his Abhidhamma opponents is a fair knowledge of the rapid development of Abhidhamma studies in contemporary Thailand. In fact, in the existing sociological studies of Thai Buddhism, there is little work dealing with the popularization of Abhidhamma studies in contemporary Thailand, even though the phenomenon is no less significant than the new Buddhist groups, such as Santi Asoke and Dhammakāya, which arose in the 1970s, became prominent in the 1980s and the 1990s, and gained much attention from a number of scholars.[3] Gabaude's and Tambiah's are the few substantial sociological studies which discuss Abhidhamma studies in contemporary Thailand. In his study on Buddhadāsa, Gabaude has a chapter on the Abhidhamma, where he mainly analyzes Buddhadāsa's interpretation of the classical theory of the Abhidhamma, and a few other chapters which contrast Buddhadāsa's unique interpretations and the doctrinal theories that his Abhidhamma opponents suggested.[4] Although in the footnotes, precise biographical information about some of Buddhadāsa's opponents is given, a comprehensive historical picture of the Abhidhamma groups in contemporary Thailand is not presented.

On the other hand, Tambiah, with regard to the propagation of *vipassanā* meditation, has mentioned Phra Phimolatham (Aat Asapho), an influential Mahanikai Order elder, who introduced *vipassanā* together with Abhidhamma studies from Burma.[5] He presented Phra Phimolatham's propagation of *vipassanā* as an element of ascetic practice much needed politically by the Mahanikai Order as a countermeasure to the indigenous ways of the ascetic forest monks, many of whom were eventually integrated into the Thammayut Order. He also contrasted the administration's effort for the expansion of *vipassanā* propagation from the capital to the provinces and urban intellectuals' spontaneous faith in forest monks. However, the activities of Phra Phimolatham alone did not account for or represent the growing popularity of Abhidhamma studies and *vipassanā* as new phenomena in Thailand. Actually, there were more popular Abhidhamma teachers, and those Abhidhamma teachers were not unanimously antagonistic to Buddhadāsa.

This chapter aims to locate the positions of Buddhadāsa and the Abhidhamma groups that opposed him in the Buddhist public sphere, and through the example of their Abhidhamma debate, to arrive at an understanding of the nature of the Thai Buddhist public sphere of their time. The chapter attempts to explore three points. First, it will present a history and grouping of contemporary Abhidhamma studies in Thailand. Second, it will examine the ideological conflict initiated by Buddhadāsa's controversial lecture on the Abhidhamma in 1965; and third, it will explore the impact of that lecture.

1. Abhidhamma Studies and Their History in Contemporary Thailand

The Abhidhamma, or *Abhidhammapiṭaka*, is one of the three baskets of the *Tipiṭaka*, the most fundamental collection of Buddhist scriptures, together with the *Suttapiṭaka* (teachings of the Buddha) and the *Vinayapiṭaka* (monastic discipline). According to Collett Cox, the development of the Abhidhamma came later than the contents of the other two collections, which were recited in the first and second councils. Two or three hundred years after the death of the Buddha, his followers seem to have developed precise definitions and an exegesis of the teachings preserved in the other collections, and they analyzed the factors of experience (Pāli: *cetasika*) and their interactions by means of a complex classification. In some schools, this analysis evolved into the third collection, the Abhidhamma. However, the Buddhist communities were far from agreement about doctrine, especially about those classifications, and various Abhidhamma texts and collections came into existence within different schools, such as Theravāda and Sarvāstivāda. Some schools did not even have an Abhidhamma collection. Even though the Abhidhamma came later and its forms in different schools differ, the content of the Abhidhamma, but not its form, has been considered attributable to the Buddha.[6] In other words, even from the time of its origin, the Abhidhamma was contentious and probably had a polemical function in its insistence on orthodoxy.

Although Thai Buddhists also inherited the Theravāda Abhidhamma as part of the *Tipiṭaka*, the popularity of Abhidhamma studies is a recent phenomenon in Thailand. Contemporary Thai Buddhists acquired methods to study the Abhidhamma from monks from Burma, where, among all the ethnic groups adhering to the Theravāda school, Abhidhamma studies have been most emphasized. In Burma, as well as in Sri Lanka, Buddhist students have mostly relied on a reworking of the material that summarized the teachings of the *Abhidhammapiṭaka*, of which the detailed classifications and discussions about the process of perception, consciousness and other Buddhist psychology are difficult. The summary, the *Abhidhammatthasaṅgaha*, or "compendium of philosophy," was written by Anuruddha, who was born in South India and lived in Sri Lanka before the 12th century but later than the eighth century C.E. Saddhatissa wrote of the *Abhidhammatthasaṅgaha*,

> For the Burmese or Sinhalese student who begins to study Abhidhamma, this book is first committed to memory. Trying to study the Abhidhamma without mastering this book is like trying to construct a house without a suitable foundation.[7]

More recently, Buddhists have been studying the Abhidhamma with the assistance of the *Abhidhammatthasaṅgaha* and its sub-commentaries, especially the *Abhidhammatthavibhāvinī-ṭīkā*, written by Sumaṅgala in the time of King Parākramabāhu (1153–1186).[8] In Burma and Sri Lanka, Abhidhamma studies are closely linked with monastic training in the *vipassanā* meditation.[9]

However, in Thailand, according to Phra Sikhamphirayan (Thawan; 1920–), a principle teacher at the Abhidhamma school at Wat Rakhang, Division 7, some portions of the *Abhidhammapiṭaka*, its *aṭṭhakathā* and Abhidhamma teachers were lost when Ayutthaya was surrendered to Burma, although the *Suttapiṭaka* and *Vinayapiṭaka* survived. He also noted that King Rama I attempted to restore the Abhidhamma when he went on an expedition to Northern Thailand and Luang Prabang, but his efforts were not totally successful.[10]

In 20th-century Thailand, the study of the Abhidhamma has also been included in the curricula of the *nak tham* ecclesiastical examinations and Pāli examinations. Studies of the Abhidhamma are included in the eighth and/or ninth, that is, the highest levels of the Pāli examination.[11] For the ninth level Pāli exam, candidates are asked to translate from the Pāli *Abhidhammatthavibhāvinī-ṭīkā* into Thai. This text is an expanded commentary on the *Abhidhammatthasaṅgaha*, which reorganized, summarized and explained material from the seven books of the *Abhidhammapiṭaka*. As long as the existing curricula of ecclesiastical examinations were followed,[12] Thai students of the Abhidhamma would be limited in number, because the Abhidhamma is only studied in the most advanced levels of the Pāli examinations, and those who pass this level have traditionally been highly respected. People were required to be experts in Pāli in order to learn the Abhidhamma; in other words, it was not designed for popular consumption.

Apart from the ecclesiastical examination system, there seems to have been a more popularized form of Abhidhamma study, in which people could study it in Thai. According to Buddhadāsa, in around 1921, when he was 15 years old, he attended an Abhidhamma class at a temple in his neighborhood, Wat Thammabucha, Phumriang, Chaiya.[13] However, little is known about those local Abhidhamma studies in early 20th-century Thailand, and they were likely to have been much less influential than the famous Abhidhamma teacher monk Phra Phatthanta Wilasa.

The Arrival of Phra Phatthanta Wilasa

The arrival of Phra Phatthanta Wilasa (1897–1936?) was an important inroad to the popularization of Abhidhamma studies in Thailand.[14] Phatthanta appears to have been an ethnic Burmese of the Pyinmana province, situated in the southern end of Upper Burma.[15] He studied the *Tipiṭaka* from the time of his ordination as a novice at the age of 12, and continued his study as a monk in Mandalay and Pahkokku for nine years. After that, he practiced *vipassanā* meditation at the meditation centre of U Chan Dun, a disciple of the renowned Mingun Hsayadaw (1869–1954).[16] In 1930, Thai gem traders invited him as a *vipassanā* teacher to Bo Phloi in the Kanchanaburi province in western Thailand, and in 1931, a group of lay supporters of Wat Prok, a known Burmese temple in Bangkok, invited him to stay there.[17]

The students of Phatthanta became the first generation of popular Thai Abhidhamma teachers. Since Phatthanta could not speak Thai very fluently, some Thai intellectuals, including Luang Praphanphatthanakan and Luang Thepdarunanusit (Thawi Thammathat, the ninth level Pāli qualification holder during the sixth reign), assisted him in translating his Burmese or Pāli into Thai when he taught his Thai students.[18] He seems to have become quite famous among eager Buddhists in search of a good teacher. Even Phraya Latphli Thammaprakhan, an important friend and supporter of Buddhadāsa, encouraged Buddhadāsa to study with Phatthanta.[19] However, the life of Phatthanta ended with what was rumored to be a mysterious murder. Some said that he was murdered when he was practicing walking meditation at midnight,[20] and others said that one morning he was found hanged in his *kuti* but was assumed to have been murdered by illegal Mon immigrants who lived in the temple and had been told to leave so that a meditation hall could be built.[21] Given a biographer's note that he stayed in Wat Prok for five years, he would have died in 1936 at the age of 39.[22] Although Phatthanta's instructions on the Abhidhamma and *vipassanā* only lasted for a short period, his students took up the work of his teaching and played an important role as Abhidhamma and *vipassanā* teachers. Among them, Naep Mahaniranon was particularly important.

Ubasika Naep Mahaniranon: A Charismatic Female Meditation Teacher

Ubasika Naep Mahaniranon (1898–1983) was born the daughter of Phraya Sattayanukun, former governor (Thai: *chao muang*) of Kanchanaburi.[23] As a woman of that time, she did not have any formal education, and throughout her life she had difficulty writing Thai. She had already married and had three sons before she became seriously interested in meditation practice at around the age of 30. In 1932, Naep was introduced to Phatthanta by Luang Praphan, who liked to visit many famous monks for *dhamma* conversations. She agreed with Phatthanta's teaching that the *dhamma* practice involved not thinking, but rather watching the present *ārammaṇa* (object of consciousness), without bringing in the past or the future.[24] Her understanding improved in a few years, and Phatthanta told her to take on the role of Abhidhamma and *vipassanā* teacher.[25] In 1944, she opened her first *vipassanā* school at Wat Rakhang,[26] and taught with Sai Saikasaem, who wrote *Abhidhamma in Summary* (*Aphitham yo*),[27] which seems to have been one of the first Abhidhamma textbooks written by a contemporary Thai. Naep became an important teacher, supervising *vipassanā* schools in 41 provinces.[28]

Dissemination of the Abhidhamma Studies by Phra Phimolatham and Burmese Monks

At the end of the 1940s, there was an effort to introduce Burmese *Abhidhamma* and *vipassanā* practice at a high level in the Thai Saṅgha. In 1948, Phra Thammatrailokachan, who is best known by his later ecclesiastical title, Phra Phimolatham (Aat Atsapho; 1903–1989; hereafter referred to as Aat),[29] then in the Saṅgha Ministry of Administration, requested the ambassador of Burma to send Burmese monks with expertise in the *Tipiṭaka*, as well as complete sets of the *Tipiṭaka*, the *aṭṭhakathā* (commentaries), and the *ṭīkā* (sub-commentaries), which had been transmitted in Burma.[30] At his request, two Burmese monks, Satthamma Chotika Thammachariya (?–1966) and Techintha Thammachariya Thammakathika[31] came to Thailand in 1949. Furthermore, in 1952, Aat sent two monks and a novice with Pāli qualifications to Burma to acquire the method of *vipassanā dhura* (the task of contemplation) and *gantha dhura* (the task of the books, i.e., of studying the scriptures). When Phra Maha Chodok Yanasit (ninth level Pāli qualification holder; 1918–1988), who had studied *vipassanā dhura* in Burma, was returning to Thailand in 1953, two Burmese *vipassanā* teacher monks, Phatthanta Atsapha Thera Pathankammathanachariya and Inthawansa Thammachariya Kammathanachariya, were invited to Thailand by Aat.[32]

These Burmese and Thai monks who studied in Burma played an important role as teachers of both Abhidhamma and *vipassanā*. The Burmese monk Chotika taught Abhidhamma at Wat Mahathat from 1950 to 1954, and also at Wat Rakhang until the time of his death in 1968.[33] Both these monasteries have a long history, dating from early in the Bangkok dynasty. Based on Burmese textbooks, Chotika and his disciples established Abhidhamma textbooks and examinations in Thai; these have nine levels (*Cuḷa abhidhammika* 3, 2, 1; *Majjhima abhidhammika* 3, 2, 1; and *Mahā abhidhammika* 3, 2, 1).[34] The Abhidhamma classes that were started by Chotika still continue to the present day, at both Wat Mahathat and Wat Rakhang. The one at Wat Mahathat was especially developed by the efforts of Aat, who opened the Abhidhamma Chotika College (Thai: *Aphitham chotika witthayalai*) in 1968 and in 1981 placed it in the administrative structure of Mahachulalongkorn Buddhist University, which had more stable sources of support.[35] Apart from his textbooks and examinations, Chotika was very important for his fostering of later generations of well-known Thai Abhidhamma teachers, including Phra Thipparinya, whose Abhidhamma textbook was once adopted as study material for the third grade *nak tham*; Bunmi Methangkun, who established the Abhidhamma Foundation; and Wannasit Waithayasewi, who established the Naep Mahaniranon Foundation. Chotika should be considered the teacher who created a significant foundation for Abhidhamma study in Thailand.[36]

The Burmese monk who came with Chotika, Techintha (or more commonly Techin; hereafter referred to as Techin), also taught the Abhidhamma at Wat Mahathat, although he seems not to have been together with Chotika, but rather resided in Division 5 of the monks' residential area in Wat Mahathat. The famous preacher Kittivuḍḍho Bhikkhu learned the Abhidhamma through the teaching of Techin, aided by Phra Khru Prakatsamathikhun, a Thai assistant monk.[37] However, Techin's lessons did not last very long. In 1961, Techin went back to Burma and never returned to Thailand.[38] It is rumored that he was arrested at the immigration bureau in Burma for bringing some gold bars from Thailand.[39]

Among the important teachers of *vipassanā* in the Burmese style was Phra Maha Chodok, a Thai returnee student from Burma.[40] With the assistance of the two Burmese *vipassanā* teachers, Chodok made Division 5 of Wat Mahathat a famous *vipassanā* training class, which exists to this day. Among his disciples was Khun Mae Siri Krinchai (1917–), who supervised *vipassanā* at the Young Buddhist Association of Thailand (Thai: *Yuwa phutthika samakhom haeng prathet thai*).[41]

However, Aat's undertakings led to difficulties because of his downfall as a result of conspiracies in ecclesiastic politics.[42] In September 1960, Aat was ordered to disrobe, being charged with a major *vinaya* offence, and in October and November respectively, his position as abbot of Wat Mahathat and his ecclesiastical title, Phra Phimolatham, were taken away. Furthermore, in April 1962 he was arrested, accused of taking part in communist activities. These charges, fabricated to remove him from power, were dismissed in August 1966, but Aat's downfall meant a serious loss of support for those monks whom he had invited. Aat returned from jail to Wat

Mahathat in November 1966, but it was not until May 1975 and October 1981 respectively that he regained his ecclesiastic title and his position as abbot.[43] During the period when Aat was out of power, one Burmese *vipassanā* teacher monk returned to Burma, and the other moved to the Chonburi province, where a lay supporter founded a place for him.[44] The Abhidhamma teacher Techin also returned to Burma in 1961, and Chotika died in Thailand in 1966. In the 1960s, Aat's project of propagation of Abhidhamma studies and *vipassanā* practice went through a difficult time.

Roles of Lay Abhidhamma Teachers and the Buddhist Association of Thailand

In the meantime, the propagation of Abhidhamma and *vipassanā* were also promoted by lay preachers who had no direct link with Aat's ecclesiastic politics. Phra Thipparinya (Thup Klamphasut; 1889–1977), who was an important lay supporter of Wat Mahathat, and had studied Abhidhamma with Chotika, published an Abhidhamma textbook, *Elementary Abhidhammatthasaṅgaha* (in Thai, *Chula Aphithammatthasangkhaha*). In 1951, this was approved by Somdet Wanrat at Wat Benchamabophit as a textbook for the third grade *nak tham* examination.[45] It was perhaps one of the first Abhidhamma textbooks written by a Thai in the 20th century. Even then, people felt that the textbook was too difficult,[46] and it did not last too long as a *nak tham* textbook.[47] Phra Thipparinya devoted himself to propagating the Abhidhamma as a supporter of the Burmese teachers, as a member of the *Tipiṭaka* translation committee specializing in the *Abhidhammapiṭaka*,[48] and as an Abhidhamma lecturer on the radio.[49] Phra Thipparinya was in fact the first person who accused Buddhadāsa of being a "communist."[50]

The most important place for lay Abhidhamma teaching activities was the Buddhist Association of Thailand. After the beginning of Naep Mahaniranon's influential regular lectures at the Buddhist Association in 1953, many lay Buddhists became interested in Abhidhamma studies.[51] After attending Naep's lectures and studying seriously, some of her followers became influential teachers and promoters of Abhidhamma studies.

Bunmi Methangkun (1909–1991) was one such teacher. Bunmi was the owner of a chalk factory in Ayutthaya province, which had made him wealthy. When he first heard Naep's lecture at the Buddhist Association by chance in 1953, he was suffering from stomach trouble resulting from work stress, but through her lecture he understood the usefulness of Buddhist teaching, which he had not realized until then. At Naep's suggestion, Bunmi began studying the Abhidhamma with Chotika at Wat Rakhang, and in September 1953, opened Abhidhamma classes at the Buddhist Association. Naep, Phra Chanbannakit, and Bunmi himself, were invited as lecturers.[52] Through their efforts, Abhidhamma teaching was developed and propagated at the Buddhist Association of Thailand. In 1957, Bunmi established the Abhidhamma Foundation (Thai: *Aphitham mulanithi*), independent of the Buddhist Association.

Maniphan Charudun, another member of Naep's audience at the Buddhist Association also expanded opportunities for Abhidhamma propagation. In 1954, Maniphan first attended Naep's lecture with his wife Utsa, and discovered the usefulness of the Abhidhamma for everyday life. Then committee member and committee secretary of the Office of Culture concerning Custom and Tradition in the National Culture Council, Maniphan proposed a project to promote Abhidhamma studies at his place of work.[53] Phibun Songkhram, then Prime Minister and president of the Council, approved the project, and Maniphan organized Abhidhamma lectures at the auditorium of the Ministry of Culture. As part of this project, he invited Naep to give a lecture, and the auditorium was filled with five to six hundred people who came to hear her. Although this project had to be abandoned at the time of Phibun's downfall in the September 1957 coup by Field Marshal Sarit Thanarat, Maniphan considered this the first case of Abhidhamma propagation officially supported by the government in the contemporary history of Thailand.[54]

The respected lay female Abhidhamma teacher Sujin Boriharnwanaket (1927–) was also one of Naep's students. According to her biographer, Sujin started her study of the Abhidhamma under Naep's instruction at the Buddhist Association of Thailand in 1953, and after a few years of study, Naep gave her opportunities to lecture.[55] From 1967 to 1976, Sujin taught *vipassanā* meditation at Tamnak Somdet in Wat Mahathat, and on several radio stations. In addition, she gave lectures to both Thais and foreigners at Mahamakut Buddhist University for many years. *Abhidhamma in Daily Life*, a book based on her Abhidhamma teaching by one of her Western disciples, Nina Van Gorkom, has been widely read among English readers outside Thailand.[56] Later, Sujin realized that it is impossible to practice the *dhamma* without having a right understanding of it, so she separated from Naep's group, which promoted *vipassanā* meditation practice as divorced from daily life.[57] In 1984, Sujin established the Dhamma Study and Support Foundation (Thai: *Mulanithi suksa lae phoei-phrae phra phutthasasana*) and developed her independent teaching activities through it.

In the early 1960s, the popularity of Naep and strong financial assistance made the Abhidhamma groups powerful in the Buddhist Association of Thailand, which was by then already prestigious in the eyes of Buddhist intellectuals. According to Sanya Dhammasakdi, one of the founding members and a key promoter of the Association's activities, the Association had few assets so the members had to buy pencils and paper by splitting donations, and brought their own food to offer to the monks. However, one Abhidhamma devotee donated 200–300 *rai* of land, from which the Association could gain several thousand baht each year as rent, and another student of the Abhidhamma donated 80 *rai* of land as a place for *dhamma* practice. Sanya said that the Abhidhamma studies group established their own committee within the Buddhist Association, and their members were involved in the Association's administration. At the same time, there was also a group for Sutta studies in the Association, and the Association's journal, *Phuttha-tham* (*Buddha-dhamma*), published a series on the Abhidhamma and on the Sutta.[58] Buddhadāsa's followers tended to appear in the series on the Sutta and their religious interests were distinct from those of the Abhidhamma group. Although in his lecture, Sanya did not clearly indicate any strife between the Abhidhamma and the Sutta groups in the Buddhist Association, significant portions of the Abhidhamma group started to leave the Association after 1962. Even though Naep and other Abhidhamma teachers, such as Khun Ying Rabiap Sunthralikhit, remained in the Buddhist Association as advisors and lecturers,[59] 1962 was the beginning of the splitting of the Abhidhamma groups from the Buddhist Association.

In December 1962, Maniphan's group for Abhidhamma studies separated from the Buddhist Association of Thailand. Prior to their split, this group proposed that the Buddhist Association establish a philological studies section to maintain, transcribe, translate and publish the ancient palm leaf manuscripts that Thailand had inherited. The Buddhist Association president, Sanya, examined their proposal at the executive meeting, but it was not approved because the Association only intended to provide lectures on the *dhamma*. The Maniphan group later moved to the Somdet Building (*Akhan tuk somdet*) at Wat Saket, and launched its own Association for the Center of Research on Buddhism (*Samakhom Sun Khonkhwa thang Phra Phutthasasana*). They upheld Naep as the president of the new Association until her death in 1983, and when those holders of high level Pāli qualifications translated old canonical texts, they sought her advice as a *vipassanā* meditator of greater achievement, even though she read neither Pāli nor Thai.[60]

In 1962, another Abhidhamma group headed by Bunmi was also asked by the Buddhist Association to find another place to give their lectures, because the old place had to be demolished for the building of a new auditorium.[61] Bunmi's group remained in the Buddhist Association even after 1962, but presumably withdrew from it in 1966, because after that, he was no longer listed as a member of the administrative committee or the *dhamma* studies committee.[62] Also, from April 1966, Bunmi started giving Abhidhamma lectures at Wat Phra Chetuphon, which is commonly known as Wat Pho, to whose abbot and vice-abbot he had been introduced by Kittivuḍḍho Bhikkhu.[63] Even after 1966, Naep and others stayed on, but Bunmi's resignation appears to have signaled the end of a financially strong Abhidhamma group in the Buddhist Association, and a shift of venue for Abhidhamma lectures.

In the Buddhist Association, Sutta studies and Abhidhamma studies groups held contrasting religious views. Contrary to the rational views of Buddhadāsa and his disciples who tended to rely on the *Suttapiṭaka*, some Abhidhamma teachers and their students, including Naep and Bunmi, put emphasis on a belief in the real existence of supernatural beings, such as spirits and deities (in Thai, *phi-sang thewada*), and life after death.[64] In particular, Bunmi's teaching at Wat Pho gained people's attention, as he "proved" the reality of reincarnation and mediumship (*rang song*). Bunmi's biographer often mentioned that Bunmi was so concerned that people would not become interested in the Abhidhamma because it involved memorizing many numbers. He seems to have used his performances as a dramatic way of attracting people to the Abhidhamma.[65] Once, his daughter Sasithon Methangkun demonstrated her power as a medium by driving a car while wearing a blindfold at Suan Lumpini Park. However, Chanai Saengthongsuk, a famous Thai conjurer, revealed that this was a trick. Bunmi was widely criticized, and that brought an end to the mediumship performances[66]. Bunmi's reputation suffered as a result of his inclusion of supernaturalism and reincarnation in his appearances. He demonstrated similarly in the provinces and in several foreign countries, but with little success, according to his biographer, incurring excessive criticism from the public and the press, who had no understanding of the Abhidhamma.[67]

In sociological studies of religion, beliefs in supernatural phenomena should not be denied or simply labeled "wrong view," just because they contradict modern rational thinking, yet it is also a reality of modern Thailand that the manipulation of such beliefs is strictly monitored by the public. It would be misleading to identify the supernatural religious beliefs of the Abhidhamma group as simply "traditional" and something endangered by modernity. Many people in contemporary Thailand persist in believing in stories of supernaturalism, and they perceive them as "real" and reliably "true." However, they know that there is a high possibility of fabrications which they find difficult to accept. When someone disappoints heightened popular expectations, they have to expect significant damage to their reputation in the public sphere. In order to fend off criticism, such people often find a scapegoat whom the people may see as problematic. Putting aside their own failure, Bunmi and some other teachers won a number of those faithful to the Abhidhamma over to their side and led an extensive negative campaign against Buddhadāsa, who had in turn been critical of Abhidhamma studies.

Kittivuḍḍho Bhikkhu: An Influential Teacher Monk

Along with the influential Phra Phimolatham (Aat) and Naep Mahaniranon, Kittivuḍḍho Bhikkhu should be counted as one of the most famous Abhidhamma teachers of Thailand. Kittivuḍḍho began propagation of the Abhidhamma in the 1960s, later than other groups; by that time, the others were already facing difficulties either in the politics within the Saṅgha or in the prestigious lay associations. Ordained in 1957 at the age of 20, Kittivuḍḍho moved to Wat Mahathat in 1960 in order to study Abhidhamma with the Burmese teacher, Techin, and to teach the *Tipiṭaka* and the Abhidhamma in the Dhamma Research Division (*Phanaek Thamma Wichai*), a propagation division of Mahachulalongkorn Buddhist University.[68] Since the Dhamma Research Division was located at Lan Asok, Kittivuḍḍho's teaching of the Abhidhamma was also of interest to people who came to discuss the *dhamma* there. His propagation activities were consolidated when he established the Foundation for the Abhidhamma (*Mulanithi Aphitham*) at Wat Mahathat in August 1965.[69] Supported by the Foundation, Kittivuḍḍho extended his radio preaching on a broadcast frequency allocated by the government, and began training young novices and monks to become preachers[70]. With such activities as a base, he began attacking Buddhadāsa in around 1964[71].

Buddhadāsa's Relationship with Abhidhamma Groups

As their history suggests, Abhidhamma groups in Thailand can be roughly divided into three groups: first, institutionalized Abhidhamma studies introduced by Phra Phimolatham (Aat)'s sponsorship and Chotika's scholarship;[72] second, lay teachers at the Buddhist Association affiliated with the charismatic figure of Naep Mahaniranon; and third, Kittivuḍḍho's Foundation, which arose later, independently from the other two.[73] After the mid-1960s, the second group further differentiated into at least four groups: the philologist group, which moved to Wat Saket;[74] Bunmi Methangkun's group, which moved to Wat Pho;[75] the group of Wannasit Waithayasewi, who established the Naep Mahaniranon Foundation (*Mulanithi Naep Mahaniranon*) in 1980; and Sujin Boriharnwanaket's Dhamma Study and Support Foundation.[76]

Among these Abhidhamma factions, those of Bunmi and of Kittivuḍḍho conducted harsh campaigns against Buddhadāsa. In those campaigns, some Abhidhamma teachers and students joined forces; for example, Phra Thipparinya, who first accused Buddhadāsa of being a "communist," worked together with Anan Senakhan, an anti-communist police officer who studied the Abhidhamma with Bunmi.[77] The Wat Saket group and Wannasit Waithayasewi's group also cooperated in defending the Abhidhamma in the face of Buddhadāsa's lecture at the Buddhist Association in 1965, but they did not commit themselves to further critical campaigns. It should be noted that Bunmi and Kittivuḍḍho, who became vicious opponents of Buddhadāsa, were the most radical and rather controversial figures among many Abhidhamma teachers in Thailand. In the course of my research on Abhidhamma study in contemporary Thailand, I heard few Abhidhamma teachers make positive remarks about Buddhadāsa; this was no doubt because they knew that he was critical of Abhidhamma studies. However, not all Abhidhamma teachers were antagonistic to Buddhadāsa.

There were several individuals and groups which accommodated both the teachings of Buddhadāsa and those of the Abhidhamma. For example, Sawai Kaewsom, the *dhamma* orator at Lan Asok, was inspired by Buddhadāsa's booklet, *Human Language and Dhamma Language* (*Phasa-khon — phasa-tham*) and also incorporated the Abhidhamma theory into his teachings.[78] Ravi Bhavirai, a famous public intellectual and astronomy teacher at Chulalongkorn University, also adopted the teaching of both Buddhadāsa and the Abhidhamma.[79] It is important to note that the Abhidhamma groups were not uniformly antagonistic to Buddhadāsa.

Furthermore, even Phra Phimolatham (Aat), one of the most influential patrons of Abhidhamma propagation in contemporary Thailand, was supportive of Buddhadāsa. According to Phra Sitthawat, who was Aat's personal secretary before his arrest in 1960, Aat highly respected Buddhadāsa as a Buddhist philosopher.[80] Aat not only visited Buddhadāsa at Suan Mokkh, but in 1954 also accorded him the honor of giving a speech at the sixth council (the *Chaṭṭasaṅgāyana*) in Burma as a representative of Thai

Buddhists.[81] The following episode, Buddhadāsa's presumably first public criticism of the Abhidhamma, affords some insight into the relationship between the Abhidhamma groups and Buddhadāsa.

The incident occurred at Wat Mahathat in 1953, at the celebration of the Burmese government's conferring on Aat of the title, *Agga-Mahāpaṇḍita* (literally "foremost great scholar." According to Sithawat, who served as Aat's private secretary, this is an honorary position next to vice-Supreme Patriarch in Burma).[82] Buddhadāsa was invited by Aat to give a speech under the title, *gantha dhura* ("the task of the books," i.e., scriptural studies).[83] In the faces of the Abhidhamma teachers and students who attended in the main hall of Wat Mahathat, Buddhadāsa rejected the Abhidhamma. Immediately, Chao Khun Phra Khamphiprichayan Thera, one of the influential monks, seized the microphone from the moderator and rebuked, "This is most destructive of Wat Mahathat, destroys the Abhidhamma most radically, and is the worst speech possible."[84]

Invited to speak at such an auspicious event, why did Buddhadāsa give a provocative speech? Sithawat, one of the witnesses and the informant of this event, could not give an answer to this question. Aat, a key promoter of *vipassanā* meditation practice together with Abhidhamma studies, may have been aware of a certain tendency in Abhidhamma teachers to teach students to just memorize numerical categories in meticulous theories and schemes instead of applying the principles in a practical sense. Inviting Buddhadāsa, who was known for promoting practical ideas that would help reduce suffering, and giving him the title, *gantha dhura*, which is a pair concept with *vipassanā dhura* meaning "the task of contemplation," Aat would have expected him to raise an alternative approach to the contemporary tendency of rote learning in Abhidhamma studies.

This story and the relationships between Buddhadāsa and individual Abhidhamma students and groups indicate that their conflicts cannot be viewed as simply ideological disagreement over the Abhidhamma itself. Because some Abhidhamma teachers and students had no problem with Buddhadāsa, and vice versa, clearly the Abhidhamma could be used together with Buddhadāsa's teaching. The most important criterion for Buddhadāsa in distinguishing the authenticity of a certain teaching was whether or not it was related to the purpose of overcoming suffering. Buddhadāsa dared to say that we should tear out some portions of the *Tipiṭaka*, if they have nothing to do with that purpose.[85] Buddhadāsa tended to say that the Abhidhamma was too philosophical and of too little use for *dhamma* practice.[86] His radical criticism of the Abhidhamma was accepted by some Abhidhamma teachers and students who shared his concerns in this regard.

In fact, the aim of studying the precise details of the Abhidhamma theory of mind is to apply them in meditation practice and to the achievement of *nibbāna*.[87] In sum, Buddhadāsa's teachings and Abhidhamma studies did have some common ground.

Positions of Abhidhamma Groups in the Buddhist Public Sphere

In summary, the history of Abhidhamma studies in contemporary Thailand suggests that two points are important for an understanding of the conflict between Buddhadāsa and the Abhidhamma groups.

First, before Abhidhamma studies prevailed in the 1950s, many Thai monks did not have much interest in Abhidhamma studies, even though it is the doctrinal core that the Theravāda school developed throughout its history. Especially after the Saṅgha reform by Prince Patriarch Wachirayan Warorot, the most prominent Buddhist "orthodoxy" enforced by the Saṅgha is doctrine consistently reaffirmed through the ecclesiastical examinations, introduced in 1913.[88] Because in ecclesiastical examination curricula doctrinal knowledge of Abhidhamma was only required in the higher level Pāli examinations, it was only studied by limited numbers of people who had already successfully passed the lower levels and were working toward higher level exams. It was widely thought in early 20th-century Thailand that not only is the Abhidhamma too difficult for the majority of Thai people to understand and discuss, while the Vinaya and the Sutta were used as a principle.

Second, Abhidhamma studies are a recently revived phenomenon in Thailand. They were re-imported from Burma around the middle of the 20th century, and the key promoters of Abhidhamma studies in Thailand were lay teachers rather than elder monks in the Saṅgha, especially after the downfall of Phra Phimolatham (Aat). Although there were also monk-teachers of the Abhidhamma, such as Kittivuḍḍho Bhikkhu, they were not in the position to exercise the authority of the Saṅgha to pass judgment in doctrinal controversies. In other words, in contemporary Thailand the Abhidhamma groups should not be seen as the adjudicators of "orthodoxy" in Thai Buddhism, but rather as prominent participants in the Buddhist public sphere.

Because of their position as newly arisen minority groups, Abhidhamma groups were criticized by powerful Thammayut monks abiding at Wat Boromniwat and Wat Bowonniwet.[89] However, because of their highly detailed systematic theories, the Abhidhamma teachers were theoretically well prepared for doctrinal disputes. In their view, one of the most respected academic monks from the Mahanikai Order, P.A. Payutto (1939–), also misunderstood Buddhist doctrine.[90] Even a monk who is respected as academics in Thailand could hardly claim authority from the Thai Saṅgha to give a definitive answer to doctrinal questions. Rather, everyone is a discussant in the Buddhist public sphere, who could only present a personal view, and the public audience of their discussion decided which one had the most convincing argument. Buddhadāsa was the most influential rival of the Abhidhamma groups in the Thai Buddhist public sphere in the 1960s.

The following section argues that the primary cause of the conflict between Buddhadāsa and the Abhidhamma groups was neither Buddhadāsa's doctrinal challenge to the "orthodox" exegesis nor their difference of doctrinal interpretations; rather, it was Buddhadāsa's ambiguous and provocative statement which could be easily misinterpreted as meaning that the Abhidhamma was not the Buddha's own words and thus it is not very authentic. The conflict suggests that the Buddhist public sphere had its own manners and concerns of discussions distinct from those of theologians and academics.

2. Buddhadāsa's Lecture at the Buddhist Association in 1965

On 21 January 1965, Buddhadāsa gave a controversial lecture, "Things That We Have Not Yet Understood" at the Buddhist Association of Thailand, a Buddhist venue for discussion and the exchange of ideas.[91] This lecture provoked extensive refutation from the lay teachers of the Abhidhamma, and was the beginning of a serious conflict with Buddhadāsa. This was only two days after the third session on empty mind at the Khurusapha auditorium, in which Buddhadāsa gave a lecture in response to criticism from Kukrit Pramoj, who had disagreed with him in the previous session and then written critical articles in his newspapers. During this time, Buddhadāsa received challenges in the Buddhist public sphere.

According to his initially stated purpose, Buddhadāsa carefully articulated that he did not intend to say who was right and who was wrong, but rather, wanted to indicate the issues that needed to be understood as a foundation. Buddhadāsa said, "Everyone should consider it their right and duty to dig into these issues so as to be clear about them for the benefit of all. I am also in the position of one among the many people who cooperate in this duty."[92] In the lecture, Buddhadāsa presented different views about each issue, and explained his understanding of them.

Buddhadāsa examined ten issues that people get caught up in and which prevent them from understanding the *dhamma*: 1) whether *lokuttara dhamma* is suitable for lay people or not; 2) whether original mind has defilements or is pure; 3) whether or not all desires are defilements; 4) whether *paṭiccasamuppāda* (dependent origination) means reincarnation or not; 5) whether we should believe in the later canonical works or not; 6) the *Abhidhammapiṭaka*; 7) *suññatā* (emptiness); 8) *kilesa* (defilements) and *bodhi* (enlightenment); 9) superstitions and dogmas in Buddhism; and 10) those who should be called "Buddhadāsa" (a slave of the Buddha).[93] Among the ten, some were related to a discussion with Kukrit in the previous year, but most topics taken up in the lecture had to do with problems that he perceived in contemporary Thai teachings referring to the Abhidhamma.

Buddhadāsa's explanations about the Abhidhamma were controversial for his audience at the Buddhist Association, in both historical and semantic terms. First, he explained historically,

> When we explore the *Abhidhammapiṭaka*, the third basket of the Pāli *Tipiṭaka*, it is not in the form of *Buddha-vacana* (the Buddha's words). It is only *Buddha-vacana* in terms of *attha*, or meaning and is only a portion of it. We have to be very careful to choose meanings for the Pāli *Abhidhammapiṭaka*, which correspond to the *Buddha-vacana*. When speaking of *vyañjana* (letters), or the characters and words of speech, the *Abhidhammapiṭaka* is not *Buddha-vacana* at all. It is not in the form of a speech by the Buddha nor in terms of form of language or literary style. The *Abhidhammapiṭaka* is composed of verses written in a later period.[94]

This statement by Buddhadāsa had a significant impact on his audience. Although Buddhadāsa carefully stated that the *Abhidhammapiṭaka* is the *Buddha-vacana* in terms of its meaning, that is, it is equivalent to the teachings of the Buddha, it sounded as if he meant that the Abhidhamma was less authentic because it was composed later, not spoken by the Buddha himself. This impression was made even stronger by his subsequent statements.

Although the Buddha actually mentioned the word, *abhi-dhamma*, Buddhadāsa suggested that by *abhi-dhamma*, the Buddha did not mean the *Abhidhammapiṭaka*, which was composed after his death, but that instead he meant the *dhamma* which was explained deeply, broadly, and completely, in the same way the compound word, *abhi-vinaya*, means precise, detailed interpretations added to the *vinaya*. Like a collection of judicial precedents, *abhi-dhamma* means detailed explanation of the *dhamma* that requires extra insight to understand. Buddhadāsa said,

> … the Buddha intended to minutely analyse the parts which need to be explained in detail, so he did not think *abhi-vinaya* and *abhi-dhamma*

> were necessary … He only spoke of the *dhamma* and *vinaya* as we can see in the [first and second] councils, which only settled [questions of] the *dhamma* and *vinaya* in the *Tipiṭaka* … There was no mention of the *Abhidhammapiṭaka*, but only of the *dhamma* and the *vinaya*.[95]

Buddhadāsa implied not only that the *Abhidhamma-piṭaka* was not composed by the Buddha, but that the *abhi-dhamma* that the Buddha mentioned was also something extra and not essential like the *dhamma* and the *vinaya*.

Furthermore, Buddhadāsa said that at a later time Buddhists turned to supernaturalism, which was more attractive for ordinary people than the religious teachings, but he considered that those aspects concealed the *dhamma* that the Buddha taught. Buddhadāsa found, for example, that the *Gambhīra Kathāvatthu* of the *Abhidhammapiṭaka* contains a lot of *micchādiṭṭhi* (wrong view) and new ideologies originating in South India.[96] He also indicated that the story of the Buddha's ascent to the *Tāvatiṃsā* (the Realm of the Thirty-Three Gods) to preach the Abhidhamma to his mother appeared only in the *Dhammapada Aṭṭhakathā*, which was written even later than the *Abhidhammapiṭaka*.[97] In this later exegesis, Buddhadāsa did not discover anything significant added to the *Suttapiṭaka* teachings of how to overcome suffering, such as the four noble truths and dependent origination.[98] When Buddhadāsa discredited the later exegesis as having nothing to do with the overcoming of suffering, his claim that the *Abhidhammapiṭaka* was not *Buddha-vacana* brought its author into question, and also suggested some doubt about whether its teaching was equivalent to that of the Buddha.

Moreover, Buddhadāsa interpreted the meaning of the word Abhidhamma in his own way. He sought a concept that would be relevant, by definition, to be called *abhi-dhamma*, which means the greatest or the highest *dhamma*, that is, for Buddhadāsa, *suññatā* (emptiness). Here he cited his favorite Pāli phrase,

> *Ye te suttantā Tathāgatabhāsitā gambhīrā gambhīratthā lokuttarā suññatapaṭisaṃyuttā* (As to those discourses uttered by the Tathāgata, deep, deep in meaning, transcendental and concerned with the Void, from time to time we will spend our days learning them).[99]

From this phrase, he deduced,

> … anything that does not indicate *suññatā* is not a discourse by the Tathāgata, is not deep, is not deep in meaning, is not transcendental. When something indicates *suññatā*, then it is the deep discourse by the Tathāgata, has deep meaning, and is transcendental.[100]

He went on to ask which one was appropriate to be called *abhi-dhamma*, the state of emptiness that does not desire anything, or the state of pursuing merit, heaven, and *mahā-kusala citta* (a mind with great merit), as some *abhi-dhamma* teachers were putting forth in their lectures. Of course, Buddhadāsa supported the former as the highest *dhamma*.[101] He criticized those inflammatory Abhidhamma teachers as creating dogma in Buddhism, because they were teaching that those who did not study the Abhidhamma would go to hell.[102] Buddhadāsa proposed before an audience of Abhidhamma teachers at the Buddhist Association that the content of the Abhidhamma be replaced by emptiness.

3. Reactions to and Implications of Buddhadāsa's Lecture

This lecture was very provocative for the Abhidhamma groups. In response, on 31 July 1965, they published a book entitled *Refuting the Lecture of Buddhadāsa*.[103] This book was a similar attempt to that of the book by Pun Chongprasoet, *What is Right? What is Wrong?* (*Arai thuk, arai phit*), which collected articles disagreeing with Buddhadāsa's concept of empty mind and some defending it. This time, one of the Abhidhamma groups headed by Bunmi Methangkun set up in the book a forum of public debate to speak against Buddhadāsa. After an introduction by Bunmi, the book begins with Buddhadāsa's controversial lecture, followed by a series of refutations by Abhidhamma lecturers at the Buddhist Association, including Phra Chanbannakit, Khun Ying Rabiap Sunthralikhit, Phra Maha Songthan, Wiset Butsapawet, and Wannasit Waithayasewi. In the book, the most serious problem that the Abhidhamma teachers perceived in Buddhadāsa's lecture was whether or not the Abhidhamma was truly the Buddha's words (Thai: *Phuttha-phot*; Pāli: *Buddha-vacana*).

The reason behind these attacks appears to lie in the strong impact on the audience made by Buddhadāsa's indication that the *Abhidhammapiṭaka* was a later exegesis and not the words by the Buddha. According to Bunmi, after his lecture every day, the Abhidhamma teachers had to answer questions as to whether or not the Abhidhamma was the words of the Buddha, and Abhidhamma teaching became very confused. Moreover, books and handbills opposing the Abhidhamma on the grounds that it was not the Buddha's words were distributed within the Buddhist Association, and the Abhidhamma school in the Association was almost ruined. This was only 12 years after the establishment of the Buddhist Association's Abhidhamma school, which Naep and Bunmi alone had established as lecturers; by then, it had already grown larger in numbers of students, classrooms, and lecturers.[104] Buddhadāsa's lecture seriously damaged the Abhidhamma studies flourishing within the Buddhist Association.

One of the reasons for such a broad reaction was the general perception of ordinary Buddhists in Thailand. It is in fact agreed by international scholars that the *Abhidhammapiṭaka* was composed later than the other two *piṭaka*, which were more or less as taught by the Buddha and recited in the first and second councils; all this is according to studies based on the chronology of early Buddhism. According to a renowned Sri Lankan Buddhist scholar, Saddhatissa, among the seven books of the *Abhidhammapiṭaka*, three were probably recited in the second council held in the fourth century B.C.E., another three were recited at the third council held during Emperor Asoka's reign (c. 269–232 B.C.E.), and the last one was most likely composed by the president of the third council.[105] However, Buddhaghosa, the late-fourth-century commentator and compiler of the *Visuddhimagga*, rejected accusations that the *Abhidhammapiṭaka* was not *Buddha-vacana* (the Buddha's words), and stated that the textual order of the Abhidhamma originated with Sāriputta, a principle follower of the Buddha, and that the Buddha himself was the first *ābhidhammika*.[106] Consequently, it is no surprise that contemporary Thai people with faith in Buddhism do not know such assessments of the historical origins of the *Abhidhammapiṭaka*, and have never dared to question whether it was the words of the Buddha or not, since it makes up a part of the revered *Tipiṭaka*. In such circumstances, Buddhadāsa's remark was too shocking for those Thai Buddhists who had just begun to be interested in the Abhidhamma.

No matter what the actual facts were, the important thing in the public sphere is image, or perception. The Thai Abhidhamma teachers had to defend the credibility of the Abhidhamma with plausible arguments. For example, Bunmi wrote,

> One [of the philosophers in Thailand] said that the seven volumes of the *Abhidhammapiṭaka* are the Buddha's words, but the *Abhidhammatthasaṅgaha* is not the Buddha's words, because it was written later, by Anuruddha.[107]

He also wrote,

> Some people say that among the seven books of the *Abhidhammapiṭaka*, there is a book which is the words of the Buddha. That is book one, the *Dhammasaṅganī*. On the other hand, the other six, including the *Vibhaṅga*, *Dhātukathā*, *Puggalapaññatti*, *Kathāvatthu*, *Yamaka*, *Tika-paṭṭhāna*, and *Duka-paṭṭhāna*, were composed later.[108]

Bunmi, by putting these suggestions in many other contexts, which had nothing to do with the main discussion, seems to have expected his readers to think of the *Abhidhammapiṭaka* as truly the Buddha's own words although he never made such an assertion directly.

Another Abhidhamma teacher, Phra Chanbannakit, pointed to several canonical texts in the *Suttapiṭaka* and the *Vinayapiṭaka* in which *abhidhamma* was discussed, and concluded,

> In the Buddha's era, there were many elder *bhikkhu* and *bhikkhunī* who studied the Abhidhamma closely. If the *Abhidhammapiṭaka* did not exist, how could they study it? Speaking of the poetic verses, they should have been written at the first council together with the *Suttapiṭaka* and the *Vinayapiṭaka*.[109]

The word *abhi-dhamma* actually occurs in the *Suttapiṭaka* and the *Vinayapiṭaka*, but this does not constitute support for the view that the *Abhidhammapiṭaka* was composed at the same time as the other two groups of texts. These defenses of the *Abhidhammapiṭaka* in the face of Buddhadāsa's lecture involved suggestions and manipulations of public perception.

Among other articles, Chao Khun Kawiworayan's lecture, which is cited in the article by Khun Ying Rabiap, presented a reasonable argument to defend the status of the Abhidhamma as *Buddha-vacana*.[110] He referred to commentaries, such as the *Atthasālinī*, which says that the seven volumes of the *Abhidhammapiṭaka* are arranged as *Buddha-bhāsita* (the Buddha's sayings), and considers the *Kathāvatthu* in the *Abhidhammapiṭaka* as *Buddha-vacana*, because it was composed in accordance with the Buddha's intent by Moggaliputta Tissa, the third council chairperson. Also, he said that the *Tipiṭaka* includes many *sutta*, such as the *Theragāthā*, *Therīgāthā*, and some spoken by Ānanda, that were not spoken by the Buddha, but which are classified as *Buddha-vacana*. He concluded that all the teachings that the Buddha gave in various *sutta* are called the *dhamma*, whilst all the explanations about the *dhamma* that the Buddha taught in various *sutta* are the *abhi-dhamma*.[111] Such an interpretation by Kawiworayan was rather moderate and reasonable enough to accept for pious Buddhists, who respected the *Abhidhammapiṭaka* as part of their religion's scriptures.

Buddhadāsa's Response to Rebuttals by the Abhidhamma Teachers

After Buddhadāsa experienced these attempted rebuttals by the Abhidhamma teachers, he responded more radically to his Abhidhamma critics in a *dhamma* lecture at Suan Mokkh on 20 March 1971, which was entitled

"What is the Abhidhamma?" (*Aphitham khu arai?*). Buddhadāsa reflected on his lecture at the Buddhist Association in 1965 and admitted that his speech might have given the impression that the Abhidhamma is not the Buddha's words. However, he reminded people that he had also said that in terms of the meaning, there were some portions of the Abhidhamma that could be considered to be the Buddha's teachings, but there were also some that could not. In the 1971 lecture, Buddhadāsa examined which portions should be regarded as the Buddha's teachings, and which ones should not.[112] This time, rather than claiming that the *Abhidhammapiṭaka* was a later exegesis, Buddhadāsa's criticism was aimed more specifically at contemporary Abhidhamma studies. He proposed to replace the "excessive and false *abhi-dhamma*" with "true *abhi-dhamma*."

Buddhadāsa sarcastically named contemporary Abhidhamma studies "the Abhidhamma of tamarind seeds" (*aphitham met makham*), which made circle diagrams in order to memorize the numbers of the mind's characteristics, as found in the *Abhidhammatthasaṅgaha*.[113] Contrary to the *abhi-dhamma* of the Buddha's period, Buddhadāsa suggested that contemporary Abhidhamma studies in Thailand explained the Abhidhamma as something to do with supernatural powers or sacred things (*khong khlang, khong saksit*). He called such Abhidhamma an excessive thing (*khong koen*), and warned that it had fallen into black *dhamma* (*thamma dam*), which was a tool for boasting and condescension. He criticized black *dhamma* Abhidhammists of "... having a mind with defilements and defensiveness, and of selling [Abhidhamma] as consumer goods," saying that such Abhidhamma, presented as an advertisement for *vipassanā*, was instead an enemy of *vipassanā*.[114]

Buddhadāsa leveled his criticism at the foundations of contemporary Thai Abhidhammists. He declared,

> Sweep away all the Abhidhamma, which we commonly know. Whatever things are attached to the Abhidhamma, such as the *Abhidhammapiṭaka*, the *Abhidhammatthasaṅgaha*, and Abhidhamma-something, sweep them away and abandon them. We will not be lacking anything, because we have the *Suttapiṭaka* left as an item of practice in order to attain *nibbāna* quickly without getting lost.[115]

Instead of being "deluded and addicted" to the so-called Abhidhamma, Buddhadāsa here again identified *suññatā* as the true *abhi-dhamma*, which literally means the highest *dhamma*, as he had done in the 1965 lecture.[116]

Abhidhamma groups also rebutted Buddhadāsa's arguments from a doctrinal point of view. In particular, they targeted his Mahāyānistic interpretation of the mind, which did not fit with the theory of Abhidhamma. In a letter from a group of Abhidhamma students questioning Buddhadāsa, which was included in the book published as a reply to his 1965 lecture, questions were asked about the specifics of his interpretation among the many subdivided types of mind according to Abhidhamma classification. On the issue of empty mind, they argued that, according to the *sabhāva dhamma* (principle of nature) in the Abhidhamma theory, the mind cannot be empty because it always perceives an *ārammaṇa* (object).[117] Also, they examined the Pāli phrase, *pabhassaram idaṃ bhikkhave cittaṃ*, by which Buddhadāsa argued that the original mind is pure and free from defilements. In their interpretation, it only indicated a mind that is not interfered with by coarse defilements. The Abhidhamma divides such states of mind into 19 kinds, including two *upekkhā santīraṇa*, eight *mahā vipāka*, and nine *mahaggata vipāka*. For example, at the time of sleeping, the mind is *pabhassara* (transparent), and there are no coarse defilements. However, delicate defilements, which are called *anusaya* (underlying tendencies), such as *kāmārāgānusaya* (the underlying tendency to lust for sensual desire) and *avijjānusaya* (the underlying tendency to ignorance), are still latent in the *khanda santāna* (continuity of aggregates, or "body"). From this theoretical foundation, they asked Buddhadāsa for evidence that the original mind was pure, and asked about the specifics of his interpretation.[118] Bunmi, Rabiap and other contributors also made the same points in their articles, and concluded that empty mind was not taught in the Abhidhamma;[119] they complained that Buddhadāsa had only picked up those phrases from the *Tipiṭaka* that fitted well with his own ideas, and discarded others.[120]

Such theoretical arguments about the mind in the Abhidhamma were a more reasonable criticism of Buddhadāsa's controversial remarks. Although Buddhadāsa presented the scriptural basis for his proposal of emptiness and empty mind, which do appear in part in the *Dhammadinna Sutta*, *Culāsuññatā Sutta*, and *Mahāsuññatā Sutta*, apparently they were not explicitly incorporated into the Abhidhamma theory of mind. Buddhadāsa interpreted the *Tipiṭaka* freely in his own way, justifying himself by the Buddha's teaching in the *Kālāma Sutta*, i.e., not to believe certain ideas merely because of tradition, a teacher, or scriptures. He did not follow traditional Theravāda exegesis strictly, starting from the *Abhidhamma-piṭaka*, *aṭṭhakathā*, *ṭīkā*, and so forth. Therefore, his interpretation was criticized as *attanomati* (personal opinion).[121] Abhidhamma should have provided its proponents with effective weapons for debate in the public sphere.

*****

Although some of Buddhadāsa's interpretations do not fit into the theoretical system of the Abhidhamma exegesis tradition, that does not mean that Buddhadāsa's teaching was completely irrelevant. People usually become interested in religious practice in order to find a clear answer to their questions about life. However, religious texts are often too difficult for them to comprehend or too general to provide answers to their personal problems. It is the role of a religious teacher to listen to individual questions and suggest an appropriate teaching for overcoming their problems. Through the intervention of a teacher, people can clarify uncertain details of Buddhist teaching and deepen their understanding in it. Until they meet a right teacher, people often visit many teachers at different temples and institutions. Some people find an appropriate answer in the Abhidhamma; others in Buddhadāsa's teaching. In the Buddhist public sphere, many contradicting interpretations can coexist and serve different personalities and religious concerns.

In Thai Buddhism, "orthodoxy" may exist, but actually "orthodoxy" and the Saṅgha have to be flexible enough to cover a variety of teachings which can lead to the same religious goal. The Elders' Council of the Thai Saṅgha seldom intervenes in doctrinal disputes to determine a winner. Some people may interpret the Elders' Council's detachment as a sign of its irresponsibility or inability to solve controversial doctrinal issues, but in a positive point of view, the Buddhist authority has to respect every individual religious teacher who can offer reasonable interpretations to people and help them understand in deep Buddhist philosophy. Even though Buddhadāsa's interpretation was criticized as not consistent with the traditional exegesis, the Thai Saṅgha never considered it seriously problematic.

The problem Buddhadāsa encountered from the conflict with the Abhidhamma groups was rather a social one — a shakeup of his reputation. The initial point of the Abhidhamma discussion — whether or not the Abhidhamma consisted of the Buddha's words — stirred up the Buddhist public and then evaporated. Some of Buddhadāsa's opponents fostered public doubt based on the suggestion that Buddhadāsa was linked to communism, then (during the Cold War period) considered the prime enemy of the Thai nation, religion and king. This sensational rumor — plausible but difficult to prove — was spread so as to upset the Buddhist public sphere.

CHAPTER 6

Buddhism Meets Marxism: Buddhadāsa and His Marxist Followers

Thailand was once known as the fortress or pending "last domino" of communist penetration into mainland Southeast Asia. Even though Thailand allied with the United States and actually accomplished its commitment to block communism at its border on the international strategic map, Thailand could never remain unaffected by communism. The communist movement reached Thailand from the adjacent Indochinese countries, as well as through its large domestic Chinese community, a part of which supported the Chinese Revolution. It is also true that the Thai communist insurgency has never remotely affected the national institutions — the monarchy and religion, but nothing else was ever more threatening or challenging than communism in the contemporary history of Thailand. Few intellectuals could avoid declaring their position vis-à-vis communism, or Marxism.[1] In Thailand, Marxism faced Buddhism, not only in its institutions, but much more significantly, in its ideological system, the essential intellectual foundation of the Thai people.

Marxism is usually seen as incompatible with religion. Karl Marx's famous phrase, "Religion is the opium of the people," has the connotation that the people should not be deluded by the temporary relief from suffering that religion offers, but should awake and take action for political and economic change to achieve real happiness in their present life.[2] The history of the 20th century also suggests that in communist countries such as the Soviet Union and China, religion was actually oppressed or critically characterized as an opponent of ideological struggle.[3] Even in the other Theravāda Buddhist countries where the communist party never gained control, communism is well remembered for its total destruction of

Buddhism in Cambodia under the Pol Pot regime, and for the restrictions placed on religious activities in Laos after 1975.[4] On the other hand, religion has always been utilized as an ideological weapon in anti-communist campaigns. In Thailand, in a radical sermon, the monk leader of a rightist mass organization said, "Killing communists does not involve demerit."[5]

However, when in Thailand, ethnic Thai Buddhist intellectuals accepted Marxism for the first time, their attitude toward Buddhism was quite different from the common formula of Marxism being opposed to religion. A number of leading Marxist intellectuals were devoted to and came to have discussions with Buddhadāsa, who had criticized people's unquestioning attachment to the façade of conventional Buddhism. Because of Buddhadāsa's presentation of the *dhamma*, not only did ordained and lay Buddhist followers come to Buddhadāsa for further study, but even Marxists who felt intellectually inspired by Buddhadāsa came to him for discussion. Buddhadāsa was one of the few monks who has been respected by, and has associated with, many of the leading Marxist intellectuals in Thailand. The meeting of Marxism and Buddhism in Buddhadāsa's and his disciples' discussion was one of the most significant events to take place in the Buddhist public sphere and in the contemporary intellectual history of Thailand.[6]

Examining the intellectual exchanges between Buddhadāsa and his Marxist followers in the period 1946–1958, this chapter explores the following four points. First, the post-Second World War social and political setting is examined with regard to ideological freedom. It was then that Marxism began to reach many ethnic Thai intellectuals under the relatively liberal political conditions of the time. Second, Buddhadāsa's encounter with Marxism is examined. Third is a discussion of the relationship between Buddhadāsa and his Marxist followers, i.e., Pridi Phanomyong, Kulap Saipradit, and Samak Burawat — some of Thailand's most respected Marxist thinkers — and their excitement at discovering a unique aspect of Buddhism that harmonizes with Marxism. The chapter closes with an examination of the rumors that Buddhadāsa was a "communist" and his position on the political map.

1. Prevalence of Marxism, 1946–1958

Marxism arrived in Thailand before the end of the Second World War. Thailand had already encountered Marxism as early as the mid-1920s through the impact of the East Asian communist movements, and the Chinese and Vietnamese communists did disseminate Marxism in Thai for the ethnic

Thai populace. However, only a very few Thais had a chance to get in touch with the new political ideology through the East Asian communists in Thailand because their activities were severely curtailed by successive Thai governments.[7] The introduction of Marxism to the ethnic Thais was the work of elite Thai intellectuals who had acquired Marxist knowledge through their overseas experiences in the pre-war period, rather than through the influence of the Communist Party of Siam. One such elite Thai intellectual was Pridi Phanomyong (1900–1983), the highly respected politician and the prime theoretician of the 1932 Constitutional Revolution. He studied Marxism while in France from 1920 to 1927, and incorporated it in his economic plan in 1933. Another is Supha Sirimanon (1914–1986), a prominent Thai Marxist intellectual. He became interested in Marxism from 1938 on his visit to Japan as a journalist and brought home many books on Marxism. Later in 1951, Supha published an exegesis of Marx's *Capital* in Thai.[8] In the pre-war period, however, the propagation of Marxism by these overseas-experienced Thai intellectuals was barred by the 1933 Anti-Communist Act, which was a reaction against Pridi's socialist economic plan.

After the end of the Second World War, the Thai public sphere gained relative freedom of expression regarding political ideologies.[9] Until the anti-communist dictator, Field Marshal Sarit Thanarat (1908–1963) seized power in 1958, the Thai government retained various diplomatic options in international politics, including choices of alliance with the United States, non-aligned countries, or even Communist China. Because of this political flexibility, expression of Marxist thought was not always strictly censored; as a result, knowledge of Marxism spread among Thai intellectuals during the post-Second World War period from 1946 to 1958.

Particularly under the regency and premiership of Pridi Phanomyong in 1945–1946, Marxism was tolerated and Thai Marxist intellectuals who associated with Buddhadāsa played active political roles.[10] In January 1946, Prasoet Sapsunthon, an MP who was elected as a member of the Democrat Party, resigned from the party after only six months and submitted a draft private bill to abolish the 1933 Anti-Communist Act; his proposal was approved in parliament in September 1946. Prasoet's proposal was successful partly because the abolishment of the Anti-Communist Act was also a condition laid down by the Soviet Union in exchange for Thailand's admission to the United Nations. Prasoet legally stood for the Communist Party in the National Assembly until the coup by Field Marshal Phibun Songkhram (1897–1964) in November 1947.[11]

After the mysterious death of King Rama VIII in June 1946, Pridi and his group were accused of being responsible for the incident, and they were expelled from the government in November 1947 by a military coup. However, even after the downfall of Pridi, the political conditions were not immediately antagonistic to Marxist discourse. Phibun, who regained power afterward, was even supportive of the Indochinese independence movement against France in the late 1940s. Thailand did not adopt its pro-American, anti-communist policy until the Chinese Revolution in October 1949 and the outbreak of the Korean War in June 1950, which resulted in the intensification of the Cold War in Asia.[12]

In September 1950, the government control over domestic communist activities began to strengthen after the Thai military's declaration that it would send troops to Korea to support the UN force. In 1951, Pridi's group of socialists also lost power as a result of the unsuccessful Manhattan coup against the Phibun regime and the Phibun coup that overthrew both the parliament and the constitution underpinning the system of parliamentary democracy.

The most damaging impact on freedom of expression of Marxist thought was the arrest of the Peace Committee members and their associates in November 1952, which totally suppressed both the communists and Pridi's group of socialists with the allegation of involvement in communist activities.[13] The Peace Committee of Thailand had begun operating in Thailand through the initiative of the Communist Party of Thailand (CPT) after the 1950 meeting of the International Peace Committee in Stockholm under the guidance of the Soviet Union.[14] The Peace Committee of Thailand included a number of leading Thai intellectuals who were critical of Thailand's participation in the Korean War and organized a campaign to collect signatures to oppose it.[15] As we shall see in later sections of this chapter, Buddhadāsa was also invited to join the Committee, along with his Marxist followers, Kulap Saipradit and Samak Burawat, who were arrested for their involvement. Their arrest came to be regarded as a significant incident in the intellectual history of Thailand; their tough experience as political prisoners gave them a chance to seriously experiment with Buddhist practice while in jail.

Into the mid-1950s, a way toward international reconciliation was sought, and Thailand took a softer line toward Marxist ideologies and communist countries. After returning from a world tour in June 1955, Phibun placed emphasis on his policy of democratizing the country. He legalized political parties, enhanced freedom of the press, and encouraged "Hyde Parks," i.e., public discussion of politics.[16] Thailand sent a representative to the Afro-Asian Conference at Bandung in April 1955, and recognized the international significance of Communist China in the region. After that, Phibun, seeking an opportunity to restore diplomatic relations with Communist China, sent a secret mission to China.[17] Even under the Anti-Communist Act, a certain degree of freedom of speech and of the press was allowed until Sarit's coup in October 1958.

Prior to the 1958 coup, post-Second World War political uncertainty provided an opportunity for Thai intellectuals to discuss Marxism and develop their social consciousness. Many Marxist writings were produced by Thai Marxists and distributed in the Thai public sphere during this period. Well-known examples include Supha Sirimanon's journal *Aksonsan* (published from April 1949 to October 1952) and Chit Phumisak's writings (most intensively produced until 1958).[18] During the time when production of these radical thoughts and publications was allowed, Buddhadāsa and his Marxist followers freely exchanged opinions with regard to Buddhism and Marxism.

2. Buddhadāsa and Prasoet Sapsunthon: Buddhists' Encounter with Marxism

Prasoet Sapsunthon (1913–1994) played the most significant role in Buddhadāsa's encounter with Marxism. Prasoet was from Surat Thani, the same province as Buddhadāsa, and Buddhadāsa first knew young Prasoet as a temple boy (*dek wat*) at Wat Rachathiwat in Bangkok, where Buddhadāsa's uncle stayed when he was a monk.[19] At first, Prasoet had little interest in politics; while studying at Chulalongkorn University, Thailand's best academic institution, he was a Buddhist poet. Prasoet was a highly educated intellectual amongst his contemporaries because he had experience as editor of a journal of the Chulalongkorn University Student Club *Mahawitthayalai* (*University*) from 1934 to 1936, and he belonged to one of the first groups to receive Bachelor of Arts degrees from Chulalongkorn University.[20] Buddhadāsa said that he heard of Marxism for the first time from Prasoet right after his graduation from the Faculty of Arts at Chulalongkorn University, while he was still boarding at Wat Rachathiwat.[21] However, the surviving records of their correspondence indicate that their initial relationship consisted mainly of exchanges on religious topics.

Correspondence between Prasoet and Buddhadāsa

14 letters exchanged by Prasoet Sapsunthon and Buddhadāsa were conserved in the Suan Mokkh Archives in Chaiya in March 1999. Those 14 letters, 13 from Prasoet to Buddhadāsa and one from Buddhadāsa to Prasoet, were

written between October 1941 and January 1972.[22] The letters suggested that Prasoet respected Buddhadāsa and held him in high regard, and wished to share his intellectual enthusiasm with the young, competent monk who was only seven years his elder. In the first six letters between Prasoet and Buddhadāsa, up to December 1944,[23] the subjects are an article contributed by Prasoet to Buddhadāsa's journal, *Buddhism*, the hiring of a tutor for Buddhadāsa's English lessons, and some concepts from Eastern philosophy and Buddhism in general. After August 1942, Prasoet expressed his interest in running his own election campaign and political activities and standing for parliament as a representative of Buddhists who were abstaining from the four vices (in Pāli, *apāyamukha*: drinking, gambling, frequenting prostitutes, and keeping bad company).[24] However, in his letters up to January 1946, Prasoet did not bring up Marxism in his discussions with Buddhadāsa.

Prasoet was an adherent of Marxism by September 1946, when in parliament he proposed the abolition of the Anti-Communist Act.[25] After achieving its abolition, Prasoet planned to establish his own Communist Party, with no knowledge about the existing Communist Party of Thailand. When Prasoet found out about the more substantial Communist Party of Thailand, he applied for membership and was admitted in December 1946. Prasoet seems to have been one of the first ethnic Thais to become a member and executive office holder of the Communist Party of Thailand (CPT), which had been established by ethnic Chinese in Thailand.[26] In his new position, Prasoet became the first and only MP who openly stood for the CPT until the November 1947 coup that overthrew the Thamrong regime. In May 1949, the Party selected Prasoet and sent him to China for further study of Marxism-Leninism. In 1952, Prasoet was appointed a member of the Central Committee of the CPT, and remained in China until August 1958, when he resigned from the Party.[27]

In his letters up to the time of his departure for China, Prasoet the communist tried enthusiastically to persuade Buddhadāsa of the value of Marxist ideology; he mentioned that he had sent Buddhadāsa some books about Marxism, including *The Communist Manifesto* and *Dialectical Materialism*.[28] Now a converted communist, Prasoet drew Buddhadāsa's attention to Marxist perspectives he had found in Buddhadāsa's Buddhist teachings. Prasoet seems to have believed that the Marxist perspective would contribute to religious reform. He criticized current Buddhist practices, which had already diverged from the original ones, as not contributing to the betterment of people's lives. Prasoet said that the Buddhism of that time did not teach self-sacrifice; rather, people only expected rewards for their good deeds. He went on to say that it was only Buddhadāsa who could revive the concept of self-sacrifice in the Buddhist religion.[29] Prasoet insisted that true morality should be pursued in a proudly Buddhist country which in fact was not moral, but rather was filled with injustices contrary to the teaching of the Buddha. He said that the true religious morality was found in poor people who maintained the religion through their daily offerings to monks, rather than those in a position to exploit others; by which Prasoet was vaguely implying the monks. Thus, he concluded, it is suitable for religion to perform practices which benefit poor people — that is true morality with *mettā* (sympathetic love) and *karunā* (compassion).[30]

In the Suan Mokkh Archives in Chaiya, there was no reply from Buddhadāsa about Prasoet's proposal to apply Marxist views to religious matters.[31] The limited sources available do not allow a clear conclusion about the nature and extent of the impact on Buddhadāsa of the Marxism introduced by Prasoet during the latter half of the 1940s.

Buddhadāsa's Reaction to Marxism

A few years after his last correspondence with Prasoet, Buddhadāsa gave a sermon entitled "Buddhism and Society" in a regular evening session for fellow monks spending the rains retreat in September 1952.[32] This was only two months before the massive arrest of Marxist intellectuals in the Peace Committee, who were accused of being "communists." In this context of increasing concern with social issues among Thai intellectuals, Buddhadāsa sought to delineate the social dimensions of Buddhism, and especially the social benefit of monks who renounced worldly society. In the sermon, Buddhadāsa contrasted the social benefit of those who have and have not attained *arahantship*. Those who have not reached *arahantship* attempt to contribute to society only within the scope of the social contract of their own rights and duties. Since they are still under the rule of defilements (*kilesa*), they can only think of repaying their social debt in the same scale as the rewards they have received from others in society. On the other hand, an *arahant* provides benefits to society with loving compassion (*mettā*) and wisdom (*paññā*), without being restricted a notion of equal reciprocal exchange within the social contract. An *arahant* only works for the benefits of others, especially with the offering of *dhamma* (*dhammadāna*) that raises people's spirituality, and expects nothing in return.[33]

According to Buddhadāsa in an interview with Phra Pracha in the mid-1980s, Buddhadāsa was interested in Marxism and communism because, as a Buddhist monk, he felt that he had to know about Marxism, which was generally regarded as an enemy of Buddhism.[34] In the interview, Buddhadāsa said that he himself had even bought a book on communism from the Home Library series in order to give it to Maha Thongsup, his friend at the Mahamakut Buddhist University. Buddhadāsa wanted to see how Maha Thongsup reacted to it, because at that time, communism was novel and was regarded as an enemy of Buddhism. Buddhadāsa said that he had read the book on communism in the Home Library series, but he understood only some parts of it since the ideas were still too new for him.[35]

Buddhadāsa remarked that his intellectual interest in Marxism did not last long. As soon as Buddhadāsa learned that Karl Marx claimed that religion was opium, he lost interest in Marxism. He thought that Marx's ideology could not be his foundation since Marx never acquired a proper understanding of Buddhism. Buddhadāsa argued that if Marx had ever understood true Buddhism, he would have known that Buddhism was not opium, but a victory over opium, for example over such things as supernatural beliefs (*saiyasat*).[36] Buddhadāsa's initial interest in Marxism was brought to an end by Sarit's coup in 1958, which strictly banned communism. Buddhadāsa had to give all his books on communism, by then a substantial collection including books in Thai and European languages by various authors, to his lawyer friend, Piu Premadittha. Buddhadāsa decided to abandon those books so as not to be accused of being a communist.[37]

Prasoet's Despair in the Communist Party

In the meantime, while he was in China, Prasoet Sapsunthon had an ideological dispute with Communist Party executives who were of Chinese origin and held pro-Chinese sentiments. Although in 1952 Prasoet became a member of the central committee of the Party, he did not agree with two elements of the Party's policy. First, in 1952 Prasoet argued that it was necessary to form a united front with Pridi Phanomyong's group of Thai Marxist intellectuals for the success of the revolution in Thailand, but his opinion was rejected. Second, in early 1958 Prasoet again argued with the Party executives when he proposed a peaceful strategy to take office through a parliamentary majority after he was influenced by Khrushchev's idea of a non-violent path to socialism. Prasoet lost both of these ideological disputes, and was accused of being elitist and of neglecting the rural masses.[38]

Although leftists tend to be skeptical of Prasoet, who left the Party and became a military advisor in 1963 after his six years of imprisonment, he was concerned that there be peaceful strategy and a non-violent approach, echoing the experience of the younger radicals also faced in their forest struggle in the late 1970s. Even after becoming a military adviser, Prasoet proposed "intellectual strategies" instead of military methods to combat the communists. At his suggestion, the military promoted public welfare in the poor, rural Northeast region in order to prevent communist penetration; at the same time, by adopting this method, the military could expect future benefits when they stood for election.[39] It is not clear that Prasoet's non-violent approach to social reform was influenced by Buddhism and Buddhadāsa, but it hints at a crossover with the Buddhist notion with which he familiarized himself through the monastic environment and his friendship with Buddhadāsa in his youth.[40]

Buddhadāsa denied that his relationship with Prasoet developed from intellectual to political. He said that Prasoet never asked him to join in communist political activities, nor did Prasoet invite him to the anti-communist campaign after his conversion.[41] Buddhadāsa chose to dispose of his Marxist books, but seems to have gained considerable knowledge of Marxism through communication with Prasoet; on the other hand, Prasoet, regardless of his work at the time — either as a communist or a military adviser — could possibly have maintained the Buddhist perspectives he received from Buddhadāsa's teaching. The early intellectual exchanges between these two men benefited each of them indirectly in their respective fields at a later time.

3. Buddhadāsa and Thai Marxist Intellectuals: A Question on Buddhism and Materialism

Buddhadāsa associated with Prasoet Sapsunthon and several other famous Marxist intellectuals during the period 1946–1958. In the relatively liberal political environment during that post-war period, those Thai intellectuals were able to absorb Marxism with little conflict with their religion; they even saw their new ideology as equivalent to Buddhism. The following is an examination of three of the most respected Thai Marxists who were in close contact with Buddhadāsa, Pridi Phanomyong, Kulap Saipradit, and Samak Burawat, and their unique understanding of "materialism" which came about as a result of their inquiry into both Marxism and Buddhism.[42]

Pridi Phanomyong

Among the prominent Thai Marxist intellectuals, Pridi Phanomyong (1900–1983) was a key political figure. At one time or another, he was the civilian leader of the 1932 Constitutional Revolution, the leader of the Free Thai movement, the Regent of King Rama VIII, and Prime Minister; and he respected Buddhadāsa's teachings and activities.

The most remarkable indicator of Pridi's serious regard for Buddhadāsa's teaching was his plan to establish a Suan Mokkh style meditation center in 1943, when he was still in power. When his mother Lukchan passed away, Pridi came up with a plan to donate 3,000 baht to make merit for her by establishing a place for *vipassanā* meditation practice at Wat Phanomyong in Ayutthaya province, a temple to which his family had given patronage for a long time. Pridi wished to invite a meditation master from Suan Mokkh, and to have Buddhadāsa as an advisor for scholarly studies.[43] Sometime between 9 January and 1 March 1943,[44] Pridi personally invited Buddhadāsa to his official residence through Wut Suwannarak, an MP from Surat Thani province and a relative of Buddhadāsa.[45] Three times, Pridi and Buddhadāsa discussed Pridi's plan to found a place for Suan Mokkh style *dhamma* practice in his home province so as to propagate the essential teachings of Buddhism. Buddhadāsa introduced his junior fellow monks, including Bo. Cho. Khemaphirat and Paññānanda Bhikkhu, to Pridi, suggesting that they preach the *dhamma* at the new place.[46] However, in the end, the project had to be abolished because no suitable forest or mountain for *dhamma* practice could be found in Ayutthaya,[47] and because Pridi had to go into exile after the coup in November 1947.[48]

Although the Ayutthaya-Suan Mokkh project was not actualized, after their first correspondence, Pridi respected Buddhadāsa for the rest of his life. In 1943, Pridi made donations for the publication of Buddhadāsa's article, "Answering the Questions of a Catholic Priest" as a propagation booklet.[49] He also offered money to support the journal *Buddhism* and offered books to the Dhammadāna Group's library.[50] Pridi officially attended Buddhadāsa's lecture entitled "Buddha-Dhamma and the Spirit of Democracy" at the Buddhist Association of Thailand in January 1947.[51] In the 1970s in Paris, where he chose to spend the latter half of his life in exile, Pridi again announced his intention to establish a Suan Mokkh style temple, by which he meant not an ordinary ritualistic temple.[52] However, the plan did not come to fruition because he could not gain enough support from the local Thai residents.[53] Pridi's wife Phunsuk Phanomyong asserted that Pridi respected Buddhadāsa and Paññānanda throughout his life. He had a booklet by Buddhadāsa, *The Buddhist Charter* (*Kotbat khong phuttha borisat*), in his pocket, even at the moment of his death.[54]

The result of the interplay between Buddhism and Marxism in Pridi's thought is most apparent in his book, *Impermanence of Society* (*Khwam-pen-anitchang khong sangkhom*), written in 1957 during his exile in Mao's China. Although in 1933 Pridi already had developed the notion of a Buddhist utopia (*phra si araya mettrai*) as the goal of his socialist economic plan, his views on Marxism and Buddhism seem to have grown more theoretically detailed after his extensive study of Marxism in China.[55]

In his book, Pridi expressed his distinctive view of the theory of materialism from the Buddhist intellectual viewpoint. First, he regarded the Buddhist law of impermanence as valid in the case of society because both Buddhist prophecy and historical materialism suggest that the conflict arising from the immoral, oppressive relationship of production will bring about a new social and political system.[56]

Second, in order to express his characteristic understandings of materialism better, Pridi translated materialism into Thai as "*sasaratham*,"[57] as distinct from both "*watthu-niyom*" and "*niyom-watthu*."[58] Pridi rejected "*watthu-niyom*" or rigid material determinism, including both the mechanical materialism of 18th-century France criticized by Marx, and the Communist Party's dogmatic materialist theory that tended to exclude all spiritual phenomena that might affect human beings. "True scientific materialism," according to Pridi, is also different from the frequently mentioned, superficial concept of *niyom-watthu* (addiction to material well-being). Although Pridi retained the most basic materialist tenet — the claim that, primarily, material conditions produce the human mind — Pridi still agreed with the Buddhist view stressing the role of human will in overcoming defilements (*kilesa*) which attached to material comfort.[59] In a veiled criticism of dogmatic materialist Marxists, Pridi urged that the ordinary worldly defiled human beings (*puthujjana*) who reject Buddhist masters as idealists needed to study what materialism and idealism actually mean.[60] For Pridi, Buddhism never contradicted materialism, or the most fundamental Marxist philosophy, because a Marxist with the right understanding of materialism would always accept the Buddhist path of overcoming suffering as idealism.

Kulap Saipradit

The second Marxist intellectual who followed Buddhadāsa was Kulap Saipradit (1905–1974), also known by the pseudonym Sriburapha.[61] Thailand's most respected humanist journalist and novelist, he openly criticized social injustice perpetrated on weaker people by privileged royalty, bureaucrat aristocracy and wealthy capitalists.[62] Buddhadāsa had been in touch with Kulap in his role as a newspaper editor from January 1939 or even earlier.[63] After Buddhadāsa started to give lectures at the Buddhist Association of Thailand in 1940, Kulap attended every lecture and wrote a summary of it in his newspaper so as to propagate Buddhadāsa's teaching.[64]

Kulap's concern with Buddhism was centered on practice. In his letters to Buddhadāsa in September and December 1951, Kulap expressed an interest in Buddhist practice in lay worldly life.[65] In Buddhadāsa's words,

> Kulap knew how to select *dhamma* that is useful for his daily life. He used it practically in his own life. Kulap studied Buddhism as a lay person, not as a temple dweller who learns Buddhism as rituals and memorizes its principles. 'As a lay person' means studying freely [without being restricted by any monastic tradition] … Kulap always studied Buddhism by reading English books and journals from foreign countries.[66]

In February 1952, Kulap traveled all the way to Chaiya in the southern province of Surat Thani in order to visit Buddhadāsa at Suan Mokkh and discuss *dhamma* practice with him. Buddhadāsa did not give any particular advice on meditation, but recommended that Kulap read his book, *Following the Footprints of the Arahant* (*Tam roi phra arahan*), in which Buddhadāsa related the story of the Buddha's path as written in the Buddhist scriptures.[67]

Kulap's concern with Buddhism continued after 10 November 1952, while he and Samak Burawat were in jail as political prisoners over the Peace Committee case. During their time in jail, Kulap and Samak received *vipassanā* meditation training from a group of monks from Wat Mahathat headed by Phra Phimolatham (Aat).[68] Kulap and Samak contributed some articles on Buddhism to *Vipassanā Journal* (*Wipatsanasan*), run by Phra Phimolatham's group.[69] Kulap's longest essay on Buddhism, "The Highest *Dhamma*" (*Udomtham*) was first published in *Vipassanā Journal*, and it attests to Kulap's continuing concern with practice in Buddhism from the time he first discussed it with Buddhadāsa. The essay also referred to Buddhadāsa[70] as well as to the monk teachers from Wat Mahathat.[71] Kulap recommended that his readers read several of Buddhadāsa's books, giving ample praise to Buddhadāsa,

> The author [Kulap] believes that any Buddhist thoughts in the time before him [Buddhadāsa] have been renewed; he [Buddhadāsa] does not consider that studies of the *dhamma* are out-dated or something to be delayed until one is advanced in years. There are many other books by other virtuous monks that should be recommended, but the author believes that it is only the two or three books listed above that can lead you [readers] to understand the core *dhamma* of Buddhism.[72]

Whilst "The Highest *Dhamma*" focused on presenting the religious ideal of pursuit of the *dhamma*, "Talks on Buddhism" (*Sonthana ruang phutthasasana*), the other series of Kulap's essays on Buddhism written in jail, included some of his understandings of Marxism and Buddhism.[73] In Chapter 9, Kulap insisted that the ideology of politics and economics, by which he implicitly meant Marxism, and the Buddhist *dhamma* have a common goal — that is, the overcoming of human suffering. The difference between the two, according to Kulap, is the scope of suffering defined by each of the ideological systems. In contrast to the many Marxists who insisted that religions were impractical idealism, Kulap understood that the scope of suffering that the *dhamma* deals with is much broader than that in a secular ideology that only looks at human suffering defined in a narrow way.[74] Kulap believed that no matter how much better material goods improve human life, suffering arises as long as human beings have defilements. At that point, he held to the notion that Buddhism is a more reliable means of improving human life.[75] In other words, Kulap valued Buddhism more highly than Marxist materialism.

Despite being a Marxist, Kulap gave priority to his intellectual liberty over the benefits of political affiliation, and thus he never aligned himself with any political group, not even the Communist Party.[76] It is not clear whether or not the reason for this was the Communist Party's coercion or expectation of its members to abandon their religious faiths; Kulap only cooperated with the Communist Party so as to form a united front (*naew ruam*). From the time of his exile in Mao's China until his death in 1974, Kulap continued his meditation practice.[77]

Samak Burawat

The third famous Marxist follower of Buddhadāsa was Samak Burawat (1916–1975). Samak was the first Thai to specialize in mining engineering,[78] and as a philosopher, he introduced European philosophy to Thailand.[79] By coming in first in the royal scholarship examinations in 1934, Samak studied natural resource development and mining, and graduated from the Royal School of Mines, Imperial College of Science and Technology at London University in 1938, obtaining a B.Sc. with first class honors.[80] After his return from Britain, Samak contributed to Thai natural resources development through his work in the government, and also taught European philosophy to the monk students at Mahamakut Buddhist University.

Buddhadāsa played a significant role at the very beginning of Samak's interest in Buddhism. In 1936, Samak wrote a book, *Buddhist Philosophy Explained by Science* (*Phuttha pratchaya athibai duai witthayasat*), integrating his Buddhist religion and his scientific knowledge. Samak said that he could only write his book thanks to the inspiration he derived from Buddhadāsa's journal *Buddhism*, to which he subscribed while he was in England.[81] Samak's father published Samak's book in Thailand for distribution to his friends; Buddhadāsa was one of its readers. According to Buddhadāsa,

> Samak Burawat wrote an interesting work relating science with Buddhism … He gave precise scientific examples that coincided with the three principles of Buddhism — impermanence (*anicca*), suffering (*dukkha*), and non-self (*anattā*).[82]

Later in 1943, Samak contributed an article to Buddhadāsa's journal *Buddhism*, relating how the three Buddhist principles coincided with the European philosophy of the "dynamism" of evolution, citing the works of Descartes, Kant, and Bergson.[83]

After indirect communication through their published works, Samak and Buddhadāsa first met in 1946 at Mahamakut Buddhist University in Bangkok, where they were introduced by Phra Siwisutthiyan (Bunrot Sujīvo), a respected young monk well-known at that time for his intellectuality.[84] Samak visited Suan Mokkh and and stayed there for a few days, and Buddhadāsa took him to some interesting geographical sites in the Chaiya area.[85]

However, later Buddhadāsa seemed not to agree very much with Samak; he said,

> Samak Burawat compared Buddhism with science, and eventually made it a philosophy. Buddhism as philosophy is not worth reading. … Samak was not interested in the overcoming of suffering. He was only interested in causal relations, not in *nibbāna* and *idappaccayatā* (dependent origination). Later, he began to be consulted about auspicious and inauspicious times (*du ruk du yam*).[86]

Samak's discussions of Buddhism and Marxism were most explicit in an article, "Buddhism in the Face of Communism" (*Phutthit phachoen na kap khommiunit*), in the intellectual Marxist journal *Aksonsan* in August 1952.[87] In this article, Samak compared and contrasted Buddhism and Marxism in terms of their ideological positions. Samak criticized the elite lay Buddhists in the Buddhist Association of Thailand and the Young Buddhist Association, as well as the famous British Buddhist, Christmas Humphreys, for using Buddhism as an ideological critique of communism in 1948. These people defined Buddhism as idealism (*chittaniyom*), which they argued cannot go together with communism, which never takes into account the spiritual aspect of human beings.

However, Samak argued that dialectical materialism does not deny spiritual aspects, as mechanical materialism does. Later in 1957, Pridi discussed this in the same way in his *Impermanence of Society*. Dialectical materialism does actually admit the existence of mind, although it places mind in a secondary position that is always dependently defined by the material. At the same time, Samak said that Buddhist philosophy was not idealism, but rather had some aspects that coincided with dialectical materialism. Samak pointed out the materialist aspect of Buddhism, referring to *The Questions of King Milinda* (Pāli: *Milinda-pañha*), a classic Buddhist scripture. According to Samak, the classical text suggests that as well as dialectical materialism, Buddhist epistemology considers that the mind comes into existence through contact with external material phenomena. For example, visual cognition (Pāli: *cakkhu viññāṇa*) arises from the eye's contact with form, and auditory cognition (Pāli: *sota viññāṇa*) arises from the ear's contact with sound, and so on for the other senses.

Nevertheless, Samak also pointed out the difference between Buddhism and dialectical materialism, which differ in their methods of overcoming suffering. Buddhism teaches an idealist method pursuing the liberation of mind by destroying defilements (*kilesa*). On the other hand, Marxism teaches an economic method of overcoming suffering: revolution that abolishes private ownership and collectivizes the economy. True Marxists who understand the philosophy of dialectical materialism, according to Samak, never refer to religion in their plans, because they regard any spiritual state as determined by material conditions, which implies that morality should be improved automatically by economic reform. For Samak, any Marxist who utilizes Buddhism for the purpose of political propagation under the pretence of Buddhism is a false Marxist. In the same way, a Buddhist who attacks Marxism as an enemy of Buddhism by arguing that Marxist materialism denies the idealist nature of Buddhism is also a false Buddhist, since such a Buddhist ignores the materialist character of Buddhism in order to polarize the ideological difference for political purposes. In summary, by indicating both the commonalities and differences between Marxism and Buddhism, the Buddhist Marxist philosopher Samak criticized the politicization of the ideological disagreement between Marxism and Buddhism.

In November 1952, three months after publishing this article, Samak was arrested and charged with being a communist involved in the Peace Committee, of which he was an elected member of the working subcommittee.[88] However, his wife Anon Burawat affirmed that he was not a communist, and was only invited by leftists from Thammasat University to give lectures and intellectual support.[89] After his release in 1957, Samak worked as a mining engineer in the private and military projects of strongmen, such as Phao Siyanon and Sarit Thanarat.[90] His wife, Anon assumed that he was avoiding communication with Marxists, and even quit teaching monks at the Buddhist University because he was afraid of making the monks communist suspects. Although Anon said that Samak hardly ever wrote books after that, his works written before his imprisonment continued to be influential throughout the 1960s, the time of the anti-communist dictators' censorship.[91] This was because his books did not have explicitly Marxist titles; however, the contents consisted of an account of the evolution of human beings based on Marxist history from ancient communism until capitalist society.[92] Samak was forgotten in the 1970s when students preferred the easy, readymade tenets of the Communist Party to complicated Marxist philosophy. Samak died in 1975 as an isolated philosopher who had not chosen either Marxism or Buddhism for his practice.[93]

Buddhadāsa's Interpretation of Materialism

Reviewing the relationships between Buddhadāsa and those three Marxist intellectuals, Pridi, Kulap and Samak, we can conclude that the three intellectuals respected Buddhadāsa highly and had some communication with him; yet in their intellectual statements about Marxism and Buddhism, the impact of Buddhadāsa's teaching is not much in evidence. Rather, the most salient point is their common interest in the question of whether Buddhism was materialism or not. Buddhadāsa, too, discussed this issue, but a cursory reading of the main body of Buddhadāsa's works shows his earliest discussion of this topic to have been in the late 1960s, more than ten years after Pridi and Samak were addressing it.

Buddhadāsa discussed social issues intensively in his lecture series *Boromatham* (*The Supreme Dhamma*), given in 1969 to a group of Chulalongkorn University students temporarily ordained as monks.[94] In those lectures, *watthuniyom* or "materialism" was one of the key issues that Buddhadāsa criticized, at least in his understanding of the term. Although originally the Thai term *watthuniyom* was coined as a specific representation of Marxism's "historical materialism," which is academically defined as "the causal primacy of men's and women's mode of production and reproduction of their natural (physical) being, or of the labour process more generally, in the development of human history,"[95] in Thai, *watthu-niyom* is easily misunderstood; for this reason, Buddhadāsa and other Thai intellectuals had to clarify its meaning in their materialism.

The Thai word *watthu-niyom* is a combination of the noun, *watthu*, which means "materials," and the suffix, *-niyom*, which indicates an ideology, analogous to the English suffix "-ism." However, since there is a homonym Thai verb, *niyom*, which means "to define, to prescribe," and "to like, to favor," *watthu-niyom* could be read as a tendency of people to indulge themselves in material happiness. In Thai, the tendency to material indulgence can be expressed more grammatically as *niyom-watthu*, since in Thai, the verb usually precedes the object.[96] For Thai Buddhist monks and practitioners who pursued happiness through working to change their spiritual attitude, a problem lay in their contemporaries' seeking of happiness only in material well-being, with little attention to the deep observation of the mind.

In the lectures of *Boromatham*, Buddhadāsa used the term *watthuniyom* more broadly than the usage of Marxism's "historical materialism," a way of thinking that gives priority to the material in decision-making. He rejected *watthuniyom* or any kind of material reductionism, including both *watthu-niyom* (Marxist idea of materialism) and *niyom-watthu* (favoring material pleasures).[97] Buddhadāsa insisted that *watthuniyom* means the system of ideas that gives rise to defilement, or one's never satisfied desire, a decisive authority to control the world. In the ideological system of *watthuniyom*, people are only concerned with the happiness coming from material satiation and sensual pleasure. Heavenly happiness, according to Buddhadāsa, also belongs to *watthuniyom* rather than *manoniyom* (Buddhadāsa's term for "idealism"), although people often took the reverse meaning, and made it a reason not to listen to religion, which is on the side of *manoniyom*. People tended to think that the notion of heaven was a lie intended to dupe people into indulging a non-existent dream. Because the materialists accordingly considered *nibbāna* as a materialistic paradise of total satisfaction of their desires, they did not believe in religion. Buddhadāsa strongly censured them,

> They do not understand what the scriptures meant. That is because they do not expect anything else but *kāmārammaṇa* (sense-desire).[98]

For Buddhadāsa, people must subscribe to the principle of *manoniyom*, or idealism, rather than *watthuniyom*. Again, Buddhadāsa's term for "idealism" — *manoniyom* — was unique; *chittaniyom* is the most common Thai translation of it, but it was commonly used with a negative connotation, particularly by anti-communist Buddhist elites. Buddhadāsa's *manomiyom* was also distinguished from the ascetic idealism that rejects the material aspects of human life. Buddhadāsa defined his term *manoniyom* as "the knowledge of mind that can control both body and mind."[99] The *manoniyom* of Buddhadāsa has to be distinguished from those of ascetics who despise the body; it should be in the "middle way" (Pāli: *majjhimā-paṭipadā*) of body and mind, always placing material and sensual desire under the control of the mind.[100]

The arguments of Buddhadāsa and his three Marxist followers, Pridi, Kulap and Samak, do not quite agree. On the one hand, Buddhadāsa never gave support to any kind of materialism or any suggestion that idealism was the principle to be upheld. On the other hand, those three Buddhist Marxists proposed commonalities in Buddhism and Marxism — particularly the aspect of materialism. Nevertheless, the ideological positions of Buddhadāsa and the Marxist intellectuals did not differ greatly. Buddhadāsa's notion of *manoniyom* was rather moderate compared to the ascetic idealism of the right; whereas his Buddhist Marxist followers' notion of historical materialism was some distance from the extreme left of mechanical materialism, which simply rejects spirituality and insists that only the material exists. Just as Buddhadāsa rejected extremist idealism but insisted on the priority of mind over the material, those Buddhist Marxists proposed historical materialism which admits the existence of mind but considers it as dependent on the material. The ideological positions of Buddhadāsa and the Buddhist Marxists were close to the center, although they never completely concurred.

It should be noted that even though the three Buddhist Marxist followers of Buddhadāsa shed light on common materialist aspects of Buddhism and Marxism, their arguments were more of intellectual interest than political propaganda to persuade Thai Buddhists to embrace Marxism. One reason for this is that until the late 1950s, none of the three became a full member of the Communist Party of Thailand (CPT) or controlled any political groups powerful enough to actualize their Marxist ideology. According to an influential CPT intellectual, Prawut Simantha, the CPT seems also to have been indifferent to such philosophical questions of materialism and Buddhism and indeed appears even to have been indifferent to Buddhism itself. Prawut said that the CPT's religious policy was influenced by that of the Chinese Communist Party; they thought that people could believe in religion and should also be allowed to criticize religion. From Prawut's point of view, the dominant Chinese executive of the Party understood neither Buddhism nor Marxist philosophy, and sometimes even believed in "superstitious spirits."[101]

Into the 1960s and 1970s, the simplistic frame of Marxist materialism versus Buddhist idealism spread among students and intellectuals. The complicated arguments made by Buddhadāsa and the Buddhist Marxist intellectuals were ignored or forgotten, except by a few non-communist Marxist disciples of Pridi Phanomyong who took up this issue in the late 1970s and the 1980s.[102] It was only after the period of tense political conflict that the philosophical comparison of Marxism and Buddhism regained intellectual attention.

4. Buddhadāsa's Political Position

As the above examination has revealed, Buddhadāsa had contacts with some of the leading Marxist intellectuals in Thailand, but the above discussion of materialism indicated that Buddhadāsa's thought cannot be simply labeled as ideologically sympathetic to Marxism. Buddhadāsa's thought may be better characterized as "radical conservatism" than in Marxist terms, which was how some of his activist followers referred to him oxymoronically.[103] However, on a number of occasions, Buddhadāsa was accused of being a "communist." Because of this labeling, Buddhadāsa acquired a controversial image and was subject to a skeptical regard, despite enjoying an outstanding reputation for disseminating long-forgotten Buddhist teachings about the overcoming of suffering. In order to articulate Buddhadāsa's political position, particularly in connection with communism, the following three points should be examined: first, the four political groups in existence in the 1950s and his relationship to them; second, his attitude toward the Peace Committee movement led by the Communist Party of Thailand; and third, the suspicion that he was a communist, as was discussed in the Buddhist public sphere.

Buddhadāsa and Political Groups in the Late 1950s

From the post-Second World War period through to the end of the 1950s, there were four main political groups in Thailand: the military group of Phibun; the anti-communist liberal royalists such as Khwan Aphaiwong and the Pramoj brothers, Seni and Kukrit; the socialists, or non-CPT Marxists, including the Pridi-Free Thai group; and the CPT.[104] The crucial question here is Buddhadāsa's relationship to or distance from these four political groups, in particular to the third and fourth groups which turned to Marxism for their political ideology.[105]

Buddhadāsa's association with the third group of socialists — including Pridi, Kulap and Samak — was widely known to the public through many booklet publications and magazine feature articles.[106] In the Thai context, so-called "socialists" were ideologically adherent to Marxism, but not Communist Party members; they were usually less radical than the communists on the left, but were more progressive than the royalists and the military on the right. Particularly, Pridi and Kulap tend to be highly regarded for their progressive stance, although they did not remain in powerful positions very long, as a result of unfortunate political incidents. The personal contacts between those socialist Marxists and Buddhadāsa hardly damaged their reputations, but rather enhanced them. The progressive image of Buddhadāsa, who sought fundamental teachings in the scriptures independently from conventional Buddhist interpretations, overlapped with that of these socialist intellectuals; it seems that their close relationships were favorable topics for inclusion in their biographies.

Among the fourth group, the CPT, there were in fact several executives who respected Buddhadāsa as a result of reading his works. Samphat Phungprasoet (1928–), who was a member of the political bureau of the CPT but quit the Party to return to his career as a lawyer in 1971, has respected Buddhadāsa and his works since around 1982. Pluang Wannasi (1922–1996), who was a central committee member, also respected Buddhadāsa from the time of his involvement in student activities. Samphat and Pluang came from Buddhist backgrounds, and did not abandon Buddhism when they became communists.[107] Wirot Amphai, one of the five supreme executives who founded the CPT, also respected Buddhadāsa, and was preparing to publish a Chinese translation of Buddhadāsa's sermons with Sukkhaphap Chai Publishing in April 2000; his Chinese translation of *Things Which We Still Pay Too Little Attention To* (*Sing thi rao yang son-chai kan noi pai*) was published together with Buddhadāsa's original Thai sermon and Phra Dr. James Ratananando's English translation.[108]

According to the attestations of the Bangkok-based Communist Party cadres, these CPT executives' respect for Buddhadāsa was a matter of personal faith in Buddhadāsa's teaching, outside Party policy. According to Prawut Simanta (a candidate for the central committee member in 1983), and Phirun Chatrawanitchakun (the central committee member in 1983), who were engaged in Party activities in Bangkok and in the jungle in the Northern region, their units never contacted Buddhadāsa for cooperation. They are not sure whether the Southern region unit contacted Suan Mokkh; the operation of the Communist Party was divided by regions, and intra-Party communication was very difficult.[109] Kanya Lilalai, one of the CPT members who worked for the Voice of the Thai People Radio Broadcasting in Yunnan, which was one of the propagation and intellectual centers of the CPT, said that Buddhadāsa could not even be regarded as a Party sympathizer. On Buddhist holidays, some monks gave sermons on the Voice of the Thai People, but none were connected to Buddhadāsa.[110]

According to Buddhadāsa, a communist monk once visited him and confessed that he was a member. The monk had thought that Buddhadāsa was a communist or a communist sympathizer from the beginning of his work. Within an hour of Buddhadāsa's denial of any communist connection, the monk left Suan Mokkh.[111] Kanya said that this visit seemed to be a personal rather than an official contact, because the monk did not disturb Buddhadāsa upon discovering his misunderstanding.

Unlike socialist Marxists, if any connection between Buddhadāsa and CPT cadre had been known to the public, it would have caused Buddhadāsa serious trouble; so it is not surprising that there was psychological constraint on the disclosure of such information. However, it should be noted that in the author's interviews, no CPT executive confirmed Buddhadāsa's involvement in their political activities, even though his reputation was potentially beneficial to the CPT's ideological propagation. Therefore, it appears safe to conclude that Buddhadāsa was not likely to have been involved in the CPT.

Buddhadāsa's Attitude toward the Peace Committee Movement

In the early 1950s in Thailand, the Peace Committee's involvement was a significant indicator of whether or not an intellectual interest in Marxism had developed into political activism. The famous Marxist intellectual Supha Sirimanon also declined to sign a pledge in support of the anti-Korean War campaign organized by the Peace Committee and through which the Communist Party intended to expand its influence. Contrary to Supha, many other Marxist contributors to Supha's journal *Aksonsan*, including Kulap Saipradit, Samak Burawat, and Atsani Phonlachan, did support the campaign, were arrested for being communists, and from November 1952 spent over four years in jail.[112] Buddhadāsa did not share the fate of those intellectuals in the Peace Committee Movement.

The strongest surviving evidence of Buddhadāsa's distance from the communist political movement was his lack of involvement in Peace Committee activities, which were developed under the guidance of the Soviet Union and led locally by the CPT. In the Suan Mokkh Archives in Chaiya, there was an invitation letter from the Peace Committee of Thailand dated July 1952. Buddhadāsa wrote a short note in the margin of a letter of invitation from Committee chair Charoen Supsaeng: "I cannot co-operate with you because [for me] the meaning of peace is different."

Buddhadāsa as a Communist Suspect in the Buddhist Public Sphere

Despite the fact that no communist leaders interviewed by the author testified to Buddhadāsa's involvement in the communist movement, on quite a few occasions in his lifetime, he was accused of being a "communist." In the face of such accusation which publicly disgraced Buddhadāsa, his followers defended him against the accusers.

The first such accusation against Buddhadāsa derived from his lecture in June 1948 at the Buddhist Association of Thailand. The lecture was titled "Mountainous Hindrance on the Way of the Buddha-Dhamma." Buddhadāsa declared in the lecture that attachment to our own views of the Buddha, the Dhamma, and the Saṅgha would block the way to reach the truth.[113] Phra Thipparinya (Thup Klamphasut), a former appeals court judge who had passed the sixth grade Pāli ecclesiastical examinations, got very angry, and said on behalf of the Lord Buddha that Buddhadāsa's lecture was irreverent.[114] Phra Thipparinya brought both civil and monastic charges against Buddhadāsa as being a communist.[115] For the civil charge, Phra Thipparinya brought the case to Luang Katsongkhram, then a confidant of Phibun Songkhram, to pressure the authorities to arrest Buddhadāsa.[116] Phra Thipparinya argued that Buddhadāsa intended to destroy Buddhism by receiving benefits from communists. However, Luang Katsongkhram did not take the charge very seriously.[117]

Phra Thipparinya brought a monastic charge against Buddhadāsa to the Supreme Patriarch and the Ecclesiastical Minister of Education.[118] The Supreme Patriarch Klom Luang Wachirayanawong, in residence at Wat Bowonniwet, never took the charge seriously. At Wat Rachathiwat, Phra Sasanasophon, the monastic head of the southern provinces, who was in a supervisory position over Buddhadāsa in the framework of the monastic administration, took him to the Supreme Patriarch to defend himself. However, the Supreme Patriarch did not pick up the charge in his conversation, but said instead, "I want to live in Suan Mokkh with you; it is busy living here."[119] On the other hand, the Ecclesiastical Minister of Education, Somdet Plot Kittisophano at Wat Benchamabophit, believed Phra Thipparinya's charge. Phra Sasanasophon at Wat Rachathiwat (then Phra Thammakosachan), again, took Buddhadāsa to Somdet Plot to defend himself. Somdet Plot reprimanded Buddhadāsa for not using the principles given in the *Visuddhimagga*, the classical Buddhist doctrinal exegetical text written by Buddhaghosa in fifth-century Sri Lanka. Somdet Plot asked for the basis of Buddhadāsa's interpretation, which identified the Buddha as an obstacle to reaching the truth. Somdet Plot listened to Buddhadāsa's defense for less than an hour, and let him go without assigning him any penalty. Buddhadāsa understood that Somdet Plot could not impose a penalty on him because there was no evidence of him being hired by communists, since the charge was solely based on a conjecture by Phra Thipparinya.[120]

The accusation that Buddhadāsa's was a communist was never seriously considered as factual by influential elder monks in the Saṅgha; in particular, the support of Phra Sasanasophon seems to have been helpful. Phra Sasanasophon knew of Buddhadāsa through Buddhadāsa's uncle, who ordained at Wat Rachathiwat, and he always gave Buddhadāsa opportunities to talk at meetings, and promoted him in the ecclesiastic echelons.[121]

It was rather Phra Thipparinya who finally lost face after ten years of his campaign. Phra Sithawat Waniwattiko, who came from the same province as Buddhadāsa and was then studying as a young monk at Wat Mahathat, and who witnessed the special *dhamma* colloquy with an audience of a thousand at Wat Mahathat in 1951, described it dramatically in an interview with the author. Chamnan Luprasoet, a notable follower of Buddhadāsa, asked in the colloquy, "I have been thinking of the issue about the accusation against Buddhadāsa, who said that the Buddha, the Dhamma, and the Saṅgha were the Himalayan Mountains, which would not allow *nibbāna* to those who were attached to them. The opponents, led by Phra Thipparinya, censured Buddhadāsa for destroying Buddhism to a greater extent than Devadatta had done. Phra Thipparinya has vehemently spent a huge amount of money and energy to destroy Buddhadāsa. I would like to know who is right and who is wrong." The chair of the colloquy was Phra Phimolatham (Aat). Aat said, "This is a big question in society, and it has been discussed for a long time. Luang Pho Suk, answer it."

The audience became completely still, waiting for an answer from Luang Pho Suk or Chao Khun Phawanaphiram, the chief respondent of the colloquy. Suk admitted that Buddhadāsa had devoted himself to work for Buddhism, and finally said, "I would say that Venerable Buddhadāsa was not wrong. He teaches high level Buddhism correctly. Everyone knows that the Buddha, the Dhamma, and the Saṅgha would be an obstacle to reach *nibbāna* if one were attached to them, but no one was ever brave enough as a monk to teach that view. This is how monks made people attached to the Buddha, the Dhamma, and the Saṅgha. Most of them teach in this way … Because the two opponents of Buddhadāsa [Phra Thipparinya and Phraya Achayachak] felt that Buddhadāsa was an enemy of Buddhism, who would work to destroy Buddhism, they dedicated their fund of 200,000 baht to fight Buddhadāsa since they had a strong belief in Buddhism. Such people are very difficult to find. Where else could we find such people who would devote a huge amount of their money and time?"

After Suk had answered, Aat the chair summarized the answer in beautiful words. He said, "We may have heard an old saying, there are some phrases of *dhamma* in the canon, and some enlightened monks are mistrusted because we do not understand the meaning deeply enough or correctly." Then, Chamnan stood up and said, "Let me add a note." Aat had to repeat his utterance several times, and Chamnan made sure of the details by repeating it loudly. Phra Thipparinya, who was then one of the most important lay supporters of Wat Mahathat, had to leave his seat. As far as Sithawat remembers, after this colloquy, Phra Thipparinya became seriously ill, and withdrew from his activities in Wat Mahathat. This colloquy was held exactly ten years after Buddhadāsa's *Phukhao* lecture at the Buddhist Association of Thailand. Sithawat recalled Buddhadāsa had said that people would understand his intentions ten years later.[122]

This story suggests that the Mahanikai elders such as Aat and Suk also understood the meaning of Buddhadāsa's radical sermon, and did not take the communist charge against him seriously. Regardless of Phra Thipparinya's charge, Buddhadāsa was on the track to wider recognition and promotion during that period. Even though the communist charge against Buddhadāsa was examined in the Saṅgha authority in 1949 and 1950, in 1949 Buddhadāsa was appointed head of the Buddhist Mission Organization of Region 5 (the southern provinces) and abbot of Wat Boromathat Chaiya, the historic temple in Buddhadāsa's hometown. In 1950, he was even promoted and given the monastic title, Phra Ariyananthamuni. These appointments in the ecclesiastic order suggest that the communist accusation was not considered serious and did not affect Buddhadāsa's reputation at that time.[123]

However, until the end of the 1970s, Buddhadāsa was suspected of being a communist by the Thai secret police and a man thought to be a CIA agent. According to Khemānanda, a famous artist monk disciple of Buddhadāsa, there was a foreign monk at Suan Mokkh who was rumored to be a CIA agent. The foreign monk was ordained in the Songkhla province and came to Suan Mokkh to conduct research in the library of Suan Mokkh and to investigate some of the monks there. The foreign monk did not deny it when someone asked him if he were from the CIA.[124] There was also a Thai secret policeman watching Suan Mokkh. Police Colonel Chalat Saengchuto was sent to watch Suan Mokkh in the 1950s. However, Chalat later became a disciple of Buddhadāsa, having been influenced by him during his work of maintaining close watch over Buddhadāsa.[125]

Buddhadāsa also had to face harsh defamatory campaigns led by some of the teachers and students of the Abhidhamma studies, people such as Kittivuḍḍho Bhikkhu and Anan Senakhan, who were also committed to anti-communist propagandizing.[126] Despite having no concrete evidence, two of Buddhadāsa's followers, Arun Wetchasuan and Suphot Dantrakun, considered the rumor of Buddhadāsa being a communist as CIA retaliation for his refusal to give propaganda sermons against communism. In the interview with Phra Pracha, they referred to a story of Buddhadāsa mentioning a visit by an American from the USIS (the United States Information Service) to seek cooperation in protecting Thailand and Buddhism from the threat of communism in exchange for material support; Buddhadāsa, however, did not accept this offer.[127] Arun and Suphot believed that the CIA, irked by Buddhadāsa's refusal to cooperate, incited anti-communist campaigners including Kittivuḍḍho and Anan, to accuse Buddhadāsa of being a communist agent.[128] Suphot also published a book, *Arguing against Phra? Anan Senakhan and His Group on the Heretical Teaching*, to defend Buddhadāsa from Anan Senakhan's attacks, writing under the pseudonym Sāvaka (a disciple of the Buddha who listened to his teaching closely).[129] Buddhadāsa spoke little about the "communist" suspicions; rather he let the Buddhist public sphere debate about them.

*****

To conclude this chapter, it can be said that the meeting of Marxism and Buddhism in post-Second World War Thailand prompted great intellectual excitement in Buddhadāsa's and his Marxist followers, and many other things, including their political despair, their religious experience and their intentions to promote and/or damage public figures' names and faces. For Thai Marxists, it was not necessarily a matter of simplistic ideological refutation of one side or the other. There were quite a few Thai Marxists — including both non-communist socialists and CPT members — who adopted Buddhadāsa's teaching for their religious lives, although some refrained from personal contact, fearing possible entanglement and trouble in the highly charged political environment. On the other hand, Buddhadāsa did study Marxism through books and information provided by his Marxist followers, and he deepened his insight into contemporary social issues without significant mention of Marxism.

It is probably too simplistic to infer that all the social aspects of Buddhism found in Buddhadāsa's ideas came from the influence of Marxism, but it is possible that Marxism inspired Buddhadāsa to develop his own Buddhist view of society. Buddhadāsa's later sermons, after the 1960s, involved several ideas reminiscent of the vocabulary of Marxist activists; his teaching frequently referred to, for instance, such notions as "non-egoism" (*khwam-mai-hen-kae-tua*), "self-sacrifice" (*sia sala*), and "usefulness for society" (*prayot to sangkhom* or *suan ruam*) — these sounded somewhat similar to the Buddhist notion of "non-self" (*anattā*) and at the same time overlapped with the catch phrases of Thai student activists who in the 1960s and 1970s left their comfortable urban homes for poor villages, so as to dedicate themselves to rural development. Whether or not it was through the influence of Marxism, Buddhadāsa shared the same concern as student activists inclined toward Marxism.

CHAPTER 7

Dhammic Socialism and Engaged Buddhism: Development of Social Aspects in Thai Buddhism[1]

Throughout the period of political turmoil in the 1970s, the Thai word for justice, *khwam-pen-tham*, frequently appeared in the daily newspapers and in leftist journals. The word *khwam-pen-tham*, which literally translates *dhamma-ness*, is used as a general noun in non-religious, secular contexts, yet Thai people readily recall the Buddhist origin of the word, the *dhamma*. Especially for Buddhadāsa's followers, who learned about the *dhamma*, the fruit of which should be obtained in the here and now, there was often concern that contemporary society and politics should be consistent with the *dhamma*. Even though Marxist tenets were generally negative about religious faith, it is not surprising that Thai student activists in the 1960s and 1970s were attracted to the notions of social justice in both Marxism and Buddhism. Buddhadāsa's notion of "Dhammic Socialism" and his followers' commitment to Buddhist social engagement arose from dialectical discussion between the two ideologies, both in search of a fair society.

Buddhadāsa's Dhammic Socialism was a Buddhist version of the just social order inspired by some Marxist concepts. Buddhadāsa indicated that in the Pāli scriptures and the early history of Buddhism, there was evidence of social, economic and political orders that coincided with the ideal society of socialism. Buddhadāsa insisted that Buddhism is practical enough to be applied to the achievement of justice in contemporary society. This promoted the public sphere of Buddhism to examine the social dimension of the *dhamma*. Buddhadāsa's Dhammic Socialism has been of interest to many scholars and activists, including Swearer, Jackson, Santikaro, Tavivat and Paisal; one aspect in need of further study is the link between the notion of Dhammic Socialism and its context in Thai intellectual history.[2]

Just as the case of Dhammic Socialism, emergence of Buddhist social engagement was brought forward in the course of the search for social justice. Internationally prominent engaged Buddhists, such as Thich Nhat Hanh of Vietnam and the 14th Dalai Lama of Tibet, each began their political protests in the contexts of enormous violence during the Vietnam War and the Chinese military advance. Many people were tortured and brutally killed; it is very doubtful that these were just and fair political actions taken by power holders. The regimes' political ideologies and strategies pointed to a realization of people's well-being and fair society; yet few people could experience them in their lives. In such circumstances, the Buddhist leaders in Vietnam and Tibet sought an alternative notion of justice in religious teaching and made it a principle for their political action.[3]

While many studies of engaged Buddhism focused on Buddhist monks' and groups' unique contributions to secular society, this chapter will focus on the ideological current which gave rise to Buddhist social engagement in Thailand.[4] Through an examination of Thai Buddhists' thoughts and experiences, this chapter will demonstrate that Thai Buddhists sought to find an element of social critique in Buddhism through dialogue with Marxism at a time when Marxist thought was absent from the public sphere.

First, the chapter will divide the second half of the 20th century into three periods and examine the development of Buddhist social concerns in each period. Particularly, examining the second period of democratic government between the 14 October 1973 and 6 October 1976 incidents, the chapter will trace shifts in the nature of Buddhadāsa's notion of Dhammic Socialism, along with the changing political landscape. Second, the chapter will focus on the experiences of Buddhadāsa's activist followers who wavered between Buddhism and Marxism and applied Buddhist concepts to real society.

1. Development of Social Thought in Thai Buddhism after the Late 1950s

Traditionally, many Thai Buddhists believed that Buddhism is a teaching for the individual's spiritual development, having not much to do with social reform; they also considered that Buddhist monks should only focus on their solitary religious practice, rather than becoming involved in secular matters. Monks' religious goal was assumed to be the other world, the state of *nibbāna* or of celestial bliss in next lives. Such traditional assumptions had to be reconsidered when Thai intellectuals lost sight of social justice in their society. The stage was set for change when Buddhist practice was introduced as a practical technique that could transform one's present life even in the secular world, and the actual change was generated under dictatorial military governments which strictly censored political expressions.

The development of Buddhadāsa's notion of Dhammic Socialism and Thai Buddhists' social engagement advanced particularly when Marxism was out of sight in the Thai public sphere. In light of the major political events that determined the rise and fall of the communist movement, the second half of the 20th century will be traced in the three periods: from 1958 to 1973; from 1973 to the end of the 1970s; and from the late 1970s onward.

Suppression of Political Expression under the Military Regimes: 1958–1973

Political speech was strictly censored from the time of the October 1958 coup led by Field Marshal Sarit Thanarat up to the 14 October 1973 student uprising, which overthrew the decade-long military regime. After his seizure of power in September 1957, Sarit needed yet another coup in October 1958 to suppress the "noise" in the democratic system, i.e., such matters as legislator corruption, the critical press, and the demand for labor welfare, which was promoted by Field Marshal Phibun Songkhram to establish the legitimacy of his government. Sarit enacted martial law, ushered in a military dictatorship, and oppressed any critical intellectuals by accusing them of being "communist."[5] This meant the end of a relatively liberal period during which a considerable volume of Marxist literature was produced by Thai intellectuals. Marxism was expelled from the public sphere of Thailand by the military dictatorship of Sarit and his successors, Thanom Kittikachon and Praphat Charusathian.

When Marxist social criticism was severely curtailed, the Thai economy and society were transformed. Under the rule of Sarit's coup government, "materialism" in the sense of consumerism was promoted in Thailand more strongly than ever. Allied with the United States, the Thai military provided the Americans with a key strategic base for the Vietnam War against the communist insurgency in Indochina, and in exchange received access to commercial opportunities based on US investment. In its domestic campaign, the anti-communist military dictatorship propagated slogans such as "Work is money, money is work which creates happiness," and advertised its success in visible material improvement with slogans such as "Flowing water, bright electricity, and good highways."[6] Thanks to the US military presence, the Thai economy rapidly expanded not only in construction but also in service sectors such as the sex industry to meet the demands of foreigners. As a result of the striking increase in investment by the United States and Japan, foreign consumer goods flooded the Thai market.[7] During the period of Sarit and the succeeding Thanom-Praphat regimes in the 1960s, great changes in material standards took place in Thailand. The social and economic transformation provoked critical opposition against these changes. Buddhism supported this trend by supplying vocabulary and concepts for use in critical discourse.[8]

In the 1950s, "Buddhist Socialism" — a concept sounding similar to "Dhammic Socialism" — was promoted in U Nu's Burma, and in the 1960s, another "Buddhist Socialism" emerged in Prince Sihanouk's Cambodia. Although a search by the author did not find mention of Buddhadāsa in Burmese and Cambodian "Buddhist Socialism," it is likely that Buddhadāsa had some knowledge of U Nu's idea; he translated and published a speech by U Nu in his journal *Buddhism* in February 1954, and visited U Nu's Buddhist Socialist regime in Burma when he attended the *Sangayanā* convocation for settling canonical questions on the *Tipiṭaka* in 1957 C.E., the year 2500 in the Buddhist calendar.[9]

Buddhadāsa's earliest mention of Dhammic Socialism was possibly sometime during the eight years after October 1958; Karuna Kusalasai reported that he and his fellow communist-charged prisoners were delighted to listen to Buddhadāsa's preaching about Dhammic Socialism when they were in jail, but no record of that sermon could be found.[10] Though the date of the first Dhammic Socialism sermon remains unclear, surely Buddhadāsa's concern with contemporary society was deepened in the 1960s.

In the late 1960s, just as seen in the lecture series *Boromatham* (*The Supreme Dhamma*), which was examined in Chapter 6, Buddhadāsa put in his sermons messages to warn the contemporary world. When the military regimes banned Marxism and attempted to satisfy people with a level of material well-being allegedly superior to that which their communist opponents could provide, Buddhadāsa pointed to the significance of mind, which should determine one's own mental state and control the material environment. He opposed both kinds of "materialism": both satisfaction with the material and sensual comfort provided by the American-allied Thai military regimes, and also Marxism's material determinism, another promise of improvement in material well-being. The critical perspective on "materialism" developed by Buddhadāsa in the 1960s became an important element of his social thought; he consistently criticized Thai society's persistent tendency toward intoxication in material pleasure.[11]

Return of Strong Marxist Influence: From 1973 to the End of the 1970s

Political freedom and Marxist discourse returned to the public sphere after the 14 October uprising in 1973. The uprising was led by students and citizens demanding a permanent constitution, the constitution having been abolished by Thanom's coup which overthrew his own government in November 1971. Public demonstrations finally saw the dictators Thanom and Praphat expelled when they were denied support by both the military and the King. The following Sanya Dhammasakdi interim government was selected and appointed by the King, and the subsequent governments established by parliamentary procedure as defined in the new constitution of October 1974. Under these democratic governments, Marxist literature written in the late 1940s and the 1950s was allowed to be republished and gained popularity amongst the Thai people, who had for some time been denied access to political critique. With the increasing popularity of Marxism, the Communist Party of Thailand (CPT) brought socially concerned students into its youth organizations through its network of student agents and intellectuals.[12]

It was in the period following the 14 October 1973 uprising that Buddhadāsa frequently mentioned Dhammic Socialism. Pocketbooks containing collections of Dhammic Socialism sermons appeared from November 1973 onward.[13] In a sermon in November 1973, only a month after the 14 October uprising, Buddhadāsa declared that all religions were "socialist" (*sangkhomniyom*) in the sense that they taught the actualization of a harmonious balance in society through a reduction of individual greed; for Buddhadāsa, individual greed is the taking of surplus profit from other people.[14] Phaisan Wongwarawisit (at present known as Phra Paisal Visalo) indicated that there are 3,500 pages of Buddhadāsa's lectures on society, originally delivered between 1973 and 1976, in the seven volumes of *Thammakhot* (*Dhamma Propagation*), the 63-volume collection of Buddhadāsa's works.[15]

It should be noted that in mid-1970s Thailand, the words *sangkhom* (society) or *sangkhomniyom* (socialism) did not refer to a subversive left; they were perceived as fashionable and progressive, but not as radical as *prachachon* or *muanchon*, which mean the "people" or the "masses."[16] In the democratic period after the 14 October 1973 uprising, Thai intellectuals and politicians liked to refer to *sangkhom* or *sangkhomniyom*, which conveyed a positive image of a welfare state giving consideration to the life of people in society — something that could hardly have been expected of the military dictatorship before the uprising. Even though he opposed communism, Seni Pramoj, the first Prime Minister in the elected parliament after 14 October, insisted that Thailand should be *sangkhomniyom*.[17] Under such circumstances, Buddhadāsa's reference to *sangkhomniyom* in combination with the *dhamma* should not necessarily be interpreted as a sign that he was inclined toward leftist ideologies.

(i) Discovery of "Socialism" in Buddhism

What Buddhadāsa found in common between "socialism" and Buddhist teaching was the aspect of non-egoism. He interpreted *sangkhomniyom* (socialism) as love of society, not loving solely oneself.[18] The love of others developed in socialism coincided with the religious teaching of the cessation of egoism (*khwam-hen-kae-tua*), which tends to follow the way of *kilesa*.[19] When people do not think of taking advantage for themselves, they can consider others (*hen kae phu-un*) in society at large. In this sense, all religions that teach against egoism are "socialistic" in that they place the community above the individual.

Dhammic Socialism was the "socialism" implied by the *dhamma*. Buddhadāsa defined the *dhamma* as having four meanings: 1) *dhammajāti* (nature) itself, or phenomena; 2) the laws of nature; 3) duty in accordance with the laws of nature; and 4) fruit from duty in accordance with the laws of nature. By nature, according to Buddhadāsa, no creature needs a surplus, that which is in excess of its requirements for living. Creatures need just the amount that can fill their stomachs. Nature has a harmonious balance of coexistence with everyone consuming just what they need. For Buddhadāsa, this is the spirit of socialism with the "*dhamma* of *dhammajāti*," the laws of nature that naturally (Thai: *doi thammachat*; Pāli: *dhammajāti*) exist.[20]

Buddhadāsa explained that this natural balance of "socialism," in which no one has to accumulate more than necessary, had already collapsed when some individuals began accumulating a surplus for their own use. This incident coincided with the birth of *kilesa* (defilement), taking advantage for oneself at the expense of others. Food and commodities became insufficient because of people's egoism, which was stimulated by *kilesa*, when people accumulated a "surplus" unnecessary for their survival.[21] Buddhadāsa argued that the way to restore the original socialism of nature was to restrict *kilesa*, the fundamental cause of problems in society. Buddhadāsa's invention was a combination of the notion of surplus value in Marxism with non-egoism in Buddhism.

(ii) The Dictatorship of the Dhamma (padetkan doi tham)

Thammika-sangkhomniyom (Dhammic Socialism) — Buddhadāsa's picture of an ideal society ruled by the *dhamma* — developed together with the rapidly radicalizing politics of the mid-1970s and shifted its emphasis in reflection of the changing political scene. In the historical event of the 14 October uprisings, King Bhumibol Adulyadej (Rama IX) played a striking role; he intervened in politics for the first time in order to halt the bloodshed led by the military firing on protesters. The King asked the military dictators Thanom and Praphat to leave the country, and replaced the Prime Minister with Sanya Dhammasakdi, who was his own selection. The King also dismissed all the members of the constitution-drafting committee appointed by the Thanom regime, and appointed a new National Assembly. The king's extralegal initiative and commitment coincided with Buddhadāsa's proposal in September 1974 for a "dictatorship of the *dhamma*" (*padetkan doi tham*).[22]

In his November 1974 lecture entitled "Socialism According to Religious Principles," Buddhadāsa pointed out that the means for the restoration of Dhammic Socialism (the harmonious balance of nature), is a dictatorship of the *dhamma*, i.e., righteousness. For Buddhadāsa, a dictatorship of righteousness was the most effective method to actualize good in this world.[23]

Buddhadāsa found the ideal dictatorship of the *dhamma* in the Buddhist scriptures and in ancient history. In the Buddhist scriptures, an ideal monarch should have ten virtues, called *dasarājadhamma*, which are, Buddhadāsa believed, filled with the spirit of Dhammic Socialism. *Dasarājadhamma* comprises the ten rules of the *dhamma* for a ruler of the world as defined in Buddhist scripture.[24] Buddhadāsa argued that there is no reason for a monarch with the *dasarājadhamma* that embodies the spirit of socialism to be abolished as was the Thai absolute monarchy in the constitutional reform of 1932; a monarch with *dasarājadhamma* would immediately actualize virtue in the world, and no misconduct would ever take place.[25] For Buddhadāsa, the system of monarchy should be maintained, but that appropriate virtue should be fostered in the person of the king.[26]

(iii) Differences between Dhammic Socialism and Worldly Socialism

Unfortunately, mid-1970s Thai politics after the 14 October uprising was never stable. The abrupt liberalization of political expression made dissident voices accessible, and drew many socially aware students toward Marxist literature and the armed struggle led by the CPT. With the rapid rise of insurgency, the military's counterinsurgency also intensified. Furthermore, the communist camp was splitting and fighting with in itself. Prior to the 6 October 1976 massacre, the political conflict in Thailand grew seriously confused as a result of the policy of brutal assassination of communist suspects; any sign of attunement to communism could endanger a person's life.[27]

At the time of chaotic political conditions, Buddhadāsa distinguished his Dhammic Socialism from "brutal, dogmatic socialisms."[28] Buddhadāsa started criticizing worldly socialism after the 1975 communist victory in Vietnam stimulated an escalation of turmoil within Thailand. Many suspected political activists were assassinated by right-wing vigilante groups and security forces until the firefight at Thammasat University on 6 October 1976. In a sermon in July 1976, Buddhadāsa scarcely mentioned "socialism" or Dhammic Socialism even though he kept teaching about righteous political rule.[29]

Buddhadāsa's mid-1970s' lectures pointed out at least three differences between Marxist "worldly socialism" and his notion of socialism supported by the law of nature and Buddhist virtues.[30]

First, Buddhadāsa's socialism is a system of morality which has little to do with the economic exploitation that Marxist socialism attempts to overcome by structural economic remedies. Any kind of disequilibrium is supposed to be caused by a lack of morality. Buddhadāsa insisted that nothing could exist normally without morality. In a system of politics, which is "concerned with many people," and thus has an inclination toward trouble, morality can exist if people can solve problems properly. Similarly, the economic system is a system of morality relating to consumption.[31] Socialism in Buddhadāsa's thought is a system of morality in every arena of human activity — a system that gives society normality or the happiness of normality.

Second, Buddhadāsa's socialism makes no mention of class conflict over the modes of production. Buddhadāsa understood that it was natural that classes come about according to people's deeds and depending upon their different capabilities and wisdoms.[32] When Buddhadāsa looked at poverty, he did not look for reasons for it in structural economic relationships or in its historical development as explored by Marxism. Rather, he considered the reason for poverty to lie in past individual deeds, such as lack of diligence, or careless spending on gambling and drinking. Buddhadāsa reduced all the causes of poverty to moral problems. Some of his followers, such as Prawase Wasi, did not agree with this, and later re-examined this issue.

Third, Buddhadāsa's socialism rejected a punishment or violent sanction (*atchaya*) that would eventually take people's lives.[33] This was in contrast to the communist strategy of armed struggle. He urged Buddhists to learn harmonious socialism arising from tradition, which was part of their very being, so as to make it their weapon with which to protect their country against the bloodthirstiness and dogmatism of worldly socialism.[34] Buddhadāsa compared his Dhammic Socialism with the back-burning of a fire around a house to protect it against a bush fire, which represented worldly socialism. The *dhamma* is the weapon to intercept this socialism which causes people to be divided at each other's throats due to conflicts over dogma.[35] Rather than an affirmation of communism, Dhammic Socialism was a counter to socialism as it was being expounded at that time.

Marxism in Decline: After the 6 October 1976 Coup

In the 6 October 1976 coup, radicals were massacred, and after that, strict anti-communist counterinsurgency measures were adopted throughout the countryside of Thailand. With the military's return to power after the 6 October 1976 incident, violence was quelled. Toward the end of the 1970s, radical students grew disappointed with the CPT executives' uncritical attitude toward the Chinese Communist Party and began returning home from the jungle struggle which they had joined after the 6 October incident. When the disappointed radical students returned to civilian life, Marxism's underground influence began to decline.

After the late 1980s, the downfall of the Communist Party in East Europe and Russia further promoted the decline of Thai confidence in Marxism. Concerned students who remained in the city needed an alternative to Marxist social critique; despairing former radicals wanted something to replace their internal loss; Buddhist intellectuals and activists developed the social dimensions of Buddhism into concrete social reform projects. Buddhist monks' and lay activists' application of Buddhist principles in practical situations became widely known as "socially engaged Buddhism." It was in the social context of the time after the 6 October massacre that Buddhism once again became an ideological pillar for the people.

Response to Dhammic Socialism and Buddhadāsa

As examined above, it seems that Buddhadāsa's intention was neither to promote socialism or communism through his proposal of Dhammic Socialism, nor to counter them by criticizing "materialism." Therefore, Buddhadāsa continued his sermons on Dhammic Socialism even after the peak of popularity of socialism.[36] Buddhadāsa's "engaged Buddhist" disciples took on the significance of Dhammic Socialism selectively from among the three characteristics of Dhammic Socialism: (1) the harmonious order of nature, which coincided with socialism; (2) the dictatorship of the *dhamma* or kingly virtues; and (3) differences with worldly socialism. They understood and accepted the first characteristic as a foundation for looking at the social order from the Buddhist philosophical perspective presented in the Pāli scriptures.[37] However, they were not totally convinced by the second, the dictatorial character of Dhammic Socialism.[38] Those who experienced the overthrow of the military dictatorship in the 14 October uprising did not weigh dictatorship against democracy, even though they understood that the *dhamma*, which is perfectly just and right, should rule the world.[39] The most significant insights of Dhammic Socialism were situated in the third characteristic, which Buddhadāsa contrasted with worldly socialism; they highlighted the significance of the necessity of morality, mind, and respect toward life, which were disregarded in the Marxist socioeconomic revolution project.

2. Ideological Struggles of Buddhism and Marxism: The Experience of Buddhadāsa's Lay Followers

In the 1960s and 1970s when Buddhadāsa developed his thoughts on the ideal society, Thai Buddhist students and intellectuals were also seriously concerned about social issues. However, Buddhadāsa's proposal of Dhammic Socialism did not immediately reach the ears of radicalizing student activists; it had to wait until the brutal conflict was calmed in the 1980s. What did Thai Buddhist student activists think and how did they act during the period of intense political conflict fortified by ideological strongholds? How did they connect to Buddhadāsa's teaching, and what message did they receive from it?

This section will look at the ideological struggles of Buddhadāsa's activist followers, who sought their own forms of social engagement, in particular the struggles of the renowned Thai public intellectuals: Sulak Sivaraksa, Pracha Hutanuwatr, Weng Tochirakan, and Kanya Lilalai. Their activities and inner experiences point to the significance of Buddhadāsa's teaching in their lives; they also constitute an ideological history that gave birth to socially engaged Buddhism in Thailand.

Buddhist Intellectuals and Students, 1958–1973

In spite of, or perhaps because of, the strict control of the military dictatorship, the public sphere of Thailand became vigorously active, especially after June 1968, when the Thanom-Praphat government promulgated the new constitution. In December 1968, students from 15 universities organized the Student Volunteer Group to Observe the National Election in order to monitor the February 1969 election, the first in 12 years. In major universities, around this time there also emerged small student groups for social and political discussions.[40] Buddhist intellectuals also influenced these students' awareness of their contemporary society and politics right up to 14 October 1973. It was not Buddhadāsa alone who discussed social issues from Buddhist perspectives. The interest and extended discussions of lay Buddhist intellectuals and students were essential for Buddhism to afford an influential critique of contemporary social issues. Sulak Sivaraksa and his group were particularly prominent. In the time leading up to the 14 October uprising, through Sulak's publications and the seminars and groups he organized, students developed their concerns about society and politics. Sulak's Buddhist networking was one of the main conduits for Marxists to return to involvement in the Buddhist public sphere.

Sulak Sivaraksa (1933–)[41] came from a well-to-do family of Chinese descent, wealthy enough to pay for his barrister studies in England, although his family fortune was not sufficient to free him from the necessity of work. Sulak always needed to make a living using his skills and talents. Like many other descendants of Chinese in Thailand, Sulak inherited Thai culture and Buddhism because of his grandparents' intermarriage with ethnic Thai women who were Buddhist. Although Sulak's connection to Buddhism began in his childhood and continued while he was in England, his contact with Buddhism belonged to the area of conventional Buddhist beliefs and practices, which often involved supernaturalism.[42] Sulak was made aware by Buddhadāsa of the role of Buddhism in social issues,[43] and later worked on social issues from Buddhist perspectives together with P.A. Payutto Bhikkhu, who taught and served as deputy secretary general at Mahachulalongkorn Buddhist University from 1961 to 1974.[44] Through his refined sensitivity toward intellectual trends, his manner of networking with high society, and his skill in communication, Sulak became an important social critic and developed his own role as an "engaged Buddhist" in the Buddhist public sphere of Thailand.

Returning from England in 1962 to Thailand under military dictatorship, Sulak demonstrated his ability as an editor of such journals as *Sangkhomsat parithat* (*Social Science Review*), and developed further opportunities to express himself as a social critic. He was also involved in promoting monastic education, especially at Mahachulalongkorn Buddhist University and Wat Thongnopphakhun, which his family continues to support. Throughout the 1960s, Sulak attempted to provide social perspectives on issues such as conservation, peace and civil society. It later became known that Sulak had used funding from anti-communist agencies such as the Asia Foundation in his work on the journal editorial board and on education in social issues for monks.[45] However, Sulak never subscribed to the ideologies of these agencies; rather, he presented his own critical view of society, sometimes intermingled with Buddhism. For example, Sulak attacked the problems of the class gap both in Thai society and in materialist Western civilization, and he insisted on the importance of morality and ethics in the actualization of social justice.[46] Although Sulak was suspected of being a CIA agent and a communist because of his funding arrangements and his critical opinions respectively, he was skilled in discovering the abilities of young people, and giving them a chance to develop.[47] This is why Sulak has been a respected mentor in student discussion groups such as Parithat Sewana (Critical Discussion Group) and Yuwachon Sayam (Young Siamese), especially before the 14 October 1973 uprising. Before the uprising, the influence of Marxism had not yet emerged, and modern Buddhist thought, such as that of Buddhadāsa and P.A. Payutto Bhikkhu, was quite influential in these discussion groups.

Parithat Sewana was established by Buddhist students and intellectuals after the seminar on "The Social and Ethical Responsibility of Youth for Siam" at the Student Christian Center in January 1966. This seminar, which was organized by a Protestant group headed by Koson Sisan, invited famous Buddhist intellectuals such as Sanya Dhammasakdi, Puey Ungphakorn, and Direk Chayanam to speak, and invited an audience of students from every university. After the seminar, some students came to Sulak for assistance in organizing a group where Buddhist students could have opportunities to discuss social issues just as the Christians had been doing. Parithat Sewana, the most famous student discussion group in the 1960s, was born from concerns with religions and society rather than with Marxism.[48]

In Parithat Sewana,[49] there were mainly three sub-groups: a group for public panel discussion, a group for editing the journal, *Social Science Review Student Edition* (*Sangkhomsat parithat chabap naksuksa*), and a group for fine art appreciation study trips to the provinces and ancient temples. For the public panel discussions, Sulak invited people who had graduated from universities in Europe to express their views. The student movement leaders after the 14 October uprising, including Seksan Prasoetkun, Weng Tochirakan, and Charan Ditthanphichai, were rather minor participants who only listened to the panel discussions. They came to the panel discussions of Parithat Sewana in order to learn about progressive ideas in foreign countries. In the group engaged in editing the journal were Khanchai Bunphan, Suchit Wongthet, Nidhi Aeusrivongse, Komon

Khimthong, and Pibhop Dhongchai. All later became famous and active in journalism and academia, and were involved in social activism. As the nature of the participants and activities suggests, the discussions in Parithat Sewana were led by the Buddhist Sulak and the Western-educated progressive elite; the influence of Marxism and the Communist Party had arrived but did not yet overwhelm discussions.[50]

Aside from Sulak, among the participants in Parithat Sewana, Weng Tochirakan (1951–)[51] was one of the most devoted promoters of Buddhadāsa. Weng took part in Parithat Sewana from the time he was in high school. He later became president of the Mahidol University Student Club and was one of the leaders of the May demonstration against General Suchinda in 1992. Weng was impressed by Buddhadāsa's book, *Why Were We Born?* (*Koet ma thammai*) when he was in junior high school, and from that time, he began propagating Buddhadāsa's teachings to his friends by distributing Buddhadāsa's books. Weng decided to take as his guiding principle Buddhadāsa's saying, "Not being egotistical, destroying egoism, and serving the people." When Weng was a Mahidol University student, he started organizing medical students for voluntary public health activities and helping people wounded in demonstrations.[52] A friend referred to Weng as "a commander of Suan Mokkh" (*mae thap haeng suan mok*). Weng's example indicates that Buddhadāsa's guiding principle for the present life was interpreted to apply to the social engagement of activist students, when Marxism was not yet dominant.

The other student discussion group, Yuwachon Sayam (Young Siamese), was established by students at Suan Kulap High School, who sought advice from Sulak Sivaraksa. Yuwachon Sayam came to exist because of Pracha Hutanuwatr (1952–) and his friends, who organized a group at a high school exhibition on society, and also held a moot student election campaign modeled on the general election of 1969, the first election in 12 years. After their experience of giving public speeches at these events, they invited students from other high schools to found an inter-high school student organization, Yuwachon Sayam.[53]

In the beginning, Marxist elements were also few in the newly founded Yuwachon Sayam, although its members aimed at devoting themselves to the good of society.[54] Pracha was interested in the life of socially concerned student activists mentioned in Komon Khimthong's cremation volume. Pracha got in touch with one of the editors of the volume, Sulak Sivaraksa, and later with the university students in Parithat Sewana. As one of the first projects of Yuwachon Sayam, Pracha organized a retreat in early 1971 at the village of Samkhok on the outskirts of Bangkok. Pracha named this retreat

"Human Potentiality Training Camp" (*Khai fuk kamlang khon*). Pracha got the idea for this project from Komon Khimthon's book, which was based on an insight from Buddhism, namely that it is important to develop the human nature of social workers themselves before working for society. Thus, this camp did not place emphasis on constructing something for the villagers, but invited lecturers to give the students a talk. The lecturers included non-communists, such as Sulak Sivaraksa and Ravi Bhavilai, as well as some university student activists connected to the Communist Party. Regardless of the original founders' intentions and concerns, the Communist Party agents came to Yuwachon Sayam to recruit students, right from the very first retreat.[55] The influence of Marxism and the Communist Party crept into these student discussion groups, and also through the CPT mobilizers and students who had parents in the CPT.[56]

Buddhadāsa's thought was significant for the students in Yuwachon Sayam as well. Pracha Hutanuwatr,[57] one of the group's founders, was a prominent follower of Buddhadāsa. Pracha became interested in Buddhadāsa's books at a time when he was bored with his elite high school life, though he was a selected student in the "King's room" at Suan Kulap High School. Pracha was deeply impressed by the book, *Empty Mind* (*Chit wang*), which was a summary of Buddhadāsa's teaching written by Pun Chongprasoet. After reading this book, Pracha bought all of Buddhadāsa's books at the Thammabucha Bookshop, and even escaped from school for a time to visit Buddhadāsa at Suan Mokkh. Pracha gave some public speeches about Buddhadāsa's teaching in his high school, and received a good response from his friends, who then developed their network into Yuwachon Sayam.

Kanya Lilalai (1955–),[58] then a schoolgirl but in a lower year than Pracha, became interested in Buddhadāsa's thought through Pracha's speech at Suan Kulap. She borrowed a book by Buddhadāsa, *Me and Mine* (*Tua ku khong ku*), from Pracha, and came to understand the essence of Buddhism. After reading this book, just like Pracha, Kanya became a regular customer of the Thammabucha Bookshop, which dealt specifically with Buddhadāsa's books.[59] Kanya also became a member of Yuwachon Sayam.

The students who took part in the discussion groups in the 1960s were very strong academically. Their intellectual pursuits went far beyond the school curriculum, and they sought new knowledge and a path in life, society, and politics. Even though Marxism was banned by the military dictatorship, they read whatever books were available.[60] They found inspiring ideas in the works of the "new left" and the student movement in Europe,[61] as well as in the life of Komon Khimthong.[62] Komon dedicated his life to serving society as a teacher in a rural area rather than in an elite career, even though he graduated from Chulalongkorn University, the top-ranking university in Thailand.[63]

For the students during their period of exploration (*yuk sawaeng ha*),[64] the influence of Buddhist intellectuals was significant. Buddhadāsa gave them an insight into life quite distanced from their success in elite high schools and universities, and he also showed them the significance of training their minds in order to develop their social engagement. Sulak Sivaraksa contributed greatly to the intellectual inquiry of these students, preparing opportunities for them to acquire and exchange knowledge outside of school. When the public sphere was energized under the military dictatorship, Buddhist intellectuals were developing a new role, largely unknown in the conventional Buddhism that had been maintained in temple activities such as rituals, scriptural studies, and meditation. However, after the 14 October 1973 uprising, with the radicalizing political conflict and the return of Marxism to the public sphere, the development of this role of Buddhism came to a halt.

Buddhist Students' Experience of Communism: From 1973 to the End of the 1970s

The rapidly changing intellectual currents after 14 October 1973 greatly affected students' and activists' views of Buddhism. The more attached they were to the Marxist tenets of the Communist Party, the more sharply Marxism and Buddhism were contrasted. Buddhism was either ignored or abandoned, even though it had developed a social dimension during Marxism's absence from the public sphere.

After the 14 October event, Sulak, rumored to be connected with the CIA, was abandoned by student activists, and Parithat Sewana never met again. A participant in Parithat Sewana, Seksan Prasoetkun suddenly became a hero of the people who had won the dramatic victory over the military dictators. Students who used to attend Parithat Sewana, including Seksan Prasoetkun, Charan Ditthanphichai, Pridi Bunsu, and even Weng, the devoted Buddhadāsa follower, began meeting outside Parithat Sewana and grew more deeply involved in reading Marxist literature. Weng felt that he could not talk about his faith in Buddhism, because his friends sarcastically called him *mae thap tham* (commander of the *dhamma*).[65] When the assassinations of students by the authorities and by rightist organizations escalated, all of these students were forced into the jungle to join the communist struggle.[66]

Though Yuwachon Sayam did not disappear after the 14 October event, it did change in character. Buddhism was either abandoned or ignored when the influence of the Communist Party rapidly penetrated Yuwachon Sayam membership, and many members became connected to the CPT youth network. Early in 1973, even before the 14 October uprising, Pracha was convinced that Marxism had a better approach to social change than Buddhism, and he became a member of the Communist Youth League (*Sannibat yaowachon khommiunit haeng prathet thai*; Thai abbr.: So. Yo. Tho.), which operated with the guidance of the Communist Party of Thailand.[67] The strong intellectual aspect of Marxism also overwhelmed Kanya's faith in Buddhism, and she chose to abandon Buddhism and become a "Maoist." She also became involved in the CPT as a full party member, and worked for the CPT's Voice of the People of Thailand radio station broadcast from Yunnan, an intellectual center of the CPT.[68]

It was not because of the religious policy of the CPT that these student followers of Buddhadāsa abandoned Buddhism for Marxism and the CPT.[69] Rather, it was because these students had perceived an ideological defect in Buddhism. Compared with the materialist theory and the actual operation of the communist revolution, Buddhism looked idealistic and thus ineffectual for social change. Even if religion could help people, these students considered that religion could only aid individuals, and had no answer to social problems.[70] Furthermore, Kanya felt that she had to abandon Buddhism when she decided to join the armed struggle of the CPT, because the act of killing contradicts Buddhist precepts. She wrote, "If I did not abandon religion, I could not become a new person for communism. Thus, I chose to be a person without religion … I offered myself as a soldier."[71]

With the powerful emergence of Marxism and the Communist movement after the 14 October uprising, students were willing to accept the prescriptions of Mao Tse-tung.[72] In the radicalizing ideological conflicts between liberalism and communism, and even within the communist camp, where they accused each other of being "revisionist," the easiest and most effective strategy in political debate was to adopt the CPT's ideological line as their own opinion. The readymade set of ideas certified by the CPT spread without being critically examined. In this context, students paid little attention to religion, which Karl Marx called "the opium of the people." They considered religion as "opium" or ineffectual idealism, and in the category of religion, they included the most rational school of Buddhism. These students did not even notice that Buddhadāsa placed an emphasis on Dhammic Socialism during the time of their student movement in the 1970s.[73] The tendency to conform to the CPT's Maoist ideology and ignore religious values had overwhelmed the Thai students by the time of the 6 October coup in 1976.

The armed conflicts escalated, particularly after the Communist victory in Indochinese countries in April 1975 and the abolition of the Lao monarchy in December 1975. Those events increased the level of fear among conservatives, including the royal family, the army, the civilian bureaucracy, and local businessmen. Especially after 1975, rightist mass organizations also grew rapidly, with the aims of countering communism and adherence to the nationalist symbols: nation, religion, and king.[74] After all the assaults on and assassinations of the leading activists, the radicalized rightist mass organizations, such as the Red Gaurs, the Village Scouts, and Naowaphon, massacred students at Thammasat University on 6 October 1976, and the military overthrew the civilian government and the parliamentary process. In order to take refuge from the reactionary violence, students had to break away from the urban mainstream and join the CPT's armed struggle in the jungle.

Buddhism for Social Change in the Late 1970s

Although during the 1970s, Buddhism was considered useless by radical student activists, and was utilized by the rightist mass organizations as a symbolic fortress against the communist invasion, Buddhism did not merely serve as anti-communist propaganda. As Buddhadāsa and Sulak had proposed in the 1960s, Buddhism had the potential to be developed as a critical discourse against existing social injustices. Even though most students rushed to the CPT's Marxist tenets, there was a small group of students who for their social action preferred Buddhism as a basis rather than the armed struggles led by the CPT.

The group was called *klum ahingsa* (*ahiṁsā* group, or non-violent group) or *klum santi withi* (group of the peaceful method). These students found that the Buddhist concept of *ahiṁsā*, or non-violence, was more significant than any goal to be achieved by violence, killing, and revolution. They were a group of Buddhist students within Yuwachon Sayam who organized themselves as the Ahiṁsā Group in 1974 in opposition to the current group of students devoting themselves to the CPT's revolutionary movement. The students in the Ahiṁsā Group included Wisit Wongwinyu,[75] Santisuk Sophonsiri,[76] Phaisan Wongwarawisit[77] (who later ordained and took the name Phra Paisal Visalo), and Pracha Hutanuwatr (also known by his ordained name Phra Pracha Pasannathammo while he was a monk from 1975 to 1986) after he withdrew from the CPT's youth organization. They remained under Sulak Sivaraksa's advisement, and developed their *ahiṁsā* movement into the "socially engaged Buddhist" movement.

The Ahiṁsā Group centered their activities on publishing the journal, *Pacharayasan*, which means "The teacher of the teacher." *Pacharayasan* came into existence in 1971 under the editorship of Pibhop Dhongchai (1945–), who at the time was an evening-course student in the Prasanmit School of Srinakharinwirot University.[78] At that time, Thanom's military government banned the publication of new journals, so people began to use the names of existing journals that were already registered. When Pibhop started *Pacharayasan*, it was officially a special edition of a journal of the Prasanmit School alumni association, *Kansuksa* (*Education*). The full name of the journal was *Kansuksa Chabap Pacharayasan* (*Education: Pacharayasan edition*). Under Pibhop's editorial board, *Pacharayasan* was a journal specializing in alternative education and introducing the Summer Hill style of education. When Pibhop graduated from university in 1974, Sulak gave the Ahiṁsā Group an opportunity to work for the editorial board of *Pacharayasan*. This was after 14 October, when the political oppression of the military dictatorship had been abolished, so the succeeding editorial board officially registered *Pacharayasan* as a new journal, and changed its editorial line to *ahiṁsā*.[79]

As the editorial board of *Pacharayasan*, the Ahiṁsā Group propagated the philosophy of non-violence. Because the students in the Ahiṁsā Group were competent in English, they were able to seek alternative views of Marxism in foreign countries through English materials. In the journal, they promoted and translated the works of non-violence movement leaders such as Gandhi[80] and Thich Nhat Hanh.[81]

While Gandhi's works had been well known in Thailand since 1938, the Ahiṁsā Group inspired their contemporary and younger student activists by introducing and translating the works of Thich Nhat Hanh, a Vietnamese Zen monk who opposed the Vietnam War using non-violent resistance. One of the most famous works of Thich Nhat Hanh, *Miracle of Being Awake*, which was first translated into Thai by Phra Pracha Pasannathammo, then ordained Pracha Hutanuwatr, has gained lasting popularity since it was first published as a pocketbook in 1976; by 1995, it had been reprinted ten times.[82] The style of political activism exemplified by Thich Nhat Hanh was strength of mind cultivated by Buddhist meditation practice, rather than physical violence. This was unique in late 1970s Thailand, in circles of both radicalized student activism and Buddhism, which most often taught that one should enter seclusion to achieve individual salvation, and was criticized from a Marxist perspective as useless idealism. In this light, Buddhism was no longer necessarily a conservative national ideology opposed to materialist communism, but rather took up the role of criticism of violence for any political purpose, either right or left.

The role of the Buddhist activists became significant especially in the absence of the radicalized students who joined in the jungle struggles (*khao pa*) of the Communist Party after the 6 October 1976 coup. The Ahiṁsā Group members had the opportunity to commit themselves to non-violent activity in the work of the Co-ordinating Group of Religion for Society (CGRS). CGRS was an ecumenical religious network which Sulak co-founded with socially conscious believers of other religions. In 1977, prior to the amnesty of thousands of political prisoners of the 6 October coup, CGRS undertook a human rights campaign; open letters were written by the chairman, Koson Sisang (a Protestant), and later by Boonluen Mansap (a Catholic bishop). As a part of CGRS activities, the Ahiṁsā Group members visited political prisoners and made reports to international organizations such as Amnesty International in order to pressure the Thai government to ensure fair trials and prompt releases. One of the CGRS and the Ahiṁsā Group members, Phaisan Wongwarawisit (1953–), currently ordained as Phra Paisal Visalo, evaluated the activities of the CGRS as meaningful both as symbolic action and as direct action in the form of the demand that the government release 600 political prisoners.[83]

Although Sulak has been a respected advisor and a mentor of the Ahiṁsā Group, initiatives in these philosophical pursuits and political actions were taken by the young activists rather than by Sulak. Sulak had been invited to the United States at the time of the 6 October coup and did not return to Thailand until the situation eased under the Kriangsak regime in the late 1970s. During Sulak's absence, the activists in the Ahiṁsā Group used Sulak's connections with international organizations. The Ahiṁsā Group appreciated Sulak for identifying the potential of young students and finding opportunities for them,[84] but at the same time, the inspiration derived from the Ahiṁsā Group seemed to be essential to Sulak's further ideological development and organization of activism as an engaged Buddhist.

Activists' Return to Buddhism in the 1980s

On the other hand, when activists involved with the Communist Party of Thailand deepened their commitment to the Party, they faced problems with its inflexible adherence to ideology. When the reality of the Communist Party disappointed them, some — including those who once abandoned Buddhism in favor of dogmatic loyalty to communism — revisited Buddhism to seek more relevant ideas and another approach to society.

(i) The Case of Pracha Hutanuwatr

In 1973, Pracha Hutanuwatr, who had been one of the founders of Yuwachon Sayam, abandoned Buddhism and became a member of a CPT youth organization. He then returned to Buddhism and was involved with the Ahiṁsā Group shortly before the 6 October 1976 military coup. Pracha withdrew from the CPT much earlier than most students, who mostly left the jungle struggle sometime after 1980. Pracha was disappointed with the CPT's revolutionary project because of its corrupt administration, its rigid, intolerant ideological adherence to the line of the Chinese Communist Party, and the absence of spiritual values in the movement.[85]

Having experienced Marxism's criticism of religion as an individual comfort and impractical idealism, Pracha discovered another dimension of Buddhist insight and meditation that actually contributed significantly to social activism. He criticized what were commonly regarded as "good" Buddhist practices, saying that they were actually egotistical. For example, a hospital whose Buddhist club of doctors and nurses were known for their eager participation in meditation practices and their devotion to their monk teachers actually gave preferential medical treatment to the rich. Pracha insisted that their religious practices should not be performed in seclusion for their individual merit, but rather should generate a right view that could distinguish good from evil in society and could through right conduct make the world better.[86] Pracha argued that the latter type of meditation practice would help activists to challenge social evils, even when doing so was at odds with the mainstream view. The *paññā*, or insight, which can arise from meditation practice, would distinguish just from unjust without conforming to the world of "materialism" that suppresses humanity.[87]

When Pracha withdrew from the Communist Youth League, he ordained as a Buddhist monk.[88] Among the members of the Ahiṁsā Group, Pracha became the closest disciple of Buddhadāsa, with whom he stayed at Suan Mokkh for six years, 1980–1986. As a capable disciple of Buddhadāsa's later years, Pracha interviewed Buddhadāsa extensively about his life and thought. This interview was published as a series of books entitled *Talking in the Twilight Years: An Autobiography of Venerable Buddhadāsa* (*Lao wai mua wai sonthaya: atchiwaprawat khong than phutthathat*). It is useful not only as a description of Buddhadāsa's personal history and thought, but also as a contemporary history of Thai Buddhism which Pracha learned from and participated in as a significant contributor.

After his experience with Marxism, Pracha summarized his view of Buddhadāsa's contribution to the Thai people and society. He said that Buddhadāsa pointed out the deepest roots of the Thai people and of human beings, or the *pumipanya* of their own civilization.[89] Pracha emphasized that what prevents individuals from realizing *sammādiṭṭhi* or "right view" and being able to distinguish the real cause of remediable social problems is *watthuniyom*, the "materialism" of both capitalist consumerism and Marxist tenets, because both give more weight to the material than the spiritual.[90] Pracha published the views he had learned from Buddhadāsa in *Pacharayasan*. His articles became popular among younger student activists, who came along when the Communist Party was in decline; they supported the non-violent approach, which respects humanity.

(ii) The Case of Kanya Lilalai

On the other hand, Kanya had a different experience when she withdrew from the Communist Party of Thailand. Kanya, who worked as a full member of the Party's radio broadcasting unit in Yunnan, had to face the many negative aspects of the CPT. She witnessed financial corruption among the CPT's executives, the Chinese faction's dominance, and the rigid ideological adherence to the Chinese Communist Party, which deserted the CPT for its own national interests in the new period of international relations.[91]

China, which had both ideologically and materially supported CPT activities from the time of the CPT's inception, adopted a pragmatic policy in the new international situation, which in effect left its Thai subsidiary stranded. Vietnam invaded Cambodia in December 1978, and in February 1979, China invaded Vietnam in retaliation. As a result of this dispute, the CPT, allied with China rather than Vietnam, lost its vital supply routes and outposts in Laos, which was allied with Vietnam. This political change made it very difficult for the CPT guerrillas to survive and struggle in the northern and northeastern jungles of Thailand. Furthermore, China sought the cooperation of the Thai government to assist the Khmer Rouge on the Thai border to block the Vietnamese advance in its southern region. China, which was cooperating with the Thai military, abruptly closed the CPT's radio station in Yunnan in July 1979. The students became critical of the CPT's old guard who were still loyal to China, which had abandoned the Thai communist movement for its own national interests.[92]

In May 1981, Kanya finally broke away from the Party, to which she had devoted herself for the higher purpose of creating a better society at the cost of her own relationships. She had to question whether or not the deaths of Thai people, including her close friends and students whom she had introduced to the Party, were in fact only a political contribution for China. She had to re-examine the value of *ahiṁsā* in Buddhism, which she had abandoned when she entered the jungle for revolutionary struggle.[93]

However, unlike the male Buddhist activists in the Ahiṁsā Group, some of whom chose to be ordained as monks, for a woman, ordination was not a choice as a return from radicalism. People do not gain as much merit from donation to women ascetics, who are usually called *mae chi* in Thailand, than to monks, so it is more difficult for *mae chi* to support their full-time religious practice. Kanya gave up the idea of renouncing the world to be an ascetic, and even rejected involvement in any group or organization. She got married and became a housewife anarchist.[94]

Kanya felt that her faith in Marxism, which used to dominate her life, was inappropriate and invalid, so she needed to sort out her beliefs. She read any book that might provide an answer. Those books included the 45 volumes of the *Tipiṭaka* and books on almost every school of Buddhism, from books on magic to sermons of famous monks and women teachers. Kanya learned *idappaccayatā*, or conditional arising, as a Buddhist way of looking at things. Everything, whether it is in the mind or in the material world, takes place because of a sequence of causes. She thought that it was more important to look at this interrelated causation of events rather than insisting that mind was dependent on matter or vice versa. If the mind is defiled by egoism, reality cannot be perceived. When she had presented herself as a Marxist or Maoist, neither of these belief systems was in fact her own view, but she put forward those ideas in order to win ideological debates. As a result, she could not take responsibility for what she had said and done. The younger students she introduced to the Party's youth organization lost their lives in the revolutionary war. Through the lessons of the CPT, she identified three principles for herself: not to tell a lie; not to do violence to other beings; and to do only whatever was useful for herself and others.[95] When she found herself following the Buddhist principles in the form of her own opinions, she thought she was no longer a person without religion. She had returned to being a Buddhist.[96]

In the process of returning to Buddhism, Kanya realized that Buddhadāsa was again significant for her. Although for a long time she had avoided reading Buddhadāsa's works so as not to succumb to his teaching, it was Buddhadāsa who best explained the meaning of the scriptural text. Among the many schools of Buddhism in Thailand that she explored in her broad reading, Buddhadāsa's insightful words touched her the most profoundly.[97]

(iii) The Case of Anut Aphaphirom

Just like Kanya, a number of intellectuals and students who returned from the communist insurgency in the jungle turned to Buddhism and Buddhadāsa's teachings in their search for the meaning of their experience and their lives.[98] Anut Aphaphirom (1940–), a CPT intellectual writer whose articles had a great impact on students' decisions to be involved in the communist struggle in the 1970s, changed his attitude toward Buddhism after he left the Party in 1981. Although Anut did not find significance in religion when he wrote his articles for the revolutionary movement, he took up the study of Buddhism after his return from China. Anut had to find an answer to his question, "Why was Marxism unsuccessful?" (*Thammai latthi mak lomleo?*) Anut did not believe that it was because capitalism was superior to socialism. Buddhism or religion must have had significant points which were lacking in Marxism. Two monk teachers were helpful to him in his search for an answer to this question. Buddhadāsa pointed out the essence of Buddhism, while P.A. Payuttho Bhikkhu defined Buddhist concepts in a manual.[99] Anut realized that the Marxist plan to radically achieve an ideal society could not be actualized, but a real change could be achieved by individuals who attained right view and used it to benefit society, as Buddhadāsa had been teaching. Even if socialist states won the revolutionary struggle, they had extensive corruption because of dictatorial structures and each individual's *kilesa*, which could not be eradicated by the revolution. Anut agreed with the analysis as proposed by Buddhism.

(iv) The Case of Weng Tochirakan

Weng, who was once a Buddhist advocate in Parithat Sewana but took part in the communist struggle, concealing his Buddhist aspect as merely an individual sentiment, also became critical of the Communist Party after his serious involvement in it. He severely criticized the leaders of socialist countries who were dominated by *kilesa* (defilements) and *avijjā* (ignorance) even though those leaders had succeeded in building up the socialist system.[100] Only after his return from the jungle in 1982 did Weng learn that Buddhadāsa had been insisting on socialism with *dhamma*. Weng said that he agreed that socialism has to be Dhammic Socialism, which is based on the *dhamma*. However, it is not clear how Dhammic Socialism developed in Weng's later intellectual and political activities. Weng said that he still respected Buddhadāsa as his highest teacher, but he did not think that Buddhism was the ideological principle behind his own leadership of the Black May demonstration.[101]

Development of Engaged Buddhism and the Handover of Dhammic Socialism

Those who took over the idea of Dhammic Socialism included those who were involved in the Ahiṁsā Group and some who claimed to be "socially engaged Buddhists." They developed their Buddhist perspectives on society in NGO activities after the 1980s.

Even in the 1980s, when those disappointed student activists left the Communist Party, the social problems that they attempted to solve using Marxism persisted or even worsened. Because of the economic boom resulting from the shift of economic orientation from agricultural products to manufacturing and service industries, the rural population shifted and became urban labor, and the gap between the urban commercially wealthy and the rural poor widened. This also resulted in the spread of "materialism" or consumerism all over the country.

With the expulsion of the Marxist critique and the decline of Marxist presence in the public sphere after 6 October 1976, Buddhist intellectuals became active in social analysis and involvement. In the sphere of university activities, the Buddhist club was one of the three student clubs allowed by the authorities, along with the Young Rotary Club and the Thai music club. Both religiously devoted students and students interested in social engagement joined the Buddhist club.[102] In the social section of the Buddhist club, the influence of Sulak Sivaraksa and the Ahiṁsā Group was expanding.[103] They advocated community development based on religious values, which appealed to student activists. Sulak developed this idea through contact with progressive Christian groups oriented toward interreligious dialogue and community development. Sulak sought a way of applying the idea of community development based on religious values to Thai Buddhism, especially in his networking of so-called *phra nak phatthana* (development monks) who had already been voluntarily supporting villagers' economic life with their religious guidance. Having some connection with Sulak, Dr. Prawase Wasi (1931–), another well-known lay follower of Buddhadāsa, developed his role as a Buddhist social critic and an organizer of rural community development, especially in the area of medical care.[104] In this situation of the expanding role of Buddhist intellectuals in social work from the 1980s onward, Buddhadāsa's Dhammic Socialism was reconsidered, and a practical application of it was sought through dialogue with Marxism.

Sulak and the Ahiṁsā Group, which expanded its scope of activities to rural development, had recently begun to call themselves "engaged Buddhists" in order to cover the wider range of social activism that they were involved in from a Buddhist perspective. Aside from promoting that idea and acting non-violently, they started organizing a network of local monk-led rural development movements, which spontaneously arose around the same time in the mid-1980s. Among many others that belong to Sulak's group, two networks should be attentioned here. One is the Thai Inter-Religious Commission for Development (*Khana kammakan sasana phua kanphatthana*) established in 1980, which is a network of lay Buddhists and intellectuals from other religions who support development. The other is Sekhiyadham (*sekhiyatham*), which was founded in 1991 to make contact between monks and *mae chi* working for development. Within these networks, the lay engaged Buddhists hold seminars, organize study trips, and publish and distribute seminar proceedings in order to share their successful experiences with monks and villagers in other villages.[105]

Those local monks, who are now organized into Sekhiyadham, are called "development monks" (*phra nak phatthana*) and have provided leadership for the betterment of the livelihood of villagers in their own local community.[106] These monks have witnessed the transformation of the rural economy in their villages in the last 40 years. According to Phra Khru Suphacharawat, a "development monk" from Yasothon Province, his village started to change in 1961 when the government introduced jute and other commercial crop cultivation for export. In the early 1970s, the government promoted high productivity rice as well as chemical fertilizers and agricultural chemicals, which severely damaged the soil and water. Practicing sales-oriented agriculture, all they got was bank debt; their profits were not even enough to buy food. Phra Khru Suphacharawat said that he had challenged this current of capitalism and consumerism in the village since 1981 by promoting the villagers' self-reliance. For the purpose of self-reliance, he introduced a village cooperative in which villagers make small deposits in and borrow money from the community funding pool.[107] This community banking system has been promoted both by a government program and by NGOs. In such a small-scale banking system with little power of enforcement, each member's morality and respect for the rules are essential for its sustainability. For that reason, the spirit of religion contributes significantly.

In the case of Phra Khru Suphacharawat, his unique idea for the villagers' self-reliance through the revival of traditional herbal medicines was shared with other village monks and leaders through a network of NGOs and Sekhiyadham seminars. In those seminars, he also learned from the experience of other villages the methods of integrated agriculture (*kasetthakam phasom phasan*) that primarily produces everything the villagers eat, including their own rice, vegetables, fruits, fish, chickens, and ducks, instead of produce for sale. Aside from such technical aspects, the engaged Buddhists or urban-educated NGO workers positively contributed to the self-respect and confidence of villagers.

Phra Khru Suphacharawat proposed the ideal of a harmonious village community as "*dhammic* community" (*thammika chumchon*), an idea he had absorbed from Buddhadāsa's "Dhammic Socialism." Working for a *dhammic* community, villagers no longer feel ashamed of their living conditions compared with those of the urban elite. The concept of the *dhammic* community stands for both an empowerment and a validation of the villagers' own way of living and wisdom, by which social reform would be achieved concretely on a small scale.

Aside from practical coordination of community development, engaged Buddhists were attempting to develop Buddhadāsa's Dhammic Socialism as the ideological basis of their social movement. On the one hand, Buddhadāsa's Dhammic Socialism was critically examined. For instance, Prawase selected some points from Marxist critiques, and examined the social problems as those of the social structure rather than those of individuals. Prawase did not believe that people became poor because they were lazy, or because they had indulged in vice, as stated by Buddhadāsa.[108] Prawase looked at the structural causes of social crisis, such as the problems of the centralized system, the unfair economic system, the structure of hidden violence, and the lack of balance in society.[109] Also, Prawase even modified the concepts of Dhammic Socialism, calling it "*dhammic* society" (*thammika sangkhom*), because he considered "socialism" to be outdated, the term "socialism" having a narrower connotation than society.[110] He said that "*dhammic* society" could avoid being misread and better promote the relevance of Dhammic Socialism in today's society.[111]

Many engaged Buddhists agreed about the value of Dhammic Socialism, which provided important spiritual values complementing contemporary society and economics that were missing in the Marxist project. What they considered significant was the presence of the *dhamma* in society. They agreed that the four meanings of the *dhamma*, nature itself, the laws of the nature, duty in accordance with the laws of nature, and the fruit from duty in accordance with the laws of nature, are valid for the case of society as well as for the human mind and individual life. An anonymous writer proposed that Dhammic Socialism provides a view of the relationship between human beings and nature, which coincided with that of the Green Movement in Europe, which has come to replace Marxist critique.[112] Furthermore, engaged Buddhists agreed with Buddhadāsa's critique of *watthuniyom*, or materialism in terms of consumerism, which should be replaced by morality. Phra Paisal Visalo stated that Dhammic Socialism could provide Western socialism, which aims at social justice and equality by emphasizing material prosperity, with a higher spiritual attitude that is not attached to the world.[113] The morality of Dhammic Socialism could free people from the problems of contemporary society, such as materialistic worldview, money worship, and purposeless, disciplineless freedom.[114]

Some engaged Buddhists were attempting to connect their understanding of Dhammic Socialism to practical reforms. Santikaro, an American disciple of Buddhadāsa, was one of the most vocal and active monk disciples in contemporary Thailand. More recently, he serves as a lay Buddhist teacher in the US and in Thailand. Through his fluent Thai sermons, he advocated the "noble twelve-fold social path" as a means of realizing Buddhadāsa's concepts: right religion, right education, right leadership, right organization and government, right communication, right culture, right sexuality and family, right ecology, right play, right monitoring, and right *saṅgha* and solidarity.[115] An anonymous writer proposed a reform of land ownership and a progressive taxation system in order to achieve a fair distribution of wealth based on the principle of Dhammic Socialism, which encourages individuals not to accumulate more property than necessary, and not to exploit other human beings or nature.[116] Phra Paisal proposed the two ways of social practice as strategies of Dhammic Socialism: support for the nurturing of civil society and reform in Buddhism by reviving the original Buddha Dhamma and by reforming the Saṅgha so that the Saṅgha administration is not an obstacle to social reform.[117] In this way, Dhammic Socialism has sought relevance to contemporary society.

*****

This chapter has examined the development of Buddhadāsa's Dhammic Socialism and the development of Buddhist social engagement based on that concept from the 1960s to the 1990s. In the face of Marxism, Buddhism was not simply divided into leftists and rightists, or labeled as an ideological weapon for the anti-communist campaign. Buddhism acquired its own critical stance toward contemporary society, a stance that sides with neither the communists nor the counter-insurgency security forces. Some of those Buddhist perspectives, such as the method of non-violence and resolution of individual defilements, were missing in the Marxist project of social transformation. These perspectives became especially important after the social criticism of Marxism weakened following the decline of the socialist regimes in the Soviet Union and Eastern Europe.

Buddhadāsa's critique of *watthuniyom*, by which he meant material determinism and consumerism, became even more important after the decline of socialism than in the 1960s when he was developing his thought through dialogue with Marxism. At the end of the 20th century, the impact of Marxist materialism decreased when capitalism became dominant, but Buddhadāsa's Buddhist social critique maintained its role as a counter to capitalism. Even today, it admonishes people who stir up endless desire for consumption in the capitalist economic system and teaches them to look into their minds. Buddhadāsa's insight has been taken up by "engaged Buddhists." Engaged Buddhists are not simply some Buddhist groups who are leading community development; they constantly serve to remind people of the significance of morality and wisdom for improving their economic life. Their projects are actual test cases for the realization of a harmonious balance of sufficiency in nature, as depicted in Buddhadāsa's Dhammic Socialism. That is to say, the Buddhism developed in the Buddhist public sphere is for people to live righteously in the real world here and now, rather than pursuing otherworldly salvation.

CHAPTER 8

Dhamma Mother: A New Female Practitioner Form Alternative to *Bhikkhunī*[1]

In his later years, Buddhadāsa attempted to improve social conditions for women practitioners' ascetic practice. Buddhadāsa's promotion of the transcendent state of *nibbāna* for everyone regardless of ordained status, gender, nationality or religious faith appeared to be encouraging for underprivileged women practitioners, yet it was not until Buddhadāsa was approaching the age of 80 that he realized that social disadvantages could be significantly hindering the spiritual development of women practitioners. He proposed an ideal for female practitioners which he named *dhammamātā*, which literally translates "*dhamma* mothers" or "mothers of *dhamma*," and a place for *dhamma* practice by *dhammamātā*, the *Dhammamātā* Hermitage. *Dhammamātā* are thus counterparts to *bhikkhunī* and alternatives to conventional renunciant female practitioners in Thailand.

The lack of opportunity for formal ordination has been one of the most noteworthy disadvantages for Buddhist women. In Theravāda tradition, the ordination lineage of Buddhist nuns called *bhikkhunī* — the female equivalents to *bhikkhu* (the ordained male monks commonly seen in contemporary Theravāda Buddhist countries, who don yellow robes and observe the 227 monastic precepts) — was disrupted in 11th-century Sri Lanka, before the prototype of present Theravāda Buddhism was transmitted to Thailand. Different from the formally ordained *bhikkhunī*, who observe the 311 monastic precepts, Thai Buddhist women practitioners commonly become *mae chi*, who have their heads shaven, don white robes, and regularly keep the eight precepts designated for pious lay people doing short-term ascetic practice in a temple. Thus *mae chi* are formally regarded as laity even though they are determined to follow a religious path for life, renouncing the secular world. Their ambiguous status — factual renunciants, yet without formal ordained status — is one of the reasons why society tends to expect *mae chi* to assist with domestic aspects of monastic life such as food preparation, rather than offering them support and opportunities of religious training equivalent to that enjoyed by *bhikkhu*. Although there are increasing efforts to raise the social status of women practitioners, there are only a small number of places providing opportunities exclusively for women's ascetic practice.[2]

Buddhadāsa's notion of *dhammamātā* is a significant topic to study for two reasons. First, it is a groundbreaking attempt by a Buddhist intellectual rooted in traditional values to solve the problem of gender inequality in Thai Buddhism. The loss of the *bhikkhunī saṅgha* is the most prominent source of gender inequality of Theravāda Buddhism, but in the tradition which highly values the continuation of traditional formality, the restoration of the lost ordination lineage is generally considered impossible.[3] In Thailand and elsewhere, people often express difficulties in accepting the ideal gender relations proposed by women's movements, even when such proposals are accompanied by a reasonable rationale. One of the reasons for such difficulties is the perception of a gap between traditional and new alternative gender norms. Buddhadāsa, rather than persuading people to make a radical change in their traditional view, by proposing *dhammamātā* appealed to a dominant local value which affords women a position of respect. This can be seen as attempted social change rooted in local tradition.

Second, among Buddhadāsa's several unique concepts, his notion of *dhammamātā* has not been studied extensively. Probably, Santikaro Bhikkhu's article is one of the few written in Western languages which mention *dhammamātā*, but it is only introduced in a paragraph in the final remarks as one of the projects of Buddhadāsa in his final years.[4] Since Buddhadāsa came to the idea of *dhammamātā* in his later years in the early 1980s, it was not included in the major studies of his thought in the late 1980s.[5] Buddhadāsa has often been regarded as one of the most prominent Buddhist thinkers who led contemporary Buddhists to engage in social works, largely because of his emphasis on *nibbāna* as being accessible in one's present psychological state in worldly circumstances. Nevertheless, even though many Buddhists who claim that their commitment to social issues was inspired by his teaching, Buddhadāsa himself planned few actual projects for social works such as rural development and public health.[6] In fact, his emphasis on the "core" of religion tended to disregard such external social phenomena as forms and rituals and social circumstances of religious practices. Thus, his teachings may be interpreted as proposing that an individual should aim at a spiritual goal, focus on spiritual training, and tolerate any social circumstances, no matter how unfavorable.

It was the question of gender inequality that prompted Buddhadāsa in his later days to reconsider his basic attitude and directed his attention to social engagement, namely by providing women with better conditions and opportunities for monastic training. His concept of the Dhammamātā Hermitage was one of the very few cases where Buddhadāsa worked to implement reformative project. This article examines the following three aspects of Buddhadāsa's thoughts on women's *dhamma* practice: first, how he shifted his attitudes toward women's rights to ordination and *dhamma* practice; second, his notion of *dhammamātā* and his appeal to motherhood; and third, the social implications of the notion of motherhood in the Thai context.

1. Shift in Buddhadāsa's Attitude toward Women's Rights in Buddhism

It seems that before the idea of *dhammamātā* dawned upon Buddhadāsa at around the age of 80, he was not particularly interested in women's opportunities to enter *dhamma* practice. Sources consulted for this article point to three main incidents which prompted Buddhadāsa to think about the gender issue in Buddhism: first, the *bhikkhunī* restoration movement in the late 1920s; second, a plea by one of his female followers in the late 1930s; and third, his sister's illness from the late 1960s onward.

Narin Phasit's Bhikkhunī Restoration Movement

One of the first incidents that stimulated Buddhadāsa to think about women's disadvantages in Buddhism was the movement for the reintroduction of female ordination in Thailand in the 1920s. In 1928, Narin Phasit (1874–1950), a provocative social critic who proposed a number of unique ideas for political and religious reforms, asked the Thai public to consider the possibility of women's ordination.[7] Narin had his two daughters ordained as *sāmaṇerī* (Buddhist female novices) and lodged them together with some other *sāmaṇerī* in a temple he had built. Narin's intention was to create a complement for the four original groups in Buddhism: *bhikkhu*, *bhikkhunī*, *upāsaka* (laymen), and *upāsikā* (laywomen) (by then *bhikkhunī* no longer existed in Theravāda Buddhism). He also hoped that the newly reintroduced ordained women would perform ideal Buddhist practices for overcoming suffering, which he could little find in practice among Buddhist monks at that time. Narin presented his plan to the public through both public print media and his own free distribution booklets; sometimes in his publications, he even bluntly criticized the existing state of Buddhism and the Saṅgha elders. A number of people accepted his claim as reasonable, yet most newspapers, along with the religious and political authorities, responded antagonistically and regarded his loud criticisms and calls for justice as the pursuit of fame.[8]

News of Narin's movement for the reform of Buddhism, including the issue of women's ordination, reached his intellectual contemporaries, young Buddhadāsa and his younger brother Dhammadāsa Phanit (1909–2000), who remained a layman. Dhammadāsa was always Buddhadāsa's important intellectual co-worker; however, the brothers had clearly differing attitudes toward Narin. In my interview with 90-year-old Dhammadāsa in 1999, in response to my question about Narin's movement for women's ordination, he smiled delightfully and said that he had faith in Narin. Dhammadāsa recalled an exciting event from his youth. He recounted that having thought that Narin was doing the right thing, he sent a letter expressing appreciation of Narin's work. Narin, in turn, responded with a gift of his books.[9] Dhammadāsa suggested that Narin visit Buddhadāsa, who was then studying Pāli in Bangkok.

Unlike Dhammadāsa, Buddhadāsa did not take Narin's criticism of laxity in monastic disciplines seriously. In an interview with a disciple, Buddhadāsa said that Narin published some large books, which contained many pictures of elder monks who were flouting rules such as the prohibition against touching money. Seeing these pictures, Buddhadāsa perceived that Narin was encouraging people to become critical of monastic misconduct and admonishing monks to take the disciplines more strictly. Nevertheless, he commented that most people thought that the examples raised by Narin were "nothing unusual."[10] Buddhadāsa seemed to be rather unhappy with Narin, because in the early 1930s when he started such activities as journal publication, some people mistrusted him, suspecting him and his group of being Narin's disciples.[11]

In an interview with his disciple Phra Pracha, Buddhadāsa did not clearly state his opinion about women's ordination, but his view of Narin's attempt was unmistakably negative. Buddhadāsa called Narin "half-crazy, half-intoxicated," and suspected that Narin wanted to cultivate a reputation as a reviver of the original four Buddhist groups through his reintroduction of *bhikkhunī*.[12] As Dhammadāsa said in my interview with him, Buddhadāsa suspected that Narin might swindle people by requesting contributions for this magnificent project. As a result, Dhammadāsa could not discuss with Buddhadāsa the possibility of formal ordination for women, because he was sure that his brother would not be interested in it. On the other hand, Dhammadāsa thought that Narin had a wonderful idea and because he had served as provincial governor (*chao muang*) of Nakhon Nayok, he was already wealthy. However, Dhammadāsa admitted that it was not just his brother, but actually the majority of people who were dissatisfied with Narin.[13] This seems to have been an opportunity for Buddhadāsa to learn how the Saṅgha authorities and the Buddhist public would react to the idea of reintroducing *bhikkhunī*, a proposal which could provoke a serious controversy. Whether or not Buddhadāsa perceived the rationale for *bhikkhunī* ordination as reasonable, the incident taught him that it would take considerable time before its revival would prove a benefit for women's *dhamma* practice. It is not difficult to imagine that Buddhadāsa had no enthusiasm for reviving the Buddhist women's ordination ritual, form, and status, because he considered these to be "outer coverings" of religion, rather than its "core."

A Question of Buddhist Women's Title: Ubasika Ki Nanayon

The second incident which raised questions for Buddhadāsa about the status of renunciant women practitioners was a call for his help from Ubasika Ki Nanayon (1901–1978), a serious female practitioner who followed his teachings.[14] Ki was highly respected as a female meditation teacher and also known for her Buddhist poetry written under the pen name, "Ko. Khaosuanluang." She often contributed her poems to Buddhadāsa's journal. There is correspondence between Ki and Buddhadāsa from 1939–1940 regarding the title of *ubasika* (Pāli: *upāsikā*) in the archives of Suan Mokkh in Chaiya, Buddhadāsa's temple, where his diaries and letters are kept.[15]

In one of her letters, Ki sought Buddhadāsa's support for the use of the title, "*Ubasika*" in certificates for Buddhist doctrinal examinations of successful women candidates, rather than "*Nang*" (used for married women, equivalent to "Mrs.") or "*Nang Sao*" (used for single women, equivalent to "Miss"), which are commonly applied to women living in the secular world.[16] It seems that Ki and her group of *ubasika* thought it inappropriate to apply to women practitioners a form of address indicating marital status, identical to the style of address for ordinary lay women living in a secular world. In fact, female practitioners in Thailand come from various states and experiences of marriage: some may have been married before they fully renounced worldly life; some may have had to shuffle between their family and the temple; and others never married. However, it was thought unnecessary to use forms of address based on marital status, because celibacy is part of ascetic practice. The most comprehensive and respectful form of address for Buddhist women practitioners who may be in various marital states is the use of the title *Ubasika* before their names. The request from Ki and her group of *ubasika* should be interpreted as a subtle demand for official recognition of their status as distinct from that of ordinary lay women living in the secular world.[17]

Ki appealed to Buddhadāsa concerning this problem, probably because he was one of her most reliable contacts who had sufficient acquaintances among the *Saṅgha* elders.[18] In response to Ki's plea in her letter dated 12 August 1939, Buddhadāsa talked with the Supreme Patriarch about this issue. According to Buddhadāsa's reply to Ki, dated 12 September, the Supreme Patriarch said that he agreed with the idea proposed by the group of *ubasika*. However, Buddhadāsa suggested instead that she bring the issue directly to the head or the deputy head of the ecclesiastical examination bureau, who was actually in charge of certification. He also urged her to hurry to make that contact as it was almost time to dispatch the list of successful candidates. In her letter dated 20 September, Ki sought further support from Buddhadāsa, because her group of *ubasika* was unable to appeal to higher ecclesiastical authorities. On 18 January 1940, Buddhadāsa replied, saying that it was already too late for that year, but expressing his wish for a possible change in the following year. Subsequently, Ki wrote at least three letters to Buddhadāsa, in which she mentioned her *ubasika* group's serious endeavor in the area of Buddhist study and practice and renewed her request for his support for the use of the title *Ubasika*.[19] Still unable to offer concrete support for this issue, in the end, Buddhadāsa encouraged Ki as follows:

> Regarding the change of title for *ubasika*, it is still in my mind, but now we have to stop working on it for a while. The reason is that we have no other way to do it but through a new law which guarantees the change. The bill for the new law has to be passed by the Parliament and needs someone to submit the bill. In fact, there should be someone who supports this idea, so there would be a possibility of success, as you wish. However, it should not be during hard times such as war or emergency, as at present. If there is anyone who goes against this current and proposes such a thing in the Parliament, that person can only receive a disappointing result, because there are many other urgent matters. We should wait until the war ends and then discuss this issue; then people would listen to us wholeheartedly, have sufficient time to think about it, and become compassionate to us. Even the same issue proposed with different timing can make a lot of difference;

> so we should wait for a while. A waiting period like now is the best opportunity for *ubasika* who wish for reform to make themselves fully useful so that politicians will feel impressed with them. It will be a way for politicians to become sympathetic, pick up the point, and examine it with a respectful attitude. If those *mae chi* wearing white robes do not do anything except begging and chanting unclearly, they are simply a burden to people. So, they may not speak to each other to be more compassionate about the point that you raise. People may consider it as unimportant whether or not they have *mae chi*; and when *mae chi* do not have a lot of practical roles, people think that they should not demand many rights and cause trouble … However, who knows, in the future *ubasika* would become a remarkable group, if there is someone to lead a revolution for improving their way of living through developing their knowledge and ability and being at the forefront of their era [*than samai*]. If the majority of people in the world still think that *mae chi* are nothing but cooks for temples, or consider their sort of renunciation as just a tradition of an unnecessary fashion, and they can simply chant with beautiful [female] voices, I am sure that no politician would be willing to waste his time on this matter. I wish for a revolution among *mae chi* and hope that a strong leader can demonstrate their usefulness very soon. This is much more important than the female Buddhist title that you want. For such a change, one should have firmness and think of preparing for the distant future, just as Martin Luther did for the Christian world.[20]

It seems that Buddhadāsa and the *Saṅgha* elders found the appeal by Ki and her *ubasika* group reasonable, but they did not offer to make an effort to help bring the issue to an appropriate administrative section of either the religious or civil authorities. For Buddhadāsa, who was a successful monk despite being still in his early 30s, it may have been quite difficult to urge the elder monks to make a political decision when they were initially unenthusiastic. The best he could do was to advise Ki, a serious practitioner, to shift her focus to the development of women's capabilities in Buddhist teaching and practice. He did not turn to political authorities to make any changes in women's position; rather, he preferred to overcome social inequalities through spiritual development, which would have the strongest religious appeal.

In the Suan Mokkh Archives in Chaiya, there is no response from Ki to this advice from Buddhadāsa. As one of his most responsive followers and co-workers, she may have taken his message to heart, and she eventually became one of the most respected female practitioners in Thailand. Yet, since she was a woman practitioner who had to face the difficulties surrounding lack of societal recognition, her aspiration had little in common with Buddhadāsa's. In fact, her attitude toward Narin's movement for *bhikkhunī* restoration was radically different from that of Buddhadāsa. She once visited Narin's ordained daughters and accepted their visit to her shop in Phetchaburi, where she used to run a business. Unlike Buddhadāsa, Ki did not consider the attempt of Narin and his daughters as simply the pursuit of fame; rather, she respected and gave moral support to their campaign for the restoration of female ordination.[21] In tandem with her conscientious endeavor toward ascetic practice, which Buddhadāsa recognized, there is evidence that she was seeking a concrete social reform to elevate the status of women practitioners in Buddhism.[22]

Probably few of Buddhadāsa's followers would disagree with his basic tenets: the overwhelming importance of religion's "essential core" rather than its "outer shells"; and a universalism that disregarded one's gender, ordained status, nationality, and religion in assessing the achievement of religious goals. However, the meaning accorded such "outer shells" of religion as monastic costumes and status would have particular weight with the socially underprivileged. The limitations of such a formulaic view are well illustrated by the following episode. Paññānanda Bhikkhu (1911–2007), one of Buddhadāsa's contemporaries and a highly respected preacher monk in contemporary Thailand, was once questioned by Sara Rongkhasuan about the possibility of reintroducing *bhikkhunī*. Sara, Narin Phasit's elder daughter, was a *sāmaṇerī* and *bhikkhunī* in the late 1920s and early 1930s; she later disrobed and married to have children. Paññānanda answered that it was not necessary to become a *bhikkhunī* because ordination is a state of mind. He said that monks were in the same situation; they did not necessarily have to become ordained as monks, because being a monk meant simply having a renunciant state of mind. Sara responded that she would invite him to disrobe so that he could learn whether lay people and those who are in the monastic form were actually the same or not.[23]

After relating this story, one of Buddhadāsa's disciples, Dutsadi Medhaṅkuro Bhikkhu, insisted that monks should not say that "ordination is not necessary; it is only a matter of one's state of mind," because they had more appropriate and convenient forms for *dhamma* practice. Referring to Buddhadāsa's words, Dutsadi said:

> If there are many precepts, religion can last long, but only a few people could reach the *dhamma*. We should examine whether we have a way for more women to reach the *dhamma* without holding on to a form of *bhikkhunī*. Otherwise, we would cling to the struggle demanding the *bhikkhunī* ordination and may end up losing the [real] point or dissolving the essential part. It may turn into a conflict; it's just a frustrating matter.[24]

The Turning Point for Buddhadāsa: The Illness of His Sister

It appears that for a long time, Buddhadāsa, grounded by his focus on philosophy, had little interest in helping women practitioners. This basic attitude is also reflected in his policy regarding women practitioners in his temple, Suan Mokkh. Initially, he did not even allow any *mae chi* to live there, because "generally speaking they say that when women or *mae chi* are staying together, there would be trouble; it is an ancient saying."[25] Later, Suan Mokkh began to accept women residents for cooking assistance. As the number of monks and novices increased, the work and cost of food preparation and delivery became a serious burden for the local villagers, and so Buddhadāsa allowed a woman volunteer to live on the temple premises in order to cook for the monastic members.

Subsequently, more women built their own huts in Suan Mokkh, so Buddhadāsa built a road to separate the women's residential area from the monastic compounds. He called the women's zone "*Ubasika* Area" (*khet ubasika*), but never considered it to be a formal *samnak chi* (a residence for *mae chi* to practice *dhamma*). He would not even agree to become a preceptor to help women become *mae chi*, nor would he allow any women to join the daily monastic activities, such as chanting, in the same place as the monks. He only accepted women he could trust not to make trouble as *mae chi* and other types of female practitioners to live in the *Ubasika* Area. Among them were both women from humble backgrounds and those who had successful careers in education and the professions.[26] Even though Buddhadāsa offered capable women practitioners such as Ranchuan Inthrakamhaeng (1921–) moral support equal to that given to monks, he seems to have been determined that male monastic members' practice must not be hindered by the presence of females.[27]

The last and the most important incident that pushed Buddhadāsa to become seriously concerned about women's *dhamma* practice was the illness of his younger sister Kimsoi (1911–89). As their family was reputable and well-to-do (what the Thai would call "*thana di*," literally of "good status") in Chaiya in southern Thailand, Kimsoi married into another good business family, the Hemakun, who had a large stationary store called Thai Watthana in the nearby town of Ban Don.[28] According to Metta Phanit, Buddhadāsa's nephew and Dhammadāsa's youngest son, after the death of her husband Kimsoi worried about her five children and how to divide the family fortune. She eventually developed insomnia and lost both her mental and physical health.[29]

In the late 1960s and early 1970s, Buddhadāsa told Kimsoi many times that she should stay at Suan Mokkh in order to overcome her suffering through *dhamma* practice. She did go to the temple a number of times, but only stayed there for a few days each time; her children took her back home before she could benefit from religious practice and health improvement. Later, Kimsoi became paralyzed and was taken care of by her children in Bangkok for many years. She died in 1989, only four years before Buddhadāsa's passing. Metta said that because Buddhadāsa could provide only a little help for his own sister's problem, his concern about women's practice deepened.[30] He would have had no doubt that the right practice of *dhamma* would lead to the overcoming of suffering, and this would have forced him to look at the social conditions which prevented women from seriously committing themselves to ascetic practice at temples.

According to Metta, Buddhadāsa started talking about *dhammamātā* as female renunciants constituting an alternative to *bhikkhunī* when land was purchased sometime in the early 1980s for the expansion of Suan Mokkh. In 1986–1987, the facilities built on the newly purchased land were opened as Suan Mokkh International, one of the government-approved projects celebrating the fifth cycle (60th birthday) of King Rama IX.[31] Dividing the premises of Suan Mokkh International into three, Buddhadāsa proposed three projects: the International Dhamma Hermitage (about 9.6 hectares), the Dhamma Missionary Training Community (about 16 hectares), and the Dhammamātā Hermitage (about 6.4 hectares).[32] The International Dhamma Hermitage offers both English and Thai retreat programs every month to 80 to 100 people from foreign countries and 40 to 80 people from Thailand.[33] The Dhamma Missionary Training Community was planned by Buddhadāsa as a place for the training of non-Thai monks and for the international propagation of *dhamma*. Santikaro Bhikkhu, an American disciple of Buddhadāsa who has translated some of his works into English, was the first resident.[34]

The Dhammamātā Hermitage was the place that Buddhadāsa reserved particularly for women in order to offer them ideal conditions for their *dhamma* practice. Unfortunately, Buddhadāsa passed away in 1993 and could not do much for the Hermitage. It was only in December 1999, six years after his death, that the Hermitage was opened to run a four-month retreat program for women entitled "Self-Training Program for a Chaste Life of Untainted Beauty" (*Khrongkan fuk-oprom ton phua khwam-mi chiwit phromachan thi mot-chot ngot-ngam*) led by Ranchuan and other female disciples.

Although Buddhadāsa was seldom directly involved in these three projects at Suan Mokkh International, he specifically wanted his disciples to carry on the work to provide access to ideal spirituality. Of the three,

Buddhadāsa's vision of women at the Dhammamātā Hermitage was quite different from that of the *Ubasika* Area. He intended the Hermitage to be a demonstration of his full support for improving conditions for women's *dhamma* practice.

2. Buddhadāsa's Notions of *Dhammamātā* and Motherhood

The main source from which we can gain insight into Buddhadāsa's thoughts about *dhammamātā* is his handwritten notes in his private diaries — each note comprising a list of items on a piece of paper or a page in his diary. After his death, among his diaries, his disciples found four short notes regarding his thoughts on *dhammamātā*. All four were printed in the handbook for the Dhammamātā Hermitage.[35] In contrast to his earlier disinterest in the social disadvantages of women practitioners, these notes on *dhammamātā* were filled with respect for their great potential to achieve the goal of Buddhism. In other words, the *dhammamātā* notes indicate a significant change in Buddhadāsa's attitude toward women's practice.

The main points of Buddhadāsa's *dhammamātā* notes are well summarized by Ranchuan, who after Buddhadāsa's passing studied his thoughts in order to launch an actual project in the Dhammamātā Hermitage. In the handbook for the Hermitage, she wrote:

> [The main points of Buddhadāsa's notes were] to give people of mother's gender full opportunities for studying and practicing *dhamma* so that they could best propagate and inherit the Buddhist traditions as female *dhammadūta* [that is, a *dhamma* missionary] who would fill the vacant post of the group of *bhikkhunī* who are still lost.[36]

Working from an image of *dhammamātā* as female practitioners and reading through Buddhadāsa's notes, however, we could not find any details about their rules and styles, which tend to develop along the lines of monastic tradition. Buddhadāsa never specified in any of his notes whether they should shave their heads or not, what types of costume they should wear, or what sort of ceremony they should go through for their initiation. He did not even mention whether they should observe the 311 precepts (like the ancient *bhikkhunī* of the Buddha's time) or only the eight precepts commonly observed by *mae chi* in contemporary Thailand. Since there is no mention of *mae chi* in Buddhadāsa's notes, we cannot tell whether he thought *dhammamātā*, who "substitute for the *bhikkhunī*," should resemble *mae chi* or not. Whatever the ordination status or styles of practice he had in mind for *dhammamātā*, the objective was to offer women practitioners who were pursuing the ultimate religious goal an essential benefit, namely the opportunity to cultivate their own spirituality and that of others.

Buddhadāsa's notes on *dhammamātā* can be read as his solution to the dilemma of the universality of religions' "essential core," which is supposed to be accessible to any group of people and able to solve any kind of problem, in any particular set of mundane conditions, depending on which one's access to the "core" could be either facilitated or hindered. His confidence in women's abilities in Buddhist practice was reaffirmed by a Pāli phrase which he quoted in one of his *dhammamātā* notes:

> *na hi sabbesuṭhānesu puriso hoti paṇḍito*
> *itthipi paṇḍita hoti tattha tattha vicakkhanā*
>
> [A man is not wise on all occasions.
> A woman is also wise, being skillful here and there.[37]]

At the same time, aware of the gender inequalities in society, Buddhadāsa clearly outlined how women should be treated. For instance, he wrote of "women's rights, which should be equal to men's," and of "fully giving human rights to those who belong to the mother gender."[38] Among the many disadvantages faced by women in Buddhism, Buddhadāsa focused on their lack of opportunity for such religious activities as studying, practicing and propagating *dhamma* — opportunities that men take for granted when they ordain as *bhikkhu*. By establishing the Dhammamātā Hermitage, Buddhadāsa intended to provide women with substantial support equal to that enjoyed by *bhikkhu* — and by *bhikkhunī* if their ordination lineages had continued to the present. Yet, he wrote that through introducing *dhammamātā*, it was possible to "provide the best benefit to people belonging to the mother gender, not necessarily through ordaining as *bhikkhunī*.[39] His compensation for women was not an opportunity for ordination equal to that of *bhikkhunī*. In other words, in line with his philosophy, he did not choose ceremonies and forms such as *bhikkhunī* as a solution to gender inequalities in Buddhism. Instead, he urged the endowment of actual benefits that could support women's spiritual development.

The next question is what Buddhadāsa thought would be the actual benefits for women practitioners. His notes on *dhammamātā* suggest that there are at least three groups of people whose practices inspired him to work on conceiving an ideal picture of women practitioners. First, it seems that he wanted his female disciples to follow his path, doing just what he did as a *bhikkhu*. Speaking metaphorically, he wrote in his notes that the Dhammamātā Hermitage should be created as if it contained a deep forest, a university, a sacred hall and a radio station, which represent an ideal environment for ascetic practice, doctrinal study, realization of religiosity, and *dhamma* propagation respectively.[40] Buddhadāsa envisioned the Hermitage as having a natural environment similar to that of his temple Suan Mokkh, and as being a place for women practitioners to pursue the highest doctrinal studies, ascetic practice, and realization of the *dhamma*. He also wrote that, if possible, the Hermitage should "publish its own journal," just as he published his *Buddhism*, "to lead the world."[41] Furthermore, he promoted "international and inter-religious activities" in the Dhammamātā Hermitage, just as he had been doing in his own work. He set "no restriction on nationality" for those who would receive training there, but he expected members to have "knowledge of Thai and at least one more foreign language" as well as "general knowledge of academics and Buddhism."[42] He may have expected that these abilities would facilitate discussion about "the essence of all religions" with those from other linguistic and religious backgrounds.

The second group of people from whom Buddhadāsa gained inspiration was other religious believers fully dedicated to their religious practices. One of his notes says that practitioners in the Dhammamātā Hermitage would be "equivalent to cloistered Christian nuns, which Buddhism does not yet have." He also wrote that as a principle of practice, women practitioners at the Hermitage should "praise virtues [*phra khun*] at least five times a day," just as Muslim people do in their daily prayers.[43] In order to concentrate on prayers and contemplation, cloistered Catholic nuns seclude themselves in convents, thus limiting their contact with secular society, while Muslims are taught to make religion their central concern by praying five times a day.

By contrast, only a small number of contemporary Buddhist women practitioners in Thailand have benefited from equivalent opportunities for ascetic practice. Especially when women live in a temple under the authority of a male abbot, their expected roles revolve around rather secular aspects of monastic life such as grocery shopping, food preparation, selling flowers and other offering items to temple visitors, and soliciting donations for temple projects. Even when women seek instruction for their religious practice, the frequent contact with monk teachers can incite vulgar gossip, hinting at possible sexual attractions. Although there are places dedicated exclusively for women practitioners, the number of such places is small and the public is less aware of female head teachers' abilities than of monks'. The religious traditions in Christianity and Islam appear to have served as a model for Buddhadāsa to provide an independent place where Buddhist women could teach one another and engage in intensive ascetic practices together as good teachers and friends following the same religious path.[44]

Mothers were the third and the most important group who contributed to Buddhadāsa's conception of *dhammamātā*. Women as mothers inspired him to work toward the full realization of their capabilities in religious practice and teaching, which are often forgotten. In his notes, Buddhadāsa repeated many times that mothers should be rewarded with gratitude, and opportunities for the mother gender to practice *dhamma* should be facilitated. One of his notes says, "As a show of loyalty and repayment of obligations to the mother gender — give equivalent [things] to their tired and difficult [contributions as mothers]" (*Pen kan-katanyu katawethi top then phaet manda — hai som kap khwam-net-nuai yak lambak*).[45] His emphasis on the repayment of debts to mothers implies that everybody has been spiritually nurtured by his or her mother's fundamental teaching during childhood, but many people are not grateful enough to their mothers and do not support women's spiritual practice.

Apart from his notes on *dhammamātā*, there were several sermons in his later life in which Buddhadāsa emphasized the importance of mothers in transmitting the most fundamental teachings and building children's basic personalities. According to Buddhadāsa:

> The mother is the creator of the children's spirit [*phu-sang-winyan hai kae luk*], more than the father. The mother contributes more than the father to the creation of children's sensitivity and extensive knowledge of their intellectuality, mentality, and spirituality. Because she teaches children to behave well from birth, she should transmit her personality to them. She teaches whatever fundamental things are required for children to be clever, modest, careful, patient, and diligent. A mother gives these things to children more than a father.[46]

In one of his sermons, by questioning why in Pāli one always says *mātā pitā* ("mother and father"), instead of "father and mother," Buddhadāsa suggested mothers' devotion and intimacy with their children:

> With what do children grow? They are brought up with the blood from their mother's breasts. Mother's milk is blood in her breasts. Blood in mother's breasts transforms itself into milk in order to bring up her children. Children can actually grow with the blood in mother's breasts. A mother undertakes much pain at the time of childbearing and raising of children. Because of these experiences, a mother feels even more fatigue and pain than a father. Therefore, in Pāli the word "mother" comes before "father" ... Children stay with their mother for a long period of time until they can be apart from each other. [Even in the case

> where] the father separates from the children when they are still young, they have their mother's milk, sleep with their mother, and stay with their mother. So, they receive lots of valuable things from the mother, even more than the father.[47]

Taking his own childhood as an example, Buddhadāsa recalled that his mother taught him to be thrifty. While cooking together in the kitchen, she often said to him, "If we don't know how to use firewood [properly], we'll be slaves to firewood; if we don't know how to use water [properly], we'll be slaves to water." She told him to use things economically in order to eliminate excess efforts acquiring them — the same with money. She also taught him how to shred coconut meat. If they did it with all their strength, they would hurt their hands but would not squeeze out much coconut milk; but if they used moderate strength, the shredded meat would be soft and could produce more milk. This was a teaching of moderation (*pho di*).[48]

In another example, Buddhadāsa's mother often said while they were gardening, "If a bird eats [fruits or vegetables in the garden], think that we are receiving a merit. If someone steals them, think that we are making an offering."[49] Buddhadāsa learned generosity from his mother's teaching; he related its significance as follows:

> let me be a bit proud of myself: no matter how and what I can do today, as my body and self, better than other people, it is all because Mother taught me to become like this. Therefore, whoever has received any useful things from me, please thank my mother as well, because she built my life to be the way it is. In a [Pāli] text entitled, *Pubbācariya* [An ancient teacher], it is said that the mother is the first teacher in the world and created individuals in this way. What should I call this? When we see things in this way, how can we be disloyal to our parents?[50]

Buddhadāsa's emphasis on repayment of one's obligations to one's mother appears to have been rooted in the gratitude which he could not sufficiently express to his own mother. He said he regretted that his knowledge of *dhamma* was not deep enough when his mother was alive. She was very interested in *dhamma* (*sonchai thamma lua praman*), so soon after his ordination, he sent her small notebooks in which he had written what he had just learned from ecclesiastical examination books. However, according to Buddhadāsa, it was "only a childish knowledge of *dhamma*." He said, "If at that time I had as much knowledge as I have now, I could have helped my mother and given her great contentment through learning the *dhamma*. But, she died before I became able to teach the *dhamma* in depth. This fact always makes me feel desolate and the feeling never disappears." Metta, his nephew, observed that this feeling of regret seems to have motivated him to work to support women's spiritual development.[51]

By using the metaphor of mothers' nurturing of children's spirituality, Buddhadāsa did not just assign women to be in charge of basic teaching; he also found motherly virtues (*phra khun khong mae*) to be equivalent to the Buddhist paths for transcendence. In a sermon entitled *dhammamātā*, while not mentioning the Hermitage or the ideal female practitioners to whom he gave the name, he talked of mothers, whose minds are motivated by *dhamma dhammamātā*. He affirmed mothers' and women's ability to achieve *dhamma* as follows:

> Mothers' virtues are supreme *dhamma* [*boromatham*]. They are the highest [virtues/teachings] for children. If they make the best effort, even your mothers can become achievers of *dhamma* [*phu-banlu-tham*]. There is a Pāli saying, "*itthipi paṇḍita hoti tattha tattha vicakkhanā*" [A woman is also wise, being skilful here and there]. If she has deep insight [*wichak*], meaning that she has a clear understanding in her mind, even a woman can become a learned person [*bandit*]; not only men can do this. Now, we praise our mothers, maternal virtues, as they can become learned people. People often say that when [men] become ordained as monks, they forget and never think about the virtues of their mothers. This is inappropriate and not right, as it is equivalent to say that women cannot do anything much. Now let me clearly indicate that a woman can also become a learned person, if she has a clear understanding of *dhamma* in mind.[52]

Buddhadāsa compared mothers' virtues to the three aspects of essential doctrine in Buddhism: *pariyatti* (textual study), *paṭipatti* (practice), and *paṭivedha* (realizable or attainable aspect).[53] Among these three, the practical aspect is most striking.[54] He explained the practical aspect of a mother's virtues as "*navārahaguṇa*," which means the nine virtues of an *arahant*. The *navārahaguṇa* are also known as "*buddhaguṇa*," the Buddha's virtues, which Thai Buddhists commonly recite as part of their morning chanting. The nine virtues of an *arahant* or Buddha include: *arahaṁ* (away from the cycle of causes and effects);[55] *sammāsambuddho* (fully self-enlightened); *vijjācaraṇa-sampanno* (perfect in theory and conduct); *sugato* (going the right path); *lokavidū* (knower of the world); *anuttaro purisadammasārathi* (incomparable leader of human beings to be tamed); *satthā devamanussānaṁ* (the teacher of both higher and lower standards of people); *buddho* (the knower, awakened and delighted one); and *bhagavā* (the distributor, who distributes *dhamma* to other people to know).[56]

Most temple residents and lay Buddhists who frequently visit temples can recite all nine virtues of the Buddha from memory. They also memorize the meaning of each Pāli word, because many temples in Thailand use the daily Pāli chanting combined with Buddhadāsa's Thai translation.[57] It seems to have been his strategy to remind people of mothers' virtues by equating them to those of the Buddha, the enlightened one. In this way, he appealed to people to pay more respect and show more gratitude to mothers and those who belonged to the "mother gender" — who were in many cases old women remaining in the countryside, less educated than their children. He concluded the sermon by stating:

> In the end, I would say that I have spoken [in this sermon] about mothers' virtues by way of suggesting that our mothers have the elements [of transcendence]. Considering the nine steps as steps together with virtues, textual studies, practices, and realizations, our mothers would advance further and attain [*nibbāna*]. They are already composed of the elements [of transcendence]. When mothers advance, they will attain [*nibbāna*]. Mothers are already composed of those virtues. They are *dhammamātā* composed of the three parts: the nine Buddha virtues, the nine *lokuttara dhamma*, and *navaṅga-satthusāsana*.[58]

In summary, Buddhadāsa had no doubt that women — the mother gender — can accomplish the transcendent path of Buddhism, as they demonstrate the virtues of the Buddha and *arahant* when they play their maternal role. He expected female practitioners, *dhammamātā*, to perform as "mothers of the world" by fully demonstrating the virtues that they already possessed and by guiding people's spiritual development. Motherhood was a strong metaphor for him in his work to recognize the potential of women's pursuits of spirituality and to remind people of its significance.

3. Motherhood: Social Appeal and a Question of Gender Roles

Although the fact tends not to be stressed much in Thailand, one of the strategies often employed for raising the status of women is to advocate the equalization of women's and men's rights. For centuries, women's movements around the world have appealed to the public about the unfairness of sex-based discrimination and certain gender role expectations, such as men functioning as breadwinners versus women as domestic caretakers. Because of those efforts, many institutional inequalities have been eradicated and many people now understand more about women's rights, but it was a long time before such notions gained general acceptance by society. Not only men but women as well often perceived a sudden change of values as overly radical, even if they felt the unfairness of gender inequality in their everyday lives. In contemporary Thailand, where people respect the hierarchical social order and prefer modest attitudes to those perceived as aggressive, many Buddhist women feel it is difficult to claim a higher social status for their own benefit. So, rather than committing themselves to a movement for social change, many of them struggle toward religious goals under the existing disadvantages, because their access to the ultimate goal of Buddhism is theoretically guaranteed.[59]

Buddhadāsa may have been one of those who felt it difficult to eradicate traditional notions of gender roles, but he did understand that the current situation was unfair for women practitioners. The aim of his *dhammamātā* proposal may not have been exactly the same as the aim of other Buddhist women's movements, but there were many commonalities in terms of giving women practitioners appropriate social conditions for their ascetic practice and making use of their achievement for the benefit of society. In order to reach this goal, Buddhadāsa gave up the reintroduction of *bhikkhunī* ordination, as it may have invited social controversy and suspicion that he was seeking fame, as was the case in the Thai public's reaction to Narin's movement. Instead, Buddhadāsa used the notion of motherhood, which had more social appeal and would provoke less conflict. In fact, many senior *mae chi* and other types of female practitioners are called *khun mae* or *mae* (both mean mother; the first being more polite), terms which convey a sense of respect for, and intimacy toward, older women. When the notion of motherhood is applied to the new model of female practitioners, *dhammamātā*, the Pāli term *mātā* is combined with *dhamma*; this suggests that the term has a deeper meaning than the colloquial term, *mae*.

Moreover, the sense of reverence conveyed by *dhammamātā* is something that can be accepted as "natural" and "appropriate" but which hardly connotes aggressiveness or challenge to superiors in the traditional hierarchy. Buddhadāsa's intention in proposing *dhammamātā* as an alternative to *bhikkhunī* seems to have been to avoid unnecessary conflict with the existing authorities of *bhikkhu* and the Thai Saṅgha, which would likely be unavoidable in the case of an attempt to restore *bhikkhunī* ordination, and which could even reduce the benefits for women. It was by use of the notion of motherhood that he could expect women practitioners to obtain the most benefit and to be granted a role equivalent to that of the ancient *bhikkhunī*.

Traditionally, motherhood is one of the resources through which Thai women can acquire prestige.[60] By giving birth, a woman in rural Thailand assumes the title of "mother" and becomes responsible for feeding her family members. As a mother, she nurtures her children by providing nutrition during her pregnancy, giving them milk after childbirth, and preparing food for them when they grow up. Because of the matrilocal tendency and high male mobility in traditional Thailand, mothers take more responsibility than fathers for the family's economic and social life. Thus, Thai people tend to feel more indebted to their mothers than to their fathers. Schoolchildren assert that the person they love the most is their mother, and many women express their satisfaction with their maternal role, saying that they want to be reborn as women.[61]

The "milk price" (*kha nom*) which Thai people owe to their mothers is repeatedly emphasized in life transition rituals such as weddings, pre-ordinations, and tonsures.[62] In particular, at a pre-ordination ceremony called *tham khwan nak* (strengthening the spirit essence of the *nāga*), a traditional singer is hired to perform a song praising maternal virtues. Because it is believed that a mother can receive great merit by her son's entrance into the monkhood, an ordination constitutes his repayment of indebtedness to his mother. Singers are expected to sing movingly so that the ordination candidates and other members of the audience will be reminded of their debt to their mothers and begin to cry. Singers who can make people cry are popular and highly paid.[63]

One of the songs for the *tham khwan nak* ceremony praises mothers' virtues as follows:

> [The preceptor] accomplishes the ordination ceremony, so the candidate can become a sprout of a victorious ascetic and holy sage, and he can thus dedicate his heart of loyalty to repay his obligation to his parents who gave him birth. No merits that have been accumulated could be compared to this great status of ordination. Despite the greatest virtues of a mother, nowadays people tend to look down on the mother's virtues as only 12, while they weigh the father's as 20. Such a saying does not agree with Buddha's words. In *Maṅgaladīpanī* [text] the Buddha appropriately said that a mother's virtue is unlimited. Even with the whole universe, her virtue is incomparably large. Even if we allot mother 16, which is equivalent to the half of the great universe, her virtue is still much heavier. For this reason, the Lord Buddha went up to the *Tāvatiṁsa* heaven of the Thirty-three Gods and said that he would show his gratitude for his mother's virtues, so his insight is fully inserted in all the Three Baskets of the *Tipiṭaka*. When picking up the virtues of both the *Suttapiṭaka* [collections of Buddha's sermons] and the *Vinayapiṭaka* [comprising the corpus of rules governing monastic discipline], they are still lighter than the virtue of the Lord Buddha's mother, but the virtue of the *Abhidhammapiṭaka* [containing philosophical and psychological issues] is equivalent to it. Therefore, the Buddha taught the *Abhidhamma* of the absolute truth and extremely

> pleased both his mother and the celestials. With this teaching, the Lord Buddha could repay his debt to his mother. So candidate, fully consider by your brilliance how much virtue your mother had. When you ordain as an ascetic *bhikkhu*, a son in Buddhism, you deserve to have it said that you are repaying an obligation to your mother once, but it is still not equivalent to her virtues. Nevertheless, whenever you have a mind seriously venerated by your diligence and study topics in the *Tipiṭaka* seriously, you can pick up something from it to explain to your mother so that she could understand clearly and be pleased blissfully. Stay on the Noble Eightfold Path by following the holy tradition, then you will repay your debt to your mother.[64]

The legend in the *Abhidhammapiṭaka* about the Buddha's ascension to the Tāvatiṁsa heaven to preach to his deceased mother is often referred to as an exemplary model for monks to follow. They are encouraged to study and practice *dhamma* diligently so that they can teach their mothers and please them with tastes of the *dhamma* — which is also considered as a repayment of their indebtedness as sons. After listening to this story repeatedly, few people can deny the significance of motherly virtues. Buddhadāsa's notion of *dhammamātā* was derived from such a cultural context, and it appealed to people's traditional sentiment toward mothers.

Nevertheless, the concept of *dhammamātā* was not simply a repetition of the commonplace idea of motherhood. Motherhood pre-eminently conveys an image of a lifegiver and nurturer.[65] By extending mothers' image as nurturers, women are often portrayed as "mothers" who feed their ordained sons daily and as important supporters of the Saṅgha.[66] The work of providing material support for monks is often considered particularly important for women. Barbara Andaya has argued that because of the traditional respect for women's nurturing role, through which they can acquire merit to improve their future state of existence, Southeast Asian women, who are said to enjoy a relatively high social status, have accepted Theravāda Buddhism even though it assigns them a low status.[67] Nevertheless, with women's role stereotyped as a supporting one, there will be little advancement of the image of women as renunciants practicing *dhamma*. Such images of women and mothers are based on the premise that they are just lay people remaining in household life and only pursuing merit accumulation as their Buddhist practice. In contrast, Buddhadāsa, by highlighting the mothers' role as children's first teachers of *dhamma*, set forth a new image of women as religious teachers. This is the very image and role that Buddhist women practitioners have wanted; by proposing the notion of *dhammamātā* Buddhadāsa conferred on them while avoiding conflict with the dominant conception of women in Thai society.

Although the notion of *dhammamātā* is an interesting attempt to enhance women's status and opportunities in ascetic Buddhist practice based on local tradition, a possible limitation should also be noted. From a feminist point of view, the notion of motherhood always places women in a dilemma. In a study based on American society, Evelyn Nakano Glenn indicated that on the one hand, some consider the function of biological reproduction as the first division of labor and the original source of women's subordination. They argue that the physical task of childbearing led to the restriction of women's mobility and to the expectation that they do domestic work. On the other hand, some women are reluctant to give up their particular experience of becoming mothers, as motherhood is a powerful bodily experience that induces an emotional link with the infant as well as creativity and insight. Furthermore, in some societies, women can gain status when they produce heirs; therefore, motherhood is a source of status and privilege. However, at the same time, this status and privilege serve to strengthen the ideology of their subordination. Thus, motherhood is a paradoxical subject for feminists. Should they perceive women indiscriminately as human beings or claim special identities and positions as women? The latter perspective tends to be romanticized and used to justify assigning them to subordinate roles.[68]

Dhammamātā who live as celibate renunciants may not be much troubled by their biological reproduction function or subordination to the patriarchal family system, yet some of Buddhadāsa's statements about mothers' duties may require careful reading. He occasionally said that mothers' nurturing role in teaching children fundamental religious notions should not disappear:

> Women's duties and rights are true and thought to exist. These are for human beings' mastery of the world; they are not for rights equal and identical to men's. Instead, women's duties and rights are to accept the duties to discipline their children so that they can obtain true and perfect humanity. Women do not have to scramble for the duties that fathers perform as people often do. If they did, the world would lose the mothers.[69]

Although Buddhadāsa expressed his support for women's rights in several places, including his notes on *dhammamātā*, he did not seem to deny traditional gender roles. I have not found in his sermon a suggestion that fathers should take more responsibility for the nurturing of children. He may have taken it for granted that mothers' roles had to be played by mothers, not by fathers. In that case, his notion of motherhood may bind women primarily to maternal roles and limit their opportunities to take up other alternatives in society outside the home. It is a task for both female and male disciples of Buddhadāsa to take best advantage of his proposal of *dhammamātā* for practical benefit. He did not instruct his disciples to rigorously follow any teaching or tradition; they are allowed to develop alternative interpretations about his notion of motherhood.[70]

*****

The Dhammamātā Hermitage has been offering retreat sessions to female practitioners since December 1999, but as yet no one has declared herself a *dhammamātā*. In order to become one, a person is required to have good qualifications and confidence in herself as an exemplary model of a renunciant female practitioner and *dhamma* teacher who well represents the late Buddhadāsa's conception. Most women can become mothers, but *dhammamātā* who embody the ideal maternal virtues that he described would probably be charismatic individuals. In Thailand — and perhaps elsewhere as well — individual practitioners' actualizations of spirituality are the most potent resources for change. The presence of capable female renunciant teachers and their demonstration of admirable spirituality can establish people's faith in female renunciants and further expand women's opportunities for *dhamma* practice.

It is clear, however, that *dhammamātā* would have less social impact than *bhikkhunī*, who don the same yellow robes as *bhikkhu* and follow almost the same monastic rules.[71] No matter how much the notion of motherhood can influence people to pay more respect to women in society, Thais will never place ordained individuals lower than their mothers. Buddhadāsa grounded his reluctance concerning the restoration of *bhikkhunī* ordination in his philosophy, but in his teaching, we can also find some ideas which could support the project. For instance, although the lineage of *bhikkhunī* precept transmission was disrupted in the Theravāda tradition, the possibility of applying the precedent of the first *bhikkhunī* ordination by the Buddha could be considered and supported by Buddhadāsa's favorite reference to *Kālāma Sutta* and the original Buddhism in the Buddha's time.[72] Just as Buddhadāsa insisted, in the contemporary debate on *bhikkhunī* restoration, many people who are opposed to *bhikkhunī* ordination also refer to the universal access of *nibbāna* without regard for gender or ordained status, arguing that it is unnecessary for women to become ordained as *bhikkhunī*. Buddhadāsa was compassionate to women practitioners in difficulty, therefore he developed his thoughts on *dhammamātā*; yet we have to conclude that as far as the issue of women's ordination rights were concerned, he was not radical enough to confront the *status quo* in present Thai Buddhism.

However, we may argue that Buddhadāsa's proposal of *dhammamātā* was significant because it led to the establishment of the Dhammamātā Hermitage, one of the few places in Thailand where women can receive full support for their doctrinal study, ascetic practice and realization of spiritual virtues. It should be noted that when one can embody overwhelming spirituality, Thai Buddhists do recognize it and pay true respect to that person, regardless of ordained status or gender. Coming to this point, Buddhadāsa and other conservative monks and *mae chi* who oppose *bhikkhunī* ordination are right: worldly status and gender difference have no meaning, as spiritual qualities of an individual transcend these matters. It is a chicken-and-egg question: which should we look at first — social conditions for ascetic practice or spiritual excellence which overwhelms any worldly circumstances? Some may argue that appropriate social conditions for ascetic practice are significant factors leading practitioners to enlightenment, while others may insist that individual religiosities which develop through ascetic practice are the most significant factor in overcoming mundane difficulties. Both are true; it is only a matter of how individuals, society, religious and civil authorities recognize the value of spirituality and how they offer support to renunciant practitioners. What Buddhadāsa offered was *dhammamātā* status and Dhammamātā Hermitage as an alternative to *bhikkhunī* ordination.

Conclusion

Buddhadāsa passed away on 8 July 1993. His cremation ceremony was conducted in the simplest way, in accordance with the will of this revered monk who found little value in excessively decorative ceremonies. Considering the teacher's preference for simplicity and afraid of the temple becoming overcrowded, Achan Pho (Phra Khru Palatsilawat, Candasaro Bhikkhu), who was appointed to succeed Buddhadāsa as abbot of Suan Mokkh, abruptly announced the date of the cremation ceremony on national radio, just the evening before the cremation ceremony on 28 September 1993. The day of the cremation started with early morning chanting by 50 monks from all over Thailand. Several hundred people listened to the sermon of Paññānanda Bhikkhu, who had worked with Buddhadāsa to spread the *dhamma*. In the afternoon, 5,000 people observed the monks' procession carrying the coffin to the Golden Buddha hill, the forested part of the Suan Mokkh compound, where the cremation actually took place.[1]

Unlike those of many other famous Thai monks, Buddhadāsa's crematory was simply made. The coffin was placed on pyres of wood brought by people from the surrounding villages. A tall bamboo pole was erected at each corner of the crematory, and a square white cloth was tied to the tops of the poles to form a canopy. The three-hour cremation was observed by people contemplating impermanence. The remaining bones and ashes were neatly collected, but unlike those of highly respected forest monks in Northeast Thailand, they were not placed in a beautiful museum-like *stupa* (tope) as an exhibit of Buddhist sainthood but rather were placed in an urn and sealed in cement under the Buddha image in Dhammaghosana Hall (Thai: *Sala Thammakhot*) where Buddhadāsa's sermon books are collected, whilst his ashes were spread in three locations in Surat Thani province — in the sea across the harbor from Ko Samui island; in the upper reaches of the Ta Pi River; and at the hilltop of Khao Prasong, which is a high landmark visible from the surrounding sea and lowland fields. According to his younger brother Dhammadāsa, Buddhadāsa intended for people to remember him and his teaching while bathing in the water or working in the paddy, from where they could see the hill which is the resting place of their teacher.[2]

The whole procedure was specified in Buddhadāsa's last words, conscientiously drawn up at his deathbed by a lawyer follower, and was materialized by his close disciples who knew what he wanted. Renowned intellectual disciples Ubasika Ranchuan Inthrakamhaeng and Dr. Prawase Wasi both pointed out that through his cremation ceremony, Buddhadāsa set an example of opposition to "materialism" (Thai: *watthuniyom*).[3] Simplicity with little material decoration was his style; he preferred that nature speak the essence of *dhamma*.

Since Buddhadāsa's passing, the world has been constantly changing, showing its impermanent nature. Several important people who lived during the same historical period as Buddhadāsa followed him in leaving this world. In 1995, his debate opponent Kukrit Pramoj died at the age of 84; in 2000, his younger brother Dhammadāsa passed away at the age of 91; in 2002, his faithful supporter Sanya Dhammasakdi left the world at the age of 95; and in November 2007, his co-worker *dhamma* orator Paññānanda Bhikkhu followed at the age of 96. In the meantime, Buddhadāsa's temple, Suan Mokkh, continues its role of teaching people the *dhamma* after the loss of the great teacher's leadership; the succeeding abbot, Achan Pho, mastered English so as to teach groups of foreigners coming to the monthly 15-day meditation retreat, and Mr. Metta Phanit, the youngest son of Dhammadāsa and the most devoted disciple of Buddhadāsa among his nephews and nieces, determined to dedicate his life as a layman, took on the administrative tasks of Suan Mokkh, the Dhammadāna Foundation, the journal *Buddhism* and Dhammamātā Hermitage that his uncle and father left as gifts to this world. Their eloquence may not be comparable to that of Buddhadāsa, yet the tasks involved in maintaining that highly reputed religious institution would never be easy without firm confidence in the role of Suan Mokkh to help people with Buddhadāsa's *dhamma* teaching.

Even after he passed away, Buddhadāsa continued to be honored, and his teaching is still highly regarded. In October 2005, UNESCO added Buddhadāsa to its list of great international personalities. Buddhadāsa was the 17th Thai to be placed on the list along with HRH the Princess Sri Nagarindra the Princess Mother, former premier Pridi Phanomyong, and respected writer Kulap Saipradit.[4]

What is more, the 100th anniversary of Buddhadāsa's birth, on 27 May 2006, was unpretentiously celebrated by many groups even outside Suan Mokkh. Whilst Suan Mokkh celebrated the teacher's centenary with peaceful fasting and meditation and without fanfare, Thai Buddhists were stirred by a sequence of commemorative events held in 2006 and 2007.[5]

In Buddha Monthon (Thai: *Phuttha-monthon*), a place established on the outskirts of Bangkok as the administrative center of the Thai Saṅgha, Buddhadāsa's centenary was officiated by UNESCO's Goodwill Ambassador Her Royal Highness Princess Maha Chakri Sirindhorn.[6] Many renowned Buddhists, including Dr. Prawase Wasi, Orasi Gnarmvittayapongse, Paññānanda Bhikkhu, Sulak Sivaraksa and Mae Chi Sansanee Satiensut spoke of Buddhadāsa's influence on their lives.[7] To mark the teacher's centenary, many governmental and non-governmental organizations, artists and musicians planned seminars, commemorative publications, essay contests, *dhamma* propagation walks, artwork productions, *dhamma* music album releases and concerts.[8] It is said that in Buddhadāsa's home province, Surat Thani, there were even plans for a boxing championship and a trade fair to celebrate Buddhadāsa's 100th birthday.[9]

In that year, the Buddhist book section in Thai bookstores was awash with books with beautiful front covers commemorating the anniversary, and with new editions of Buddhadāsa's sermons. Some publishers printed his sermon books' front covers with cheerful, colorful pictures probably meant to attract the younger generations who were too young to have met Buddhadāsa yet. It was reported, "Dhamma books became more widely available than ever before, not just in the big bookshops but in petrol stations and 7-Elevens too."[10] To afford urban people easy access to Buddhadāsa's teaching, the Buddhadāsa Indapañño Archives was opened in Bangkok on 1 August 2010; the budget for its construction was reported to be some 185 million baht.[11]

Among the abovementioned events, even if some had more to do with commercial promotion than Buddhadāsa's teaching, the festivities of May 2006 and thereafter were not totally unrelated to what Buddhadāsa intended to convey to contemporary Thai Buddhists: the overcoming of suffering here and now.

The surge of renewed interest in Buddhadāsa indicated that his "*dhamma*" is still alive and helping people, just as he related in his poem:

> Buddhadāsa will continue to live; he never dies
> Even if the body should vanish and never hear a sound
> The body follows the way of the body, with no exception
> It is simply matter which perpetually changes as time goes by
>
> Buddhadāsa will continue to live; he never dies
> Good or bad, he lives along with religion

It is just like him having been dedicating his body and
mind for services
In accordance to the Buddha's command, never stopping

Buddhadāsa will continue to live; he never dies
Lives to serve his human being friends, never stopping
With the *Thammakhot*[12] which has been already made
Oh, dear friends, do you see what is dying?[13]

*****

Reflecting Buddhadāsa's life and work, his delightful independent pursuit of the essence of Buddhism and all religions was highly appreciated as a work to revive the Buddha's original teaching in the present time; at the same time, Buddhadāsa developed a parallel negative reputation as unorthodox, even heretic. Reviewing the development of Buddhadāsa's thought and people's discussions as examined in the main chapters here, it can be seen that the reasons for these contradictory reputations were intermingled.

Buddhadāsa's initial impact on the Buddhist public sphere was through the teaching of *lokuttara dhamma* (supramundane teaching), retrieved from classical scriptures when he launched the tri-monthly journal *Buddhism* in 1933. For general Thai Buddhists, at a time of suffering, merit-making (Thai: *tham bun*) was the way to make up for their past evil actions which caused the arising of suffering and also to lead to future happiness. In opposition, the *dhamma* rediscovered by Buddhadāsa taught them to overcome suffering through realizing the nature, the cause, the cessation and the way of overcoming suffering. Traditionally, this was known as a way to achieve the transcendent state of *nibbāna* to become an *arahant*, whereas Buddhadāsa promoted its practical use in daily life to realize peacefulness. Touched by the remarkable result, people highly appreciated Buddhadāsa's uncovering of that buried Buddhist teaching.

Controversies developed for several reasons. One reason was Buddhadāsa's independent development of thought through his own critical perspective and active intellectual exchanges with other schools of thought, such as Zen and Christianity, although it is mentioned little in this book. When the notion of empty mind and stories of Zen monks' wit were dedicated to the purpose of overcoming suffering, *nibbāna* became even more accessible in the here and now. On the one hand, those who pursued spiritual peace for their present lives appreciated the notions and interpretations presented by Buddhadāsa; on the other hand, his unconventional ideas were debatable. Similarly, Buddhadāsa's critical remarks about the emerging contemporary Abhidhamma studies, traditional exegesis in Theravāda Buddhism, were positively understood by those who put emphasis on the common goal of overcoming suffering, but it did offend those who promoted the Abhidhamma studies in Thailand, and invoked a strong retort criticizing his doctrinal deviance.

In some cases, Buddhadāsa's controversy was extended by interpretations of his followers. For the purpose of *dhamma* propagation, Buddhadāsa never exercised his copyright, so that any of his impressive words and thoughts could be freely reorganized and published. As a result, some works were published in Buddhadāsa's name, but in fact, they were his disciples' random collections of their favorite parts or even rephrased summaries. Some reworkings, such as *Handbook for Humankind* (Thai: *Khumu manut*) by Pun Chongprasoet, became one of Buddhadāsa's long-term bestsellers; but in other cases, Buddhadāsa's careful phrasing about polemical issues was translated into straightforward expressions, and the latter came to be propagated as Buddhadāsa's teaching. For example, on the traditional theme of Buddhist debate, "after death whether reborn or extinct" (Thai: "*tai laew koet*"), Buddhadāsa followed the Buddha's double-edged attitude of never affirming nor denying rebirth after death, since conventional belief in rebirth could benefit people by helping them to observe moral codes in the present life, even if it has not so much to do with the overcoming of suffering. However, Buddhadāsa's disciples were confident that Buddhadāsa's emphasis was placed on the overcoming of suffering, so some of them unhesitatingly denied rebirth in the name of Buddhadāsa's teaching; consequently, Buddhadāsa became a target of criticism by adherents to conventional beliefs.

Most momentously, Buddhadāsa's controversies became more acute through uproars intentionally aroused by his opponents. As early as the late 1940s, Buddhadāsa was accused of being a "communist" for the reason that his radical phrase in a 1948 lecture, "attachment to our own views of the Buddha, the Dhamma, and the Saṅgha would block the way to the truth"[14] was perceived as damaging of the traditional Buddhist conception. The accuser brought the case to the Saṅgha elders and further compounded the problem by spreading handbills accusing Buddhadāsa. Similarly, Buddhadāsa's sarcasm about a popular Abhidhamma study was responded to harshly by Abhidhamma teachers. Some teachers went beyond defending the merits of Abhidhamma study; speeches, publications and other actions aimed at damaging Buddhadāsa's reputation, including burning his books in front of a crowd, were witnessed. Their negative campaign did not completely destroy Buddhadāsa's public face, but it prompted some unsure people to refrain from positive comments about Buddhadāsa. The effect of that backbiting by opponents was somewhat similar to that of contemporary defamation commonly seen on website message boards; even when libel and slanders are proven to be groundless, the targeted individual has to incur a certain loss of social confidence. Therefore, Buddhadāsa could not dispel that distorted image, even though his teaching continued to inspire spiritual seekers, for whom he was a modern Buddhist saint.

No matter how people gossiped about him, Buddhadāsa kept aloof and confidently taught what he found to be true; critical intellectuals and young radicals revered his resolute attitude as much as his teaching, and their support may have made him look even more radical. As indicated in Chapters 6 and 7, Buddhadāsa did associate with Thailand's most famous "socialist" (in the Thai social context, socialists were Marxists who were not Communist Party members) intellectuals and his sermons were widely read by later generations of student activists. In fact, Buddhadāsa's actual political commitments were few and he was reluctant to support the controversial social change campaigns led by Narin Phasit and the Peace Committee; yet his temple was watched by the secret police from the 1950s through to the late 1970s.[15] Buddhadāsa was considered to be more radical than was the actual case.

*****

Reviewing the scenes of the Buddhist public sphere in 20th-century Thailand, there were many lay Buddhists seriously involved in doctrinal studies and meditation practice, which were traditionally the pursuits of ordained Buddhists in monasteries. Both Buddhadāsa and his opponent Abhidhamma teachers propagated the supra-mundane doctrines widely among mass audiences including lay Buddhists, and they directed every Buddhist to the common goal of attaining *nibbāna*, pointing to examples in the scriptures of lay people's enlightenment. Such a phenomenon looks like it is hinting at a change in the roles of monks and lay people.

However, it is not quite right to jump to the conclusion that the distinctions between the two had become blurred or that they were equalized. The traditionally higher status of monks continued to be respected, and the traditional lay Buddhist practice of merit making was also enduring. When monks attended as students at lay teachers' lectures or *dhamma* preacher training sessions, lay teachers humbly called their acts "a dedication of knowledge" rather than "teaching." Lay people usually experimented with meditation practice under a monk teacher's guidance at a retreat in a monastery for a week, a month or longer. In a retreat, lay people experienced a temporary renunciation, observing eight precepts, following daily monastic practices such as morning and evening chanting, and practicing meditation, rather than performing regular lay Buddhist activities such as offering morning meals to monks. If they found spiritual benefits in meditation practice, they might consider lifelong full renunciation from the mundane world. Aiming at the same religious goal as ordained Buddhists and becoming fully convinced of the religious path, some lay Buddhists moved on to full renunciation, i.e., to a religiously more committed stage, as an extension of their religious practice.

Looking at the situation of women practitioners, it was revealed that a blurring of the monk-lay distinction was rather unwelcome. In conventional Buddhism, because of women's lack of fully ordained status equal to that of male monks (*bhikkhu*), women had to do monastic practice as *mae chi*, i.e., renounced female practitioners with lay status. That obscure religious status was of little help for *mae chi* to follow a religious path; most lay Buddhists considered that supporting *mae chi* did not make as much merit as supporting monks, and in a monastery, *mae chi* were often expected to contribute to the monastery particularly through cooking for the monks rather than secluding themselves for meditation, since they were allowed free accommodation and free meals through people's donations to the monks. In order to support women practitioners to concentrate on *dhamma* practice, Buddhadāsa established the Dhammamātā Hermitage, and other Buddhist groups campaigned for the reintroduction of *bhikkhunī* ordination, by which women practitioners could enjoy the same religious status and support from the Buddhist community as monks received. In other words, even in the contemporary world, there was a desire for the Theravāda style of practice to be supported by an apparent ordained status rather than an obscure status neither ordained nor lay.

*****

Reflection on Buddhadāsa and his decades of teaching in the Thai Buddhist public sphere reveals that Buddhadāsa's insight into the profound messages of the Buddha and Buddhism served as a beacon for people who were seriously in search of the purpose of life. An important point to bear in mind here is that Thai Buddhists never accepted Buddhadāsa's teaching as infallible doctrine, nor did they worship Buddhadāsa uncritically as a modern Buddhist saint. Under the surface of rather diplomatic admiration or avoidance of fault-finding, people seriously considered the question as to whether his teaching was a proper religious reference point for their lives. Among Buddhadāsa's followers who found his interpretation to be the most appropriate expressions that made sense of the world, some even had the great joy of speaking their opinions based on his sermons and winning over their opponents in debates about "true" Buddhism and the "essential nature" of problems in contemporary Buddhism, society and politics. Obviously, it is debatable whether Buddhadāsa's thought as cited in his followers' arguments was exactly in accord with the content of his own sermons; yet even if minor inaccuracies did arise, people were taking his essential message into their hearts when they reinterpreted and discussed it in reference to their own lives.

A rich diversity of doctrinal interpretations and practices in contemporary Buddhism is examined by serious Buddhist practitioners who are motivated to see satisfactory outcomes in their own lives, even if there are some who are occasionally caught up in secular concerns of status and fame, just as ordinary people outside religious circles are. Contemporary social historians do not commit themselves to judging an authentic original Buddhist teaching from unreliable interpretations; they would even be hesitant to speak of an "absolute truth" in religion. Yet, the notion of validity of every variety presented in the Buddhist public sphere is inevitably censored deliberately by many individual Buddhist practitioners in their practices. As far as meeting people's religious demands, a teaching should survive as a reference for next generations. According to a common Buddhist saying, there are many paths, but all aim at the same goal, *nibbāna*. Lasting varieties may not be too many, nor too few. The free Buddhist public sphere serves as a democratic sphere for testing the practicality of Buddhist teachings for living Buddhists.

Among the many renowned contemporary Buddhist teachers in Thailand, voices of the people interviewed for this research suggested that Buddhadāsa was one of the most open-minded teachers, ready for discussion with people from any background. Throughout his lifetime at Suan Mokkh, Buddhadāsa was usually seen sitting on a bench surrounded by chickens of rough nature and waiting for guests to approach him for *dhamma* conversations. After his physical passing, his spirit is surely still there and elsewhere, just as he related in his poem, cited earlier. His sincere scriptural readings and philosophical interpretation of the world constitute a striving to provide ever deeper insight into the *dhamma*, i.e., the nature of existence, and his work and thought continue to welcome further challenges.

Notes

Introduction

1. Their publications include: Jack Kornfield, "Achaan Buddhadasa," in *Living Buddhist Masters* (Santa Cruz: Unity Press, 1977), pp. 117–29; Louis Gabaude, *Une herméneutique bouddhique contemporaine de Thaïlande: Buddhadāsa Bhikkhu* (Paris: École Française d'Extrême-Orient, 1988); Peter A. Jackson, *Buddhadāsa: A Buddhist Thinker for the Modern World* (Bangkok: The Siam Society, 1988), which is reprinted in 2003 as *Buddhadāsa: Theravāda Buddhism and Modernist Reform in Thailand* (Chiang Mai: Silkworm Books); Donald K. Swearer, trans., ed., *Me and Mine: Selected Essays of Bhikkhu Buddhadāsa* (Albany: State University of New York Press, 1989); Sulak Sivaraksa *et al.*, eds., *Radical Conservatism: Buddhism in the Contemporary World, Articles in Honour of Bhikkhu Buddhadāsa's 84th Anniversary* (Bangkok: Thai Inter-Religious Commission for Development, and International Network of Engaged Buddhists, 1990); Santikaro Bhikkhu, "Buddhadāsa Bhikkhu: Life and Society through the Natural Eyes of Voidness," in *Engaged Buddhism: Buddhist Liberation Movements in Asia*, eds. Christopher S. Queen and Sallie B. King (Albany: State University of New York Press, 1996), pp. 147–94; Buddhadāsa Bhikkhu, *Heartwood of the Bodhi Tree: The Buddha's Teaching on Voidness*, ed. Santikaro Bhikkhu, trans. Dhammavicayo (Boston: Wisdom Publications, 1994); and Kamala Tiyavanich, *Sons of the Buddha: The Early Lives of Three Extraordinary Thai Masters* (Boston: Wisdom Publications, 2007).
2. Donald S. Lopez, *A Modern Buddhist Bible: Essential Readings from East and West* (Boston: Beacon Press, 2002).
3. David L. McMahan, *The Making of Buddhist Modernism* (Oxford: Oxford University Press, 2008), p. 152.
4. Lopez, "Introduction," in *A Modern Buddhist Bible*, p. xxxix.
5. Sulak, ed., *Radical Conservatism*.
6. Those opponents included Anan Senakhan and Bunmi Methangkun, discussed in Chapter 5.
7. See Peter A. Jackson, *Buddhism, Legitimation, and Conflict: The Political Functions of Urban Thai Buddhism* (Singapore: Institute of Southeast Asian Studies, 1989); Apinya Fuengfusakul, "Empire of Crystal and Utopian

Commune: Two Types of Contemporary Theravāda Reform in Thailand," *Sojourn* 8, 1 (February 1993): 153–83.

8. Thai Buddhist intellectuals are seriously concerned about the recent current of consumerism. See, for example, Phra Phaisan Wisalo (Paisal Visalo Bhikkhu), *Phutthasatsana thai nai anakhot: naew-nom lae thang-ok chak wikrit* (*Thai Buddhism in the Future: The Sign of Crisis and the Way Out*) (Bangkok: Mulanithi Sotsi-Saritwong, 2003).
9. Venerable Paññānanda Bhikkhu (1911–2007), a revered Thai monk who worked alongside Buddhadāsa to popularize higher Buddhist doctrines, explained in the author's interview in 1998 that with such notions as *paṭiccasamppāda* (dependent origination) and *idappaccayatā* (conditionality), Buddhadāsa pointed to a key Buddhist doctrinal notion of causality which Thai people knew only as *kamma* in their conventional Buddhism. Paññānanda Bhikkhu, interview, Nonthaburi, 7 October 1998.
10. Jürgen Habermas, *The Structural Transformation of the Public Sphere: An Inquiry into a Category of Bourgeois Society*, trans. Thomas Burger (Cambridge, Mass.: MIT Press, 1989).
11. Habermas, *The Structural Transformation of the Public Sphere*, pp. 55–6.
12. Ibid., pp. 36–7.
13. Regarding the Thai Saṅgha's centralized governance structure, see Yoneo Ishii, *Saṅgha, State, and Society: Thai Buddhism in History* (Honolulu: University of Hawai'i Press, 1986).
14. Justin Thomas McDaniel, *Gathering Leaves and Lifting Words: Histories of Buddhist Monastic Education in Laos and Thailand* (Seattle: University of Washington Press, 2008), p. 15.
15. Studies on the Santi Asoke and the Dhammakāya Foundation include: Edwin Zehner, "Reform Symbolism of a Thai Middle-Class Sect: The Growth and Appeal of the Thammakai Movement," *Journal of Southeast Asians Studies* 21, 2 (September 1990): 402–26; Marja-Leena Heikkilä-Horn, *Buddhism with Open Eyes: Belief and Practice of Santi Asoke* (Bangkok: Fah Apai Co., Ltd., 1997); Rory Mackenzie, *New Buddhist Movements in Thailand: Towards an Understanding of Wat Phra Dhammakāya and Santi Asoke* (Abingdon, Oxon: Routledge, 2007).
16. The Santi Asoke is a rare case which broke away from the Thai Saṅgha's affiliation after all the conflicts, whereas the Dhammakāya still remains as a part of the Thai Saṅgha despite the fact that heightened public criticism on its chief abbot's land ownership, suspected affairs and doctrinal interpretation led to the deliberation of the Saṅgha's Elders' Council, which amicably settled the case with rather quiet admonition. A question should be asked why some cases are dealt rigorously while others are tolerated.
17. A more concrete process of the dissemination of religious knowledge is described in Chapter 2.
18. See Michael Walzer, *Politics and Passion: Toward a More Egalitarian Liberalism* (New Haven: Yale University Press, 2004).

19. John Brewer, "'The Most Polite Age and the Most Vicious': Attitudes towards Culture as a Commodity, 1660–1800," in *The Consumption of Culture 1600–1800: Image, Object, Text*, eds. Ann Bermingham and John Brewer (London: Routledge, 1995), pp. 341–61.
20. Shawn Frederick McHall, *Print and Power: Confucianism, Communism, and Buddhism in the Making of Modern Vietnam* (Honolulu: University of Hawai'i Press, 2004).
21. Phra Pracha Pasannathammo (Pracha Pasannadhammo Bhikkhu), *Lao wai mua wai sonthaya: atchiwaprawat khong than phutthathat* (*Talking in the Twilight Years: An Autobiography of Venerable Buddhadāsa*) (Bangkok: Mulanithi Komon Khimthong, 1988). Chapter 7 will discuss Buddhadāsa's teaching learned in Pracha's life.

Chapter 1

1. Phra Pracha Pasannathammo (Pracha Pasannadhammo Bhikkhu), *Lao wai mua wai sonthaya: atchiwaprawat khong than phutthathat* (*Talking in the Twilight Years: An Autobiography of Venerable Buddhadāsa*) (Bangkok: Mulanithi Komon Khimthong, 1988).
2. See Yoneo Ishii, *Saṅgha, State, and Society: Thai Buddhism in History* (Honolulu: University of Hawai'i Press, 1986), pp. 65, 83; Donald K. Swearer and Sommai Premchit, "The Relationship between the Religious and Political Orders in Northern Thailand (14th–16th Centuries)," in *Religion and Legitimation of Power in Thailand, Laos, and Burma*, ed. Bardwell L. Smith (Chambersburg, PA: ANIMA Books, 1978), pp. 20–33; John W. Butt, "Thai Kingship and Religious Reform (18th–19th Centuries)," in *Religion and Legitimation of Power*, ed. Smith, pp. 34–51.
3. Peter A. Jackson, *Buddhism, Legitimation, and Conflict: The Political Functions of Urban Thai Buddhism* (Singapore: Institute of Southeast Asian Studies, 1989), p. 43; Louis Gabaude, *Une herméneutique bouddhique contemporaine de Thaïland: Buddhadāsa Bhikkhu* (Paris: École Française d'Extrême-Orient, 1988), p. 367; Peter A. Jackson, *Buddhadāsa: Theravāda Buddhism and Modernist Reform in Thailand* (Chiang Mai: Silkworm Books, 2003), pp. 37–9.
4. For instance, Reynolds indicated that Chao Phraya Thiphakorawong's work published in 1867, *Kitchanukit* (*A Book Explaining Various Things*), represented a shift of Buddhist worldview replacing the one in *Traiphum Phra Ruang* (*Three Worlds Cosmography of Phra Ruang*) compiled in the 14th century. According to Reynolds, the most remarkable aspect of change in the 19th century was skepticism toward supernatural premise of the traditional Buddhist cosmography and empiricism inspired by modern Western science. See Craig J. Reynolds, "Buddhist Cosmography in Thai History, with Special Reference to Nineteenth Century Culture Change," *Journal of Asian Studies* 35, 2 (February 1976): 203–20.

5. R. Lingat, "La vie religieuse du roi Mongkut," *Journal of the Siam Society* 20 (1926–1927): 129–49; R. Lingat, "History of Wat Pavaraniveca," *Journal of the Siam Society* 26 (1932): 73–102.
6. Lingat, "La vie religieuse du roi Mongkut," pp. 140–1; Lingat, "History of Wat Pavaraniveca," pp. 77–83.
7. Lingat, "History of Wat Pavaraniveca," p. 84.
8. Phra Pracha, *Lao wai mua wai sonthaya*, p. 573.
9. Ibid., p. 120.
10. Ibid., p. 63.
11. Ibid., p. 572.
12. A.B. Griswold, "King Mongkut in Perspective," *Journal of the Siam Society* 45 (1957): 18–9.
13. Craig J. Reynolds, "Buddhist Cosmography in Thai History," p. 215.
14. Phra Phaisan Wisalo (Paisal Visalo Bhikkhu), *Phutthasasana Thai nai anakhot: naew-nom lae thang-ok chak wikrit* (*Thai Buddhism in the Future: Tendency of Crisis and Exit from It*) (Bangkok: Mulanithi Sotsi-saritwong, 2003), p. 24; translated by Ito. Paisal's argument was based on the reform by Prince Patriarch Wachirayan Warorot, rather than the one by Mongkut. Regarding Buddhadāsa's view on Wachirayan's work, see the quotation on p. 39, footnote 120.
15. Regarding Wachirayan's biography, see Craig Reynolds, ed., trans., *Autobiography: The Life of Prince-Patriarch Vajirañāṇa* (Athens, Ohio: Ohio University Press, 1979).
16. Phra Pracha, *Lao wai mua wai sonthaya*, p. 59.
17. Rong Prathan Phong Samaloek, vice-president of the Laotian Fellowship of Buddhists (this position is equivalent to the vice-Supreme Patriarch in the Thai Saṅgha, and in Laos under the socialist regime; the Laotian Fellowship of Buddhists is equivalent to the Saṅgha in Thailand) interview, Vientiane, 29 April 2000.
18. Stephen Zack, "Buddhist Education under Prince Wachirayan Warorot," PhD diss., Cornell University, 1977, p. 105.
19. Yoneo Ishii, *Saṅgha, State, and Society: Thai Buddhism in History* (Honolulu: The University of Hawai'i Press, 1986), pp. 88–91; Zack, "Buddhist Education," p. 169.
20. Phra Maha Thongsup, "Pathakatha ruang nak tham" (A Public Lecture on *Nak Tham*), *Thammachaksu* 20, 3 (December 1934): 259–74. This article was originally broadcast on radio on 15 June 1934.
21. Phra Maha Thongsup, "Pathakatha nak tham," pp. 265–6.
22. In 1933, 20,397 passed the examinations, 21,111 failed, and 12,871 withdrew from sitting the examinations. See Phra Maha Thongsup, "Pathakatha nak tham," p. 272. According to the statistics that Ishii cited, by 1967, the *nak tham* candidates had grown to 144,765, among whom 35,744 passed the examinations. See Ishii, *Saṅgha, State, and Society*, p. 96.
23. Phra Maha Thongsup added that included in these figures were some lay people who were to be teachers to teach Buddhism at elementary school.

He said that these people should also be assisted. See Phra Maha Thongsup, "Pathakatha nak tham," p. 273.

24. Suksanti Chirachariyawet, ed., *7 rop achan sanya* (*Seventh 12-Year Cycle [i.e., 84 years] of Achan Sanya*) (Bangkok: Mulanithi Nitthisat, Mahawitthayalai Thammasat, 1991), p. 137.
25. About K.S.R. Kulap, see Craig Reynolds, "The Case of K.S.R. Kulap: A Challenge to Royal Historical Writing in Late Nineteenth Century Thailand," *The Journal of the Siam Society* 61, 2 (July 1973): 63–90.
26. About Thianwan, see Chai'anan Samutwanit, ed., *Sanniphon khong thianwan* (*Writings of Thianwan*) (Bangkok: Ongkan Naksuksa Mahawitthayalai Ramkhamhaeng, 1974); Walter F. Vella, "Thianwan of Siam: A Man who Fought Giants," in *Anuson Walter Vella*, ed. Ronald D. Renard (Chiang Mai: Walter F. Vella Fund, Phayap University, 1986), pp. 78 91.
27. About Narin Phasit, see Sakdina Chatrakun na Ayutthaya, *Chiwit, naewkhit lae kantosu khong 'narin klung' ru narin phasit: khon khwang lok* (*Life, Thought and Struggle of 'Narin Klung' or Narin Phasit: A Person who Blocked the World*) (Bangkok: Samnakphim Matichon, 1993).
28. Reynolds, "The Case of K.S.R. Kulap," p. 75.
29. Vella translated the title of the journal as "The Equal Share Journal," or "Fair Deal Journal." See Vella, "Thianwan of Siam," p, 81. One of Thianwan's articles on Buddhism, "Rok khong sasana" (Illness of Religion), was selected from *Tulawiphak Phochanakit* 4, 147 (16 April 1904) and reprinted in Buddhadāsa's journal, *Phutthasasana* (*Buddhism*) 20 (1952): 23–6. It criticized as "illness of religion" any world-renunciates, either *bhikkhu*, *sāmaṇera*, *ta then* (old ascetics), *yai chi* (old female ascetics), *upāsaka* (lay men), or *upāsikā* (lay women), who did not understand the purpose of religion, but sought instead to benefit their social status as renunciates. Thianwan indicated that the medicine for such illness is in Buddhism.
30. Phra Pracha, *Lao wai mua wai sonthaya*, p. 113.
31. Sakdina, *Chiwit, naewkhit lae kantosu khong 'narin klung'*, pp. 10–3, 32–45.
32. Phra Pracha, *Lao wai mua wai sonthaya*, pp. 114–5.
33. About his life and the works of Dharmapāla, see Ananda Guruge, ed., *Return to Righteousness: A Collection of Speeches, Essays and Letters of Anagārika Dharmapāla* (Ceylon: Government Press, 1965).
34. Phra Pracha, *Lao wai mua wai sonthaya*, pp. 126–7.
35. The volumes of these journals that I looked through were in the collections in the main library and the subsidiary library of the Faculty of Arts, the University of Kyoto. The following analyses of articles in these journals are based on the volumes that I looked at. They included: *The Mahā Bodhi* 39, 1 (January 1931) to 41, 12 (December 1933); *Buddhist Annual of Ceylon* 1, 1 (1920) to 4, 2 (1932); *The British Buddhist* 4, 1 (October 1929) to 8 Conference and Farewell Number (1934); and *The Young East* 1, 3 (August 1925) to 10, 2 (1942).
36. The British Mahā Bodhi Society was established with the object of "the extension of the knowledge of the tenets of Buddhism, the establishment of a

Vihāra in London and the promotion of the cause of Buddhism in the West." See *The British Buddhist* 4, 1 (October 1929), advertisement page for the British Mahā Bodhi Society.

37. Prince Wan was the President of the British Mahā Bodhi Society from July 1929 until October 1930. From 1926, his appointment was as His Majesty's envoy extraordinary and Minister Plenipotentiary to Great Britain. From 1928, he was also Siam's Permanent Delegate to the League of Nations and Siamese Minister in London. Prince Wan resigned from the Society's Presidency because of returning to Siam in October 1930. See The Editor, "Democratic Prince," *The British Buddhist* 4, 8–9 (May–June 1930); "Yet Another Departure," *The British Buddhist* 5, 1 (October 1930): 194. In *The British Buddhist*, the name of Prince Wan is Romanized as "Varnvaidya," but his name is more commonly written as "Wan Waithayakon."
38. Prince Damras was President of the Society after 1932. In 1929, he had been appointed as His Siamese Majesty's envoy extraordinary and Minister Plenipotentiary to the Court of St. James and Permanent Representative to the League of Nations, in addition to being Siamese Minister in London. See *The British Buddhist* 6, 11 (August 1933).
39. *The British Buddhist* 7, 11 (August 1933), advertisement for the British Mahā Bodhi Society.
40. The Editor, "Democratic Prince."
41. "Democratic Siam," *The Mahā-Bodhi* 40, 8 (August 1932): 390–1. There was a reply from Chao Phya Mahadhasa, Principal Private Secretary of King Prajadhipok as well.
42. "New Siamese Constitution: Highest Power Belongs to People," *The Mahā-Bodhi* 40, 9 (September 1932): 415–22.
43. *The British Buddhist* 8, 2 (January–March 1934).
44. For example, when a Siamese Buddhist journal, *Thammachaksu*, translated the news of some Buddhist mission and converts in Europe from the *Mahā Bodhi Journal*, the editor of *Thammachaksu* wrote, "I hope that these news will bring a sense of pride to Buddhists everywhere." See "Thalaengkan buang ton" (Announcement in the Beginning), *Thammachaksu* 23, 4 (January 1937).
45. In Buddhadāsa's journal, they wrote, "These days, some foreigners who are philosophers having high knowledge, study Buddhism and try to practice it for overcoming suffering by expecting the fruit of *lokuttara* happiness, because overcoming suffering is not possible in modern academic studies, such as science. However, they want to see a model of practice, or someone who has already done the practice. How should we, who are placed in the position of the owners of Buddhism in the present time, advise and help them, if we do not have any *bhikkhu* and *sāmaṇera* who does good and right practice, at an authentic level (*suppaṭipanno*), as examples to show?" See "Thalaengkan khong khana thammathan" (An Announcement from the Dhammadāna Group), *Phutthasasana* 1, 1 (May 1933): 8; translated by Ito.
46. Phuwa Ratchakan Changwat lae Khana Kromkan Changwat Surat Thani (Provincial Governor and Administrative Council of Surat Thani), ed., *Changwat*

surat thani — kan-chalong 25 phutthasattawat (*Surat Thani Province — Celebration for the 25th Buddhist Century*) (Bangkok: 1957), p. 12.

47. *Changwat surat thani — kan-chalong 25 phutthasattawat*, p. 14.
48. Prathum Chumphenphan, ed., *Chaiya — surat thani* (Bangkok: Krung Sayam Kanphim, 1972, 1976), pp. 4–5.
49. For example, Buddhadāsa's grandfather (father's father), Kho Yiko (許二哥?), was from China, and married a local third-generation Chinese woman. Those Chinese who married Thais became assimilated, especially when they accepted Theravāda Buddhist culture, including ordination and education at temples, as seen in the examples of Buddhadāsa's father and brother. When local Chinese married newer migrants from China, they resumed Chinese ancestor worship at home, as in the case of Buddhadāsa's cousin, Damri Phanit (a son of Buddhadāsa's father's brother, Uncle Siang). Damri Phanit, interview, Chumphon, 6 March 1999. According to Buddhadāsa, there were many Chinese descendants in the area, and on some of the Chinese was conferred the title "Phraya." See Phra Pracha, *Lao wai mua wai sonthaya*, pp. 14–5.
50. Prathum, *Chaiya — surat thani*, pp. 4–5.
51. Ibid., pp. 73–5.
52. Phra Pracha, *Lao wai mua wai sonthaya*, pp. 45–6, 697. In 1935, the regional center moved from Phumriang to the Talat Chaiya area when the railway station was built and the district office moved to be near the railway. See Phra Pracha, *Lao wai mua wai sonthaya*, p. 697.
53. According to Dhammadāsa, his name Yikoei is a Chinese name, which means "the second chicken" (二鷄). Dhammadāsa did not learn Chinese from his father, but he studied it from textbooks by himself after he quit Chulalongkorn University and returned home in order to run the family business in place of Buddhadāsa, who had been ordained at the age of 20. Dhammadāsa believed that the names, Nguam and Kimsoi, were both Chinese, but he was not sure what those names meant. He also considered himself as almost Chinese. Dhammadāsa Phanit, interview, Chaiya, 4 March 1999. According to Buddhadāsa, his own name was originally Nguam with *mai-tho* (the second tone marker in Thai script; in this case pronouncing in high tone), which was a word of poetic expression meaning "high" or "eldest," but at his school, his name was somehow registered as Nguam with *mai-ek* (the first tone marker; in this case pronouncing in falling tone). The name of his younger brother, Dhammadāsa, was originally Yikoei ("Yi" with *mai-ek*, "koei" without any tone marker), which was an old Thai word meaning "second unit," but at school, his name was registered as Yikoei ("Yi" with *mai-ek*, "koei" with *mai-tho*), which meant "second chicken" in Chinese, because people thought his name was Chinese. The youngest sister's name was originally Soi, probably named after Thao Soi, a female governor who was born as the youngest sibling. But at school, her name was registered as Kimsoi, because there were many Chinese women whose names were Kimsoi, so people understood that the name must be Chinese. See Phutthathat Inthapanno (Buddhadāsa) and Thammathat (Dhammadāsa) Phanit, "Khon la kham song kham nam-cai luk"

(One or Two Words by Each Person Considerate of Children), in *Watthu-anuson 100 wan morana: nang kimsoi hemakun* (*Commemoration of the 100th day After Passing: Mrs. Kimsoi Hemakun*) (Chaiya: Suan Mokkhabalarama, 14 October 1989).

54. "Dhammadāsa" is a Pāli spelling of his name. In Thai, his name is pronounced as "Thammathat."
55. The following family history is based on the interview with Damri Phanit (1916–), the eldest son of Uncle Siang.
56. Buddhadāsa and Dhammadāsa, who lost their father in their youth, believed that their grandfather was from Hokkien. Phra Pracha, *Lao wai mua wai sonthaya*, p. 5; Dhammadāsa Phanit, interview with author, Chaiya, 4 March 1999. However, according to Damri Phanit, a cousin of theirs and a son of Uncle Siang, their grandfather was actually born in Taechew, but he emphasized his background in Hokkien in order to marry Somchin, whose family originated in Hokkien.
57. Phra Pracha, *Lao wai mua wai sonthaya*, p. 5.
58. Buddhadāsa's father's name, Siang, and his uncle's name, Siang, is different in script and tone in Thai, but it cannot be Romanized in English. Buddhadāsa's father's name is written in Thai, *so-so* and *mai-tho*, and pronounced with the high tone; while his uncle's name is written *so-sua* and *mai-tho*, and pronounced with the falling tone. In this chapter, I call Buddhadāsa's father "Father Siang," and his uncle "Uncle Siang."
59. *Phra baidika* is the lowest of the *thananukrom* (honorary positions) that elder monks at the level of *phra rachakhana* (those monks on whom have been conferred ecclesiastical titles above the level of *phra khru*) can appoint. The higher the ecclesiastical title conferred, the more *thananukrom* monks a monk can appoint. For example, in 1912, when on future Somdet Phra Phutthakhosachan (Charoen Yanawaro; 1872–1951) was conferred the ecclesiastical title, Phra Ratchamuni, he was allowed to appoint three *thananukrom* monks: *phra khru palat*, *phra khru samu*, and *phra khru baidika*. In 1926, when the title of Somdet Phra Phutthakhosachan at the level of *somdet rachakhana* was conferred, he was allowed to appoint ten *thananukrom* monks: *phra khru plat samphiphatthana silachan yanawimon sakon khani-sason utdon sangkhanayok pidok thamma rakkhit*, *phra khru winaithon*, *phra khru thammathon*, *phra khru methangkon phra khru khu suat*, *phra khru warawong phra khru khu suat*, *phra khru thammarat*, *phra khru thammaruchi*, *phra khru sangkhawichan*, *phra khru samu*, and *phra khru baidika*. In the rank of *thananukrom*, *baidika* is the lowest. See the headings, "thananukrom," "baidika," and "rachakhana" in *Photchananukrom chabap ratchabandit sathan pho. so. 2525* (*A Thai Dictionary: The Royal Academy*, 1982 edition). See also "Prawat chao phra khun somdet phra phutthakhosachan yanawara thera" (A History of Somdet Phra Phutthakhosachan), in Chao Phra Khun Somdet Phra Phutthakhosachan Yanawara Thera, *Phra mongkhon wisesakatha* (A Commemoration book Distributed by his Disciples at his Cremation) (1952), pp. (1)–(28).

60. Wat Pathumkhongkha was the temple where Buddhadāsa stayed when he studied Pāli on Uncle Siang's advice. Uncle Siang took a novice when he went to study in Bangkok. The novice, Maha Klan or later Phra Khru Chayaphiwat, was to become Buddhadāsa's teacher of Pāli. Damri Phanit, interview. Uncle Siang's connections and advice were important for the path of the young monk, Buddhadāsa.
61. Buddhadāsa's father did not speak Chinese except for a few words, but he studied Thai at the temple when he was a temple boy. In Buddhadāsa's house, his father celebrated Chinese New Year (*trut chin*) and the Chinese autumn festival (*sat chin*), but the Chinese holidays were not celebrated after his father died when Buddhadāsa was 16. Uncle Siang never performed Chinese ancestor worship at home. According to Damri, Uncle Siang's son, Uncle Siang could not speak Chinese, but did speak some English for his business, and read Pāli fluently because of his long monastic education. Uncle Siang was even capable of writing *bailan*. Both Buddhadāsa's father and uncle were talented in making Thai poems. See Phra Pracha, *Lao wai mua wai sonthaya*, p. 15, 43; Damri, interview. These facts indicate that Thai cultural elements were stronger than the influence of Chinese culture even in Buddhadāsa's father's generation.
62. Kittivuḍḍho Bhikkhu, interview, Chonburi, 29 April 1999.
63. Suchip Punyanuphap, interview, Bangkok, 17 August 1998.
64. Dhammadāsa, interview. According to Buddhadāsa in his interview with Phra Pracha, his mother was born in Tha Chang, another district in the Chaiya region, and her mother and grandparents were from Tha Chang. See Phra Pracha, *Lao wai mua wai sonthaya*, p. 6. Dhammadāsa said that their mother's father worked as the first district governor (*nai amphoe*) of Kanchanadit District (Nai Amphoe Kanchanadit), and then the family moved to Tha Chang District.
65. Dhammadāsa, interview; Siri Phanit, interview, Chaiya, 4 March 1999.
66. Eiji Murashima, *Kanmuang chin sayam* (*Politics of the Chinese in Siam*) (Bangkok: Sathaban esia suksa, Chulalongkon mahawitthayalai, 1996), p. 39.
67. Although Buddhadāsa said that his family did not have the same status or wealth as Chao Muang or Chinese merchants (Phra Pracha, *Lao wai mua wai sonthaya*, p. 6), Dhammadāsa and other members of the Phanit Family agreed that they were in the higher level, better off than ordinary local farmers or shopowners. Dhammadāsa, interview; Siri, interview; Metta Phanit, the youngest son of Dhammadāsa, interview, Chaiya, 4 March 1999.
68. Some of the members of the Phanit family did well in their education. For example, among the five children of Dhammadāsa, one studied abroad in Britain and the United States, two graduated from Chulalongkorn University, the other two also graduated from college and university. In Uncle Siang's family, one of the most accomplished children is Dr. Wichan Phanit, or a grandson of Uncle Siang and the eldest son of Damri, who held the position of the Director of the Research Funding Council (*phu amnuaikan samnakngan kongthun sanap sanun kanwichai*) in the late 1990s.

69. Phra Pracha, *Lao wai mua wai sonthaya*, pp. 16, 43.
70. Damri, interview.
71. Arun Wetchasuan, interview, Bangkok, 2 March 1999.
72. Many books on Buddhadāsa's life have been published, but I refer to Phra Pracha, *Lao wai mua wai sonthaya*. Since Buddhadāsa himself talked about his experiences and opinions in it, *Lao wai mua wai sonthaya* is in all likelihood the most reliable work to be examined for Buddhadāsa's life and work.
73. For Dhammadāsa's life, I have referred mainly to three sources: an interview with Dhammadāsa; "Song si phra phutthasasana, song phu-sathapana mokkhaphalaram — khana thammathan" (Two Outstanding Contributors to Buddhism, Two Founders of [Suan] Mokkh Phalaram — Dhammadāna Group), a leaflet on the lives and work of Buddhadāsa and Dhammadāsa, which was published by the Dhammadāna Group; and an MA thesis on Dhammadāsa: Wira Phaengyang, "Suksa chiwaprawat lae phonngan khong thammathat phanit" (A Study on the Life History and Works of Dhammadāsa Phanit), MA thesis, Mahawitthayalai Sinakharin Wirot Phak Tai, 1996. Dhammadāsa fell ill on 21 November 1999 because of bleeding in the esophagus, but just as Buddhadāsa had wished, his family did not take him to a hospital for modern medical treatment to prolong his life. His strength gradually decreased, and he finally breathed his last on 18 February 2000. See "Ramluk khun khru thammathat phanit, phu chak pai" (A Remembrance of the Teacher, Dhammadāsa Phanit, who Departed from Us), *Phutthasasana* 68, 2 (May, June, July 2000): 103. See also *Phutthasasana* (Chabap phiset: sadudi khru thammathat phanit) (Special Issue: Tribute to the Teacher, Dhammadāsa Phanit) 68, 3 (August, September, October 2000).
74. Up until December 1940, or 2483 Buddhist Era, the Thai calendar started its year from April and ended in March. According to the Thai calendar, Buddhadāsa was born in May 2449 (1906), and Dhammadāsa was born in March 2451 (1909), so their age difference is only two years, but in the modern calendar, it is three.
75. Phra Pracha, *Lao wai mua wai sonthaya*, pp. 22–9.
76. According to a report of the Ministry of Public Instruction in 1926–1927, those who continued studying at secondary school moved on to the first grade in secondary school from the third grade in primary school, instead of completing the fifth grade in primary school. See Ministry of Public Instruction, *Report on the Work of the Ministry of Public Instruction of the Siamese Government B.E. 2469 (1926–27)* (Bangkok: Bangkok Times Press, 1931).
77. Phra Pracha, *Lao wai mua wai sonthaya*, p. 41.
78. Ibid., pp. 41–2.
79. According to Dhammadāsa, the brothers never talked about Buddhism in their childhood. Dhammadāsa said that he was not able to explain why Buddhadāsa became interested in Buddhism, but assumed it was because of Buddhadāsa's experience as a temple boy because the temple abbot was capable in preaching the *dhamma*. Dhammadāsa, interview. However, Buddhadāsa did

not mention the *dhamma* he studied when he talked about his experience as a temple boy in the interview with Phra Pracha. It was rather during the time when Dhammadāsa was away from home for his education, and Buddhadāsa was running his shop that Buddhadāsa started to be interested in Buddhist *dhamma*.

80. Dhammadāsa, interview.
81. Ministry of Public Instruction, *Report on the Work of the Ministry of Public Instruction*.
82. Ibid.
83. Phra Pracha, *Lao wai mua wai sonthaya*, pp. 51–2.
84. Ibid., pp. 70–1.
85. Ibid., pp. 74–6.
86. Ibid., pp. 78–87.
87. Kim'nguan, or Nguan for short, was one of the wives of Phraya Patinanphumirak, a very wealthy Chinese merchant in Surat Thani. She donated 5,000 baht for building the *nak tham* school in the historic Sri Vijaya temple for the merit of her dead parents. Buddhadāsa was already famous in the region for his ability to explain the *dhamma* in his sermons and for serious study of Buddhism, so his aunt recruited Buddhadāsa to be a teacher in her newly opened school. Buddhadāsa taught two classes of students, and all students passed the third and second grade of *nak tham* examinations except one whose answer sheet was lost by the examiners. This result must be far better than the old *nak tham* school in Phumriang. His aunt Nguan offered a reward for Buddhadāsa's teaching work, a set of one *piṭaka* of the three. Buddhadāsa instead requested a Thai typewriter, which he was to use throughout his life, because he could borrow and read *Tipiṭaka* volumes in the temple. See Phra Pracha, *Lao wai mua wai sonthaya*, pp. 89–90.
88. Phra Pracha, *Lao wai mua wai sonthaya*, pp. 94–103, 111–4.
89. Ibid., pp. 110–1.
90. Phutthathat Phikkhu, *Phra phutthasatsana chan phuthuchon* (Bangkok: Klum Suksa lae Patibat Tham, reprint edition).
91. Phra Pracha, *Lao wai mua wai sonthaya*, p. 300.
92. Dhammadāsa, interview; Phra Pracha, *Lao wai mua wai sonthaya*, pp. 87–8, 126–7.
93. Phra Pracha, *Lao wai mua wai sonthaya*, p. 204.
94. Ibid., p. 127; "Bannathikan thalaeng" (Editor's Announcement), *Phutthasasana* 1, 3 (November 1933): 106.
95. Buddhadāsa said that the *Krunthep Deli me* did not put his penname Phutthathat with his article. See Phra Pracha, *Lao wai mua wai sonthaya*, p. 156. The pseudonym, Phutthathat or Buddhadāsa, became more known to people through his articles in the journal, *Phutthasasana* (*Buddhism*), which was launched in May 1933.
96. Narin visited Buddhadāsa at his temple in Bangkok, Wat Pathumkhongkha, on advice from Dhammadāsa. The group of Dhammadāsa agreed with Narin because Narin wanted monks to be strict, instead of being superstitious as was

common then. Dhammadāsa seemed to believe that his brother Buddhadāsa was a strict monk who was critical of superstitions so that both Narin and Buddhadāsa should agree with and help each other. However, Buddhadāsa did not agree with Narin. See Phra Pracha, *Lao wai mua wai sonthaya*, pp. 121–2.

97. Buddhadāsa's first meeting with Phra Lokanatha involved the assistance of Sanya Dhammasakdi, one of Lokanatha's supporters in Thailand (see more details in Chapter 2). After the unsuccessful first tour and the decline in Lokanatha's popularity, Dhammadāsa asked Buddhadāsa to visit the house of Phra Aphaiwong, which Phra Lokanatha announced in *The Mahā Bodhi Journal* as a place he stayed in Bangkok. However, no one seemed to be living in the house, and Buddhadāsa did not meet Phra Lokanatha. See Phra Pracha, *Lao wai mua wai sonthaya*, pp. 129–30. A biography of Lokanatha and his mission are reported in: Karuna Kusalasai, *Chiwit thi luak mai dai* (*Life Without Choice*) (Bangkok: Mae Kham Phang, 1986), pp. 69–93, 240–2, 260–1; Phra Maha Chanya Sutthiyano, *Chiwit lae ngan khong than panyanantha* (*The Life and Work of Ven. Panyanantha*) (Bangkok: Borisat Amarin, 1991), pp. 63–88. According to Karuna, who was one of the novices involved in the tour, Lokanatha, or Salvatore Cioffi before his ordination, was born in Italy and was raised as a Roman Catholic. He completed a bachelor's degree in science at Columbia University in the United States, and in 1925, he was ordained as a Buddhist monk in Burma. In the journal, *The Mahā Bodhi* in January 1933 (2435 Buddhist Era), he advertised three Buddhist world missions, by a Burmese group in 1933, by a Thai and Cambodian group in 1934, and by a Sinhalese group in 1935. This was translated and reported as "Phiksu doen pai phae sasana tang prathet" (A Monk Who Goes to Propagate Buddhism in Foreign Countries), *Phutthasasana* 1, 3 (November 1933): 64–73. Buddhadāsa's journal, *Phutthasasana*, reprinted newspaper and journal articles about Lokanatha's mission in: Vol. 1 Nos. 2, 3, 4; Vol. 2 Nos. 1, 2, 3, 4; Vol. 3 Nos. 1+2, 3; Vol. 4 No. 1; Vol. 5 Nos. 2, 3, 4; Vol. 6 No. 1; and Vol. 7 No. 2.
98. Phra Pracha, *Lao wai mua wai sonthaya*, pp. 112–3; translated by Ito.
99. Ibid., pp. 123–4; translated by Ito.
100. Aside from the case of Narin that I examine in the text, Buddhadāsa's view on K.S.R. Kulap was also rather closer to the royalist elite who discredited Kulap. When Buddhadāsa learned of some works of Kulap and heard a story from Uncle Siang, who actually had had a chance to talk with Kulap, Buddhadāsa agreed that Kulap's works enabled people in the provinces to gain a wider knowledge and were in opposition to the establishment circle. However, Buddhadāsa concluded that Kulap was boasting of his achievement against the king and wanted to become famous so that he insisted unverified information was in fact true. See Phra Pracha, *Lao wai mua wai sonthaya*, p. 43.
101. Phra Pracha, *Lao wai mua wai sonthaya*, p. 121.
102. Not only Dhammadāsa, but many Thai intellectual Buddhists were excited by Lokanatha. The founders of the Buddhist Association of Thailand, such as Phra Ratchathamnithet and Sanya Dhammasakdi, supported the

campaign of Lokanatha who wanted to take Thai monks and novices on the tour. Panyanantha Bhikkhu and Bunchuan Khemaphirat, who later became Buddhadāsa's co-workers of *dhamma* propagation, also accompanied Lokanatha to Burma and India. However, Buddhadāsa did not agree to go on the world tour with Lokanatha, and was rather skeptical about the popularity of Lokanatha. See Phra Pracha, *Lao wai mua wai sonthaya*, pp. 129–30.

103. This article (The Thai title is "Thammai mai pai kap phra lokkanat") was also reprinted in his journal, *Phutthasasana* 2, 1 (May 1934): 210–2.

104. The second of the four points that Buddhadāsa indicated was that it was difficult to practice the *dhamma* on a world tour if one was attracted by the catchy advertisement of traveling the world. The third was that Phra Lokanatha was not trustworthy enough, since he named himself Lokanatha, which can really only indicate the Buddha. The fourth was similar to the third, Lokanatha claimed in a Visakha conference that he would not have taught other people if he was not yet in one of the streams of *arahantship*. That means that Lokanatha, who had already started preaching, had accomplished *arahantship*, but Buddhadāsa could not believe in his claim. See "Parian Dek," "Thammai mai pai kap phra lokkanat," pp. 211–2.

105. Phra Pracha, *Lao wai mua wai sonthaya*, pp. 128–9. Buddhadāsa's critical comment on Dharmapāla's belief in rebirth referred to Dharmapāla's famous words at his death, "Let me be reborn … I would like to be born again twenty-five times to spread Lord Buddha's Dhamma." See Ananda Guruge, ed., *Return to Righteousness*, p. xliii.

106. Prince Damrong first met Dharmapāla when he was visiting India in 1891. Dharmapāla explained his plan of restoring Buddhism in India by making the historical site of Buddhism in Bodhgaya a center for propagating the *dhamma*. However, the Hindu landowner of the Bodhgaya site did not sell the land to Dharmapāla so Dharmapāla sought assistance from Prince Damrong to talk to the governor-general of India to pressure the owner. Damrong declined his cooperation, first because he was a guest of the government of India and unable to intervene in politics. Second, Damrong indicated that propagation of the *dhamma*, which had primary importance over land ownership, could be started from anywhere, so he questioned why they had to start with strife over land. Dharmapāla seemed to be unhappy with Damrong's response and never sought contact to him. See Somdet Krom Phraya Damrong Ratchanuphap, *Nithan borankhadi* (*Ancient Stories*) (Published as a cremation volume for Nang Nian Laphanukrom, 1968), pp. 57–8.

107. Buddhadāsa found in the premises of the abandoned temple that there were many trees of *mok* and *phla*. By those names of the trees, he named the temple Suan Mokkh Phalaram, "a garden of *mok* and *phla* trees," which can also mean "a place having a power for liberation (Pāli: *mokkha*)." See Phra Pracha, *Lao wai mua wai sonthaya*, pp. 155–6.

108. Dhammadāsa, interview.

109. "Prawat nang khluan phanit" (A History of Mrs. Khluan Phanit), *Phutthasasana* 16, 3 (August 1948): 86.

110. "Matu buchanuson" (Commemoration for Mother), *Phutthasasana* 16, 3 (August 1948): 80.
111. "Thalaengkan khong khana thammathan," *Phutthasasana* 3, 1–2 (May– August 1935): 639.
112. See Phutthathat Phikkhu, *Sip pi nai suan mok: lao ruang chiwit nai wai num* (*Ten Years in Suan Mokkh: Talking About the Life When Young*) (Nonthaburi: Kong Thun Wutthi Tham).
113. Buddhadāsa's letter to Dhammadāsa upon his return from Bangkok was reprinted in his biographies: Chit Phibanthaen, *Chiwit lae ngan khong phutthathat* (*Life and Work of Buddhadāsa*) (Bangkok: Sinlapabannakhan, 1977), pp. 38–42; Phra Pracha, *Lao wai mua wai sonthaya*, pp. 106–8.
114. Phra Pracha, *Lao wai mua wai sonthaya*, p. 153; "Thalaengkan khong khana thammathan" (Announcement of the Dhammadāna Group), *Phutthasasana* 1, 1 (May 1933): 12. Later, they stopped paying the rent for the land and temple of Suan Mokkh, because when Buddhadāsa had an audience with Supreme Patriarch Wachirayanawong, he laughed at their over-carefulness of legally hiring a temple in order to let a monk abide there. See Phra Pracha, *Lao wai mua wai sonthaya*, p. 154.
115. "Thalaengkan khong khana thammathan" (Announcement of the Dhammadāna Group), *Phutthasasana* 1, 2 (August 1933): 55.
116. About Narin, see Sakdina Chatrakun Na Ayutthaya, *Chiwit, naew khit, lae kan to su khong 'narinklung' ru narin phasit: khon khwang lok* (*Life, Thought, and Struggle of 'Narinklung' or Narin Phasit: A Man Blocks the World*) (Bangkok: Samnak-phim Matichon, 1993).
117. Although Buddhadāsa and the Dhammadāna Group tried to avoid conflict, some members of the Dhammadāna Group believed strongly in Narin's movement and made Buddhadāsa's teacher Phra Khru Chayaphiwat angry by proposing Narin's ideas. See Phra Pracha, *Lao wai mua wai sonthaya*, p. 136. In the beginning of their activities, troubles were inevitable, for example, some actually distrusted the Dhammadāna Group as "disciples of Narin," and the monk in Suan Mokkh as "crazy." See "Matu buchanuson" (Commemoration and Respect for the Late Mother), *Phutthasasana* 16, 3 (August 1948): 82.
118. Phutthathat Phikkhu, *Sip pi nai suan mok*, p. 2; translated by Ito.
119. Phra Pracha, *Lao wai mua wai sonthaya*, p. 134; translated by Ito.
120. Ibid., pp. 137–8; translated by Ito.
121. Ibid., p. 459; translated by Ito.
122. See Phutthathat, *Sip pi nai suan mok*.
123. Phra Pracha, *Lao wai mua wai sonthaya*, p. 650; translated by Ito.
124. Buddhadāsa recorded reflections of his body and mind in the early days at Suan Mokkh. His notebook was published as: *Anuthin patibat tham: suksa chiwit yang pen witthayasat; banthuk rai wan khana fuk-fon ton yang khem-khon nai wai num* (*Diary of Dhamma Practice: A Scientific Study of Life; Daily Records During the Young days of Strict Training of Self*) (N.p.: Published by people in Nakhon Si Thammarat province as a dedication on the day of Venerable Buddhadāsa's ceasing of his bodily aggregates, n.d.).

Chapter 2

1. The Thai title is *Thai khasem ruam khao*. The wife of the owner of *Thai Khasem*, Khun Ying Khachaseni, was from the Chaiya area, and married a man with the title of Phraya. Dhammadāsa contacted the owner of *Thai Khasem* to place the advertisement for his journal, and the *Thai Khasem* agreed to publish the free coupon of *Buddhism*. See Phra Pracha Pasannathammo (Pracha Pasannadhammo Bhikkhu), *Lao wai mua wai sonthaya: atchiwaprawat khong than phutthathat* (*Talking in the Twilight Years: An Autobiography of Venerable Buddhadāsa*) (Bangkok: Mulanithi Komon Khimthong, 1988), p. 212.
2. "Thalaengkan khong khana thammathan" (News of Dhammadāna Group), *Phutthasasana* (*Buddhism*) 1, 2 (August 1933): 57.
3. According to Metta Phanit, the youngest son of Dhammadāsa who is now responsible for the Dhammadāna Foundation (in Thai, Mulanithi Thammathan), during Buddhadāsa's lifetime, the print run peaked at 2,500 copies. *Buddhism* most recently published 5,000 copies, and retailed in bookshops through book distributors. Metta Phanit, interview, 4 March 1999.
4. "Thalaengkan khong khana thammathan," *Phutthasasana* 1, 2 (August 1933): 58.
5. "Chotmai naksuksa num: chak nakrian thai nai muang manila (Philippines)" (A Letter of a Young Student: From a Thai Student in Manila [Philippines]), *Phutthasasana* 2, 3 (November 1934): 354–7.
6. Karuna contributed 11 articles from August 1935 to May–August 1942.
7. Samak Burawat was inspired by *Buddhism*, and wrote *Phutthapratchaya athibai duai witthayasat* (*Buddhist Philosophy Explained by Science*) (Bangkok: Rongphim Song Tham, 1937) while he was studying in England. See Phra Pracha, *Lao wai mua wai sonthaya*, p. 554; Samak Burawat, "Suan mokkhaphalaram," in *Ha-sip pi suan mok: phak nung mua khao phut thung rao* (*Fifty Years of Suan Mokkh: Part I When They Spoke of Us*) (Bangkok: Suan Usom Mulanithi, 1982), p. 1157. Sot Kuramarohit contributed three articles in *Buddhism*: "Top a'ngun on ruang kanbuat" (Answering A'ngun On about Ordination), *Phutthasatsana* 2, 4 (February 2477/1935): 418–30; "Chotmai naksuksa num" (A Letter of a Student), *Phutthasatsana* 3, 1–2 (May–August 1935): 469–76; and "Anatta kap atta" (Non-Self and Self), *Phutthasatsana* 3, 4 (February 2478/1936): 701–10.
8. Phra Maha Thongsup Charuwanno, "Thalaengkan buang ton" (Foreword), *Thammachaksu* 22, 2 (November 1936): ko.–kho.
9. The original Thai title is "Tam roi phra arahan."
10. The original Thai title is "Phuttha prawat chak phra ot."
11. Thammathat, "Samrap naksuksa num," *Phutthasasana* 1, 2 (August 1933): 39.
12. The announcement did not openly say that there existed some opposing opinions against foreign articles, but it attempted to explain the editorial policy

of including various kinds of articles, such as scriptural translation, sermons, and translations of foreign articles. See "Thalaengkan," *Thammachaksu* 27, 4 (January 1942). *Thammachaksu* resumed publishing translated articles from foreign journals after the end of the Second World War.

13. Details introduced in Chapter 1 also support this view. See also footnotes 44 and 45, Chapter 1.
14. "From Siam," *The British Buddhist* 8, 2 (January–March 1934): 114–5.
15. The same editorial style can be found in a journal, *Suksa Thammada*, which was published from 1919 until at least 1924 by a lay Buddhist group, and from which Dhammadāsa said that he gained an idea for his journal, *Buddhism*. Dhammadāsa, interview. The *Suksa Thammada* is held in the National Library of Thailand from vol. 2 (1920) to vol. 6 (1924).
16. Buddhadāsa mentioned that A'ngun On was actually Dhammadāsa in his interview with Phra Pracha. See Phra Pracha, *Lao wai mua wai sonthaya*, p. 216.
17. A'ngun on (under the pseudonym Dhammadāsa), "Ruang samrap naksuksa num: chotmai naknangsuphim num" (For Young Students: A Letter from a Young Newspaper Reporter), *Phutthasasana* 2, 1 (May 1934): 172–5.
18. Khaisaeng, "Chotmai top naknangsuphim num," *Phutthasasana* 2, 2 (August 1934): 296–9.
19. Sot Kuramarohit, "Top a'ngun on ruang kanbuat," *Phutthasasana* 2, 4 (February 2477/1935): 418–30.
20. *Buddhism* issued only one volume of 38 pages on bad-quality paper in the two-year period 1944–1945, and another volume of 21 pages in 1946. It got back to normal production of one issue every three months after February 1947. *Thammachaksu* was also affected by the war and reduced publication from a monthly basis to every four months from October 1945, and the paper used for the two volumes in 1945 and 1946 (vol. 31 nos. 1–4 [October 1945–January 1946], vol. 31 nos. 5–8 [February–May 1946]) were of very bad quality. The paper quality of *Thammachaksu* returned to normal during the period June–September 1946, but appeared every three to two months after that.
21. "Lak 12 kho haeng phra phutthasasana khong nai khritmat hamfre, nayok ho phutthasasanik haeng krung london" (The Twelve Principles of Buddhism by Mr. Christmas Humphreys, the President of London Buddhist Lodge), *Thammachaksu* 31, 9–12 (June–October 1946): 77–84. No translator's name was given.
22. Phutthathat Indapañño, "Lak Phutthasasana 12 kho khong hamfre" (The Twelve Principles of Buddhism by Humphreys), *Phutthasasana* 15, 1 (February 1947): 5–33.
23. According to a biographer of Chitti Tinsaphat (1909–1995), Chitti started following the teachings of Buddhadāsa, because he reached a deep understanding of the book through Buddhadāsa's translation of it, although he had gained neither much understanding nor a strong impression from another translation of the same book by an elder monk. See Khana Nittisat lae

Mulanithi Nittisat Mahawitthayalai Thammasat (The Faculty of Law and the Foundation for the Faculty of Law, Thammasat University), ed., "Prawat lae phonngan sastrachan chitti tinsaphat" (A History and Work of Professor Chitti Tinsaphat), 23 January 1990 (A commemoration video for the 80th anniversary of Prof. Chitti Tinsaphat). Chitti served as a judge, the dean of the Faculty of Law at Thammasat University, and a member of the Privy Council.

24. Phutthathat Phikkhu, "Kho khuan sap kiao kap lak phutthasasana rawang nikai tang tang," *Phutthasasana* 15, 1 (February 1947): 35–48.
25. Wong Mu Lam, "Sut khong wei lang" (Sutra of Wei Lang), *Phutthasasana* 15, 2 (May 1947): 96–123. The *Jeng Yan Daily News* (正言日報), a Chinese-language newspaper published for the local Chinese community in Bangkok, announced Buddhadāsa's Thai translation of *Sutra of Wei Lang* as a "prelude to cross-cultural exchanges between Chinese and Siamese." See *Jeng Yan Daily News*, 28 April 1947. Prof. Eiji Murashima, who discovered this article in his research on political movements in the ethnic Chinese community in Siam, suggested that *Jeng Yan Daily News* is a daily publication of the Kuomingtang (Chinese Nationalist Party); it published Lian Sathiansut's regular column on Buddhism and reported on the activities of the Institute for Studies of Chinese Buddhism (中華佛學研究社), such as Tan Mo Siang's Zen lecture supported by Sathian Phothinantha's translation and the active participation of Kuomintang cadre. See *Jeng Yan Daily News*, 23 August 1947.
26. Phra Pracha, *Lao wai mua wai sonthaya*, p. 501.
27. Sawami Sathayananthaburi (Swami Satyananda Puri), "Ruang winyan" (About *viññāṇa*), *Thammachaksu* 26, 8 (May 1941): 890–902; Sawami Sathayananthapri, "Khwam-kao-na haeng sasana" (Progress in Religion), *Thammachaksu* 26, 11 (August 1941): 1184–8; Sawami Sathayananthapri, "Kala haeng sasana" (Time in Religion), *Thammachaksu* 27, 10 (July 1942): 879–84.
28. See Chapter 2, footnote 84.
29. The date of the speech is uncertain. His speech was given in English, and published in D.N. Das, ed., *Speeches and Writings of Swami Satyananda* (Bangkok: Thai-Bharata Cultural Lodge, 1940), pp. 1–38.
30. M.C. Varnvaidya Varavarn (Wan Waithayakon), "My Impressions of Swami Satyananda Puri's Lecture on the 'Origin of Buddhistic Thoughts,'" *Maha-witthayalai* (*University*) 10, 5 (1932): 630–3.
31. Phra Ratchathamnithet, "Khwam-nuk chua khana" (A Thought in a Moment), *Mahawitthayalai* 10, 6 (1932): 813–9.
32. Phutthathat Phikkhu, "Top panha batluang," *Phutthasasana* 7, 3–4 (November 1939–February 1940): 280–335.
33. Mom Chao Chatchawarit Kasemsan, "Kham-top panha khong batluang khong mom chao chatchawarit," *Thammachaksu* 24, 10 (February 2482/1940): 959–73.
34. Suchip Punyanuphap, "Khamnam nai kanphim khrang thi raek" (Introduction for the First Printing), in *Sasana Priap Thiap* (*Comparative Religions*) (Bangkok: Mahamakut Ratchawitthayalai, 1961, 1997), p. kho.

35. "Sut-thai lua khon diaw" (At the End, Being Left Alone), *Phutthasasana* 16, 3 (August 1948).
36. Prayun Wathayanakun, "Wan idilawat ha," *Phutthasasana* 21, 3–4 (August–November 1953): 127–32.
37. Phutthathat Phikkhu, "Thamma khu phra chao?" (Is the *Dhamma* 'God'?), *Phutthasasana* 31, 3–4 (August–November 1963).
38. For examples, Khukrit Pramot (Kukrit Pramoj), "Chalachon nai wiatnam tai" (Uprisings in South Vietnam), *Thammachaksu* 48, 11 (August 1963); Khukrit Pramot, "Hetkan nai wiatnam tai" (Incidents in South Vietnam), *Thammachaksu* 48, 12 (September 1963); Khukrit Pramot, "Khwam-wunwai thi wiatnam tai" (Confusions in South Vietnam), *Thammachaksu* 49, 1 (October 1963); Khukrit Pramot, "Phuttha borisat nai wiatnam tai" (Buddhists in South Vietnam), *Thammachaksu* 49, 2 (November 1963); Khukrit Pramot, "Ratthaban wiatnam tai kap phuttha borisat" (South Vietnamese Government and Buddhists), *Thammachaksu* 49, 2 (December 1963).
39. Before the 14 October uprising in 1973, Sulak's articles in *Phutthachak* included in the special issue, "Khrongkan oprom phra phikkhusu phua songsoem kan-phatthana thongthin" (The Project of Training Monks for Promoting Rural Development), *Phutthachak* 23, 7 (July 1969); Sulak Siwarak (Sulak Sivaraksa), "Wat kap kan-anurak sinlapakam lae saphap waetlom" (Temples and Fine Arts and Environment Conservation), *Phutthachak* 26, 12 (December 1972); So. Siwarak (Sulak Sivaraksa), "Champen tong mi sasana ru mai" (Is it Necessary for Us to Have Religion or Not?), *Phutthachak* 27, 2 (February 1973): 22–6; So. Siwarak, "Damrong chiwit yu phua arai" (For What Do We Live?), *Phutthachak* 27, 3 (March 1973): 12–6. The articles of Sulak and his group of engaged Buddhists often appeared again near to the 6 October coup in 1976. Their articles included: Tit Nat Han (Thich Nhat Hanh), "Baep fuk hat samrap charoen sati," *Phutthachak* 30, 4–5 (April–May 1976): 5–11; Nikolat Bennet (Nicolas Bennett?), "Santi withi kap kan-sawaeng-ha thang thi sam" (The Peaceful Method and Pursuit of the Third Way), *Phutthachak* 30, 6–7 (June–July 1976); Prawet Wasi (Prawase Wasi), "Thammai son tham mai dai phon" (Why Do We Not Receive a Result?), *Phutthachak* 30, 7 (July 1976); Sulak Siwarak, "An nuang ma chak kham samphat than kittiwuttho phikkhu" (In Relation to the Interview of Venerable Kittivuḍḍho Bhikkhu), *Phutthachak* 30, 7 (July 1976): 23–5. From around August 1976 when the 6 October coup was approaching, and the violence of counter-insurgency escalated, articles that were related to politics and society disappeared from *Phutthachak*, and by 1977, the journal only published articles on Pāli study and English literature.
40. Phra Pracha, *Lao wai mua wai sonthaya*, p. 217.
41. Chao Khun Chonlathopmakhunnamuni once ordained as a monk by the then monk, Prince Mongkut, who established the Thammayut Order. After he disrobed, he worked for the Office of the Royal Page. After he retired, he once again ordained as a monk, and became the abbot of Wat Khao Bang Sai. When King Chulalongkorn traveled in Chonburi, and learned the background of the

abbot, he raised the ecclesiastical title of the abbot to the level of *phra racha khana*. See "Prawat chao phra Khun somdet phra phutthakhosachan yanawara thera," pp. (1)–(2).

42. The principal was Phra Khru Winaithonchai, a *thananukrom* of Phra Ong Chao Phra Arunniphakkhunakon. See "Prawat chao phra khun somdet phra phutthakhosachan yanawara thera," p. (2). About the meaning of *thananukrom*, see footnote 59, Chapter 1.
43. "Prawat chao phra khun somdet phra phutthakhosachan yanawara thera," pp. (3)–(4).
44. Ibid., pp. (17)–(18); Ubasika Unchit Tirattana, interview, Bangkok, 21 March 1999. According to Unchit, who used to be a high school teacher and later became a co-founder of Suan Usom, or Buddhadāsa's followers' women's place for *dhamma* practice, Somdet Phra Phutthakhosachan (Charoen) directly taught practical *dhamma*. Later, she read Buddhadāsa's journal *Buddhism* and thought that the teachings of Charoen and Buddhadāsa were along the same line. Phra Dunlayaphaksuwaman, one of the judges who assisted Buddhadāsa, also highly respected Charoen as a disciple who had been ordained by him. Thipphawan Patthomsathan (a daughter of Phra Dunlayaphaksuwaman), interview, 22 August 1998; Phra Pracha, *Lao wai mua wai sonthaya*, p. 221.
45. Phra Pracha, *Lao wai mua wai sonthaya*, p. 122.
46. After the change of the Saṅgha Act in 1941 under the Phibun government, in July 1941, Charoen became chair of the ecclesiastical assembly, and in May 1950, he became chair of the ecclesiastical cabinet. He filled many important positions in the Saṅgha throughout his life. See "Prawat chao phra khun somdet phra phutthakhosachan yanawara thera," pp. (4)–(27).
47. "Somdet phra phutthakhosachan yiam lae phak raem nai suan mok" (Somdet Phra Phutthakhosachan Visited and Stayed Overnight at Suan Mokkh), *Phutthasasana* 5, 2 (August 1937): kho.–cho.; Phra Pracha, *Lao wai mua wai sonthaya*, p. 187.
48. Phra Pracha, *Lao wai mua wai sonthaya*, pp. 383–6.
49. Thongsup told Buddhadāsa to expand the book by investigating further the social conditions in India at the time of the Buddha. Buddhadāsa felt that he had clearer understandings in the topic when he visited India in 1955, but by then, Thongsup had already disrobed. At that time, according to Buddhadāsa, Buddhadāsa's work at Suan Mokkh did not allow him to seclude himself to write a book, so the book was left incomplete: only a chapter of the book was done. See Phra Pracha, *Lao wai mua wai sonthaya*, p. 300.
50. Phra Pracha, *Lao wai mua wai sonthaya*, pp. 301–2.
51. Ibid., p. 301.
52. Ibid., p. 463.
53. Ibid., pp. 371–2. About the position of the Propagation Unit under the 1941 Saṅgha Act, see Ishii, *Saṅgha, State, and Society*, p. 105.
54. Karuna Kusalasai, *Chiwit thi luak mai dai* (*Life Without Choice*) (Bangkok: Mae kham phang, 1986), pp. 69–79.

55. The consequence of Lokanatha's mission that I describe here is based on newspaper articles that the Dhammadāna Group reprinted in their journal: "Khao phra lokanat nam phikkhu thai ok pai chak prathet sayam" (News About Phra Lokanatha, Who Leads Thai Monks Out of Siam), *Phutthasasana* 2, 2 (August 1934): 284–94.
56. Chalong Cheyakhom, *Than Bo. Cho. Khemaphirat* (*Venerable Bunchuan Khemaphirat*) (Bangkok: Somsan), p. 43; Phra Maha Chanya, *Chiwit lae ngan khong than panyanantha*, p. 21.
57. Phra Maha Chanya, *Chiwit lae ngan khong than panyanantha*, pp. 63–84.
58. Ibid., pp. 87–8.
59. Ibid., p. 99; translated by Ito.
60. Bo. Cho. (abbr. Bunchuan) Khemaphirat, "Khwam-suam-sun khong phra phutthasasana nai india" (Decline of Buddhism in India), *Phutthasasana* 4, 1 (May 1936): 11–26.
61. "Bannathikan thalaeng" (Editor's Announcement), *Phutthasasana* 4, 2 (August 1936): 217–8.
62. Phra Maha Chanya, *Chiwit lae ngan khong than panyanantha*, pp. 104–5, 108.
63. Ibid., p. 106; translated by Ito.
64. Karuna, *Chiwit thi luak mai dai*, p. 73.
65. Ibid., pp. 76–93.
66. Ibid., pp. 94–103.
67. Karuna Kusalasai, interviews, Bangkok, 6 and 29 November 1998; "Thalaengkan khana thammathan" (Announcement by the Dhammadāna Group), *Phutthasasana* 3, 4 (February 1936/2478): 747.
68. These 11 articles of Karuna were: "Chotmai chak samanen thai nai india" (A Letter from a Thai Novice in India), *Phutthasasana* 3, 4 (February 2478/1936): 711–8; "Ngan chalong mulakan kutti wihan nai prathet india" (A Celebration in India for the Foundation of a *Vihāra* Where There Used to Be a *Kuti* [Monk's Hut] Used by the Buddha) 4, 1 (May 1936): 59–64; "Khao di thung phuttha mamaka sayam" (Good News for Siamese Buddhists) 4, 3 (November 1936): 336; "Khao Kan-khluang-wai khong phra phutthasasana nai india" (News about Buddhist Movements in India) 5, 1 (May 1937): 122–6; "Phra maha wihan phutthakhaya" (A *Vihāra* in Bodhgaya) 5, 2 (August 1937): 194–203; "Phutthasasana nai prathet yipun" (Buddhism in Japan) 5, 4 (February 1938): 341–6; "Wanna sut nai india" (Untouchables in India) 6, 1 (May 1938): 41–8; "Phonsawadan khong phra wihan phutthakhaya" (History of the Bodhgaya Temple) 6, 3 (November 1938): 195–202; "Horyoyi — pathom phuttha wihan khong yipun" (Horyoji — The First Temple of Japan) 7, 2 (August 1939): 130–8; "Nam thiao namasakan sathan thi saksit nai india" (Visiting Holy Places in India) 8, 3–4 (November 1940): 183–90; "Kan-phoeiphrae phutthasasana" (Propagation of Buddhism) 10, 1 (February 1942): 93–4.
69. Karuna, interview, 29 November 1998.
70. Karuna published the letters from Buddhadāsa to commemorate his memory. They are collected in: *Phutthathat ramluk: likhit than 'phutthathat' thung*

nong-chai doi tham, 'karuna kusalasai' (*A Memory of Buddhadāsa: Letters from Venerable Buddhadāsa to a Younger Brother in the Dhamma, Karuna Kusalasai*) (Bangkok: Mae Kham Phang, 1993). Karuna also published *Than phutthathat nai khwam-song-cham khong phom: kho to sai so prawatisat khong phutthathat lae suan mok* (*Venerable Buddhadāsa in My Memory: A Chain of History about Buddhadāsa and Suan Mokkh*) (Chaiya: Dhammadāna Foundation, 1998).

71. "Phra phutthasasana sun hai pai chak india yang-rai?" (How Did India Lose Buddhism?), *Thammachaksu* 27, 7 (April 1939): 652–63 and 27, 8 (May 1939): 748–58; "Mahatma nichiren," 27, 10 (July 1939): 935–43 and 27, 11 (August 1939): 1035–42; "Phra phutthasasana nai india patchuban" (Buddhism in Present Day India), 28, 1 (October 1939): 39–51.
72. Karuna, *Chiwit thi luak mai dai*, pp. 104–5.
73. Suksanti Chirachariyawet, ed., *7 rop achan sanya* (Seventh 12-Year Cycle [i.e., 84 years] of Achan Sanya) (Bangkok: Mulanithi Nitthisat, Mahawitthayalai Thammasat, 1991), p. 141.
74. Ibid., pp. 141–2.
75. "Prawat phraya latphli thammaprakhan" (Biography of Phraya Latphli Thammaprakhan), in *Mahawitthayalai chiwit khong phutthathat phikkhu, panya nai phutthasasana nikai sen khong khun prachak* (*A University of Life by Buddhadāsa Bhikkhu, and Insight in the Zen School of Buddhism by Khun Prachak*), ed. Khana Thammathan lae Phu thi Khaorop nai Khunnatham khong Phraya Latphli Thammaprakhan (The Dhammadāna Group and a group which respect the moral principles of Phraya Latphli Thammaprakhan) (A cremation volume for Phraya Latphli Thammaprakhan, 19 September 1968), pp. ko.–tho.
76. Sanya Thammasak (Sanya Dhammasakdi), "Kham ramluk" (A Note of Memory), in *Anuson nai ngan sadet phra-ratcha-damnoen phra-ratcha-than phloeng sop: phraya latphli thammaprakhan (wong latphli)* (*Commemoration for the Cremation: Phraya Latphli Thammaprakhan [Wong Latphli]*) (19 September 1968).
77. Phutthathat Inthapanyo, "Anumothana" (Blessing), in *Mahawitthayalai chiwit khong phutthathat phikkhu*, p. (4); translated by Ito.
78. Ibid., pp. (4)–(5).
79. Phra Pracha, *Lao wai mua wai sonthaya*, p. 184; Phutthathat Inthapanyo, "Anumothana," p. (5).
80. Phraya Pharotratchasuphit was also an important member of the Buddhist Association of Thailand. He was the Association's president and vice-president several times. He is also known as the first contemporary Thai to write a book on vegetarianism through the influence of Phra Lokanatha. See *Thammabannakan nai ngan phra-ratcha-than phoeng sop phraya pharotratchasuphit-thammaphiwitthepsuphabodi (choi hemachan)* (*A Writing on the Dhamma at the Cremation of Phraya Pharotratchasuphit [Choi Hemachan]*) (1970); Phraya Pharotratchasuphit, *Witthi prakop ahan*

mangsawirat (*Recipes for Vegetarian Dishes*) (Bangkok: Chomrom Phim Thammathan Pao Keng Teng).

81. Phra Pracha, *Lao wai mua wai sonthaya*, p. 196.
82. Phutthathat Inthapanyo, "Anumothana," p. (6).
83. Phra Pracha, *Lao wai mua wai sonthaya*, pp. 389, 515.
84. Phutthathat Inthapanyo, "Anumothana," p. (6); *Phutthathat ramluk*, pp. 33, 41, 45; Phra Pracha, *Lao wai mua wai sonthaya*, pp. 509–12, 515–7.
85. Phra Pracha, *Lao wai mua wai sonthaya*, p. 501.
86. Phutthathat Inthapanyo, "Anumothana," p. (8); translated by Ito.
87. Ibid.
88. Ibid., pp. (8)–(9); translated by Ito.
89. Ibid., p. (7).
90. Suksanti Chirachariyawet, ed., *7 rop achan sanya*, p. 149; translated by Ito.
91. The following history of the Buddhist Association of Thailand is based on: Sanya Thammasak (Sanya Dhammasakdi), "Prawat kan-kotang, phonngan, lae khwam-pen-ma nai 35 pi khong phutthasamakhom haeng prathet thai nai phra boromarachupatham" (The History of Establishment, Works, and Transition in the 35 Years of the Buddhist Association of Thailand under Royal Patronage), in *Kham thalaeng kitchakan nai rop pi phutthasakkarat 2533 khong phutthasamakhom haeng prathet thai nai phra boromarachupatham* (*The Announcement of the Activities in the Year 1990 of the Buddhist Association of Thailand under Royal Patronage*) (Bangkok: Samnakngan khong Phutthasamakhom haeng Prathet Thai, 1992), pp. 5–30; Sanya Thammasak, *Nathi khong phutthasamakhom* (*The Duty of the Buddhist Association*) (Bangkok: Phutthasamakhom haeng Prathet Thai, 1961).
92. *Anuson nai ngan phra-ratcha-than phloeng sop: phra ratchathamnithet (phian ratchathamnithet)* (*Commemoration for the Cremation: Phra Ratchathamnithet [Phian Ratchathamnithet]*) (11 April 1966). I am grateful to Prof. Eiji Murashima for his advice as to some of these people's political affiliation to the People's Party.
93. Sanya Thammasak, "Prawat kan-kotang, phonngan, lae khwam-pen-ma ...," pp. 7–8.
94. Ibid., p. 6.
95. Ibid., p. 7.
96. Kamala Tiyavanich, *Forest Recollections: Wandering Monks in Twentieth-Century Thailand* (Chiangmai: Silkworm Books, 1997), p. 187.
97. Sanya Thammasak, "Prawat kan-kotang, phonngan, lae khwam-pen-ma ...," p. 16; translated by Ito.
98. Ibid., p. 10.
99. Ibid., pp. 18–20.
100. This also began in 1934, and was probably the first activity for youth in Thailand, according to Sanya. See Sanya Thammasak, "Prawat kan-kotang, phonngan, lae khwam-pen-ma ...," pp. 12–3.
101. The Buddhist Association was given an opportunity to propagate the *dhamma* on the radio by the Department of Publicity who offered to send a monthly

article on Buddhism "for the propagation and promotion of good morality of people." See Sanya Thammasak, "Prawat kan-kotang, phonngan, lae khwam-pen-ma ...," p. 17; quotation translated by Ito. In 1965, the Buddhist Association broadcasted *dhamma* lectures and *dhamma* conversations 67 times, for a total of 40 hours; in 1966, 53 times for 27 hours; and in 1967, 42 times for 30 hours. See Sanya Thammasak, "Prawat kan-kotang, phonngan, lae khwam-pen-ma ...," p. 17.

102. Sanya Thammasak, "Prawat kan-kotang, phonngan, lae khwam-pen-ma ...," p. 18.
103. Ibid., p. 12. Aside from the journals, the Buddhist Association published and distributed books on the *dhamma*: 36,489 copies in 1965, 43,000 copies in 1966, and 36,610 copies in 1967.
104. Sanya Thammasak, *Nathi khong phutthasamakhom*, p. 10.
105. Sanya Thammasak, "Prawat kan-kotang, phonngan, lae khwam-pen-ma ...," p. 15; translated by Ito.
106. Ibid., p. 15.
107. Ibid., p. 28.
108. The Buddhist Association still called itself in Thai "Phuttha-tham samakhom" then, instead of "Phuttha-samakhom haeng prathet thai" as it is at present.
109. Phra Pracha, *Lao wai mua wai sonthaya*, p. 321.
110. Phikkhu Phutthathat Inthapanyo (Buddhadāsa Indapañño Bhikkhu), "Witthi haeng kan-khao thung phuttha-tham, patthakatha phiset," in *Chumnum patthakatha phuttha-tham* (*Collection of Lectures on the Buddha Dhamma*) (Bangkok: Samnakphim Sukkhaphap Chai, 1992), pp. 1–2; translated by Ito.
111. Ibid., pp. 2–3.
112. Ibid., p. 5; translated by Ito.
113. Ibid., pp. 10–30.
114. Ibid., pp. 41–58.
115. Ibid., p. 40; translated by Ito.
116. About Chao Phraya Thammasakmontri, see Chonthila Sattayawatthana, ed., *Khru thep* (Bangkok: Thai Watthana Phanit, 1992).
117. Phra Pracha, *Lao wai mua wai sonthaya*, p. 321; quotation translated by Ito.
118. In Thai, the lecture's title is *Phuttha-tham kap chettanarom khong prachatipatai*. Phra Pracha, *Lao wai mua wai sonthaya*, p. 322.
119. Phra Pracha, *Lao wai mua wai sonthaya*, pp. 321–2. Some of Kulap's summary of Buddhadāsa's lecture are collected in *Ha-sip pi suan mok: mua khao phut thung rao* (*Fifty Years of Suan Mokkh Volume I: When They Talked about Us*) (Bangkok: Suan Usom Mulanithi, 1982). For example, Isarachon (a pseudonym of Kulap Saipradit), "Thi-ni lae thi-nan" (Here and There), originally published in *Prachamit* (10 March 1946), collected in *Ha-sip pi suan mok*, pp. 1201–4; Isarachon, "Phuttha-tham lae santiphap" (The Buddha's *Dhamma* and Peace), originally published in *Suphap Burut* (6 June 1946), collected in *Ha-sip pi suan mok*, pp. 1205–9.
120. Wilat's biographical information here is based on: Wilat Maniwat, interview, Bangkok, 1 February 1999; Chuai Phulaphoem, "Chom na phu-praphan:

wilat maniwat" (The Face of the Writer: Wilat Maniwat), Wilat Maniwat, *Thamma samrap khon nok wat* (*The Dhamma for the People Outside Temples*) (Bangkok: Samnakphim Dok Ya, 1995).

121. Manop (a pseudonym of Wilat Maniwat), "Thamma parithat phutthathat phikkhu" (The *Dhamma* Critique of Buddhadāsa Bhikkhu), originally published in *Nikon Wan Atthit* (9 April 1944), *Ha-sip pi suan mok*, pp. 1166–200.
122. In Thai, the lecture's title is *Phukhao haeng witthi phuttha-tham*. Phra Pracha, *Lao wai mua wai sonthaya*, p. 324.
123. Phra Pracha, *Lao wai mua wai sonthaya*, p. 324.
124. Ibid.

Chapter 3

1. About Chao Khun Ubalikhunupamachan (his name is often referred to by the shortened "Chao Khun Ubali"), see Phra Ubalikhunupamachan (Siricando Chan), *Attanoprawat, thamma banyai lae khirimannatha sut* (*Autobiography, Dhamma Lecture, and Girimaṇḍa Sutta*) (Bangkok: Chomrom Phutthasat Ko. Fo. Pho., 1988). Also, Kamala's study examined Ubali's and other Saṅgha officials' relations with forest monks, especially in "Chapter 7 Relation with Saṅgha Officials," in *Forest Recollections: Wandering Monks in Twentieth-Century Thailand* (Chiangmai: Silkworm Books, 1997), pp. 172–97. Regarding Phra Achan Man and other Thammayut forest monks, see Tambiah, *The Buddhist Saints of the Forest and the Cult of Amulets* (Cambridge: Cambridge University Press, 1984); J.L. Taylor, *Forest Monks and the Nation-state: An Anthropological and Historical Study in Northeastern Thailand* (Singapore: Institute of Southeast Asian Studies, 1993); Kamala, *Forest Recollections*.
2. The following description of Chao Chun's life history is based on Chao Chun Sirorot, *Chiwaprawat nai chun sirorot thi chao-khong khian lao wai eng: pho. so. 2439–2529* (*A Life History of Mr. Chun Sirorot, Which is Written by Himself: 1896–1986*); Dr. Phra Maha Chanya Suddhiñāño, ed., *Chiwit, kho-khit lae ngan khong chao chun* (*Life, Thoughts, and Works of Chao Chun*) (Bangkok: Borisat Amarin). The biography in the latter book was written from interviews with Chao Chun by Phra Maha Chanya. Phenchai Sirorot, interview, Chiang Mai, 15 March 1990.
3. Phra Maha Chanya, *Chiwit, kho-khit lae ngan khong chao chun*, p. 20.
4. Ibid., p. 69.
5. *Phutthacharanuson nai ngan phra-ratcha-than phloeng sop phra yanasitthachan (Luang Pu Sim Phutthacharo)* (*Commemoration of Buddhācāro in the Cremation Ceremony for Phra Yanasitthachan [Luang Pu Sim Buddhācāro]*) (Chiang Mai: Samnak Song Tham Pha Plong, Amphoe Chiang Dao, 1993), pp. 22–3; *Prawat wat santitham, amphoe muang, changwat chiang mai, thi raluk nai ngan chaloeng phra ubosot, phra chedi* (*A History of Wat Santitham, Muang District, Chiang Mai Province, to Commemorate the Celebration of the Hall and the Pagoda*) (1997).

6. Phra Maha Chanya, *Chiwit, kho-khit lae ngan khong chao chun*, pp. 80–1, 83.
7. Ibid., p. 83; quotations translated by Ito.
8. Phra Maha Chanya, *Chiwit, kho-khit lae ngan khong chao chun*, p. 82.
9. Phenchai Sirorot, interview.
10. Ibid.
11. Hans Penth, *History of Wat Umong* (Chiang Mai: Buddhanikom), p. 3. The first article in this booklet was reprinted from: Hans Penth, "A Note on the History of Wat Umong Thera Jan (Chiang Mai)," *The Journal of the Siam Society* 62, 2 (July 1974). The booklet includes another article by the same author: Hans Penth, "Additional Notes on Wat Umong" (February 1987).
12. Hans Penth, *A Brief History of Lan Na: Civilisations of North Thailand* (Chiang Mai: Silkworm Books, 1994), pp. 11–22.
13. *Prawat wat umong suan phuttha-tham* (*A History of Wat Umong Suan Phuttha-tham*) (Chiang Mai: Khana Phuttha Nikhom), pp. 15–20. The English- and Thai-language editions of the Phuttha Nikhom Group's booklets on the history of Wat Umong do not have identical contents. The English edition gives a historian's academic account on the history of the origins of the temple, whereas the Thai edition is based on the tradition that local people have handed down from the past, as well as a translated article of Hans Penth, the history of the Khana Phuttha Nikhom, and Buddhist sayings.
14. *Prawat wat umong suan phuttha-tham*, p. 41.
15. Pathumuttara Phikkhu, "Phikkhu kap kan-riarai," *Phutthasasana* 15, 3–4 (August–November 1947): 155–60.
16. Phra Maha Chanya, *Chiwit, kho-khit lae ngan khong chao chun*, pp. 94–5.
17. Dr. Phra Maha Chanya Suddhiñāño, ed., *Chiwit lae ngan khong than panyanantha* (*Life and Work of Venerable Paññānanda*) (Bangkok: Borisat Amarin Printing Group, 1991), p. 145.
18. The following account of the biography of Paññānanda Bhikkhu is based on: Phra Maha Chanya, *Chiwit lae ngan khong than panyanantha.*
19. About Lokanatha, see Chapter 1, footnote 97 and Chapter 2, pp. 55–8.
20. Details of their meeting are discussed in Chapter 2, p. 57.
21. Phra Maha Chanya, *Chiwit lae ngan khong than panyanantha*, p. 108; quotation translated by Ito.
22. Ibid., p. 125.
23. Ibid., pp. 126–7.
24. Ibid., pp. 129–39.
25. Phra Maha Chanya, *Chiwit, kho-khit lae ngan khong chao chun*, p. 96.
26. Phra Maha Chanya, *Chiwit lae ngan khong than panyanantha*, p. 165.
27. Paññānanda and Phra Ratchawisutthimori, an assistant monk of Paññānanda, interview, Nonthaburi, 7 October 1998. They think that the first standing sermon of Paññānanda was at the train station of Nakhon Si Thammarat before leaving for Bangkok to join the world mission of Phra Lokanatha in 1934.
28. Phenchai Sirorot, interview.

29. Phra Maha Chanya, *Chiwit, kho-khit lae ngan khong chao chun*, p. 97.
30. Phenchai Sirorot, interview.
31. Phra Maha Chanya, *Chiwit, kho-khit lae ngan khong chao chun*, p. 97.
32. Phenchai Sirorot, interview.
33. "Mua than panyanantha phut thung chao chun sirorot" (When Venerable Paññānanda Talked About Chao Chun Sirorot) (Interview with Paññānanda Bhikkhu by Dr. Phra Maha Chanya Suddhiñāño on 2 Februrary 1992), Phra Maha Chanya, *Chiwit, kho-khit lae ngan khong chao chun*, pp. 190, 198.
34. Phenchai Sirorot, interview.
35. Phra Maha Chanya, *Chiwit lae ngan khong than panyanantha*, pp. 165–6; translated by Ito.
36. Ibid., p. 166.
37. Ibid., pp. 227–8; translated by Ito.
38. In Thai, the title was "Than panya ao khon lek ti khanot hang nak Rat." Phra Maha Chanya, *Chiwit lae ngan khong than panyanantha*, pp. 227–8.
39. Phra Maha Chanya, *Chiwit, kho-khit lae ngan khong chao chun*, p. 102.
40. Phra Maha Chanya, *Chiwit lae ngan khong than panyanantha*, p. 220.
41. Phra Maha Chanya, *Chiwit, kho-khit lae ngan khong chao chun*, p. 106.
42. Sanya Thammasak, "Kamnoet phuttha sathan chiang mai" (The Birth of the Chiang Mai Buddhist Hall), in *Phuttha sathan chiang mai* (*A Volume Commemorating the Establishment of the Chiang Mai Buddhist Hall*), ed. Khana Kammakan Klang Chat Tang Phuttha Sathan Chiang Mai (Central Committee for the establishment of the Chiang Mai Buddhist Hall) (1958), pp. 11–7.
43. Sanya Thammasak, "Kamnoet phuttha sathan chiang mai," p. 13; "Rai phra nam — nam phu borichak sang phuttha sathan chiang mai" (The List of Donors' Names to the Chiang Mai Buddhist Hall), in *Phuttha sathan chiang mai*, pp. 203–234.
44. "Kham thalaeng" (Announcement), in *Phuttha sathan chiang mai*, p. 2.
45. Sanya Thammasak, "Phuttha sathan khu arai?" (What is the Buddhist Hall?), in *Phuttha sathan chiang mai*, p. 52; translated by Ito.
46. Udom Bunyaprasop, "Kham rap saraphap" (Confession), in *Phuttha sathan chiang mai*, p. 31.
47. Sanya Thammasak, "Phuttha sathan khu arai?," p. 52. In the commemoration book, there are congratulatory speeches from the Supreme Patriarch and the Ecclesiastical Primate (*Sangkha Nayok*), as well as an article contributed by the ecclesiastical head of Region 5 (*Chao Khana Truatkan Phak 5*) that expressed his approval in the project of the Buddhist Hall. See Somdet Phra Wachirayanawong (the Supreme Patriarch), "Phra owat kham khwan," pp. 5–8; Somdet Phra Wanrat (the Ecclesiastical Primate), "Kham khwan," pp. 9–10; Phra Thammaratchanuwat, "Ruang kiao duai phuttha sathan chiang mai," in *Phuttha sathan chiang mai*, pp. 18–27.
48. Chao Phuttha Nikhom, "Phuttha nikhom kap phuttha sathan" (the Phuttha Nikhom and the Buddhist Hall), in *Phuttha sathan chiang mai*, p. 66; translated by Ito.

49. "Rai phra nam — nam phu borichak sang phuttha sathan chiang mai," in *Phuttha sathan chiang mai*, p. 203; Sanya Thammasak, "Kamnoet phuttha sathan chiang mai," p. 16.
50. See Chapter 6, pp. 175–6.
51. Phra Maha Chanya, *Chiwit lae ngan khong than panyanantha*, pp. 239–40.
52. Phra Khru Sukhanthasin, interview, Chiang Mai, 15 March 1999.
53. Phenchai Sirorot, interview; Dr. Phra Maha Chanya Sutthiyano (Suddhiñāṇo), "Chao chun sirorot: phu mi lom haichai pen thamma" (Chao Chun Sirorot: A Person Who Has Breathed the *Dhamma*), in *Thammaphinanthanakan nai ngan chapanakit sop: chao chun sirorot* (*A Cremation Volume for Chao Chun Sirorot*) (1995), p. 14.
54. Phra Maha Chanya, *Chiwit, kho-khit lae ngan khong chao chun*, p. 107.
55. Sa'at worked as assistant director of the reception division in the Parliament Office. During his work there, Sa'at read books by Buddhadāsa, and with Kiti Sihanon, his friend from Law School, visited Buddhadāsa in Suan Mokkh. As a result of contacting Buddhadāsa's teaching, he quit his job and opened the Suwichan Bookshop. The details about Sa'at Watcharaphai are based on *Anuson nai ngan phra-ratcha-than phloeng sop: nai sa'at watcharaphai* (*Commemoration for the Cremation: Mr. Sa'at Warcharaphai*) (1987); Phra Pracha, *Lao wai mua wai sonthaya: atchiwaprawat khong than phutthathāt* (*Talking in the Twilight Years: An Autobiography of Venerable Buddhadāsa*) (Bangkok: Mulanithi Komon Khimthong, 1988), pp. 314–5, 539; Phra Pracha Pasannathammo and Santisuk Sophonsiri, eds., *Phap chiwit 80 pi phutthathat phikkhu* (*Pictorial Biography of 80 Years of Buddhadāsa Bhikkhu*) (Bangkok: Mulanithi Sathian Koset — Nakhaprathip and Samnakphim Mulanithi Komon Khimthong, 1986), pp. 202, 208–9; and Suvimol Vajrabhaya (Suwimon Watcharaphai), the eldest daughter of Sa'at, interview, Bangkok, 29 August 2000.
56. Phutthathat Inthapanyo, "Anumothana" (Benediction), in *Anuson: nai sa'at watcharaphai*; quotation translated by Ito.
57. Suvimol Vajrabhaya, interview; Arunwati Suwannakanit, "Ngan phoei-phrae phutthasasana ruam thawai than phra achan 'phutthathat phikkhu'" (Cooperative Propagation Activities to Commemorate the Life of Venerable Master Buddhadāsa Bhikkhu), in *Anuson: nai sa'at watcharaphai.*
58. Among the customers were Fak na Songkhla, a famous lawyer defending the man suspected of murdering King Rama VIII; Kuang, then a Singaporean engineer and later ordained as Buddhadāsa's disciple, Phra Kuang Muttibhaḍḍo; Haj Prayun Wathayanakun, the most devoted Muslim follower of Buddhadāsa; and Arunwati Suwannakanit, then a school inspector and one of the founders of Suan Usom, the place for Buddhadāsa's women disciples' *dhamma* practice. See Phra Pracha, *Lao wai mua wai sonthaya*, pp. 314–5, 539; Arunwati Suwannakanit, "Ngan phoei-phrae phutthasasana."
59. "Pho khong rao," in *Anuson: nai sa'at watcharaphai*; Phra Pracha and Santisuk, *Phap chiwit 80 pi phutthathat phikkhu*, p. 202.

60. Pun Chongprasoet's birthdate and career at the Ministry of Foreign Affairs appear in the Ministry's archival document which estimated his pension after his retirement. See "Bamnan khong nai pun chongprasoet" (Pension of Mr. Pun Chongprasoet), NAT (2) ko. to. 2.2.3/53. Pun's close friends, Wirot Siriat and Phra Sithawat Vanivattiko both said that Pun died in 1980. Wirot Siriat, interview, Bangkok, 12 March 1999; Phra Sithawat Vanivattiko, interview, Nonthaburi, 30 April 1999.
61. These years of his graduation were located in the name list of students at Chulalongkorn University and Thammasat University by Prof. Eiji Murashima. I am grateful for his provision of this information. Pun was one of the 33 students who received the Bachelor of Arts in Buddhist Era (B.E.) 2478 (i.e., C.E. April 1935–March 1936) as the first generation of graduates from Chulalongkorn University after it started conferring bachelor degrees. See "Prospectus Faculty of Arts and Science, Chulalankankarana University Session B.E. 2480 (A.D. 1937–38)" (Bangkok: Bangkok Times Press), p. 89. This is Chulalongkorn University's prospectus booklet written in English. As Pun used to write in his signature, O. Bo., Po. Mo., and Tho. Bo., he had degrees and qualification of *Aksonsat bandit* (Bachelor of Arts), *Prakatniyabat khru matthayom* (high-school teacher qualification), and *Thammasat bandit* (Bachelor of Law). See Phutthathat, *Sunyata — chit wang — chit doem thae* (*Emptiness, Empty Mind, and the True, Original Mind*) (Samutprakan: Ongkan Funfu Phutthasasana).
62. "Bamnan khong nai pun chongprasoet," NAT (2) ko. to. 2.2.3/53. According to this archival document, when Pun started his career in May 1933 as the third-class teacher of the Formal Education Department in the Ministry of Education (*Khru-tri, Krom saman suksa, Krasuang thammakan*), his monthly salary was 80 baht; when he retired from the Ministry of Foreign Affairs in November 1961, his monthly salary was 3,800 baht. The amount of his salary also indicates his high socioeconomic status.
63. Pun Chongprasoet, "Naenam nangsu 'khwam-ngom'ngai'" (Book Recommendation, "Superstitious Belief"), in *Tai di kwa yu ru* (*Is it Better to Die Than to Live?*) (Samutprakan: Ongkan Funfu Phutthasasana, 1964), p. 7; Sawai Kaewsom, interview, Bangkok, 21 March 1999.
64. Pun Chongprasoet, "Naenam nangsu 'khwam-ngom'ngai,'" pp. 7–9.
65. Phra Pracha and Santisuk, eds., *Phap chiwit 80 pi phutthathat phikkhu*, p. 216.
66. Pun Chongprasoet, "Kham kho-rong" (A Request), in Phutthathat Phikkhu, *Khu mu manut*, p. 169. I am not sure who the authors of these works that Pun mentioned were. *Khum sap chak phra ot* is a work by Buddhadāsa, but the abridged edition was most possibly a summarization by Pun.
67. Pun found out that people often did not find any value if his books were free. Thus, he later decided to sell his books at cost. See Pun Chongprasoet, "Kham kho-rong," p. 170.
68. Sawai said that Pun asked to sell his publications at Suwichan Bookshop. Sawai Kaewsom, interview, 21 March 1999.

69. Wirot wrote that he bought Buddhadāsa's books that were published by the Organization for the Restoration of Buddhism at the bookshop of Mahamakut Buddhist University in 1958. See Wirot Siriat, "Tai di kwa yu?" (Better to Die Rather Than Live?), in *Tai di kwa yu ru*, p. 5.
70. Pun Chongprasoet, "Kham kho-rong," p. 168.
71. The English edition, *A Handbook for Humankind* and its translations into other languages are based on Pun's summary rather than Buddhadāsa's own sermon. In 1988, the Thammasapha Publisher published a book, *Khu mu manut chabap sombun* (*A Handbook for Humankind: Complete Edition*), which was Buddhadāsa's whole unsummarized preaching to the assistant judges in 1956, even though the title, *Khu mu manut*, was originally given by Pun to his own summary. Thammasapha's *Khu mu manut chabap sombun* is in turn identical to *Lak Phra Phutthasasana*, which was published by Dhammadāna Foundation, and is still published by Sukkhaphap Chai. See Phutthathat Inthapanyo, *Khu mu manut chabap sombun* (Bangkok: Thammasapha, 1988, 1992); Phra Ariyananthamuni (Phutthathat Inthapanyo), *Lak phra phutthasasana: oprom phuchuai phuphiphaksa run raek, pho. so. 2499* (*The Principles of Buddhism: Preaching for the First Generation of Assistant Judges, 1956*) (Bangkok: Sukkhaphap Chai, 1990).
72. Although the volume of *Khu mu manut* that I referred to was printed in April 1959, the book was very likely first published in 1958. This is because the forewords by Buddhadāsa and Pun are dated January 1958, and Wirot Siriat, who was deeply impressed by the book, remembers that he read *Khu mu manut* at the end of 1958. Wirot Siriat, a co-worker of Pun for the *dhamma* propagation, interview, Bangkok, 12 March 1999.
73. Phutthathat Phikkhu, "Anumothana" (Benediction), Phutthathat Phikkhu, in *Khu mu manut* (Bangkok: Ongkan Funfu Phutthasasana, 1959), p. ko; translated by Ito.
74. For instance, Buddhadāsa's instructions on meditation practice, including *Khu mu anapanasai phawana yang sombun baep* (*A Handbook for ānāpānasati bhāvanā: A Complete Manual*) and *Wipatsana rabop lat san* (*Vipassanā: A Shortcut Style*) were summarized by someone under the pseudonym, "Chen-nan-eng" (which literally means "suchness" or "the way it is"; one of the famous expressions of Buddhadāsa) and published by Sukkhaphap Chai in 1990 and 2000, respectively.
75. Pracha Hutanuwatr, personal conversation, May 2005.
76. "Phra ratcha prarop khong phra bat somdet phra mongkut klao chao yu hua (Khat ma chak bot phra ratcha niphon kan thi 9, thetsana sua pa)" (A Statement by King Vajiravudh [Selected from his writing in Chapter 9, Preaching to the Wild Tiger Corps]), in Phutthathat Phikkhu, *Tamra du phra lae winai khong phiksu* (originally published from: Bangkok: Ongkan Funfu Phutthasasana, 1959; the volume referred to here was published in Bangkok by Thammasapha in 1994).
77. "Phiksu o e" (An Idle/Inactive/Inefficient Monk), in Phutthathat Phikkhu, *Tamra du phra lae winai khong phiksu*, p. 12.

78. Pun Chongprasoet, "Phuttha phot: kan hai thamma pen than yom chana kan hai than thang puang" (The Buddha's Saying: Giving the *Dhamma* is the Alms That Would Win Any Kind of Alms), in Phutthathat, *Thamma thi khrai khan mai dai* (*The Dhamma That No One Can Oppose*) (Samutprakan: Ongkan Funfu Phutthasasana).
79. Pun Chongprasoet, "Mahorasop thang winyan," p. 171.
80. Pun listed the titles of his slides as: "Sangwetchaniyasathan" (Four Holy Places of Buddhism: The Places of Birth, Enlightenment, First Preaching, and Final *Nibbāna* of the Buddha), "Thewalok" (The World of Gods), "Rusi chi pluai" (Naked Ascetics), "Khantha kuti phra phuttha chao" (The Buddha's Scented Room), "Phutthakhaya" (Bodh Gaya), "Saranatha" (Sarnath), "Nalantha" (Nalanda), and "Pa himmaphan" (Himavant Forest, or a Forest in the Himalayas). See Pun Chongprasoet, "Mahorasop thang winyan," p. 171.
81. A friend of Sawai Kaewsom, who interrupted my interview with Sawai, a comment, Bangkok, 21 March 1999.
82. A friend of Sawai Kaewsom, a comment.
83. Phra Sithawat Vanivattiko , interview, Bangkok, 30 April 1999.
84. Ibid.
85. *Chiwit lae phon ngan khong achan phon rattanasuan* (*Life and Works of Achan Phon Rattanasuan*) (Bangkok: Rongphim Winyan, 1993), p. 14.
86. Ibid., pp. 13–4.
87. Sawai Kaewsom, interview, Bangkok, 21 March 1999.
88. Phra Phimolatham, "Anuson khun phra thipparinya" (Commemoration for Phra Thipparinya), in *Anuson ngan phra ratcha than phloeng sop: phra thipparinya (thup klamphasut)* (*Commemoration of Phra Thipparinya's Cremation*) (21 May 1977), pp. 13–4.
89. Kittivuḍḍho Bhikkhu, interview, Chonburi, 29 April 1999.
90. *Chiwit lae phon ngan khong achan phon rattanasuan*, p. 14.
91. Sawai Kaewsom, interview, Bangkok, 21 March 1999, 22 August 2000; Kittivuḍḍho Bhikkhu, interview, Chonburi, 29 April 1999; Phra Sithawat Vanivattiko, interview, Nonthaburi, 30 April 1999; Wannasit Waithayasewi, interview, Bangkok, 3 May 1999; Samana Phothirak, interview, Nakhon Phathom, 6 May 1999.
92. The following story about Sawai is based on interviews with him on 21 March 1999 and 22 August 2000.
93. A man who came to talk when I was interviewing Sawai at Thamma Sathan, a place of his *dhamma* talk behind the main library of Chulalongkorn University, on 21 March 1999.
94. See, for example, Phutthathat Phikkhu (Buddhadāsa Bhikkhu), *Phasa khon, phasa tham* (*Human Language and Dhamma Language*) (Bangkok: Thammasapha, n.d.); Donald K. Swearer, trans., ed., *Me and Mine: Selected Essays of Bhikkhu Buddhadāsa* (Albany: State University of New York Press, 1989). Regarding Buddhadāsa's unique interpretation method, Louis Gabaude and Peter A. Jackson have already discussed that in their books. See Gabaude,

"La Théorie Herméneutique," Louis, *Une herméneutique bouddhique contemporaine de Thaïlande: Buddhadāsa Bhikkhu* (Paris: École Française d'Extrême-Orient, 1988); Jackson, "*Phasa khon–phasa tham*: Buddhadāsa's Method of Scriptural Interpretation" and "Buddhadāsa on Rebirth and *paṭicca-samppāda*," in *Buddhadāsa: Theravāda Buddhism and Modernist Reform in Thailand* (Chiang Mai: Silkworm Books, 2003).

95. Phra Pracha, *Lao wai mua wai sonthaya*, pp. 315, 493–4.
96. Pun Chongprasoet, "Maihet" (An Endnote), in *'Rian-ru phutthasasana phai-nai 15 nathi' khong pun chongprasoet, kayai-khwam duai ruang 'tai laew ca koet ru mai' khong than phutthathat* (*Learn Buddhism in 15 Minutes, Expanded Interpretation of 'Is There Rebirth After Death or Not' by Venerable Buddhadāsa*) (Samutprakan: Ongkan Funfu Phutthasasana, n.d.), p. 18; translated by Ito.
97. Sawai Kaewsom, *Tai koet, tai sun, panha lok taek ru?* (*Is It a Problem That Could Divide the World: After Death, Are We Reborn or Do We Disappear?*) (A Cremation Volume for Phirawut Kaewsom, 18 Feruary 1990) (Bangkok: Somchai Kanphim, 1990), p. 18; translated by Ito. Round brackets are Sawai's notes; square brackets are Ito's.
98. Sawai Kaewsom, interview, Bangkok, 21 March 1999.
99. Phra Pracha, *Lao wai mua wai sonthaya*, pp. 315–6; translated by Ito.
100. Sathiangphong Wannapok, interview, Bangkok, 30 April 1999.
101. Sathiangphong Wannapok, interview, 30 April 1999. See Sathiangphong Wannapok, "Tai-koet chua khana chit" (Death and Birth in a Moment of Mind), in *Thamma khong luang pho phutthathat* (*Dhamma of Venerable Buddhadāsa*) (Bangkok: Thammasapha, 1994), pp. 67–9.
102. Sawai Kaewsom, interview, 21 March 1999.
103. Sawai Kaewsom, "Krai? khu phu-ko-kanrai," Kaptan Samut (pseudonym of Samak Burawat), *Phutthit phachoen na kap kommiunit* (*Buddhism in the Face of Communism*) (Klum yaowachon itsara, 1974), pp. 81–94. According to Sawai, this book was published by a group of students at Thammasat University. Sawai, interview, 22 August 2000.
104. About Prasoet Sapsunthon, see Chapter 6, pp. 166–70.
105. Sawai, interview, 21 March 1999.
106. The following story about Wirot's life is based on an interview on 12 March 1999, and his article, "Tai di kwa yu?," in a booklet, *Tai di kwa yu ru* (*Is it Better to Die Rather Than to Live?*) (Samutprakan: Ongkan Funfu Phutthasasana, 1964).
107. Wirot Siriat, "Tai di kwa yu?," pp. 3–4.
108. Ibid., p. 4.
109. Phutthathat Phikkhu, *Khu mu manut*, pp. 35–8; translated by Ito.
110. Wirot Siriat, "Tai di kwa yu?," p. 5; translated by Ito.
111. Wirot, interview, 12 March 1999.
112. There is a prose attached to the picture. See Figure 3.3 and its caption.
113. Wirot, interview, 12 March 1999.

114. The first printing of the second volume, *Ekkasan Chut Mong Dan-nai Andap 2: Ruang Phai Khong Phutthasasana Khong Phutthathat Phikkhu* (*The Series of Documents Looking Inside No. 2: Danger to Buddhism by Buddhadāsa Bhikkhu*), does not give the year of its publication. However, it should be sometime after late 1966, because Buddhadāsa's sermon was given on 23 January 1966. 100,000 copies of this book were printed. Another example: 500,000 copies of the second printing of the seventh volume, *Tham Bun Sam Baep* (*Three Kinds of Merit Making*), were printed in 1968. These examples of the early printings indicate that the Sublime Life Mission vigorously published a great many copies of Buddhadāsa's works within a very short period.
115. Khana phoei phrae phuttha-tham (The *dhamma* propagation group), "Krap rian than phu borichak" (A Report for the Donors), in *Phai khong phutthasasana*.
116. Pracha Hutanuwatr, interview, Bangkok, 1 May 1999.
117. Weng Tochirakan, interview, Bangkok, 31 August 1999.
118. Phra Pracha, *Lao wai mua wai sonthaya*, p. 316.
119. Ibid.; Khana thammathan lae phu thi khaorop nai khunnatham khong phraya latphlithammaprakhan (The Dhammadāna Group and a Group Which Respects the Moral Principles of Phraya Latphlithammaprakhan), ed., *Mahawitthayalai chiwit khong phutthathat phikkhu, panya nai phutthasasana nikai sen khong khun prachak* (*A University of Life by Buddhadāsa Bhikkhu, and Insight in the Zen School of Buddhism by Khun Prachak*) (A Cremation Volume for Phraya Latphlithammaprakhan, 19 September 1968); Phutthathat Inthapanyo (Buddhadāsa), "Kham prarop" (Preface; dated 22 January 1970), "Phutthaprawat chak phra ot" (The Life of the Buddha in His Own Words) in *Thammakhot khong phutthathat* (*The Dhamma Propagation of Buddhadāsa*), series no. 1, 12th edition (Chaiya: Thammathan Muranithi, 1992).
120. Phra Pracha, *Lao wai mua wai sonthaya*, p. 317; Upāsikā Chalo Kengrangwat, interview, Suan Usom, Bangkok, 20 August 1998.
121. Metta Phanit, interview, Suan Mokkh, 9 May 2005.
122. In English, for example, "Buddhadāsa Bhikkhu — Handbook for Mankind," at <http://www.buddhanet.net/budasa.htm> [accessed 26 December 2006]; Ven. Buddhadāsa Bhikkhu, "Anapanasati — Mindfulness of Breathing," at <http://www.buddhanet.net/ebooks_m.htm> [26 December 2006]; Buddhadāsa Bhikkhu, "The Dhamma Truth of Samatha-Vipassana for the Nuclear Age," "The Prison of Life," at <http://www.dharmaweb.org/index.php/Category:Buddhadāsa_Bhikkhu> [accessed 26 December 2006]. In Chinese, for example, 佛使比丘、「人类手册」、「上座部佛教的某些殊胜特色」 at <http://www.mba.net.my/BuddDatabase/FoXueWenJi/Buddhadasa/Index.htm> [accessed 26 December 2006].
123. Metta Phanit, interview, Suan Mokkh, 9 May 2005.
124. See S.J. Tambiah, "The Ideology of Merit and the Social Correlates of Buddhism in a Thai Village," in *Dialectic in Practical Religion*, ed. E.R. Leach (Cambridge: Cambridge University Press, 1968), pp. 41–121.

Chapter 4

1. Louis Gabaude, *Une herméneutique bouddhique contemporaine de Thaïlande: Buddhadāsa Bhikkhu* (Paris: École Française d'Extrême-Orient, 1988), pp. 119–21.
2. Peter Jackson, *Buddhadāsa: Theravada Buddhism and Modernist Reform in Thailand* (Chiang Mai: Silkworm Books, 2003), especially "Cit-wang and the Abolition of the Monk-Lay Distinction," pp. 129–53; "The Practice of Cit-Wang," pp. 155–75; "Cit-Wang and Zen," pp. 177–200.
3. For instance, Jackson, *Buddhadāsa*, pp. 180–1.
4. Wong Mu Lam (Phutthathat Phikkhu trans.), "Sut khong wei lang," *Phuttha-sasana* 15, 2 (May 1947): 96–123.
5. *The Sutra of Wei Lang* was first translated to English by Wong Mou-lam in 1930 and published by Yu Ching Press in Shanghai, and a new edition was published in 1944 by Christmas Humphreys in London. See "Forward to New Edition," Luzac & Co., p. 5.
6. Phra Pracha Pasannathammo, *Lao wai mua wai sonthaya: atchiwaprawat khong than phutthathat* (*Talking in the Twilight Years: An Autobiography of Venerable Buddhadāsa*) (Bangkok: Mulanithi Komon Khimthong, 1988), p. 501.
7. Phutthathat Inthapanyo, "Anumothana," in *Mahawitthayalai Chiwit*, pp. (3)–(4).
8. The biographical information of Tan Mo Siang here is based on his cremation volume, *Anuson ngan phra ratchathan phloeng sop nai phaet tan mo siang (chanwang)* (*Commemoration at the Cremation Ceremony for Dr. Tan Mo Siang [Chanwang]* [his family name in Thai — note by Ito]), cremation date: 19 January 1995.
9. Tan Mo Siang was a Chinese migrant who as a young boy followed his parents to Thailand from mainland China. He studied Thai for two years at a school in Thailand; after that, he returned to China and completed high school study in Shantou, Guangdong province (広東省汕頭). In China, he gained expertise in classical Chinese literature and traditional Chinese medicine. At the age of 25, Tan Mo Siang returned to Thailand and started his career as a doctor of traditional Chinese medicine. As a doctor, Tan Mo Siang served poor people without charging any fees. As an exceptional Chinese intellectual living in Thailand, aside from the Thai-Chinese Buddhist Association, of which he was one of the co-founders, and another local Chinese Buddhist association called Pao Keng Teng (保宮亭), Tan Mo Siang delivered speeches and published articles about the philosophies of Chinese Zen and *bodhisattva* in many prestigious religious and academic institutions in Thailand, including the Buddhist Association of Thailand, the Young Buddhist Association of Thailand, Mahamakut Buddhist University, and Royal Academy of Thailand. His biographer wrote that Tan Mo Siang was loved among both the local Chinese migrant community and Thai intellectuals and royal family members, because of his humble and friendly personality. See "Prawat nai phaet tan mo siang" (Biography of Dr. Tan Mo Siang), in *Anuson ngan phra ratchathan phloeng sop nai phaet tan mo siang*, pp. 7–21.

10. "Prawat nai phaet tan mo siang," p. 15.
11. Phra Pracha, *Lao wai mua wai sonthaya*, pp. 501–2.
12. Later, Tan Mo Siang further helped Buddhadāsa to find traditional Chinese Buddhist pictures for the Spiritual Amusement Hall (*Rong mahorasop thang winyan*) in Suan Mokkh. See "Prawat nai phaet tan mo siang," p. 16.
13. Along with several other publishers, those translation by Buddhadāsa of Mahāyāna texts have been reprinted many times by "Thirathat" (Thira Wongphophra), a local Chinese Zen Buddhist teacher living in Bangkok and have been distributed free for propagation purposes by Phutthasamakhom Pao Keng Teng (保宫亭).
14. The *Dhammadinna Sutta* is in *Mahā-vagga, Saṃyutta-nikāya, Sutta-piṭaka.* See M. Léon Feer, ed., *Saṃyutta-nikāya Part V Mahā-vagga* (London: Pāli Text Society, 1960), pp. 406–8.
15. These *sutta* are in the *Suññatāvagga, Uparipaṇṇāsa, Majjhima-nikāya*. The Pāli text is in Robert Chalmers, ed., *The Majjhima-nikāya* vol. III (London: The Pāli Text Society, 1960), pp. 104–18. For the discussion here, the following two English translations were referred to: I.B. Horner, trans., *The Collection of the Middle Length Sayings* (*Majjhima-nikāya*) vol. III (London: The Pāli Text Society, 1959), pp. 147–62; and Bhikkhu Ñānamoli, trans., and Bhikkhu Bodhi, trans., ed., rev., *The Middle Length Discourse of the Buddha* (Boston: Wisdom Publications, 1995), pp. 965–78.
16. Including one occurrence in the *Dhammadinna Sutta*, this phrase is mentioned altogether four times in the *Suttapiṭaka*, according to Lamotte's study on emptiness in certain Buddhist scriptures. It appears in "Aṇi," in *Saṃyutta-nikāya Part II Nidāna-vagga*, ed. M. Léon Feer (London: The Pāli Text Society, 1960), p. 267; Richard Morris and A.K. Warder, eds., *Aṅguttara-nikāya Part I* (London: The Pāli Text Society, 1961), p. 72; Richard Morris and A.K. Warder, eds., *Aṅguttara-nikāya Part III* (London: The Pāli Text Socity, 1961), p. 107. See Étienne Lamotte, *Le traité de la grande vertu de sagesse de Nāgārjuna*, p. 2004.
17. Étienne Lamotte, "Les Dix-Huit Vacuités," in *Le traité de la grande vertu de sagesse de Nāgārjuna: Mahāprajñāpāramitāśāstra: Avec une étude sur la vacuité*, Volume IV (Louvain: Institut Orientaliste, Université de Louvain, 1974), pp. 1995–2013. I thank Dr. Royce Wiles for translating from and discussing Lamotte's philological study.
18. Phutthathat, *Kan-tham-ngan duai chit wang phua sangkhom khong than phutthathat* (*Working with the Empty Mind for the Sake of Society by Venerable Buddhadāsa*) (Samutprakan: Ongkan Funfu Phutthasasana), pp. 7–8; Phutthathat, *Sunyata — chit wang — chit doem thae khong than phutthathat* (*Suññatā, Empty Mind, and Original Mind by Venerable Buddhadāsa*) (Samutprakan: Ongkan Funfu Phutthasasana), p. 2.
19. Phutthathat, *Kan-tham-ngan duai chit wang phua sangkhom*, pp. 7–8; translated by Ito.
20. The bracketed phrase was given by either Buddhadāsa or Pun Chongprasoet, the editor of the book, Phutthathat, *Sunyata — chit wang — chit doem thae*, p. 17.

21. Phutthathat, *Sunyata — chit wang — chit doem thae*, p. 17; Ito's translation from Buddhadāsa's words in Thai. Buddhadāsa often mentioned this phrase in his sermons. In Pāli, the latter half of the phrase seems to be *Sabbe dhammā nālam abhinivesāya*. See Ranchuan Inthrakamhaeng, *Suan mok thammai? Thammai suan mok?* (*Why Suan Mokkh? Suan Mokkh, Why?*) (Bangkok: Attamayo, 1991), p. 32.
22. Phutthathat, *Sunyata — chit wang — chit doem thae*, p. 10. This is Ito's English translation of Buddhadāsa's Thai translation of the Pāli phrase.
23. Phutthathat, *Sunyata — chit wang — chit doem thae*, pp. 11–2; translated by Ito.
24. Ibid., pp. 14–5.
25. Ibid., pp. 3–4.
26. The *Dhammadinna Sutta* is in *Mahā-vagga, Saṃyutta-nikāya, Sutta-piṭaka*. See M. Léon Feer, ed., *Saṃyutta-nikāya Part V Mahā-vagga* (London: Pāli Text Society, 1960), pp. 406–8.
27. F.L. Woodward, ed., *The Book of the Kindred Sayings (Saṃyutta-nikāya) or Grouped Suttas: Part V (Mahā-vagga)* (London: The Pāli Text Society, 1965), p. 348.
28. Arun, *Wiwattha*, pp. 114–21.
29. Phutthathat, *Kan-tham-ngan duai chit wang phua sangkhom*, p. 17.
30. Phutthathat, *Sunyata — chit wang — chit doem thae*, pp. 7–8.
31. According to Paññānanda Bhikkhu, a co-worker of Buddhadāsa's *dhamma* propagation, Buddhadāsa said, "I used to think that it would take 20 years for people to understand *suññatā*, but nowadays it looks like it will not take so long. This is because Kukrit helped very much. He helped by criticizing it and making people interested in it. People will be able to read and study in various newspapers, which helps to stimulate them to study." See Panyanantha Phikkhu (Paññānanda Bhikkhu), "Chiwit lae phonngan khong than phutthathat" (Life and Work of Venerable Buddhadāsa) (originally spoken on 2 February 1986), in *Chiwit lae phonngan khong than phutthathat* (Bangkok: Atammayo), p. 20.
32. Sanya Thammasak (Sanya Dhammasakdi), "Phutth-tham kap chiwit kan-ngan" (Buddha *Dhamma* and a Life of Work), in *Arai thuk, arai phit*, ed. Pun Chongprasoet (originally published by Ongkan Funfu Phutthasasana, 1973; reprinted by Mulanithi Phoei Phrae Chiwit Prasoet, 1982), p. 165. According to Sanya, King Bhumibol used the term "empty mind" many times when speaking to him. When Sanya, a member of the Privy Council, was worrying that he did not have a good idea about something that the king wished to discuss, King Bhumibol told him to have empty mind.
33. The Thai title was "Thamma nai thana pen khruang mu sang khon, sang chat, lae sang lok." There are several books that collect Buddhadāsa and Kukrit's discussions at the Khurusapha. Here I refer to Arun Wetchasuan's edition, one of the large-circulation editions. Arun wrote that the version that Pun Chongprasoet's Organization for the Restoration of Buddhism prepared had been widely read, but it was an incomplete record of the whole discussion, omitting the beginning and the end. See Arun Wetchasuan,

"Kham nam" (Introduction), in *Wiwattha: khwam-hen mai trong kan rawang mom ratchawong khukrit pramot kap than phutthathat phikkhu* (*Dispute: Disagreement of Opinions between M.R.W. Kukrit Pramoj and Venerable Buddhadāsa Bhikkhu*), ed. Arun Wetchasuan (Bangkok: Arun Witthaya, 1977, 1996), p. 8. Also, Pun's edition only contained the second of the three Khurusapha events, while Arun's provides all three with precise details of time and date.

34. Although their reputations could have been different in the 1960s, in an opinion poll, both Kukrit and Buddhadāsa were elected to the list of "Ordinary citizens [i.e., non-royal family] too precious to leave the world" (*Kan-chak-pai khong samanchon thi khon sia-dai mak thi sut*) and were in the top ten of its ranking in 1999. Kukrit was in third place, winning 31.5% of the votes, while Buddhadāsa was in sixth place, with 20.9% of the votes. See "Khrongkan samruat prachamati phua sathon phap ruam sangkhom, kanmuang, watthanatham thai kon pi 2000" (Public Opinion Survey for Reflecting a Total Picture of Thai Society, Politics, and Culture before 2000), in *Thai phot* (*Thai Post*, a daily newspaper), 13 December 1999, p. 2.
35. Kasaem Sirisamphan, Sunthari Asawai, Atcharaphon Kamutthaphisamai, Sathaban Thai Khadi Suksa, eds., "Prawat mom ratchawong khukrit pramot" (A Life History of M.R.W. Kukrit Pramoj), in *Anuson nai ngan phra ratcha than phloeng sop satstrachan phon tri mom ratchawong khukrit pramot, po. cho., mo. po. cho., mo. wo. mo.* (*Commemoration at the Cremation of Professor Major General Mom Ratchawong Kukrit Pramoj, Pathom Chulachomklao, Maha Paramaphon Chang phuak, Maha Wachira Mongkut* [these three are decorations that Kukrit received from the king]) (23 December 1995), pp. 43–51.
36. Arun, "Kham nam," in *Wiwattha*, p. 6.
37. Arun, *Wiwattha*, pp. 15–6.
38. Ibid., p. 59; the quotations translated by Ito.
39. Ibid., p. 65; translated by Ito. For this argument, the definition of the *dhamma* that Buddhadāsa explained should be noted. He said on another occasion, "The word, *dhamma*, according to Pāli or Sanskrit, has four meanings. [First,] it is all nature, earth, water, wind, fire, mind, form; anything that is nature itself is called the *dhamma*. [Second,] all nature has the laws of nature (Pāli: *dhammajāti*). For example, it has impermanence, suffering, non-self, and so on. These are called laws of nature. [Third,] it is the duty of human beings to practice. Morality, meditation, wisdom, or the duties of human beings in whatever occupation they do for a living are called the *dhamma*. [Fourth,] various fruits that arise from doing duties, for example, happiness, suffering, money or whatever, are called the *dhamma* just as they are." See Phinit Rakthongko, ed., *Thammanukrom thammakhot* (*Thammakhot* [this literally means "*dhamma* propagation"; it is a title of the collection of Buddhadāsa's works] *Dictionary of the Dhamma*) (Chaiya: Thammathan Mulanithi, 1994), p. 132. This book, *Thammanukrom thammakhot*, is a dictionary of important Buddhist concepts that one of Buddhadāsa's lay disciples codified from the 12 books in the *Thammakhot*, the collection of Buddhadāsa's works.

40. Arun, *Wiwattha*, pp. 66–7; the quotation translated by Ito.
41. Ibid., p. 71; translated by Ito.
42. The article was later reprinted in a collection of Kukrit's columns, *Phutthasasana kap khukrit* (*Buddhism and Kukrit*), cited in Arun, "Kham nam," p. 6.
43. Although here I focus on their discussion on empty mind, there were in fact two major issues of conflict. Apart from the relevance of empty mind for lay people, Kukrit and Buddhadāsa did not agree on the role of faith (Thai: *sattha*; Pāli: *saddhā*). Kukrit argued that people should first have faith in the triple gem: the Buddha, the Dhamma, and the Saṅgha, and then believe in what the Buddha taught: *dukkha* (suffering), *samudaya* (origin), *nirodha* (cessation), and *magga* (path). Without this first basic faith and understanding of doctrines, Kukrit asserted that people would misunderstand or lose themselves in the world of attachment and suffering. See Arun, *Wiwattha*, p. 109. Buddhadāsa partially agreed with Kukrit in the second session, but after experiencing an escalation of conflict in Kukrit's critical columns, Buddhadāsa took up this point to criticize Kukrit in the third session of the Khurusapha. In it, Buddhadāsa said that Kukrit was trying to bring dogma into Buddhism. According to Buddhadāsa, Buddhism is a religion of *paññā* (wisdom), not of faith, so unlike in religions of faith, dogma does not exist in the religion of *paññā*. Buddhadāsa explained that *saddhā* in Buddhism cannot be faith or belief in religions with dogma. In Buddhism, people should examine everything, then have faith afterward. He referred to the Buddha's teaching to be free (Thai: *itsara*) in thinking, examining and understanding, and in each practice, and also to be self-reliant at all times. Thus, Buddhadāsa said, "To believe in the Buddha, the Dhamma, the Saṅgha, *kamma*, or anything else before having *paññā*, only depends on a person's necessity. It is not a principle of Buddhism at all." See Arun, *Wiwattha*, p. 146.
44. Arun, *Wiwattha*, pp. 81–5.
45. According to *Photchananukrom chabap ratchabandit sathan pho. so. 2525* (*A Thai Dictionary: The Royal Academy 1982 edition*), p. 362, *tai thao* is defined as "A pronoun used for those whom we respect. A personal pronoun." As far as I understand, the second person pronoun, *tai thao*, seems to be equivalent to the third person pronoun, *chao khun*, which is used for those on whom has been conferred a *bandasak* (court title) above the level of *phraya*, or a *samanasak* (ecclesiastical title) above *phra ratcha khana*. See the definition of "chao khun" in *Photchananukrom chabap ratchabandit sathan pho. so. 2525*, p. 219. At the time of this discussion, Buddhadāsa held the ecclesiastical title, Phra Ratchachaikawi, which is the level of *phra ratcha khana*.
46. Arun, *Wiwattha*, pp. 122–4.
47. Ibid., pp. 123–4; translated by Ito.
48. Ibid., p. 133; translated by Ito.
49. As well as empty mind, Buddhadāsa also promoted the application to lay life of some other ideas belonging to *lokuttara dhamma* taught for the purpose of liberation. For example, he said of the four *iddhipāda* (roads to power):

chanda (zeal), *viriya* (will to strive), *citta* (concentration), and *vīmaṃsā* (investigation) for the attainment of *nibbāna*, that farmers can also be mindful of and use these concepts in their daily activities. See Arun, *Wiwattha*, pp. 179–80.

50. Pun Chongprasoet, "Thung than phu an" (To Readers), in *Wiwattha (khwam-mai-hen-trong-kan) rawang mom ratchawong khukrit pramot kap than phutthathat phikkhu* (*A Dispute: Disagreement of Opinions between M.R.W. Kukrit Pramoj and Venerable Buddhadāsa Bhikkhu*) (Ongkan Funfu Phutthasasana, 1 April 1964; reprinted by Bangkok: Pho. Cho. Po., 1986), pp. 5–6.
51. Pun Chongprasot, "Khwam-hen khong mom ratchawong khukrit nai ruang 'chit wang'" (The View of M.R.W. Kukrit on 'Empty Mind'), in Phutthathat, *Sunyata — chit wang — chit doem thae*, p. 22.
52. Ibid., pp. 22–3; translated by Ito. The phrase in parentheses seems to have been added by Pun rather than by Kukrit.
53. Arun, "Kham nam," p. 7.
54. Pun Chongprasot, "Kham nam" (Introduction), in *Arai thuk, arai phit*, ed. Pun Chongprasoet (originally published by Ongkan Funfu Phutthasasana, 1973; reprinted by Mulanithi Phoei Phrae Chiwit Prasoet, 1982). In the book, Pun's summary of Kukrit's article was published as "Khwam-hen bang ton khong mom ratchawong khukrit pramot" (Some Parts of the View of M.R.W. Kukrit Pramoj), in *Arai thuk, arai phit*, ed. Pun Chongprasoet, pp. 1–8.
55. "Khwam-hen bang ton khong mom ratchawong khukrit pramot," pp. 3–4.
56. Ibid., p. 4.
57. Ibid., p. 5; translated by Ito.
58. Ibid., p. 5.
59. Phra Pracha, *Lao wai mua wai sonthaya*, p. 341. Mom Chao Suphasawat is a grandson of King Mongkut, and a son of Prince Sawat. Mom Chao Suphasawat was an elder brother of Queen Rambhai Barni of King Prajadhipok. His father, Prince Sawat, was a younger brother of the grandmother of King Ananda and King Bhumibol. Although by blood, King Bhumibol is closer to Mom Chao Suphasawat than Kukrit, he sought political support from Kukrit rather than Mom Chao Suphasawat. Mom Chao Suphasawat played an important political role as a leader of the Free Thai movement in England, and he supported Pridi Phanomyong, whose downfall was brought about by Kukrit through the mysterious death of King Ananda Mahidol. This personal background indicates that Mom Chao Suphasawat was in opposition to Kukrit in real politics, as well as in the discussion over empty mind in Buddhism. The royal family members are not necessarily aligned against commoners either in politics or discussions of Buddhism. I thank Prof. Eiji Murashima who kindly explained to me these biographical facts about Mom Chao Suphasawat.
60. The fact that in 1960 the Queen Mother recommended inviting Buddhadāsa to give a lecture at Chulalongkorn University indicates that she was in favor of Buddhadāsa's teaching. See Sanya Thammasak (Sanya Dhammasakdi), *Nathi*

khong phutthasamakhom (*The Duty of the Buddhist Association*) (Bangkok: Phutthasamakhom haeng Prathet Thai, 1961), pp. 25–6.

61. Khukrit Pramot (Kukrit Pramoj), "Soi suan phlu," in *Sayam rat rai wan* (*Siamese Nation Daily Newspaper*) (10 July 1993), p. 5. Although this article mainly discussed expressions for death in Thai and the news of Buddhadāsa's death was the introduction of his main argument, Kukrit clearly expressed his respect to Buddhadāsa and his teachings as "... free from superstitious beliefs, containing only scrupulous rationality, the true *dhamma* of the Buddha is unrestricted by time and is provable by ourselves"; translated by Ito.
62. In the publication list of the Organization for the Restoration of Buddhism that was attached to one of its booklets (Than Phutthathat, *Sunyata — chit wang — chit doem thae*), there are at least four relating to Kukrit: *Sunyata — chit wang — chit doem thae*; *Khwam-long-phit khong sangkhom nai ruang kan tham bun* (*The Delusion of Society in Making Merit*); *Arai thuk, arai phit; Wiwattha nai ruang 'chit wang'* (*Disputes About Empty Mind*). Apart from this list, there is: Than Phutthathat, *Kan-tham-ngan duai chit wang phua sangkhom*, which seems to be Pun's summary of Buddhadāsa's third session at the Khurusapha and some other sermons of Buddhadāsa in response to Kukrit.
63. [Pun Chongprasoet], "Maihet khong ongkan funfu phutthasasana" (A Note by the Organization for the Restoration of Buddhism), in Pun Chongprasoet, "Khwam-hen khong mom ratchawong khukrit nai ruang 'chit wang,'" in Than Phutthathat, *Sunyata — chit wang — chit doem thae*, p. 30; translated by Ito.
64. Usually, Pun published booklets, which consisted of a sermon of Buddhadāsa accompanied by his own essay and some supplementary comments on recent incidents and discussions which had taken place in the Thai Buddhist public sphere.
65. Pun Chongprasoet, "Cha tham yang rai chung cha riak wa tham-ngan duai chit wang" (What Should We Do to be Said to be Working with Empty Mind?), in Than Phutthathat (Venerable Buddhadāsa), *Kan-tham-ngan duai chit wang phua sangkhom* (*Working with Empty Mind for Society*) (Samutprakan: Ongkan Funfu Phutthasasana, 1975), pp. 23–9.
66. Ibid., pp. 25–6; translated by Ito.
67. Ibid., p. 29; translated by Ito.
68. Kukrit's argument was first published in *Duang Prathip* in May 1972. Pun's summary of Kukrit's argument is summarized here in this chapter.
69. Phutthathat Phikkhu (Buddhadāsa Bhikkhu), "Uppasak haeng kan phoei phrae tham" (Obstacles in the Propagation of the *Dhamma*) (A lecture given at Wat Mahathat on 28 November 1967), in *Arai thuk, arai phit*, ed. Pun Chongprasoet, pp. 9–71; Phutthathat Phikkhu, "Uppasak haeng kan khao chai thamma" (Obstacles to Understanding of the *Dhamma*) (A sermon at Wat Noranatthasuntharikkaram, Bangkok, on 4 February 1968), pp. 72–109; Pun Chongprasoet, ed., "Chit praphatson — chit doem thae — chit wang (Yo chak kham banyai khong than phutthathat phikkhu)" (A Pure Mind, a True Original Mind, an Empty Mind [A Summary of a Lecture by Venerable Buddhadāsa Bhikkhu]) (A sermon at Suan Mokkh on 28 July 1969), pp. 110–21.

70. Pun Chongprasoet, "Maihet" (An Endnote), in *Arai thuk, arai phit*, ed. Pun Chongprasoet, p. 8.
71. Pun wrote in his note that the handbill was brought to him by a supporter of Sawai Kaewsom at Lan Asok, Wat Mahathat, and that he was publishing it in order for other people with *paññā* to examine what is right and what is wrong. See Pun Chongprasoet, "Maihet" (An Endnote), Kittivuḍḍho Bhikkhu, "Ruang chit wang nok phra traipidok mi khwam samkham nai patchuban mak lae ruang phra phuttha chao son lokkuttara tham nai thammathinna kho plian thamma mai" (About [the teaching of] Empty Mind Which is Not in the *Tipiṭaka* and Places a Lot of Emphasis on the Present Time; and About [the story of how] the Buddha Taught *Lokuttara Dhamma* to Dhammadinna Who Asked for a New *Dhamma*) (Originally published as a mimeographed handbill on Māgha Pūjā 1973), in *Arai thuk, arai phit*, ed. Pun Chongprasoet, p. 131.
72. Charles F. Keyes, "Political Crisis and Militant Buddhism in Contemporary Thailand," in *Religion and Legitimation of Power in Thailand, Laos, and Burma*, ed. Bardwell L. Smith (Chambersburg, PA: ANIMA Books, 1978), pp. 147–64; Kittivuḍḍho Bhikkhu, *Kha khommiunit mai bap* (*Killing Communists is Not Demeritorious*) (Bangkok: Mulanithi Aphitham Mahathat Witthayalai, 1976).
73. Buddhadāsa's grandfather on his father's side came to Thailand, while Kittivuḍḍho's family settled in Thailand during his father's generation. Thus, Buddhadāsa was third-generation Chinese, and Kittivuḍḍho second. Buddhadāsa's mother was ethnic Thai, while Kittivuḍḍho's mother was an ethnic Chinese born in Thailand; her family also originated in Hokkien province. The biographical information about Kittivuḍḍho is based on an interview with Kittivuḍḍho Bhikkhu in Chonburi on 29 April 1999.
74. The training project is called "Nuai kan phatthana thang chit" (A Unit to Develop Mind). It started in 1965 at Wat Mahathat, and in 1968 it moved to Djitthabhawan College, which was then newly built in Chonburi province. Kittivuḍḍho, interview.
75. Phra Sithawat Vanivattiko, interview, Nonthaburi, 30 April 1999. Sithawat has been a follower of Buddhadāsa since he was a novice in Surat Thani in the early 1940s, and he helped Pun Chongprasoet's propagation activities in Wat Mahathat, and later for a long time he cooperated with Wirot Siriat's Sublime Life Mission. Although Kittivuḍḍho was notorious for his defamatory campaign against Buddhadāsa, Sithawat had a fair view about Kittivuḍḍho's intellectual ability.
76. Phra Maha Khachit Siriwattho (The abbot of Suan Mokkh Chiang Rai), interview, Chiang Rai, 16 March 1999.
77. Arun Wetchasuan was born and brought up in Chaiya, the same city where Buddhadāsa originated. Arun was in monastic robes since he was 16, and he disrobed at the age of 38. Arun published many articles and books about Buddhism and Buddhadāsa. Arun Wetchasuan, interview, Bangkok, 2 March 1999.

78. Arun Wetchasuan, interview, Bangkok, 2 March 1999.
79. Here I have summarized the story of the *Dhammadinna Sutta* from Kittiwuttho [Kittivuḍḍho], "Ruang chit wang nok phra traipidok," pp. 126–8, and F.L. Woodward, ed., *The Book of the Kindred Sayings*, pp. 347–9. Kittivuḍḍho's story is basically the same as that in the English edition of the Pāli Text Society's *Tipiṭaka*.
80. Kittiwuttho, "Ruang chit wang nok phra traipidok," pp. 128–9.
81. Ibid., p. 129. Kittivuḍḍho wrote that these phrases appear in page 402 of *Sārattathappakāsinī* (probably one of the Thai script editions), but I was unable to access the Thai script edition. I thank Royce Wiles for finding the text in the *Sārattathappakāsinī* in a Roman script edition, and clarifying the meaning of the original Pāli phrases. English translations of Kittivuḍḍho's Thai translation from Pāli are by Ito.
82. Kittiwuttho, "Ruang chit wang nok phra traipidok," pp. 129–30. *Khajjanika sutta* is located under the title, *Khajjanīya sutta*, in *Saṃyutta-nikāya*, Vol. III (London: Pāli Text Society, 1960), pp. 86–91. An English translation of it is available in "The Prey," in *Kindred Sayings on Elements*, Vol. III (London: Pāli Text Society, 1960), pp. 72–6.
83. Kittiwuttho, "Ruang chit wang nok phra traipidok," p. 130; quotation translated by Ito. Jackson also indicated the inaccurate claim of Kittivuḍḍho. Quoting Kittivuḍḍho's statement, Jackson wrote that Buddhadāsa's critics "mistakenly claim that this [the notion of emptiness — note inserted by Ito] is solely a Mahayana and not a Theravada concept." See Buddhadāsa, *Theravada Buddhism and Modernist Reform in Thailand*, p. 180.
84. Phutthathat Phikkhu, "'Sunyata': huachai khong Phutthasasana" (Emptiness: The Heart of Buddhism), in *Phuttha-tham kam mu diao: ruam botkhwam lae patthakatha khong than phutthathat phikkhu lae khun pun chongprasoet* (*A Handful of the Buddha Dhamma: Collections of Essays and Lectures by Venerable Buddhadāsa Bhikkhu and Mr. Pun Chongprasoet*), ed. Klum Watcharaphon (Bangkok: Klum Watcharaphon).
85. Ibid., pp. 37–8; quotation translated by Ito.
86. The Buddha said, "However, Ānanda, there is this abiding discovered by the Tathāgatha: to enter and abide in voidness internally by giving no attention to all signs." See Robert Chalmers, *The Majjhima-Nikāya* Vol. III, p. 111; Bhikkhu Ñānamoli and Bhikkhu Bodhi, *The Middle Length Discourse of the Buddha*, p. 972, and he explained each level of *jhāna* and *nibbāna*. This passage is also cited in Rune E.A. Johansson, "Nibbāna as Emptiness," in *The Psychology of Nirvāna* (London: George Allen and Unwin, 1969), p. 34.
87. See the phrase quoted by Kittivuḍḍho from *Sārattathappakāsinī*, earlier in this chapter, p. 125, with footnote 81.
88. F.L. Woodward, ed., *The Book of the Kindred Sayings*, p. 75.
89. Bhikkhu Buddhadāsa, "Me and Mine," in *Me and Mine: Selected Essays of Bhikkhu Buddhadāsa*, trans., ed. Donald K. Swearer (Albany: State University of New York Press, 1989), pp. 80–114.

90. A comment from a Thai lecturer at the Australian National University when I asked the meaning of the Thai phrase that Kittivuḍḍho translated from Pāli.
91. "Prayut" (This name looks like either a first name or a pseudonym), "Samnao chotmai thung kittiwuttho phikkhu" (The Draft of a Letter to Kittivuḍḍho Bhikkhu) (The letter is dated 6 February 1965), in *Arai thuk, arai phit*, ed. Pun Chongprasoet, pp. 132–7.
92. Pun, "Maihet," Kittiwuttho, "Ruang chit wang nok phra praipidok," in *Arai thuk, arai phit*, ed. Pun Chongprasoet, p. 131.
93. Prayut, "Samnao chotmai thung kittiwuttho phikkhu," p. 134.
94. Ibid., p. 135.
95. Pun Chongprasoet, "Maihet" (An Endnote), Khamhuno, "Tua ku lae khong ku" (Me and Mine), in *Arai thuk, arai phit*, ed. Pun Chongprasoet, p. 150.
96. Chamrat confirmed that "Khamhuno" was his pseudonym. Chamrat Duangthisan, interview, Bangkok, 31 July 1998.
97. Pun Chongprasoet, "Maihet," Khamhuno, "Tua ku lae khong ku" (Me and Mine), p. 150.
98. Khamhuno, "Chao na 'phu chit wang'" (A Farmer with Empty Mind) (originally published in Sayam rat sapda wichan, 18 October 1964), in *Arai thuk, arai phit*, ed. Pun Chongprasoet, pp. 139–44.
99. Khamhuno, "Tua ku lae khong ku" (originally published in *Sayam rat sapda wichan*, 29 November 1964), in *Arai thuk, arai phit*, ed. Pun Chongprasoet, pp. 145–9.
100. Khamhuno, "Chao na 'phu chit wang'" pp. 141–2.
101. Ibid., p. 142; translated by Ito.
102. Ibid., p. 144.
103. Pun, "Maihet," Khamhuno, "Chao na 'phu chit wang,'" p. 144.
104. Khamhuno, "Tua ku lae khong ku," p. 146; translated by Ito.
105. Pun, "Maihet," Khamhuno, "Tua ku lae khong ku," p. 150; translated by Ito.
106. Wai, "Samnao chomai thung 'Khamhuno'" (The Draft of a Letter to 'Khamhuno') (The letter is dated 25 January 1965), in *Arai thuk, arai phit*, ed. Pun Chongprasoet, pp. 151–62.
107. Ibid., p. 158; translated by Ito.
108. Ibid., pp. 161–2; translated by Ito. Although in the book, *Arai thuk, arai phit*, Khamhuno is given the role of an opponent of Buddhadāsa, he later changed his attitude toward Buddhadāsa, perhaps following the change in Kukrit. In my interview with Khamhuno on 31 July 1998, he explained that Buddhadāsa had only the third grade of Pāli qualification, but he was competent in English and was engaged in respected intellectual pursuit, and his teaching was "scientific Buddhism" without superstition. He said that Buddhadāsa learned the ideology of *suññatā* from Mahāyāna Buddhism, but it does not contradict Theravāda Buddhism. Chamrat Duangthisan (Khamhuno), interview.
109. Suksanti Chirachariyawet, ed., *7 rop achan sanya* (*Seventh 12-Year Cycle* [i.e., 84 years] *of Achan Sanya*) (Bangkok: Mulanithi Nitthisat, Mahawitthayalai Thammasat, 1991), pp. 181–2.

110. Sanya Thammasak (Dhammasakdi), "Phuttha-tham kap chiwit kan-ngan" (The Buddhist *Dhamma* and Work Life), in *Arai thuk, arai phit*, ed. Pun Chongprasoet, pp. 166–7; translated by Ito.
111. Ibid., p. 168; translated by Ito.
112. Ibid., p. 169; translated by Ito. The passage in round brackets was given by Sanya, whereas that in square brackets is by Ito.
113. Chakradharm Dhammasakdi (Chakkatham Thammasak), interview, Bangkok, 12 October 1998.
114. Pun Chongprasoet, "Patchima likhit" (Epilogue), in *Arai thuk, arai phit*, ed. Pun Chongprasoet, p. 178; translated by Ito.
115. Ibid., p. 179; translated by Ito.
116. Ibid., pp. 181–2; translated by Ito.
117. In the mid-1980s, Buddhadāsa's propagation of *lokuttara dhamma* and empty mind was further challenged by Samana (Phra) Phothirak, the leader of the Santi Asoke, a new Buddhist group that separated from the Thai Saṅgha. Phothirak criticized the elite followers of Buddhadāsa, as usually being absorbed in greediness in luxurious living, but who only apply the method of empty mind by releasing attachment when they feel suffering. From the perspective of an ordinary commoner, Phothirak proposed what he considered more practical teachings for people in general. For example, the Santi Asoke is known for their strict adherence to moral precepts, which they think more realistic for people to train themselves, and by establishing a Buddhist community of common ownership supported by the members' moral precepts. Phothirak wrote that he truly respected Buddhadāsa, but he critically examined Buddhadāsa's teachings in order to help people in worldly society. See Satcha Wimuttinan, edited from a public lecture by Phra Phothirak, *Panha sangkhom thi kae mai dai phro kansuksa phutthasasana phit phlat* (*Social Problems That Cannot be Solved Because of Wrong Education in Buddhism*) (Bangkok: Rongphim Mulanithi Thamma Santi, 1985). Phothirak confirmed such views of him in my interview with him on 6 May 1999.

Chapter 5

1. Jackson wrote, for instance, "The criticisms of conservative Buddhists like Anan Senakhan and Bunmi Methangkun can be taken as an indicator of Buddhadāsa's failure to develop a popular acceptable reform of Theravāda Buddhism." See Peter Jackson, *Buddhadāsa: Theravāda Buddhism and Modernist Reform in Thailand* (Chiang Mai: Silkworm Books, 2003), p. 126. He also wrote, "In criticizing Buddhadāsa, Anan Senakhan summarizes this traditional interpretation ...." See Jackson, *Buddhadāsa*, p. 193.
2. Gabaude, "Le langage scolastique: l'Abhidhamma," and "Le langage animiste: les esprits," in *Une herméneutique bouddhique contemporaine de Thaïlande: Buddhadāsa Bhikkhu* (Paris: École Française d'Extrême-Orient, 1988), pp. 126–74, 279–344.

3. For instance, Peter A. Jackson, *Buddhism, Legitimation, and Conflict: The Political Functions of Urban Thai Buddhism* (Singapore: Institute of Southeast Asian Studies, 1989); Suwanna Satha-Anand, "Review of Buddhism, Legitimation, and Conflict: The Political Functions of Urban Thai Buddhism, by Peter A. Jackson," *Crossroads* 5, 1 (1990): 105–8; Edwin Zehner, "Reform Symbolism of a Thai Middle-Class Sect: The Growth and Appeal of the Thammakai Movement," *Journal of Southeast Asian Studies* 21, 2 (September 1990): 402–26; Apinya Fuengfusakul, "Empire of Crystal and Utopian Commune: Two Types of Contemporary Theravāda Reform in Thailand," *Sojourn* 8, 1 (February 1993): 153–83; Heikkilä-Horn, Marja-Leena, *Buddhism with Open Eyes: Belief and Practice of Santi Asoke* (Bangkok: Fah Apai Co., Ltd., 1997); Rory Mackenzie, *New Buddhist Movements in Thailand: Towards an Understanding of Wat Phra Dhammakāya and Santi Asoke* (London: Routledge, 2007).
4. *Une herméneutique bouddhique contemporaine de Thaïlande: Buddhadāsa Bhikkhu* contains "Le langage scolastique: l'Abhidhamma," pp. 126–74; "Le langage classique: la production conditionnée," pp. 175–241; "Le langage magique: la prolongation de la vie," pp. 242–79; and "Le langage animiste: les esprits," pp. 279–344.
5. S.J. Tambiah, "The Center-Periphery Dialectic: The Mahathat and Bovonnivet Sponsorship of Meditation Compared," in *The Buddhist Saints of the Forest and the Cult of Amulets* (Cambridge: Cambridge University Press, 1984), pp. 183–99.
6. Collett Cox, "Buddhism, Ābhidharmika Schools of," in *Routledge Encyclopedia of Philosophy*, ed. Edward Craig (London and New York: Routledge, 1998), pp. 53–8.
7. Hammalawa Saddhatissa, "Introduction: The Abhidhammatthasaṅgaha," in Hammalawa Saddhatissa, *The Abhidhammatthasaṅgaha of Bhadantācariya Anurudda and the Abhidhammatthavibhāvinī-ṭīkā of Bhandantācariya Sumangalasāmi* (Oxford: The Pāli Text Society, 1989), p. xv.
8. Hammalawa Saddhatissa, "Introduction: The Abhidhammatthasaṅgaha," p. xix.
9. According to Collett Cox, "Abhidharma enables the practitioner to discriminate those aspects of experience that are defiling and so lead to suffering from those that are virtuous; through this discriminating insight, one can remove the defilements, cultivate virtue, and thereby emulate the Buddha and attain enlightenment." See Cox, "Buddhism, Ābhidharmika schools of," p. 54.
10. Phra Sikhamphirayan, interview, Bangkok, 28 December 1998. I have not yet located evidence of this information in historical documents.
11. Sathianphon Wannaphok, a ninth level Pāli qualification holder, said in an interview that the Abhidhamma is asked about in the eighth and ninth levels (Bangkok, 30 April 1999), but two other ninth level qualification holders, Suchip Phunyanuphap (interview, Bangkok, 10 March 1999) and Siri Phetchai (The head of the academic division, Association for the Research Centre of Buddhism [*Samakhom sun khonkwa thang phra phutthasasana*]), said that

the Abhidhamma is only examined in the ninth level. Siri Phetchai, interview, Bangkok, 11 March 1999. According to Ishii's list of canonical texts for each level of the Pāli examination, the eighth level requires translation from the *Samantapāsādika* (a sub-commentary on the *Vinayapiṭaka*) from Thai to Pāli, and from the *Visuddhimagga* from Pāli to Thai. See Yoneo Ishii, *Saṅgha, State, and Society: Thai Buddhism in History* (Honolulu: The University of Hawai'i Press, 1986), p. 95. The *Visuddhimagga* is a para-canonical text, which is abstracted from the entire *Tipiṭaka*, rather than an *aṭṭhakathā* which depends on a base text. It includes Abhidhamma material as well. Perhaps the eighth level sometimes requires translation of sections relating to the Abhidhamma in the *Visuddhimagga*.

12. A textbook on the Abhidhamma, *Chula aphithammatthasangkhaha* (*Culā abhidhammatthasaṅgaha*), written by Phra Thipparinya, was approved in 1951 for use in the third, or the lowest, grade *nak tham*, however, it was not used for a long time. See *Anuson ngan phra ratcha than phloeng sop phra thipparinya* (*Commemoration of Phra Thipparinya's Cremation*) (21 May 1977), p. 14; Kittivuḍḍho Bhikkhu, interview, Chonburi, 29 April 1999.
13. Phutthathat phikkhu, *Aphitham khu arai?* (*What is Abhidhamma?*) (Bangkok: Samnak nangsu thammabucha khong khana phoei phrae witthi kan damnoen chiwit an prasoet, 1978), pp. 5–6. Buddhadāsa said that people were excited to talk about *kāmāvacara* (the world of pleasure) or *rūpāvacara* (world of form), even though they did not know the meaning well, given the many unfamiliar concepts. Buddhadāsa seems not to have become too deeply involved in the Abhidhamma, as he said that he did not know how to use it.
14. Phra Phadungsulakkarit (A *thayok* of Wat Prok), "Prawat phra phatthanta wilasa" (A History of Phra Phatthanta Wilasa), in Phra Phatthanta Wilasa, *Thamma bet talet* (*Small Piece of the Dhamma*) (Bangkok: Samakhom sun khonkhwa thang phra phutthasasana, 1982), pp. 6–7. The name of this Burmese monk, which I transcribe here in accordance with Thai pronunciation, can also be transcribed using Pāli spelling as Bhaddanta Vilāsa. Although in Pāli Bhaddanta, meaning "venerable" or "reverend," is used to refer to a monk, my impression is that Thai people seem to use it as the name of the Burmese monk. See T.W. Rhys Davids and William Stede, eds., "Bhadanta (Bhaddanta)," in *Pāli-English Dictionary* (Oxford: The Pāli Text Society), pp. 497–8.
15. Because of his parents' names (U Kyaung and Daw Hla Win) and the place of his birth, he was most likely an ethnic Burmese. I thank Professor Kei Nemoto for his advice on the ethnic and geographical situation in Burma, as well as the possible English spellings of Burmese names, which were found in Thai materials.
16. Mingun Hsayadaw is respected as the preceptor of the famous meditation teacher, Mahasi Hsayadaw. For Mingun Hsayadaw's biography and work, see Madhav M. Deshpande, trans., ed., *Milindapañhā-aṭṭhakathā by Thaton Mingun Zatawun Sayadaw alias U Narada Mahathera* (Tokyo: The International Institute for Buddhist Studies of the International College for Advanced Buddhist Studies, 1999).

17. Phra Phadungsulakkarit, "Prawat phra phatthanta wilasa," pp. 5–8.
18. Ibid., p. 7; Siri Phetchai, interview, Bangkok, 11 March 1999.
19. Phutthathat Inthapanyo, "Anumothana" (Blessing), in *Mahawitthayalai chiwit khong phutthathat phikkhu, panya nai phutthasasana nikai sen khong khun prachak* (*A University of Life* by Buddhadāsa Bhikkhu, and *Insight in Zen School of Buddhism* by Khun Prachak), ed. Khana thammathan lae phu thi khaorop nai khunnatham khong phraya Latphli Thammaprakhan (The Dhammadāna Group and a Group which Respects the Moral Principles of Phraya Latphli Thammaprakhan) (A Cremation Volume for Phraya Latphli Thammaprakhan, 19 September 1968), p. (6).
20. Siri Phetchai, interview.
21. Wannasit Waithayasewi, interview, Bangkok, 3 May 1999.
22. Phra Phadungsulakkarit, "Prawat phra phatthanta wilasa," p. 7.
23. "Chiwit lae ngan khong achan naep mahaniranon" (Life and Work of Naep Mahaniranon), *Panyasan* (*Journal of Paññā*) 15 (21 September 1983): 1. In English, Jack Kornfield introduced Naep's brief biography and sermon in his book: "Achaan Naeb," in *Living Buddhist Masters* (Santa Cruz: Unity Press, 1977), pp. 131–58.
24. Wannasit, interview.
25. "Chiwit lae ngan khong achan naep mahaniranon," p. 2.
26. Ibid., p. 3. The year might be 1934. Wannasit, who was one of the closest disciples of Naep, said in an interview that Phatthanta died soon after the school at Wat Rakhang opened. He also said that Sai Saikasaem, who used to work at the Department of Forestry in Chiang Mai and who could speak Burmese, assisted by translating Phatthanta's teaching at the school. Wannasit, interview.
27. Wannasit, interview.
28. "Chiwit lae ngan khong achan naep mahaniranon," p. 3.
29. Aat Asapho is best known by his second to last ecclesiastical title, Phra Phimolatham. The title Phra Phimolatham was given to him on 4 December 1959 and he was known by this title until his next elevation, to Somdet Phra Phutthachan on 5 December 1985, even though it was withdrawn from 11 November 1960 to 31 May 1975 on account of a false charge against him. See "Somdet phra phutthachan (at atsapha maha thera)," in *Maha thera prawat: somdet phra phutthachan (at atsapha maha thera)* (*A History of the Great Elder: Somdet Phra Phutthachan [Aat Atsapha Maha Thera]*) (Bangkok: Mahachulalongkon Ratcha Witthayalai, 1990), pp.120–2.
30. In 1950, three sets of scriptures were dedicated by the Buddhist Congress of the Burmese Union (this is a translation of the term, *Sapha kan phutthasasana haeng sahaphap phama*, which appears in a Thai source). One set was sent to Mahachulalongkon Buddhist University at Wat Mahathat, one to Mahamakut Buddhist University at Wat Bowonniwet, and one to the Abhidhamma School at Wat Rakhang. See "Somdet phra phutthachan (at atsapha maha thera)," pp. 116–7.
31. Here I gave their names in accordance with Thai pronunciation and transliteration. Thai people usually call the former Achan Chotika, and the latter

Achan Techin. The Pāli transliterations of their names are Saddhamma Jotika Dhammācariya and Tejinda Dhammācariya Dhammakathika, respectively.

32. "Somdet phra phutthachan (at atsapha maha thera)," pp. 118–9; "Prawat lae phonngan doi yo: phra thammathiraratmahamuni (chodok yanasit thera, parien tham 9 prayok)" (Life and Work in Summary: Phra Thammathiraratmahamuni [Chodok Yanasit Thera, Ninth Level Pāli qualification]), in Phra Thammathiraratmahamuni, *Phet nai duang chai* (*A Jewel in the Mind*) (Bangkok: Samnak ngan klang kong kan wipatsana thura, 1996), pp. 242–3. The names of these monks in Pāli transliteration are Bhaddanta Āsabha Thera Padhānakammaṭṭhānācariya and Indavaṃsa Dhammācariya Kammaṭṭhānāchariya.
33. "Somdet phra phutthachan (at atsapha maha thera)," pp. 115–6; "Aphitham chotika witthayalai, mahachulalongkon ratcha witthayalai," in *Ngan mop prakatniyabat apitham bandit run 34/2540* (*The Ceremony to Confer the Qualification of Apitham Bandit*), ed. Aphitham Chotika Witthayalai (Bangkok: Aphitham Chotika Witthayalai, Mahachulalongkon Ratcha Witthayalai, 1998), p. 13. Chotika may have started his teaching at Wat Mahathat in 1951, because publications from the Abhidhamma Chotika College refer to its time of origin as Chotika's arrival in Thailand, which they say was in 1951. I assume that compared with the rough overview of the school history of the Abhidhamma Chotika College, the data in "Somdet phra phutthachan (at atsapha maha thera)" are more reliable. This is because the latter provides more detailed information about Aat's works, which must have been recorded by Aat himself or surveyed by his disciples.
34. Phra Sikhamphirayan, interview.
35. "Aphitham chotika witthayalai, mahachulalongkon ratcha witthayalai," p. 13.
36. According to a brochure I received in 1999, the Abhidhamma Chotika College has expanded its branches to 21 in Central Thailand, four in the North, 11 in the Northeast, 14 in the East, and two in the South. See "Aphitham chotika witthayalai, mahachulalongkon ratcha witthayalai nai phra boromarachupatham" (The Abhidhamma Chotika College, Mahachulalongkon Ratcha Witthayalai under Royal Patronage). The data indicate an expansion of Abhidhamma study from Chotika's work in Bangkok into provincial Thailand.
37. Kittivuḍḍho Bhikkhu, interview.
38. "Somdet phra phutthachan (at atsapha maha thera)," p. 117.
39. Wannasit, interview.
40. For Chodok's brief bio-data, see "Prawat lae phonngan doi yo: phra thammathiraratmahamuni (chodok yanasit thera, parien tham 9 prayok)."
41. About Khun Mae Siri, see *Thammathan khong khun mae siri: thi raluk nuang nai wara charoen chansa khrop 6 rop (72 pi)* (*Khun Mae Siri's Gift of the Dhamma: Commemoration for her Sixth 12-year Cycle [72 Years Old]*) (22 August 1988).
42. About Aat's downfall and its related political dispute, see Krachang Nanthaphot, *Mahanikai — thammayut* (*Mahanikai Order and Thammayut Order*)

(Nonthabri: Santi tham, 1985), pp. 175–253; Peter Jackson, "Persecution of Phra Phimontham (Vimaladhamma) Bhikkhu," in Peter Jackson, *Buddhism, Legitimation, and Conflict: The Political Functions of Urban Thai Buddhism* (Singapore: Institute of Southeast Asian Studies, 1989), pp. 94–112.

43. "Somdet phra phutthachan (at atsapha maha thera)," pp. 120–2.
44. Ibid., pp. 118–9. The one who returned to Burma was Inthawansa; the other was Phatthanta Atsapha.
45. *Anuson ngan phra ratcha than phloeng sop phra thipparinya*, p. 14.
46. Kittiwuttho Phikkhu (Kittivuḍḍho Bhikkhu), "Dae phra thipparinya" (To Phra Thipparinya), in *Anuson ngan phra ratcha than phloeng sop phra thipparinya*, p. 26.
47. Wannasit, interview. As far as Wannasit could remember, the textbook was only used for a year or so.
48. Phra Phimolatham, "Anuson khun phra thipparinya" (Memory of Khun Phra Thipparinya), in *Anuson ngan phra ratcha than phloeng sop phra thipparinya*, pp. 13–4.
49. Kittiwuttho Phikkhu, "Dae phra thipparinya," p. 26.
50. Phra Pracha, *Lao wai mua wai sonthaya*, p. 322; *Ha sip pi suan mok: phak nung mua khao phut thung rao* (*Fifty Years of Suan Mokkh: Part I When They Spoke of Us*) (Bangkok: Suan usom mulanithi, 1982), pp. 747–62.
51. "Chiwit lae ngan khong achan naep mahaniranon," p. 3.
52. "Phra achan bunmi methangkuro: duang prathip duang ek haeng phra aphitham" (Phra Achan Bunmi Methangkuro: The Number One Light of the Abhidhamma), in *Alai phra achan bunmi methangkun* (*In Memory of Phra Achan Bunmi Methangkun*), ed. Aphitham Mulanithi lae Khana Sit (The Abhidhamma Foundation and a group of disciples) (Bangkok: 6 June 1992), pp. 1–3; "Mulanithi Aphitham Mulanithi" (Foundation for the Abhidhamma Foundation) (A brochure given to the author at the time of her visit on 9 October 1998).
53. In Thai, the committee member and committee secretary of the Office of Culture concerning Custom and Tradition is *Kammakan lekhanukan samnak watthanatham thang rabiap prapheni*, and the National Culture Council is *Sapha watthanatham haeng chat*.
54. Maniphan and Utsa Charudun, "Than achan naep kap pathom haet hai koet samakhom sun khonkhwa thang phra phutthasasana lae mulanithi phumiphalo phikkhu" (Teacher Naep and the Origins of the Association for Centre of the Research on Buddhism and the Phumiphalo Bhikkhu Foundation), in *Thang bamphen kuson phua ok chak thuk haeng kan koet: anuson nai kan chapanakit sop achan naep mahaniranon* (*The Way to Make Merit in Order to Exit from the Suffering of Births: Commemoration at the Cremation of Achan Naep Mahaniranon*) (Bangkok: Samakhom sun khonkhwa thang phra phutthasasana, 14 December 1983), pp. 1–4.
55. Khana Kammathikan Sasana Sinlapa lae Watthanatham (Committee for Religion, Art and Culture), "Prawat than achan suchin borihanwannakhet" (Biography of Respected Teacher Sujin Boriharnwanaket), in *Prawat achan*

suchin borihanwannakhet (*Biography of Teacher Sujin Boriharnwanaket*) (Bangkok: Dhamma Study and Support Foundation, 2002), pp. 2–5.

56. Nina Van Gorkom, *Abhidhamma in Daily Life* (London: Zolag, 1992).
57. Sujin Boriharnwanaket and her disciple, conversation with the author at the regular weekend *dhamma* discussion session, Dhamma Study and Support Foundation, Bangkok, 10 March 2007.
58. Sanya Thammasak (Sanya Dhammasakdi), *Nathi khong phutthasamakhom* (*The Duty of the Buddhist Association*; originally given on 18 February 1961) (Bangkok: Phutthasamakhom haeng Prathet Thai, 1961), pp. 13–6. In fact, available data indicate that Bunmi was a member of the administration committee and the *dhamma* studies committee at least from 1957 to 1964; Naep and Khun Ying Rabiap Sunthralikhit, another Abhidhamma teacher, were on the advisory board as long as from 1957 to 1967; and Naep and Bunmi were elected to the group of six vice-presidents in 1963 and 1965, respectively. The data here are based on the lists of the executive committee members and advisors of the Buddhist Association published in the Association's journal, *Phuttha-tham*, from 1957 until 1967, which I was able to access at the National Library of Thailand. They might also have been on the committees before 1957, and may have continued to be on them after 1967.
59. See footnote 58 (about the membership of the executive committees in the Buddhist Association).
60. Maniphan and Utsa Charudun, "Than achan naep kap pathom haet hai koet," pp. 13–4; Maniphan Charudun and Siri Phetchai, interview, Bangkok, 11 March 1999.
61. "Mulanithi Aphitham Mulanithi" (A brochure).
62. See footnote 58 (about the membership of the executive committees in the Buddhist Association).
63. "Mulanithi Aphitham Mulanithi" (A brochure).
64. Some said that the teachings of Bunmi and Naep were the same, but others said they differed somewhat. Bunmi's biographer proudly wrote a comment by Naep, who heard Bunmi's remarks about his feelings in *vipassanā*, "Let me bless Bunmi. I entrust him to look after the Abhidhamma." See "Phra achan bunmi methangkuro: duang prathip duang ek haeng phra aphitham," p. 5. Wannasit, who used to be an Abhidhamma teacher at Bunmi's school at Wat Pho but resigned later, said that the understandings of Naep and Bunmi were basically the same, however Bunmi placed too much emphasis on supernaturalism in order to gain popular attention, whereas Naep never performed "miracles." Wannasit, interview. Sawai Kaewsom and his friend stated that their understandings about *viññāṇa* (this Pāli word means consciousness, but in Thailand can often mean "a soul") after death. They said that Naep understood that *viññāṇa* flows in the air after the death of a person, while Bunmi insisted that there is no *viññāṇa* after death, but an energy of *kamma* continues to exist and leads to rebirth. Sawai Kaewsom and his friend, interview, Bangkok, 21 March 1999.

65. "Phra achan bunmi methangkuro: duang prathip duang ek haeng phra aphitham," pp. 3–5.
66. "Kitchakan ngan khong than achan bunmi methangkun" (Activities of Teacher Bunmi Methangkun), in Aphitham Mulanithi lae Khana Sit, *Alai phra achan bunmi methangkun*, p. 8; Sawai Kaewsom and his friend, interview, 21 March 1999.
67. "Phra achan bunmi methangkuro: duang prathip duang ek haeng phra aphitham," p. 4. Issues related to supernaturalism and reincarnation were points about which Bunmi and Buddhadāsa's disciples disagreed with each other. Sawai Kaewsom was once invited by Bunmi to give a talk at Wat Pho, and he opposed Bunmi's depiction of *kamma*. Criticizing Bunmi, who explained the concept of *kamma* as life after death, Sawai insisted that *kamma* is intention to perform good and evil, and thus it is only an element of the present life. Sawai Kaewsom, interview, 21 March 1999. Since the Buddha said those who believe in reincarnation of a soul and those who deny it are both *micchādiṭṭhi* (wrong view), Buddhadāsa was careful enough in his teaching not to deny reincarnation, but to encourage the overcoming of suffering in this lifetime. See, for example, Than Phutthathat (Venerable Buddhadāsa), "Tai laeo koet ik ru mai" (Are We Reborn Again or Not), in Pun Chongprasoet, *Rian ru phutthasasana phai nai 15 nathi* (*Studying Buddhism Within Fifteen Minutes*) (Samutprakan: Ongkan Funfu Phutthasasana), pp. 19–24. However, some of Buddhadāsa's followers, such as Pun Chongprasoet and Sawai Kaewsom, interpreted his teaching as saying that there is no rebirth after death, and that the idea of rebirth is not Buddhist but Brahmanist. See for example, Pun Chongprasoet, "Rian ru phutthasasana phai nai 15 nathi," in Pun Chongprasoet, *Rian ru phutthasasana phai nai 15 nathi*, pp. 5–18; Sawai Kaewsom, *Tai koet, tai sun, panha lok taek ru?* (*Reincarnation, or Extinction After Death: Is It a Problem that Divides the World?*) (1991). Bunmi's Abhidhamma group and Buddhadāsa's disciples had opposing views on this issue; this opposition was the source of a conflict in the Buddhist public sphere in Thailand.
68. Kittivuḍḍho, interview.
69. Than Chao Phra Khun Somdet Phra Wanrat, "Kham klao nai phithi poet mulanithi aphitham mahathat witthayalai" (A Speech at the Opening Ceremony of Mulanithi Aphitham Mahathat Witthayalai), *Chofa* 1, 1 (October 1965): 5.
70. Kittivuḍḍho, interview.
71. Pun Chongprasoet, "Maihet" (An Endnote), to Kittiwuttho Phikkhu (Kittivuḍḍho Bhikkhu), "Ruang chit wang nok phra traipidok," in *Arai thuk, arai phit*, p. 131.
72. This group includes two educational institutions. One is the Abhidhamma school at Wat Rakhang, Division 7, where Chotika used to teach, and which has been handed down to Phra Sikhamphirayan (Thawan). The other is the Aphitham Chotika Witthayalai in Wat Mahathat, which is now run as a part of Mahachulalongkorn Buddhist University. These two were institutionalized as colleges rather than being centered on an individual's charisma.

73. For conducting activities, Kittivuḍḍho established the Foundation for the Abhidhamma (*Mulanithi Aphitham*) and Djitthabhawan College, which was founded in 1967 in Chonburi province. However, Kittivuḍḍho's training project for novices and young monks does not specialize in the Abhidhamma, but provides wider and more general knowledge so that those monks, who otherwise have few chances for formal education, may become capable preachers. Kittivuḍḍho, interview.
74. This group established the Association for the Center of Research on Buddhism in Wat Saket. Apart from philological studies, the group has an Abhidhamma class at their weekend school. The staff includes Maniphan and Utsa Charudun, and Sujin Boriharnwanaket, a well-known female Abhidhamma teacher.
75. The institutional body of this group is the Abhidhamma Foundation, which was established by Bunmi Methangkun. After Bunmi apparently left the Buddhist Association in 1966, he continued his activities at Wat Pho until the death of his patron Somdet Wanrat in 1987, at which time he was asked to return to the temple premises. In 1987, the Abhidhamma Foundation moved to Phutthamonthon Sai 4. Since Bunmi's death in 1991, his daughter has been in charge of those activities.
76. Wannasit used to be a teacher at Bunmi's Abhidhamma school at Wat Pho, but he withdrew over disagreement with Bunmi's excessive emphasis on supernaturalism. He now teaches Abhidhamma and *vipassanā* at Wat Bowonniwet, but only to lay people, not to the monks and novices living there, who are not allowed to receive instruction from outside teachers. Wannasit, interview.
77. For instance, Phiksu Chayanantho (Phra Anan Senakhan), ed., *Kham son khong diarathi* (*Teachings of a Heretic*) (Bangkok: Borisat Bophit, 1979); Bunmi Methangkun, *To than phutthathat!: ruang cit wang*, lem 1 (*Refuting Venerable Buddhdasa!: Regarding Empty Mind*), Volume 1 (Bangkok: Suthisan Kan-phim, 1979); Bunmi Methangkun, *To than phutthathat!: ruang awitcha lae phi-sang thewada*, lem 2 (*Refuting Venerable Buddhdasa!: Regarding Ignorance, Ghost, and Celestial Beings*), Volume 2 (Bangkok: Suthisan Kan-phim, 1980); Bunmi Methangkun, *To than phutthathat!: ruang awitcha patchaya sangkhan*, lem 3 (*Refuting Venerable Buddhdasa!: Regarding Ignorance Caused by Compounded Things [Avijjā Paccayā Saṅkhāra]*), Volume 3 (Bangkok: Suthisan Kan-phim, 1981).
78. Sawai Kaewsom interview, Bangkok, 21 March 1999.
79. Ravi Bhavirai (Rawi Phawirai), interview, Bangkok, 4 May 1999.
80. Phra Sithawat Vanivattiko, interview, Nonthaburi, 30 April 1999.
81. Phra Pracha Pasannathammo, *Lao wai mua wai sonthaya: atchiwaprawat khong than phutthathat* (*Talking in the Twilight Years: An Autobiography of Venerable Buddhadāsa*) (Bangkok: Mulanithi Komon Khimthong, 1988), pp. 377–9.
82. Sithawat, interview. The year of the incident that Sithawat mentioned in his interview was confirmed in "Somdet phra phutthachan (at atsapha maha

thera)," p. 120. As far as Sithawat knew, this speech by Buddhadāsa was not recorded.

83. Sithawat, then a monk secretary of Aat, sent a telegram to Buddhadāsa to ask him to give a speech under this title on behalf of Aat. Sithawat, interview.
84. Sithawat, interview.
85. Phra Pracha, *Lao wai mua wai sonthaya*, pp. 472–3.
86. Ibid., p. 486.
87. The content of Abhidhammatthasaṅgaha, the traditional exegesis of the Abhidhamma, lends support to this view. See Bhikkhu Bodhi, ed., *A Comprehensive Manual of Abhidhamma: The Abhidhammattha Sangaha of Ācariya Anuruddha* (Onalaska: BPS Pariyatti Editions, 2000).
88. See Ishii, "The Establishment and Significance of the Ecclesiastical Examination System," in *Saṅgha, State, and Society*, pp. 81–99.
89. For example, Wannasit mentioned that Pemangkharo Bhikkhu at Wat Boromniwat had harshly criticized the Abhidhamma. Also, he said that Phra Thepdilok (Rabaep Chittayano) at Wat Bowonniwet used to criticize it, but at one point Rabaep changed his mind; he recently requested their textbooks for study. Wannasit, interview. Rabaep is an academic monk at Mahamakut Buddhist University, and well known for his critical campaign against the Catholic Church, which he claimed was plotting to destroy Buddhism. Concerning his campaign, see Phra Ratchathamnithet (Rabaep Chittayano), *Phaen thamlai phra phutthasasana* (*The Plot to Destroy Buddhism*) (Bangkok: Sun Songsoem Phra Phutthasasana haeng Phrathet Thai, 1994).
90. For example, when I interviewed Kittivuḍḍho Bhikkhu on 29 April 1999, we happened to speak of a contemporary debate between the Dhammakāya group and P.A. Payutto about whether *nibbāna* is *attā* (self) or *anattā* (non-self). Kittivuḍḍho said both the Dhammakāya and Payutto were wrong. If *nibbāna* is *anattā* as Payutto insisted, *nibbāna* should have the *sāmañña lakkhaṇa* (general characteristics: impermanence, suffering, and not-self), which belongs to the *saṅkhata dhamma* (conditioned *dhamma*). If it is *attā* as the Dhammakāya group insisted, it is suffering, which also has the *sāmañña lakkhaṇa* of the *saṅkhata dhamma*. Kittivuḍḍho explained, following the Abhidhamma theory, that *nibbāna* is neither *attā* nor *anattā*, but it is the *asaṅkhata dhamma* (unconditioned *dhamma*), which has the characteristic of tranquillity. Kittivuḍḍho, interview. Another Abhidhamma teacher Wannasit Waithayasewi said that those who study only the *Suttapiṭaka* did not understand the reasonable principles of *sabhāva* (individual essence). In Wannasit's view, Payutto was one of them, and had analyzed the *dhamma* incorrectly. However, Wannasit also said that if Payutto studied the Abhidhamma, he would be very good. Wannasit, interview.
91. This lecture is published as: Phutthathat phikkhu, *Sing thi rao yang khaochai kan mai dai* (*The Things That We Have Not Yet Understood*) (Samutprakan: Ongkan Funfu Phutthasasana). This same lecture by Buddhadāsa was also examined in Gabaude's study, yet his focus was the contrast of doctrinal

interpretations of Buddhadāsa and what he called "Abhidhammists." See "Le langage scolastique: l'Abhidhamma," pp. 126–74. My focus here is on the lecture's effect on the Abhidhamma groups and their reactions to it.

92. Phutthathat, *Sing thi rao yang khaochai kan mai dai*, p. 2; translated by Ito.
93. These ten issues are discussed in the following pages in Phutthathat, *Sing thi rao yang khaochai kan mai dai*: 1) pp. 2–5; 2) pp. 5–8; 3) pp. 9–15; 4) pp. 15–9; 5) pp. 20–3; 6) pp. 23–31; 7) pp. 32–41; 8) pp. 42–4; 9) pp. 44–6; and 10) pp. 46–50.
94. Phutthathat, *Sing thi rao yang khaochai kan mai dai*, pp. 23–4; translated by Ito.
95. Ibid., pp. 28–9; translated by Ito.
96. Ibid., pp. 27–8.
97. Ibid., p. 24.
98. Ibid., p. 27.
99. Ibid., p. 30. According to Lamotte's study on emptiness in Buddhist scriptures, this Pāli phrase appears at least four times in the *Suttapiṭaka*. For more details, see Chapter 4, footnote 16, p. 280. The translation of this Pāli phrase here is cited from: F.L. Woodward, *The Book of the Kindred Sayings (Saṃyutta-nikāya) or Grouped Suttas: Part V (Mahā-vagga)* (London: The Pāli Text Society, 1965), p. 348.
100. Phutthathat, *Sing thi rao yang khaochai kan mai dai*, pp. 30–1; translated by Ito.
101. Ibid., pp. 31–2.
102. Ibid., pp. 45–6.
103. Bunmi Methangkun, ed., *To top patthakatha phutthathat phikkhu* (Bangkok: Aphitham Mulanithi, 1965, 1980). The second edition, which was published in 1980, was in cooperation with the Ongkan Phithak Phutthasasana (Organization to Protect Buddhism), which was headed by Anan Senakhan, who studied the Abhidhamma with Bunmi at Wat Pho. See Bunmi Methangkun, "Thoi thalaeng" (Postscript), in *To top patthakatha phutthathat phikkhu*, p. (ngo.).
104. Bunmi Methangkun, "Kham prarop" (Forward), in *To top patthakatha phutthathat phikkhu*, pp. 13–4.
105. Hammalawa Saddhatissa, "Introduction: The Abhidhammatthasaṅgaha," pp. xiii – xxiii.
106. K.R. Norman, *Pāli Literature Including the Canonical Literature in Prakrit and Sanskrit of All the Hīnayāna Schools of Buddhism* (Wiesbaden: Otto Harrassowitz, 1983), p. 98.
107. Bunmi Methangkun, "Kham prarop," p. 8; translated by Ito.
108. Ibid., p. 10; translated by Ito.
109. Phra Chanbannakit, "Sing thi yang mai at khaochai kan dai" (Things That Still Might Not Be Able to Be Understood), in *To top patthakatha phutthathat phikkhu*, pp. 196–7; translated by Ito.
110. Khun Ying Rabiap Sunthralikhit, "Kham to top" (A Retort), in *To top patthakatha phutthathat phikkhu*, pp. 203–25. This lecture by Chao Khun

Kawiworayan was given in February 1963, which was before Buddhadāsa's controversial lecture, and not directly critical of Buddhadāsa.

111. Ibid., pp. 204–9.
112. Phutthathat, *Aphitham khu arai?*, p. 4.
113. Ibid., pp. 29, 32, 117.
114. Ibid., pp. 33–9.
115. Ibid., p. 102; translated by Ito.
116. Ibid., p. 109.
117. Naksuksa Phra Aphitham (Students of the Abhidhamma; including Sa'nga Suphat, Suphani Wirawat, Chaluai Phenphaibun, Suchit Sa'nganmu, and Chuai Kannawat), "Samnao chotmai: kho khongchai khong naksuksa" (A Draft of a Letter: Some Students' Concerns), in *To top patthakatha phutthathat phikkhu*, p. 87.
118. Ibid., pp. 87–8.
119. For example, Bunmi Methangkun, "Phra aphithampidok pen bot suksa thi wa duai ruang arai" (What Kind of Lesson is It to Study the Abhidhammapiṭaka?), in *To top patthakatha phutthathat phikkhu*, pp. 115–9; and Rabiap, "Kham to top," pp. 213–9.
120. Rabiap, "Kham to top," p. 222.
121. Siri Phetchai, interview.

Chapter 6

1. In the following discussion, the term "Marxism" is used for the theory delivered by Marx, from which derived both communism and socialism. While the term, "communist," is used "… to describe the parties that accepted violent revolution and the dictatorship of the proletariat as the means of transition to communism," "socialism" is used to describe "those who rejected it." See Eero Loone, "Communism" in *The Blackwell Dictionary of Twentieth-Century Social Thought*, eds. William Outhwaite and Tom Bottomore (Oxford: Blackwell, 1993), p. 98.
2. Karl Marx, "Contribution to the Critique of Hegel's Philosophy of Law. Introduction," in Karl Marx and Frederich Engels, *Collected Works Volume 3: Marx and Engels 1843–44* (London: Lawrence & Wishart, 1975), p. 175.
3. See J.M. Bochenski, "Marxism-Leninism and Religion," in *Religion and Atheism in the U.S.S.R. and Eastern Europe*, eds. Bohdan R. Bociurkiw and John W. Strong (London: Macmillan Press Ltd., 1975), pp. 1–17; Holmes Welch, *Buddhism under Mao* (Cambridge, Massachusetts: Harvard University Press, 1972).
4. See Charles F. Keyes, "Communist Revolution and the Buddhist Past in Cambodia," in *Asian Visions of Authority: Religion and the Modern States of East and Southeast Asia*, eds. Charles F. Keyes, Laurel Kendall, and Helen Hardacre (Honolulu: University of Hawai'i Press, 1994), pp. 43–73; Martin Stuart-Fox, *Buddhist Kingdom, Marxist State: The Making of Modern Laos* (Bangkok: White Lotus, 1996).

5. Kittiwuttho Phikkhu (Kittivuḍḍho Bhikkhu), *Kha khommiunit mai bap* (*Killing Communists is Not Demeritorious*) (Bangkok: Mulanithi Aphitham Mahathat Witthayalai, 1976); Charles F. Keyes, "Political Crisis and Militant Buddhism in Contemporary Thailand," in *Religion and Legitimation of Power in Thailand, Laos, and Burma*, ed. Bardwell L. Smith (Chambersburg, PA: ANIMA Books, 1978), pp. 147–64. About the political events and their background in the 1970s, see David Morell and Chai-anan Samudavanija, *Political Conflict in Thailand: Reform, Reaction, Revolution* (Cambridge: Oelgeschlager, Gunn & Hain, Publishers, Inc., 1981); and Benedict Anderson, "Withdrawal Symptoms," in *The Spectre of Comparison: Nationalism, Southeast Asia and the World* (London: Verso, 1998), pp. 139–73. About the counter-insurgency, see Katharine A. Bowie, *Rituals of National Loyalty: An Anthropology of the State and the Village Scout Movement in Thailand* (New York: Columbia University Press, 1997).
6. A concise review of the studies of Marxism in Thailand before 1983 is given by Craig Reynolds and Hong Lysa, "Marxism in Thai Historical Studies," *Journal of Asian Studies* 43, 1 (November 1983): 77–104. One of the few studies that paid attention to the Buddhist influence on Thai Marxist thought is: Yuangrat (Pattanapongse) Wedel, "Modern Thai Radical Thought: The Siamization of Marxism and its Theoretical Problems," PhD diss., University of Michigan, 1981. Wedel argued the Buddhist elements appeared in the thoughts of Thai Marxist thinkers as a part of "Siamization" of Marxism, considering those represented by Pridi Phanomyong and his disciples. Another important study examined Marxism's influence on Buddhist monks, particularly the radicalized movement of the Young Monks (*yuwasong*) connected to the Communist Party in the 1970s is: Somboon Suksamran, *Buddhism and Politics in Thailand: A Study of Socio-Political Change and Political Activism of the Thai Saṅgha* (Singapore: Institute of Southeast Asian Studies, 1982). Looking more closely at individual experiences, this chapter attempts to trace Buddhadāsa's and other prominent Thai intellectuals' encounters with Marxism and their comparative discussions on Buddhism and Marxism.
7. The early history of the Chinese communist movement in Siam is extensively examined in Eiji Murashima, *Kanmuang chin sayam: kan-khluan-wai thang kanmuang khong chaw chin phon thale nai prathet thai kho. so. 1924–1941* (*Politics of the Chinese in Siam: The Political Activities of Overseas Chinese in Thailand in 1924–1941*) (Bangkok: Sun Chin Suksa, Sathaban Esia Suksa, Chulalongkon Mahawitthayalai, 1996). Also, Vietnamese communists' activities which were the important elements of the early communist movement in Siam/Thailand are precisely examined in Christopher E. Goscha, *Thailand and the Southeast Asian Networks of the Vietnamese Revolution, 1885–1954* (Surrey: Curzon Press, 1999).
8. Murashima, *Kanmuang chin sayam*, p. 68; Kasian Tejapira, "Commodifying Marxism: The Formation of Modern Thai Radical Culture, 1927–1958," PhD diss., Cornell University, 1992, pp. 16–7.

9. In Fineman's study on political and diplomatic history after Phibun's returning coup in November 1947 to Phibun's downfall in 1958, he divided the period into four using the Thai relationship with the United States: 1947–1948; 1948–1950; 1950–1954; and 1955–1958. See Daniel Fineman, *A Special Relationship: The United States and Military Government in Thailand, 1947–1958* (Honolulu: University of Hawai'i Press, 1997). Whereas, in Kasian's analysis on post-Second World War communist activities, he divided the period between 1945 and 1958 into three: (1) 1945–1947; (2) 1948–1952; and (3) 1952–1958. See Kasian Tejapira, "Commodifying Marxism," p. 269. Kasian considered the fall of the Pridi Free Thai regime in 1947 as the end of relative tolerance toward communists. However, the Phibun coup government was not tough toward communism until the beginning of the Cold War in Asia. Also, as Kasian argued, the Anti-Communist Act in 1952 affected the Communist Party's activities and forced them to be recognized, but the enforcement of the Act in the public sphere became rather loosened after 1955 when the Thai government contacted Communist China at the Bandung Conference. The Thai government toughened its control of Marxist speech during 1950 and 1954, in which are included the massive arrests of the participants in the Peace Committee. Therefore, in accordance with the governments' policy toward communism and the degree of freedom of expression, the period between 1946 and 1958 can be characterized by three subdivided periods: (1) 1946–1950; (2) 1950–1954; and (3) 1955–1958.
10. Although a socialist civilian politician Pridi once fell into disgrace for the proposal of an economic plan in 1933, he returned to power after the war for his merit of leadership in the anti-Japanese Free Thai Movement, which in turn permitted Thailand to escape from being internationally sanctioned as an allied nation of the defeated Japan. He was the regent of King Ananda Mahidol (Rama VIII) in 1945–1946, and the Prime Minister in 1946. See Eiji Murashima, *Pibun: dokuritsu tai okoku no rikken kakumei* (*Phibun: Constitutional Revolution in the Independent Kingdom of Thailand*) (Tokyo: Iwanami Shoten, 1996), in Japanese; Chris Baker and Pasuk Phongpaichit, trans., *Pridi by Pridi: Selected Writings on Life, Politics and Economy* (Chiang Mai: Silkworm Books, 2001).
11. *Anuson nai ngan phra ratcha than phloeng sop: nai prasoet sapsunthon* (*Commemoration for the Cremation: Mr. Prasoet Sapsunthon*) (2 April 1995), p. (8); Prasoet Patthamasukhon, *Ratthasapha thai nai rop 42 pi* (*42 Years of the Thai Parliament*) (Bangkok: Ratthakit Seri, 1974), p. 557; Kasian, "Commodifying Marxism," pp. 135–6, 557.
12. Eiji Murashima, "Opposing French Colonialism: Thailand and the Independence Movements in Indo-China in the Early 1940s," *South East Research* 13, 3 (October 2005): 333–5.
13. Along with the Peace Committee's arrest, the Anti-Communist Act was again proclaimed on 13 November 1952 and enforced on the next day. The anti-communist mood in Thailand was further heightened by Thailand becoming the headquarters of the Southeast Asia Treaty Organization (SEATO) in 1954.

See David K. Wyatt, *Thailand: A Short History* (Chiangmai: Silkworm Books, 1982, 1984), pp. 260–75.

14. See Somsak Jeamteerasakul, "The Communist Movement in Thailand," PhD diss., Monash University, 1991, pp. 334–53.
15. The Peace movement was organized by the Soviet Union after 1949, and the detailed theory was published by Stalin as *Economic Problem of Socialism* in 1952. See David Wilson, "China, Thailand and the Spirit of Bandung (Part I)," *The China Quarterly* 30 (April–June 1967): 155. About the Peace Committee of Thailand, see Wiwat Catithammanit, *Kabot santhiphap* (*Peace [Committee's] Revolt*) (Bangkok: Khrongkan Chat Phim Khop Fai, 1996); Chonthira Sattayawatthana (Cholthira Satyawadhna), ed., *Kung satawat khabuankan santhiphap* (*Half Century of the Peace Campaign*) (Bangkok: Mek Khao, 2002).
16. David Wilson, "China, Thailand and the Spirit of Bandung (Part I)," p. 99.
17. Fineman, *A Special Relationhip*, p. 224; Ari Phirom, *Thai-chin* (*Thailand-China*) (Bangkok: Mitranara Kanphim, 1981), p. 51; Karuna Kusalasai, *Chiwit thi luak mai dai* (*Life Without Choice*) (Bangkok: Mae Kham Phang, 1986, 1997), p. 204. Ari and Karuna were members of this secret delegation to China.
18. Regarding *Aksonsan*, see Kasian, "Commodifying Marxism," pp. 449–94. About Chit Phumisak's life and one of his most famous works, see Craig Reynolds, *Thai Radical Discourse: The Real Face of Thai Feudalism Today* (Ithaca: Cornell Southeast Asia Program, 1994).
19. Prasoet was a temple boy at that temple from when he was an eight-year-old schoolboy until he graduated from Chulalongkorn University. See *Anuson Prasoet Sapsunthon*, p. (7); Phra Pracha Pasannathammo (Pracha Pasannadhammo Bhikkhu), *Lao wai mua wai sonthaya: atchiwaprawat khong than phutthathat* (*Talking in the Age of Twilight: An Autobiography of Ven. Buddhadāsa*) (Bangkok: Mulanithi Komon Khimthong, 1988), p. 377.
20. Prasoet graduated from the Faculty of Arts and Science in early 1937. See "Prospectus Faculty of Arts and Science, Chulalankankarana University Session B.E. 2480 (A.D. 1937–1938)" (Bangkok: Bangkok Times Press), p. 89. This is Chulalongkorn University's prospectus booklet written in English; it includes a list of the first two generations of alumni who obtained Bachelor degrees in the years 2478 and 2479 of the Buddhist Era. (According to the then Thai calendar, Buddhist Era [B.E.] 2478 started in April 1935 and ended in March 1936; B.E. 2479 was from April 1937 to March 1938). In B.E. 2478, there were seven people conferred Bachelors of Science and 33 Bachelors of Arts; in B.E. 2479 four Bachelors of Science and 17 Bachelors of Arts. Prasoet was one of the 17 Bachelors of Arts in B.E. 2479. Previously, in order for Thai people to obtain a Bachelor's degree, they had to study abroad; Chulalongkorn University, established as Thailand's first academic institution, started to confer diplomas and later gave Bachelor's degrees. In such a circumstance, Prasoet was one of the small numbers of best educated intellectuals in Thailand.

21. Phra Pracha, *Lao wai mua wai sonthaya*, p. 340. According to the cremation volume of Prasoet, he graduated from Chulalongkorn University in 1936. See *Anuson Prasoet Sapsunthon*, p. (7). Buddhadāsa recalled that Prasoet was not totally devoted to communist ideas at that time. See Phra Pracha, *Lao wai mua wai sonthaya*, p. 340.
22. The letters from Prasoet to Buddhadāsa are dated: 8 October 1941, 24 July 1942, 26 August 1942, 31 July 1944, 22 December 1944, 8 January 1945, 5 October 1945, 15 January 1946, 22 November 1946, 3 September 1947, 3 May 1948, 1 November 1948, and 3 January 1972. The letter from Buddhadāsa to Prasoet is dated 2 December 1944.
23. The six letters are dated: 8 October 1941, 24 July 1942, 26 August 1942, 31 July 1944, and 22 December 1944.
24. Prasoet's wish appeared in his letters to Buddhadāsa dated 26 August 1942, 8 January 1945, 5 October 1945, and 15 January 1946.
25. *Anuson prasoet sapsunthon*, p. 8.
26. Prasoet Sapsunthon, interview by Eiji Murashima, Bangkok, 16 June 1981; Prasoet Sapsunthon, *Kolam prasoet sapsunthon* (*Column Prasoet Sapsunthon*) (Bangkok: publisher unknown, 1983). I am grateful to Prof. Murashima for this information.
27. In the interview with Prof. Eiji Murashima on 16 June 1981 in Bangkok, Prasoet said that he stayed in China from 1949 until 1958. He was formally elected as a CPT Central Committee member in 1952 at the second Party Congress. However, at the second Party Congress, the CPT adopted the strategy of armed struggle, and Prasoet strongly opposed it. In 1958, he returned to Thailand and was arrested and imprisoned. At the third Party Congress in 1962, the CPT disaffiliated Prasoet.
28. Those letters of Prasoet included the ones dated 22 November 1946, 3 September 1947, 3 May 1948, and 1 November 1948.
29. Prasoet Sapsunthon, letter to Buddhadāsa, 3 September 1947, Suan Mokkh Archives, Chaiya.
30. Prasoet Sapsunthon, letter to Buddhadāsa, 3 May 1948, Suan Mokkh Archives, Chaiya.
31. Buddhadāsa usually kept a copy of his own letters to his friends and disciples, and collected them together with his friends' letters to him. These letters were recently all filed by his disciples, and they are available for access, with appropriate permission.
32. Phra Ariyananthamuni (the then ecclesiastical title of Buddhadāsa Bhikkhu), "Phutthasasana kap sangkhom" (Buddhism and Society), *Phutthasasana* 29, 3–4 (August–November 1961): 60–76. The same sermon was published by Mahachulalongkorn Buddhist University in 1956 in order to congratulate nine monks who had been elevated to ecclesiastical titles in that year. See Phutthathat Phikkhu, *Phutthasasana kap sangkhom* (Bangkok: Khana Kammatan Mahachulalongkon Ratcha Witthayalai, 1956). This sermon of Buddhadāsa seems to have been chosen for that occasion, probably because of the increasing concerns with social aspects of Buddhism among the monks

in Wat Mahathat, in which premises the Buddhist University is located. There were several monks who had been involved in the Peace Committee movement and who had been arrested in 1952 at Wat Mahathat.

33. Phra Ariyananthamuni, "Phutthasasana kap sangkhom," p. 73.
34. According to Pracha, he conducted his interview with Buddhadāsa between 1984 and 1986. Pracha Hutanuwatr (previously ordained as Phra Pracha Pasannadhammo), interview, Bangkok, 1 May 1999. Phra Pracha, *Lao wai mua wai sonthaya*, pp. 337, 564.
35. Phra Pracha, *Lao wai mua wai sonthaya*, pp. 301–2.
36. Ibid., pp. 544–5.
37. Ibid., pp. 337–8.
38. Kasian Tejapira, "Commodifying Marxism," pp. 404–6, 558.
39. Prasoet intellectually supported the strategies of military politicians ranging from Thanom Kittikhachon in the 1960s to Chaovalit Yongchaiyut in the early 1990s. See *Anuson prasoet sapsunthon*, p. (10). Prasoet was the one who systematized *Prachatipatai baep thai* (*Thai Way of Democracy*) in the 1960s. See Eiji Murashima, "Tai ni okeru seiji taisei no shuki teki tenkan: gikai sei minshushugi to gunbu no seiji kainyu" (The Periodical Cycle of the Political Regime in Thailand: Parliamentary Democracy and Military Intervention in Politics), in *ASEAN shokhoku no seiji taisei* (*The Political Regime in the ASEAN States*), eds. Yoshiyuki Hagiwara and Eiji Murashima (Tokyo: Ajia Keizai Kenkyu-sho, 1987), pp. 151–3. Later, Prasoet also systematized the theoretical foundation of the constitution draft by the military, supposedly in the name of democracy in 1983. See Murashima, "Tai ni okeru seiji taisei no shuki teki tenkan," p. 171.
40. Regarding Prasoet's thought after becoming a military advisor, see his discussion with Sawai Kaewsom in Chapter 3, p. 98.
41. Phra Pracha, *Lao wai mua wai sonthaya*, p. 340.
42. In addition to these three, probably Supha Sirimanon (1914–1986) and Chit Phumisak (1930–1966) were also important Thai Marxist intellectuals. In fact, both Supha and Chit had read Buddhadāsa's works; however, their contact with Buddhadāsa was much less than that of Pridi, Kulap and Samak. Possibly they never met Buddhadāsa. According to Phra Pracha, who gave a public lecture at Supha's cremation ceremony, Supha was a Marxist journalist and at the same time a pious Buddhist who used to make merit at Wat Phra Kaew, and who always followed the works of Buddhadāsa. Phra Pracha Pasannathammo (Pasannadhammo), "Phutthasasana kap khwam-yuttitham thang sangkhom" (Buddhism and Justice in Society), *Pacharayasan* 13, 4 (September–October 1986): 114. Chit Phumisak also mentioned that some monks such as Paññānanda and Buddhadāsa agreed with his understanding of Buddhism. According to Sutcharit Satchawichan, Chit referred to Paññānanda's sermon, "Thammakatha ruang phra phutthasasana thi thae" (Verses of Dhamma on the True Buddhism), and Buddhadāsa's "Silapphattaparamat" (Pāli: "Sīlabbata-parāmāsa") in his draft of the famous speech on Buddhism at the 23 October incident of "throwing on to the ground" (*karani yon bok 23 Tula*). Sutcharit

Satchawichan, "Phuttha pratchaya nai thatsana 'nakhon that'" (Buddhist Philosophy in the View of 'City Slave'), *Aksonsat phichan* 3, 11–2 (April–May 1976): 50. Chit's speech was published as: Nakhon That (City Slave; pseudonym Chit Phumisak), "Phuttha pratchaya kae saphap sangkhom trong kilet, watthuniyom daialektik kae saphap thi tua sangkhom eng, mi chai patirup tam baep khong sitthantha, pratchaya watthuniyom daialektik kap pratchaya khong sitthantha phit kan yang chakan thi trong ni" (Buddhist Philosophy Solves Social Problems at the Place of Defilement, While the Philosophy of Dialectical Materialism Solves It in Society Itself, and Thus Differs from the Reform of Siddhartha; Dialectical Materialism is Thus Totally Different from the Philosophy of Siddhartha in This Sense), in Chit Phumisak, *Karani 'yon bok' 23 tula* (*The 23 October Incident of 'Throwing onto the Ground'*), ed. Samnakphim Nok-huk (Samnakphim Nok-huk, 1986), pp. 27–45. This article of Chit was translated by Craig J. Reynolds as: City Slave, "Phi Tong Luang/ The Spirit of Yellow Leaves" (For the Echols Collection, Olin Library, Cornell University, 1980).

43. A letter from Pridi's personal secretary to Buddhadāsa on 9 January 1943, Suan Mokkh Archives, Chaiya.
44. There is a letter from Pridi's personal secretary to Buddhadāsa on 9 January 1943 to inform Buddhadāsa about this plan. In his letter to Regent Pridi on 1 March 1943, Buddhadāsa discussed the selection of the place for *dhamma* practice in Ayutthaya because Wat Phanomyong was not large enough (a letter from Buddhadāsa to Regent Pridi Phanomyong on 1 March 1943, Suan Mokkh Archives, Chaiya). Buddhadāsa and Pridi met to discuss the plan sometime between the dates of these two pieces of correspondence.
45. *Wut Suwannarak* (A Cremation Volume for Wut Suwannnarak, 1 March 1998), p. 51.
46. A letter from Buddhadāsa to Pridi on 1 March 1943; Phra Thammakosachan (Paññānanda Bhikkhu), *Phutthathat khu khrai, than tham arai* (*Who is Buddhadāsa? What Did He Do?*) (Bangkok: Mulanithi Phra Dulayaphak-suwaman-chaluai-thiphawan Patthamassathan, 1998), pp. 23–4; Arun Wetchasuan, *Rattha burut awuso pridi phanomyong* (*Senior Statesman Pridi Phanomyong*) (Bangkok: Arunwithaya, 1983, 1999), p. 211.
47. In the letter from Buddhadāsa to Pridi on 1 March 1943, Buddhadāsa wrote that it was difficult to find a good forest in Ayutthaya, and suggested a new place on the Phu Khao Thong mountain, which is quite far from Wat Phanomyong. In Buddhadāsa's letter to Pho. Siriwat, Pridi's secretary, dated 20 June 1943, Buddhadāsa wrote that the monks in Ayutthaya who were supposed to be in charge of the project had not contacted him. See Buddhadāsa, letter to Pho. Siriwat, 20 June 1943, Suan Mokkh Archives, Chaiya.
48. Phra Pracha, *Lao wai mua wai sonthaya*, pp. 402–3; Phra Thammakosachan, *Phutthathat khu khrai, than tham arai*, pp. 23–4; Arun Wetchasuan, *Rattha burut awuso pridi phanomyong*, p. 211; Wani Saipradit (Pridi's daughter), interview, Bangkok, 12 October 1998.

49. According to a letter dated 7 June 1943 from Phoem Siriwat, a personal secretary of the Regent Pridi, to Buddhadāsa, Pridi selected this article for a cremation volume for Leng Sisamuang's father. Leng, who was a member of the People's Party and the manager of the Siam Commercial Bank at that time, asked Pridi to sponsor publishing the cremation volume for his father. See Phoem Siriwat, letter to Buddhadāsa, 7 June 1943, Suan Mokkh Archives, Chaiya.
50. The details about Pridi's contributions to Buddhadāsa's journal and his group are in *Phutthasasana* 11 (1943). This information is also cited in Arun Wetchasuan, *Rattha burut awuso pridi phanomyong*, p. 208.
51. Phra Pracha, *Lao wai mua wai sonthaya*, p. 322. In Phra Pracha's interview, Buddhadāsa said that in the lecture a special seat was arranged for Pridi as the Regent of King Rama VIII, but either the lecture date or Pridi's position was mistaken. Pridi was regent between 16 December 1941 and 15 December 1945, and he was the prime minister from 24 March– 9 May 1946; 8–9 June 1946; and 10 June–20 August 1946. At the time of the lecture in January 1947, Pridi was still an influential patron of the Thamrong regime, although he had stepped down from the prime ministership because of the mysterious death of King Rama VIII on 9 June 1946. Pridi's political power was ended by the military coup that overthrew the Thamrong regime on 8 November 1947. The coup also saw him exiled from his country. See Pridi Phanomyong, *Chiwaprawat yo khong nai pridi phanomyong* (*A Short Biography of Mr. Pridi Phanomyong*) (Mulanithi Pridi Phanomyong, 1983, 1992).
52. This project was in process in October 1970 when Phra Maha Sathianphong Punyawanno visited England. Phra Maha Sathianphong attended Pridi's lecture at the Samakkhi Samakhom (Solidarity Association) speaking about this project to establish a Thai Buddhist temple in France. Pridi invited Pantarato Bhikkhu (Phra Kramon Chonlasuk) in England to wait until the temple would be ready in France. However, Pantarato Bhikkhu passed away before the temple was prepared. See Phra Maha Sathianphong Punyawanno, "Than pridi sang wat thai nai pari" (Pridi Builds a Thai Temple in Paris), in *Chut suan thuang* (*The Center of Gravity*) (Bangkok: Hang Hun Suan Chamkat, 1972), pp. 125–33.
53. Wani Saipradit, interview.
54. Ibid. Wani learned this story from Than Phuying Phunsuk Phanomyong, Pridi's wife and Wani's mother. Phunsuk exhibited the book by Buddhadāsa as "Than Pridi's favorite book" at the opening exhibition of the Pridi Banomyong Library at Thammasat University on 27 June 1998.
55. Yuangrat Wedel, "Modern Thai Radical Thought," pp. 63–85.
56. In the book, *Khwam-pen-anitchang khong sangkhom*, citing commonalities to Buddhist notions, Pridi introduced Marxist notions of class, dialectics, scientific materialism, and the coming of the dark age of suppression (in Thai, he called *yuk mikkha-sanyi*), followed by the age of the Buddhist Maitreya (in Thai, *yuk si-arayamettrai*). See Pridi Phanomyong, *Khwam-pen-anitchang khong sangkhom* (*Impermanence of Society*) (Bangkok: Warasan Mo Khwam-yuttitham, 1988), particularly the final chapter in pages 88–90.

57. See Chapter 5, "Samutthan khong manut lae manutsaya sangkhom" (Origins of Human Beings and Human Society), in Pridi Phanomyong, *Khwam-pen-anitchang khong sangkhom*.
58. In Thai, *sasara* means "materials" and *-tham* is the suffix used to form an abstract noun, as in terms such as *watthanatham* or *arayatham*. See *Photchananukrom chabap ratchabandit sathan pho. so. 2525* (*A Thai Dictionary: The Royal Academy 1982 Edition*), p. 809, p. 421. For its counter concepts, Pridi translated "idealism" as *chittatham*, which is defined as an ideology that denies the significance of all material aspect. See Pridi, *Khwam-pen-anitchang*, p. 45. Pridi seems to have avoided the Thai suffix *-niyom* which indicates some kind of ideology, as the English suffix "-ism," because the Thai suffix *-niyom* is often confused with the Thai verb *niyom*, which means "be fond of." Because of this confusion, *watthuniyom*, a Thai translation of "materialism" has been often confused as *niyom-watthu*, or indulgence in material pleasure. However, the suffix, *-tham* in *sasaratham* that Pridi coined as an alternative translation for materialism, is also ambiguous; it is not clear whether Pridi intended to integrate *sasara* (material) and *tham* (the *dhamma* of Buddhism), or simply chose another suffix that implied the abstract nature of the compound word.
59. Pridi said, "The Buddha taught human beings to destroy their defilements, and not to be infatuated by materials. The true materialist (Thai: *sasarathammik*) will accept the teaching method which prevents people from becoming too intoxicated with happiness, as taught in Buddhism." See Pridi, *Khwam-pen-anitchang*, p. 45.
60. Pridi, *Khwam-pen-anitchang*, p. 90.
61. Kulap came from a not very wealthy urbanite family in Bangkok. His father was a clerk in the Railway Department, and could speak English. After his father died when Kulap was six, Kulap's mother raised her children — Kulap and his elder sister — by working as a tailor. Although his family was not very wealthy, Kulap was highly educated at an elite high school Thepsirin and at Thammasat University. Because of his radical articles on humanity criticizing the upper class, the daily newspaper *Thai Mai* (*New Thai*) abandoned his series in December 1931; another daily newspaper he wrote for, *Si Krung* (*Glorious Capital*), was temporarily closed in January 1932. After the Constitutional Revolution in June 1932, Kulap's intellectual excellence was recognized by Prince Wan Waithayakon (who was a part of the royal intellectual elite but who supported the Revolution), and he entrusted Kulap with the job of editor of *Prachachat*, a daily newspaper that he owned. See "Banthuk chiwit lae ngan khong kulap saipradit: banthuk chak chanit saipradit phu pen panraya" (A Note on the Life and Work of Kulap Saipradit: A Note By Chanit Saipradit, His Wife), *Lok Nangsu* (*Book World*) (November 1978): 29–34; "Banthuk chak phaet ying suraphin thanasophon — but-sao: lao doi nang chamrat nimaphat – phi-sao" (A Note by Kulap's Daughter, Dr. Suraphin Thanasophon: A Story By Mrs. Chamrat Nimaphat, Kulap's Elder Sister), *Lok Nangsu* (*Book World*) (November 1978): 35–7; Eiji Murashima, *Pibun: dokuritsu tai okoku no rikken*

kakumei, pp. 93–4. Kulap pursued Marxism most intensively when he studied in Australia. He had individual lessons on political science from a junior lecturer at Melbourne University, and he collected Marxist literature during his stay in Australia. For details of Kulap's life and the English translation of his works written while he was in Australia, see Scot Barmé, ed., trans., *Kulap in Oz: A Thai View of Australian Life and Society in the Late 1940s* (Clayton: Monash Asia Institute, 1995), especially "Introduction" by Barmé. A series of his articles, "Pratchaya khong latthi maksit" (The Philosophy of Marxist Ideology) in the journal *Aksonsan* in 1950 suggests that Kulap had become a Marxist. See Suphat Sukhonthaphirom, "Ramruk thung khun kulap saipradit" (A Memory of Kulap Saipradit), in *Ramluk thung 'siburapha' – kulap saipradit doi phuan ruam khuk 2495–2500 lae saha thammic* (*Memories of Kulap Saipradit by His Friends Together in Jail in 1952–1957 and His Friends in the Dhamma*), ed. Suphot Dantrakun (Nonthaburi: Samnakphim Santi Tham, 1985), pp. 6, 8. About Kulap's life and work in English, see B.A. Batson, "Kulap Saipradit: The War of Life," *Journal of the Siam Society* 69, 1 & 2 (January–July 1981): 58–73; and David Smyth, "Introduction," in Siburapha, *Behind the Painting and Other Stories* (Singapore: Oxford University Press, 1990), pp. 1–44.

62. Eiji Murashima, *Pibun: dokuritsu tai okoku no rikken kakumei*, pp. 93–4.
63. In a letter from Buddhadāsa to Kulap dated 3 January 1939, Buddhadāsa asked Kulap to publish his article, "Chiwit kap nipphan" (Life and *Nibbāna*) in the daily newspaper *Prachachat* of which Kulap was then the editor. However, Kulap's reply to Buddhadāsa's request could not be found in Suan Mokkh Archives in Chaiya. The correspondence between Buddhadāsa and Kulap were first published in the journal *Pacharayasan* (December 1986) and reprinted in various books. For example, Siburapha, *Udomtham kap phon-ngan chut phutthasasana* (*The Highest Dhamma and the Works on Buddhism*) (Bangkok: Samnakphim Dok Ya, 1988, 1993), pp. 255–76.
64. Buddhadāsa was not sure whether or not Kulap attended his first lecture in 1940 at the Buddhist Association. See Phra Pracha, *Lao wai mua wai sonthaya*, pp. 320–2, 400. Two examples of Kulap's summaries under the pseudonym Itsarachon are collected in *Ha sip pi suan mok: phak nung mua khao phut thung rao* (*Fifty Years of Suan Mokkh: Part I When They Spoke of Us*) (Bangkok: Suan Usom Mulanithi, 1982), pp. 1201–9.
65. Kulap Saipradit, letter to Buddhadāsa, 5 September 1951, 3 December 1951, 31 May 1952, Suan Mokkh Archives, Chaiya. Buddhadāsa, letter to Kulap, 19 October 1951, Suan Mokkh Archives, Chaiya.
66. Phra Pracha, *Lao wai mua wai sonthaya*, pp. 400–1; Ito's translation.
67. Ibid., p. 400.
68. About their religious training, see Suphot Dantrakun, ed., *Ramluk thung 'siburapha.'*
69. In the journal, Kulap and Samak used the title, "Kho. Cho." or *phu tong khang chai*, which means a male prisoner, until they were released. Their title in the journal became "Nai" (Mr.) after Volume 3, No. 4 (July 1957). See

Chuai Phulaphoem, "Chak samnakphim" (From the Publisher), in Siburapha, *Udomtham kap phon-ngan chut phutthasasana*. Kulap wrote a series of "Udomtham" (The Highest Dhamma) in *Wipatsanasan* from Volume 2, No. 4 (July 1956), and Samak wrote "Nung duan nai wipatsana" (A Month of Vipassanā Meditation), *Wipatsanasan* 2, 1 (January 1956), "Khun kha thang sukkhaphap khong wipatsana kammathan" (Health Advantage of Vipassanā Meditation), *Wipatsanasan* 2, 5 (September 1956), *Wipatsanasan* 2, 6 (November 1956), and "Thatsana thang pratchaya lang khao phra kammathan laeo" (A View on Philosophy After Experiencing Meditation), *Wipatsanasan* 3, 4 (July 1957).

70. Siburapha, *Udomtham kap phon-ngan chut phutthasasana*, pp. 24, 30, 43.
71. Ibid., pp. 43, 64.
72. Ibid., p. 24; Ito's translation. Kulap listed the following books written by Buddhadāsa: *Kiatikhun khong phra phuttha chao* (*The Buddha's Honor*), *Panha kiao kap phra phu pen chao, kam, anatta* (*Questions About Gods, Kamma, and Anattā*), *Nipphan* (*Nibbāna*), *Withi haeng kan khao thung phutthatham* (*The Way to Reach the Buddhist Dhamma*), and *Phuttha-prawat chak phra ot* (*The Buddha's History From His Own Speech*).
73. This series of essays was first published in the journal, *Kadung thong* (*Gold Wind-Bell*) in 1956 under the pseudonym "Ubasok" (A lay Buddhist male). These essays are collected and republished in: Siburapha, *Udomtham kap phon-ngan chut phutthasasana*, pp. 71–226. In some sections of the series of "Sonthana ruang phutthasasana," Kulap mentioned Marxist tenets, such as utopian socialism, idealism, the contrast between metaphysical and dialectical methods, and formal and dialectical logic. See Siburapha, *Udomtham kap phon-ngan chut phutthasasana*, pp. 76, 82, 136, 139. However, they are not argued in relation to Buddhism. Unlike Pridi and Samak, Kulap did not systematically discuss Marxist materialism and Buddhism.
74. Siburapha, *Udomtham kap phon-ngan chut phutthasasana*, p. 196.
75. Ibid., pp. 207–8.
76. According to Chanit Saipradit, Kulap's wife, Kulap declined politicians' offers of cooperation a number of times because he thought that it would hamper his freedom to express his opinion about what was just. For example, Kulap declined all of the following invitations: to join the People's Party after the 1932 Constitutional Revolution; to cooperate in a project for the nation by Field Marshal Phibun; to run a lawyer's office with Direk Chayanam, a famous former ambassador and former Minister for Foreign Affairs; and to become an editor of a government newspaper run by Phao Siyanon. See "Banthuk chiwit lae gnan khong kulap saipradit," p. 33.
77. After he was released from imprisonment related to the Peace Committee case in 1957, Kulap returned to his journalistic career, and was invited to visit socialist countries several times as a representative of the Thai group. While Kulap was visiting China as head of a Thai cultural exchange delegation of writers and journalists, Field Marshal Sarit Thanarat overthrew the government in a military coup in October 1958, and imposed martial law for the purposes

of countering the communist threat. Since Sarit arrested everyone who had ever visited China as a communist, Kulap decided not to return to Thailand, and he spent the rest of his life in China. See Rudi Roengchai, *Yot nung nai krasae than* (*A Drop of Water in the Stream*) (Bangkok: Samnakphim Ming Mit, 1996), p. 181.

78. The top science student in Thailand, Samak was requested by then Prime Minister Phraya Phahon to major in natural resources in earth science because there was no Thai engineer who could work for resource development, and thus all aspects of mining were monopolized by foreigners. Samak fulfilled this expectation. After his return from England, he did not choose to work in foreign companies which promised him twice the salary that the government could offer. For the details of Samak's life, see his cremation volume: *Anuson nai ngan phra ratcha thang phloeng sop phan ek samak burawat to. cho. to. mo.* (*Commemoration in the Cremation of Colonel Samak Burawat — The Third Class Order of the Thai Crown, and the Third Class Order of the White Elephant*) (15 November 1975).
79. Samak also introduced European philosophies, including Marxism and social Darwinism, in Thailand. In 1942, he was appointed a philosopher member of the Royal Academy (*Ratcha bandit nai wicha pratchaya*) at the age of 26. See *Anuson phan ek samak burawat*, p. [4].
80. NAT ko. to. 43.10/257. This is a set of archival documents reporting Samak's completion of his studies in England and boarding a ship returning to Thailand in September 1938. It says Samak (in the document his name is spelled as "Smagr Burawas") passed the final examinations for the Special B.Sc. and obtained first class honors in the B.Sc. and A.R.S.M. in June 1938. Although in the educational career column of his cremation commemoration book, *Anuson phan ek samak burawat*, it says that his study at Royal School of Mines in London University was the three years from 1935 to 1937 (p. [2]), the date of the archival documents should be considered more accurate.
81. Samak Burawat, "Suan mokkhaphalaram" (Suan Mokkhabalārāma), *Nangsuphim rai sapda ekachon* (*Weekly Magazine Private*) 4, 16 (31 May 1947); reprinted in *Ha sip pi suan mok*, pp. 1156–65.
82. Phra Pracha, *Lao wai mua wai sonthaya*, p. 545; Ito's translation.
83. Samak Burawat, "Ruang phratchaya wa duai kan-plian-plaeng" (About the Philosophies of Dynamism), *Phutthasasana* (Special issue for the tenth anniversary, 1943): 112–20.
84. Samak Burawat, "Suan mokkhaphalaram," p. 1157.
85. Phra Pracha, *Lao wai mua wai sonthaya*, p. 548.
86. Ibid., pp. 546, 554–5; Ito's translation.
87. Kaptan Samut (pseudonym Samak Burawat), "Phutthit phachoen na kap khommiunit," *Aksonsan* 4, 5 (August 1952): 10–45.
88. Kasian, "Commodifying Marxism," p. 477.
89. Anon Burawat, interview, Bangkok, 23 December 1999.
90. Mining was a boom industry in the 1960s. Employment in mining increased from 30,000 to 87,000 (+290%) between 1960 and 1970. See Table 1.2 in

World Bank, "Thailand" II (14 November 1975), quoted in Benedict Anderson, "Withdrawal Symptoms," in *The Spectre of Comparisons: Nationalism, Southeast Asia and the World* (London: Verso, 1998), p. 146.

91. Important communist intellectuals, such as Prawut Simanta and Anut Aphaphirom, said that they studied Marxism through Samak's books. Prawut Simanta, interview, Bangkok, 16 August 1999; Anut Aphaphirom, interview, Bangkok, 17 August 1999.
92. For example, Samak Burawat, *Panya wiwat phak 1, 2* (*The Evolution of Human Intellect Part 1, 2*) (Bangkok: Phrae Phitthaya, second edition 1982).
93. As his career suggests, Samak was never involved in the political communist movement after his release from the Peace Committee case. Samak also practiced *vipassanā* meditation when he was imprisoned over the Peace Committee case, and wrote his experiences of *vipassanā* in the journal, *Wipatsanasan*. However, when interviewed, Anon said that Samak did not practice meditation at home because he was busy working as an engineer.
94. The record of the *Boromatham* lecture series is published in two volumes of Buddhadāsa's series of works, *Thammakhot*: Phutthathat Phikkhu, *Boromatham: oprom phiksu nisit chulalongkon mahawitthayalai phansa pi 2512* (*Supreme Dhamma: Training for Student Monks from Chulalongkorn University in the 1969 Rains Retreat*) (Chaiya: Mulanithi Thammathan, 1982), part I, II. The *Boromatham* series includes the lecture "Ruang watthuniyom kap manoniyom" (On Materialism and Idealism), in Volume I, pp. 41–60.
95. Roy Bhaskar, "Materialism," in *A Dictionary of Marxist Thought: Second Edition*, eds. Tom Bottomore, Laurence Harris, V.G. Kiernan and Ralph Miliband (Oxford: Blackwell, 1991), p. 369.
96. See Pridi's discussion of *sasaratham*, which he viewed as distinct from both *watthu-niyom* and *niyom-watthu*. See footnote 58.
97. Buddhadāsa's understanding of *watthuniyom* was criticized as easily confused with *niyom-watthu*, which means favoring material pleasure. Some of Buddhadāsa's followers who had contact with Marxism, such as Suphot Dantrakun, Naowarat Phongphaibun, and Prasoet Sapsunthon pointed out that Buddhadāsa mistranslated the Marxist notion of "materialism" as *niyom-watthu*, or "favoring materials." Naowarat wrote a letter to Buddhadāsa to suggest this mistranslation, but Buddhadāsa did not reply. Suphot Dantrakun, interview, Bangkok, 8 October 1998; Naowarat Phongphaibun, interview, Kanchanaburi, 2 February 1999. See also Naowarat Phongphaibun, "Watthuniyom — chittaniyom kap phutthasasana" (Materialism — Spiritualism and Buddhism) in Naowarat Phongphaibun, *Dap thi mok yu nai chiwon* (*A Sword Hidden Under the Yellow Robe*) (Bangkok: Suan nangsu, 1978), pp. 231–7. Buddhadāsa mentioned this suggestion of Prasoet in his interview with Phra Pracha. See Phra Pracha Pasannathammo, *Lao wai mua wai sonthaya*, p. 340. On the other hand, Phra Pracha supported Buddhadāsa's criticism of *watthuniyom* including the notion of Marxism and addiction to material satisfaction. See Phra Pracha Pasannathammo, "Than phutthathat kap

kanpatiwat watthanatham" (Ven. Buddhadāsa and Revolution in Culture), in *Phutthathat kap khon run mai*, pp. 161–2.

98. Phutthathat Phikkhu, *Boromatham phak ton*, pp. 50–1; Ito's translation.
99. Ibid., p. 46.
100. Ibid., pp. 46, 60, 174. Buddhadāsa presented a concept of *thamma-niyom* (Dhamma-ism) as the middle way of the body and mind, or of materialism and spiritualism. The concept of *thammaniyom* can be represented by *manoniyom* because through the concept of *thammaniyom*, Buddhadāsa insisted on the position of *manoniyom*, which did hold both the material or body and the mind in control under the supervision of the mind. However, Marxists and social thinkers questioned Buddhadāsa's idea of material poverty, which is reducible to a mental attitude such as idleness. See Phutthathat Phikkhu, *Boromatham phak ton*, pp. 175–6.
101. Prawut Simanta, interview, Bangkok, 16 August 1999. Prawut was nominated to be a candidate for a member of the central committee (Thai: *kammakan klang samrong*) of the Communist Party of Thailand (CPT) in 1983, and was the number two man at the CPT's capital area division for bringing intellectuals into the Party. Prawut said that he himself had a different view from those Buddhist Marxist thinkers who had never become members of the CPT. Although Prawut was from an ethnic Thai Buddhist village in Yasothon Province, he found it unnecessary to adhere to Buddhism after he became fully enlightened about the relationship between matter and ideas through the study of the law of conservation of matter. Since Prawut was convinced by materialist philosophy and became a full Marxist, he no longer believed in Buddhism, which had disappointed him as a result of the indulgent practices of Buddhist monks. In Prawut's own words, "I respect religion, but I do not believe in religion. I completely believe in Marxism."
102. There were at least two Buddhist Marxist thinkers, Suphot Dantrakun and Suphat Sukhonthaphirom, who were never Communist Party members, but rather disciples of Pridi Phanomyong. Suphot first discussed the issues between Marxism and Buddhism in his book, *Lok khommiunit* (*Communist World*), which was first published in 1975, but this book was banned and confiscated after the 6 October reactionary coup in 1976. Suphot republished it in 1986, changing its title to *Phutthasasana kap khommiunit* (*Buddhism and the Communist*) and using the pseudonym, Sawok, which means a male Buddhist disciple. The third edition of this book is published as: Suphot Dantrakun, *Phutthasasana kap khommiunit* (Bangkok: Samnakphim Sukkhaphap Chai, 2000). See Suphot Dantrakun, "Kham khun ton" (Forward), in *Phutthasasana kap khommiunit*, p. 3. In the book, Suphot responded to the question of whether communism would destroy religion, as anti-communist government propaganda had been proclaiming. Suphot developed his argument on the philosophical question of Marxism and Buddhism by referring to Pridi Phanomyong and Samak Burawat. The other Buddhist Marxist, Suphat Sukhonthaphirom, published a book, *Phutthapratchaya kap pratchaya maksit* (*Buddhist Philosophy and Philosophy of Marxism*) in 1981; it was reprinted in

1998. See Suphat Sukhonthaphirom, *Phuttha pratchaya kap pratchaya maksit* (Nonthaburi: Sathaban Witthayasat Sangkhom, 1998). In this book, Suphat detailed the relationship between mind and matter in Buddhist and Marxist philosophy, and also referred to Buddhadāsa's works.

103. Sulak Sivaraksa *et al.*, eds., *Radical Conservatism: Buddhism in the Contemporary World* (Bangkok: Thai Inter-Religious Commission for Development, and International Network of Engaged Buddhists, 1990). This book, dedicated to Buddhadāsa, consists of contributions by Buddhist activists and scholars who subscribe to Buddhadāsa's thought.
104. See Kasian Tejapira, "Commodifying Marxism," p. 259.
105. It is not surprising to find followers of Buddhadāsa's teaching belonging to either the first or second group; however, my research concern was focused on Buddhadāsa's relationship with the third and fourth groups, which I perceived to be given more emphasis in the Thai Buddhist public sphere than the first and second groups. It is also widely known that Kukrit Pramoj, who represented the second group, disagreed with Buddhadāsa. For more detailed discussions about Kukrit and Buddhadāsa, see Chapter 4.
106. For example, Arun Wetchasuan, *Rattha burut awuso pridi phanomyong; Pacharayasan* (December 1986); Siburapha, *Udomtham kap phon-ngan chut phutthasasana.*
107. Samphat Phungprasoet, interview, Bangkok, 6 April 2000; Khana Kammakan Chat Ngan Ramluk Pluang Wannasi, ed., *Prawat phon-ngan lae kham ramluk pluang wannasi: kwi-nakkhian-naksu* (*History, Work of and Word of Condolence for Pluang Wannasi: A Poet, Writer, and Fighter*) (Bangkok: Chonniyom, 1597), p. 20.
108. Bancha Chaloemchaikit, the owner of the Sukkhaphap Chai publishing, telephone conversation, April 2000; Phutthathat Phikkhu, *Sing thi rao yang son-chai kan noi pai: chabap 3 phasa — thai, angkrit, cin* (*Things Which We Still Pay Too Little Attention to: Three Language Edition — Thai, English and Chinese*) (Bangkok: Sukkhaphap Chai, 2006).
109. Prawut, interview; Phirun Chatrawanitchakun, interview, Bangkok, 1 September 1999.
110. Kanya Lilalai, interview, Bangkok, 18 December 1999.
111. Phra Pracha, *Lao wai mua wai sonthaya*, p. 339.
112. See Kasian Tejapira, "Commodifying Marxism," pp. 449–94.
113. Phutthathat Inthapanyo, "Phukhao haeng withi phuttha-tham" (Mountainous Hindrance on the Way of the Buddha-Dhamma), in *Chumnum patthakatha chut phuttha-tham* (*The Collection of Lectures on the Buddha Dhamma*) (Bangkok: Sukkhaphap Chai, 1992), pp. 126–69.
114. The title "Phra" of Phra Thipparinya does not indicate that he was a monk; rather, it was a *bandasak* (a non-hereditary title conferred by the sovereign mostly on government officials). Phra Thipparinya (Thup Klamphasut) (1890–1977) had been a monk at Wat Rakhang and Wat Mahathat. After disrobing at the age of 22, he studied law and became a judge. As a judge, he was socially respected, and earned a good salary so that he was able to

be an influential supporter of Wat Mahathat. He was also one of the first generation of Abhidhamma teachers in Thailand. Later, he and Kittivuḍḍho Bhikkhu cooperated to attack Buddhadāsa's concept of *chit wang* (empty mind). See *Anuson ngan phra ratcha than phloeng sop: phra thipparinya (thup klamphasut)* (*Commemoration for the Cremation: Phra Thipparinya*) (21 May 1977); Phra Sithawat Vanivattiko interview, Nonthaburi, 30 April 1999.

115. Excerpts from Phra Thipparinya's leaflet which attacked Buddhadāsa were reprinted in *Ha sip pi suan mok: phak nung mua khao phut thung rao* (*Fifty Years of Suan Mokkh: Part I When They Spoke of Us*) (Bangkok: Suan Usom Mulanithi, 1982), pp. 747–62. According to his leaflets, Phra Thipparinya worked intensively to criticize Buddhadāsa. First, he sent a letter containing questions to Buddhadāsa in July 1948, a month after his lecture. On 4–6 August 1948, at Wat Thammathipatai, he gave lectures on meditation, which contained an accusation against Buddhadāsa. Those lectures were published in *Phutthacak*, the journal of the Mahachulalongkorn Buddhist University. On 28 August 1948, he produced a leaflet, "Sarup yo naew wipatsana" (Summary of Styles of Vipassanā Meditation), containing excerpts from his lectures. On 17 July 1949, he produced a leaflet containing seven questions and his answers regarding Buddhadāsa's interpretation. In 1949, Phra Thipparinya and Phraya Achayachak distributed a leaflet, "Raboet phukhao himalai: khan kho thi phutthathat phikkhu klao thet sai rai phra phut, phra tham, phra song wa pen phu khao himalai bang mai hai hen phra nipphan" (Blasting the Himalayan Mountains: Opposing Buddhadāsa Bhikkhu's Wrong Argument Which Said That the Buddha, the Dhamma and the Saṅgha are Himalayan Mountains That Hinder to Attainment of Nibbāna). They sent the leaflet to the monastic head of each province, and to the public at Wat Samphraya in Bangkok.

116. Luang Katsongkhram, a military member of the People's Party, participated in the Constitutional Revolution in 1932. He was the ringleader of the coup of November 1947, which brought Phibun Songkhram back to power after the Second World War. As a result of his actions, Luang Katsongkhram was appointed the deputy chief commander of the military. However, some years later, Luang Katsongkhram fled into exile because of a suspected attempt to overthrow Phibun. Eiji Murashima, personal communication, 16 July 1999.

117. Phra Pracha, *Lao wai mua wai sonthaya*, p. 322.

118. In 1948–1951, when Buddhadāsa was sued by Phra Thipparinya, the Supreme Patriarch was Krom Luang Wachirayanawong at Wat Bowonniwet, and the Ecclesiastical Ministry of Education was Somdet Plot Kittisophano at Wat Benchamabophit. After Wachirayanawong died in 1958, Somdet Plot succeeded to the position of the Supreme Patriarch.

119. Supreme Patriarch Wachirayanawong knew of Buddhadāsa through Maha Thongsup Suphamak at the textbook bureau of the Mahamakut Buddhist University. Buddhadāsa had once met the Supreme Patriarch before this defense. The Supreme Patriarch had already made a positive comment about Buddhadāsa's work. See Phra Pracha, *Lao wai mua wai sonthaya*, p. 301.

120. In the defense, Chamnan Luprasoet, a celebrity follower of Buddhadāsa, attended to assist Buddhadāsa, as did Phra Sasanasophon. See Phra Pracha, *Lao wai mua wai sonthaya*, p. 323. According to Sanya Dhammasakdi, Sanya sent Buddhadāsa to defend himself before Somdet Plot at Wat Benchamabophit, the latter had not yet become the Supreme Patriarch. Sanya was so afraid that he could not attend the meeting in Buddhadāsa's defense since he anticipated Plot's severe criticism of Buddhadāsa. However, Plot agreed with Buddhadāsa's opinion in the end, saying that Buddhadāsa's talk was too progressive for people to take in, and no penalty was given to him. See Thammakriat Kan'ari, "Samphat sanya thammasak" (Interview with Sanya Thammasak), *Matichon sut sapda* (*Weekly Matichon*) 8, 403 (22 May 1988): 18–20.
121. Although Phra Sasanasophon belonged to the Thammayut Order and Buddhadāsa belonged to the Mahanikai Order, Phra Sasanasophon supervised Buddhadāsa under the 1941 Saṅgha Act, which integrated the two separate administrations into one administrative unit. See Phra Pracha, *Lao wai mua wai sonthaya*, p. 377; Phra Pracha and Santisuk Sophonsiri, *Phap chiwit 80 pi phutthathat phikkhu: miti mai khong phra phutthasasana* (*Pictorical Biography of 80 Years of Buddhadāsa Bhikkhu: A New Dimension of Buddhism*) (Bangkok: Satiankoset-Nakhaprathip Foundation, 1986, 2530), p. 113.
122. Phra Sithawat Vanivattiko, interview, 30 April 1999.
123. See the biographical calendar in Phra Pracha, *Lao wai mua wai sonthaya*, p. 701; *Ha sip pi suan mok: phak nung*, p. 762.
124. Kowit Kemānanda, interview, 29 January 1999. Kemānanda stayed at Suan Mokkh from 1967 to 1971.
125. Phra Sithawat Vanivattiko, interview, Bangkok, 30 April 1999.
126. For instance, Phra Anan Chayanantho, or ordained Anan Senakhan, published a book, *Khamson khong diarathi* (*Teachings of a Heretic*) (Bangkok: Ongkan Phithak Phutthasat, 1979), which includes Bunmi and other authors' articles criticizing Buddhadāsa's teaching. In the book, Anan criticized Buddhadāsa for attracting the "New Left" of materialism, characterized as socialist rather than democratic idealism. See *Khamson khong diarathi*, p. 2. In 1975 and 1976, Arun Wetchasuan, who was in robes from 1962 to 1974, often saw handbills at his temple, the Wat Chiangwai in Bangkok, accusing Buddhadāsa of being a communist. He said that those monks who relied on superstitious magic had posted those handbills on the notice board of their temple because Buddhadāsa's teachings went against their activities. Those handbills were believed to be produced by Kittivuḍḍho, although Arun does not have any concrete evidence of that. Arun Wetchasuan, interview, Bangkok, 2 March 1999.
127. The American man from USIS explained to Buddhadāsa that Thailand had a duty to resist communism, and that Thailand would lose its Buddhism if communists took over the country. Buddhadāsa answered the American, "We are more afraid of *kilesa* (defilement) than communists," but the American did

not give up easily. The American stayed overnight, and continued negotiating with several offers, such as loudspeakers and paper for printing. However, Buddhadāsa declined the American's offers politely so as to avoid further communication with him. After the American left, Buddhadāsa received no further offers of that kind. See Phra Pracha, *Lao wai mua wai sonthaya*, p. 338. USIS was an American agency for anti-communist propagation in Thailand in operation since 1949. It hired a "fairly prominent Thai" to translate anti-communist literature from the Buddhist Society of London, for example. See Daniel Fineman, *A Special Relationship*, p. 120.

128. Arun and Suphot said that they inferred this from the connections of Buddhadāsa's opponents and their anti-communist campaign, although they have no evidence. Arun Wetchasuan, interview; Suphot Dantrakun, interview, Bangkok, 8 October 1998. However, in my interview with Kittivuḍḍho, he denied any assistance or cooperation from American agencies. He believed that Americans were happy to find that he taught people the danger of communism, and the principles for maintaining social order. He said that there was something that he could not propagate at that time. He thought that his devotion to protecting the country should be appreciated because it prevented the country from falling into the confusion experienced by Laos and Cambodia. He said that he did his duty without receiving any benefit from anyone, and that as a monk he spent less than other people. Kittivuḍḍho Bhikkhu, interview, Chonburi, 29 April 1999.

129. Sawok (Sāvaka), *To phra? anan senakhan lae khana ruang khamson diarathi* (*Arguing Against Phra? Anan Senakhan and His Group on the Heretical Teaching*) (Bangkok: Rongphim Suwannaphum, n.d.).

Chapter 7

1. A part of this chapter has been published as "Sulak and Engaged Buddhists in Contemporary Thai History," in *Socially Engaged Spirituality: Essays in Honor of Sulak Sivaraksa on His 70th Birthday*, ed. David W. Chappell (Bangkok: Sathirakoses-Nagapradipa Foundation, 2003), pp. 241–50.
2. Donald K. Swearer, "Introduction: The Vision of Bhikkhu Buddhadāsa," in *Bhikkhu Buddhadāsa, Dhammic Socialism*, ed., trans. Donald K. Swearer (Bangkok: Thai Inter-Religious Commission for Development, 1986), pp. 13–43; Peter A. Jackson, *Buddhadāsa: Theravāda Buddhism and Modernist Reform in Thailand* (Bangkok: Silkworm Books, 1988, 2003); Santikaro Bhikkhu, "Four Noble Truths of Dhammic Socialism," in *Entering the Realm of Reality: Towards Dhammic Societies*, eds. Jonathan Watts, Alan Senauke, and Santikaro Bhikkhu (Bangkok: INEB, 1997), pp. 89–161; Tavivat Puntarigvivat, "Bhikkhu Buddhadāsa's Dhammic Socialism in Dialogue with Latin American Liberation Theology," PhD diss., Temple University, 1994; Phaisan Wongwarawisit (currently known as Phra Paisal Visalo), "Than phutthathat kap thammika sangkhomniyom" (Buddhadāsa and Dhammic Socialism), in *Phutthathat kap khon run mai: mua khon num sao tham thung rak khong khwam-pen-thai*

(*Buddhadāsa and the New Generation: When Youth Asks about the Root of Thainess*) (Bangkok: Mulanithi Komon Khimthong, 1983), pp. 60–93.

3. Thich Nhat Hanh, *Vietnam: Lotus in a Sea of Fire* (New York: Hill and Wang, 1967); Chan Khong (Cao Ngoc Phuong), *Learning True Love: How I Learned and Practiced Social Change in Vietnam* (Berkeley: Parallax Press, 1993); The 14th Dalai Lama (Tenzin Gyatso), *Freedom in Exile* (New York: HarperCollins Publishers, 1990).
4. Studies on engaged Buddhism include the following literature: Christopher S. Queen and Sallie B King, eds., *Engaged Buddhism: Buddhist Liberation Movement in Asia* (Albany: State University of New York Press, 1996); Christopher S. Queen, ed., *Engaged Buddhism in the West* (Boston: Wisdom Publications, 2000); Christopher S. Queen, Charles Prebish and Damien Keown, eds., *Action Dharma: New Studies in Engaged Buddhism* (London: RoutledgeCurzon, 2003); Sallie B King, *Being Benevolence: The Social Ethics of Engaged Buddhism* (Honolulu: University of Hawai'i Press, 2005).
5. Thak Chaloemtiarana, *Thailand: The Politics of Despotic Paternalism* (Bangkok: Social Science Association of Thailand, Thai Khadi Institute, Thammasat University, 1979); David K. Wyatt, *Thailand: A Short History* (Chiangmai: Silkworm Books, 1982, 1984), pp. 278–85.
6. Pasuk Phongpaichit and Chris Baker, *Thailand: Economy and Politics* (Kuala Lumpur: Oxford University Press, 1995), p. 130.
7. Pasuk and Baker, *Thailand: Economy and Politics*, pp. 137–8.
8. In fact, Buddhadāsa's sermon about *dhamma*'s relevance to contemporary society was found prior to 1958, the beginning of the military regimes. In 1947, Buddhadāsa gave a lecture entitled "Buddha-Dhamma and the Spirit of Democracy" at the Buddhist Association of Thailand with an audience of Pridi Phanomyong, then the regent of King Rama VIII. In this lecture, Buddhadāsa extended his interpretation of the *Buddha-Dhamma* through the concepts of "democracy" consisting of liberty, equality, and brotherhood. He was trying to call people's attention to the essence of Buddhism by comparing the meanings of democracy and *dhamma* for those who were concerned with democracy. At the time of this lecture, Dhammic Socialism had not yet appeared, yet the lecture interestingly indicates Buddhadāsa's sources of ideas on society in the *Aggañña sutta*, a Buddhist scripture which he continued referring to in his Dhammic Socialism. See Phutthathat Phikkhu (Buddhadāsa Bhikkhu), *Phuttha-tham kap chetanarom khong prachathipatai* (*Buddha-Dhamma and the Spirit of Democracy*) (Nonthaburi: Kong thun wutthi tham).
9. U Nu, "Kanbanru makphon samai kung phutthakan" (the original English title: "Accomplishing the Enlightenment in the Half Buddhist Era"), *Phutthasasana* 22, 1 (February 1954): 33–4. The original title of this speech of U Nu was given as "a new method," and it was delivered on 29 November 1953 at the Conference for International Buddhist Culture.
10. Karuna Kusalasai, interview, Bangkok, 6 November 1998.
11. Buddhadāsa kept placing emphasis on "retrieving the world from the power of materialism" as one of the three wishes (Thai: *panithan 3 prakan*) that he

would like himself and other people to pursue in his later years. According to Seri Phongphit, Buddhadāsa's famous three wishes were first presented in the preface of a book, *Phut-khrit nai thatsana than phutthathat: chaikhwam haeng sasana khrit thi chaw phut khwan ruchak* (*Buddhist and Christian in the View of Venerable Buddhadāsa: The Meaning of Christianity that Buddhists Have to Know*) (Bangkok: Samnakphim Thianwan, 1984), which was transcribed and published from Buddhadāsa's lecture in 1979. Seri Phongphit, interview, Bangkok, 5 May 1999. The three wishes include: 1) Each person, without asking whether they are a Buddhist or believer of other religion, should understand his/her own religion most deeply; 2) People in different religions should understand each other well; and 3) They should rescue friend human beings from the influence of materialism. See *Phut-khrit nai thatsana than phutthathat*, p. (5).

12. David Morell and Chai-anan Samudavanija, *Political Conflict in Thailand: Reform, Reaction, Revolution* (Cambridge: Oelgeschlager, Gunn & Hain, 1981), pp. 137–80.
13. For example, there are such pocketbooks as: Phutthathat Phikkhu, *Kanmuang khu thamma* (*Politics is the Dhamma*) (Bangkok: Arun Withaya); and Phutthathat Inthapanyo, *Thammika sankhomniyom* (Bangkok: Sayam Prathet, 1995).
14. Phutthathat Phikkhu, "Prachathipatai baep sangkhomniyom" (*Democracy in the Style of Socialism*), in *Kanmuang khu thamma*, p. 149. This was originally spoken in November 1973.
15. Paisal pointed to *Mua thamma khrong lok* (*When Dhamma Rules the World*), *Silatham kap manusayalok* (*Morality and the Human World*), *Thamma sacca songkhro* (*Truth of Dhamma Helps*), *Ariyasilatham* (*Saint Morality*), *Kan-klap-ma haeng silatham* (*Return to Morality*), *Thamma kap kanmuang* (*Dhamma and Politics*), and *Yaowachon kap silatham* (*Youth and Morality*). See Phaisan Wongwarawisit, "Than Phutthathat kap thammika sangkhomniyom" (Venerable Buddhadāsa and Dhammic Socialism) in *Phutthathat kap khon run mai*, p. 61.
16. Anut Aphaphirom, interview, Bangkok, 17 August 1999.
17. Another politician, Kukrit Pramoj, who became the Prime Minister after Seni Pramoj, preferred the word *sangkhom*, even though he opposed communism from a liberal conservative point of view. Kukrit named his party *Phak Kit Sangkhom* or the Social Action Party, which was modeled after the People's Action Party in Singapore. In order to give a progressive, welfare-oriented meaning to his party, but to avoid the radical connotation of the word "people," Kukrit chose the word *sangkhom* for the name of his party. The example of Kukrit also suggests that the word *sangkhom* or *sangkhomniyom* was perceived as having a good progressive image even by a conservative politician. Anut Aphaphirom, interview.
18. Phutthathat Phikkhu, "Thamma nai thana latthi kanmuang" (Dhamma as an Ideology of Politics), in *Kanmuang khu thamma*, p. 85. This was originally spoken in 1979. As Pricha indicated, the "socialism" that Buddhadāsa meant

was a kind of collectivism (*latthi suan ruam*), an antonym of individualism (*latthi ekkathet*). Buddhadāsa preached that socialism should place emphasis on society rather than individuals. See Pricha Changkhwanyun, *Khwam-khit thang kanmuang khong than phutthathat phikkhu* (*Buddhadāsa's Thoughts on Politics*) (Bangkok: Samnakphin Chulalongkon Mahawitthayalai, 1993), p. 93.

19. Phutthathat Phikkhu, "Prachathipatai baep sangkhomniyom," p. 149.
20. Ibid., p. 153.
21. Phutthathat Phikkhu, "Sangkhomniyom chanit thi chuai lok dai" (A Kind of Socialism That Can Help the World), in *Thammika sankhomniyom*, p. 124. This was originally spoken in May 1975.
22. Phutthathat Phikkhu, "Sangkhomniyom tam lak haeng phra sasana" (Socialism According to the Principle of Religion), in *Thammika sankhomniyom*, pp. 57–110. This lecture was translated into English and given the title "A Dictatorial Dhammic Socialism" by Donald K. Swearer; it is published in Bhikkhu Buddhadāsa, *Dhammic Socialism* (Bangkok: Inter-Religious Commission for Development, 1986), pp. 77–100. This was originally spoken in September 1974. In this lecture, Buddhadāsa gave a clearer definition to his 1973 sermon about Dhammic Socialism, which entailed simply adding the "*dhamma*" to his idea of "socialism" to distinguish it from communism and its negative associations. See Phutthathat Phikkhu, "Prachathipatai baep sangkhomniyom," originally spoken in November 1973.
23. Phutthathat Phikkhu, "Sangkhomniyom tam lak haeng phra sasana," pp. 74, 91.
24. Ibid., pp. 84–8, 92–3. The ten rules include almsgiving (Pāli: *dāna*), morality (*sīla*), liberality (*pariccaga*), straightness (*ajjava*), gentleness (*maddava*), self-restriction (*tapo*), non-anger (*akkodha*), non-hurtfulness (*avihimsa*), forbearance (*khanti*), and non-opposition (*avirodhana*).
25. Ibid., pp. 97–9.
26. Ibid., pp. 102, 104.
27. See Morell and Chai-anan, *Political Conflict in Thailand*; Gawin Chutima, *The Rise and Fall of the Communist Party of Thailand (1973–1987)*, University of Kent at Canterbury, Centre of South-East Asian Studies, Occasional Paper No. 12 (1990).
28. Phutthathat Phikkhu, "Sangkhomniyom chanit thi chuai lok dai" (A Kind of Politics That Can Help the World), in *Kanmuang khu thamma*, pp. 111–50.
29. Phutthathat Phikkhu, "Thamma kap kanmuang, kanmuang kap thamma" (*Dhamma* and Politics, Politics and *Dhamma*), in *Kanmuang khu thamma*, pp. 1–76; Phutthathat Phikkhu, "Kanmuang chanit thi chuai lok dai," pp. 89–135. These lectures were originally given in July 1976.
30. There is actually a fourth difference between Buddhadāsa's socialism and orthodox Marxism, concerned with historical materialism, which was already argued in Chapter 6. In short, Buddhadāsa's socialism is not economic determinism in accordance with the historical materialism of Marx. Buddhadāsa's socialism is even distinct from the common definition of "socialism" among

Thai intellectuals, which usually means justice in distribution without threatening the monarchy and religion. Buddhadāsa's socialism aims at a fundamental order of righteousness without favoring either the poor or the rich.

31. Phutthathat Inthapanyo, "Sangkhomniyom tam lak haeng phra sasana," pp. 59–63.
32. Phutthathat Phikkhu, *Kan to tan kae khai khwam-wiparit khong lok (2519)* (*Facing up to the World Disorder for Solution, 1976*; a booklet for free distribution; 27 May 1977), p. 4.
33. Phutthathat Phikkhu, "Kanmuang chanit thi chuai lok dai," p. 90; Phutthathat Phikkhu, "Thamma nai thana latthi kanmuang," pp. 85–6.
34. Phutthathat Inthapanyo, "Sangkhomniyom chanit thi chuai lok dai," p. 115.
35. Ibid., p. 130.
36. For instance, in September 1979, Buddhadāsa spoke about Dhammic Socialism in a public radio broadcast. See Phutthathat Phikkhu, "Thamma nai thana latthi kanmuang," pp. 77–88. This was originally spoken in 1979.
37. Santikaro Bhikkhu, "Four Noble Truths of Dhammic Socialism".
38. Sulak Sivaraksa, Bangkok, 19 March 1999; Phra Paisal Visalo, Bangkok, 25 August 1999.
39. Some agree that Buddhadāsa was able to govern Suan Mokkh in a dictatorial method, and everybody approved his decisions as consistent with the *dhamma*, but no one except Buddhadāsa is confident or respected enough to administer such a group of people. Phra Kittisak Kittisophano, Bangkok, 25 August 1999.
40. Morell and Chai-anan, *Political Conflict in Thailand*, pp. 139–43.
41. About Sulak's biography, see Sulak Sivaraksa, *Loyalty Demands Dissent: Autobiography of an Engaged Buddhist* (Berkeley: Parallax Press, 1998); So. Siwarak, *Chuang haeng chiwit* (*A Period of My Life*) (Bangkok: Khlet Thai); So. Siwarak, *Chuang lang haeng chiwit* (*The Latter Period of My Life*) (Bangkok: Khlet Thai, 1997).
42. Sulak, *Loyalty Demands Dissent*, pp. 14–7. Sulak gradually became interested in the "modern Buddhism" discussed in Buddhadāsa's journal, *Phutthasasana*, as well as in Sujīvo Bhikkhu's sermons, and the works of Phra Phimolatham (Choi Thanathatto). See Sulak, *Loyalty Demands Dissent*, pp. 26, 32. However, Sulak at first did not like Buddhadāsa because of his radical teaching that the Buddha image could become a hindrance to reach the *dhamma*. When he returned from England, Sulak read a book of Buddhadāsa's, *Tam roi phra arahan* (*Following the Footprints of Arahant*) in a new light. See Sulak, *Loyalty Demands Dissent*, p. 89.
43. Sulak, *Loyalty Demands Dissent*, pp. 87–92. Although Sulak's role in promoting Buddhadāsa's social thought has been significant, Buddhadāsa was not the only mentor of Sulak. In terms of personal relationship, Sulak has had stronger ties with monks at Wat Thongnopphakhun and Mahachulalongkorn Buddhist University. Sulak does not hesitate to take a different view from Buddhadāsa, and sometimes he makes critical comments about Buddhadāsa's views. Before their first meeting in the mid-1960s, when Sulak had just

started the *Social Science Review*, both Buddhadāsa and Sulak were impressed by each other's reading of their respective works. See Phra Pracha Pasannathammo, *Lao wai mua wai sonthaya: atchiwaprawat khong than phutthathat* (*Talking in the Twilight Years: An Autobiography of Venerable Buddhadāsa*) (Bangkok: Mulanithi Komon Khimthong, 1988), p. 401; Sulak, *Loyalty Demands Dissent*, p. 89. Sulak's writings on, and interviews with Buddhadāsa are collected in several books such as: S. Sivaraksa, "Buddhadāsa Bhikkhu: A Religious Innovator of Undying Fame," in *Siam in Crisis* (Bangkok: Thai Inter-Religious Commission for Development, 1990), pp. 224–48; So. Siwarak, "Than phutthathat phikkhu" (Venerable Buddhadāsa Bhikkhu), *Phra di thi na ruchak* (*Good Monks Who Are Worth Knowing*) (Bangkok: Samnakphim Khlet Thai, 1967, 1987), pp. 149–76; So. Siwarak, *Itthiphon phutthathat to sangkhom* (*The Influence of Buddhadāsa to Society*) (Bangkok: Khana Kammakan Sasana Phua Sangkhom, 1990); So. Siwarak, *Sonthana kap than phutthathat phikkhu* (*Interview with Buddhadāsa Bhikkhu*) (Bangkok: Khana Kammakan Sasana Phua Sangkhom, 1993).

44. P.A. Payutto (1939–) is also known by his ecclesiastical titles, Phra Siwisutthimoli (1969–73); Phra Ratchawaramuni (1973–1987); Phra Thepweti (1987–1993); Phra Thammapidok (1993–2004); and Phra Brahmagunabhorn (2004–present). According to Phra Paisal Visalo, who has been working closely with Sulak since he was a student, Sulak was the one who brought P.A. Payutto into social issues. Payutto was famous for his intelligence, passing the highest level of Pāli ecclesiastical examination while he was a novice. In the late 1960s, Payutto was invited by Sulak to give a talk in a seminar on Buddhism and society held at the Siam Society; that was the first time for Payutto to perform his role outside the Saṅgha circle. Phra Paisal Visalo, email correspondence, 17 July 2002. Socially engaged Buddhists, including Phra Paisal Visalo, Sulak Sivaraska, Prawase Wasi, and Wira Sombun, wrote their articles about P.A. Payutto in: *Patthakatha khrop rop 60 pi phra thammapidok (po. o. payutto): phuttha-tham kap udomkan samrap sattawat thi 21* (*The Memorial Lecture for 60 Years of Phra Thammapidok: Buddha-Dhamma and the Aim for the 21st century*) (Bangkok: Mulanithi Komon Khimuthong, 1999).
45. Sulak, *Loyalty Demands Dissent*, p. 87.
46. For examples of Sulak's critiques in the 1960s, see S. Sivaraksa, *Siam in Crisis*, part III.
47. Pracha Hutanuwatr, interview, Bangkok, 1 May 1999.
48. Sulak Sivaraksa, *Loyalty Demands Dissent*, pp. 108–10; So. Siwarak, *Chuang lang haeng chiwit*, pp. 103–16.
49. The following descriptions of Parithat Sewana are based on an interview with Pibhop Dhongchai, a regular member of Parithat Sewana from the beginning. Pibhop Dhongchai, interview, Bangkok, 24 August 1999.
50. Although in Parithat Sewana there were people such as Charan who had connection with the Communist Party of Thailand, neither Marxism nor the Communist Party was influential.

51. When Weng entered the medical school of Mahidol University in 1968, he was 17 years old. Since Weng entered primary school when he was five, he graduated from his high school at the age of 16. Weng's experience described here is based on interviews of him by the author, Bangkok, 23 December 1998 and 31 August 1999.
52. Weng started voluntary activities from his first year in Mahidol University in 1968. In his first year, he was a secretary of the student body. In his second year, Weng became the president of the Buddhist club at Mahidol University. He said that he was not very active as its president because he did not want to be involved in activities for Buddhist ceremonies, to which he did not want to be attached. However, it was his third year when Weng started a social activity outside university. He organized a medical volunteer group of medical students to go to Khlong Toei slum. They gave children vaccinations, took physical measurements, and gave advice on how to avoid drug addiction. In his fourth year, Weng coordinated a group ordination of 20 medical students. They had an ordination ceremony at Wat Chonlaprathan by receiving precepts from Paññānanda Bhikkhu, and then had training by Buddhadāsa at Suan Mokkh. Buddhadāsa's teaching to these medical student monks is collected in Phutthathat Phikkhu (Buddhadāsa Bhikkhu), *Mahidon tham* (*Mahitala dhamma*) (Chaiya: Mulanithi Thammatham). The Thai word *mahidon* is linked to two Sanskrit words *mahitala* (surface of the earth) and *mahidhara*, literally a mountain but by extension meaning something indestructible and strong. In his fifth year in medical school, Weng was the secretary general of the Medical Student Club of Thailand (*Chomrom nisit naksuksa phaet haeng prathet thai*). He organized medical students from Chulalongkorn University, Sirirat Hospital, and Ramathibodi Hospital to do medical examinations at Khong Toei slum every Saturday and Sunday. Weng, interview, 23 December 1998.
53. Apart from Pracha, the original members of Yuwachon Sayam included Santisuk Sophonsiri and Wisit Wongwinyu, who later established the Ahiṁsā Group, which launched a journal, *Pacharayasan*. Pracha Hutanuwatr, interview, Bangkok, 1 May 1999.
54. The later generations of Yuwachon Sayam became more radical in political activism, and one member, Thongchai Winichakul, became a student leader of 6 October 1976. Another member, Phaisan Wongwarawisit, chose the non-violent approach for his activism and worked with the Ahiṁsā Group. Pracha Hutanuwatr, interview.
55. Pracha Hutanuwatr, interview.
56. Phra Paisal Visalo, interview, Bangkok, 25 August 1999. Paisal (1953–) was a member of Yuwachon Sayam; he is a year younger than Pracha.
57. The story of Pracha's experience is based on an interview with him by the author on 1 May 1999.
58. The story of Kanya's experience is based on: Kanya Lilalai, interview, Bangkok, 18 December 1999; and Rudi Roengchai (pseudonym of Kanya Lilalai), *Yot nung nai krasae than* (*A Drop of Water in the Stream*) (Bangkok: Ming Mit, 1996).

59. About Thammabucha Bookshop, see Chapter 3, p. 103.
60. Kanya Lilalai, interview.
61. Ibid.
62. Pracha Hutanuwatr, interview; Weng Tochirakan, interview, 31 August 1999; Rudi Roengchai, *Yot nung nai krasae than*, p. 104.
63. Pracha, who received the highest marks in his university entrance examination among those who applied for the social science and humanities, chose to study in the Faculty of Education at Chulalongkorn University in order to follow the path of Komon. See Rudi Roengchai, *Yot nung nai krasae than*, p. 104. Even after Komon's tragic murder, his aim and path has been respected by his junior student activists, and Sulak founded the Komon Khimthong Foundation for publishing books and organizing public lectures with the same purpose. See Sulak Sivaraksa, *Loyalty Demands Dissent*, pp. 116–8.
64. My impression is that this Thai phrase is used to refer to young people in the late 1960s in the period before student activism, and so prior to the strong influence of Marxism. Marxism was banned at that time; they were working for a way to improve the world but they had not yet found a means of doing so.
65. Weng, interview, 31 August 1999.
66. Weng Tochirakan, interview, 23 December 1998 and 31 August 1999.
67. Pracha was already a member of the League before the 14 October uprising. During that time, Pracha and his cell members were able to escape to the provinces because they received information from the Party in advance.
68. Rudi Roengchai, *Yot nung nai krasae than*, p. 147.
69. The CPT did not demand that its followers abandon religion as a prerequisite for party membership. In fact, the CPT was tolerant of its members' faith in Buddhism to a certain extent. Phirun Chatrawanitchakun, interview, Bangkok, 1 September 1999; Chonthira Satyawatthana, interview, Bangkok, 25 August 1999; Prawut Simanta, interview, 16 August 1999, etc. Although the intellectual members were criticized for participating in superstitious rituals to protect themselves from *phi* or evil spirits, members were not criticized for having an interest in Buddhist philosophy and for respecting "good monks" such as Phra Phimolatham and Buddhadāsa Bhikkhu. Phirun, interview. There were even some CPT leaders such as Pluang Wannasi (1922–1996) and Prasit Thiansiri who acknowledged the significance of religion. Pluang was a former MP from Surin Province and a central committee member of the CPT, and was also known for his poems. He respected Buddhadāsa and P.A. Payutto Bhikkhu until his death in China. See Khana Kammakan Chat Ngan Ramluk Pluang Wannasi (The Committee for the Memory of Pluang Wannasi), ed., *Prawat phon ngan lae kham ramluk pluang wannasi: kwi, nak khit, nak khian, nak su* (*The History of Works and Memories of Pluang Wannasi: Poet, Thinker, Writer, and Fighter*) (Bangkok: Khana Kammakan Chat Ngan Ramluk Pluang Wannasi, 1997), p. 20. Prasit was the leader of the CPT in the southern provinces, which had been the most powerful and self-supportive army of the CPT, requiring no assistance from China or other foreign countries. When he was confronted by and disappointed with the dominant Chinese Party's policy,

and sent on to the northern bases, he was reading the *Tipiṭaka* in the jungle. Seksan Prasoetkun, interview, Bangkok, 31 August 1999. Seksan was together with Prasit in the jungle in the north for six months. Prasit had been in jail from 1952 to 1957 for involvement in the Peace Committee case, and practiced *vipassanā* meditation and studied the Abhidhamma with Phra Phimolatham. See Suphat Sukhonthaphirom, "Raluk thung kulap saipradit" (The Memory of Kulap Saipradit), in *Ramluk thung 'siburapha' — kulap saipradit doi phuan ruam khuk 2495–2500 lae saha thammic* (*Memories of Kulap Saipradit by His Friends Together in Jail in 1952–1957 and His Friends in the Dhamma*), ed. Suphot Dantrakun (Nonthaburi: Samnak-phim Santi Tham, 1985), p. 10. In the CPT, however, no one called him/herself a *phutthasasanikachon* or a Buddhist. Phirun, interview.

70. Pracha Hutanuwatr, interview. ; Rudi Roengchai, *Yot nung nai krasae than*, p. 147.
71. Rudi Roengchai, *Yot nung nai krasae than*, p. 170.
72. Ibid., pp. 143–4, 148.
73. Weng, interview, 23 December 1998; Anut Aphaphirom, interview, Bangkok, 17 August 1999.
74. Bowie, *Rituals of National Loyalty*, pp. 19–33.
75. Wisit was the practical editor of *Pacharayasan* in the second half of 1974. The nominal editor (*bannathikan*) of the journal was Sulak Sivaraksa for official purposes. Wisit was officially in the position of sub-editor (*phu chuai saraniyakon*) to the main editor, Pibhop Dhongchai, but it was Wisit who was in charge of presenting the volumes in line with the principle of *ahiṁsā*.
76. Santisuk was the editor (*saraniyakon*) in 1975.
77. Paisal was the editor (*saraniyakon*) in 1975–1977.
78. At that time, Pibhop was working daytime as the secretary of Sulak Sivaraksa and pursuing his studies in the evenings. He was also involved then in work at the instructional materials company Thai Wathana Phanit and on the editorial board of *Social Science Review* (*Sangkhomsat parithat*). Pibhop Dhongchai, interview, Bangkok, 24 August 1999.
79. Pibhop Dhongchai, interview.
80. Gandhi's life and work was known in Thailand at least since 1938 through Sawami Satthayanantha Buri's (Swami Satyananda Puri's) *Mahatama khanthi: phu patthiwat india* (*Mahatma Gandhi: An India's Revolutionary*) (Bangkok: Dharmashrama, 1938). Gandhi became more popular among recent generations through the translations of Karuna Kusalasai and Ruan'urai Kusalasai, the Thai scholars of Indian literature in Hindi and Sanskrit. *Pacharayasan* also propagated the ideas and activities of Gandhi and his followers from the mid-1970s onward.
81. Pracha Hutanuwatr, interview. Thich Nhat Hanh's thought and approach became very influential among Thai student activists through the works of the Ahiṁsā Group in *Pacharayasan*. About Thich Nhat Hanh, see Sallie B. King, "Thich Nhat Hanh and the United Buddhist Church: Nondualism in Action," in *Engaged Buddhism: Buddhist Liberation Movements in Asia*, eds. Christopher

S. Queen and Sallie B. King (Albany: State University of New York Press, 1996), pp. 321–63.

82. Thit Nat Han (Thich Nhat Hanh), *Patihan haeng kan tun yu samoe* (*Miracle of Being Awake*), trans. Phra Pracha Pasannathammo (Bangkok: Mulanithi Komon Khimthong, 1995).
83. The announcement of the CGRS establishment is in "Thalaengkan" (Announcement), *Pacharayasan* 5, 17 (March–April 1976); Pracha Hutanuwatr, interview; Phra Paisal Visalo, interview, Bangkok, 25 August 1999; Phra Paisal Visalo, email correspondence, 17 July 2002.
84. Pracha Hutanuwatr, interview.
85. Ibid.
86. Phra Pracha Pasannathammo, *Phawana kap kan-rap-chai sangkhom* (*Meditation Practice and Serving Society*) (Bangkok: Mulanithi Komon Khimthong, 1981), pp. 5–9.
87. Ibid., pp. 42–5.
88. Pracha's ordained name was Phra Pracha Pasannathammo. Pracha remained a monk for 11 years, and disrobed in 1986. Pracha Hutanuwatr, interview.
89. Phra Pracha Pasannathammo, "Than phutthathat kap kan-patiwat watthanatham" (Venerable Buddhadāsa and Revolution in Culture) in *Phutthathat kap khon run mai*, p. 154.
90. Ibid., pp. 148, 154, 160–70.
91. Kanya Lilalai, interview.
92. Gawin Chutima, *The Rise and Fall of the Communist Party of Thailand (1973–1987)*, University of Kent at Canterbury, Centre of South-East Asian Studies, Occasional Paper No. 12 (1990), pp. 37–41; Pasuk and Baker, *Thailand: Economy and Politics*, pp. 311–2.
93. Kanya Lilalai, interview.
94. Rudi Roengchai, *Yot nung nai krasae than*, p. 282.
95. Kanya Lilalai, interview.
96. Rudi Roengchai, *Yot nung nai krasae than*, pp. 288–9.
97. Kanya Lilalai, interview.
98. Apart from Buddhadāsa's, several other schools of Buddhism fulfilled the internal demands of former communists. According to some of the former CPT members, such as Charan Ditthanphichai and Phirun Chatrawanitchakun, there were many former party comrades and villagers in the Buddhist communities of Santi Asoke, which resembled the ideal of communism. Charan Ditthanphichai, interview, 21 August 1999; Phirun Chatrawanitchakun, interview, 1 September 1999. Suthep Lakkhanawichian, one of the most influential underground mobilizers of university and high school students throughout the 1970s, became ordained in 1988 as a monk, Phra Suthep Chinawaro. Suthep followed a meditation teacher, Luang Pho Thian. Phra Suthep Chinawalo, interview, 26 August 1999.
99. Anut Aphaphirom, interview, 17 August 1999.
100. For example, Weng stated that Stalin killed his political enemies through his *dosa* (anger) and *moha* (ignorance), and Mao Tse-tung killed people for

the sake of his Cultural Revolution, and acquired many pretty women as his "wives". Weng, interview, 23 December 1998.

101. Weng, interview, 31 August 1999.
102. Phra Dutsadi Medhāṅkuro, interview, 6 March 1999. Dutsadi entered Thammasat University in 1977, and became the president of the Buddhist club in his third year. Throughout and after his activities in the Buddhist club, Dutsadi worked closely with Sulak Sivaraksa and the Buddhist activists who sought Sulak's advice. After graduating from university and working for NGOs for four years, Dutsadi was ordained as a monk in 1985, and stayed at Suan Mokkh for eight years, 1987–1995.
103. In Thammasat University, the Buddhist club was differentiated into three sub-groups: the group undertaking the traditional Buddhist ceremonies; the meditation group; and the social work group. The members of the social work group organized a camp to help develop rural communities and urban slum areas. They had contact with Sulak and some NGOs as well. Phra Dutsadi, interview.
104. Compared with Sulak, a public intellectual who basically does not have a position in academia, Prawase belongs to more elite circles. Prawase studied in the United States and in England on a Royal Scholarship, and became an expert on hematology. He has had important positions in Sirirat Hospital, Mahidol University, and the Doctors Council. When Prawase started reading Sulak's journal, *Social Science Review* (*Sangkhomsat Parithat*), and was involved in an extensive research on thalassemia (a blood disease) in rural areas in the 1960s, he began to pay attention to the villagers' diseases and poverty. Around the same time, Prawase became interested in Buddhism through the influence of Dr. Uai Ketsing at Sirirat Hospital. However, Prawase preferred Buddhadāsa's sermons to those of the forest monks whom Uai respected. For Prawase's biography, see Prawet Wasi, *Bon sen thang chiwit* (*On the Road of Life*) (Bangkok: Mo Chaoban), Vols. 1–7.
105. Waraphong Wetchamalinon, a secretary at the Thai Inter-Religious Commission for Development, interview, Bangkok, 23 August 1999.
106. About development monks, see Seri Phongphit, *Religion in a Changing Society: Buddhism, Reform and the Role of Monks in Community Development in Thailand* (Hong Kong: Arena Press, 1988).
107. Phra Khru Suphacharawat, interview, Yasothon, 25 December 1999; Prida Ruangwichithon, *Phlik fun khun chiwit: chiwit lae ngan khong phra khru suphacharawat* (*Restoring Life: Life and Work of Phra Khru Suphacharawat*) (Bangkok: Khana Kammakan Sasana phua Kanphatthana, 1992).
108. Prawase Wasi, interview, Bangkok, 29 April 1999.
109. Prawet Wasi (Prawase Wasi), *Thammika sangkhom* (Bangkok: Mulanithi Komon Khimthong, 1995), pp. 34–59.
110. Ibid., pp. 3–4.
111. Prawase Wasi, interview.
112. "Bot nam: thammika sangkhomniyom si khiao" (Introduction: Green Dhammic Socialism), *Pacharayasan* 20, 4 (October– December 1993): 7–15.

113. Phra Phaisan Wisalo (Paisal Visalo), "Yutthasat thammika sangkhomniyom lae thang ok haeng phuttha-tham" (The Strategy of Dhammic Socialism and an Exit [i.e., solution of a problem] at the Buddha Dhamma), *Pacharayasan* 25, 3 (March–June 1999): 33.
114. Ibid., p. 35.
115. Santikaro Bhikkhu, "The Four Noble Truths of Dhammic Socialism," in *Entering the Realm of Reality*, eds. Watts, Senauke, and Santikaro, pp. 89–161.
116. "Bot nam: thammika sangkhomniyom si khiao," pp. 12–3.
117. Phra Phaisan, "Yutthasat thammika sangkhomniyom," p. 36.

Chapter 8

1. This chapter was originally published as "Dhammamātā: Buddhadāsa Bhikkhu's Notion of Motherhood in Buddhist Women Practitioners," *Journal of Southeast Asian Studies* 38, 3 (October 2007): 409–32.
2. See Tomomi Ito, "Buddhist Women in Dhamma Practice in Contemporary Thailand: Movements Regarding Their Status as World Renunciates," *Journal of Sophia Asian Studies* 17 (1999): 147–81; and Monica Lindberg Falk, *Making Fields of Merit: Buddhist Nuns Challenge Gendered Orders in Thailand* (Göteborg: Department of Social Anthropology, Göteborg University, 2002).
3. See Karma Lekshe Tsomo, ed., *Śakyadhītā: Daughters of the Buddha* (Delhi: Sri Satguru Publications, 1988); Chatsumarn Kabilsingh, *Thai Women in Buddhism* (Berkeley: Parallax Press, 1991); Tessa J. Bartholomeusz, *Women under the Bo Tree: Buddhist Nuns in Sri Lanka* (Cambridge: Cambridge University Press, 1994); Karma Lekshe Tsomo, ed., *Buddhist Women Across Cultures: Realizations* (Delhi: Sri Satguru Publications, 1999); Karma Lekshe Tsomo, ed., *Innovative Buddhist Women: Swimming Against the Stream* (Surrey: Curzon Press, 2000); Charles S. Prebish, "Varying the *Vinaya*: Creative Responses to the Modernity" in *Buddhism in the Modern World: Adaptations of an Ancient*, eds. Steven Heine and Charles S. Prebish (New York: Oxford University Press, 2003), pp. 45–74.
4. Santikaro Bhikkhu, "Buddhadāsa Bhikkhu: Life and Society through the Natural Eyes of Voidness," in *Engaged Buddhism: Buddhist Liberation Movements in Asia*, eds. Christopher S. Queen and Sallie B. King (Albany: State University of New York Press, 1996), p. 185.
5. Buddhadāsa's thought has been extensively studied and is widely known in Western languages through the publications of three scholars: Bhikkhu Buddhadāsa, *Me and Mine: Selected Essays of Bhikkhu Buddhadāsa*, ed., trans. Donald K. Swearer (Albany: State University of New York Press, 1989); Peter A. Jackson, *Buddhadāsa: A Buddhist Thinker for the Modern World* (Bangkok: The Siam Society, 1988); Louis Gabaude, *Une herméneutique bouddhique contemporaine de Thaïlande: Buddhadāsa Bhikkhu* (Paris: École Française d'Extrême-Orient, 1988). With a new preface and epilogue, Jackson's book was reprinted in 2003 as *Buddhadāsa: Theravāda Buddhism*

and Modernist Reform in Thailand (Chiang Mai: Silkworm Books). However, it does not include Buddhadāsa's thoughts on women practitioners. I also did not deal with this topic in Tomomi Ito, "Discussions in the Buddhist Public Sphere in Twentieth-Century Thailand: Buddhadāsa Bhikkhu and His World," PhD diss., The Australian National University, 2001.

6. For instance, the following studies refer to Buddhadāsa as a significant Buddhist thinker pertaining to rural development work and engaged Buddhism: Seri Phongphit, *Religion in a Changing Society: Buddhism, Reform and the Role of Monks in Community Development in Thailand* (Hong Kong: Arena Press, 1988), pp. 8–11, 28; Christopher Queen, ed., *Engaged Buddhism in the West* (Boston: Wisdom Publications, 2000), pp. 4–5.
7. On Narin, see Sakdina Chatrakun na Ayutthaya, *Chiwit, naew khit, lae kan-to-su khong 'narinklung' ru narin phasit: khon khwang lok* (*The Life, Thought, and Struggle of 'Narinklung' or Narin Phasit: A Man Blocks the World*) (Bangkok: Samnakphim Matichon, 1993).
8. Ito, "Buddhist Women in Dhamma Practice," pp. 152–3.
9. Dhammadāsa Phanit, interview, Chaiya, 4 March 1999.
10. Phra Pracha Pasannathammo (Pasannadhammo Bhikkhu), *Lao wai mua wai sonthaya: Atchiwa prawat khong than Putthathat* (*Talking in the Twilight Years: An Autobiography of Venerable Buddhadāsa*) (Bangkok: Mulanithi Komonkhimthong, 1992), pp. 121–2; all translations from Thai are Ito's.
11. Luk lae lan (Offspring) (probably written by Buddhadāsa on behalf of his siblings), "Matubuchanuson" (Commemoration of Mother), *Phutthasasana* (*Buddhism*) 16, 3 (1948): 82.
12. Pracha, *Lao wai mua wai sonthaya*, p. 121.
13. Dhammadāsa, interview, 4 March 1999.
14. On Ki's background, see Ito, "Buddhist Women in *Dhamma* Practice," pp. 166–7.
15. In March 1999 in the Suan Mokkh Archives in Chaiya, I had access to 14 letters between Buddhadāsa and Ki Nanayon dated 16 January 1939 through 3 December 1940. In the contemporary Thai context, *ubasika* is used to refer to pious lay women dedicated to Buddhist practices, often indicating renunciant female practitioners, including *mae chi* and those who subscribe to other styles.
16. Ki Nanayon, letter to Buddhadāsa, dated 12 August 1939.
17. In the area surrounding Ratchaburi Province, where Ki was based, people usually call renunciant female practitioners *ubasika* (Thai pronunciation of Pāli *upāsikā*). They call both *mae chi* who don white robes and those who take other costumes *ubasika*, so it was a convenient concept which could comprehensively cover various types of female practitioners. In fact, Ki observed the eight precepts and had her head shaved, just as *mae chi* do, but she did not take the white robes of *mae chi*, instead wearing a white blouse and a black skirt. In Thai, those who wear an outfit such as Ki are commonly called *ubasika*, not *mae chi*.

18. An evidence of the high credit given to Buddhadāsa was the then Acting Supreme Partiarch's visit to his forest temple in southern Thailand in 1937. Buddhadāsa was only 31 years old and had no ecclesiastical title, but his intellectual prowess was widely recognized by both monastic and lay Buddhist intellectuals who read his tri-monthly Buddhist journal, *Phutthasasana*, launched in 1933. See details in Chapter 2.
19. Ki Nanayon, letters to Buddhadāsa, dated 23 January 1940, 19 May 1940, and 17 July 1940.
20. Buddhadāsa, letter to Ki Nanayon, dated 3 December 1940; Ito's translation.
21. Ito, "Buddhist Women in *Dhamma* Practice," p. 175, footnote 48.
22. Buddhadāsa expressed appreciation for Ki's religious pursuit and practice in an interview by his disciple monk. See Pracha, *Lao wai mua wai sonthaya*, pp. 398–9.
23. Ranchuan Inthrakamhaeng, *Sitthi satri, withi phut: ranchuan inthrakamhaeng patthakatha* (*Women's Rights, Buddhist Methods: Lecture by Ranchuan Inthrakamhaeng*), ed. Sompong Phrompiam (Nonthaburi: Gender Press, 1994), p. 65. Although in the comment by Dutsadi Medhaṅkuro Bhikkhu, in this book, the names of the monk and the woman are not specified, the same story was told as a dialogue between Bhikkhu Paññānanda and Sara by one of Sara's daughters. Utsa Rongkhasuan, interview, Bangkok, January 1999.
24. Ranchuan, *Sitthi satri, withi phut*, p. 65; Ito's translation.
25. Pracha, *Lao wai mua wai sonthaya*, pp. 279–80; the quotation is Ito's translation.
26. Ibid., pp. 279–80, 367–8.
27. Ranchuan said that when she lived in Suan Mokkh, Buddhadāsa made her forget her gender, because he gave her the same opportunities as monks for studying, practicing and asking him questions about *dhamma*. He recognized her ability to teach, so he let her take the task of teaching other practitioners without considering her gender. She said that such wise teachers as Buddhadāsa hardly made women feel inferior. See Ranchuan, *Sitthi satri, withi phut*, pp. 16–7. Regarding her background, see Ito, "Buddhist Women in *Dhamma* Practice," p. 167; and *Chiwit lok, chiwit tham: prawat chiwit thammada khong ranchuan inthrakamhaeng* (*Secular Life and Dhamma Life: Biography of Ranchuan Inthrakamhaeng*) (Bangkok: Kong-thun Thamma Sawatdi, 2004).
28. *Watthu-anuson 100 wan morana: nang kimsoi hemakun* (*Commemoration of the 100th Day After Passing: Mrs. Kimsoi Hemakun*) (Chaiya: Suan Mokkha-balarama, 14 October 1989).
29. Metta Phanit, interviews, Suan Mokkh, 5 March 1999, 9 May 2005. According to Metta, Kimsoi had had six children, but one of them died very young.
30. Metta, interview, 5 March 1999.
31. Ibid. In his book *Moradok thi kho fak wai* (*Legacies to be Bequeathed*), Buddhadāsa's eighth legacy was as follows: "Suan Mokkh International is particularly for friends of different nations and different languages to be illuminated in their spirituality. I came to this idea when they were struggling to search for their true self." See Phutthathat Inthapanyo (Buddhadāsa

Indapañño), *Moradok thi kho fak wai* (Bangkok: Thammasapha, 1997), p. 14; the quotation is Ito's translation.

32. In the Thai standard measurement of area, the three plots of land are respectively 60 *rai*, 100 *rai*, and *40* rai. One *rai* is equivalent to 1,600 square meters.
33. Ubasika Dr. Soemsap Damrongrat (a teacher at the Dhammamātā Hermitage), interview, Suan Mokkh, 8 May 2005.
34. Santikaro was a monk when he stayed at the Dhamma Missionary Training Community. He later moved to the United States. Although presently no longer a monk, Santikaro still uses his ordained name and teaches Buddhism. Santikaro, email correspondence, 15 December 2005.
35. *Thammasom thammamata* (*Dhammamātā Hermitage*) (Chaiya: Dhammadāna Foundation, 2001).
36. Ibid., p. 11; Ito's translation. In the following, quotations from Buddhadāsa's notes are translated by Ito.
37. I am grateful to Dr. Mark Allon at the University of Sydney for suggesting this English translation.
38. Quotations from Buddhadāsa, "Thammasom thammamata" (The First Note) and "Thammamata" (The Third Note) in *Thammasom thammamata* (Chaiya: Dhammadāna Foundation, 2001).
39. "Thammamata" (The Third Note) in *Thammasom thammamata* (Chaiya: Dhammadāna Foundation, 2001).
40. Buddhadāsa, "Asom thammamata" (The Fourth Note) in *Thammasom thammamata* (Chaiya: Dhammadāna Foundation, 2001).
41. Buddhadāsa, "Asom thammamata" (The Second Note) in *Thammasom thammamata* (Chaiya: Dhammadāna Foundation, 2001).
42. Buddhadāsa, "Asom thammamata" (The Fourth Note) in *Thammasom thammamata* (Chaiya: Dhammadāna Foundation, 2001).
43. Buddhadāsa, "Asom thammamata" (The Second Note) in *Thammasom thammamata* (Chaiya: Dhammadāna Foundation, 2001). Although in his note, Buddhadāsa did not mention Muslim prayers, Ubasika Soemsap Damrongrat, who studied closely with him in his later years at Suan Mokkh and is currently a teacher at the Dhammamātā Hermitage, said in an interview (8 May 2005) that he was inspired by Muslim prayers.
44. Buddhadāsa wrote in one of his *dhammamātā* notes, "It is better, more appropriate and more convenient for women to teach women with each other, so we should have *dhammamātā*." See "Thammamata" (The Third Note), in *Thammasom thammamata* (Chaiya: Dhammadāna Foundation, 2001).
45. Ibid.
46. Phra Thammakosachan (Phutthathat phikkhu) (Buddhadāsa Bhikkhu), "Mae thi than yang mai ru-chak: Lok ca mi santiphap, tha ru-chak mae thi thae ching" (Motherhood That You Have Not Yet Known: The World Would Have Peace, If It Knows the True Mother), in Phutthathat Phikkhu and Panyanantha Phikkhu (Paññānanda Bhikkhu), *Mae phra nai ban: Phra*

thamma-thetsanaphiset (*Mother is a Monk at Home: Special Dhamma Sermons*) (Bangkok: Thammasapha, n.d.), p. 49; Ito's translation.

47. Phutthathat Phikkhu (Buddhadāsa Bhikkhu), *Phra khun khong mae khu santiphap khong lok* (*Mothers' Virtues are World Peace*) (Bangkok: Atammayo, n.d.), p. 4; the original sermon was delivered on 12 August 1989. The translation is by Ito. The analogy of mother's milk as her blood seems to be common in Thailand. Jane Hanks, based on her research in Central Thailand, quoted a saying that "[mother's] blood was purified to a white color to become the milk of the breast"; Hanks, *Maternity and Its Rituals in Bang Chan* (Ithaca: Cornell Southeast Asia Program Data Paper, 1963), p. 72.
48. Phutthathat, *Phra khun khong mae*, p. 14. According to a friend, if we use too much strength in shredding coconut meat, the meat will crumble into big pieces which cannot be properly shredded and are unsuitable for squeezing out milk.
49. Phot Yangphonkhan, ed., *Mae son wai: Ruap ruam kham son khong mae Phutthathat Phikkhu* (*Mother Taught: A Collection of Teachings by the Mother of Buddhadāsa Bhikkhu*) (Bangkok: Sukkhaphap Chai, 2002), pp. 19–20, 37.
50. Phutthathat, *Phra khun khong mae*, p. 18; Ito's translation.
51. Metta, interview, 9 May 2005. The quotation is from Phutthathat, *Phra khun khong mae*, pp. 18–9. A similar story appears in another Buddhadāsa's sermon "Mae thi than yang mai ru-chak" (Aspects of Mothers You Do Not Know Yet), in *Mae phra nai ban*, p. 45.
52. Phutthathat Phikkhu (Buddhadāsa Bhikkhu), "Thammamata" (Dhammamātā), in *Anuson ngan phra ratcha than phloem sop: nang phitsamai kamalamen (im'udom)* (*Commemoration for the Cremation Ceremony: Mrs. Phitsamai Kamalamen [Im'udom]*) (28 November 1994), p. 44; Ito's translation. On the other hand, in his notes on the Dhammamātā Hermitage, Buddhadāsa metaphorically described women practitioners as mothers who have *dhamma*.
53. Phutthathat, "Thammamata" (Dhammamātā), in *Anuson ngan phra ratcha than phloeng sop nang phitsamai*, p. 37. See Phra Thepwethi (P.A. Payutto Bhikkhu; now known as Phra Phromkhunaphon), *Dictionary of Buddhism* (Bangkok: Mahachulalongkon Ratchawitthayalai, 1992), p. 125.
54. Buddhadāsa explained each of the three by means of nine attributes. Concerning textual study, he quoted *navaṅga-sathusāsana* (the Teacher's nine-factored dispensation), including *sutta* (discourses), *geyya* (discourses mixed with verses), *veyyākarana* (prose-expositions), and others. See Phutthathat, "Thammamata," pp. 37–9; Phra Thepwethi, *Dictionary of Buddhism*, pp. 261–2. These nine seem to be composite styles of teaching. Regarding the realizable or attainable aspect, or realization aspect, he said that it corresponds with the nine *lokuttara dhamma*, consisting of four *magga* [paths], four *phala* [results], and one *nibbāna*. However, in this sermon, he did not give precise details about the realizable aspect. See Phutthathat, "Thammamata," pp. 41–2.
55. The cycle of causes and effects is called *saṁsāravaṭṭa* in Pāli. Buddhadāsa explained that because of the transcendence from the cycle, *arahaṁ* is the

one who should be paid respect and who has no secret to hide, while Phra Thepwethi translates *arahaṁ* as "holy; worthy; accomplished." See *Dictionary of Buddhism*, p. 262. In the Thai translation of morning chanting, Buddhadāsa translated it as "the prospered one who is away from defilements"; *Tham wat chao yen lae suat mon phiset bang bot plae Thai khong Samnak Suan Mokphalaram Chaiya* (*Morning and Evening Chants and Some Special Chants, Thai Translation, by Suan Mokkhabalarama, Chaiya*), p. 2.

56. Phra Thepwethi, *Dictionary of Buddhism* translates the last three terms respectively as "the teacher of gods and men," "awakened," and "blessed; analyst" (p. 262). In Buddhadāsa's Thai translation of the morning chants, *bhagavā* is rendered as "the prosperous one who distributes *dhamma* to teach living beings." See *Tham wat chao yen*, p. 3.
57. *Tham wat chao yen*.
58. Phutthathat, "Thammamata," p. 47; Ito's translation.
59. I have written about Buddhist women's opinions on movements to raise their status in Ito, "Buddhist Women in *Dhamma* Practice" and Tomomi Ito, "Ordained Women in Yellow Robes: An Unfamiliar "Tradition" in Contemporary Thailand," in *Out of the Shadows: Socially Engaged Buddhist Women*, ed. Karma Lekshe Tsomo (Delhi: Sri Satguru Publication, 2006), pp. 168–71.
60. Marjorie A. Muecke, "Make Money Not Babies: Changing Status Makers of Northern Thai Women," *Asian Survey* 24, 4 (1984): 461–2.
61. Marjorie A. Muecke, "Thai Conjugal Family Relationships and Hsu Hypothesis," *Journal of the Siam Society* 71, 1–2 (1983): 25–41; A. Thomas Kirsch, "Development and Mobility among the Phu Thai of Northeast Thailand," *Asian Survey* 6, 7 (1966): 370–8; Hanks, *Maternity and Its Rituals*, pp. 72–3; Charles F. Keyes, "Mother or Mistress But Never a Monk: Buddhist Notions of Female Gender in Rural Thailand," *American Ethnologist* 11, 2 (1984): 229; and Penny Van Esterik, "Nurturance and Reciprocity in Thai Studies," in *State Power and Culture in Thailand*, Monograph 44, ed. E. Paul Durrenberger (New Haven: Yale Southeast Asia Studies, 1996), pp. 24–5. On the schoolchildren's and women's views, see Muecke, "Thai Conjugal Family Relationships," p. 32; Hanks, *Maternity and Its Rituals*, pp. 76–7.
62. Van Esterik, "Nurturance and Reciprocity in Thai Studies," p. 27. Jane Hanks cited mothers' virtues sung in tonsure-chants. See *Maternity and Its Rituals in Bang Chan*, p. 32. Ms. Chintana Sandiland, a Thai lecturer at the Australian National University, mentioned that the bride price paid by the groom to the bride's mother is called *kha nam nom* (milk price). Chintana, personal communication, 3 February 2006.
63. Chintana, personal communication, 3 February 2006. On the *tham khwan nak* ceremony, see Stanley J. Tambiah, *Buddhism and the Spirit Cults in North-East Thailand* (Cambridge: Cambridge University Press, 1970), p. 105; the term "*nāga*" (*nak*) in this context designates the candidate for ordination. Tambiah's discussion uses the term "*su khwan*," which replaces "*tham khwan*" in northeastern Thailand and Laos.

64. Than Wat Thanontaeng (probably an abbot of Wat Thanontaeng), "*Tham khwan nak chaloei sak*" (Ceremony for Strengthening the Spirit Essence for an Ordination Candidate), in Kasem Bunsi, *Prapheni tham bun nai Phutthasasana* (*Merit-Making Customs in Buddhism*) (Bangkok: Khurusapha, 1961), pp. 137–8; Ito's translation.
65. In Thai, this image appears as the title "Mother" in the names of goddesses, such as the Earth (*Mae Thorani*) and Rice (*Mae Phosop*) Goddesses. See Jane Hanks, "Reflections on the Ontology of Rice," in *Culture in History: Essay in Honor of Paul Radin*, ed. Stanley Diamond (New York: Octagon Press, 1981), pp. 298–301; and John P. Ferguson, "The Great Goddess Today in Burma and Thailand: An Exploration of Her Symbolic Relevance to Monastic and Female Roles," in *Mother Worship: Theme and Variations*, ed. James J. Preston (Chapel Hill: University of North Carolina Press, 1982), pp. 283–303. Lucien and Jane Hanks quoted a ceremonial dialogue between two monks about the Rice Goddess, in which one monk asked the other why we do not call her "Father." The response was, "Mother means one who is our benefactor, but father means a person who has power. Things having power, influence and hardness are supposed to be masculine. Rice has no power or influence. On the contrary, it feeds all creatures in the world and lengthens their lives; so it is placed on the side of female." See Lucien M. Hanks and Jane Richardson Hanks, "Thailand: Equality Between the Sexes," in *Women in the New Asia: The Changing Social Roles of Men and Women in South and South-East Asia*, ed. Barbara E. Ward (Paris: UNESCO, 1963), pp. 439–40.
66. Keyes, "*Mother or Mistress*," p. 233; Barbara Andaya, "Localising the Universal: Women, Motherhood and the Appeal of Early Theravāda Buddhism," *Journal of Southeast Asian Studies* 33, 1 (2002): 1–30; and Penny Van Esterik, "Feeding Their Faith: Recipe Knowledge Among Thai Buddhist Women," *Food and Foodways* 1 (1986): 197–215.
67. Andaya writes, "Despite inherent contradictions between the alleged "high status" of women in Southeast Asia and their ambiguous position in Theravāda traditions, "female agency" has never been an issue in the region's religious historiography … Moving into Southeast Asia at a time when its basic receptivity to lay involvement had been enhanced, Theravāda Buddhism offered continuing opportunities for all women to acquire merit through gift-giving and thereby counter their relegation to an inferior position." See "Localising the Universal," p. 29. For discussions of women's status in Southeast Asia, see, for instance: Hanks and Hanks, "Thailand: Equality Between the Sexes"; Ferguson, "Great Goddess Today," p. 295; Anthony Reid, *Southeast Asia in the Age of Commerce 1450–1680, Vol. 1: The Lands below the Winds* (New Haven: Yale University Press, 1988), p. 146; Penny Van Esterik, "Introduction," in *Women of Southeast Asia*, ed. Penny Van Esterik (Northern Illinois University, Center for Southeast Asian Studies Occasional Paper, 1982), pp. 1–15; Penny Van Esterik, *Materializing Thailand* (Oxford: Berg, 2000); and Suwanna Satha-Anand, ed., *Women's Studies in Thailand: Power, Knowledge and Justice* (Seoul: Ewha Womans University Press, 2004).

68. Evelyn Nakano Glenn, "Social Constructions of Mothering: A Thematic Overview," in *Mothering: Ideology, Experience, and Agency*, eds. Evelyn Nakano Glenn, Grace Chang, and Linda Rennie Forcey (New York: Routledge, 1994), pp. 1–29.
69. Phutthathat phikkhu (Buddhadāsa Bhikkhu), "Moradok thi 158" (Legacy Number 158), in *Moradok thi kho fak wai*, p. 169. For another statement on women's rights and duties, see Phutthathat, "Mae thi than yang mai ru-chak," pp. 48–9; Ito's translation.
70. Buddhadāsa often referred to the ten principles of *Kālāma Sutta*; Phutthathat, "Moradok thi 35" (Legacy Number 35), in *Moradok thi kho fak wai*, p. 41.
71. Social responses toward those recently ordained as either *bhikkhunī* or *sāmaṇerī* (female Buddhist novices) are discussed in Ito, "Ordained Women in Yellow Robes."
72. In *Kālāma Sutta*, the Buddha taught, "Do not go upon what has been acquired by repeated hearing; nor upon tradition; nor upon rumor; nor upon what is in a scripture; nor upon surmise; nor upon an axiom; nor upon specious reasoning; nor upon a bias towards a notion that has been pondered over; nor upon another's seeming ability; nor upon the consideration, 'The monk is our teacher'. Kalamas, when you yourselves know [that] 'These things are good; these things are not blamable; these things are praised by the wise; undertaken and observed, these things lead to benefit and happiness', enter on and abide in them." See *Kālāma Sutta: The Buddha's Charter of Free Inquiry*, trans. Soma Thera (Kandy: Buddhist Publication Society, 1981).

Conclusion

1. The episodes and descriptions of Buddhadāsa's cremation ceremony are based on a video CD, *Satchatham bot sut-thai: mua phutthathat klap su thammachat* (*The Last Chapter of Truth: When Buddhadāsa Returned to the Nature*) (Bangkok: Komon Khimthong Foundation, 2005). At the time of his cremation, the author had not yet started her study about Buddhadāsa, so she did not attend to observe the ceremony.
2. Dhammadāsa Phanit, comment in the video CD, *Satchatham bot sut-thai*. In the video CD, Dhammadāsa also said that when his and Buddhadāsa's father died, his monk teacher told them to place their father's ashes at the hilltop of Khao Prasong so that they could always remember their father when looking up the hill. Since ashes of their mother and younger sister are also there, Dhammadāsa said that Buddhadāsa left a will to bring part of his ashes to the same place.
3. Ranchuan Inthrakamhaeng and Prawase Wasi, comments in the video CD, *Satchatham bot sut-thai*.
4. "Late Phra Buddhadāsa Honoured by Unesco," *The Nation*, 22 October 2005.
5. See "A Century of Spirituality," *The Nation*, 24 May 2006.

6. UNESCO Bangkok Office, "UNESCO News and Events: 100th Anniversary of the Birth of the Venerable Buddhadāsa Bhikkhu (1906–1993)," at <http://www.unescobkk.org/information/news-and-events/unesco-news-and-events-details/100th-anniversary-of-the-birth-of-the-venerable-buddhadasa-bhikkhu-1906-1993/> [accessed 21 May 2009].
7. "Simple Truths," *The Nation*, 28 May 2006.
8. According to *The Nation*, the Culture Ministry and Foreign Affairs Ministry were to jointly organize an international event entitled "Dialogue among Civilisations"; the Culture Ministry had a plan to publish and distribute a commemorative book with a one million baht budget; the Sathirakoses-Nagapradeepa Foundation planned to translate "Dhammic Socialism" into ten Asian languages; the Foundation for Children hosted high school students' essay contest to write about Buddhism in their lives; and university groups organized seminars. See "Making the Centenary of a Great Teacher," *The Nation*, 19 March 2006. A respected female practitioner Mae Chi Sansanee Satiensut led a series of *dhamma* propagation walks, "Dhamma Khot Dhamma Yatra" walk from Suan Mokkh, passing through nine provinces to her meditation center, Sathira Dhammasathan. See "Youth Walk to Promote *Dhamma*," *The Nation*, 29 September 2006. Dr. Suchart Vongthong, an honorary advisor to the Thailand Watercolour Association, held an exhibition "Buddhadāsa: The Lantern of Life" after spending two years in Suan Mokkh. See "Art and the Deconstruction of Self," *The Nation*, 21 January 2007. Three spiritual music albums are released under the title "Buddhadāsa Song — Open the Eyes of Dhamma," and concerts with the same title were held in Thammasat University's main auditorium. See "Dhamma Poetry in Motion," *The Nation*, 1 November 2006; "Body & Soul: Chill-out Dharma," *The Nation*, 14 April 2007; "Musical Maelstrom," *The Nation*, 1 May 2007; and "Songs for the SOUL," *The Nation*, 1 July 2007.
9. "A Century of Spirituality," *The Nation*, 24 May 2006.
10. "Salvation in Print," *The Nation*, 26 March 2006.
11. See The Buddhadāsa Indapañño Archives Foundation website at <http://www.bia.or.th>, and a news article provided by Thai-ASEAN News Network at <http://www.tannetwork.tv/tan/ViewData.aspx?DataID=1033578>. *The Nation* reported that there were plans to build a three-storied building containing exhibition rooms, seminar rooms, a digital database, research-service zone and a theatre for spiritual entertainment, surrounded by trees and ponds. See "Buddhadāsa Treasure Trove for City," *The Nation*, 2 June 2007; "Become Spiritually Fit," *The Nation*, 14 September 2008.
12. The *Thammakhot* means "Dhamma propagation"; it is the title of the collected series of Buddhadāsa's sermons.
13. Phutthathat Phikkhu (Buddhadāsa Bhikkhu), a poem without a title, quoted from: Suwinai Phonnawalai, *Phutthabucha chiwaprawat phutthathat, chabap tha phra chan* (*Buddhist Veneration: Biography of Buddhadāsa, Tha Phra Chan edition*) (Bangkok: Openbooks, 2007), p. 533; Ito's translation.

14. Phutthathat Inthapanyo (Buddhadāsa Indapañño), "Phukhao haeng withi phuttha-tham" (Mountainous Hindrance on the Way of the Buddha-Dhamma), in *Chumnum patthakatha chut phuttha-tham* (*The Collection of Lectures on the Buddha Dhamma*) (Bangkok: Sukkhaphap Chai, 1992), pp. 126–69.
15. See Chapter 6, p. 185. Kowit Kemānanda, interview, 29 January 1999; Phra Sithawat Vanivattiko, interview, Bangkok, 30 April 1999.

Bibliography

*List of interviews and personal communication**

** All the interviews below were conducted by the author in person, unless otherwise stated. She expresses her sincerest gratitude to Prof. Eiji Murashima and Ms. Malinee Kumsupha, who accompanied her to these interviews, and greatly complemented her research with their insightful questions and deeper understandings about the Thai socio-historical context.*

Anon Burawat, Bangkok, 23 December 1999.
Anut Aphaphirom, Bangkok, 17 August 1999.
Arun Phet'urai, Mae Chi, Bangkok, 20 December 1998.
Arun Wetchasuan, Bangkok, 2 March 1999.
Bancha Chaloemchaikit, Bangkok, 1 August 1998.
Bancha Chaloemchaikit, telephone conversation, April 2000.
Banchong Santisuknirandon, Father, Bangkok, 5 April 2000.
Barkat bin Faiz Muhammad Siamwalla (Barakat Sayamwala), Bangkok, 28 August 2000.
Bunchan Tejadhammo (Tetchathammo), Phra, Vientiane, 27 March 2000.
Bunluan Mansap, Bishop, Ubon Ratchathani, 26 December 1999.
Chaiwat Satha-Anand, Bangkok, 27 August 1999.
Chakradharm Dhammasakdi, Bangkok, 12 October 1998.
Chalo Kengrangwat, Ubasika, Bangkok, 21 March 1999.
Chamnong Thongprasoet, Bangkok, 30 August 2000.
Chamrat Duangthisan, Bangkok, 31 July 1998.
Chaowarit Ghosādhammo (Khosathammo), Phra, Bangkok, 19 December 1998.
Charan Ditthanphichai, 21 August 1999.
Chatsumarn Kabilasingh, Bangkok, 30 November; Nakhon Phathom, 26 December 1998.
Chik Chela, Chiang Mai, 15 March 1999.
Chintana Sandiland, personal communication, 3 February 2006.
Chitsai Padungrat, conversation, Chaiya, 21 May 1998; Chaiya, 29 August 1999.
Choem Suvaco (Suwacho), Phra Maha, Bangkok, 16 October 1998.
Chonthira Satyawatthana, Bangkok, 25 August 1999.
Dhammadāsa Phanit (Thammathat Phanit), Chaiya, 4 March 1999.

Damri Phanit, Chumphon, 6 March 1999.
Damrongsak Liangphibun, Bangkok, 10 March 1999.
Dej Tulavardhana, Maj. Gen. (Phon Tri Det Tulawanthana), Bangkok, 15 October 1998.
Dutsadi Medhāṅkuro, Phra, 6 March 1999.
Ekkawit na Thalang, Bangkok, 20 March 1999.
Kanittha Wichiancharoen, Mae Chi Khun Ying, Bangkok, 30 January 1999, 11 March 1999, 30 August 1999, 30 August 2000.
Kanya Lilalai, Bangkok, 18 December 1999.
Karuna Kusalasai, Bangkok, 6 November 1998, 29 November 1998.
Kasem Sirisamphan, Bangkok, 15 October 1998.
Khachit Sirivaḍḍho (Siriwattho), Phra Maha, Chiang Rai, 16 March 1999.
Khamchan Wirachit Thera, Sathu, Luang Praban, 31 March 2000.
Khemachit Bhikkhu, 15 December 1998.
Kirti Bunchua (Kirati Bunchua), Bangkok, 7 May 1999.
Kittisak Kittisobhaṇo (Kittisophano), Phra, Bangkok, 25 August 1999.
Kittivuḍḍho Bhikkhu, Chonburi, 29 April 1999.
Kittiyansunthon, Phra Khru, Sakon Nakhon, 24 December 1999.
Kowit Kemānanda, 29 January 1999.
Lakkhano, Samana (Somlak Losimuang), Nakhon Phathom, 9 October 1998.
Manat Changopsamai, Bishop, Bangkok, 21 August 1999.
Maniphan Charudun and Siri Phetchai, Bangkok, 11 March 1999.
Metta Phanit, Chaiya, 4 March 1999, 5 March 1999, 29 August 1999, 9 May 2005.
Mitsuo Gavesako (Khawesako), Phra, Kanchanaburi, 25 December 1998.
Muangchai Wannaphut, Mae Chi, Chonburi, 9 March 1999.
Murashima, Eiji, personal communication, 16 July 1999.
Nan Suddhasīlo (Sutthasilo), Phra (Phra Khru Phiphithaprachanat), Surin, 26 December 1999.
Naowarat Phongphaibun, Kanchanaburi, 2 February 1999.
Nikhom Chetcharoenrak, Bangkok, 19 August 1998.
Paisal Visalo (Phaisan Wisalo), Phra, Bangkok, 25 August 1999.
Paññānanda Bhikkhu, Nonthaburi, 7 October 1998.
Parinya Thewanarumittrakun, Bangkok, 23 August 1999.
Pethai Pathumchantarat (Phethai Pathumchantharat) *et al.* at the Soon Klang Thewa Credit Union Cooperative Limited, Bangkok, 28 December 1999.
Phawanaphirat, Phra Khru, Chiang Mai, 17 March 1999.
Phenchai Sirorot, Chiang Mai, 15 March 1999.
Phengphan Wongwiwat, Chiang Mai, 17 March 1999.
Phirun Chatrawanitchakun, Bangkok, 1 September 1999.
Phisanthammaphani, Phra Khru, Udon Thani, 24 December 1999.
Pho Candasaro (Chanthasaro), Phra (Phra Khru Palatsilawat), Chaiya, 4 March 1999.
Phong Samaloek, Rong Prathan, Vientiane, 29 April 2000.
Phothirak, Samana, Nakhon Pathom, 6 May 1999.

Phum Detchawongsa Bhikkhu, Vientiane, 28 March 2000.
Pibhop Dhongchai (Phiphop Thongchai), Bangkok, 24 August 1999.
Plian Paññāpadīpo (Panyapathipo), Phra, Chiang Mai, 17 March 1999.
Pracha Hutanuwatr, Bangkok, 1 May 1999, May 2005.
Prani Thammasophinkun, conversation with author, Chaiya, 29 August 1999.
Praphat Uaichai, Bangkok, 14 October 1998.
Prathin Khwan'on, Mae Chi, Paktho, 24 December 1998.
Prawase Wasi (Prawet Wasi), Bangkok, 29 April 1999.
Prawut Simanta, Bangkok, 16 August 1999.
Prayun Wathayanakun, Haji, Family of, Bangkok, 13 March 1999.
Rabaep Ṭhitañāṇo (Thitayano), Phra Maha (Phra Ratchathammnithet, Phra Thepdilok), Bangkok, 14 October 1998, 21 August 2000.
Ranchuan Inthrakamhaeng, Ubasika Khun, Sakon Nakhon, 15 December 1998.
Ravi Bhavirai (Rawi Phawirai), Bangkok, 4 May 1999.
Rotrung Suannasut, Bangkok, 14 October 1998.
Samphat Phungprasoet, Bangkok, 6 April 2000.
Samroen Kosum, Samutprakan, 9 March 1999.
Sangdao Siamwalla (Saengdao Sayamwala), Khun Ying, Bangkok, 7 April 2000.
Sansani Sathiansut, Mae Chi, 12 February 1999.
Santikaro Bhikkhu, Bangkok, 10 April 1999; Chaiya, 29 August 1999.
Santisuk Sophonsiri, Bangkok, 16 October 1998.
Sathianphon Wannaphok, Bangkok, 30 April 1999.
Sawaeng Bunchaloemwiphat, Bangkok, 19 November 1998.
Sawai Kaewsom, Bangkok, 21 March 1999, 22 August 2000.
Sawai Kaewsom and his friend, Bangkok, 21 March 1999.
Seksan Prasoetkun, Bangkok, 31 August 1999.
Seri Phongphit, Bangkok, 5 May 1999.
Sikhamphirayan, Phra, Bangkok, 28 December 1998.
Siri Muangbunmi, Mae Chi, Phetchaburi, 26 December 1998.
Siri Phanit, Chaiya, 4 March 1999.
Siri Phetchai, Bangkok, 11 March 1999.
Sithawat Vanivattiko, Phra, Nonthaburi, 30 April 1999, 20 August 1999.
Soemsap Damrongrat, Upasika, Dr, Chaiya, 29 August 1999, 8 May 2005.
Somporn Thepsithar (Somphon Thepsittha), Bangkok, 8 April 2000.
Somsong Punyarit, Bangkok, 22 March 1999.
Sophon Rattanakon, Bangkok, 21 December 1998.
Subin Paṇīto (Panito), Phra, Trat, 21 August 1999.
Suchip Phunyanuphap, Bangkok, 17 August 1998, 10 March 1999.
Sukhanthasin, Phra Khru, Chiang Mai, 15 March 1999.
Sulak Sivaraksa, Bangkok, 19 March 1999.
Sulan Pabhassaso (Paphatsaso), Phra, Udon Thani, 18 December 1998.
Sumana Hengsawat, Mae Chi, Ratchaburi, 21 November, 24 December 1998.
Sunthoramongkhonwat, Phra Khru, Bangkok, 22 July 1998.
Suphacharawat, Phra Khru, Yasothon, 25 December 1999.
Suphaphan na Bangchang, Mae Chi, Bangkok, 15 January 1999.

Suphot Dantrakun, Bangkok, 8 October 1998, 19 August 1999, 17 December 1999.
Suthep Jinavaro (Chinawaro), Phra, 26 August 1999.
Sutthatsi Wongduan, Silacharini, Bangkok, 27 December 1998.
Suvimol Vajrabhaya (Suwimon Watcharaphai), Bangkok, 29 August 2000.
Suwanna Satha-Anand, Bangkok, 4 December 1998.
Thammadilok, Phra, Chiang Mai, 15 March 1999.
Thammanun Latphli, 10 October 1998.
Thapani Nakhonthap, Bangkok, 1 February 1999.
Thawan Phonprasoet, Phra, Vientiane, 1 April 2000.
Thepsinghakhanachan, Phra, Chiang Mai, 15 March 1999.
Thipphawan Patthomsathan, Bangkok, 22 August 1998.
Thira Wongphophra, Bangkok, 27 July 1998.
Thongchua, Mae Chi, Phetchaburi, 26 December 1998.
Unchit Tirattana, Ubasika, Bangkok, 21 March 1999.
Utsa Rongkhasuan, Bangkok, 22 December 1998.
Wani Saipradit, Bangkok, 12 October 1998.
Wannasit Waithayasewi, Bangkok, 3 May 1999.
Weng Tochirakan, Bangkok, 23 December 1998, 31 August 1999.
Wilat Maniwat, Bangkok, 1 February 1999.
Wimolsiri Jamanarnwej (Wimonsiri Chamnanwet), Bangkok, 23 December 1999.
Wirot Siriat, Bangkok, 12 March 1999, 31 August 1999, 15 December 1999.
Wisutthikhunrangsi, Phra Khru, Nong Khai, 18 December 1998.

Email correspondence

Paisal Visalo (Phaisan Wisalo), Phra, 17 July 2002.
Santikaro, 15 December 2005.

Unpublished personal correspondence with Buddhadāsa Bhikkhu†

†*All were found in the Suan Mokkh archives, in Chaiya in 1999.*

Buddhadāsa, letter to Ki Nanayon, 21 April 1939, 21 May 1939, 12 September 1939, 18 January 1940, 3 December 1940.
Buddhadāsa, letter to Phoem Siriwat, 20 June 1943.
Buddhadāsa, letter to Prasoet Sapsunthon, 2 December 1944.
Buddhadāsa, letter to Pridi Phanomyong, 1 March 1943.
Buddhadāsa, letter to Kulap, 19 October 1951.
Ki Nanayon, letter to Buddhadāsa, dated 16 January 1939, 5 April 1939, 26 May 1939, 16 June 1939, 12 August 1939, 20 September 1939, 23 January 1940, 19 May 1940, 17 July 1940,
Kulap Saipradit, letter to Buddhadāsa, 5 September 1951, 3 December 1951, 31 May 1952.

Lotthanan (One of Pridi Phamonyong's personal secretaries), letter to Buddhadāsa, 9 January 1943.

Phoem Siriwat (One of Pridi Phamonyong's personal secretaries), letter to Buddhadāsa, 7 June 1943.

Prasoet Sapsunthon, letters to Buddhadāsa, 8 October 1941, 24 July 1942, 26 August 1942, 31 July 1944, 22 December 1944, 8 January 1945, 5 October 1945, 15 January 1946, 22 November 1946, 3 September 1947, 3 May 1948, 1 November 1948, and 3 January 1972.

Archival documents at the National Archives of Thailand

"Bamnan khong nai pun chongprasoet" (Pension of Mr. Pun Chongprasoet), NAT (2) ko. to. 2.2.3/53.

Video and audio tapes

Khana Nittisat lae Mulanithi Nittisat Mahawitthayalai Thammasat (The Faculty of Law and the Foundation for the Faculty of Law, Thammasat University), ed. "Prawat lae phon-ngan sastrachan chitti tinsaphat" (A History of, and the Works of Professor Chitti Tinsaphat) (23 January 1990) (A commemoration video for the 80 year anniversary of Prof. Chitti Tinsaphat).

Mulanithi Komon Khimthong lae Thammathan Mulanithi (Komol Keemthong Foundation and Dhammadāna Foundation), ed. "Satcha-tham bot sut thai mua phutthathat klap su thammachat" (The Last Lesson of Truth when Buddhadāsa Returned to the Nature) (May 2005) (A video CD about Buddhadāsa's cremation ceremony).

Sawai Kaewsom, "Thammathipatai" (Dhammocracy), Vols. 1–4 (Bangkok: Thammacharoen) (Tape-recording of Sawai's speech).

__________. "Thang mai, chiwit mai" (A New Way, A New Life), Vols. 1–3 (Bangkok: Thammacharoen) (Tape-recording of Sawai's speech).

__________. "Than phutthathat son tai sun" (Ven. Buddhadāsa Taught Extinction After Death), Vols. 1–3 (Bangkok: Thammacharoen) (Tape-recording of Sawai's speech).

__________. "Winyan lang tai mai chai chao phut" ([The Teaching About] the *Viññāṇa* after Death is not Buddhist), Vols. 1–2 (Bangkok: Thammacharoen) (Tape-recording of Sawai's speech).

Websites

Buddhadāsa Bhikkhu, Venerable, "Anapanasati — Mindfulness of Breathing." Available at <http://www.buddhanet.net/ebooks_m.htm> [accessed 26 December 2006].

"Buddhadāsa Bhikkhu — Handbook for Mankind." Available at <http://www.buddhanet.net/budasa.htm [accessed 26 December 2006].

Buddhadāsa Bhikkhu, "The Dhamma Truth of Samatha-vipassana for the Nuclear Age." Available at <http://www.dharmaweb.org/index.php/Category:Buddhadasa_Bhikkhu> [accessed 26 December 2006].

The Buddhadāsa Indapañño Archives Foundation. <http://www.bia.or.th>.

UNESCO Bangkok Office, "UNESCO News and Events: 100th Anniversary of the Birth of the Venerable Buddhadāsa Bhikkhu (1906–1993)." Available at <http://www.unescobkk.org/information/news-and-events/unesco-news-and-events-details/100th-anniversary-of-the-birth-of-the-venerable-buddhadasa-bhikkhu-1906-1993/> [accessed 21 May 2009].

佛使比丘、「人类手册」、「上座部佛教的某些殊胜特色」 Available at <http://www.mba.net.my/BuddDatabase/FoXueWenJi/Buddhadasa/Index.htm> [accessed 26 December 2006].

Thai-language materials

A'ngun on (pseudonym Thammathat). "Ruang samrap naksuksa num: chotmai nak-nangsuphim num" (For Young Students: A Letter from a Young Newspaper Reporter). *Phutthasatsana* 2, 1 (May 1934): 172–5.

Anuson nai ngan phra ratcha than phloeng sop: nai prasoet sapsunthon (*Commemoration for the Cremation: Mr. Prasoet Sapsunthon*), 2 April 1995.

Anuson nai ngan phra ratcha than phloeng sop: nai sa'at watcharaphai (*Commemoration for the Cremation: Mr. Sa'at Warcharaphai*), 23 April 1987.

Anuson nai ngan phra ratcha than phloeng sop: nang phitsamai kamalamen (im'udom) (*Commemoration for the Cremation Ceremony: Mrs. Phitsamai Kamalamen [Im'udom]*), 28 November 1994.

Anuson nai ngan phra ratcha thang phloeng sop: phan ek samak burawat, to. cho. to. mo. (*Commemoration for the Cremation of Colonel Samak Burawat — Third Class Order of the Thai Crown, and Third Class Order of the White Elephant*), 15 November 1975.

Anuson nai ngan phra ratcha than phloeng sop: phra ratchathamnithet (phian ratchathamnithet) (*Commemoration for the Cremation: Phra Ratchathamnithet [Phian Ratchathamnithet]*), 11 April 1966.

Anuson nai ngan sadet phra ratcha damnoen phra ratcha than phloeng sop: phraya lapphlithammaprakhan (wong latphli) (*Commemoration for the Cremation: Phraya Latphlithammaprakhan [Wong Latphli]*), 19 September 1968.

Anuson ngan phra ratcha than phloeng sop: phra thipparinya (*Commemoration for the Cremation: Phra Thipparinya*), 21 May 1977.

Anuthin patibat tham: suksa chiwit yang pen witthayasat; banthuk rai wan khana fuk fon ton yangkhem khon nai wai num (*Diary of Dhamma Practice: A Scientific Study of Life; Daily Records During the Young Days of Strict Training of Self*). Published by people in Nakhon Si Thammarat province as a dedication on the day of Venerable Buddhadāsa's ceasing of his bodily aggregates, n.d.

Aphitham Chotika Witthayalai, ed. *Ngan mop prakatniyabat aphitham bandit run 34/2540* (*Ceremony to Confer the Qualification of Aphitham Bandit*).

Aphitham Chotika Witthayalai, Maha Chulalongkon Ratchawitthayalai, Bangkok, 1998.

"Aphitham chotika witthayalai, maha chulalongkon ratchawitthayalai nai phra boromarachupatham" (The Abhidhamma Chotika College, Maha Chulalongkon Ratchawitthayalai under Royal Patronage). A brochure, n.d.

"Aphitham chotika witthayalai, maha chulalongkon ratchawitthayalai." In *Ngan mop prakatniyabat aphitham bandit run 34/2540*, ed. Aphitham chotika witthayalai, pp. 13–7.

Aphitham mulanithi lae khana sit (The Abhidhamma Foundation and a Group of Disciples), ed. *Alai phra achan bunmi methangkun* (*In Memory of Phra Achan Bunmi Methangkun*). Bangkok: 6 June 1992.

Ari Phirom, *Thai-chin* (*Thailand-China*). Bangkok: Mitranara Kanphim, 1981.

Ariyananthamuni, Phra (Buddhadāsa Bhikkhu). *Lak phra phutthasasana: oprom phuchuai phuphiphaksa run raek, pho. so. 2499* (*The Principles of Buddhism: Preaching for the Assistant Judges of the First Generation, 1956*). Bangkok: Sukkhaphap Chai, 1990.

________. "Phutthasasana kap sangkhom" (Buddhism and Society). *Phutthasasana* 29, 3–4 (August–November 1961): 60–76.

Arun Wetchasuan, ed. *Rattha burut awuso pridi phanomyong* (*Senior Statesman Pridi Phanomyong*). Bangkok: Arunwithaya, 1983, 1999.

________. *Wiwattha: khwam hen mai trong kan rawang mom ratchawong khukrit pramot kap than phutthathat phikkhu* (*Dispute: Disagreement of Opinions between M.R.W. Kukrit Pramoj and Ven. Buddhadāsa Bhikkhu*). Bangkok: Arun Witthaya, 1977, 1996.

Arunwati Suwannakanit. "Ngan phoei phrae phutthasasana ruam thawai than phra achan 'phutthathat phikkhu'" (Cooperative Propagation Activities to Commemorate Venerable Master Buddhadāsa Bhikkhu). In *Anuson: nai sa'at watcharaphai*.

Atchalathammaphibucha nai thi raluk nuang nai ngan tham bun khlai wan koet khrop 66 pi lae chalong samanasak phat yot phra khru phawanaphirat (sang sangkitcho) (*Worshipping Atchalathammo in Commemoration of the Merit Making Ceremony for the Approaching 66th Birthday and the Promotion in Ecclesiastical Title of and [awarding of an] Honorary Fan to Phra Khru Phawanaphirat (Sang Sangkitcho) [current abbot of Wat Pa Achan Tu]*). Chiang Mai: Wat Pa Achan Tu, Amphoe Mae Taeng, 1996.

"Bannathikan thalaeng" (Editor's Announcement). *Phutthasasana* 1, 3 (November 1933): 106.

"Bannathikan thalaeng" (Editor's Announcement). *Phutthasasana* 4, 2 (August 1936): 217–8.

"Banthuk chak phaet ying suraphin thanasophon — but-sao: lao doi nang chamrat nimaphat — phi-sao" (A Note by Kulap's daughter, Dr. Suraphin Thanasophon: A Story by Mrs. Chamrat Nimaphat, Kulap's Elder Sister). *Lok nangsu* (*Book World*) (November 1978): 35–7.

"Banthuk chiwit lae gnan khong kulap saipradit: banthuk chak chanit saipradit phu pen panraya" (A Note on the Life and Work of Kulap Saipradit: A Note by Chanit Saipradit, His Wife). *Lok nangsu* (*Book World*) (November 1978): 29–34.

Bo. Cho. (abbr. Bunchuan) Khemaphirat. "Khwam suam sun khong phra phutthasasana nai india" (The Decline of Buddhism in India). *Phutthasasana* 4, 1 (May 1936): 11–26.

"Bot nam: thammika sangkhomniyom si khiao" (Introduction: Green Dhammic Socialism). *Pacharayasan* 20, 4 (October–December 1993): 7–15.

Buddhadāsa Bhikkhu. See Phutthathat Phikkhu.

Bunmi Methangkun. "Kham prarop" (Forward). In *To top patthakatha phutthathat phikkhu*, pp. 1–29.

________. "Phra aphithampidok pen bot suksa thi wa duai ruang arai" (What Kind of Lesson is it to Study the *Abhidhammapiṭaka*?). In *To top patthakatha phutthathat phikkhu*, pp. 93–179.

________. "Thoi thalaeng" (Postscript). In *To top patthakatha phutthathat phikkhu*, pp. (ko.)–(so.).

________. *To than phutthathat!: ruang cit wang*, lem 1 (*Refuting Venerable Buddhadāsa!: Regarding Empty Mind*), Vol. 1. Bangkok: Suthisan Kan-phim, 1979.

________. *To than phutthathat!: ruang awitcha lae phi-sang thewada*, lem 2 (*Refuting Venerable Buddhadāsa!: Regarding Ignorance, Ghost, and Celestial Beings*), Vol. 2. Bangkok: Suthisan Kan-phim, 1980.

________. *To than phutthathat!: ruang awitcha patchaya sangkhan*, lem 3 (*Refuting Venerable Buddhadāsa!: Regarding Ignorance Caused by Compounded Things [avijjā paccayā saṅkhāra]*), Vol. 3. Bangkok: Suthisan Kan-phim, 1981.

________. ed. *To top patthakatha phutthathat phikkhu* (*Refuting the Lecture of Buddhadāsa*). Bangkok: Aphitham Mulanithi, 1965, 1980.

Chai'anan Samutwanit, ed. *Sanniphon khong thianwan* (*Writings of Thianwan*). Bangkok: Ongkan Naksuksa Mahawitthayalai Ramkhamhaeng, 1974.

Chalong Cheyakhom, *Than bo. cho. khemaphirat* (*Ven. Bunchuan Khemaphirat*). Bangkok: Somsan.

Chanbannakit, Phra, "Sing thi yang mai at khaochai kan dai" (Things That Still Might Not be Able to be Understood). In *To top patthakatha phutthathat phikkhu*, pp. 180–202.

Chanya Sutthiyano (Suddhiñāño). Dr. Phra Maha, "Chao chun sirorot: phu mi lom haichai pen thamma" (Chao Chun Sirorot: A Person Who Breathed of the *Dhamma*). In *Thammaphinanthanakan nai ngan chapanakit sop: chao chun sirorot*, pp. 11–5.

________. ed. *Chiwit, kho-khit lae ngan khong chao chun* (*Life, Thoughts, and Works of Chao Chun*). Bangkok: Borisat Amarin.

________. *Chiwit lae ngan khong than panyanantha* (*The Life and Work of Venerable Paññānanda*). Bangkok: Borisat Amarin, 1991.

Chao Phuttha Nikhom, "Phuttha nikhom kap phuttha sathan" (The Phuttha Nikhom and the Phuttha Sathan). In *Phuttha sathan chiang mai*, pp. 65–6.

Chatchawarit Kasemsan, Mom Chao. "Kham top panha khong batluang khong mom chao chatchawarit." *Thammachaksu* 24, 10 (February 2482/1939): 959–73.

Chatthip Natsupha (Chatthip Nartsupha), "Naew-khit ruang kansuksa, prapheni lae watthanatham" (Thoughts on Education, Custom and Culture). In *Watthanatham thai kap khabuankan plian plaeng sangkhom* (*Thai Culture *and Movements of Social Change*). Bangkok: Samnakphim Chulalongkon Mahawitthayalai, 1991, pp. 3–15.

Chayanantho, Phikkhu (Phra Anan Senakhan), ed. *Khamson khong diarathi* (*Teachings of a Heretic*). Bangkok: Ongkan Phithak Phutthasat, 1979.

"Chen-nan-eng" (pseudonym). *Khu mu anapanasai phawana yang sombun baep* (*A Handbook for ānāpānasati bhāvanā: A Complete Manual*). Bangkok: Sukkhaphap Chai in 1990.

________. *Wipatsana rabop lat san* (*Vipassanā: A Shortcut Style*). Bangkok: Sukkhaphap Chai, 2000.

Chit Phibanthaen. *Chiwit lae ngan khong phutthathat* (*Life and Work of Buddhadāsa*). Bangkok: Sinlapabannakhan, 1977.

Chit Phumisak (Samnakphim nok huk ed.). *Karani 'yon bok' 23 tula* (*The 23 October Incident of 'Throwing onto the Ground'*). Samnakphim Nok Huk, 1986.

"Chiwaprawat than phra achan tu atchalathammo" (Life History of Than Phra Achan Tu Atchalathammo). In *Atchalathammaphibucha nai thi raluk nuang nai ngan tham bun khlai wan koet khrop 66 pi lae chalong samanasak phat yot phra khru phawanaphirat (sang sangkitcho)*, pp. 1–86.

"Chiwit lae ngan khong achan naep mahaniranon" (Life and Work of Naep Mahaniranon). *Panyasan* (*Journal of paññā*) 15 (21 September 1983): 1–6.

Chiwit lae phon-ngan khong achan phon rattanasuan (*Life and Works of Achan Phon Rattanasuan*). Bangkok: Rongphim Winyan, 1993.

Chiwit lok, chiwit tham: prawat chiwit thammada khong ranchuan inthrakamhaeng (*Secular Life and Dhamma Life: Biography of Ranchuan Inthrakamhaeng*). Bangkok: Kong-thun Thamma Sawatdi, 2004.

Chonlatee Yangtrong. "Khwam khit thang kanmuang khong phutthathat phikkhu" (The Political Thoughts of Buddhadāsa Bhikkhu). M.A. thesis, Department of Government, Graduate School, Chulalongkorn University, 1990.

Chonthila Sattayawatthana (Cholthira Satyawadhna), ed. *Khru thep*. Bangkok: Thai Watthana Phanit, 1992.

________. ed. *Kung satawat khabuankan santhiphap* (*Half Century of the Peace Campaign*). Bangkok: Mek Khao, 2002.

Chotika Thammachariya, Phra Satthamma. *Paramattha chotika paritchet thi 1-2-3: chit, chettasik, rup, nipphan* (*Chotika's Supreme Teaching Lesson 1-2-3: Citta, Cetasika, Rūpa, Nibbāna*). Bangkok: Mulanithi Satthamma Chotika, 1997.

"Chotmai naksuksa num: chak nakrian thai nai muang manila (philippines)" (A Letter of a Young Student: From a Thai Student in Manila [Philippines]). *Phutthasasana* 2, 3 (November 1934): 354–7.

Chuai Phulaphoem. "Chak Samnakphim" (From the Publisher). In Siburapha, *Udomtham kap phon-ngan chut phutthasasana*.

________. "Chom na phu-praphan: wilat maniwat" (The Face of the Writer: Wilat Maniwat). In Wilat Maniwat, *Thamma samrap khon nok wat*.

Chun Sirorot, Chao. *Chiwaprawat nai chun sirorot thi chao-khong khian lao wai eng: pho. so. 2439–2529* (*A Life History of Mr. Chun Sirorot, Which is Written by Himself: 1896–1986*).

Damrong Rachanuphap, Somdet Krom Phraya. *Nithan Borankhadi* (*Ancient Stories*). Published as a cremation volume for Nang Nian Laphanukrom, 1968.

Ha-sip pi suan mok: phak nung mua khao phut thung rao (*Fifty Years of Suan Mokkh: Part I When They Spoke of Us*). Bangkok: Suan Usom Mulanithi, 1982.

Itsarachon (pseudonym Kulap Saipradit). "Phuttha-tham lae santiphap" (The Buddha's *Dhamma* and Peace). In *Ha-sip pi suan mok: phak nung*, pp. 1205–9.

________. "Thi-ni lae Thi-nan" (Here and There). Originally published in *Prachamit* (10 March 1946), *Ha-sip pi suan mok: phak nung*, pp. 1201–4.

Kaptan Samut (pseudonym Samak Burawat). "Phutthit phachoen na kap khommiunit." (Buddhism in the Face of Communism). *Aksonsan* 4, 5 (August 1952): 10–45.

________. *Phutthit phachoen na kap kommiunit* (*Buddhism in the Face of Communism*). Klum Yaowachon Itsara, 1974.

Karuna Kusalasai. *Chiwit thi luak mai dai* (*Life Without a Choice*). Bangkok: Mae Kham Phang, 1986.

________, ed. *Phutthathat ramluk: likhit than 'phutthathat' thung nong chai doi tham, 'karuna kusalasai'* (*A Memory of Buddhadāsa: Letters from Ven. Buddhadāsa to a Younger Brother in the Dhamma, Karuna Kusalasai*). Bangkok: Mae Kham Phang, 1993.

Karuna Kusalasai, see also Samanen Thai nai Saranat.

Kasem Bunsi. *Prapheni tham bun nai phutthasatsana* (*Merit-Making Customs in Buddhism*). Bangkok: Khrusapha, 1961.

Kasem Sirisamphan, Sunthari Asawai, Atcharaphon Kamutthaphisamai, Sathaban Thai Khadi Suksa, eds. "Prawat mom ratcha wong khukrit pramot" (A Life History of M.R.W. Kukrit Pramoj). In *Anuson nai ngan phra ratcha than phloeng sop satstrachan phon tri mom ratcha wong khukrit pramot, po. cho., mo. po. cho., mo. wo. mo.* (*Commemoration at the Cremation of Professor Major General Mom Ratcha Wong Kukrit Pramoj, Pathom Chulachomklao, Maha Paramaphon Chang phuak, Maha Wachira Mongkut* [these three are decorations that Kukrit received from the King]), 23 December 1995, pp. 43–51.

Khaisaeng, "Chotmai top nak-nangsuphim num." *Phutthasasana* 2, 2 (August 1934): 296–9.

"Kham thalaeng" (Announcement). In *Phuttha sathan chiang mai*, p. 2.

Kham thalaeng kitchakan nai rop pi phutthasakkarat 2533 khong Phutthasamakhom haeng prathet thai nai phra boromarachupatham (*The Announcement of the Activities in the Year 1990 of the Buddhist Association of Thailand under Royal Patronage*). Bangkok: Samnakngan khong Phutthasamakhom haeng Prathet Thai, 1992.

Khamhuno (pseudonym Chamrat Duangthisan). "Chao na 'phu chit wang'" (A Farmer With 'Empty Mind'). In Pun, *Arai thuk, arai phit*, pp. 139–44.

________. "Tua ku lae khong ku" (Me and Mine). In Pun, *Arai thuk, arai phit*, pp. 145–50.

Khana Kammakan Chat Ngan Ramluk Pluang Wannasi, ed. *Prawat phon ngan lae kham ramluk pluang wannasi: kwi-nakkhian-naksu* (*History and Work of, and Word of Condolence for Pluang Wannasi: Poet, Writer, and Fighter*). Bangkok: Chonniyom, 1597.

Khana Kammakan Klang Chat Tang Phuttha Sathan Chiang Mai (Central Committee for the establishment of the Chiang Mai Buddhist Hall), ed. *Phuttha sathan chiang mai* (*A Volume Commemorating the Establishment of the Chiang Mai Buddhist Hall*), 1958.

Khana Luksit (a group of disciples). *Rom ngao wat nongpaphong* (*Shadow of Wat Nongpaphong*), 1989.

Khana Phoei Phrae Phuttha-tham (The *dhamma* propagation group). "Krap rian than phu borichak" (A Report for the Donors). In *Phai khong phutthasasana.*

Khana Thammathan lae Phu thi Khaorop nai Khunnatham khong Phraya Latphli Thammaprakhan (The Khana Thammathan and a group which respects the moral principles of Phraya Latphli Thammaprakhan), ed. *Mahawitthayalai chiwit khong phutthathat phikkhu, panya nai phutthasasana nikai sen khong khun prachak* (*'A University of Life' by Buddhadāsa Bhikkhu, and 'Insight in the Zen School of Buddhism' by Khun Prachak*). A cremation volume for Phraya Lapphli Thammaprakhan, 19 September 1968.

Khanungnit Chanthabut. *Sathana lae botbat khong phra phutthasasana nai prathet thai* (*The Situation and the Role of Buddhism in Thailand*). Bangkok: Klum Prasan'ngan Sasana Phua Sangkhom, 1989.

"Khao phra lokanat nam phikkhu thai ok pai chak prathet sayam" (News about Phra Lokanatha, who Leads Thai Monks out of Siam). *Phutthasasana* 2, 2 (August 1934): 284–94.

"Khrongkan sanruat prachamati phua sathon phap ruam sangkhom, kanmuang, watthanatham thai kon pi 2000" (Public Opinion Survey for Reflecting a Total Picture of Thai Society, Politics, and Culture before 2000). *Thai phot* (*Thai Post*), 13 December 1999, p. 2.

Khukrit Pramot (Kukrit Pramoj). "Chalachon nai wiatnam tai" (Uprisings in South Vietnam). *Thammachaksu* 48, 11 (August 1963).

________. "Hetkan nai wiatnam tai" (Incidents in South Vietnam). *Thammachaksu* 48, 12 (September 1963).

________. "Khwam wunwai thi wiatnam tai" (Confusions in South Vietnam). *Thammachaksu* 49, 1 (October 1963).

________. "Phuttha borisat nai wiatnam tai" (Buddhists in South Vietnam). *Thammachaksu* 49, 2 (November 1963).

________. "Ratthaban wiatnam tai kap phuttha borisat" (The South Vietnamese Government and Buddhists). *Thammachaksu* 49, 2 (December 1963).

________. "Soi suan phlu." In *Sayam rat rai wan* (*Siam rath*), 10 July 1993, p. 5.

"Kitchakan ngan khong than achan bunmi methangkun" (Activities of Ven. Bunmi Methangkun). In Aphitham mulanithi lae khana sit, *Alai phra achan bunmi methangkun*, pp. 7–8.

Kittiwuttho Phikkhu (Kittivuḍḍho Bhikkhu). "Dae phra thipparinya" (To Phra Thipparinya). In *Anuson ngan phra ratcha than phloeng sop phra thipparinya*, pp. 26–8.

________. *Kha khommiunit mai bap* (*Killing Communists is Not Demeritorious*). Bangkok: Mulanithi Aphitham Mahathat Witthayalai, 1976.

________. "Ruang chit wang nok phra traipidok mi khwam samkhan nai patchuban mak lae ruang phra phuttha chao son lokkuttara tham nai thammathinna kho plian thamma mai" (About [the teaching of] Empty Mind Which is Not in the *Tipiṭaka* and Which Places a Lot of Emphasis on the Present Time; and About [the story that] the Buddha Taught *Lokuttara Dhamma* to Dhammadinna Who Asked For a New *Dhamma*). In Pun, *Arai thuk, arai phit*, pp. 126–31.

Krachang Nanthaphot, *Mahanikai — thammayut* (*Mahanikai Order and Thammayut Order*). Nonthabri: Santi Tham, 1985.

Kukrit Pramoj, see Khukrit Pramot.

Kulap Saipradit, see Itsarachon; Siburapha.

"Lak 12 kho haeng phra phutthasasana khong nai khritmat hamfre, nayok ho phutthasasanik haeng krung london" (The Twelve Principles of Buddhism by Mr. Christmas Humphreys, the President of the London Buddhist Lodge). *Thammachaksu* 31, 9–12 (June–October 1946): 77–84.

Luang pu wean suchinno. Chiang Mai: Wat Doi Mae Teang, Amphoe Phrao.

Luk lae lan (Offspring) (probably written by Buddhadāsa on behalf of his siblings). "Matubuchanuson" (Commemoration of Mother). *Phutthasasana* (*Buddhism*) 16, 3 (August 1948): 79–84.

Maha thera prawat: somdet phra phutthachan (at atsapha maha thera) (*A History of the Great Elder: Somdet Phra Phutthachan [At Atsapha Maha Thera]*). Bangkok: Mahachulalongkon Ratchawitthayalai, 1990.

Maniphan and Utsa Charudun, "Than achan naep kap pathom haet hai koet samakhom sun khonkhwa thang phra phutthasasana lae mulanithi phumiphalo phikkhu" (Naep and the Origins of the Association for Centre of the Research on Buddhism and the Phumiphalo Bhikkhu Foundation). In *Thang bamphen kuson phua ok chak thuk haeng kan koet*, pp. 1–16.

Manlika Watcharaphai. Untitled condolence. In *Anuson: Nai sa'at watcharaphai*.

Manop (pseudonym Wilat Maniwat). "Thamma parithat phutthathat phikkhu" (The *Dhamma* Critique of Buddhadāsa Bhikkhu). In *Ha-sip pi suan mok: phak nung*, pp. 1166–200.

"Matu buchanuson" (Commemoration for Mother). *Phutthasassana* 16, 3 (August 1948): 79–84.

"Mua than panyanantha phut thung chao chun sirorot" (When Venerable Paññānanda Talked about Chao Chun Sirorot). In Phra Maha Chanya, *Chiwit, kho khit lae ngan khong chao chun*, pp. 187–205.

"Mulanithi aphitham mulanithi" (Foundation for the Abhidhamma Foundation). A brochure.

Mulanithi Phoei Phrae Chiwit Prasoet, "Thoi thalaeng" (Preface). In *Khu mu banchi thanakhan mu ban*, ed. Phairot Sisakunwong, *et al*., pp. 3–7.

Murashima, Eiji. *Kanmuang chin sayam: kan-kluan-wai thang kanmuang khong chao chin phon thale nai prathet thai kho. so. 1924–1941* (*Politics of the Chinese in Siam: The Political Activities of Overseas Chinese in Thailand*). Bangkok: Sun Chin Suksa, Sathaban Esia Suksa, Chulalongkorn University, 1996.

Nakhon That (City Slave; pseudonym Chit Phumisak). "Phuttha pratchaya kae saphap sangkhom trong kilet, watthuniyom daialektik kae saphap thi tua sangkhom eng, mi chai patirup tam baep khong sitthantha, pratchaya watthuniyom daialektik kap pratchaya khong sitthantha phit kan yang chakan thi trong ni" (Buddhist Philosophy Solves Social Problems at the Place of Defilement, While the Philosophy of Dialectical Materialism Solves it in Society Itself, Unlike the Reform by Siddhartha. The Philosophy of Dialectical Materialism and the Philosophy of Siddhartha Are Totally Different in This Sense). In *Chit Phumisak, Karani 'yon bok' 23 tula*, pp. 27–45.

Naksuksa Phra Aphitham (Students of the Abhidhamma; including Sa'nga Suphat, Suphani Wirawat, Chaluai Phenphaibun, Suchit Sa'nganmu, and Chuai Kannawat). "Samnao chotmai: kho khongchai khong naksuksa" (A Draft of a Letter: Some Students' Worries). In *To top patthakatha phutthathat phikkhu*, pp. 81–92.

Naowarat Phongphaibun, "Watthuniyom — chittaniyom kap phutthasasana" (Materialism — Spiritualism and Buddhism). In Naowarat Phongphaibun, *Dap thi mok yu nai chiwon* (*A Sword Hidden under the Yellow Robe*). Bangkok: Suan Nangsu, 1978, pp. 231–7.

Narin Phasit. *Chuai bamrung chat* (*Assist Nurturing the Nation*), 1914.

Nikolat Bennet (Nicolas Bennett?). "Santi withi kap kan sawaeng ha thang thi sam" (The Peaceful Method and Pursuit of the Third Way). *Phutthachak* 30, 6–7 (June–July 1976).

Paññānanda, see Panyanantha Phikkhu; Pathumuttara Phikkhu; Thammakosachan, Phra.

Panyanantha Phikkhu (Paññānanda Bhikkhu). *Chiwit lae phon-ngan khong than phutthathat*. Bangkok: Atammayo.

Parien dek (A boy with the Pali qualification; a pseudonym of Buddhadāsa). "Thammai mai pai kap phra lokkanat" (Why I Did Not Go With Lokanatha). *Phutthasasana* 2, 1 (May 1934): 210–2.

Pathumuttara Phikkhu (Paññānanda Bhikkhu). "Phikkhu kap kanriarai." *Phuttha-sasana* 15, 3–4 (August–November 1947): 155–60.

Phadungsulakkarit, Phra (A *thayok* of Wat Prok). "Prawat phra phatthanta wilasa" (A History of Phra Phatthanta Wilasa). In Phra Phatthanta Wilasa, *Thamma bet talet*, pp. 5–8.

Phairot Sisakunwong, Charoen Sisaeng, and Chamnong Somprasong. *Khu mu banchi thanakhan mu ban* (*A Handbook for Village-Bank Accounting*). Bangkok: Mulanithi Phoei Phrae Chiwit Prasoet, 1994.

Phaisan Wisalo, Phra. *Phutthasatsana thai nai anakhot: naew-nom lae thang ok chak wikrit* (*Thai Buddhism in the Future: The Sign of Crisis and the Way Out*). Bangkok: Mulanithi Sotsi-Saritwong, 2003.

________. "Yutthasat thammika sangkhomniyom lae thang ok haeng phuttha-tham" (The Strategy of Dhammic Socialism and an Exit [i.e., solution of a problem] at the Buddha Dhamma). *Pacharayasan* 25, 3 (March–June 1999): 32–7.

Phaisan Wisalo, Phra, So. Siwarak, Prawet Wasi, and Wira Sombun. *Patthakatha khrop rop 60 pi phra thammapidok (po. o. payutto): phuttha-tham kap udomkan samrap sattawat thi 21* (*The Memorial Lecture for the 60th Anniversary of Phra Thammapidok: Buddha-Dhamma and the Aim of the 21st Century*). Bangkok: Mulanithi Komon Khimuthong, 1999.

Phaisan Wongwarawisit (Phaisan Wisalo, Phra). "Than phutthathat kap thammika sangkhomniyom" (Buddhadāsa and Dhammic Socialism). In *Phutthathat kap khon run mai*, pp. 60–93.

Pharotratchasuphit, Phraya. *Witthi prakop ahan mangsawirat* (*Recipes for Vegetarian Dishes*). Bangkok: Chomrom Phim Thammathan Pao Keng Teng.

Phatthanta Wilasa, Phra. *Thamma bet talet* (*A Small Piece of the Dhamma*). Bangkok: Samakhom Sun Khonkhwa Thang Phra Phutthasasana, 1982.

"Phiksu doen pai phae satsana tang prathet" (A Monk Who Goes to Propagate Buddhism in Foreign Countries). *Phutthasasana* 1, 3 (November 1933): 64–73.

"Phiksu o e" (An idle/inactive/inefficient monk). In Phutthathat Phikkhu, *Tamra du phra lae winai khong phiksu*, pp. 12–3.

Phimolatham, Phra. "Anuson khun phra thipparinya" (In Memory of Khun Phra Thipparinya). In *Anuson ngan phra ratcha than phloeng sop phra thipparinya*, pp. 13–4.

Phinit Rakthongko, ed. *Thammanukrom thammakhot* (*Thammakhot Dictionary of the Dhamma*). Chaiya: Thammathan Mulanithi, 1994.

"Pho khong rao" (Our Father). *Anuson: nai sa'at watcharaphai.*

Phot Yangphonkhan, ed. *Mae son wai: Ruap ruam kham son khong mae phutthathat phikkhu* (*Mother Taught: A Collection of Teachings by the Mother of Buddhadāsa Bhikkhu*). Bangkok: Sukkhaphap Chai, 2002.

Photchananukrom chabap ratchabandit sathan pho. so. 2525 (*A Thai Dictionary: The Royal Academy 1982 edition*).

"Phra achan bunmi methangkuro: duang prathip duang ek haeng phra aphitham" (Phra Achan Bunmi Methangkuro: The Number One Light of the Abhidhamma). In *Alai phra achan bunmi methangkun*, ed. Aphitham Mulanithi lae Khana Sit, pp. 1–6.

"Phra ratcha prarop khong phra bat somdet phra mongkut klao chao yu hua (Khat ma chak bot phra ratcha niphon kan thi 9, *thetsana sua pa*)" (A Statement by King Vajiravudh [Selected from His Writing in Chapter 9, Preaching to the Wild Tiger Scouts]). In Phutthathat Phikkhu, *Tamra du phra lae winai khong phiksu.*

Phutthacharanuson nai ngan phra ratcha than phloeng sop phra yanasitthachan (luang pu sim phutthacharo) (*Commemoration of Buddhācāro in the Cremation Ceremony for Phra Yanasitthachan [Luang Pu Sim Buddhācāro]*). Chiang Mai: Samnak Song Tham Pha Plong, Amphoe Chiang Dao, 1993.

Phutthakhosachan Yanawara Thera, Chao Phra Khun Somdet Phra. *Phra mongkhon wisetkatha* (A commemoration book distributed by his disciples at his cremation), 1952.

Phuttha sathan chiang mai (*A Commemoration Volume for the Establishment of the Phuttha Sathan Chiang Mai*), 1958.

Phutthasasana (chabap phiset: sadudi khru thammathat phanit) (*Special Issue: Tribute to the Teacher, Thammathat Phanit*) 68, 3 (August–October 2000).

Phutthathat kap khon run mai: mua khon num sao tham thung rak khong khwam pen thai (*Buddhadāsa and the New Generation: When Youth Asks About the Root of Thainess*). Bangkok: Mulanithi Komon Khimuthong, 1983.

Phutthathat Phikkhu (Buddhadāsa Bhikkhu), or Phutthathat Inthapanyo (Buddhadāsa Indapañño). "Anumothana" (Benediction). In *Anuson: nai sa'at watcharaphai.*

________. "Anumothana" (Benediction). In *Mahawitthayalai chiwit khong phutthathat phikkhu, panya nai phutthasasana nikai sen khong khun prachak* (*'A University of Life' by Buddhadāsa Bhikkhu, and 'Insight in the Zen School of Buddhism' by Khun Prachak*), eds. Khana Thammathan *et al.*, pp. (3)–(11).

________. "Anumothana" (Benediction). In *Khu mu manut*, pp. ko.–kho.

________. *Aphitham khu arai?* (What is *Abhidhamma*?). Bangkok: Samnak Nangsu Thammabucha Khong Khana Phoei Phrae Witthi Kan Damnoen Chiwit An Prasoet, 1978.

________. *Ariya sat chak phra ot* (*Four Noble Truths from the Buddha's Words*). Chaiya: Mulanithi Thammathan, 1998.

________. "Asom thammamata" (The Second Note). In *Thammasom thammamata.* Chaiya: Dhammadāna Foundation, 2001.

________. "Asom thammamata" (The Fourth Note). In *Thammasom thammamata.* Chaiya: Dhammadāna Foundation, 2001.

________. *Boromatham: oprom phiksu nisit chulalongkonmahawitthayalai phansa pi 2512* (*Supreme Dhamma: Training for Student Monks from Chulalongkorn University in the 1969 Rain Retreat*). Chaiya: Mulanithi Thammathan, 1982, parts I, II.

________. *Chumnum patthakatha chut phuttha-tham* (*The Collection of Lectures on the Buddha Dhamma*). Bangkok: Sukkhaphap Chai, 1992.

________. "Kanmuang chanit chuai lok dai" (A Kind of Politics that Can Help the World). In *Kanmuang Khu Thamma*, pp. 89–135.

________. *Kanmuang khu thamma* (*Politics is the Dhamma*). Bangkok: Arunwithaya.

________. *Kan tham ngan duai chit wang phua sangkhom* (*Working for Society with Empty Mind*). Samutprakan: Ongkan Funfu Phutthasatsana, 1975.

________. *Kan tham ngan duai chit wang phua sangkhom khong than phutthathat* (*Working with Empty Mind for the Sake of Society by Venerable Buddhadāsa*). Samutprakan: Ongkan Funfu Phutthasasana.

________. *Kan to tan kae khai khwam wiparit khong lok (2519)* (*Facing Up to the World Disorder for Solution, 1976*). A booklet for free distribution, 27 May 1977.

________. "Kho khuan sap kiao kap lak phutthasasana rawang nikai tang tang." *Phutthasasana* 15, 1 (February 1947): 35–48.

________. *Khu mu manut* (*A Handbook for Humankind*). Bangkok: Ongkan Funfu Phutthasasana, 1959.

________. *Khu mu manut chabap sombun* (*A Handbook for Humankind: Complete Edition*). Bangkok: Thammasapha, 1988, 1992.

________. *Khumsap chak phra ot* (*A Treasure Trove From the Buddha's Words*). Chaiya: Mulanithi Thammathan.

________. "Lak phutthasasana 12 kho khong hamfre" (The Twelve Principles of Buddhism by Humphreys). *Phutthasasana* 15, 1 (Febrauary 1947): 5–33.
________. *Mahidon tham* (*Mahitala Dhamma*). Chaiya: Mulanithi Thammatham.
________. "Makhapunnamikatha." *Chumnum thamma banyai ruang chit wang* (*Collection of Dhamma Lectures on Empty Mind*). Bangkok: Arun witthaya, 1992.
________. *Moradok thi kho fak wai* (*Legacies to be Bequeathed*). Bangkok: Thammasapha, 1997.
________. "Moradok thi 8" (Legacy Number 8). In *Moradok thi kho fak wai*, p. 14.
________. "Moradok thi 35" (Legacy Number 35). In *Moradok thi kho fak wai*, p. 41.
________. "Moradok thi 158" (Legacy Number 158). In *Moradok thi kho fak wai*, p. 169.
________. *Phai khong phutthasasana* (*Danger to Buddhism*). Bangkok: Mulanithi Phoei Phrae Chiwit Prasoet, 1966.
________. *Phra khun khong mae khu santiphap khong lok* (*Mothers' Virtues are World Peace*). Bangkok: Atammayo, n.d.
________. *Phra phutthasasana chan phuthuchon* (*Buddhism at the Level of the Unenlightened Ordinary People*). Bangkok: Klum Suksa lae Patibat Tham, reprint edition.
________. "Phukhao haeng withi phuttha-tham" (Mountainous Hindrance on the Way of the Buddha-Dhamma). In *Chumnum pathakatha chut phuttha-tham*, pp. 126–69.
________. *Phut-khrit nai thatsana than phutthathat: chaikhwam haeng sasana khrit thi chaw phut khwan ruchak* (*Buddhist and Christian in the View of Venerable Buddhadāsa: The Meaning of Christianity That Buddhists Have to Know*). Bangkok: Samnakphim Thianwan, 1984.
________. *Phutthaprawat chak phra ot* (*The Life of the Buddha in His Own Words*). Chaiya: Mulanithi Thammathan, 1936, 1982.
________. *Phutthasasana kap sangkhom*. Bangkok: Khana Kammakan Mahachulalongkon Ratchawittayalai, 1956.
________. *Phuttha-tham kap chetanarom khong prachathipatai* (*Buddha-Dhamma and the Spirit of Democracy*). Nonthaburi: Kong thun wutthi tham.
________. A poem without a title. In Suwinai Phonnawalai, *Phutthabucha chiwaprawat phutthathat, chabap tha phra chan*, p. 533.
________. "Prachathipatai baep sangkhomniyom" (Democracy in the Style of Socialism). In Phutthathat Phikkhu, *Kanmuang khu thamma*, pp. 136–74.
________. *Rian Phutthasasana nai 15 nathi* (*Studying Buddhism in 15 Minutes*). Bangkok: Sukkhaphap Chai, 1998.
________. "Ruang watthuniyom kap manoniyom" (On Materialism and Idealism). In *Boromatham phak ton*, pp. 41–60.
________. "Sangkhomniyom chanit thi chuai lok dai" (A Kind of Socialism That Can Help the World). In *Thammika sankhomniyom*, pp. 111–50.
________. "Sangkhomniyom tam lak haeng phra sasana" (Socialism According to the Principle of Religion). In *Thammika sankhomniyom*, pp. 57–110.

________. *Sing thi rao yang khaochai kan mai dai* (*The Things That We Have Not Yet Understood*). Samutprakan: Ongkan Funfu Phutthasasana.

________. *Sing thi rao yang son chai kan noi pai: chabap 3 phasa — thai, angkrit, cin* (*Things Which We Still Pay Too Little Attention To: Three Language Edition — Thai, English and Chinese*). Bangkok: Sukkhaphap Chai, 2006.

________. *Sip pi nai suan mok: lao ruang chiwit nai wai num* (*Ten Years in Suan Mokkh: Talking About the Life When Young*). Nonthaburi: Kong Thun Wutthit Tham.

________. *Sunyata — chit wang — chit doem thae khong than phutthathat* (*Suññatā, Empty Mind, and Original Mind by Venerable Buddhadāsa*). Samutprakan: Ongkan Funfu Phutthasasana.

________. "'Sunyata' huachai khong phutthasasana" (Suññatā [Emptiness]: The Heart of Buddhism). In *Phuttha-tham kam mu diao*, ed. Klum Watcharaphon, pp. 33–64.

________. "Tai laeo koet ik ru mai" (Are We Reborn Again or Not?). In Pun Chongprasoet, *Rian ru phutthasasana phai nai 15 nathi*, pp. 19–24.

________. *Tam roi phra arahan* (*Following the Footprints of Arahant*). Chaiya: Mulanithi Thammathan.

________. *Tamra du phra lae winai khong phiksu* (*A Field-Guide to Monks and Their Precepts*). Bangkok: Thammasapha, 1994.

________. *Tham bun sam baep* (*Three Kinds of Merit Making*). Bangkok: Mulanithi Phoei Phrae Chiwit Prasoet, 1968.

________. "Thamma kap kanmuang, kanmuang kap thamma" (Dhamma and Politics, Politics and Dhamma). In *Kanmuang khu thamma*, pp. 1–76.

________. "Thamma khu phra chao?" (Is the *Dhamma* God?). *Phutthasasana* 31, 3–4 (August–November 1963).

________. "Thamma nai thana latthi kanmuang" (Dhamma as an Ideology of Politics). In *Kanmuang khu thamma*, pp. 77–88.

________. *Thamma thi khrai khan mai dai* (*The Dhamma That No One Can Oppose*). Samutprakan: Ongkan Funfu Phutthasasana.

________. "Thammamata" (Dhammamātā). In *Anuson ngan phra ratchathan phloeng sop nang phitsamai kamalamen (im'udom)*, pp. 37–50.

________. "Thammamata" (The Third Note). In *Thammasom thammamata*. Chaiya: Dhammadāna Foundation, 2001.

________. "Thammasom thammamata" (The First Note). In *Thammasom thammamata*. Chaiya: Dhammadāna Foundation, 2001.

________. *Thammika sankhomniyom*. Bangkok: Sayam Prathet, 1995.

________. "Top panha batluang." *Phutthasasana* 7, 3–4 (November 1939–February 1940): 280–335.

________. "Uppasak haeng kan khao chai thamma" (Obstacles in the Understanding of the *Dhamma*). A sermon at Wat Noranatthasunthrikkaram, Bangkok, 4 February 1968). In Pun, *Arai thuk, arai phit*, pp. 72–109.

________. "Uppasak haeng kan phoei phrae tham" (Obstacles in the Propagation of the Dhamma). A lecture given at Wat Mahathat, 28 November 1967). In Pun, *Arai thuk, arai phit*, pp. 9–71.

________. "Witthi haeng kan-khao thung phuttha-tham, patthakatha phiset." In *Chumnum patthakatha chut phuttha-tham*, pp. 1–70.

Phutthathat Phikkhu, see also Ariyananthamuni, Phra; Thammakosachan, Phra; and Buddhadāsa Bhikkhu.

Phutthathat Phikkhu and Panyanantha Phikkhu (Paññānanda Bhikkhu). *Mae phra nai ban: phra thamma thetsana phiset* (*Mother is a Monk at Home: Special Dhamma Sermons*). Bangkok: Thammasapha, n.d.

Phutthathat Inthapanyo (Buddhadāsa Indapañño) and Thammathat (Dhammadāsa) Phanit. "Khon la kham song kham nam cai luk" (One or Two Words Per Person Considerate of Children). *Watthu anuson 100 wan morana: nang kimsoi hemakun* (*Commemoration of the 100th Day After Passing: Mrs. Kimsōi Hēmakun*). Chaiya: Suan Mokkhabalarama, 14 October 1989).

Phuwa Ratchakan Changwat lae Khana Kromkan Changwat Surat Thani (Provincial Governor and Administrative Council of Surat Thani), ed. *Changwat surat thani — kan chalong 25 phutthasattawat* (*Surat Thani Province — Celebration for the 25th Buddhist Century*). Bangkok, 1957.

Pracha Pasannathammo, Phra (Pasannadhammo Bhikkhu; Pracha Hutanuwatr). *Lao wai mua wai sonthaya: atchiwaprawat khong than phutthathat* (*Talking in the Twilight Years: An Autobiography of Venerable Buddhadāsa*). Bangkok: Mulanithi Komon Khimthong, 1988.

________. *Phawana kap kan rap chai sangkhom* (*Meditation Practice and Serving Society*). Bangkok: Mulanithi Komon Khimthong, 1981.

________. "Phutthasasana kap khwam yuttitham thang sangkhom" (Buddhism and Justice in Society). *Pacharayasan* 13, 4 (September–October 1986): 114–9.

________. "Than phutthathat kap kan patiwat watthanatham" (Venerable Buddhadāsa and Revolution in Culture). In *Phutthathat kap khon run mai*, pp. 161–2.

Pracha Pasannathammo, Phra, and Santisuk Sophonsiri, eds. *Phap chiwit 80 pi phutthathat phikkhu* (*Pictorial Biography of 80 years of Buddhadāsa Bhikkhu*). Bangkok: Mulanithi Sathian Koset — Nakhaprathip and Samnakphim Mulanithi Komon Khimthong, 1986.

Prathum Chumphenphan, ed. *Chaiya — surat thani*. Bangkok: Krung Sayam Kanphim, 1972, 1976.

"Prawat Chao Phra Khun Somdet Phra Phutthakhosachan Yanawara Thera" (A History of Somdet Phra Phutthakhosachan). In Chao Phra Khun Somdet Phra Phutthakhosachan Yanawara Thera, *Phra mongkhon wisetkatha*. A commemoration book distributed by his disciples at his cremation, 1952, pp. (1)–(28).

Prawat khong phra khruba chao siwichai: nakbun haeng lanna thai (*Biography of Khruba Siwichai: A Meritorious Person in Lanna Thai*). A commemoration book for the opening of the Phra Khruba Chao Siwichai Museum, 1994.

"Prawat lae phon-ngan doi yo: phra thammathiraratmahamuni (chodok yanasit thera, parien tham 9 prayok)" (Life and Work in Summary: Phra Thammathiraratmahamuni [Chodok Yanasit Thera, Ninth Level Pali Qualification]). In Phra Thammathiraratmahamuni, *Phet nai duang chai*, pp. 242–3.

"Prawat nang khluan Phanit" (A History of Mrs. Khluan Phanit). *Phutthasasana* 16, 3 (August 1948): 85–8.

"Prawat phraya lapphlithammaprakhan." In *Mahawitthayalai chiwit khong phutthathat phikkhu, panya nai phutthasatsana nikai sen khong khun prachak* (*'A University of Life' by Buddhadāsa Bhikkhu, and 'Insight in the Zen School of Buddhism' by Khun Prachak*), eds. Khana Thammathan *et al.*, pp. ko.–tho.

Prawat wat santitham, amphoe muang, changwat chiang mai, thi raluk nai ngan chaloeng phra ubosot, phra chedi (*A History of Wat Santitham, Muang District, Chiang Mai Province, to Commemorate the Celebration [for the opening] of the Hall and the Pagoda*), 1997.

Prawat wat umong suan phuttha-tham (*A History of Wat Umong Suan Phutthatham*). Chiang Mai: Khana Phutthanikhom.

Prawet Wasi (Prawase Wasi), *Bon sen thang chiwit* (*On the Road of Life*). Bangkok: Samnakphim Mo Chawban, Vols. 1–7.

________. "Thammai son tham mai dai phon" (Why Do We Not Get a Result?). *Phutthachak* 30, 7 (July 1976).

________. *Thammika sangkhom*. Bangkok: Mulanithi Komon Khimuthong, 1995.

Prayun Wathayanakun, "Wan idilawat ha." *Phutthasasana* 21, 3–4 (August–November 1953): 127–32.

"Prayut" [This name appears to be either a first name or a pseudonym]. "Samnao chotmai thung kittiwuttho phikkhu" (The Draft of a Letter to Kittivuḍḍho Bhikkhu) Pun. In *Arai thuk, arai phit*, pp. 132–7.

Prasoet Patthamasukhon. *Ratthasapha thai nai rop 42 pi* (*42 Years of the Thai Parliament*). Bangkok: Ratthakit seri, 1974.

Pricha Changkhwanyun. *Khwam khit thang kanmuang khong than phutthathat phikkhu* (*Buddhadāsa's Thoughts on Politics*). Bangkok: Samnakphim Chulalongkon Mahawitthayalai, 1993.

Pridi Phanomyong. *Chiwaprawat yo khong nai pridi phanomyong* (*A Short Biography of Mr. Pridi Phanomyong*). Mulanithi Pridi Phanomyong, 1983, 1992.

________. *Khwam pen anitchang khong sangkhom*. Bangkok: Warasan mo khwam yuttitham, 1988.

Pun Chongprasoet, ed. *Arai thuk, arai phit*. Originally published by Ongkan Funfu Phutthasasana, 1973; reprinted by Mulanithi Phoei Phrae Chiwit Prasoet, 1982.

________. "Cha tham yang rai chung cha riak wa tham-ngan duai chit wang" (What Should We Do to be Called Working with Empty Mind?). In Phutthathat, *Kan tham ngan duai chit wang phua sangkhom*, pp. 23–9.

________. ed. "Chit praphatson — chit doem thae — chit wang (Yo chak kham banyai khong than phutthathat phikkhu)" (A Pure Mind, a Truly Original Mind, an Empty Mind [Summary of a Lecture by Venerable Buddhadāsa Bhikkhu]). In Pun, *Arai thuk, arai phit*, pp. 110–21.

________. "Kham kho rong" (A Request). In Phutthathat Phikkhu, *Khu mu manut*, pp. 167–70.

________. "Khwam hen khong mom ratchawong khukrit nai ruang 'chit wang'" (The View of M.R.W. Kukrit on 'Empty Mind'). In Phutthathat, *Sunyata — chit wang — chit doem thae*, pp. 19–32.

________. "Mahorasop thang winyan" (Amusement for the Soul). In Phutthathat Phikkhu, *Khu mu manut*, p. 171.

________. "Maihet" (An Endnote). In Kittiwuttho Phikkhu (Kittivuḍḍho Bhikkhu), "Ruang chit wang nok phra traipidok." In *Arai thuk, arai phit*, p. 131.

________. "Maihet" (An Endnote). In *Rian ru phutthasasana phai nai 15 nathi*, p. 18.

________. "Naenam Nangsu 'Khwam ngom'ngai'" (Book Recommendation, 'Superstitious Belief'). In *Tai di kwa yu ru*, pp. 7–12.

________. "Patchima likhit" (*Pacchima likhit*; Epilogue). In Pun, *Arai thuk, arai phit*, pp. 174–85.

________. "Phuttha phot: kan hai thamma pen than yom chana kan hai than thang puang" (The Buddha's Saying: Giving the *Dhamma* is the Alms that Would Win Any Kind of Alms). In Phutthathat, *Thamma thi khrai khan mai dai.*

________. "Rian ru phutthasasana phai nai 15 nathi." In Pun Chongprasoet, *Rian ru phutthasassana phai nai 15 nathi*, pp. 5–18.

________. *'Rian ru phutthasasana phai nai 15 nathi' khong pun chongprasoet, khayai khwam duai ruang 'tai laew ca koet ru mai' khong than phutthathat* (*Learn Buddhism in 15 Minutes, Expanded Interpretation of 'Is There Rebirth After Death or Not" by Venerable Buddhadāsa*). Samutprakan: Ongkan Funfu Phutthasasana, n.d.

________. *Wiwattha (Khwam mai hen trong kan) rawang mom ratcha wong khukrit pramot kap than phutthathat phikkhu* (*A Dispute: Disagreement of Opinion between M.R.W. Kukrit Pramoj and Venerable Buddhadāsa Bhikkhu*). Ongkan Funfu Phutthasasana, 1 April 1964; reprinted in Bangkok: Pho. cho. po., 1986.

Rabiap Sunthralikhit, Khun Ying. "Kham to top" (A Retort). In *To top patthakatha phutthathat phikkhu*, pp. 203–25.

"Rai phra nam — nam phu borichak sang phuttha sathan chiang mai" (The List of Donor Names for the Phuttha Sathan Chiang Mai). In *Phuttha sathan chiang mai*, pp. 203–34.

"Ramluk khun khru thammathat phanit, phu chak pai" (A Remembrance of the Teacher, Thammathat Phanit, Who Has Left [the world]). *Phutthasasana* 68, 2 (May, June, July 2000): 103.

Ranchuan Inthrakamhaeng. *Sitthi satri, withi phut: ranchuan inthrakamhaeng patthakatha* (*Women's Rights, Buddhist Methods: Lecture by Ranchuan Inthrakamhaeng*), ed. Sompong Phrompiam. Nonthaburi: Gender Press, 1994.

________. *Suan mok thammai? Thammai suan mok?* (*Why Suan Mokkh? Suan Mokkh, Why?*). Bangkok: Attamayo, 1991.

Ratchathamnithet, Phra. "Khwam-nuk chua khana" (A Thought in a Moment). *Mahawitthayalai* 10, 6 (1932): 813–9.

Ratchathamnithet, Phra (Rabaep Chittayano). *Phaen thamlai phra phutthasasana* (*The Plot to Destroy Buddhism*). Bangkok: Sun Songsoem Phra Phutthasasana haeng Phrathet Thai, 1994.

100 [Roi] pi anuson amonritthamrong (*100 Years' Anniversary of Amonritthamrong*). Khana luk lan phim pen thi raluk nai ngan tham bun chalong khrop rop 100 pi wan khlai wan koet phraya amonritthamrong (phrom na thalang), 28 February 1993 (The group of children and grandchildren publish to commemorate on the occasion of the merit making ceremony approaching 100 years since his birthday).

"Ruang cak bot sonthana kap 'Phutthathat phikkhu' wa duai phutthasasana kap sangkhom thai" (Stories From a Conversation with Buddhadāsa Bhikkhu Talking About Buddhism and Thai Society; Chatthip Nartsupha's Interview with Buddhadāsa). *Lok nangsu* (*Book world*) 39, 11 (August 1980): 50–64.

Rudi Roengchai (pseudonym Kanya Lilalai). *Yot nung nai krasae than* (*A Drop of Water in the Stream*). Bangkok: Samnakphim Ming Mit, 1996.

Sakdina Chatrakun na Ayutthaya. *Chiwit, naewkhit lae kantosu khong 'narin klung' ru narin phasit: khon khwang lok* (*Life, Thought and Struggle of 'Narin Klung' or Narin Phasit: A Person Who Blocked the World*). Bangkok: Samnakphim Matichon, 1993.

Samak Burawat. "Khun kha thang sukkhaphap khong wipatsana kammathan" (Health Advantages of *Vipassanā* Meditation). *Wipatsanasan* 2, 5 (September 1956)–2, 6 (November 1956).

________. "Nung duan nai wipatsana" (A Month of *Vipassanā* Meditation). *Wipatsanasan* 2, 1 (January 1956).

________. *Panya wiwat phak 1, 2* (*The Evolution of Human Intellect Part 1, 2*). Bangkok: Phrae phitthaya, second edition 1982.

________. *Phutthapratchaya athibai duai witthayasat* (*Buddhist Philosophy Explained by Science*). Bangkok: Rongphim Song Tham, 1937.

________. "Ruang phratchaya wa duai kan-plian-plaeng" (About the Philosophies of Dynamism). *Phutthasasana* (Special Issue for the Tenth Anniversary, 1943): 112–20.

________. "Suan Mokkhaphalaram." In *Ha-sip pi suan mok: phak nung*, pp. 1156–65.

________. "Thatsana thang pratchaya lang khao phra kammathan laeo" (A View on Philosophy After Experiencing Meditation). *Wipatsanasan* 3, 4 (July 1957).

________. See also Kaptan Samut.

Samanen Thai nai Saranat (pseudonym Karuna Kusalasai). "Chotmai chak samanen thai nai india" (A Letter from a Thai Novice in India). *Phutthasasana* 3, 4 (February 1936): 711–8.

________. "Horyoyi — pathom phuttha wihan khong yipun" (Horyoji — The First Temple of Japan). *Phutthasasana* 7, 2 (August 1939): 130–8.

________. "Kan-phoeiphrae Phutthasasana" (Propagation of Buddhism). *Phutthasasana* 10, 1 (February 1942):. 93–4.

________. "Khao di thung phuttha mamaka sayam" (Good News for Thai Buddhists). *Phutthasasana* 4, 3 (November 1936): 336.

________. "Khao kan khluang wai khong phra phutthasasana nai india" (News About Buddhist Movements in India). *Phutthasasana* 5, 1 (May 1937): 122–6.

________. "Mahatma Nichiren." *Thammachaksu* 27, 10 (July 1939): 935–43.

________. "Mahatma Nichiren" (Continued from the previous issue). *Thammachaksu* 27, 11 (August 1939): 1035–42.

________. "Nam thiao namasakan sathan thi saksit nai india" (Visiting Holy Places in India). *Phutthasasana* 8, 3–4 (November 1940): 183–90.

________. "Ngan chalong mulakan kutti wihan nai prathet india" (A Celebration in India for the Foundation of a *Vihāra* Where There Used to be a *Kuti* [monk's hut] Used by the Buddha). *Phutthasasana* 4, 1 (May 1936): 59–64.

________. "Phonsawadan khong phra wihan phutthakhaya" (History of the Bodh Gaya Temple). *Phutthasasana* 6, 3 (November 1938): 195–202.

________. "Phra maha wihan phutthakhaya" (A *Vihāra* in Bodh Gaya). *Phutthasasana* 5, 2 (August 1937): 194–203.

________. "Phra phutthasasana nai india patchuban" (Buddhism in Present Day India). *Thammachaksu* 28, 1 (October 1939): 39–51.

________. "Phra phutthasasana sun hai pai chak india yang-rai?" (How Did India Lose Buddhism?). *Thammachaksu* 27, 7 (April 1939): 652–63.

________. "Phra phutthasasana sun hai pai chak india yang rai?" (Continued from the previous issue). *Thammachaksu* 27, 8 (May 1939): 748 58.

________. "Phutthasasana nai prathet yipun" (Buddhism in Japan). *Phutthasasana* 5, 4 (February 1938): 341–6.

________. "Wanna sut nai india" (Untouchables in India). *Phutthasasana* 6, 1 (May 1938): 41–8.

Sanya Thammasak (Sanya Dhammasakdi). "Kamnoet phuttha sathan chiang mai" (The Birth of the Phuttha Sathan Chiang Mai). In *Phuttha sathan chiang mai*, ed. Khana Kammakan Klang Chat Tang Phuttha Sathan Chiang Mai, pp. 11–7.

________. "Kham ramluk" (A Rememberance). In *Anuson: phraya lapphlithamma-prakhan*.

________. *Nathi khong phutthasamakhom* (*The Duty of the Buddhist Association*). Bangkok: Phutthasamakhom haeng Prathet Thai, 1961.

________. "Phuttha tham kap chiwit kan ngan" (Buddha Dhamma and a Life of Work). In Pun, *Arai thuk, arai phit*, pp. 163–9.

________. "Phuttha sathan khu arai?" (What is the Phuttha Sathan?). In *Phuttha sathan chiang mai*, pp. 50–9.

________. "Prawat kan kotang, phonngan, lae khwam pen ma nai 35 pi khong phutthasamakhom haeng prathet thai nai phra boromarachupatham" (The History of the Establishment, Works, and Transitions in the 35 Years of the Buddhist Association of Thailand Under Royal Patronage). In *Kham thalaeng kitchakan nai rop pi phutthasakkarat 2533 khong Phutthasamakhom haeng prathet thai nai phra boromarachupatham*, pp. 5–30.

Satcha Wimuttinan (edited from a public lecture of Phra Phothirak). *Panha sangkhom thi kae mai dai phro kansuksa phutthasasana phit phlat* (*Social Problems That Cannot Be Solved Because of Wrong Education in Buddhism*). Bangkok: Rongphim Mulanithi Thamma Santi, 1985.

Sathianphong Punyawanno, Phra Maha. "Than pridi sang wat thai nai pari" (Pridi Builds a Thai Temple in Paris). In *Chut suan thuang* (*The Centre of Gravity*). Bangkok: Hang Hun Suan Chamkat, 1972, pp. 125–33.

Sathiangphong Wannapok. "Tai-koet chua khana chit" (Death and Birth in a Moment of Mind). In *Thamma khong luang pho phutthathat*, pp. 67–9.

________. *Thamma khong luang pho phutthathat* (*Dhamma of Venerable Buddhadāsa*). Bangkok: Thammasapha, 1994.

Sawai Kaewsom. "Krai? Khu phu ko kanrai" (Who is a Terrorist?). In Kaptan Samut, *Phutthit phachoen na kap kommiunit*, pp. 81–94.

________. *Tai koet, tai sun, panha lok taek ru?* (*Is it a Problem that Could Divide the World: After Death, Are We Reborn or Do We Disappear?*) (A cremation volume for Phirawut Kaewsom, 18 February, 1990). Bangkok: Somchai Kanphim, 1990.

Sawami Satthayanantha Buri (Swami Satyananda Puri). "Kala haeng sasana" (Time in Religion). *Thammachaksu* 27, 10 (July 1942): 879–84.

________. "Khwam kao na haeng sasana" (Progress in Religion). *Thammachaksu* 26, 11 (August 1941): 1184–8.

________. *Mahatama khanthi: phu patthiwat india* (*Mahatma Gandhi: India's Revolutionary*). Bangkok: Dharmashrama, 1938.

________. "Ruang winyan" (About Viññāṇa). *Thammachaksu* 26, 8 (May 1941): 890–902.

Sawok. *To phra? anan senakhan lae khana ruang khamson diarathi* (*Arguing Against Phra? Anan Senakhan and His Group on the Heretical Teaching*). Bangkok: Rongphim Suwannaphum.

Siburapha. *Udomtham kap phon-ngan chut Phutthasasana* (*The Highest Dhamma and Works on Buddhism*). Bangkok: Samnakphim Dok Ya, 1988, 1993, pp. 255–76.

So. Siwarak (Sulak Sivaraksa). "Champen tong mi sasana ru mai" (Is it Necessary for Us to Have Religion or Not?). *Phutthachak* 27, 2 (February 1973): 22–6.

________. *Chuang haeng chiwit* (*A Period of My Life*). Bangkok: Samnakphim Khlet Thai.

________. *Chuang lang haeng chiwit* (*The Later Period of [My] Life*). Bangkok: Samnakphim Khlet Thai, 1997.

________. "Damrong Chiwit yu phua arai" (For What Do We Live?). *Phutthachak* 27, 3 (March 1973): 12–6.

________. *Itthiphon phutthathat to sangkhom* (*The Influence of Buddhadāsa on Society*). Bangkok: Khana Kammakan Sasana Phua Sangkhom, 1990.

________. *Sonthana kap than phutthathat phikkhu* (*Interview with Buddhadāsa Bhikkhu*). Bangkok: Khana Kammakan Sasana Phua Sangkhom, 1993.

________. "Than phutthathat phikkhu" (Venerable Buddhadāsa Bhikkhu). In *Phra di thi na ruchak* (*Good Monks Who Are Worth Knowing*). Bangkok: Samnakphim Khlet Thai, 1967, 1987, pp. 149–76.

Sombat Chanthraong. *Rai'ngan kansuksa ruang chumchon pathom asok, kansuksa phuttha yuthopia* (*A Report on the Pathom Asok Community, A Study of a Buddhist Utopia*). Bangkok: the Faculty of Political Science, Thammasat University, 1988.

"Somdet phra phutthachan (at atsapha maha thera)." In *Maha thera prawat*, pp. 107–61.

"Somdet phra phutthakhosachan yiam lae phak raem nai suan mok" (Somdet Phra Phutthakhosachan Visited and Stayed Over One Night at Suan Mokkh). *Phutthasasana* 5, 2 (August 1937): kho.–cho.

"Song si phra phutthasasana, song phu-sathapana mokkhaphalaram — khana thammathan" (Two Outstanding Contributors to Buddhism, Two Founders of [Suan] Mokkh Phalaram — Dhammadāna Group) (A leaflet published by the Dhammadāna Group).

Sot Kuramarohit. "Anatta kap atta" (Non-Self and Self). *Phutthasasana* 3, 4 (February 2478/1937): 701–10.

________. "Top A'ngun On ruang Kanbuat" (Answering A'ngun On About Ordination). *Phutthasasana* 2, 4 (February 2477/1935): 418–30.

________. "Chotmai naksuksa num" (A Letter of a Student). *Phutthasasana* 3, 1–2 (May–August 1936): 469–76.

Suchip Punyanuphap. "Khamnam nai kanphim khrang thi raek" (Introduction for the First Printing). In *Sasana priap thiap* (*Comparative Religions*). Bangkok: Mahamakut Ratchawitthayalai, 1961, 1997.

Suksan Chirachariyawet, ed. *7 rop achan sanya* (*Seventh Twelve-Year Cycle* [i.e., 84 years] *of Achan Sanya*). Bangkok: Mulanithi Nitthisat, Mahawitthayalai Thammasat, 1991.

Sulak Sivaraksa. See So. Siwarak; Sulak Siwarak.

Sulak Siwarak (Sulak Sivaraksa). "An nuang ma chak kham samphat than kittiwuttho phikkhu" (In Relation to the Interview of Ven. Kittivuḍḍho Bhikkhu). *Phutthachak* 30, 7 (July 1976): 23–5.

________. "Khrongkan oprom phra phikkhusu phua songsoem kanphatthana thong thin" (The Project of Training Monks for Promoting Rural Development). *Phutthachak* 23, 7 (July 1969).

________. "Wat kap kan anurak sinlapakam lae saphap waetlom" (Temples and Fine Arts and Environment Conservation). *Phutthachak* 26, 12 (December 1972).

Suphat Sukhonthaphirom. *Phuttha pratchaya kap pratchaya maksit* (*Buddhist Philosophy and Marxist Philosophy*). Nonthaburi: Sathaban Witthayasat Sangkhom, 1998.

________. "Ramruk thung khun kulap saipradit" (A Memory of Kulap Saipradit). In Suphot, *Ramluk thung 'siburapha'*, pp. 1–13.

Suphot Dantrakun. "Kham khun ton" (Forward). In *Phutthasasana kap khommiunit.*

________. *Phutthasatsana kap khommiunit*. Bangkok: Samnakphim Sukkhaphap Chai, 2000.

________. ed. *Ramluk thung 'siburapha' — kulap saipradit doi phuan ruam khuk 2495–2500 lae saha thammic* (*Memories of Kulap Saipradit by his Friends Together in Jail in 1952–1957 and His Friends in the Dhamma*). Nonthaburi: Samnakphim Santi Tham, 1985.

Sutcharit Satchawichan. "Phuttha pratchaya nai thatsana 'nakhon that'" (Buddhist Philosophy in the View of 'City Slave'). *Aksonsat phichan* 3, 11–12 (April–May 1976): 45–59.

Suwanna Sathanan (Suwanna Satha-Anand). *Pratchaya phutthathat kap mahayan tham* (*Buddhadāsa's Philosophy and Mahāyāna Dhamma*). Bangkok: Khrongkan phoei phrae phon-ngan wichai Chulalongkon Mahawitthayalai, 1993.

Suwinai Phonnawalai. *Phutthabucha chiwaprawat phutthathat, chabap tha phra chan* (*Buddhist Veneration: Biography of Buddhadāsa, Tha Phra Chan edition*). Bangkok: Openbooks, 2007.

Tai di kwa yu ru (*Is it Better to Die Rather Than to Live?*). Samutprakan: Ongkan Funfu Phutthasasana, 1964.

"Thalaengkan" (Announcement). *Thammachaksu* 27, 4 (January 1942).

"Thalaengkan" (Announcement). *Pacharayasan* 5, 17 (March–April 1976).

"Thalaengkan Buang Ton" (Announcement in the Beginning). *Thammachaksu* 23, 4 (January 2480/1937).

"Thalaengkan khong khana thammathan" (An Announcement from the Khana Thammathan). *Phutthasasana* 1, 1 (May 1933): 6–17.

"Thalaengkan khong khana thammathan" (An Announcement from the Khana Thammathan). *Phutthasasana* 1, 2 (August 1933): 54–8.

"Thalaengkan khong khana thammathan" (An Announcement from the Khana Thammathan). *Phutthasasana* 3, 1–2 (May–August 1935): 636–41.

"Thalaengkan khana thammathan" (An Announcement from the Khana Thammathan). *Phutthasasana* 3, 4 (February 1936/2478): 745–8.

"Thalaengkan mulanithi phoei phrae chiwit prasoet" (An Announcement of the Foundation for the Sublime Life Mission). In *Thalaengkan trasan mulanithi phoei phrae chiwit prasoet (pho. cho. po.) chabap pho. so. 2522*, pp. 1–12.

Thalaengkan trasan mulanithi phoei phrae chiwit prasoet (pho. cho. po.) chabap pho. so. 2522 (*An Announcement Document of the Foundation for the Sublime Life Mission, 1979 edition*).

Tham wat chao yen lae suat mon phiset bang bot plae thai khong samnak suan mokphalaram chaiya (*Morning and Evening Chants and Some Special Chants, Thai translation, by Suan Mokkhabalarama, Chaiya*).

Thammabannakan nai ngan phra ratcha than phoeng sop phraya pharotratchasuphit-thammaphiwitthepsuphabodi (choi hemachan) (*A Writing on the Dhamma at the Cremation of Phraya Pharotratchasuphit [Choi Hemachan]*), 1970.

Thammadilok, Phra (Chan Kusalo), ed. *Nam chom wat chedi luang: chabap somphot 600 pi phra that chedi luang* (*A Guide to Wat Chedi Luang: The 600th Anniversary of the Grand Pagoda*).

Thammakriat Kan'ari. "Samphat sanya thammasak" (Interview with Sanya Dhammasakdi). *Matichon sut sapda* (*Weekly Matichon*) 8, 403 (22 May 1988): 18–20.

Thammakosachan, Phra (Paññānanda Bhikkhu). *Phutthathat khu khrai, than tham arai* (*Who was Buddhadāsa? What Did He Do?*). Bangkok: Mulanithi Phra Dulayaphaksuwaman-Chaluai-Thiphawan Patthamassathan, 1998.

Thammakosachan, Phra (Phutthathat phikkhu) (Buddhadāsa Bhikkhu). "Mae thi than yang mai ruchak: lok ca mi santiphap, tha ruchak mae thi thae ching"

(Motherhood That You Have Not Yet Known: The World Would Have Peace, If it Knows the True Mother). In Phutthathat Phikkhu and Panyanantha Phikkhu, *Mae phra nai ban*, pp. 25–59.

Thammaphinanthanakan nai ngan chapanakit sop: chao chun sirorot (*A Cremation Volume for Chao Chun Sirorot*), 1995.

Thammapidok, Phra (Po. O. Payuttho). *Photchananukrom phutthasat chabap pramuan sap* (*Dictionary of Buddhist Studies: Edition for Glossary of Dhamma Terms*). Bangkok: Mahachulalongkon Ratchawitthayalai, 1995.

________. *Photchananukrom phutthasat chabap pramuan tham* (*Dictionary of Buddhist Studies: Edition for Explanation of Dhamma Terms*). Bangkok: Mahachulalongkon Ratchawitthayalai, 1995.

Thammaratchanuwat, Phra. "Ruang kiao duai phuttha sathan chiangm mai." In *Phuttha sathan chiang mai*, pp. 18–27.

Thammasom thammamata (*Dhammamātā Hermitage*). Chaiya: Dhammadāna Foundation, 2001.

Thammathan khong khun mae siri: thi raluk nuang nai wara charoen chansa khrop 6 rop (72 pi) (*Khun Mae Siri's Gift of the Dhamma: Commemoration For Her Sixth Twelve Year Cycle [72 years old]*), 22 August 1988.

Thammathat (Dhammadāsa). "Samrap naksuksa num." *Phutthasasana* 1, 2 (August 1933): 34–41.

Thammathiraratmahamuni, Phra. *Phet nai duang chai* (*A Jewel in the Mind*). Bangkok: Samnak ngan klang kong kan wipatsana thura, 1996.

Thang bamphen kuson phua ok chak thuk haeng kan koet: anuson nai kan chapanakit sop achan naep mahaniranon (*The Way to Make Merit in Order to Exit from the Suffering of Births: Commemoration at the Cremation of Achan Naep Mahaniranon*). Bangkok: Samakhom sun khonkhwa thang phra *Phutthasatsana*, 14 December 1983.

Thianwan. "Rok khong sasana." *Phutthasasana* (*Buddhism*) 20 (1952): 23–6.

Thipparinya, Phra. "Ruang rao klao sanoe hai long thot." In *Ha-sip pi suan mok: phak nung*, pp. 747–62.

Thit Nat Han (Thich Nhat Hanh). *Patihan haeng kan tun yu samoe* (*The Miracle of Being Awake*), trans. Phra Pracha Pasannathammo. Bangkok: Mulanithi Komon Khimuthong, 1995.

Thongsup, Phra Maha. "Pathakatha ruang nak tham" (A Public Lecture on Nak Tham). *Thammachaksu* 20, 3 (December 1934): 259–74.

Thongsup Charuwanno, Phra Maha. "Thalaengkan buang ton." *Thammachaksu* 22, 2 (November 1936): ko.–kho.

U Nu. "Kanbanru makphon samai kung phutthakan" (Accomplishing Enlightenment Half Way through the Buddhist Era). *Phutthasasana* 22, 1 (February 1954): 33–4.

Ubalikhunupamachan, Phra (Siricando Chan). *Attanoprawat, thamma banyai lae khirimannatha sut* (*Autobiography, Dhamma Lecture, and Girimaṇḍa Sutta*). Bangkok: Chomrom Phutthasat Ko. Fo. Pho., 1988.

Udom Bunyaprasop. "Kham rap saraphap" (Confession). In *Phuttha sathan chiang mai*, pp. 28–43.

Ulliana, John. "Sut-thai lua khon diaw" (At the End, Being Left Alone). *Phuttha-sasana* 16, 3 (August 1948).

Wachirayanawong, Somdet Phra (the Supreme Patriarch). "Phra owat kham khwan." In *Phuttha sathan chiang mai*, pp. 5–8.

Wai. "Samnao chomai thung 'khamhuno'" (The Draft of a Letter to 'Khamhuno'). In Pun, *Arai thuk, arai phit*, pp. 151–62.

Wannasit Waithayasewi. "Kham to top" (A Retort). In *To top patthakatha phutthathat phikkhu*, pp. 250–307.

Wanrat, Somdet phra. "Kham khwan." In *Phuttha sathan chiang mai*, pp. 9–10.

Wanrat, Than chao phra khun somdet phra. "Kham klao nai phithi poet mulanithi aphitham mahathat witthayalai" (A Speech at the Opening Ceremony of Mulanithi Aphitham Mahathat Witthayalai). *Chofa* 1, 1 (October 1965): 5–7.

Wat Thanontaeng, Than (probably an abbot of Wat Thanontaeng). "Tham khwan nak chaloei sak" (Ceremony for Strengthening the Spirit Essence for an Ordination Candidate). In Kasem Bunsi, *Prapheni tham bun nai phutthasasana*, pp. 130–43.

Watcharaphon, Klum, ed. *Phuttha-tham kam mu diao: ruam botkhwam lae patthakatha khong than phutthathat phikkhu lae khun pun chongprasoet* (*A Handful of the Buddha Dhamma: Collections of Essays and Lectures by Venerable Buddhadāsa Bhikkhu and Mr. Pun Chongprasoet*). Bangkok: Klum Watcharaphon.

Watthu-anuson 100 wan morana: nang kimsoi hemakun (*Commemoration of the 100th Day After Passing: Mrs. Kimsoi Hemakun*). Chaiya: Suan Mokkhabala-rama, 14 October 1989.

Wilat Maniwat. *Thamma samrap khon nok wat* (*The Dhamma for the People Outside Temples*). Bangkok: Samnakphim Dok Ya, 1995.

Wira Phaengyang. "Suksa chiwaprawat lae phonngan khong thammathat phanit" (A Study on the Life History and Works of Dhammadāsa Phanit). M.A. thesis, Mahawitthayalai Sinakharin Wirot Phak Tai, 1996.

Wirot Siriat, "Tai di kwa yu?" (Better to Die Rather Than to Lve?). In *Tai di kwa yu ru*, pp. 3–6.

Wiwat Catithammanit. *Kabot santhiphap* (*Peace* [Committee's] *Revolt*). Bangkok: Khrongkan Chat Phim Khop Fai, 1996.

Wong Mu Lam. "Sut khong wei lang" (Sutra of Wei Lang), trans. Phutthathat Phikkhu. *Phutthasasana* 15, 2 (May 1947): 96–123.

Wut suwannarak (*A Cremation Volume for Wut Suwannnarak*), 1 March 1998.

Thai Periodicals

Chao Phut (*Buddhists*) 1, 1 (May 1952)–26, 6 (April–May 1973).

Mahawitthayalai (*University*) 2, 1 (1924)–17, 3 (1939).

Phutthachak (*Buddhist Realm*) 3, 1 (January 1949)–31, 12 (December 1973).

Phutthasasana (*Buddhism*) 1, 1 (May 1933)–68, 3 (August, September, November 2000).

Phuttha-tham (*Buddha Dhamma*) 1, 1 (January 1942)–25, 11 (November 1972).

Suksa Thammada (*Ordinary Education*) 2 (1920)–6 (1924).

Thammachaksu (*Eye of the Dhamma*) 19, 1 (October 1933)–62, 4 (Mahapawarana 1973).
Wipatsanasan (*Journal of Vipassanā*) 2, 1 (January 1956)–23, 6 (November 1973).

Non-Thai Language Materials (including Chinese, English, French, Japanese, and Pali)

Akin Rabibhadana. "Clientship and Class Structure in the Early Bangkok Period." In *Change and Persistence in Thai Society: Essays in Honor of Lauriston Sharp*, eds. G. William Skinner and A. Thomas Kirsch. Ithaca and London: Cornell University Press, 1975, pp. 93–123.
Andaya, Barbara. "Localising the Universal: Women, Motherhood and the Appeal of Early Theravāda Buddhism." *Journal of Southeast Asian Studies* 33, 1 (February 2002): 1–30.
Anderson, Benedict. *The Spectre of Comparison: Nationalism, Southeast Asia and the World*. London: Verso, 1998.
Apinya Fuengfusakul. "Empire of Crystal and Utopian Commune: Two Types of Contemporary Theravada Reform in Thailand." *Sojourn* 8, 1 (February 1993): 153–83.
"Art and the Deconstruction of Self." *The Nation*, 21 January 2007.
Aung-Thwin, Michael. *Pagan: The Origins of Modern Burma*. Honolulu: University of Hawai'i Press, 1985.
Baker, Chris and Pasuk Phongpaichit, trans. *Pridi by Pridi: Selected Writings on Life, Politics and Economy*. Chieng Mai: Silkworm Books, 2001.
Bareau, André. "Review of *Une herméneutique bouddhique contemporaine de Thaïlande: Buddhadāsa Bhikkhu*, by Louis Gabaude." *Revue de l'histoire de religions* CCIX, 1 (Janvier–Mars 1992): 92–4.
Barmé, Scot, ed., trans. *Kulap in Oz: A Thai View of Australian Life and Society in the Late 1940s*. Clayton: Monash Asia Institute, 1995.
Bartholomeusz, Tessa J. *Women under the Bo Tree: Buddhist Nuns in Sri Lanka*. Cambridge: Cambridge University Press, 1994.
Batson, B.A. "Kulap Saipradit: The War of Life." *Journal of the Siam Society* 69, 1 and 2 (January–July 1981): 58–73.
"Become Spiritually Fit." *The Nation*, 14 September 2008.
Bhaskar, Roy, "Materialism." In *A Dictionary of Marxist Thought*, eds. Tom Bottomore, Laurence Harris, V.G. Kiernan, and Ralph Miliband, pp. 369–73.
Bochenski, J.M. "Marxism-Leninism and Religion." In *Religion and Atheism in the U.S.S.R. and Eastern Europe*, eds. Bociurkiw and Strong, pp. 1–17.
Bociurkiw, Bohdan R. and John W. Strong, eds. *Religion and Atheism in the U.S.S.R. and Eastern Europe*. London: Macmillan Press Ltd., 1975.
Bodhi, Bhikkhu, ed. *A Comprehensive Manual of Abhidhamma: The Abhidhammatha Sangha of Ācariya Anuruddha*. Onalaska: BPS Pariyatti Editions, 2000.
"Body & Soul: Chill-out Dharma." *The Nation*, 14 April 2007.
Bottomore, Tom, Laurence Harris, V.G. Kiernan, and Ralph Miliband, eds. *A Dictionary of Marxist Thought*, second edition. Oxford: Blackwell, 1991.

Bowie, Katharine A. *Rituals of National Loyalty: An Anthropology of the State and the Village Scout Movement in Thailand.* New York: Columbia University Press, 1997.

Brewer, John, "'The Most Polite Age and the Most Vicious': Attitudes Towards Culture as a Commodity, 1660–1800." In *The Consumption of Culture 1600–1800: Image, Object, Text*, eds. Ann Bermingham and John Brewer. London: Routledge, 1995, pp. 341–61.

Buddhist Annual of Ceylon 1, 1 (1920)–4, 2 (1932).

Buddhadāsa, Bhikkhu. *Heartwood of the Bodhi Tree: The Buddha's Teaching on Voidness*, ed. Santikaro Bhikkhu, trans. Dhammavicayo. Boston: Wisdom Publications, 1994.

________. *Me and Mine: Selected Essays of Bhikkhu Buddhadāsa*, ed., trans. Donald K. Swearer. Albany: State University of New York Press, 1989.

________. *Mindfulness with Breathing: A Manual for Serious Beginners*, ed. Santikaro Bhikkhu. Boston: Wisdom Publications, 1988.

"Buddhadāsa Treasure Trove for City." *The Nation*, 2 June 2007.

Bunnag, Jane. *Buddhist Monk, Buddhist Layman: A Study of Urban Monastic Organization in Central Thailand.* Cambridge: Cambridge University Press, 1973.

Cabezón, José Ignacio. "Buddhist Studies as a Discipline and the Role of Theory." *Journal of the International Association of Buddhist Studies* 18, 2 (Winter 1995): 231–68.

"A Century of Spirituality." *The Nation*, 24 May 2006.

Chalmers, Robert, ed. *The Majjhima-nikāya*, vol. III. London: The Pali Text Society, 1960.

Chatsumarn Kabilsingh. *Thai Women in Buddhism*. Berkeley: Parallax Press, 1991.

Chatthip Nartsupha. "The Community Culture School of Thought." In *Thai Constructions of Knowledge*, eds. Manas and Turton, pp. 118–41.

________. "The Ideology of Holy Men Revolts in North East Thailand." In *History and Peasant Consciousness in South East Asia*, eds. Turton and Tanabe, pp. 111–34.

Collins, Steven. *A Pāli Grammar for Students*. Chiang Mai: Silkworm Books, 2005.

________. *Selfless Persons: Imagery and Thought in Theravāda Buddhism*. Cambridge: Cambridge University Press, 1982.

Cox, Collett. "Buddhism, Ābhidharmika Schools of." In *Routledge Encyclopedia of Philosophy*, ed. Edward Craig. London and New York: Routledge, 1998, pp. 53–8.

Das, D.N., ed. *Speeches and Writings of Swami Satyananda*. Bangkok: Thai-Bharata Cultural Lodge, 1940.

"Democratic Prince." *The British Buddhist* 4, 8–9 (May–June 1930).

"Democratic Siam." *The Maha-Bodhi* 40, 8 (August 1932): 390–1.

Deshpande, Madhav M., "Introduction." In *Milindapañhā-aṭṭhakathā by Thaton Mingun Zatawun Sayadaw alias U Narada Mahathera*, ed., trans. Madhav M. Deshpande. Tokyo: The International Institute for Buddhist Studies of the International College for Advanced Buddhist Studies, 1999, pp. 1–23.

"Dhamma Poetry in Motion." *The Nation*, 1 November 2006.

Dharma-vijava (*Triumph of Righteousness or the Revolt in the Temple*). Colombo: Sinha Publications, 1953.

Dongieux, Henri. "Institutionalization and Change at Suan Mokkhabalaram: Rationalist Buddhism and the Micro-Social Context." M.A. diss., Universiteit van Amsterdam, 1999.

Falk, Monica Lindberg. *Making Fields of Merit: Buddhist Nuns Challenge Gendered Orders in Thailand.* Göteborg: Göteborg University, Department of Social Anthropology, 2002.

Feer, M. Léon, ed. *Saṃyutta-nikāya Part II Nidāna-vagga* and *Part V Mahā-vagga*. London: The Pali Text Socity, 1960.

Ferguson, John P. "The Great Goddess Today in Burma and Thailand: An Exploration of Her Symbolic Relevance to Monastic and Female Roles." In *Mother Worship*, ed. James J. Preston, pp. 283–303.

Fineman, Daniel. *A Special Relationship: The United States and Military Government in Thailand, 1947–1958*. Honolulu: University of Hawai'i Press, 1997.

"From Siam." *The British Buddhist* 8, 2 (January–March 1934): 114–5.

Gabaude, Louis. *Une herméneutique bouddhique contemporaine de Thaïlande: Buddhadāsa Bhikkhu*. Paris: École Française d'Extrême-Orient, 1988.

________. "Thai Society and Buddhadāsa: Structural Difficulties." In *Radical Conservatism*, eds. Sulak Sivaraksa *et al.*, pp. 211–29.

Gawin Chutima. "The Rise and Fall of the Communist Party of Thailand (1973–1987)." University of Kent at Canterbury, Centre of South-East Asian Studies, Occasional Paper No. 12, 1990.

Glenn, Evelyn Nakano. "Social Constructions of Mothering: A Thematic Overview." In *Mothering*, eds. Evelyn Nakano Glenn, Grace Chang, and Linda Rennie Forcey, pp. 1–29.

Glenn, Evelyn Nakano, Grace Chang, and Linda Rennie Forcey, eds. *Mothering: Ideology, Experience, and Agency*. New York: Routledge, 1994.

Gokhale, Balkrishna Govind. "Anagarika Dharmapala: Toward Modernity through Tradition in Ceylon." In *Contributions to Asian Studies*, vol. 4. Leiden: E.J. Brill, 1973, pp. 30–9.

Gombrich, Richard, and Gananath Obeyesekere. *Buddhism Transformed: Religious Change in Sri Lanka*. Princeton: Princeton University Press, 1988.

Gorkom, Nina van. *Abhidhamma in Daily Life*. London: Triple Gem Press, 1969, 1997.

Goscha, Christopher E. *Thailand and the Southeast Asian Networks of the Vietnamese Revolution, 1885–1954*. Surrey: Curzon Press, 1999.

Guruge, Ananda, ed. *Return to Righteousness: A Collection of Speeches, Essays and Letters of Anagārika Dharmapāla*. Ceylon: Government Press, 1965.

Habermas, Jürgen. *The Structural Transformation of the Public Sphere: An Inquiry into a Category of Bourgeois Society*, trans. Thomas Burger. Cambridge, Mass.: MIT Press, 1989.

Hagiwara, Yoshiyuki and Eiji Murashima, eds. *Asean shokhoku no seiji taisei* (*The Political Regime in the ASEAN States*). Tokyo: Ajia Keizai Kenkyu Sho, 1987.

Hanks, Jane. *Maternity and Its Rituals in Bāng Chan*. Ithaca: Cornell Southeast Asia Program Data Paper, 1963.

________. "Reflections on the Ontology of Rice." In *Culture in History: Essay in Honor of Paul Radin*, ed. Stanley Diamond. New York: Octagon Press, 1981, pp. 298–301.

Hanks, Lucien M. and Jane Richardson Hanks. "Thailand: Equality between the Sexes." In *Women in the New Asia*, ed. Barbara E. Ward, pp. 424–59.

Heikkilä-Horn, Marja-Leena. *Buddhism with Open Eyes: Belief and Practice of Santi Asoke*. Bangkok: Fah Apai Co., Ltd., 1997.

Heine, Steven and Charles S. Prebish, eds. *Buddhism in the Modern World: Adaptations of an Ancient Tradition*. New York: Oxford University Press, 2003.

Hinüber, O. von, "Pāli Manuscripts of Canonical Texts from North Thailand — A Preliminary Report." *Journal of the Siam Society* 71 (1983): 75–88.

Hong Lysa. "Warasan Setthasat Kanmuang Critical Scholarship in Post-1976 Thailand." In *Thai Constructions of Knowledge*, eds. Manas and Turton, pp. 99–117.

Horner, I.B., trans. *The Collection of the Middle Length Sayings (Majjhima-nikāya)*, vol. III. London: The Pali Text Society, 1959.

Ileto, Reynaldo Clemeña. *Pasyon and Revolution: Popular Movements in the Philippines, 1840–1910*. Manila: Ateneo de Manila University Press, 1979.

Ishii, Yoneo. "Church and State in Thailand." *Asian Survey* VIII, 10 (1968): 864–71.

________. *Jozabu bukkyo no seiji shakai gaku* (*Political Sociology of Theravada Buddhism*). Tokyo: Sobunsha, 1975.

________. "A Note on Buddhistic Millenarian Revolts in Northeastern Siam." *Journal of Southeast Asian Studies* 6, 2 (1975): 121–6.

________. *Sangha, State, and Society: Thai Buddhism in History*, trans. Peter Hawkes. Honolulu: University of Hawai'i Press, 1986.

Ito, Tomomi. "Buddhist Women in Dhamma Practice in Contemporary Thailand: Movements Regarding Their Status as World Renunciates." *Journal of Sophia Asian Studies* 17 (1999): 147–81.

________. "Dhammamātā: Buddhadāsa Bhikkhu's Notion of Motherhood in Buddhist Women Practitioners." *Journal of Southeast Asian Studies* 38, 3 (October 2007): 409–32.

________. "Discussions in the Buddhist Public Sphere in Twentieth-Century Thailand: Buddhadāsa Bhikkhu and His World." PhD diss., The Australian National University, 2001.

________. "Ordained Women in Yellow Robes: An Unfamiliar 'Tradition' in Contemporary Thailand." In *Out of the Shadows: Socially Engaged Buddhist Women*, ed. Karma Lekshe Tsomo. Delhi: Sri Satguru Publication, 2006), pp. 168–71.

________. "Sulak and Engaged Buddhists in Contemporary Thai History." In *Socially Engaged Spirituality: Essays in Honor of Sulak Sivaraksa on His 70th Birthday*, ed. David W. Chappell. Bangkok: Sathirakoses-Nagapradipa Foundation, 2003, pp. 241–50.

Jackson, Peter A. *Buddhadāsa: A Buddhist Thinker for the Modern World*. Bangkok: The Siam Society under Royal Patronage, 1988. Reprinted as *Buddhadāsa: Theravāda Buddhism and Modernist Reform in Thailand*. Chiang Mai: Silkworm Books, 2003.

________. *Buddhism, Legitimation, and Conflict: The Political Functions of Urban Thai Buddhism*. Singapore: Institute of Southeast Asian Studies, 1989.

________. "The Enchanting Spirit of Thai Capitalism: The Cult of Laung Phor Khoon and the Post-Modernization of Thai Buddhism." *South East Asian Research* 7, 1 (March 1999): 5–60.

________. "The Hupphaasawan Movement: Millenarian Buddhism Among the Thai political Elite." *Sojourn* 3, 2 (1988): 134–70.

________. "Royal Spirits, Chinese Gods, and Magic Monks: Thailand's Boom Time Religious Prosperity." *South East Asia Research* 7, 3 (November 1999): 245–320.

Jeng Yan Daily News (正言日報), 28 April 1947 and 23 August 1947.

Johansson, Rune E.A. *The Psychology of Nirvāna*. London: George Allen and Unwin, 1969.

Kamala Tiyavanich, *Forest Recollections: Wandering Monks in Twentieth-Century Thailand*. Honolulu: University of Hawai'i Press, 1997.

________. *Sons of the Buddha: The Early Lives of Three Extraordinary Thai Masters*. Boston: Wisdom Publications, 2007.

Kasian Tejapira. "Commodifying Marxism: The Formation of Modern Thai Radical Culture, 1927–1958." PhD diss., Cornell University, 1992.

Keyes, Charles F. "Communist Revolution and the Buddhist Past in Cambodia." In *Asian Visions of Authority*, eds. Keyes, Kendall, and Hardacre, pp. 43–73.

________. "Millennialism, Theravāda Buddhism, and Thai Society." *Journal of Asian Studies* 36, 2 (February 1977): 238–302.

________. "Mother or Mistress But Never a Monk: Buddhist Notions of Female Gender in Rural Thailand." *American Ethnologist* 11, 2 (May 1984): 223–41.

________. "Political Crisis and Militant Buddhism in Contemporary Thailand." In *Religion and Legitimation of Power in Thailand, Laos, and Burma*, ed. Bardwell L. Smith, pp. 147–64.

Keyes, Charles F., Laurel Kendall, and Helen Hardacre, eds. *Asian Visions of Authority: Religion and the Modern States of East and Southeast Asia*. Honolulu: University of Hawai'i Press, 1994.

King, Sallie B. *Being Benevolence: The Social Ethics of Engaged Buddhism*. Honolulu: University of Hawai'i Press, 2005.

________. "Thich Nhat Hanh and the United Buddhist Church: Nondualism in Action." In *Engaged Buddhism*, eds. Queen and King, pp. 321–63.

Kirsch, A. Thomas. "Development and Mobility Among the Phu Thai of Northeast Thailand." *Asian Survey* 6, 7 (July 1966): 370–8.

________. "Modernizing Implications of 19th Century Reforms in the Thai Saṅgha." *Contributions to Asian Studies* VIII (1975): 8–23.

Kornfield, Jack. "Achaan Buddhadasa." In *Living Buddhist Masters*, pp. 117–29.

________. "Achaan Naeb." In *Living Buddhist Masters*, pp. 131–58.

________. *Living Buddhist Masters*. Santa Cruz: Unity Press, 1977.

________. *Living Dharma: Teachings of Twelve Buddhist Masters*. Boston: Shambhala Publications, 1977.

Lamotte, Étienne. "Les dix-huit vacuités." In *Le traité de la grande vertu de sagesse de Nāgārjuna: Mahāprajñāpāramitāśāstra: avec une étude sur la vacuité*, Volume IV. Louvain: Institut Orientaliste, Université de Louvain, 1974, pp. 1995–2013.

Landon, K.P. *Thailand in Transition: A Brief Survey of Cultural Trends in the Five Years since the Revolution of 1932*. Chicago: The University of Chicago Press, 1939.

"Late Phra Buddhadāsa Honoured by Unesco." *The Nation*, 22 October 2005.

Leach, E.R., ed. *Dialectic in Practical Religion*. Cambridge: Cambridge University Press, 1968.

Leach, E.R. "Introduction." In *Dialectic in Practical Religion*, ed. E.R. Leach, pp. 1–6.

Lerki, George Jan. *Origins of Trotskyism in Ceylon: A Documentary History of the Lanka Sama Samaja Party, 1935–1942*. Stanford: Hoover Institution on War, Revolution, and Peace, 1968.

Leuke. *Gautama Buddha and Karl Marx: A Critical and Comparative Study of Their System of Philosophy*. Colombo: Vijaya Publishing House, 1943.

Loone, Eero. "Communism." In *The Blackwell Dictionary of Twentieth-Century Social Thought*, eds. Outhwaite and Bottomore, pp. 96–8.

Lopez, Donald S. *A Modern Buddhist Bible: Essential Readings from East and West*. Boston: Beacon Press, 2002.

Mackenzie, Rory. *New Buddhist Movements in Thailand: Towards an Understanding of Wat Phra Dhammakāya and Santi Asoke*. London: Routledge, 2007.

Maen Pongudom. "Apologetic and Missionary Proclamation: Exemplified by American Presbyterian Missionaries to Thailand (1828–1978), Early Church Apologists: Justin Martyr, Clement of Alexandria and Origen, and the Venerable Buddhadasa Bhikkhu, a Thai Buddhist Monk-Apologist." PhD diss., The University of Otago, Dunedin, New Zealand, 1979.

"Making the Centenary of a Great Teacher." *The Nation*, 19 March 2006.

Manas Chitakasem and Andrew Turton, eds. *Thai Constructions of Knowledge*. London: School of Oriental and African Studies, University of London, 1991.

Marx, Karl. "Contribution to the Critique of Hegel's Philosophy of Law. Introduction." In *Collected Works Volume 3*, eds. Marx and Engels, pp. 174–87.

Marx, Karl and Frederich Engels. *Collected Works Volume 3: Marx and Engels 1843–44*. London: Lawrence & Wishart, 1975.

McCargo, Duncan. *Chamlong Srimuang and the New Thai Politics*. London: C. Hurst & Co., 1997.

McDaniel, Justin Thomas. *Gathering Leaves and Lifting Words: Histories of Buddhist Monastic Education in Laos and Thailand*. Seatle: University of Washington Press, 2008.

McHall, Shawn Frederick. *Print and Power: Confucianism, Communism, and Buddhism in the Making of Modern Vietnam*. Honolulu: University of Hawai'i Press, 2004.

McMahan, David L. *The Making of Buddhist Modernism*. Oxford: Oxford University Press, 2008.

Ministry of Public Instruction. *Report on the Work of the Ministry of Public Instruction of the Siamese Government B.E. 2469 (1926–27)*. Bangkok: Bangkok Times Press, 1931.

Morell, David and Samudavanija, Chai-anan. *Political Conflict in Thailand: Reform, Reaction, Revolution*. Cambridge: Oelgeschlager, Gunn & Hain, Publishers, Inc., 1981.

Morris, Richard and A.K.Warder, ed. *Aṅguttara-nikāya Part I and Part III*. London: The Pali Text Society, 1961.

Muecke, Marjorie A. "Make Money Not Babies: Changing Status Makers of Northern Thai Women." *Asian Survey* 24, 4 (April 1984): 459–70.

________. "Thai Conjugal Family Relationships and Hsu Hypothesis." *Journal of the Siam Society* 71, 1–2 (1983): 25–41.

Mulder, Niels. "Review of *Une herméneutique bouddhique contemporaine de Thaïlande: Buddhadāsa Bhikkhu*, by Louis Gabaude." *Bijdragen tot de taal-land-en volkenkunde* 150, 1 (1994): 234–5.

Murashima, Eiji. "1940 nen dai ni okeru tai no shokuminchi taisei dakkyakuka to indoshina no dokuritsu undo: tai futsuin funso kara reisen no kaishi made" (Thailand's 'Decolonisation' of Its System and the Indochinese Independence Movement in the 1940s: From the Thai-French Indochina Conflict to the Beginning of the Cold War). In *Betonamu to tai*, eds. Shiraishi, Murashima *et al*., pp. 110–219.

________. "Opposing French Colonialism: Thailand and the Independence Movements in Indo-China in the Early 1940s." *South East Research* 13, 3 (October 2005): 333–83.

________. *Pibun: dokuritsu tai okoku no rikken kakumei* (*Phibun: Constitutional Revolution in the Independent Kingdom of Thailand*). Tokyo: Iwanami Shoten, 1996.

________. "Tai kindai kokka no keisei" (The Formation of the Modern State of Thailand). In *Tonan ajia shi I — tairiku-bu* (*History of Southeast Asia Vol. I — Mainland*), eds. Yoneo Ishii and Yumio Sakurai. Tokyo: Yamakawa Shuppansha, 1999, pp. 397–439.

________. "Tai ni okeru seiji taisei no shuki teki tenkan: gikai sei minshushugi to gunbu no seiji kainyu" (The Periodical Cycle of the Political Regime in Thailand: Parliamentary Democracy and Military Intervention in Politics). In *Asean shokhoku no seiji taisei*, eds. Hagiwara and Murashima, pp. 135–90.

"Musical Maelstrom." *The Nation*, 1 May 2007.

Ñāṇamoli, Bhikkhu, trans. *The Middle Length Discourses of the Buddha*, ed., trans., rev. Bhikkhu Bodhi. Boston: Wisdom Publications, 1995.

"New Siamese Constitution: Highest Power Belongs to People." *The Maha-Bodhi* 40, 9 (September 1932): 415–22.

Norman, K.R. *Pāli Literature Including the Canonical Literature in Prakrit and Sanskrit of All the Hīnayāna Schools of Buddhism*. Wiesbaden: Otto Harrassowitz, 1983.

________. "Pāli Philology and the Study of Buddhism." *Collected Papers Volume IV*. Oxford: The Pāli Text Society, pp. 80–91.

________. "The Present State of Pāli Studies, and Future Tasks." In *Collected Papers, Volume VI*. Oxford: The Pāli Text Society, pp. 68–9.

O'Connor, Richard A. "Interpreting Thai Religious Change: Temples, Sangha Reform and Social Change." *Journal of Southeast Asian Studies* 24, 2 (September 1993): 330–9.

Olson, Grant A. "Cries Over Spilled Holy Water: 'Complex' Responses to a Traditional Thai Religious Practice." *Journal of Southeast Asian Studies* 22, 1 (March 1991): 75–85.

________. "From Buddhadasa Bhikkhu to Phra Debvedi: Two Monks of Wisdom." In *Radical Conservatism*, eds. Sulak Sivaraksa *et al.*, pp. 251–67.

________. "A Person-Centered Ethnography of Thai Buddhism: The Life of Phra Rajavaramuni (Prayudh Payutto)." PhD diss., Cornell University, 1989.

Outhwaite, William and Tom Bottomore, eds. *The Blackwell Dictionary of Twentieth-Century Social Thought*. Oxford: Blackwell, 1993.

Paisal Visalo, Phra. "The Forest Monastery and Its Relevance to Modern Thai Society." In *Radical Conservatism*, eds. Sulak Sivaraksa *et al.*, pp. 288–300.

Pasuk Phongpaichit. *Civilising the State: State, Civil Society and Politics in Thailand*. Amsterdam: Centre for Asian Studies, 1999.

Pasuk Phongpaichit and Chris Baker. *Thailand: Economy and Politics*. Kuala Lumpur: Oxford University Press, 1995.

Pataraporn Sirikanchana. "Buddhadāsa Bhikkhu and the Buddhist Hermeneutics." In *Radical Conservatism*, eds. Sulak Sivaraksa *et al.*, pp. 245–50.

________. "The Concept of Dhamma in Thai Buddhism: A Study in the Thought of Vajirañāṇa and Buddhadāsa." PhD diss., The University of Pennsylvania, 1985.

Payutto Bhikkhu, P.A. See Thepwethi, Phra.

Peerachat Saccavadit. "Citwaang as an Adequate Aim of Education." PhD diss., Indiana University, 1979.

Penth, Hans. *A Brief History of Lan Na: Civilisations of North Thailand*. Chiang Mai: Silkworm Books, 1994.

________. *History of Wat Umong*. Chiang Mai: Buddhanikom, n.d.

Prebish, Charles S., "Varying the Vinaya: Creative Responses to the Modernity." In *Buddhism in the Modern World: Adaptations of an Ancient*, eds. Steven Heine and Charles S. Prebish. New York: Oxford University Press, 2003, pp. 45–74.

Preston, James J., ed. *Mother Worship: Theme and Variations*. Chapel Hill: University of North Carolina Press, 1982.

"Prospectus Faculty of Arts and Science, Chulalankankarana University Session B.E. 2480 (A.D. 1937–38)." Bangkok: Bangkok Times Press.

Queen, Christopher S., ed. *Engaged Buddhism in the West*. Boston: Wisdom Publications, 2000.

Queen, Christopher S. and Sallie B. King, eds. *Engaged Buddhism: Buddhist Liberation Movements in Asia*. Albany: State University of New York Press, 1996.

Queen, Christopher S., Charles Prebish and Damien Keown, eds. *Action Dharma: New Studies in Engaged Buddhism*. London: RoutledgeCurzon, 2003.

Redfield, Robert. *Peasant Society and Culture*. Chicago: University of Chicago Press, 1956.

Reid, Anthony. *Southeast Asia in the Age of Commerce 1450–1680, Vol. 1: The Lands Below the Winds*. New Haven: Yale University Press, 1988.

Reynolds, Craig J., ed. *Autobiography: The Life of Prince-Patriarch Vajirañāṇa of Siam, 1860–1921*. Athens, Ohio: Ohio University Press, 1979.

________. "The Buddhist Monkhood in Nineteenth Century Thailand." PhD diss., Cornell University, 1973.

________. "The Case of K.S.R. Kulap: A Challenge to Royal Historical Writing in Late Nineteenth Century Thailand." *The Journal of the Siam Society* 61, 2 (July 1973): 63–90.

________. trans. City Slave. "Phi Tong Luang/The Spirit of Yellow Leaves." For the Echols Collection, Olin Library, Cornell University, 1980.

________. *Thai Radical Discourse: The Real Face of Thai Feudalism Today*. Ithaca: Cornell Southeast Asia Program, 1987.

Reynolds, Craig and Hong Lysa. "Marxism in Thai Historical Studies." *Journal of Asian Studies* XLIII, 1 (November 1983): 77–104.

Reynolds, Frank E. "Legitimation and Rebellion: Thailand's Civic Religion and the Student Uprising of October, 1973." In *Religion and Legitimation of Power in Thailand, Laos, and Burma*, ed. Bardwell L. Smith, pp. 134–46.

Rhys Davids, T.W., and William Stede, eds. *Pāli-English Dictionary*. Oxford: The Pāli Text Society.

Saddhatissa, Hammalawa. "Introduction: The Abhidhammatthasaṅgaha." In *The Abhidhammatthasaṅgaha of Bhadantācariya Anurudda and the Abhidham matthavibhāvinī-ṭīkā of Bhandantācariya Sumangalasāmi*, ed. Hammalawa Saddhatissa. Oxford: The Pāli Text Society, 1989, pp. xiii–xxiii.

"Salvation in Print." *The Nation*, 26 March 2006.

Santikaro Bhikkhu. "Buddhadāsa Bhikkhu: Life and Society through the Natural Eyes of Voidness." In *Engaged Buddhism: Buddhist Liberation Movements in Asia*, eds. Christopher S. Queen and Sallie B. King. Albany: State University of New York Press, 1996, pp. 147–94.

________. "Four Noble Truths of Dhammic Socialism." In *Entering the Realm of Reality*, eds. Watts, Senauke, and Santikaro, pp. 89–161.

________. "The Future of Suan Mokkh." In *Radical Conservatism*, eds. Sulak Sivaraksa *et al.*, pp. 268–87.

________. ed., trans. *Keys to Natural Truth*. Bangkok: Mental Health Publishing, 1988.

Sarkisyanz, E. *Buddhist Background of Burmese Revolution*. Hague: Martinus Nijhoff, 1965.

________. "Buddhist Background of Burmese Socialism." In *Religion and Legitimation of Power in Thailand, Laos, and Burma*, ed. Smith, pp. 87–99.

Satyananda Puri, Swami. "The Origin of Buddhist Thoughts." In *Speeches and Writings of Swami Satyananda*, ed. Das, pp. 1–38.

Seri Phongphit. "The Problem of Religious Language: A Study of Buddhadāsa Bhikkhu and Ian Ramsey as Models for a Mutual Understanding of Buddhism and Christianity." Inaugural-dissertation zur Erlangung des Doktorgrades an der Hochschule für Philosophie/Philosophische Fakultät SJ, München, 1978.

________. *Religion in a Changing Society: Buddhism, Reform and the Role of Monks in Community Development in Thailand.* Hong Kong: Arena Press, 1988.

Shiraishi, Masaya, Eiji Murashima *et al. Betonamu to tai* (*Vietnam and Thailand*). Tokyo: Daimeido, 1998.

Siapno, Jacqueline. "Alternative Filipina Heroines: Contested Tropes in Leftist Feminisms." In *Bewitching Women, Pious Men: Gender and Body Politics in Southeast Asia*, eds. Aihwa Ong and Michael G. Peletz. Berkeley: University of California Press, 1995.

"Simple Truths." *The Nation*, 28 May 2006.

Skilling, Peter. *Buddhism and Buddhist Literature of South-East Asia: Selected Papers*. Bangkok and Lumbini: Fragile Palm Leaves Foundation, Lumbini International Research Institute, 2009.

Smith, Bardwell L., ed. *Religion and Legitimation of Power in Thailand, Laos, and Burma*. Chambersburg, PA: ANIMA Books, 1978.

Smyth, David. "Introduction." In *Behind the Painting and Other Stories*, ed. Siburapha. Singapore: Oxford University Press, 1990, pp. 1–44.

Soma Thera, trans. *Kālāma Sutta: the Buddha's Charter of Free Inquiry*. Kandy: Buddhist Publication Society, 1981.

Somboon Suksamran. *Buddhism and Politics in Thailand: A Study of Socio-Political Change and Political Activism of the Thai Sangha*. Singapore: Institute of Southeast Asian Studies, 1982.

________. *Political Buddhism in Southeast Asia: The Role of the Sangha in the Modernization of Thailand*. London: G. Hurst, 1977.

Somsak Jeamteerasakul. "The Communist Movement in Thailand." PhD diss., Monash University, 1991.

"Songs for the SOUL." *The Nation*, 1 July 2007.

Spiro, Melford E. *Buddhism and Society: A Great Tradition and Its Burmese Vicissitude*. Berkeley: University of California Press, 1970, 1982.

Stuart-Fox, Martin. *Buddhist Kingdom, Marxist State: The Making of Modern Laos*. Bangkok: White Lotus, 1996.

Suchira Payulpitack. "Buddhadāsa's Movement: An Analysis of Its Origins, Development, and Social Impact." Dissertation zur Erlangung des Grades eines Doktors der Sozialwissenschaften, Universität Bielefeld, 1991.

________. "Changing Provinces of Concern: A Case-Study of the Social Impact of the Buddhadāsa Movement." *Sojourn* 7, 1 (February 1992): 39–68.

Sulak Sivaraksa. *Loyalty Demands Dissent: Autobiography of an Engaged Buddhist*. Berkeley: Parallax Press, 1998.

Sulak Sivaraksa *et al.*, eds. *Radical Conservatism: Buddhism in the Contemporary World, Articles in Honour of Bhikkhu Buddhadāsa's 84th Anniversary*. Bangkok: Thai Inter-Religious Commission for Development, and International Network of Engaged Buddhists, 1990.

Suwanna Satha-Anand. "Review of *Buddhism, Legitimation, and Conflict: The Political Functions of Urban Thai Buddhism*, by Peter A. Jackson." *Crossroads* 5, 1 (1990): 105–8.

________. ed. *Women's Studies in Thailand: Power, Knowledge and Justice*. Seoul: Ewha Womans University Press, 2004.

Swearer, Donald K., "Bhikkhu Buddhadāsa's Interpretation of the Buddha." *Journal of the American Academy of Religion* LXIV, 2 (Summer 1996): 313–36.

________. "Buddha, Buddhism and Bhikkhu Buddhadāsa." In *Radical Conservatism*, eds. Sulak Sivaraksa *et al.*, pp. 230–44.

________. "Buddhism, Christianity and Bhikkhu Buddhadāsa." In *Visakha Puja 2511*. Bangkok: Buddhist Association, 1968, pp. 77–90.

________. *Buddhism and Society in Southeast Asia*. Chambersburg, PA: ANIMA Books, 1981.

________. *Buddhism in Transition*. Philadelphia: The Westminster Press, 1970.

________. "Buddhist Virtue, Voluntary Poverty, and Extensive Benevolence." *Journal of Religious Ethics* 26, 1 (Spring 1998): 71–103.

________. *The Buddhist World of Southeast Asia*. Albany: State University of New York Press, 1995.

________. ed., trans. *Dhammic Socialism*. Bangkok: Inter-Religious Commission for Development, 1986.

________. "Fundamentalism in Theravada Buddhism." In *Fundamentalisms Observed*, eds. Martin E. Marty and R. Scott Appleby. Chicago: University of Chicago Press, 1991, pp. 628–90.

________. ed., trans. *Me and Mine: Selected Essays of Bhikkhu Buddhadāsa*. Albany: State University of New York Press, 1989.

________. "Thai Buddhism: Two Responses to Modernity." *Contributions to Asian Studies* IV (1973): 79–92.

________. ed., trans. *Toward the Truth*. Philadelphia: The Westminster Press, 1971.

________. "Three Legacies of Bhikkhu Buddhadāsa." In *The Quest for a Just Society: The Legacy and Challenge of Buddhadāsa Bhikkhu*, ed. Sulak Sivaraksa. Bangkok: International Network of Engaged Buddhists, 1994, pp. 1–26.

Tambiah, S.J. *Buddhism and the Spirit Cults in North-East Thailand*. Cambridge: Cambridge University Press, 1970.

________. *The Buddhist Saints of the Forest and the Cult of Amulets*. Cambridge: Cambridge University Press, 1984.

________. "The Ideology of Merit and the Social Correlates of Buddhism in a Thai Village." In *Dialectic in Practical Religion*, ed. E.R. Leach, pp. 41–121.

________. *World Conqueror and World Renouncer: A Study of Buddhism and Polity in Thailand Against a Historical Background*. Cambridge: Cambridge University Press, 1976.

Tanabe, Shigeharu. "Ideological Practice in Peasant Rebellions: Siam at the Turn of the Twentieth Century." In *History and Peasant Consciousness in South East Asia*, eds. Turton and Tanabe, pp. 75–110.

Tannenbaum, Nicola. "Protest, Tree Ordination, and the Changing Context of Political Ritual." *Ethnology* 39, 2 (Spring 2000): 109–27.

Tavivat Puntarigvivat. "Bhikkhu Buddhadāsa's Dhammic Socialism in Dialogue with Latin American Liberation Theology." PhD diss., Temple University, 1994.

Taylor, Jim. "Buddhist Revitalization, Modernization, and Social Change in Contemporary Thailand." *Sojourn* 8, 1 (February 1993).

________. *Forest Monks and the Nation-State: An Anthropological and Historical Study in Northeastern Thailand.* Singapore: Institute of Southeast Asian Studies, 1993.

________. "New Buddhist Movements in Thailand: An Individualistic Revolution, Reform and Political Dissonance." *Journal of Southeast Asian Studies* 21, 1 (March 1990): 135–54.

________. "Social Activism and Resistance on the Thai Frontier: The Case of Phra Prajak Khuttajitto." *Bulletin of Concerned Asian Scholars* 25, 2 (April–June 1993): 3–16.

Terwiel, B.J. *Monks and Magic: An Analysis of Religious Ceremonies in Central Thailand.* London: Curzon Press, 1979.

Thak Chaloemtiarana. *Thailand: The Politics of Despotic Paternalism.* Bangkok: Social Science Association of Thailand, Thai Khadi Institute, Thammasat University, 1979.

The British Buddhist 4, 1 (October 1929)–Vol. 8 Conference and Farewell Number (1934).

The Mahā Bodhi 39, 1 (January 1931)–41, 12 (December 1933).

The Young East 1, 3 (August 1925)–10, 2 (1942).

Thepwethi, Phra (P.A. Payutto Bhikkhu; now known as Phra Phromkhunaphon). *Dictionary of Buddhism.* Bangkok: Mahachulalongkon Ratchawitthayalai, 1992.

Thongchai Winichakul. *Siam Mapped: A History of the Geo-Body of a Nation.* Chiang Mai: Silkworm Books, 1994.

Tsomo, Karma Lekshe. ed. *Buddhist Women Across Cultures: Realizations.* Delhi: Sri Satguru Publications, 1999.

________. ed. *Innovative Buddhist Women: Swimming Against the Stream.* Surrey: Curzon Press, 2000.

________, ed. *Śakyadhītā: Daughters of the Buddha.* Delhi: Sri Satguru Publications, 1988.

Tsui, Chak Wing David. *China and the Communist Armed Struggle in Thailand.* London: Sangam Books Limited, 1995.

Turton, Andrew and Shigeharu Tanabe, eds. *History and Peasant Consciousness in South East Asia.* Osaka: National Museum of Ethnology, 1984.

Van Esterik, Penny. "Feeding Their Faith: Recipe Knowledge Among Thai Buddhist Women." *Food and Foodways* 1 (1986): 197–215.

________, "Introduction." In *Women of Southeast Asia*, ed. Penny Van Esterik, pp. 1–15.

________. *Materializing Thailand.* Oxford: Berg, 2000.

________. "Nurturance and Reciprocity in Thai Studies." In *State Power and Culture in Thailand*, Monograph 44, ed. E. Paul Durrenberger. New Haven: Yale Southeast Asia Studies, 1996, pp. 22–46.

________, ed. *Women of Southeast Asia*. Detroit, Mich.: Northern Illinois University, Center for Southeast Asian Studies, 1982.

Varnvaidya Varavarn (Wan Waithayakon), M.C. "My Impressions of Swami Satyananda Puri's Lecture on the 'Origin of Buddhistic Thoughts.'" *Mahawitthayalai* (*University*) 10, 5 (1932): 630–3.

Vella, Walter F. "Thianwan of Siam: A Man who Fought Ggiants." In *Anuson Walter Vella*, ed. Ronald D. Renard. Chiang Mai: Walter F. Vella Fund, Phayap University, 1986, pp. 78–91.

Walzer, Michael. *Politics and Passion: Toward a More Egalitarian Liberalism*. New Haven: Yale University Press, 2004.

Ward, Barbara E., ed. *Women in the New Asia: The Changing Social Roles of Men and Women in South and South-East Asia*. Paris: UNESCO, 1963.

Watts, Jonathan, Alan Senauke, and Santikaro Bhikkhu, eds. *Entering the Realm of Reality: Towards Dhammic Societies*. Bangkok: INEB, 1997.

Welch, Holmes. *Buddhism under Mao*. Cambridge, Massachusetts: Harvard University Press, 1972.

Wilson, Constance M. "The Holy Man in the History of Thailand and Laos." *Journal of Southeast Asian Studies* 28, 2 (September 1997): 345–64.

Wilson, David A. "China, Thailand and the Spirit of Bandung (Part I)." *The China Quarterly* 30 (April–June 1967):149–69.

________. "China, Thailand and the Spirit of Bandung (Part II)." *The China Quarterly* 31 (July–September 1967): 96–127.

Wong Mou-lam, ed., trans. *The Sutra of Wei Lang*. London: Luzac & Co., 1944.

Woodward, F.L., ed. *The Book of the Kindred Sayings (Saµyutta-nikāya) or Grouped Suttas: Part V (Mahā-vagga)*. London: The Pali Text Society, 1965.

Wyatt, David K. *Thailand: A Short History*. Chiangmai: Silkworm Books, 1982, 1984.

"Yet Another Departure." *The British Buddhist* 5, 1 (October 1930): 194.

"Youth Walk to Promote Dhamma." *The Nation*, 29 September 2006.

Yuangrat (Pattanapongse) Wedel. "Modern Thai Radical Thought: The Siamization of Marxism and Its Theoretical Problems." PhD diss., University of Michigan, 1981.

Yuangrat Wedel. *The Thai Radicals and the Communist Party: Interaction of Ideology and Nationalism in the Forest, 1975–1980*. Singapore: Maruzen Asia, 1983.

Yuangrat Wedel and Paul Wedel. *Radical Thought, Thai Mind: The Development of Revolutionary Ideas in Thailand*. Bangkok: ABAC, 1987.

Zack, Stephan J. "Buddhist Education under Prince Wachirayan Warorot." PhD diss., Cornell University, 1977.

Zehner, Edwin. "Reform Symbolism of a Thai Middle-class Sect: The Growth and Appeal of the Thammakai Movement." *Journal of Southeast Asians Studies* 21, 2 (September 1990): 402–26.

Index